KS3 Maths Progress θ THREE

Confidence • Fluency • Problem-solving • Progression

θ

θ

Series editors:
Dr Naomi Norman • Katherine Pate

ALWAYS LEARNING PEARSON

Published by Pearson Education Limited, Edinburgh Gate, Harlow, Essex, CM20 2JE.

www.pearsonschoolsandfecolleges.co.uk

Text © Pearson Education Limited 2014
Typeset by Tech-Set Ltd, Gateshead
Original illustrations © Pearson Education Limited 2014
Cover photo/illustration by Robert Samuel Hanson
Index by Martin Brooks

The rights of Nick Asker, Lynn Byrd, Andrew Edmondson, Catherine Murphy, Katherine Pate and Mary Pardoe to be identified as authors of this work have been asserted by them in accordance with the Copyright, Designs and Patents Act 1988.

First published 2014

17 16 15 14
10 9 8 7 6 5 4 3 2 1

British Library Cataloguing in Publication Data
A catalogue record for this book is available from the British Library.

ISBN 978 1 447 96237 3

Copyright notice
All rights reserved. No part of this publication may be reproduced in any form or by any means (including photocopying or storing it in any medium by electronic means and whether or not transiently or incidentally to some other use of this publication) without the written permission of the copyright owner, except in accordance with the provisions of the Copyright, Designs and Patents Act 1988 or under the terms of a licence issued by the Copyright Licensing Agency, Saffron House, 6–10 Kirby Street, London EC1N 8TS (www.cla.co.uk). Applications for the copyright owner's written permission should be addressed to the publisher.

Printed in Italy by Lego S.p.A

Acknowledgements
The publisher would like to thank the following individuals and organisations for permission to reproduce photographs:
(Key: b-bottom; c-centre; l-left; r-right; t-top)
Corbis: Ken Sutton / Colorsport 34; **Fotolia.com:** Benjamin Haas 25, David Harding 28, Hellen Sergeyeva 138, Ilya Andreev 113, LaCozza 133, lunamarina 4, Markus Mainka 250, paul prescott 165; **Getty Images:** Lonely Planet Images 107bc, 109, 119, 122, 131; **Pearson Education Ltd:** David Sanderson 201, Gareth Boden 93, Jörg Carstensen 84, Stuart Cox 65; **PhotoDisc:** 37; **Photos.com:** Archiwiz 140, macroart 231, Rafal Olkis 225, simon askham 234; **Rovio Entertainment Ltd:** 198; **Science Photo Library Ltd:** Adam Hart-Davis 192; **Shutterstock.com:** Carolina K. Smith MD 81, Dalibor Sevaljevic 167, hxdbzxy 253, isak55 143, Milolika 261, Vit Kovalcik 170; **Veer / Corbis:** Brian Jackson 59, c 136, Corepics 162, Dmitrijs Dmitrijevs 228, Emilia Ungur 195, EpicStockMedia 206, eyematrix 56, gud 1, 256, 259, JanMika 116, Lev Kropotov 90, Lightpoet 53, luchschen 10, Maridav 146, Markus Mainka 189, michaeljung 62, rufar 173, stevemeese 31, Valeri Potapova 107tl, william87 87, Zbyněk Buřival 7, Zhenikeyev 110
All other images © Pearson Education Ltd.

We are grateful to the following for permission to reproduce copyright material:
GDP data (p65) from 'GDP per capita', accessed March 2013, The World Bank; UK population data (p69, p77) from 'National Population Projections 2012-based', Office for National Statistics licensed under the Open Government Licence v.2.0; Average weekly earnings in Wales (p88), https://statswales.wales.gov.uk/, Welsh Government; Data on oil use in the UK (p104) from 'Energy Consumption in the UK', Department of Energy and Climate Change licensed under the Open Government Licence v.2.0; Crime data (p226, p243 and p246) from 'Recorded crime tables 2011-12', Office for National Statistics licensed under the Open Government Licence v.2.0.

Every effort has been made to contact copyright holders of material reproduced in this book. Any omissions will be rectified in subsequent printings if notice is given to the publishers.

α

KS3 Maths Progress

Confidence • Fluency • Problem-solving • Progression

Pedagogy at the heart – This new course is built around a unique pedagogy that's been created by leading mathematics educational researchers and Key Stage 3 teachers. The result is an innovative learning structure based around 10 key principles designed to nurture confidence and raise achievement.

Pedagogy – our 10 key principles

- Fluency
- Mathematical Reasoning
- Multiplicative Reasoning
- Problem Solving
- Progression
- Concrete-Pictorial - Abstract (CPA)
- Relevance
- Modelling
- Reflection (metacognition)
- Linking

Progression to Key Stage 4 – In line with the 2014 National Curriculum, there is a strong focus on fluency, problem-solving and progression to help prepare your students' progress through their studies.

Stretch, challenge and support – Catering for students of all abilities, these Student Books are structured to deliver engaging and accessible content across three differentiated tiers, each offering a wealth of worked examples and questions, supported by key points, literacy and strategy hints, and clearly defined objectives.

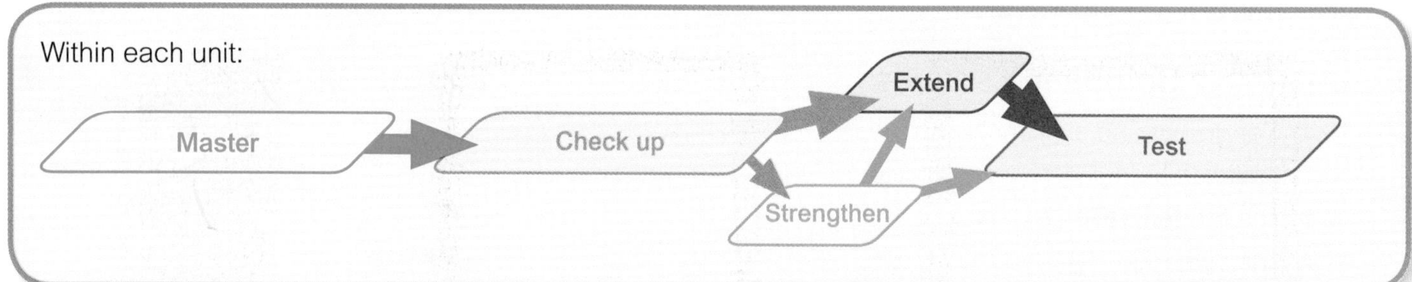

Differentiated for students of all abilities:

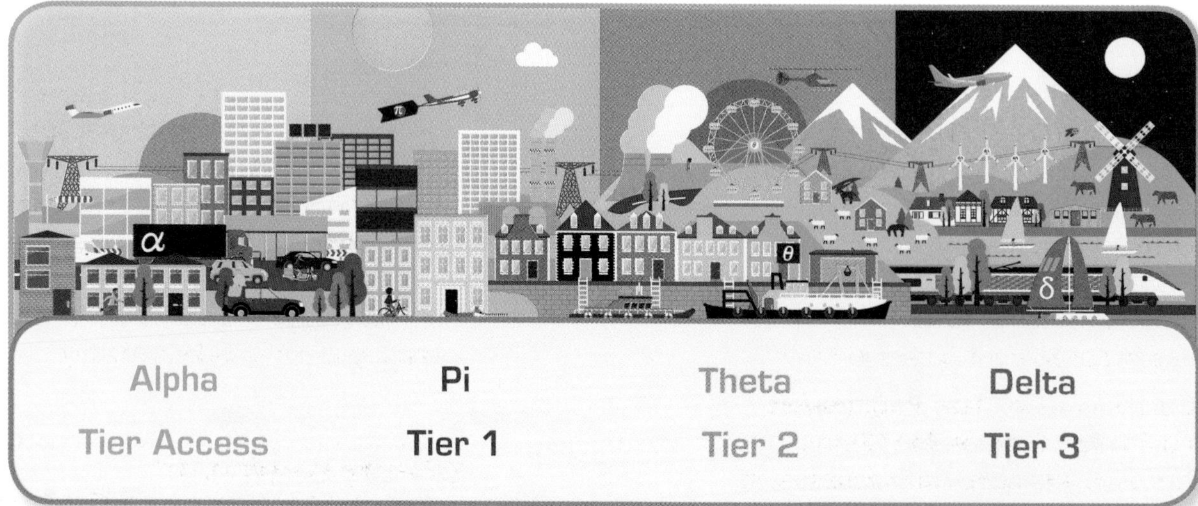

Progress with confidence!

This innovative Key Stage 3 Maths course embeds a modern pedagogical approach around our trusted suite of digital and print resources, to create confident and numerate students ready to progress further.

Help at the front-of-class – **ActiveTeach Presentation** is our tried and tested service that makes all of the Student Books available for display on a whiteboard. The books are supplemented with a range of videos and animations that present mathematical concepts along a concrete - pictorial - abstract pathway, allowing your class to progress their conceptual understanding at the right speed.

Learning beyond the classroom – Focussing on online homework**, ActiveCourse** offers students unprecedented extra practice (with automarking) and a chance to reflect on their learning with the confidence-checker. Powerful reporting tools can be used to track student progression and confidence levels.

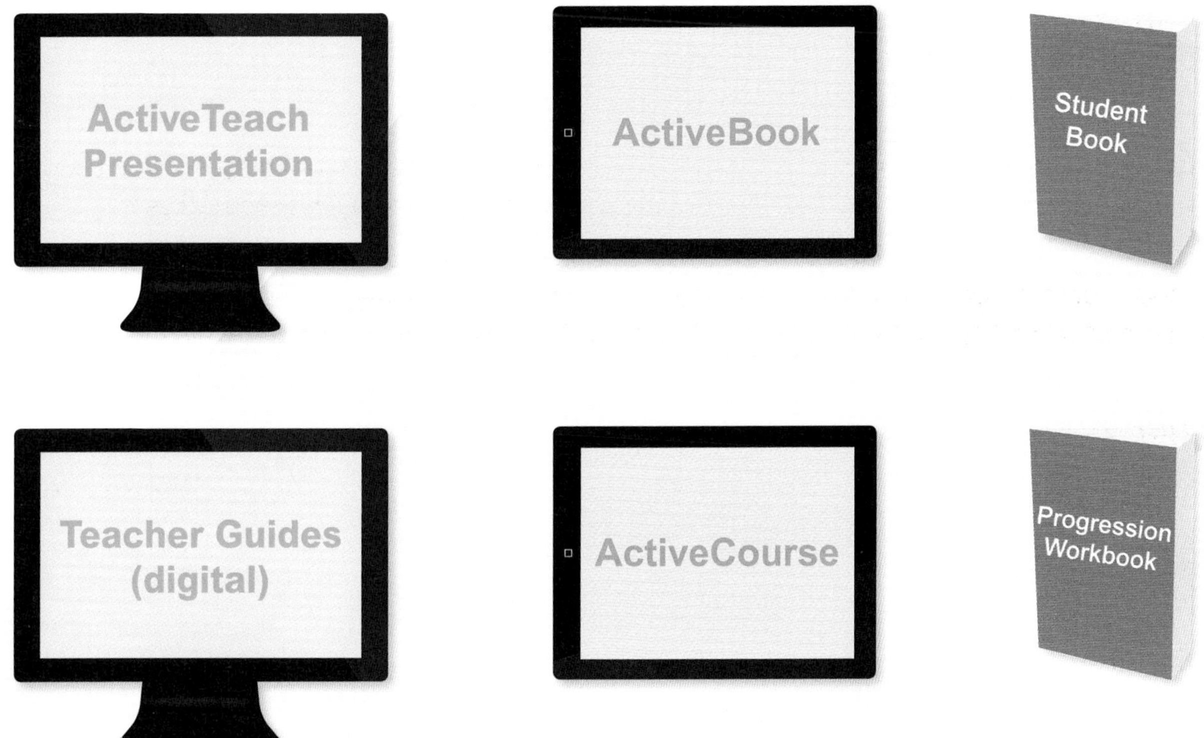

Easy to plan, teach and assess – Downloadable **Teacher Guides** provide assistance with planning through the Schemes of Work. Lesson plans link both front-of-class **ActiveTeach Presentation** and **ActiveCourse** and provide help with reporting, functionality and progression. Both **Teacher Guides** and **ActiveTeach Presentation** contain the **answers** to the Student Book exercises.

Teacher Guides include **Class Progression Charts** and **Student Progression Charts** to support formative and summative assessment through the course.

Practice to progress – KS3 Maths Progress has an extensive range of practice across a range of topics and abilities. From the **Student Books** to write-in **Progression Workbooks** through to **ActiveCourse**, there is plenty of practice available in a variety of formats whether for in the classroom or for learning at home independently.

For more information, visit www.pearsonschools.co.uk/ks3mathsprogress

Welcome to KS3 Maths Progress student books!

Confidence • Fluency • Problem-solving • Progression

Starting a new course is exciting! We believe you will have fun with maths, at the same time nurturing your confidence and raising your achievement.

Here's how:

Extend helps you to apply the maths you know to some different situations. *Strengthen* and *Extend* both include *Enrichment* or *Investigations*.

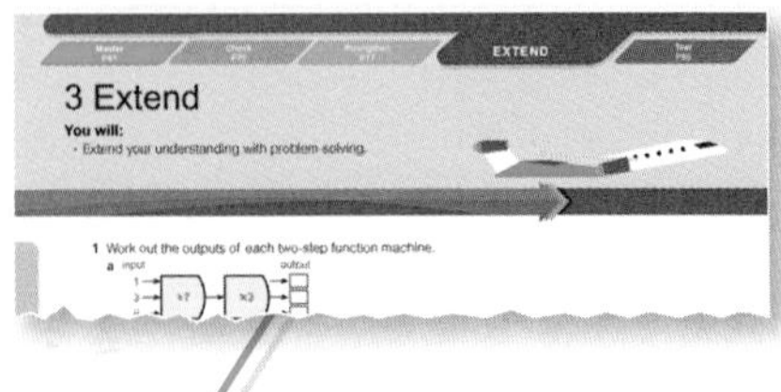

At the end of the *Master* lessons, take a *Check up* test to help you decide to *Strengthen*, or *Extend* your learning. You may be able to mark this test yourself.

6 Check up

Choose only the topics in *Strengthen* that you need a bit more practice with. You'll find more hints here to lead you through specific questions. Then move on to *Extend*.

10 Strengthen

When you have finished the whole unit, a *Unit test* helps you see how much progress you are making.

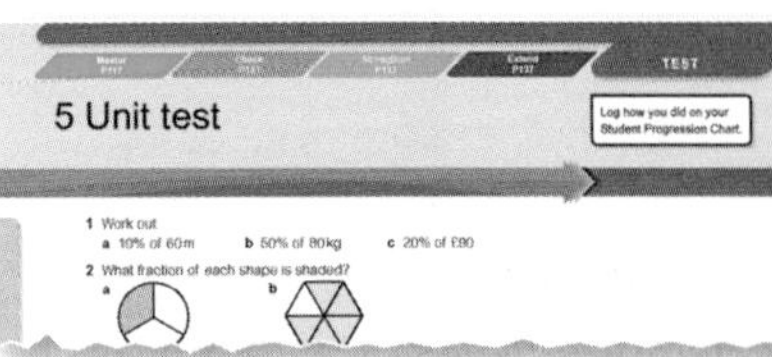

Clear *Objectives,* showing what you will cover in each lesson, are followed by a *Confidence* panel to boost your understanding and engage your interest.

Have a look at *Why Learn This?* This shows you how maths is useful in everyday life.

Improve your *Fluency* – practise answering questions using maths you already know.

The first questions are *Warm up*. Here you can show what you already know about this topic or related ones…

…before moving on to further questions, with *Worked examples* and *Hints* for help when you need it.

Your teacher has access to Answers in either ActiveTeach Presentation or the Teacher Guides.

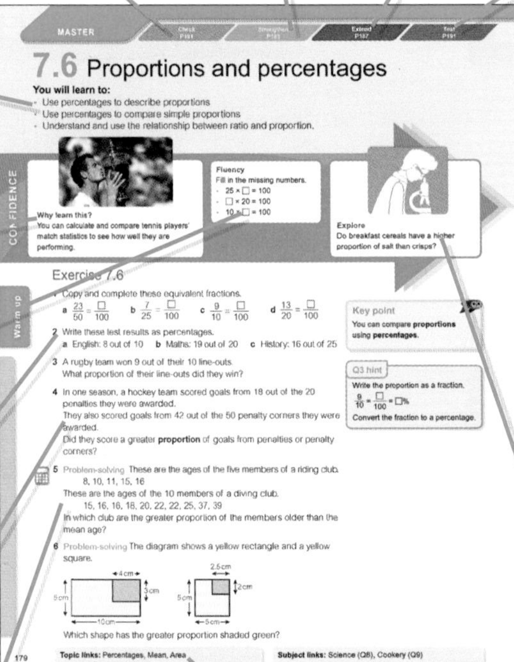

Topic links show you how the maths in a lesson is connected to other mathematical topics. Use the *Subject links* to find out where you might use the maths you have learned here in your other lessons, such as science, geography and computing .

Explore a real-life problem by discussing and having a go. By the end of the lesson you'll have gained the skills you need to start finding a solution to the question using maths.

At the end of each lesson, you get a chance to *Reflect* on how confident you feel about the topic.

STEM and Finance lessons

Context lessons expand on *Real*, *STEM* and *Finance* maths. Finance questions are related to money. STEM stands for Science, Technology, Engineering and Maths. You can find out how charities use maths in their fundraising, how engineers monitor water flow in rivers, and why diamonds sparkle (among other things!)

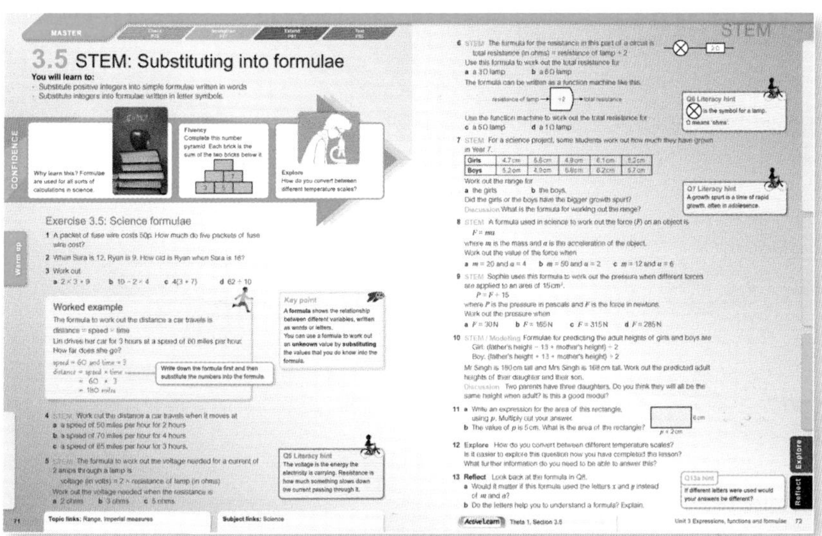

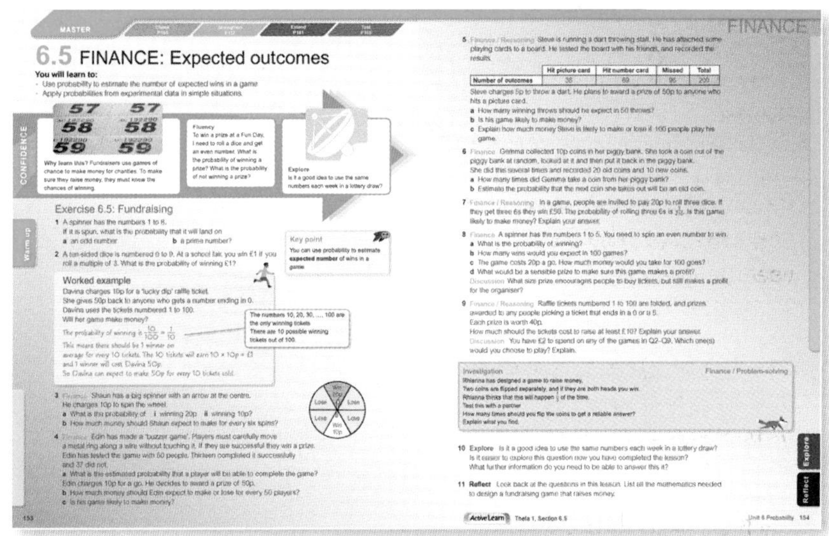

You can improve your ability to use maths in everyday situations by tackling *Modelling*, *Reasoning*, *Problem-solving* and *Real* questions. *Discussions* prompt you to explain your reasoning or explore new ideas with a partner.

As well as hints that help you with specific questions, you'll find *Literacy hints* (to explain some unfamiliar terms) and *Strategy hints* (to help with working out).

Some questions are tagged as *Finance* or *STEM*. These questions show how the real world relies on maths. Follow these up with whole lessons that focus on how maths is used in the fields of finance, science and technology.

Your teacher may give you a Student Progression Chart to help you see your progression through the units.

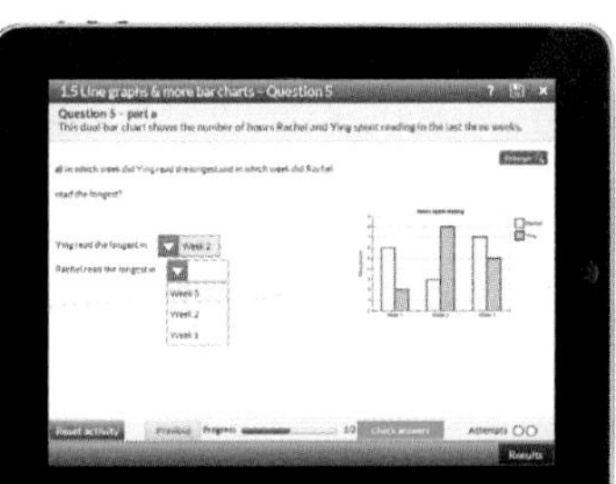

Further support

You can easily access extra resources that tie in to each lesson – look for the ActiveLearn icon on the lesson pages for ActiveCourse online homework links. These are clearly mapped to lessons and provide fun, interactive exercises linked to helpful worked examples and videos.

The Progression Workbooks, full of extra practice for key questions will help you reinforce your learning and track your own progress.

Enjoy!

1 Indices and standard form

MASTER | Check P13 | Strengthen P15 | Extend P19 | Test P23

1.1 Indices

You will learn to:
- Calculate combinations of indices, fractions and brackets
- Use index laws to simplify expressions.

CONFIDENCE

Why learn this?
Computers work with the binary number system, which uses powers of 2.

Fluency
- Work out
  3^3 5^3 10^3
- Work out
  -3×-3 4×-4
- Work out $(2 + 3)^2$

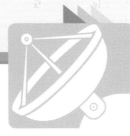

Explore
How much working memory (RAM) does a modern home computer have, compared with the first home computers?

Exercise 1.1

Warm up

1 Work out
a 2^4 b $(-4)^2$ c $3^2 \times 3$ d $2^3 \times 2$
e $2 \times 3^2 \times 5$ f $3^2 \times 10^3$ g 0.7^2 h 0.02^2

Key point
Index is the name for the small raised number in a power. Indices is the plural of index.

Q1g hint
Work out $7^2 \times 0.1^2$

2 Work out
a $\frac{2}{2}$ b $\frac{2 \times 9}{2 \times 3}$ c $\frac{3 \times 3 \times 3}{3}$
d $\frac{5 \times 5 \times 5}{5 \times 5}$ e $\frac{7 \times 7 \times 7 \times 7 \times 7}{7 \times 7 \times 7}$

3 Use the priority of operations to calculate
a $3 + 4^3$ b 2×3^2 c $2(1 + 3^2)$ d $(2 \times 5)^2$

4 a Work out
i $2^2 \times 2^3$ ii 2^5 iii $2^2 \times 2^4$
iv 2^6 v $2^3 \times 2^4$ vi 2^7
b How can you work out the answers to part **a** by using the indices of the powers you are multiplying?
c Copy and complete the multiplication grid of powers of 3.
Write your answers as powers of 3.

Q4a hint
Use the power key on your calculator.

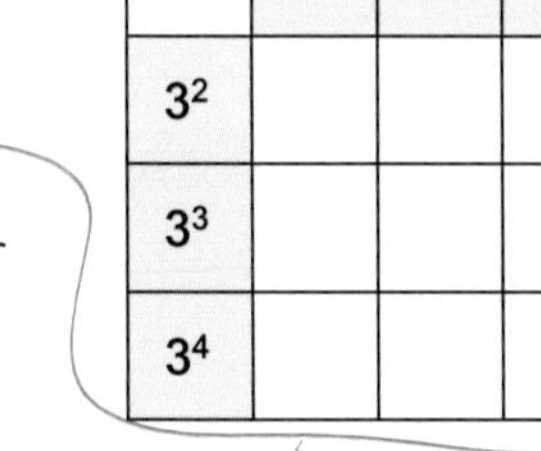

×	3^4	3^5	3^6
3^2			
3^3			
3^4			

Discussion Simplify $a^2 \times a^3$.
Do powers of letters follow the same rules for multiplying as powers of numbers?

5 Write each product as a single power.
a $2^5 \times 2^3$ b $4^3 \times 4^3$ c 3×3^4
d $5^3 \times 5^2$ e $7^2 \times 7^3 \times 7$ f $2^3 \times 2^4 \times 2^2$

Q5c hint
3 can be written as 3^1 (3 to the power 1).

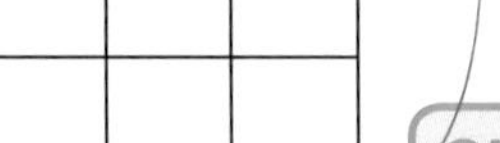

Topic links: Geometry and measures

Subject links: Computing (Q7, Q11, Q17)

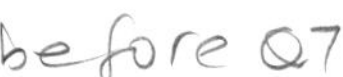

6 Write these calculations using powers of a single number. Give your answers in index form.

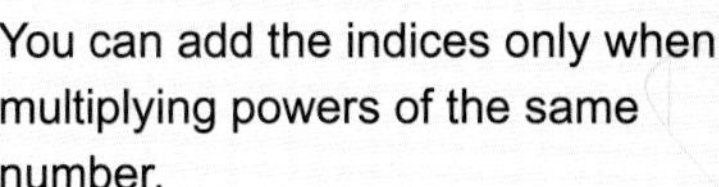

a $8 \times 2^4 = 2^{\square} \times 2^4 = 2^{\square}$ **b** $9 \times 3^3 = 3^{\square} \times 3^3 = 3^{\square}$

c 64×4^2 **d** 3×27

e 25×125 **f** $16 \times 4 \times 8$

g $27 \times 27 \times 27$ **h** $16 \times 16 \times 16$

Key point

You can add the indices only when multiplying powers of the same number.

7 Real / STEM One byte of computer memory is 8 bits of data.

a Write 8 as a power of 2.

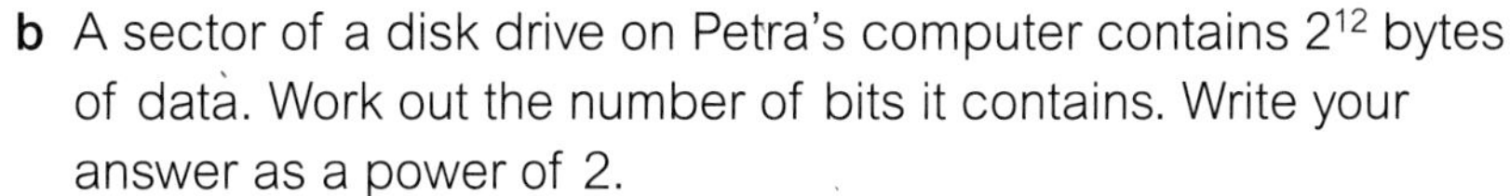

b A sector of a disk drive on Petra's computer contains 2^{12} bytes of data. Work out the number of bits it contains. Write your answer as a power of 2.

c Write your answer to part **b** as a simple number (not using powers).

8 a Work out $\frac{2 \times 2 \times 2 \times 2 \times 2 \times 2 \times 2}{2 \times 2 \times 2 \times 2}$ by cancelling.

b Write your answer to part **a** as a power of 2.

c Copy and complete $\frac{2 \times 2 \times 2 \times 2 \times 2 \times 2 \times 2}{2 \times 2 \times 2 \times 2} = \frac{2^{\square}}{2^{\square}} = 2^{\square}$

d Copy and complete $2^5 \div 2^3 = \frac{2^5}{2^3} = \frac{\square \times \square \times \square \times \square \times \square}{\square \times \square \times \square} = 2^{\square}$

e How can you work out the answers using the indices?

Discussion Do powers of letters follow the same rules for division as powers of numbers?

9 Write each division as a single power.

a $5^5 \div 5^2$ **b** $4^6 \div 4$ **c** $3^{10} \div 3^7$

d $2^8 \div 2^7$ **e** $5^3 \div 5$ **f** $6^8 \div 6^5$

Key point

You can subtract the indices when dividing powers of the same number.

10 Write these calculations using powers of a single number. Give your answers in index form.

a $16 \div 2^2 = 2^{\square} \div 2^2 = 2^{\square}$ **b** $32 \div 2^2$ **c** $3^3 \div 9$

11 Real / STEM A USB memory stick holds up to 2^{28} bytes of data. The hard drive of Alan's computer holds up to 2^{40} bytes. How many memory sticks would you need to back up a full hard drive?

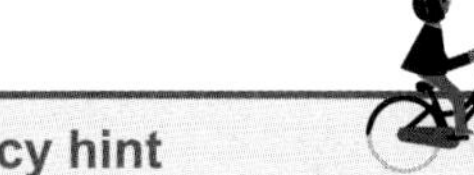

Q11 Literacy hint

Backing up a hard drive means copying its contents onto another storage device.

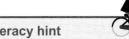

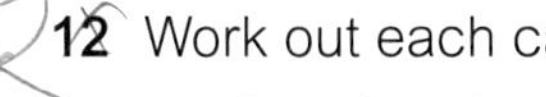

12 Work out each calculation as a single power.

a $3^2 \times 3^4 \div 3^3$ **b** $4^5 \div 4^3 \times 4^2$ **c** $5^2 \times 5^3 \div 5$

d $2^5 \times 2^4 \div 2^3 \div 2$ **e** $2^7 \div (2^2 \times 2^3)$ **f** $4^8 \div (4^2 \times 4^3)$

Q12a hint

Work from left to right.

Discussion Are the brackets necessary in the calculation $2^8 \div (2^7 \div 2^5)$? What about $(2^8 \div 2^7) \div 2^5$?

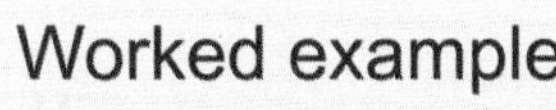

Worked example

Work out $[10 - (5 - 2)]^2$.

$[10 - 3]^2 = 7^2 = 49$

Work out the inner brackets first. $(5 - 2) = 3$

13 Work out these. Check your answers using a calculator.

a $[2 \times (1 + 2)]^2$
b $[(6 + 10) \div 2]^2$
c $[11 - (9 - 3)]^3$
d $[(3 + 5) \times 2]^2$
e $[(3 + 12) \div 5]^2$
f $[12 \div 2 - (8 - 7)]^2$
g $10 - [10 - (10 - 1)^2]$
h $[48 \div (5 - 3)^3 - 4] \div 2$

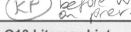

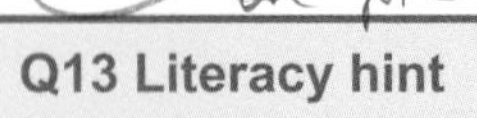

Q13 Literacy hint

Square brackets [ ] make the inner and outer brackets easier to see. Input them as round brackets on your calculator.

14 The diagram shows three squares.

3 cm 5 cm 5 cm

Which one of these calculations gives the total area?

A $(3 + 5 + 5)^2$
B $3^2 + (2 \times 5)^2$
C $3^2 + 2 \times 5^2$
D $[3 + (2 \times 5)]^2$

15 Work out

a $6 + (-3)^2$
b $6 - 3^2$
c $(-5)^2 - 5$
d $-2 - 2^2$
e $(-4)^2 - 4^2$
f $5 - (-5)^2$

Q15a hint

$(-3)^2 = -3 \times -3$

16 Write each of these using a single power.

a $(-3)^2 \times (-3)^3$
b $-2 \times (-2)^2$
c $(-2)^3 \times (-2)^3$
d $(-3)^4 \div (-3)^3$
e $(-2)^3 \div -2$
f $(-2)^5 \div (-2)^2$

Discussion Do the index laws work for negative numbers?

Investigation — Reasoning

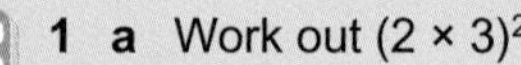

1 a Work out $(2 \times 3)^2$ b Work out $2^2 \times 3^2$ c What do you notice?
2 a Work out $(2 \times 3)^3$ b Work out $2^3 \times 3^3$ c What do you notice?
3 Write a rule for calculating a power of a product.
4 Check that your rule works for
a $(2 \times 3)^4$ b $(2 \times 3 \times 4)^2$
5 a Work out $(6 \div 3)^2$. b Work out $6^2 \div 3^2$.
c What do you notice?
6 a Write a rule for calculating a power of a division.
b Check that your rule works for powers higher than 2.

Part 3 Literacy hint

Multiplying two numbers together gives their **product**.

Explore

17 Explore How much working memory (RAM) does a modern home computer have, compared with the first home computers?
Is it easier to explore this question now you have completed the lesson?
What further information do you need to be able to answer this?

Reflect

18 Reflect For each statement **A**, **B** and **C**, choose a score:

1 – strongly disagree 2 – disagree 3 – agree 4 – strongly agree

A I always try hard in mathematics.
B Doing mathematics never makes me worried.
C I am good at mathematics.

For any statement you scored less than 3, write down two things you could do so that you agree more strongly in future.

1.2 Calculations and estimates

You will learn to:
- Calculate combinations of powers, roots, fractions and brackets
- Estimate answers to calculations.

CONFIDENCE

Why learn this?
The time for a pendulum to swing back and forth can be estimated using a formula involving a square root.

Fluency
- What is the square root of 64?
- What is the cube root of 64?
- Round 23.4 cm to the nearest centimetre.

Explore
What is a safe speed for a spacecraft to fire its thrusters when landing on Mars?

Exercise 1.2

Warm up

1 Use the priority of operations to work out these.

a $6 \times \sqrt{81}$ b $\sqrt{5^2 + 12^2}$ c $\sqrt{1600} = \sqrt{\square \times 100} = \sqrt{\square} \times \sqrt{100}$

d $\sqrt{4900}$ e $\sqrt{\frac{125}{5}}$ f $\sqrt[3]{4 \times 16}$

g $\frac{4^2 + 4}{1 + \sqrt{16}}$ h $(-3)^3$ i $(-2)^3 \times 4$

2 Work out these. Write each answer in its simplest form.

a $\frac{4}{5} \times \frac{4}{5}$ b $\frac{25 \times 8}{10}$ c $\frac{7 \times 27}{9 \times 14}$ d $\frac{16 \times 12}{6 \times 4}$

3 a Estimate the cost of 9 tickets at £19.80 each.
b Is your answer an underestimate or an overestimate?

4 Work out

a $\sqrt[3]{125}$ b $\sqrt[3]{8}$ c $\sqrt[3]{-8}$ d $\sqrt[3]{-27}$

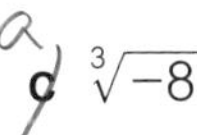

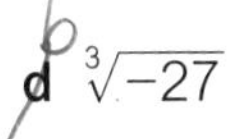

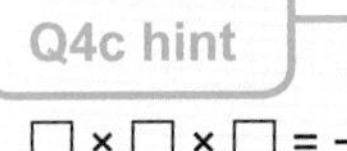

Q4c hint
$\square \times \square \times \square = -8$

5 Problem-solving A cube has a volume of 64 cm^3.
a Work out the length of one side of the cube.
b Work out the surface area of the cube.
c One face of another cube has an area of 25 cm^2.
Work out the volume of the cube.
d The diagram shows a cuboid bar of silver. It is melted down and made into five identical silver cubes.
Work out the side length of one of the cubes.

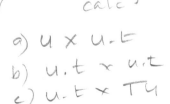

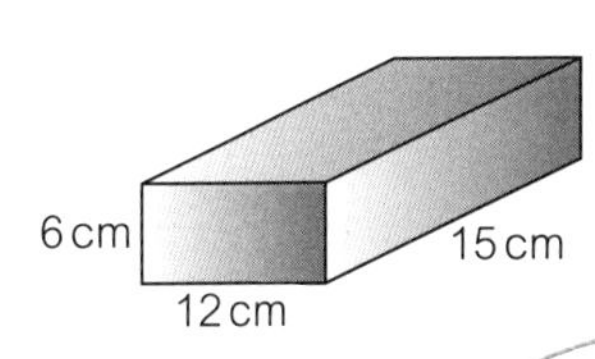

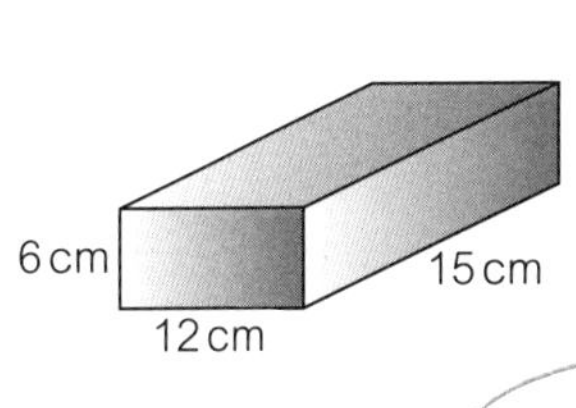

6 STEM / Modelling The approximate time T seconds a pendulum takes to swing back and forth is given by the formula $T = 2\sqrt{l}$ where l m is the length of the pendulum.
Work out the value of T
a when $l = 9$ m
b for a pendulum that has a length of 225 cm.

7 a $a = \sqrt{b^2 + c^2}$

Find the value of a when

i $b = 3$ and $c = 4$

ii $b = 30$ and $c = 40$

iii $b = 7$ and $c = 9$, correct to one decimal place.

b $d = \sqrt{a^2 + b^2 + c^2}$

Find the value of d when

i $a = 1$, $b = 2$ and $c = 2$

ii $a = 2$, $b = 6$ and $c = 9$

iii $a = 3.4$, $b = 2.7$ and $c = 5.1$, correct to three decimal places.

8 Modelling / Reasoning The length L cm of a Dover sole fish can be estimated from its mass m grams using the formula $L = \sqrt[3]{10m}$.

a Estimate the length of a Dover sole with a mass of 100 g.

b Work out the value of L when $m = 20$ g

i correct to the nearest cm

ii correct to two decimal places

iii as accurately as possible.

c Pris says that the most accurate way to write the answer to part **b** is $\sqrt[3]{200}$.

Is she correct? Explain your answer.

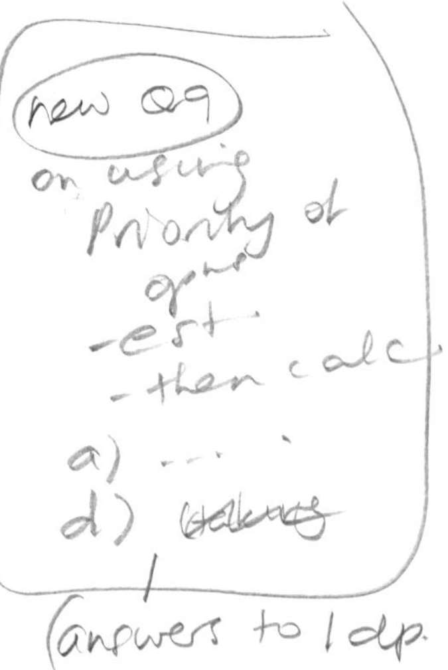

Investigation **Reasoning**

To estimate a multiplication or addition, Sally says, 'It is best to round one number up and the other number down.'

To estimate a division or subtraction, Sally says, 'It is best to round both numbers up or both numbers down.'

For each of these calculations, work out an estimate using Sally's 'rule'. Then work it out another way.

Which estimate is closer to the accurate answer? What do you think of Sally's rules?

1 11.6 × 12.3 **2** 58.1 ÷ 11.5 **3** 71.1 − 52.2

4 2778 + 1217 **5** 9.5×10.85^2 **6** 577 ÷ 171

9 a Estimate the answers to these.

i (429 − 17.3) ÷ (15.1 + 6.7)

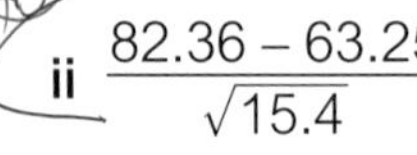

ii $\dfrac{82.36 - 63.25}{\sqrt{15.4}}$

iii $(14.8 - \sqrt[3]{124}) \times 2.1992$

iv $(24.49 + \sqrt{15}) \div 0.09$

b Use a calculator to work out each answer.

Give your answers correct to one decimal place.

10 Real A roll of carpet is 4 m wide. It costs £8.98 per square metre.

You can buy any length of carpet.

a Estimate the cost of carpet required for each of these rooms.

i 3.6 m by 1.2 m

ii 4.65 m by 3.71 m

iii 8.15 m by 6.35 m

b Use a calculator to work out each answer.

How good were your estimates?

Discussion Is it better to overestimate or underestimate a cost?

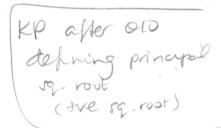

Q10a hint

Think about how many widths of carpet you need for one side of the room.

11 **a** **i** Work out $\left(\frac{2}{3}\right)^2$ as a fraction in its simplest form.

ii Work out $\frac{2^2}{3^2}$ as a fraction in its simplest form.

iii What do you notice?

b **i** Work out $\left(\frac{2}{3}\right)^3$ as a fraction in its simplest form.

ii Work out $\frac{2^3}{3^3}$ as a fraction in its simplest form.

iii What do you notice?

c Reasoning Copy and complete this rule:
To find a power of a fraction, work out ____________

d Work out these as fractions in their simplest form.

i $\left(\frac{4}{5}\right)^3$ **ii** $\left(\frac{3}{4}\right)^3$ **iii** $\left(\frac{7}{2}\right)^2$ **iv** $\left(2\frac{1}{3}\right)^2$

e Discussion Is the square of a fraction bigger or smaller than the original fraction?

> **Q11a i hint**
> Work out $\frac{2}{3} \times \frac{2}{3}$.

> **Q11d iv hint**
> Write $2\frac{1}{3}$ as an improper fraction.

Worked example

Work out $\frac{(4 \times 5)^2}{5 \times 2^2}$

$$\frac{(4 \times 5)^2}{5 \times 2^2} = \frac{4^2 \times 5^2}{5 \times 2^2}$$
$$= \frac{4 \times 4 \times 5 \times 5}{5 \times 2 \times 2}$$
$$= \frac{{}^2\cancel{4} \times {}^2\cancel{4} \times {}^1\cancel{5} \times 5}{{}_1\cancel{2} \times {}_1\cancel{2} \times {}_1\cancel{5}}$$
$$= 2 \times 2 \times 1 \times 5$$
$$= 20$$

Cancel the common factors.
5 × 2 × 2 is the same as 2 × 2 × 5

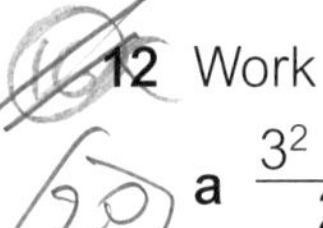

12 Work out

a $\frac{3^2 \times 4^2}{2^2}$ **b** $\frac{(6 \times 2)^2}{3^2}$ **c** $\frac{16 \times 18}{(2 \times 3)^2}$

d $\frac{(3 \times 4)^3}{3^2 \times 4^2}$ **e** $\frac{6^2 \times 2^3}{2^2 \times 3}$ **f** $\frac{(2 \times 5)^3}{5^2 \times 2}$

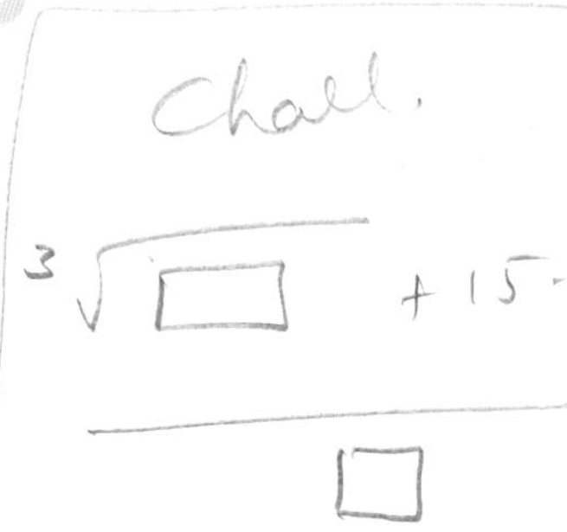

13 **Explore** What is a safe speed for a spacecraft to fire its thrusters when landing on Mars?
Is it easier to explore this question now you have completed the lesson?
What further information do you need to be able to answer this?

14 **Reflect** Antony looks back at Q9a in this lesson. He says, 'For question 9a i, I wanted to divide by a nice number, so first I looked at the calculation in the second bracket. I estimated this to be 20.'
What do you think Antony estimated for the first bracket? Explain.
What do you think of Antony's method? Explain.
Look back at Q9a iv.
What did you do first to estimate this calculation? Why?
Could you have done it a better way? Explain.

Explore

Reflect

1.3 More indices

You will learn to:

- Understand negative and 0 indices
- Use powers of 10 and their prefixes.

CONFIDENCE

Why learn this?
Radioactive decay can be described using negative indices.

Fluency

- Work out

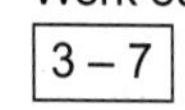

3 – 7 | −2 − −6 | −3 − 5

- What is the reciprocal of these numbers?

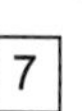
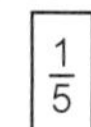

2 | 7 | $\frac{1}{5}$

Explore
How long will it take for 99% of a piece of radioactive krypton to decay?

Exercise 1.3

Warm up

1 Write each calculation as a single power.

a $5^2 \times 5^2$ b $10^3 \times 10^4$ c $2^5 \div 2^2$
d $10^6 \div 10^3$ e $10^5 \div 1000$ f 8×2^2

2 Convert

a 45 m to kilometres b 250 mm to metres.

3 a Copy and complete the sequence.
Write your answers as whole numbers or as decimals or fractions for numbers less than 1.

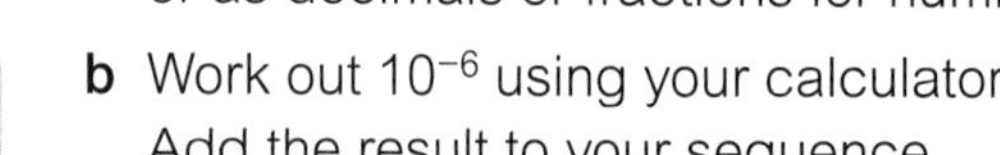

b Work out 10^{-6} using your calculator.
Add the result to your sequence.

10^5 = 100 000
10^4 = 10 000 (÷10)
10^3 = (÷10)
10^2 =
10^1 =
10^0 =
10^{-1} =
10^{-2} =
10^{-3} =
10^{-4} =
10^{-5} =

4 a To write 10^{-2} as a fraction, copy and complete

$10^{-2} = \frac{1}{10^{\square}}$

b Copy and complete these statements.

i $10^{-3} = \frac{1}{10^{\square}}$ ii $10^{-1} = \frac{1}{10^{\square}}$

iii $\frac{1}{10^6} = 10^{\square}$ iv $\frac{1}{10^9} = 10^{\square}$

v The reciprocal of 10^4 is $10^{\square}$.

c Copy and complete the rule: $10^{-n} = \frac{1}{10^{\square}}$

Topic links: Converting units

Subject links: Science (Q10, Q15)

5 Copy and complete the table of prefixes.

Prefix	Letter	Power	Number
tera	T	10^{12}	1 000 000 000 000
giga	G		1 000 000 000
mega	M	10^6	
kilo	k		1000
deci	d	10^{-1}	
centi	c		0.01
milli	m	10^{-3}	
micro	μ		0.000 001
nano	n	10^{-9}	
pico	p		0.000 000 000 001

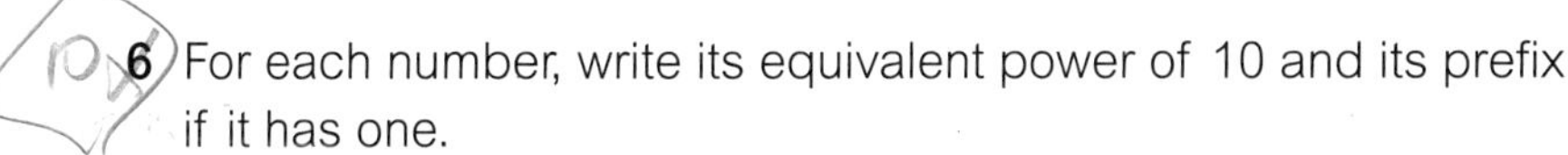

6 For each number, write its equivalent power of 10 and its prefix, if it has one.

a million **b** $\frac{1}{100}$ **c** billion

d $\frac{1}{10}$ **e** $\frac{1}{10\,000}$ **f** trillion

g $\frac{1}{100\,000}$ **h** one billionth **i** $\frac{1}{1000}$

7 Work out these conversions.

a 1 kilometre (km) = □m **b** 1 microsecond (μs) = □s

c 1 megatonne (Mt) = □t **d** 1 picogram (pg) = □g

e 1 terahertz (THz) = □Hz **f** 1 nanometre (nm) = □m

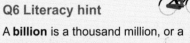

8 How many

a μg in a gram **b** pm in a metre

c d*l* in a litre **d** nanoseconds in a second?

9 Convert

a 5 m to μm **b** 2.5 g to mg

c 4 GW to watts **d** 1.9 s to nanoseconds

e 4.23 g to picograms **f** 5000 μg to grams.

10 STEM A nanorobot that can repair scar tissue is 1 μm wide. How many nanorobots can fit across a scar 2.5 mm wide?

11 Copy and complete the sequence. Write your answers as whole numbers and fractions.

Discussion What do you notice about 10^0 (in Q3) and 2^0?
Use your calculator to work out n^0 for other values of n.
What do you notice?
What can you say about the size of a whole number raised to a negative power?

2^5 = 32) ÷2
2^4 = 16) ÷2
2^3 =
2^2 =
2^1 =
2^0 =
2^{-1} =
2^{-2} =
2^{-3} =
2^{-4} =
2^{-5} =

Key point

Some powers of 10 have a name called a **prefix**.
Each prefix is represented by a letter. For example, mega means 10^6 and is represented by the letter M, as in MW for megawatt.

Q5 Literacy hint

μ, the letter for the prefix micro, is the Greek letter mu.

Q6 Literacy hint

A **billion** is a thousand million, or a 1 followed by 9 zeros.
A **trillion** is a thousand billion, or a 1 followed by 12 zeros.

Q7e Literacy hint

Hertz (Hz) is the unit of frequency. The highest frequency sound a human can hear is about 20 000 Hz.

Q8a hint

From the prefix table,
1 μg = 10^{-6} g = $\frac{1}{1\,000\,000}$ g.

Q9a hint

How many μm are in a metre?

Q10 Strategy hint

Convert both measurements to the same units first.

12 **a** **i** Write 2^{-3} as a fraction.

ii Copy and complete $2^{-3} = \frac{1}{2^{\square}}$

b Copy and complete

i $2^{-4} = \frac{1}{2^{\square}}$ **ii** $2^{-1} = \frac{1}{2^{\square}}$ **iii** $\frac{1}{2^2} = 2^{\square}$

iv $\frac{1}{2^6} = 2^{\square}$ **v** The reciprocal of 2^5 is $2^{\square}$.

c Copy and complete the rule: $2^{-n} = \frac{1}{2^{\square}}$.

d Evaluate

i 3^{-2} **ii** 5^{-3} **iii** 6^{-1} **iv** 8^0

Q12d Literacy hint

Evaluate means 'find the value of'.

13 Write each calculation as a single power.

a $10^5 \times 10^{-2}$ **b** $4^{-5} \times 4^3$

c $2^{-5} \times 2^{-2}$ **d** $10^3 \times 10^{-8}$

e $10^3 \div 10^5$ **f** $2^{-5} \div 2^{-2}$

g $5^{-2} \div 5^3$ **h** $3^3 \div 3^{-4}$

Q13a hint

Add the indices when multiplying powers.

Q13e hint

Subtract the indices when dividing powers.

14 Work out these.
Write each answer as a whole number or a fraction.

a $2^3 \div 2^5$ **b** $4^3 \times 4^{-4}$

c $2^3 \times 2^3 \div 2^7$ **d** $3^5 \div 3^5$

e $1 \div 2^{-3}$ **f** $\frac{3^4 \times 3^2}{3^3}$

g $\frac{1}{2^3 \times 2^2}$ **h** $\frac{4^2 \times 4^6}{4^5}$

Investigation 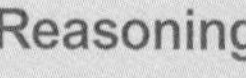 **Reasoning**

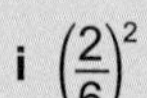

1 **a** Work out

i $\left(\frac{2}{6}\right)^2$ **ii** $\left(\frac{6}{2}\right)^{-2}$ **iii** $\left(\frac{10}{5}\right)^2$ **iv** $\left(\frac{5}{10}\right)^{-2}$

b What do you notice?

2 Repeat part 1 using powers of 3 and −3.

3 Copy and complete the rule:
A negative power of a fraction is the same as ____________________

or

$\left(\frac{a}{b}\right)^{-n} = \left(\frac{\square}{\square}\right)^n$

4 Use your calculator to test the rule with other negative powers of fractions.

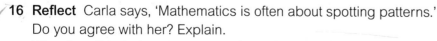

Explore

15 **Explore** How long will it take for 99% of a piece of radioactive krypton to decay?
It is easier to explore this question now you have completed the lesson? What further information do you need to be able to answer this?

Reflect

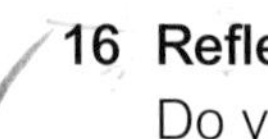

16 **Reflect** Carla says, 'Mathematics is often about spotting patterns.'
Do you agree with her? Explain.
Why does it help to spot patterns in mathematics? Explain.

Q16 hint

Look back at this lesson and the previous lesson. Can you find any questions where you were spotting a pattern? Where else in mathematics have you used pattern spotting?

1.4 STEM: Standard form

You will learn to:
- Write large and small numbers using standard form
- Enter and read standard form numbers on your calculator
- Order numbers written in standard form.

CONFIDENCE

Why learn this?
Standard form is used to write very small quantities used in nanotechnology and very large distances used in astronomy.

Fluency
- Which is bigger: 10^{-5} or 10^{2}?
- What is $\frac{1}{1000}$ as a power of 10?
- What does µm mean?

Explore
Can you see a virus through an optical microscope? What about bacteria?

Exercise 1.4 Telescopes and microscopes

Warm up

1 Write in full
a 10^3 b 10^6 c 10^{-2}

2 Copy and complete
a 2 300 000 = □ million b 8 440 000 = □ million

3 Work out
a 2×10^3 b 6×10^6 c 7.1×10^7 d 3.9×10^9

4 Work out
a 7×10^{-2} b 5×10^{-3} c 3.8×10^{-5} d 7.1×10^{-9}
e 1.2×10^{-4} f 3×10^{-6} g 4×10^{-1} h 1×10^{-9}

Discussion Does multiplying a number by a negative power of 10 make it bigger or smaller?

Key point
Multiplying by a negative power of 10 is the same as dividing by a positive power of 10.
For example, $3 \times 10^{-4} = 3 \times \frac{1}{10^4}$
$= 3 \div 10^{-4} = 3 \div 10\,000 = 0.0003$.

5 **Reasoning**
a i Write $7^3 \times 7^3 \times 7^3$ as a single power. ii Write $7^3 \times 7^3 \times 7^3$ as $(7^3)^{\square}$.
b i Write $3^2 \times 3^2 \times 3^2 \times 3^2 \times 3^2$ as a single power. ii Write $3^2 \times 3^2 \times 3^2 \times 3^2 \times 3^2$ as $(3^2)^{\square}$.
c Use your answers to parts **a** and **b** to complete the rule: $(p^a)^b = p^{\square\square}$.

6 a Write each of these as a single power.
i $(11^2)^6$ ii $(10^3)^8$ iii $(2^4)^7$ iv $(6^7)^4$
b Write 125^4 as a power of 5.

Key point
A number written in **standard form** is a number between 1 and 10 multiplied by 10 to a power.
For example, 3.5×10^5 is written in standard form because 3.5 is between 1 and 10.
35×10^5 is *not* in standard form because 35 does not lie between 1 and 10.

7 Using algebra, standard form is $A \times 10^n$ where $1 \leqslant A < 10$ and n is an integer. Which of these numbers are written in standard form?
A 9.3×10^5 B 25×10^7 C 6×10^{-5}
D 0.83×10^{-7} E 10×10^6 F 7.2 million

Worked example

Write each number using standard form.

a 230 000

230 000 = 2.3×10^5

> 2.3 lies between 1 and 10.
> Multiply by the power of 10 needed to give the original number.
> 2 3 0 0 0 0

b 0.000 453

0.000 453 = 4.53×10^{-4}

> 4.53 lies between 1 and 10.
> Multiply by the power of 10 needed to give the original number.
> 0 · 0 0 0 4 5 3

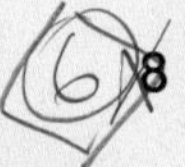

8 Write each number using standard form.

a 4200 **b** 9 000 000 **c** 27

d 0.0064 = $6.4 \times 10^{\square}$ **e** 0.000 000 7 **f** 0.3

g 0.000 000 000 099

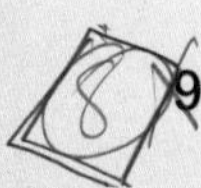

9 STEM Write each quantity using standard form.

a Quasar SDSS_1044_0125 is one of the furthest known objects in space at a distance of 240 000 000 000 000 000 000 000 000 m from Earth.

b One of the smallest known particles is the neutron of an atom, with an estimated diameter of 0.000 000 000 000 0018 m.

c The temperature of the Sun at its core is 15 million °C.

d Botulin is the main ingredient of Botox. It is so poisonous that just 0.000 000 075 g is enough to kill a person.

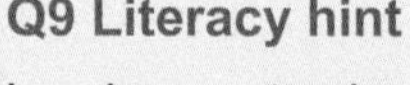

Q9 Literacy hint

In science, standard form is sometimes called scientific notation.

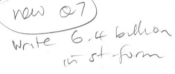

10 STEM Write each answer

i as an ordinary number ii using standard form.

a The mass of the Hubble space telescope is 11 000 kg. Convert this to grams.

b The distance of the Sun from the Earth is 149 600 000 000 m. Convert this to kilometres.

c The diameter of the red supergiant star Betelgeuse is 1350 Gm. Convert this to metres.

d The diameter of a human hair is 25 μm. Convert this to metres.

e A granule of quartz has a mass of 1.4 mg. Convert this to grams.

11 STEM / Reasoning

a The maximum distance of Pluto from Earth is 7.38×10^{12} m.

i Is the number 7.38×10^{12} written using standard form?

ii Write 7.38×10^{12} as an ordinary number.

iii Enter the number into your calculator and press the = key. Compare your calculator display with the standard form number. Explain how your calculator displays a number in standard form.

b Gold leaf is approximately 1.25×10^{-7} m thick.

i Write 1.25×10^{-7} m as an ordinary number.

ii Enter the number into your calculator and press the = key. Compare your calculator display with the standard form number.

12 STEM The distance of each space object from Earth is shown here. Write the objects in order, from closest to furthest from Earth.

Mercury (at its closest) 7.7×10^{10} m

Alpha Centauri 4.1×10^{16} m

Horsehead nebula 1.5×10^{19} m

GPS satellite 2×10^7 m

Pole star 4×10^{18} m

Pisces galaxy 4×10^{22} m

Discussion Vega is 2.39×10^{17} m from Earth and Pollux is 3.2×10^{17} m from Earth. Which is closer?

Subject links: Science (Q9, Q10, Q11, Q12, Q13, Q14, Q15)

Topic links: Substitution

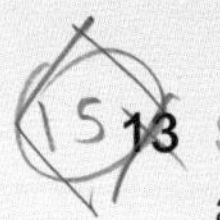

STEM

13 STEM An optical microscope can be used to see objects as small as 2×10^{-7} m.

a Which of these objects can be seen with it?

Discussion The smallest transistor in a computer chip is 2.6×10^{-7} m. Can this be seen using the microscope?

b Write the objects in order of size, from smallest to largest.

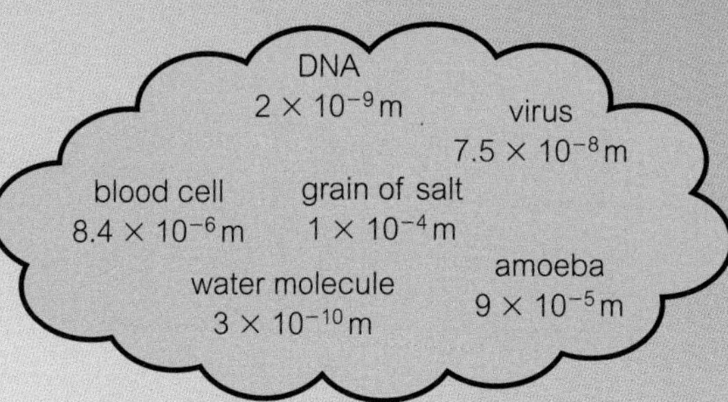

DNA
2 × 10⁻⁹ m
virus
7.5 × 10⁻⁸ m
blood cell
8.4 × 10⁻⁶ m
grain of salt
1 × 10⁻⁴ m
amoeba
9 × 10⁻⁵ m
water molecule
3 × 10⁻¹⁰ m

14 STEM A 3D electron microscope magnifies 100 000 times. The diameter of a molecule of insulin appears to be 0.5 mm when viewed using the microscope. Work out the actual diameter. Give your answer in metres using standard form.

Investigation — **Modelling / STEM**

The number of intelligent civilisations, N, in the Milky Way galaxy has been estimated using Drake's equation:

$$N = R \times F \times L \times S \times I \times C \times T$$

Scientists disagree about the values to substitute into the formula. The table shows the ranges of values they have suggested.

R	F	L	S	I	C	T
1 to 7	0.4 to 1	0.2	10^{-11} to 0.13	10^{-9} to 1	0.1 to 0.2	10^9 to 10^{11}

1 Work out the largest possible value of N.

2 a Work out the smallest possible value of N.

b Does this equation predict that there are other intelligent civilisations in the Milky Way?

3 The Milky Way is just one of 100 billion galaxies in space. Does Drake's equation suggest there are other intelligent civilisations in space?

Part 3 hint
A billion is 10^9.

Discussion Do you think Drake's equation is a useful model for predicting intelligent life in the Milky Way? Explain your answer.

15 **Explore** Can you see a virus through an optical microscope?
What about bacteria?
Is it easier to explore this question now you have completed the lesson?
What further information do you need to be able to answer this?

16 **Reflect** Sophie and Jamie discuss how they used the worked example in this lesson.
Sophie says, 'I read the whole worked example before starting Q8. I read each question and its answer. If I wasn't sure how to get the answer, then I read the note box.'
Jamie says, 'I went straight to Q8. Then, I looked back at the questions, answers and note boxes in the worked example to help me when I needed to.'
Write a sentence explaining how you used the worked example in this lesson. How did it help you? Compare with other people in your class.

Explore

Reflect

1 Check up

Log how you did on your Student Progression Chart.

Indices and powers of 10

1 Write each calculation as a power of a single number.

a $5^3 \times 5^2$ b $3^{10} \div 3^7$ c $7^4 \times 7 \times 7^3$

d $4^4 \times 4^3 \div 4^2$ e 8×2^7 f 9×3^7

2 Convert

a 3.8 GW to watts

b 7 milligrams to grams.

3 Write each calculation as a single power.

a $10^{-3} \times 10^{-2}$ b $2^{10} \div 2^{-5}$ c $3^{-7} \div 3^{-9}$

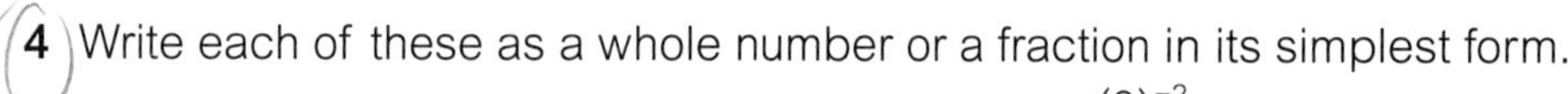

4 Write each of these as a whole number or a fraction in its simplest form.

a 3^{-2} b 2^0 c $\left(\frac{3}{4}\right)^{-2}$

Powers and roots

5 Which two calculations give the same answer?

A $3^2 \times 4^2$ B $3^2 \times 4$ C $(3 \times 4)^2$ D 3×4^2

6 Insert brackets in the calculation to give the answer 35.

$5 + 3 \times 1 + 3^2$

7 Work out $\sqrt[3]{1000} - \sqrt[3]{-8}$.

8 Work out

a $(-2)^3$ b $10 \times 3^2 - (-3)^2$

9 Work these out as whole numbers or fractions in their simplest form.

a $\left(\frac{3}{5}\right)^2$ b $\frac{2^3 \times 6^2}{2}$ c $\frac{(2 \times 5)^2}{8 \times 50}$

10 Work out a good estimate for each calculation.

a $(9.6 - 15.3) \times (8.6 + 9.8)$

b $(56.4 + \sqrt[3]{30}) \div (7.8 \times 4.12)$

c $(\sqrt{69} - 3.5) \times 3.4$

Standard form

11 Write each number as an ordinary number.

a 4.5×10^4 b 1.2×10^{-3}

12 Which of these numbers is written using standard form?

A 10×10^4 B 5.2×10^{-4} C -2.5×10^2 D 43×10^{-3}

13 Write each number using standard form.

a 750 000 b 0.000 000 02 c 8.3 billion

14 It has been estimated that the Arctic could hold 14 000 000 000 000 litres of oil. Write this

a using a suitable prefix **b** using standard form.

15 The recommended adult daily intake for vitamin B12 is 2.4×10^{-6} g and for iodine is 1.5×10^{-4} g.
Which does an adult need most of – B12 or iodine?

16 How sure are you of your answers? Were you mostly

Just guessing **Feeling doubtful** **Confident**

What next? Use your results to decide whether to strengthen or extend your learning.

Reflect

Challenge

17 Keith writes the numbers 1 to 16 on cards and begins to lay them out.

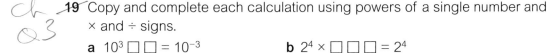

Two cards next to each other always add up to make a square number.
For example, 8 + 1 = 9.
Lay out the rest of the cards so that this rule continues.

18 a Copy and complete the pattern.

$4 + 2^2 = \square$

$4 + 2^2 + 2^3 = \square$

$4 + 2^2 + 2^3 + 2^4 = \square$

b What do you notice about the answers?

c Write down the answer to

i $4 + 2^2 + 2^3 + 2^4 + 2^5$ **ii** $2 + 2^2 + 2^3 + 2^4 + 2^5$

d Write an algebraic expression that gives the sum of the first n powers of 2.

19 Copy and complete each calculation using powers of a single number and × and ÷ signs.

a $10^3 \square\square = 10^{-3}$ **b** $2^4 \times \square\square\square = 2^4$

c $5^8 \square\square\square\square\square\square = 5^{-8}$ **d** $10^5 \square 10^6 \square\square\square 10^{-5} \square\square \div \square = 10^5$

20 These three factor trees for the number 120 start in different ways.

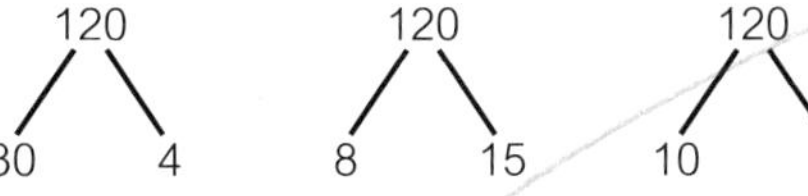

a i Copy and complete the factor trees.

ii Use each factor tree to write 120 as the product of its prime factors using powers.

iii What do you notice about your three answers to part **ii**?

iv Does it matter which starting numbers you use for a factor tree?

b Test your answer to part **a iv** using other numbers.

1 Strengthen

You will:
- Strengthen your understanding with practice.

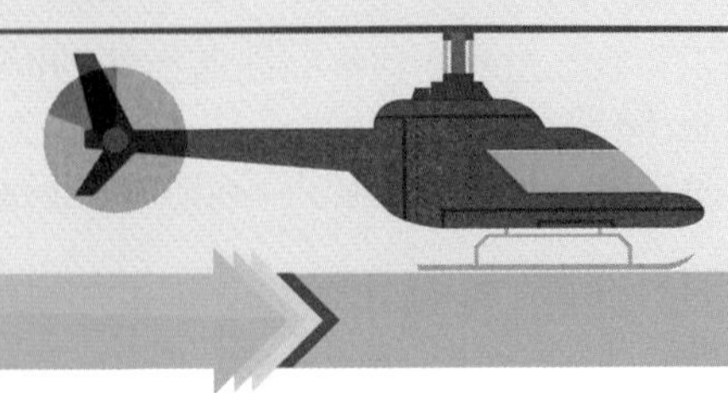

Indices and powers of 10

1 Write each product as a single power.
 a $3^2 \times 3^4 = 3^{\square + \square} = 3^{\square}$
 b $5^2 \times 5^3 = 5^{2 \square 3}$
 c $2^3 \times 2^3$
 d $7^3 \times 7$
 e $5^2 \times 5^3 \times 5^4 = 5^{\square + \square + \square} = 5^{\square}$
 f $10^4 \times 10 \times 10^3$

2 Write each division as a single power.
 a $6^5 \div 6^2 = 6^{\square - \square} = 6^{\square}$
 b $5^7 \div 5^5 = 5^{7 \square 5}$
 c $2^7 \div 2^3$
 d $7^3 \div 7$

3 a To work out $2^4 \times 2^3$, Asifa said, 'Four times three is twelve' and wrote '2^{12}'. Explain why she is wrong.
 b To work out $10^8 \div 10^2$, Jeremy said, 'Eight divided by two is four' and wrote '10^4'. Explain why he is wrong.

4 Write each product as a single power. Work from left to right.
 a $2^4 \times 2^3 \div 2^5 = 2^{\square} \div 2^5 = 2^{\square - \square} = 2^{\square}$
 b $10^7 \times 10^2 \div 10^4 = 10^{\square} \div 10^4 = 10^{\square - \square} = 10^{\square}$
 c $8^5 \div 8^2 \times 8^3 = 8^{\square} \times 8^3$
 d $4^5 \div 4 \times 4^2$
 e $3^5 \div 3^2 \div 3^2$

Q1a hint

$3^2 \times 3^4 = \underbrace{3 \times 3}_{2} \times \underbrace{3 \times 3 \times 3 \times 3}_{4}$

How many 3s are multiplied together?

Q1d hint

Write 7 as the power 7^1.

Q2a hint

$6^5 \div 6^2 = \frac{6^5}{6^2} = \frac{\overbrace{\cancel{6} \times \cancel{6} \times 6 \times 6 \times 6}^{5}}{\underbrace{\cancel{6} \times \cancel{6}}_{2}}$

How many 6s are left after cancelling two of them?

Q4a hint

Work out $2^4 \times 2^3$ first.

Q4c hint

Work out $8^5 \div 8^2$ first.

Key point

← To convert bigger units to smaller units, multiply

pm ⇄ nm ⇄ µm ⇄ mm ⇄ m ⇄ km ⇄ Mm ⇄ Gm ⇄ Tm

(×1000 for each step right to left; ÷1000 for each step left to right)

To convert smaller units to bigger units, divide →

5 Convert the units.
 a 0.25 Tm to km b 0.034 m to mm c 0.000 000 8 mm to nm

6 Convert the units.
 a 4500 mm to m b 80 000 nm to mm c 3500 km to Mm

Q5 Strategy hint
Multiply to convert bigger units to smaller units.

Q6 Strategy hint
Divide to convert smaller units to bigger units. How many times do you have to divide by 1000?

Topic links: Converting units

Subject links: Science (Indices and powers of 10, Q8b, Standard form Q2, Q7), Computing (Indices and powers of 10, Q8a)

7 Convert the units.

a 0.46 GHz to MHz
b 530 µg to mg
c 0.000 007 MW to W
d 270 000 l to ml

Q7 hint
Use the key point to decide whether to multiply or divide.

8 STEM **a** Andrea's computer processor has a speed of 4.2 MHz. Convert this speed to kHz.

b STEM The wavelength of red light is 680 nm. Convert this to µm.

9 **a** Copy and complete $4^2 \div 4^2 = \frac{4^2}{4^2} = \frac{\square}{\square} = \square$

b Copy and complete $4^2 \div 4^2 = 4^{\square - \square} = 4^{\square}$

c Use your answers to parts **a** and **b** to find the value of 4^0.

d **i** Repeat parts **a** and **b** for $5^2 \div 5^2$.

ii What is the value of 5^0?

e Copy and complete the rule:
When you write a number to the power 0, the answer is _______.

10 **a** **i** Copy and complete $4^3 \div 4^5 = 4^{\square}$

Q10a i hint
Which rule can you use?

ii Copy and complete

$$4^3 \div 4^5 = \frac{4^3}{4^5} = \frac{\not{4} \times \not{4} \times \not{4}}{\not{4} \times \not{4} \times \not{4} \times 4 \times 4} = \frac{1}{4^{\square}}$$

iii Use your answers to copy and complete $4^{-2} = \frac{1}{4^{\square}}$

b **i** Copy and complete $10^4 \div 10^7 = 10^{\square}$

ii Copy and complete

$$10^4 \div 10^7 = \frac{10^4}{10^7} = \frac{10 \times 10 \times 10 \times 10}{10 \times 10 \times 10 \times 10 \times 10 \times 10 \times 10} = \frac{1}{10^{\square}}$$

iii Use your answers to copy and complete $10^{-3} = \frac{1}{10^{\square}}$

c Copy and complete

i $2^{-3} = \frac{1}{2^{\square}}$
ii $10^{-4} = \frac{1}{10^{\square}}$
iii $\frac{1}{10^2} = 10^{\square}$
iv $\frac{1}{10} = 10^{\square}$

Q10c iv hint
$10 = 10^{\square}$

11 Reasoning Four students each work out 4^{-3} as shown.

Paul $4^{-3} = 4 \times -3 = \ldots$
Terri $4^{-3} = 4 - 3 = \ldots$
Sandhu $4^{-3} = \frac{1}{4^3} = \ldots$
Marcia $4^{-3} = -4^3 = \ldots$

Who is correct?

Q12c hint
$2 = 2^{\square}$

12 Write each of these as a single power.

a $10^3 \times 10^{-1} = 10^{3 + -1} = 10^{\square}$
b $10^{-2} \times 10^{-4} = 10^{\square + \square} = 10^{\square}$
c 2×2^{-4}
d $10^4 \div 10^7 = 10^{\square - \square} = 10^{\square}$
e $10^{-4} \div 10^2$
f $\frac{10^2}{10^6}$

Q12f hint
Work out $10^2 \div 10^6$.

13 Write each of these as a single power. Work from left to right.

a $10^3 \times 10^{-5} \times 10^{-1}$
b $10^{-4} \times 10^2 \div 10^{-3}$
c $10^2 \div 10^6 \times 10^{-3}$
d $10^{-3} \div 10^{-5} \times 10^2$

Q13a hint
Work out $10^3 \times 10^{-5}$ first.

14 **a** Write 8 as a power of 2.

b Use your answer to write each product as a single power of 2.

i $8 \times 2^5 = 2^{\square} \times 2^5$

ii $2^6 \times 8$

iii 8×8

Q14a hint
$8 = 2 \times 2 \times \ldots$ How many 2s are multiplied together to make 8?

Powers and roots

1 Work out
a $(2 \times 3)^2$
b $(5 \times 4)^2$
c $(4 \times 10)^2$

Q1a hint
Work out the calculation inside the brackets first.

2 Work out these. Calculate the inside brackets first.
a $[10 - (5 - 3)] = [10 - \square] = \square$
b $[10 - (5 - 3)]^2 = \square^2 = \square$
c $[(5 + 9) \div 2]^2 = [\square \div 2]^2 = \square^2 = \square$
d $[2 \times (8 - 3)]^2$

Q2 Strategy hint
Write out the priority of operations to help you with Q2 to Q5.

Q2b hint
Use your answer to part **a**.

3 Use the priority of operations to work out these.
a $[4 \times (2 + 3)]^2$
b $(2 \times 5 + 1)^2$

4 **Reasoning** **a** Use the x^2 key of your calculator to work out -4^2 and $(-4)^2$.
b Explain why you get two different answers.
c Use your answers to work out
i $20 + (-4)^2$ **ii** $20 - -4^2$
iii $(-4)^2 - 4^2$ **iv** $-4^2 - (-4)^2$
v $10 - (-3)^2$ **vi** $15 - 2^2$
vii $(-5)^2 - 3^2$ **viii** $-5^2 - (-3)^2$

5 **a** Sally estimates $\frac{12.5}{4.2} + 3.9$ as $\frac{12}{4} + 4 = 3 + 4 = 7$.
Why did she round 12.5 down and not up?
b Estimate
i $\frac{18.3}{6.8} - 1.5$ **ii** $\sqrt{78} + 30.4$ **iii** $\sqrt{11.3 + 3.4}$

Q5b i hint
Round the numerator and denominator up or down to give an easy division.

Standard form

1 Work out
a 2.3×10^3
b 1.6×10^2
c 3.9×10^4
d 7.3×10^9

Q1a hint
2 . 3 → 2 3 0 0 . $\times 10^3$ means multiply by 10 three times.

2 **STEM** The temperature of the Sun at its core is 1.5×10^7 °C.
Write this as an ordinary number.

3 Work out
a 1.7×10^{-3}
b 7.2×10^{-2}
c 8×10^{-6}
d 9.4×10^{-8}

Q3a hint
1 . 7 → 0 . 0 0 1 7 $\times 10^{-3}$ means $\div 10^3$, so divide by 10 three times.

4 A number written using standard form looks like this. $A \times 10^n$
(A: number between 1 and 10; ×: times sign; 10^n: power of 10)
Write each number using standard form.
a $5300 = 5.3 \times 10^{\square}$
b 49 000
c 63 000 000
d 700 000
e 56 000 000 000

Q4a hint
5.3 lies between 1 and 10.
5 . 3 → 5 3 0 0 . Multiply by how many 10s to get 5300?

5 Write each number using standard form.

a $0.0029 = 2.9 \times 10^{\square}$ b 0.057

c 0.000063 d 0.000000007

e 0.00000000000012

> **Q5a hint**
>
> 2.9 lies between 1 and 10.
>
> 2 · 9
> 0 · 0 0 2 9 Divide by how many 10s to get 0.0029?.

6 Which one of these numbers is written using standard form?

A 54×10^4 B 5.4×10^{-4} C 0.54×10^{-4} D $5.4 \div 10^4$

7 STEM Write each quantity using standard form.

a The circumference of the Earth at the equator is approximately 40000000 m.

b A molecule of sugar has a diameter of 0.0000000014 m.

8 Write each of these sets of standard form numbers in order, from smallest to largest.

a 2.7×10^{-4} 7.3×10^2 4.3×10^7 9×10^{-6}

b 7.3×10^6 3.5×10^7 5×10^7 1.2×10^6

> **Q8 hint**
>
> Look at the powers of 10 first.

Enrichment

1 Problem-solving

a Follow these steps to find out how thick a page of this textbook is.

i Use a ruler to measure the thickness of the book in mm.

ii Work out the number of sheets of paper.

iii Use your calculator to divide the thickness by the number of sheets.

iv Round your answer to two decimal places.

v Write your answer in mm using standard form.

vi Convert your answer to part **v** to μm.

b Repeat the question for different books or glossy magazines. What can you say about the thickness of the paper used?

2 In spreadsheets, these symbols are used to enter calculations.

/ instead of ÷

* instead of ×

10^2 instead of 10^2

SQRT (16) instead of $\sqrt{16}$

Write these calculations using spreadsheet notation.

a $5 \times 2 + 3^2$ b $(5 - 2)^3$ c $\sqrt{4 + 12}$

d $20 \div 2^2$ e $\frac{4^2}{\sqrt{16}}$ f $\frac{3^2}{2 \times 9}$

> **Q2c hint**
>
> Use brackets.

3 **Reflect** Luke says, 'Working with indices, powers and roots is all about adding, subtracting, multiplying and dividing.'

Look back at the questions you answered in these Strengthen lessons. Describe when you had to

- add
- subtract
- multiply
- divide.

Do you agree with Luke's statement?

Give some examples to explain why.

Reflect

1 Extend

You will:
- Extend your understanding with problem-solving.

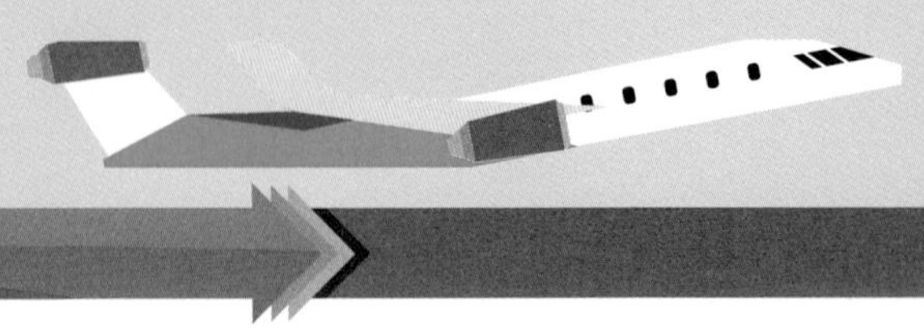

1 Reasoning **a** Work out

i $(-2)^4$ **ii** $(-2)^5$ **iii** $(-2)^6$ **iv** $(-2)^7$

b **i** What do you notice about the signs of the answers?

ii Write a rule that gives the sign of a power of a negative number.

c Test that your rule works for other negative numbers and powers.

d Does the rule work for negative indices?

2 **a** How many

i m^2 are in a km^2 **ii** m^3 are in a km^3?

b Convert

i 500 000 m^2 to km^2 **ii** 0.027 km^2 to m^2

iii 4.8 km^3 to m^3 **iv** 400 million m^3 to km^3

c

1 yard = 0.9144 m
1 acre = 4840 square yards
1 square mile = 640 acres

Convert

i 1 square yard to m^2 **ii** 1 acre to m^2

iii 1 square mile to m^2 **iv** 1 square mile to km^2

Q2 hint

1 km^2 | 1000 m | 1000 m

3 Real / Problem-solving The Eiffel Tower is 324 m tall.

a The height was halved repeatedly to make a model around 30 cm tall. What power of 2 was the height divided by?

b A computer-controlled laser was used to engrave the Eiffel Tower onto the head of a pin. The laser was programmed to make an engraving 100 times smaller than the model. How tall was the engraving?

c How many times taller is the real Eiffel Tower than the engraving? Write your answer using standard form.

4 Reasoning Insert brackets so that each calculation gives the target number. If necessary, use square brackets for outer brackets.

a $3 \times 2 + 3^2$ Target 75

b $10 - 5 - 3^2$ Target 64

c $2 \times 6 - 2^2 - 2$ Target 28

d $2\sqrt{81} - \sqrt{25}$ Target 8

(SE:) (ensure it goes beyond content in lesson 1.1)

5 Problem-solving / Reasoning Some 56 cm by 27.5 cm rectangular stone slabs are used to cover a rectangular courtyard measuring 12 m by 18 m. Find the best way to estimate the number of slabs. State whether your answer is an overestimate or an underestimate.

Q5 Strategy hint
Make some sketches. Why is your way the best?

Topic links: Substitution, Ratio, Units, Scale factors, Percentages

Subject links: Science (Q11, Q17, Q24), Geography (Q25)

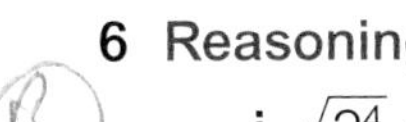

6 Reasoning a Work out

i $\sqrt{2^4}$ and 2^2 ii $\sqrt{2^6}$ and 2^3 iii $\sqrt{2^8}$ and 2^4

b i What do you notice?

ii Write a rule for finding the square root of an even power.

iii Test that your rule works for even powers of other numbers.

7 The diagram shows the floor plan of a building made using three squares. Rooms A and B each have an area of $50\,\text{m}^2$. Room C has an area of $120\,\text{m}^2$. Which one of the following expressions gives the length of the building?

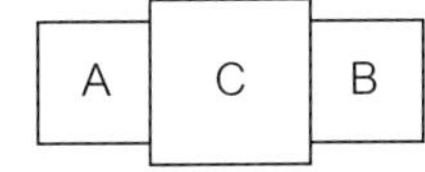

A $\sqrt{2 \times 50 + 120}$

B $2 \times \sqrt{50 + 120}$

C $2 \times \sqrt{50} + \sqrt{120}$

D $\sqrt{2 \times 50} + \sqrt{120}$

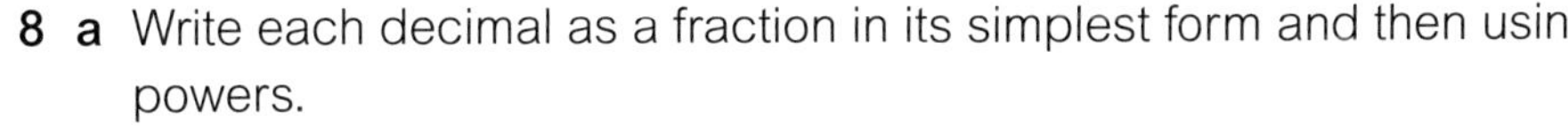

8 a Write each decimal as a fraction in its simplest form and then using powers.

i 0.25

ii 0.125

iii 0.015625

b Use your answer to part **a iii** to write 2^{-5} as a decimal.

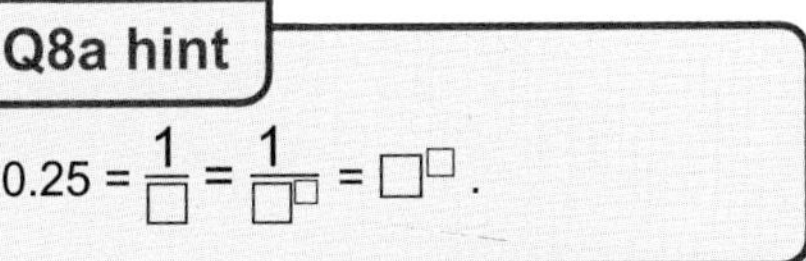

Q8a hint

$0.25 = \frac{1}{\square} = \frac{1}{\square^{\square}} = \square^{\square}$.

9 a Problem-solving / Finance A computer that cost £613.50 new was sold on an internet marketplace at a loss of 39%. Estimate the sale price.

b An earth digger removed 117 000 kg of earth using 25 buckets. The operator had a break after removing 13 buckets of earth. Estimate the weight of earth she removed before her break.

c A square anti-slavery memorial had an area of $246\,000\,\text{m}^2$ and was surrounded by a chain. The chain was divided equally between 18 different countries to make smaller square memorials. Estimate the side length of a small square memorial.

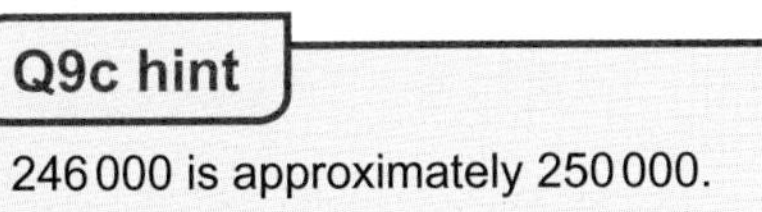

Q9c hint

246 000 is approximately 250 000.

10 Modelling An estimate for the ideal number of ornaments on a Christmas tree is given by the formula $N = \frac{\sqrt{17}}{20} \times h$, where h is the height of the tree in centimetres.

a Estimate the ideal number of ornaments for a tree of height 2.6 m.

b Is your answer an underestimate or an overestimate?

11 STEM / Modelling A pile driver is a machine that repeatedly drops a heavy ram to drive heavy metal beams into the ground to support buildings.

This formula gives the load L that a pile can support when it is made from a 3000 lb ram dropped from 8.5 feet.

$$L = 51.52 \times \frac{3000 \times \sqrt[3]{8.5}}{4}$$

Estimate L.

12 Reasoning a i Work out $(2 \times 5)^{-2}$ as a fraction.

ii Work out $2^{-2} \times 5^{-2}$ as a fraction.

iii What do you notice?

b i Work out $(2 \times 5)^{-3}$

ii Work out $2^{-3} \times 5^{-3}$

iii What do you notice?

c i Write a rule for calculating a negative power of a product.

ii Use a calculator to test if the rule works for other negative powers of products.

13 Write these quantities using an appropriate prefix.

a 8.3×10^{6} m
b 5.2×10^{-3} g
c 6×10^{12} J
d 9.44×10^{-6} A

14 An imaginary circle around the Earth that passes through the North and South Poles is called a great circle and is approximately 4×10^{7} m long.

a One of the great circles passes over land and sea in the ratio 11 : 20. How many metres of the circle are over land?

b 15% of another great circle passes over land. How many metres of this circle are over land?

Q14a hint

Write the standard form number as an ordinary number.

15 Write each of these as a simplified product of powers.

a $6^{4} \times 2^{3} \times 3^{2}$
b $15^{3} \times 3^{2} \times 5^{4}$
c $12^{2} \times 2^{4} \times 3^{3}$
d $6^{-2} \times 3^{4}$

Q15a i hint

$6^{4} = (2 \times 3)^{4}$

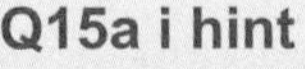

16 Solve the equation $3p^{5} \times 2p^{-3} = 150$.

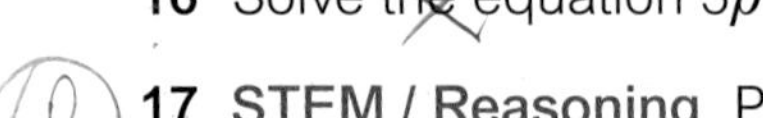

17 STEM / Reasoning People who practise homeopathy claim that very tiny amounts of a substance can treat illness.

a One drop of the substance is mixed with 9 drops of water to make a Potency 1 remedy. What fraction of the Potency 1 remedy is the substance? Write your answer as a power of 10.

b To make a Potency 2 remedy, one drop of Potency 1 remedy is mixed with 9 drops of water. What fraction of the Potency 2 remedy is the substance? Write your answer as a power of 10.

c What fraction of these remedies is the substance? Write each answer as a power of 10.

i Potency 5 **ii** Potency 10 **iii** Potency 100

d People who practise homeopathy claim that the more times a remedy is diluted, the more effective it becomes. There are about 1.7×10^{22} molecules in 10 drops of a remedy. Is it likely that a Potency 100 remedy contains any molecules of the original substance? Explain your answer.

18 Here are some incorrect answers given by students when asked to write numbers in standard form. Rewrite each answer correctly.

a 55×10^{11}

b 0.732×10^{8}

c 102×10^{-9}

d 0.045×10^{-15}

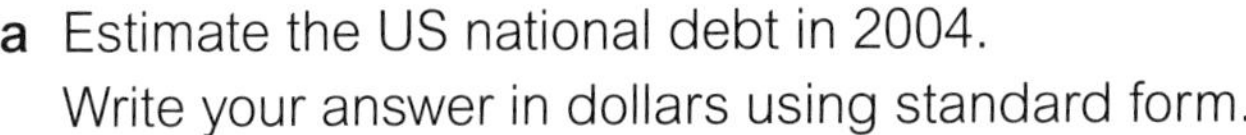

19 **Finance / Modelling** The graph shows the national debt of the USA between 2000 and 2010.

a Estimate the US national debt in 2004.
Write your answer in dollars using standard form.

b Work out the increase in the US national debt between 2000 and 2010.
Give your answer as an ordinary number.

c Estimate the US national debt in 2009.
Give your answer as a number of millions of dollars.

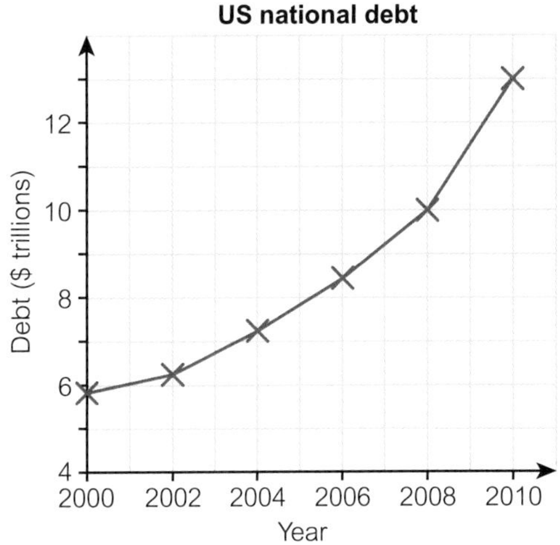

20 **Problem-solving / Modelling**

a A mouse runs 1 m every second.
How long does it take to complete a 100 m race?

b A hare starts the race at the same time as the mouse.
It takes 10 seconds to run half the distance.
It then takes another 10 seconds to run half the remaining distance. And so on. How far does the hare run in

i 20 seconds **ii** 30 seconds?

c Estimate how long it takes for the mouse to overtake the hare.

d Write an expression for the distance the hare runs in the last 10 seconds. Your expression must involve a negative power of 2.

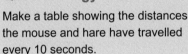

Q20c Strategy hint
Make a table showing the distances the mouse and hare have travelled every 10 seconds.

21 Write these as a single power of the smallest possible integer.

a $(7^3)^{33}$ **b** $[(13^5)^3]^4$ **c** $10\,000^{12}$ **d** $(27^6)^5$

22 Write these numbers using standard form.

a 7.2 million **b** 295 thousand **c** 0.62 million
d 17 millionths **e** 32 thousandths **f** 350 billion
g 1.9 trillion **h** 24 billionths **i** 32 trillionths

Q22c hint
Watch out! $0.62 \times 10^{\square}$ is not in standard form.

23 **a** The observable universe contains about 10 billion trillion stars arranged in about 100 billion galaxies.
How many stars are there in a galaxy? Write your answer using standard form.

b The volume of a water molecule is approximately 3×10^{-26} litres.
Work out the volume of a trillion trillion water molecules.

Q23a hint
A billion is 1000 million.
A trillion is 1000 billion.

24 **STEM / Modelling** The distance of Jupiter from Earth is approximately 9.3×10^8 km.
Use the formula time $= \frac{\text{distance}}{\text{speed}}$ to estimate the time it would take a rocket travelling at 10^3 km/h to reach Jupiter.

25 **Reflect** Imagine you are writing a maths textbook.
Write a definition of

- a power
- a root.

Q25 hint
Make sure your definitions explain all kinds of powers (positive, negative, 0 and powers of fractions), and all kinds of roots (square root, cube root etc.).

Reflect

1 Unit test

Log how you did on your Student Progression Chart.

1 Write each calculation as a power of a single number.

a $10^3 \times 10^4$ **b** $4^{10} \div 4^8$

2 Convert

a 4.3 m to mm **b** 5.4 μs to s **c** 3.16 GW to W

3 Six square wooden panels were used to make a wooden packing case with volume $8\,m^3$.
Work out the area of each square panel.

4 Write each calculation as a single power.

a $2^5 \times 2 \div 2^2$ **b** 9×3^4

5 Work out $3^0 - 2^0$

6 Which one of these calculations gives the answer 144?

A $4 \times (1 + 2)^2$
B $4 \times 1 + 2^2$
C $[4 \times (1 + 2)]^2$
D $(4 \times 1 + 2)^2$

7 Work out $5^2 - (-2)^2$

8 Work out a good estimate for each calculation.

a 3.6×5.7 **b** $7.4 \div \sqrt{14}$

9 A can of paint covers $48\,m^2$.
Jon wants to paint an area of $244\,m^2$. He needs to estimate the calculation $\frac{244}{48}$ to find the number of cans of paint to buy.

a Which of these two estimates gives the closer answer: $\frac{250}{50}$ or $\frac{240}{50}$? Explain why.

b Jon wants to make sure he overestimates the number of cans to buy. Work out an overestimate.

10 A power station can produce 3.2 gigawatts (GW) of power.

a How many watts is this?

b How many kilowatts (kW) is this?

11 a What is a nanometre (nm)?

b A night vision device picks up infrared radiation with a wavelength of 1200 nm. Convert 1200 nm to μm.

12 Write each of these as a single power.

a $5^{-2} \times 5^{-1}$ **b** $3^8 \div 3^{-4}$

13 Write each of these as an ordinary number.

a 2.7×10^5 **b** 6×10^{-4}

14 Work out

a $\left(\frac{12}{3}\right)^2$ b $\frac{2^2 \times 2^2}{2}$ c $\frac{18 \times 4}{(2 \times 3)^2}$

15 Write $\left(\frac{2}{3}\right)^{-2}$ as a fraction in its simplest form.

16 The distance of the Sun from Earth is approximately 150 000 000 000 m.
Write this distance
a using a suitable prefix b using standard form.

17 Write $(5^7)^6$ as a single power.

18 Write each number using standard form.
a 0.000 000 047 b 12 billion

19 A protein has a width of 5.3×10^{-8} m and a virus has a width of 2.5×10^{-7} m.
Which is bigger?

Challenge

20 **Modelling** A 5 cm cube is removed from a 10 cm plastic cube.

a Work out the volume of the remaining shape.

b Can you mould the remaining volume into

i a cube with integer sides

ii a cuboid with integer sides?

Show your working.

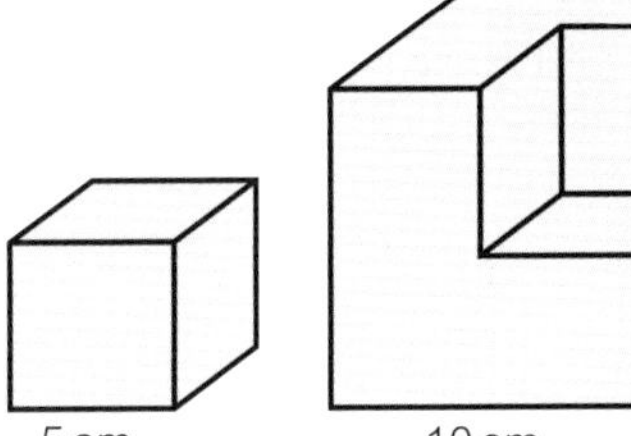

Q20 hint
An integer is a whole number.

21 What is the smallest size of square table top you could cover exactly using a combination of 2 cm and 3 cm square mosaic tiles?

22 a Choose any word on this page, for example the word 'page'.
Use the positions of the letters in the alphabet to make a number.

a	b	c	d	e	f	g	h	i	j	k	l	m	n	o	p	q	r	s	t	u	v	w	x	y	z
1	2	3	4	5	6	7	8	9	10	11	12	13	14	15	16	17	18	19	20	21	22	23	24	25	26

The number for the word 'page' is 16 175.

b Write the number using standard form.

c Repeat for another nine words.

d Write the words in order, from the smallest standard form number to the largest.

e Can you use the length of a word to predict its position in your list from part **d**?
Use the previous sentence to test your prediction.

f Find a word with a standard form number containing 10^{12}.

23 **Reflect**

- Which of the questions in this unit test took the shortest time to answer? Why?
- Which of the questions in this unit test took the longest time to answer? Why?
- Which of the questions in this unit test took the most thought to answer? Why?

Reflect

2 Expressions and formulae

MASTER

Check P39 | Strengthen P41 | Extend P46 | Test P51

2.1 Substituting into expressions

You will learn to:
- Use the priority of operations when substituting into algebraic expressions
- Substitute integers into expressions involving powers and roots.

CONFIDENCE

Why learn this?
Some courier companies substitute the dimensions of a parcel into an expression to decide if the customer has to pay an extra fee for the parcel to be delivered.

Fluency
What is x^2 when the value of x is
- 2
- 5
- 9
- 12?

Explore
What size parcel would a courier charge an extra fee to deliver?

Exercise 2.1

Warm up

1 Work out
a $12 + 3 \times 5$ b $20 - \frac{8}{2}$ c $3 \times 4 + 4 \times 5$
d 2×3^2 e $4(9 - 2)$ f $16 - 4 \times 3$

2 When $x = 3$ and $y = -5$, work out
a $2x + 3$ b $4y - 5$ c $8x + 2y$ d xy

3 Write the missing lengths.

a
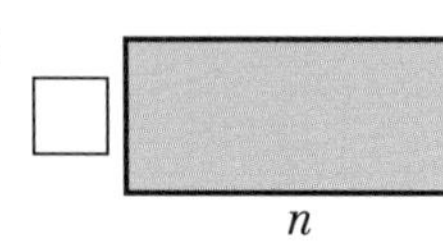

area = $2n$

b
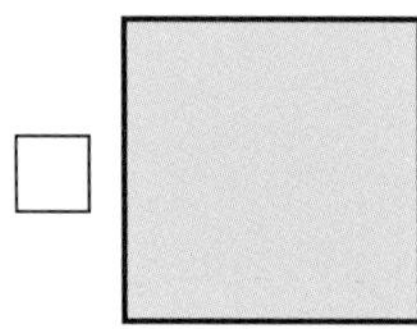

area = n^2

c
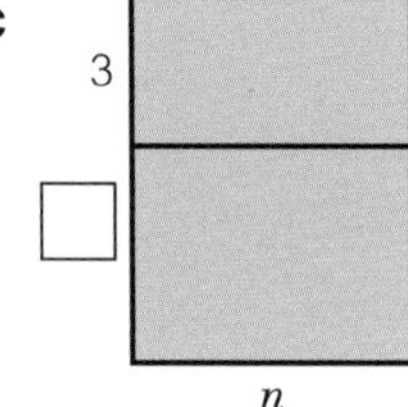

area = $3n + \square n = 7n$

d
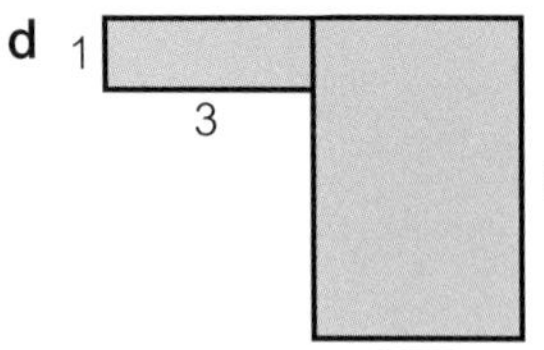

area = $3 + 4n$

4 Work out the value of these expressions.
a x^2 when $x = 40$ b y^2 when $y = 10$ c z^2 when $z = 0.6$

5 Work out the area of each shape in Q3 when $n = 9$

Topic links: Area, Priority of operations, Sequences, Negative numbers

Worked example

Work out the value of $a + (2b + c)^2$ when $a = 4$, $b = 2$ and $c = 3$

$a + (2b + c)^2 = 4 + (2 \times 2 + 3)^2$ — Substitute the values of a, b and c.

$= 4 + (4 + 3)^2$

$= 4 + 7^2$ — Work out the brackets.

$= 4 + 49$ — Work out the index (power).

$= 53$ — Add to get the final value.

6 Work out the value of these expressions when $c = 3$ and $d = 2$

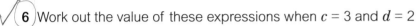

a $4d + c^2$ **b** $4c^2$ **c** $3d^3$

d $5c^3 + 2d^3$ **e** $10d^3 - 6c$ **f** $2c^3 - 9$

g $-5c + 2d^2$ **h** $(5d)^2$ **i** $(2c + d)^2$

j $(5d - c)^2 + 1$ **k** $cd + (2c - d)^3$ **l** $(4d - 2c)^2 - cd$

Discussion Is $(5d)^2 = 25d^2$ always, sometimes or never true?

7 Work out the value of these expressions.

a $3a^2b$ when $a = 3$ and $b = 4$

b $35 - (b^3 - a)$ when $a = 2$ and $b = 3$

c $(a + b)^2 - c$ when $a = 5$, $b = 2$ and $c = 1$

d $\dfrac{ab + cd}{b + c}$ when $a = 6$, $b = 3$, $c = 1$ and $d = 4$

Q7d hint

$\dfrac{ab + cd}{b + c}$ is the same as $(ab + cd) \div (b + c)$.

8 **Real / Modelling** The cards show two different expressions that you can use to estimate the mass of a child aged between 1 and 5

$2(A + 4)$ $2.5A + 8$

where A is the age of the child in years, and the mass is in kilograms.

a Use the expressions to give two estimates for the mass of a 3-year-old child.

b Copy and complete this table showing the estimates of the mass of a child, from both expressions.

Age	$2(A + 4)$	$2.5A + 8$
1	10 kg	10.5 kg
2		
3		
4		
5		

c Danny is 4 years old and has a mass of 15.5 kg. Which expression is the better mathematical model for his mass? Explain your answer.

d Write the term-to-term rule for the sequence of numbers generated by each expression.

Discussion What does the term-to-term rule represent?

9 Find the value of each expression when $x = 4$, $y = 2$ and $z = -5$

a $3(x^3 + y)$

b $3x(x + z)$

c $y^2(z + x^3)$

d $4x(3 - z) + y$

e $5(x^2 + y) + x(3x + 2)$

f $5y(x + y^3 + z) + 3y^2(x + 3z)$

g $y\sqrt{x}$

h $\sqrt[3]{xy} + z^2$

i $\sqrt{xyz + 76}$

10 Using the values of the letters in the table, is A, B or C the correct answer for each of these expressions?

Letter	a	b	c	d	e	f
Value	2	−1	7	−4	6	16

a $e + (ad)^2$	A −58	B 38	C 70
b $a(c - d)^2$	A 18	B 78	C 242
c $(c + d)^3 - 2f$	A −23	B −5	C 1299
d $e\sqrt{f} - 3bd$	A 12	B 36	C 52
e $\sqrt[3]{4f} - a^3$	A −4	B −2	C 13

Investigation **Problem-solving**

Use the values $x = 4$, $y = 9$, $u = -6$, $v = -2$ to write three expressions that will give each of these answers.

- 18
- 24
- 12
- 40

For example, $\frac{xy}{2}$ is one expression that gives an answer of 18.

$$\frac{xy}{2} = \frac{4 \times 9}{2} = \frac{36}{2} = 18$$

At least one of your expressions should involve a square or square root.

Explore

11 **Explore** What size parcel would a courier charge an extra fee to deliver?
Is it easier to explore this question now you have completed the lesson?
What further information do you need to be able to answer this?

Reflect

12 **Reflect** Helga writes,

When substituting into expressions, watch out for
- Brackets (HINT: work out whatever is in the brackets first)
-

Look back at the questions you answered in this lesson.
Write your own 'watch out for' list.
Write a short hint for each point in your list.

Q12 hint
You could begin with the same point as Helga.

2.2 Writing expressions and formulae

You will learn to:
- Write expressions and formulae.

CONFIDENCE

Why learn this?
Formulae can help describe situations that work in the same way for different numbers. The cost of hiring a vehicle depends on its type, how long you have it and how far you travel.

Fluency
Which of these are formulae and which are expressions?
- $A = 2x + 2y$
- $4x^2$
- $6y - 3x$
- $V = lbh$
- $2A(B - 7)$

Explore
How long does it take to walk up a mountain?

Exercise 2.2

1 Match each statement to the correct expression.

A	2 more than x	1	$\frac{x}{2}$
B	twice x	2	$2x + 2$
C	2 less than x	3	$2 - x$
D	half x	4	$x + 2$
E	x less than 2	5	$2x$
F	2 more than double x	6	$x - 2$

Warm up

Key point
A **formula** is a rule that shows a relationship between two or more variables (letters). You can use substitution to find each unknown value.

2 Modelling A plumber charges a call-out fee of £35, plus £20 per hour.
a How much does he charge for a 2-hour job?
b Write a **formula** to work out the total charge, C, when the plumber is called out for h hours.

3 Modelling A riding stables charges £32 for an adult and £25 for a child to go riding.
a How much does it cost a family of 2 adults and 2 children to go riding?
b Write a formula for the total cost, T, for A adults and C children to go riding.

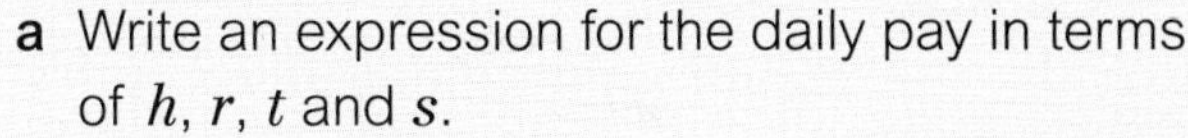

Worked example

You can work out a waiter's daily pay using the number of hours worked, h, the hourly rate of pay, r, the total amount of tips, t, and the number of staff who share the tips, s.

a Write an expression for the daily pay in terms of h, r, t and s.

$hr + \frac{t}{s}$

hourly rate × number of hours worked + $\frac{\text{total amount of tips}}{\text{number of staff who share the tip}}$

b Write a formula for the daily pay, P, in terms of h, r, t and s.

$P = hr + \frac{t}{s}$

The formula has 'P =' in front of the expression.

4 Modelling A worker's daily pay depends on the number of hours worked, h, the hourly rate of pay, r, and a travel allowance, t. The travel allowance is the same however many hours worked.

a Work out how much a worker is paid for working a 7-hour day at an hourly rate of £7.50 and a travel allowance of £8.

b Write an expression for his daily pay in terms of h, r and t.

c Write a formula for his daily pay, P, in terms of h, r and t.

d Use your formula to work out P when $h = 6$, $r = £9.50$ and $t = £12.50$.

5 Real / Modelling To cook a joint of beef takes 20 minutes per $\frac{1}{2}$kg, plus an extra 30 minutes.

a How long does it take to cook a 2.5 kg joint of beef?

b Write an expression for the number of minutes it takes to cook a joint of beef that weighs x kg.

c Write a formula to work out the number of minutes, M, it takes to cook a joint of beef that weighs x kg.

d Use your formula to work out M when $x = 3.8$ kg.

e What time should you put a 3 kg joint in the oven for lunch at 1 pm?

Discussion What assumptions did you make when writing this formula?

Q5b hint

How much time for every kilogram?

6 Real / Modelling Wooden flooring costs £35 per square metre. The floor is then edged with a narrow wooden strip which costs £4 per metre.

a How much does it cost for a 6 m by 4 m room, including the edging?

b Write a formula for the cost, C, of a wooden floor in a rectangular room of width w and length l (remember to include the edging).

c Use your formula to work out C when $w = 3.5$ m and $l = 5$ m.

Discussion What assumptions did you make when writing this formula?

Q6 Strategy hint

Draw a diagram.

7 Real / Modelling The graph shows the amount an electrician charges his customers.

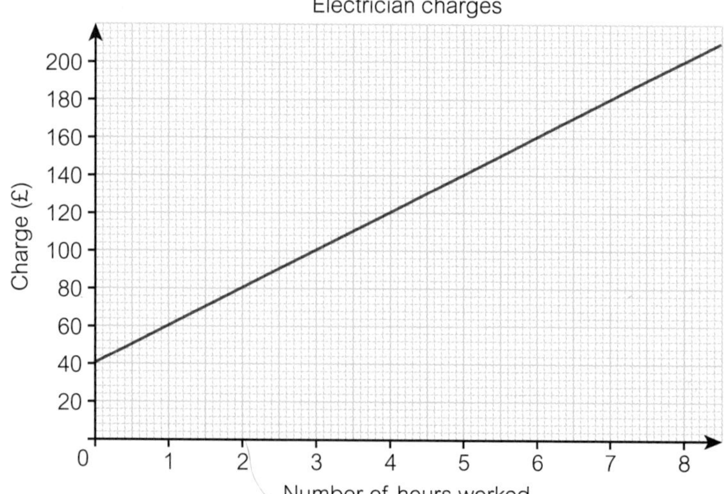

a How much does the electrician charge for

i 1 hour's work ii 4 hours' work?

Topic links: Real-life graphs, Fractions, Decimals

Subject links: Science (Q9)

b The electrician charges a call-out fee. How much is it?

c Write a formula for the total amount, C, that the electrician charges his customers for h hours' work.

d Use your formula to work out C when $h = 2\frac{3}{4}$ hours.

Discussion How is your formula linked to the equation of the line?

8 Modelling / Problem-solving The graph shows the amount it costs to hire a bicycle.

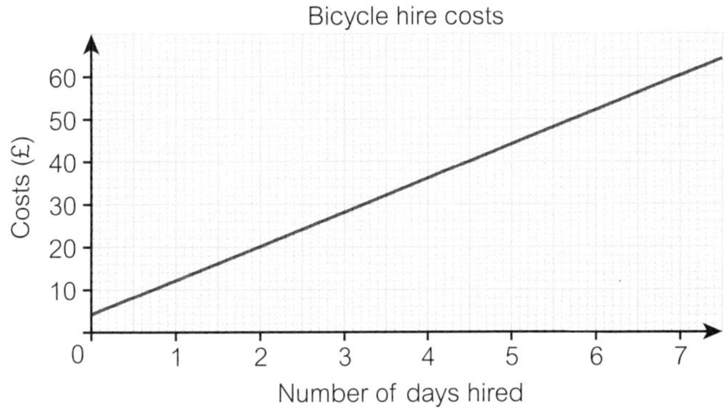

Write a formula for the total cost, C, to hire a bicycle for d days.

9 STEM / Modelling In an experiment a metal bar was heated. At 0 °C, the bar was exactly 10 m long. The increase in length of the bar was measured as the temperature increased. The results are shown in the table.

Temperature of metal bar (°C)	0	1	2	3	4	5	6	7
Increase in length (mm)	0	0.12	0.24	0.36	0.48	0.60	0.72	0.84

a How much does the length of the bar increase with every 1 °C rise in temperature?

b Copy and complete the table showing how to work out the increase in length after a temperature increase of t °C.

Temperature of metal bar (°C)	0	1	2	3	t
Increase in length (mm)	0	0.12 × 1	0.12 × 2	0.12 × □	0.12 × □

c Write a formula for the total length of the bar in millimetres, L, after a temperature increase of t °C.

d Use your formula to work out the total length of the bar at a temperature of 15 °C.

Q9c hint

Add the increase in length to the original length of the bar.

10 **Explore** How long does it take to walk up a mountain?
Is it easier to explore this question now you have completed the lesson?
What further information do you need to be able to answer this?

11 **Reflect** What is different and what is the same about formulae and equations?

Explore

Reflect

2.3 STEM: Using formulae

You will learn to:
- Solve equations by substituting into formulae
- Change the subject of a formula.

CONFIDENCE

Why learn this?
Project managers for developments such as this wind farm, use formulae to work out the total cost of a project.

Fluency
Work out
- −7 + 9
- −4 × −3
- 8 × 2 − 25
- $(-4)^2$

Explore
How do formula triangles work?

Exercise 2.3: Science formulae

Warm up

1 Use the formula $S = 5n$ to work out the value of S when
a $n = 5$ b $n = 0$ c $n = -4$

2 Use the formula $T = u^2 - v$ to work out the value of T when
a $u = 7$ and $v = 3$ b $u = 0$ and $v = 9$ c $u = 2$ and $v = 7.5$

3 Solve these equations.
a $x + 12 = 25$ b $3x - 4 = 11$ c $\frac{x}{3} = 12$

4 **STEM / Modelling** You can use this formula to work out the distance, s, travelled by an object.

$$s = \frac{(u + v)t}{2}$$

where
s = distance travelled (metres, m)
u = starting speed (metres per second, m/s)
v = finishing speed (metres per second, m/s)
t = time (seconds, s).
Work out the value of s when
a $u = 0$, $v = 20$ and $t = 8$ b $u = 12$, $v = 25$ and $t = 5$

Q4a hint
$s = \frac{(0 + 20) \times 8}{2}$

5 **STEM / Modelling** You can use this formula to work out the elasticity value, e, of two objects that collide.

$$e = \frac{v - V}{U - u}$$

where
e = elasticity value
U = starting speed of first object (m/s)
V = finishing speed of first object (m/s)
u = starting speed of second object (m/s)
v = finishing speed of second object (m/s).
Work out the value of e when
a $U = 6$, $V = 5$, $u = 4$ and $v = 15$ b $U = 8$, $V = 12$, $u = 2$ and $v = 30$

Q5 Literacy hint
Elasticity is the property that some objects have, where they return to their original shape and size after being stretched.

Topic links: Decimals, Negative numbers

Subject links: Science (Q4–Q10)

6 STEM / Modelling You can use this forumla to calculate the force acting on a body.

$F = ma$

where

F = force (newtons, N)

m = mass of body (kg)

a = acceleration (metres per second per second, m/s^2).

Work out the value of F when

a $m = 6$ and $a = 5$

b $m = 2$ and $a = -4$

c $m = 0.6$ and $a = -9.8$

Discussion What does a negative acceleration mean?

7 STEM / Modelling You can use this formula to work out the height of a ball when it is thrown upwards.

$s = ut + \frac{1}{2}at^2$

where

s = height (m)

u = starting speed (m/s)

a = acceleration (m/s^2)

t = time (s).

Work out the value of s when

a $u = 30$, $t = 6$ and $a = -10$

b $u = 40$, $t = 8$ and $a = -9.8$

8 STEM The formula $E = mc^2$ gives the energy E (joules) contained in a mass m kg.
The speed of light, c, is approximately 300 000 000 m/s.
Calculate the energy contained in a mass of 20 kg.
Write your answer using standard form.

Part 8 hint

m/s means metres per second.

Worked example

Use the formula $v = u + at$ to work out the value of t when $v = 30$, $u = 10$ and $a = 4$

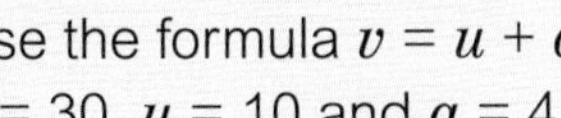

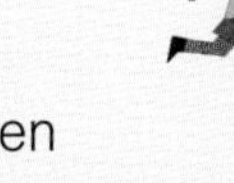

$v = u + at$

$30 = 10 + 4t$

$30 - 10 = 4t$

$20 = 4t$

$\frac{20}{4} = t$

$t = 5$

Substitute the numbers that you know into the formula.
Solve the equation, one step at a time, to find the value of t.

Key point

The **subject** of a formula is always the letter on its own on one side of the equation.
For example:
the subject of $k = \frac{1}{2}mv^2$ is k.

9 STEM Use the formula $F = ma$ to work out the value of

a m when $F = 24$ and $a = 10$

b a when $F = 54$ and $m = 12$

10 STEM Use the formula $v = u + at$ to work out the value of

a u when $v = 34$, $a = 5$ and $t = 3$

b t when $v = 50$, $u = 20$ and $a = 5$

c a when $v = 22$, $u = 8$ and $t = 7$

Worked example

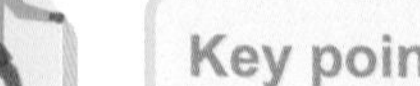

Make m the subject of the formula $F = ma$.

$F = m \times a$

$\frac{F}{a} = m$

or $m = \frac{F}{a}$

$m \rightarrow$ [$\times a$] $\rightarrow F$

$\frac{F}{a} \leftarrow$ [$\div a$] $\leftarrow F$

Key point

You **change the subject** of a formula by rearranging the formula to get the letter that you want on its own on one side of the equation.

11 Make x the **subject** of these formulae.

a $P = xh$

b $A = x + y$

c $F = x - r$

d $t = x - 2v$

e $r = \frac{x}{2}$

f $Y = x + np$

Q11a hint

Rearrange the formula $P = xh$ so it starts '$x =$ '.

Q11d hint

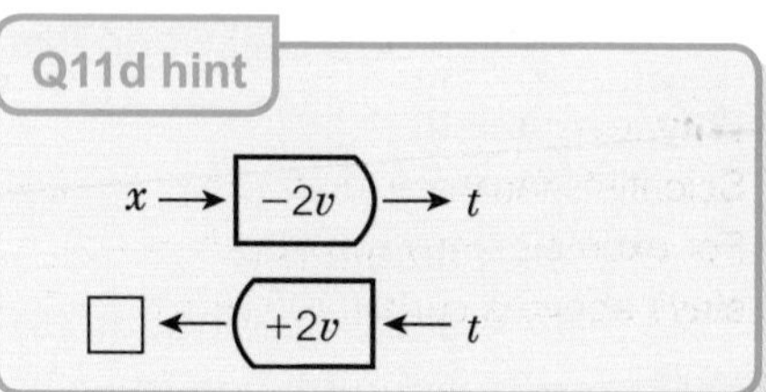

12 Make the letter in brackets the subject of each of these formulae.

a $D = ST$ (T)

b $F = T + R$ (T)

c $h = m - n$ (m)

d $k = 2l + n$ (n)

e $v = u + at$ (u)

f $F = T - mg$ (T)

g $K = \frac{m}{t}$ (m)

h $D = \frac{M}{V}$ (V)

Investigation — Problem-solving

1 Use the formula cards to work out the value of each letter.

$I = 12$	$K + I = G$	$4H = I$	$G + 4 = 2I$
$N = H^3 - I$	$A = (W - H)^2$	$K + I = 4W$	

2 Write the letters in order of value from the smallest to the biggest.
What famous scientist's surname do they spell?

13 The number of office chairs, N, that an online business should regularly order is given by the formula $N = \sqrt{\frac{2AP}{H}}$, where A is the number sold each year, H is the storage cost and P is the cost of processing an order.
Work out N, when $A = 100$, $P = £10$ and $H = £5$.

Explore

14 Explore How do formula triangles work?
Is it easier to explore this question now you have completed the lesson?
What further information do you need to be able to answer this?

Reflect

15 Reflect In this lesson, you have met or used some formulae used by scientists.
Who else uses formulae?
Why do you think formulae are useful?

2.4 Rules of indices and brackets

You will learn to:

- Simplify expressions involving brackets
- Use the rules for indices for multiplying and dividing
- Factorise an expression by taking out an algebraic common factor.

CONFIDENCE

Why learn this?
Scientists factorise expressions to solve equations. For example, they work out how long an object stays above a certain height when it is kicked.

Fluency
Write these numbers in order of size, starting with the smallest.
3^3 2^5 4^2 1^8 5^2 12^0

Explore
What expressions will simplify to x^{-2}?

Exercise 2.4

Warm up

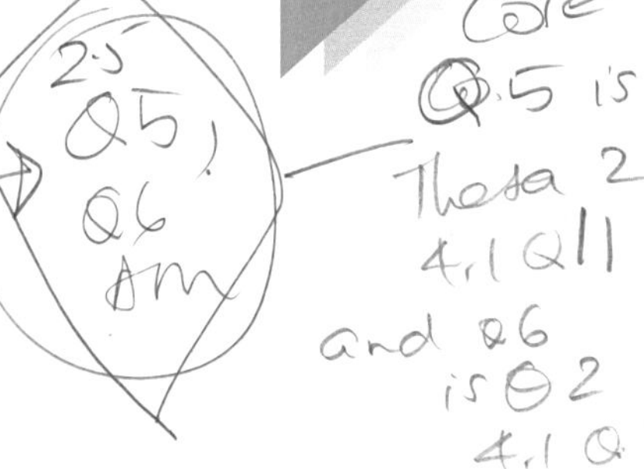

1 Simplify

a $p^3 \times p^2$
b $a^5 \times a$
c $5e^4 \times -3e^3$
d $e^5 \div e^2$
e $3d^8 \div d^5$
f $8m^4 \div -4m^3$

2 Expand and simplify

a $3(x + 5) + 4(x - 1)$
b $8(p - 7) - 3(p + 2)$
c $5m^2 + m(7m - 2)$
d $2y(y + 4) + 6(5 - 3y)$

Worked example

Expand $x(x^2 + 2x - 4)$.

$x(x^2 + 2x - 4) = x^3 + 2x^2 - 4x$

$x \times x^2 = x^3$
$x \times 2x = 2x^2$
$x \times -4 = -4x$
$x(x^2 + 2x - 4)$

Key point
When you expand brackets, you multiply every term inside the brackets by the term outside the brackets.

3 Expand these brackets.

a $y(y^2 + 5y)$
b $x(x^3 + 3x + 7)$
c $a(a^2 - 8a + 1)$
d $b(b^3 + 5b^2 - 6)$
e $2p(4 + 5p + p^2)$
f $3y(8y - 2y^3)$
g $6z(z^3 - 4z^2 + 9)$
h $a^2(2a^2 + 3a - 4)$
i $3k(k^3 - 6k - 7)$

Q3e hint
$2p \times 4 + 2p \times 5p + 2p \times p^2$

Q4 hint
Expand both sets of brackets separately, then simplify by collecting like terms.

4 Expand and simplify

a $x(x^2 + 3x) + 2x(x^2 + 4x)$
b $4b(b^2 + 7b) - b(b^2 + 9b)$
c $5d(d^3 - 3) - d(2d^3 - 9)$
d $y(y^2 + 4y + 5) + y(2y^2 - 7)$
e $z(z^3 + 8z^2 - 3) + 4z(z^3 - 3z^2 - 1)$
f $4p(p^2 + 5p + 12) - p(3p^2 + 17p - 2)$
g $7q(8 + 4q - 3q^2) - 2q(5 - 3q + 12q^2)$
h $6a(2a + 3a^2 - 1) + 4(a^2 - 3a^3 + a)$

5  Problem-solving / Reasoning
Show that $3x^3 + x(4x^2 + 9x) = 7x^2(x + 3) - 12x^2$.

6 Reasoning / Modelling The diagram shows a cuboid.

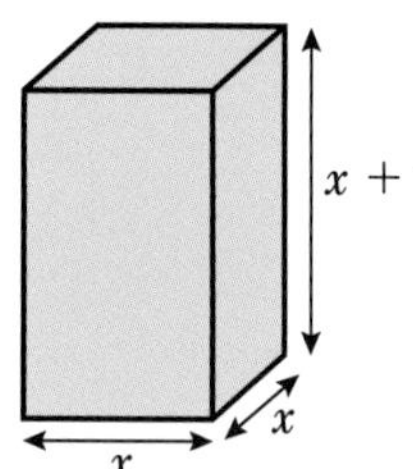

Show that an expression for the volume of the cuboid is $x^3 + 7x^2$.

7 Simplify these terms. Two have been started for you.

a $(2a)^2 = 2a \times 2a = 4a^2$ b $(5x)^2$ c $(4y)^3$

d $\left(\frac{a}{3}\right)^3 = \frac{a}{3} \times \frac{a}{3} \times \frac{a}{3} =$ e $\left(\frac{x}{6}\right)^2$ f $\left(\frac{y}{2}\right)^3$

Discussion Which of these are the same? $(3x)^2$, $-3x^2$, $-(3x)^2$, $(-3x)^2$

8 Reasoning

a i Work out the answers to these divisions.

$\frac{5}{5}$, $\frac{9}{9}$, $\frac{12}{12}$, $\frac{350}{350}$, $\frac{x}{x}$, $\frac{x^5}{x^5}$

ii What do you notice about your answers?

iii Complete this statement.
'When you divide a number by itself the answer is always □.'

b i Copy and complete this pattern.

$\frac{x^5}{x^1} = x^4$, $\frac{x^5}{x^2} = x^3$, $\frac{x^5}{x^3} = x^{\square}$, $\frac{x^5}{x^4} = x^{\square}$, $\frac{x^5}{x^5} = x^{\square}$

ii What do you notice about your answers to $\frac{x^5}{x^5}$ in part **a i** and part **b i**?

iii Complete this statement.
'Any number or letter to the power of 0 = □.'

9 Write true (T) or false (F) for each of these statements.

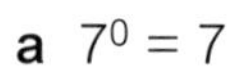

a $7^0 = 7$ b $16^0 = 1$ c $x^0 = 0$

d $y^0 = 1$ e $4p^0 = 1$ f $3q^0 = 3$

10 Simplify these expressions.

a $\frac{9x^2}{3x^2} = 3x^0 = \square$ b $\frac{24y^7}{4y^7}$ c $\frac{3p^5}{2p^5}$

d $\frac{4q^2 \times 5q^6}{10q^8}$ e $\frac{8r^5 \times 2r^9}{20r^{14}}$ f $\frac{3t^4 \times 4t^6}{15t^{10}}$

11  Reasoning Copy and complete

a $6^{-2} = \frac{1}{6^{\square}}$ b $3^{-3} = \frac{1}{3^{\square}}$ c $5^{-1} = \frac{1}{5^{\square}}$

d $x^{-2} = \frac{1}{x^{\square}}$ e $y^{-4} = \frac{1}{y^{\square}}$ f $z^{-1} = \frac{1}{z^{\square}}$

Q5 Strategy hint
Expand and simplify each side of the equation to show that both expressions are the same.

Q5 Literacy hint
'Show that' means 'Show your working'.

Q9e hint
$4p^0 = 4 \times p^0$

Q10d hint
First simplify $4q^2 \times 5q^6$, then divide the answer by $10q^8$.

Q10e hint
Write your answer as a fraction in its simplest form.

Topic links: Fractions, Volume

12 a Copy and complete these division patterns.

i $\frac{3^2}{3^5} = 3^{2-5} = 3^{\square}$ and $\frac{3^2}{3^5} = \frac{3 \times 3}{3 \times 3 \times 3 \times 3 \times 3} = \frac{1}{3^{\square}}$, so $3^{\square} = \frac{1}{3^{\square}}$ and $\frac{1}{3^{\square}} < 1$

ii $\frac{x^3}{x^4} = x^{3-4} = x^{\square}$ and $\frac{x^3}{x^4} = \frac{x \times x \times x}{x \times x \times x \times x} = \frac{1}{x^{\square}}$, so $x^{\square} = \frac{1}{x^{\square}}$ and $\frac{1}{x^{\square}} < \square$

iii $\frac{y^8}{y^{11}} = y^{8-11} = y^{\square}$ and $\frac{y^8}{y^{11}} = \frac{1}{y^{\square}}$, so $y^{\square} = \frac{1}{y^{\square}}$ and $\frac{1}{y^{\square}} < \square$

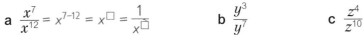

b Complete this statement.
'Any number or letter to a negative power can be written as a fraction which has a value smaller than □.'

13 Simplify these expressions. Write each one as a negative power and as a fraction. The first one has been started for you.

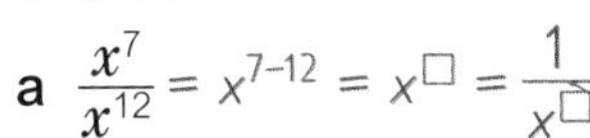

a $\frac{x^7}{x^{12}} = x^{7-12} = x^{\square} = \frac{1}{x^{\square}}$ **b** $\frac{y^3}{y^7}$ **c** $\frac{z^4}{z^{10}}$

d $\frac{w^2}{w^9}$ **e** $\frac{v}{v^3}$ **f** $t^5 \div t^{11}$ **g** $m^6 \div m^8$

Q13e hint

$v = v^1$

14 Problem-solving / Reasoning Hannah and Barney both simplify the expression $\frac{6x^7}{3x^9}$.
Hannah says that the answer is $2x^{-2}$. Barney says that the answer is $\frac{1}{2x^2}$.
Only one of them is correct. Who is it? Explain your answer.

Worked example

Factorise $6x^2 + 12x$. Check your answer.

$6x^2 + 12x = 6x(x + 2)$

Check: $6x(x + 2) = 6x^2 + 12x$

The HCF of $6x^2$ and $12x$ is $6x$.
$6x \times x = 6x^2$ and $6x \times 2 = 12x$

Key point

To **factorise** an expression completely, take out the **highest common factor** (HCF) of its terms.

15 **Factorise** each expression completely. Check your answers.

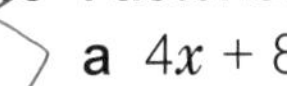

a $4x + 8$ **b** $4x^2 + 8x$ **c** $4x^3 + 8x^2$ **d** $6x - 2x^3$

e $y^2 + 5y^3$ **f** $9y^5 - 3y^3$ **g** $10y^4 - 5y^2$ **h** $12y^7 + 9y^5$

16 Factorise each expression completely. Check your answers.

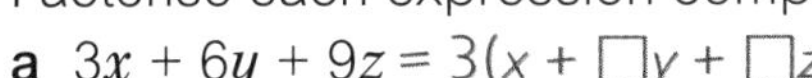

a $3x + 6y + 9z = 3(x + \square y + \square z)$ **b** $xy + 5y + yz$

c $x^2 + 6xy + 9xz$ **d** $5x^2 + 10xy + 15xz$

e $x^3 + 2x^2y + 5x^2z$ **f** $12xy - 4x^2y^2 + 8yz$

Q16b hint

What is the HCF of xy, $5y$ and yz?

17 Problem-solving / Reasoning

a Work out the missing terms from this factorised expression.
$\square x^2y + \square y^2 + 9\square = 3x\square(\square + 4y + \square)$

b Is there only one answer to this problem? Explain your answer.

18 **Explore** What expressions will simplify to x^{-2}?
Is it easier to explore this question now you have completed the lesson?
What further information do you need to be able to answer this?

19 **Reflect** Look back at Q17.
Roland says, 'I worked from left to right. I thought about what could go in the box before x^2y first.'
Rachel says, 'I began with the $3x\square$ outside the bracket and the $4y$ inside the bracket. This meant I was only working with one box.'
What did you do first?
Which is the best first step, Roland's, Rachel's or yours? Why?

Explore

Reflect

2.5 Expanding double brackets

You will learn to:

- Multiply out double brackets and collect like terms.

CONFIDENCE

Why learn this?
Scientists expand double brackets to help them work out the equation of the path of a moving object.

Fluency
Work out

- 4 × −3
- −8 × −4
- −7 × 5
- −2 × −3 × −6

Explore
How do you square $x + 1$?

Exercise 2.5

Warm up

1 Simplify

a $a \times a$ b $x \times x$ c $4 \times a$

d $-2 \times x$ e $3a - a$ f $7x - 2x$

g $x^2 + 4x + 7x + 1$ h $x^2 - 3x + 5x + 12$ i $a^2 + 2a - 5a - 7$

2 Expand and simplify

a $4(x + 2) + 3(x + 7)$ b $6(y + 9) + 8(y - 1)$ c $3(p - 7) - 4(4 + p)$

d $2(11 + w) - 3(w - 9)$ e $z(z + 4) + z(z - 3)$ f $m(7 + m) - m(m - 4)$

3 i Write down an expression for length × width = area of each rectangle. Write each expression in its simplest form.

ii Work out the area of each small rectangle.

iii Write the area in two ways.

a

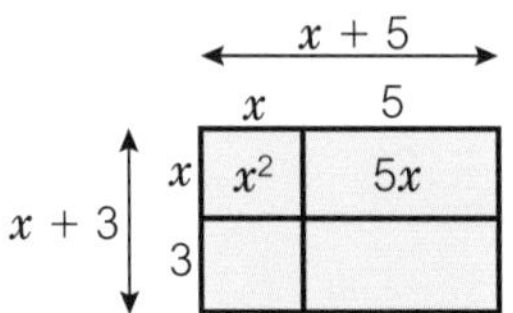

$(x + 3)(x + 5) = x^2 + 5x + \square + \square$

b

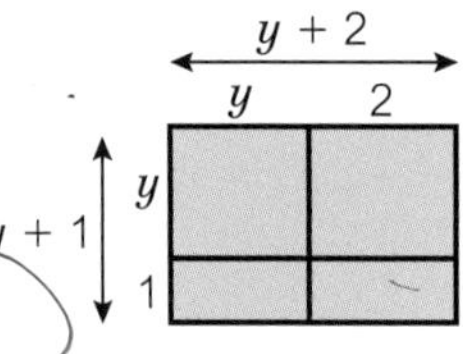

c

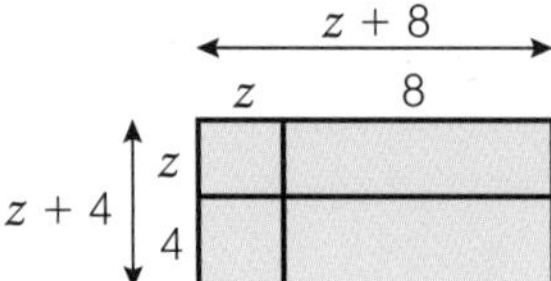

d

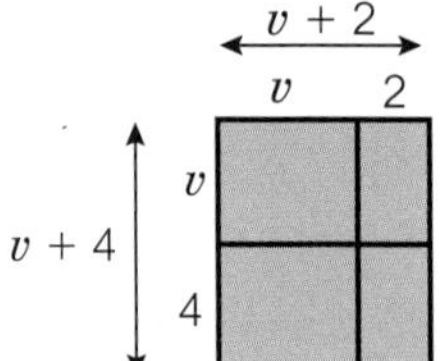

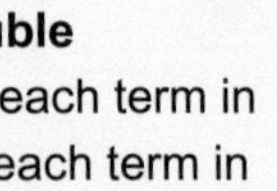

Key point

When you **expand double brackets**, you multiply each term in one set of brackets by each term in the other brackets.

$(a + b)(c + d) = ac + ad + bc + bd$

4 **Problem-solving / Modelling**
Work out an expression for the area of this rectangle.

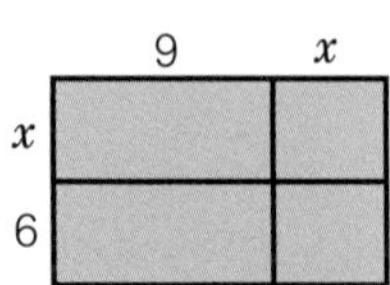

Discussion Is $(x + 6)(x + 9)$ the same as $(x + 6)(9 + x)$?

Topic links: Area

Worked example

Expand and simplify $(w + 6)(w + 12)$.

$$(w + 6)(w + 12) = w^2 + 12w + 6w + 72$$
$$= w^2 + 18w + 72$$

$$(w + 6)(w + 12) = w^2 + 12w + 6w + 72$$
$$= w^2 + 18w + 72$$

Key point

A **quadratic** expression is one that contains an x^2 and no higher powers of x.

5 Expand and simplify these double brackets.

a $(x + 3)(x + 7)$ **b** $(y + 1)(y + 9)$ **c** $(m + 4)(m + 6)$

d $(p + 8)(p + 11)$ **e** $(q + 15)(q + 3)$ **f** $(n + 5)(n + 12)$

6 Expand and simplify

a $(x + 3)(x - 5)$ **b** $(y + 5)(y - 3)$ **c** $(p - 7)(p + 12)$

d $(q - 9)(q + 8)$ **e** $(m - 4)(m - 2)$ **f** $(n - 1)(n - 5)$

Q6a hint

Watch out for the minus sign.

Q6e hint

$-4 \times -2 = +8$

7 Problem-solving / Reasoning Kaira and Pawel both expand and simplify the **quadratic** expression $(x - 4)(3 + x)$.
Kaira says that the answer is $x^2 + x - 12$.
Pawel says that the answer is $x^2 - x - 12$.
Only one of them is correct. Who is it? What mistake was made?

8 Copy and complete these expansions. Simplify each answer.

a $(x + 6)(x - 3) + x(2x - 5)$

b $(n - 5)(n - 8) - 12(n - 2)$

Q8a hint

Work out $(x + 6)(x - 3)$
Expand $x(2x - 5)$
Add them together.

9 Problem-solving / Reasoning Show that $n(n + 4) - 2(n + 7) = (n + 2)(n - 6) + 2(3n - 1)$.

10 **Explore** How do you square $x + 1$?
Is it easier to explore this question now you have completed the lesson?
What further information do you need to be able to answer this?

11 **Reflect** Larry says, 'When expanding brackets, I like to draw "Horace".'

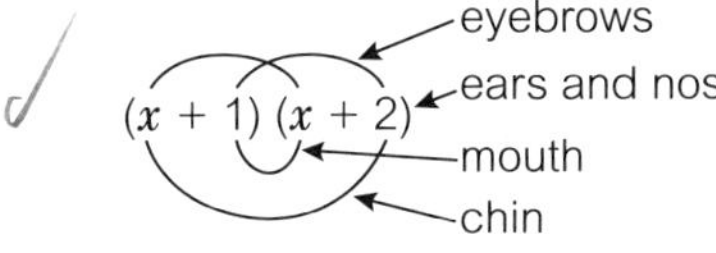

Q11 hint

Are all terms multiplied together?

Does this work for expanding brackets?
Could 'Horace' help you to remember how to expand brackets?
If not, how might you remember?
What pictures (on paper or in your head) do you use to remember mathematics?
Compare with others in your class.

Explore

Reflect

2 Check up

Log how you did on your Student Progression Chart.

Substituting into expressions

1 Work out the value of these expressions.

a $5ab^2$ when $a = 2$ and $b = 3$

b $4 + (a^3 - b)$ when $a = 3$ and $b = 7$

c $(a - b)^2 + 2c$ when $a = 13$, $b = 6$ and $c = 5$

d $\frac{2a + 3b}{c - d}$ when $a = 7$, $b = 2$, $c = 7$ and $d = 3$

2 Find the value of each expression when $x = 2$, $y = -3$ and $z = 4$

a $5(x^2 + y)$

b $y^2(4 + 2x^3)$

c $5z(6 - x) - y$

d $y(x + \sqrt{z})$

Writing and using formulae

3 Use the formula $P = mgh$ to work out the value of P when

a $m = 8$, $g = 10$ and $h = 2.5$

b $m = 3$, $g = 9.8$ and $h = -4$

4 Use the formula $T = \frac{kx}{l}$ to work out the value of T when

a $k = 20$, $x = 0.6$ and $l = 3$

b $k = 50$, $x = -0.5$ and $l = 4$

5 A car hire company charges £x per day to hire a car for d days. They also charge a one-off fuel cost of £f.

a Work out the total cost to hire a car for 7 days that costs £15 per day with a one-off fuel cost of £55.

b Write an expression for the total amount a customer pays in terms of x, d and f.

c Write a formula for the total amount a customer pays, T, in terms of x, d and f.

d Use your formula to work out T when $x = 18$, $d = 10$ and $f = 65$.

6 Use the formula $L = \frac{5x^2}{v}$ to work out the value of L when $x = 4$ and $v = 10$

7 Use the formula $P = mv + t$ to work out the value of

a t when $P = 50$, $m = 6$ and $v = 5$

b v when $P = 28$, $m = 10$ and $t = 12$

8 Use the formula $A = \frac{(a + b)h}{2}$ to work out the value of a when $A = 30$, $b = 7$ and $h = 6$

Expanding, factorising and indices

9 Expand

a $y(y^3 + 7y)$

b $x^2(2x^2 + 5x - 7)$

10 Expand and simplify $x(x^2 + 5x) + 3x(x^2 + 9x)$.

11 Simplify

a $(7y)^2$

b $\left(\frac{x}{5}\right)^3$

12 Simplify these expressions.

a $\frac{x^8}{x^{10}}$

b $y^2 \div y^3$

c $\frac{15z^7}{3z^7}$

d $\frac{2a^2 \times 6a^3}{3a^6}$

13 Factorise each expression completely. Check your answers.

a $9x - 3x^3$

b $20y^6 + 15y^4$

c $9x + 12y + 18z$

d $x^2 + 8xy + 2xz$

14 This is how Alisha factorises the expression $8x^2y^2 - 4xy^2z$ completely.

$8x^2y^2 - 4xy^2z = 2xy(4xy - 2yz)$

a Explain the mistake that she has made.

b Factorise the expression correctly and completely.

15 Expand and simplify

a $(x + 4)(x + 8)$

b $(x + 9)(x - 3)$

c $(p - 6)(p + 3)$

d $(m - 5)(m - 4)$

16 **How sure are you of your answers? Were you mostly**

Just guessing **Feeling doubtful** **Confident**

What next? Use your results to decide whether to strengthen or extend your learning.

Reflect

Challenge

17 Write down three expressions that simplify to give an answer of x^{-3}.

18 In this spider diagram, the four expressions with brackets expand to give the expression in the middle.

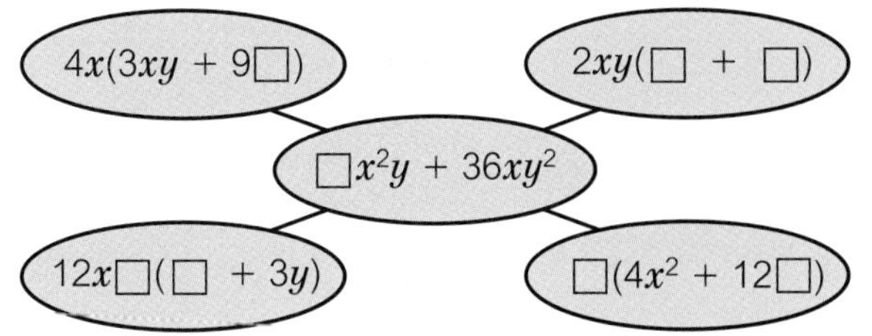

6x	3y	x
	y² xy	
y	12	18y

Use the terms in the box to fill in the spider diagram.

2 Strengthen

You will:

- Strengthen your understanding with practice.

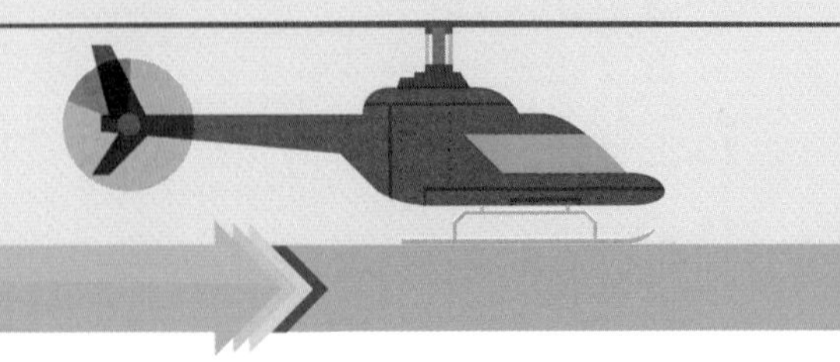

Substituting into expressions

1 Work out

a 4^2 and 4×2 **b** 6^2 and 6×2

Check your answers with a calculator.

c Is 5^2 the same as 5×2?

2 Use priority of operations to write these calculations in order of size.

A $6(12 - 5)$ **B** $4^2 + 3 \times 6$ **C** $20 + \frac{3^3}{2}$ **D** $(4 \times 5 - 7 \times 2)^2$

3 Copy and complete the workings to find the value of these expressions when $a = 7$ and $b = 2$

a $8a^2 = 8 \times \square^2 = 8 \times \square \times \square$ **b** $4b^3 = 4 \times \square^3 = 4 \times \square \times \square \times \square$

c $2b^4$ **d** $(a - b)^2 = (\square - \square)^2 = \square^2 = \square$

e $(5b)^3 = (5 \times \square)^3 = \square^3 = \square$

f $2(3a + b) = 2(3 \times \square + \square) = 2(\square + \square) = 2 \times (\square) = \square$

g $\frac{2a + 3b}{a - b} = \frac{2 \times \square + 3 \times \square}{\square - \square} = \frac{\square + \square}{\square} = \frac{\square}{\square} = \square$

Q3d hint

Brackets before powers.

4 Work out the value of these expressions when $x = 3$ and $y = 4$

a $2x + y^2$ **b** $5x^2$ **c** $6x^3 - 12$ **d** $2y^3 - 15x$

e $3xy - y^2$ **f** $2(x + y)$ **g** $3(4x - y)$ **h** $4(y^2 - x^2)$

Q4a hint

$2 \times \square + \square^2 = \ldots$

5 This is how Adam and Beth substitute $c = 4$ and $d = 5$ into the expression $3(c^2 + 6d)$:

Adam

$3(c^2 + 6d) = 3(4^2 + 6 \times 5)$

$= 3(8 + 30)$

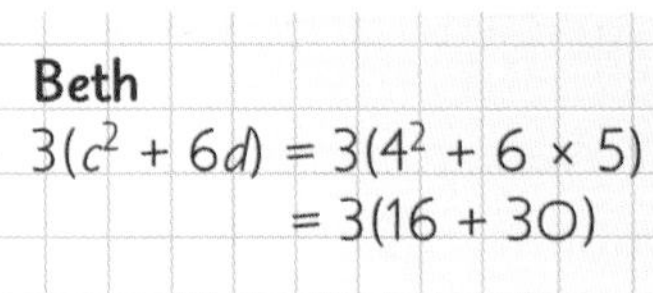

a Who is correct so far?

b Explain the mistake that the other one has made.

c Work out the final correct answer.

6 This is how Carrie and Dai substitute $a = -2$ and $b = -3$ into the expression $6a^2 - 4b$:

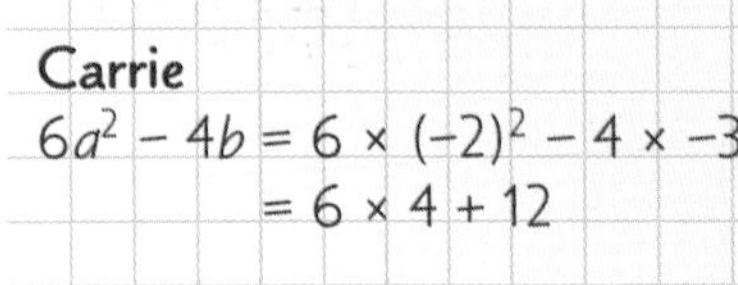

Dai

$6a^2 - 4b = 6 \times (-2)^2 - 4 \times -3$

$= 6 \times -4 - 12$

a Who is correct so far?

b Explain the mistakes that the other one has made.

c Work out the final correct answer.

7 Work out

a $4 + -1$ b $-5 - -2$ c 3×-2

d -6×5 e -3×-5 f $(-1)^2 = -1 \times -1 =$

Check your answers with a calculator.

8 Copy and complete the workings to find the value of these expressions when $a = 2$ and $b = -1$

a $2a + b = 2 \times 2 + -1 = 4 - 1 = \square$

b $6a - 4b = 6 \times \square - 4 \times \square = \square + \square = \square$

c $a^2 - b = \square^2 - \square = \square + \square = \square$

d $3b^2 = 3 \times (\square)^2 = 3 \times \square = \square$

e $4(b - a) = 4(\square - \square) = 4 \times \square = \square$

f $6(b^3 + 2a) = 6((\square)^3 + 2 \times \square) = 6(\square + \square) = 6 \times \square = \square$

9 Find the value of each expression when $x = 5$, $y = 4$ and $z = -3$

a $xy + 2z$ b $z^2 + 3xy$ c $5y^2 - xz$

d $6(4x - 9z)$ e $3(y^3 + 4xz)$ f $\frac{x - z}{2y}$

Q8d hint

$(-1)^2 = -1 \times -1 = +1$

Q8f hint

$(-1)^3 = -1 \times -1 \times -1 = \square$

Q9a hint

$5 \times 4 + 2 \times -3 = 20 + -6 = 20 - 6 = \square$

Q9b hint

$z^2 = (-3)^2 = -3 \times -3 = \square$

Q9d hint

Work out the brackets first, then multiply the answer by 6.

Writing and using formulae

1 Use the formula $M = Fd$ to work out the value of M when

a $F = 12$ and $d = 6$ b $F = 25$ and $d = 3$ c $F = 8.5$ and $d = 0.2$

2 STEM / Modelling The formula to change a temperature in degrees Celsius to degrees Fahrenheit is

$F = 1.8C + 32$

where

C = temperature in degrees Celsius

F = temperature in degrees Fahrenheit.

Work out the value of F when

a $C = 10°C$ b $C = 28°C$ c $C = -5°C$ d $C = -20°C$

3 Use the formula $T = 2P + 3R$ to work out the value of T when

a $P = 12$ and $R = -7$

b $P = -2$ and $R = 14$

c $P = -6$ and $R = -1$

4 Use the formula $M = \frac{rg}{h}$ to work out the value of M when

a $r = 8$, $g = -10$ and $h = 5$ b $r = 2$, $g = -12$ and $h = 4$

c $r = -6$, $g = 9$ and $h = 3$ d $r = -4$, $g = 15$ and $h = -12$

5 Modelling A bicycle hire company charge an amount per day to hire a bicycle. The amount depends on the size and quality of the bicycle.

a Work out the total cost to hire a bicycle for

i 3 days at £8 per day ii 5 days at £12 per day.

b Write an expression for the total cost to hire a bicycle for d days at £c per day.

c Write a formula for the total cost, T, in terms of d and c.

d Use your formula to work out T when $d = 10$ and $c = £9.50$.

Q1a hint

Replace the letters with numbers.

$M = F \times d = \square \times \square = \square$

Q2a hint

$F = 1.8 \times 10 + 32 = \square + \square = \square$

Q2c hint

$F = 1.8 \times -5 + 32 = \square$

Q4a hint

$M = \frac{8 \times -10}{5} = \frac{\square}{5}$

Q5b hint

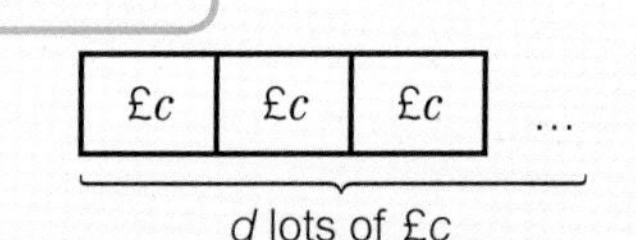

Q5c hint

Write 'T =' in front of the expression you wrote in part **b**, to make it a formula.

6 Modelling A surf shop charge an amount per hour to hire a surfboard. They also charge a one-off cost to hire a wetsuit.

a Work out the total cost to hire a surfboard for 3 hours at £6 per hour when the one-off wetsuit cost is £12.

b Write an expression for the total cost to hire a surfboard for h hours at £x per hour when the one-off wetsuit cost is £w.

c Write a formula for the total cost, T, in terms of h, x and w.

d Use your formula to work out T when $h = 6$, $x = 5$ and $w = 8$.

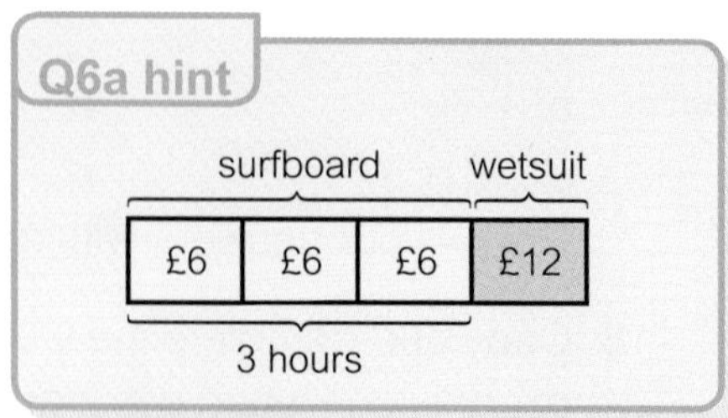

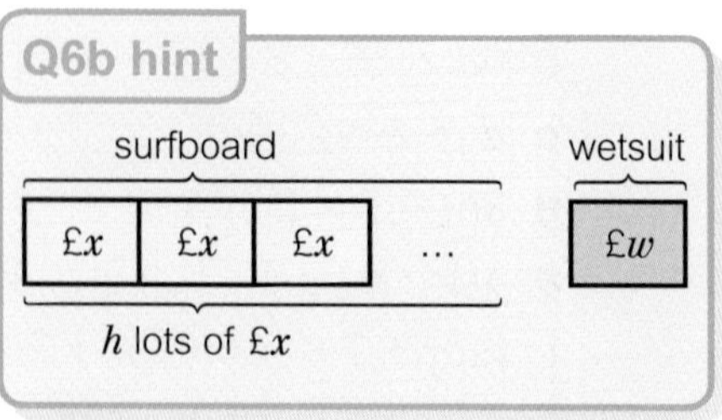

7 Modelling A dance club charge their members £12 for the first evening they attend, then £3 for each evening after that.

a Work out the total amount a member pays for
i 2 evenings ii 5 evenings iii 9 evenings.

b Write an expression for the total amount a member pays for e evenings.

c Write a formula for the total amount a member pays, T, in terms of e.

d Use your formula to work out T when $e = 30$.

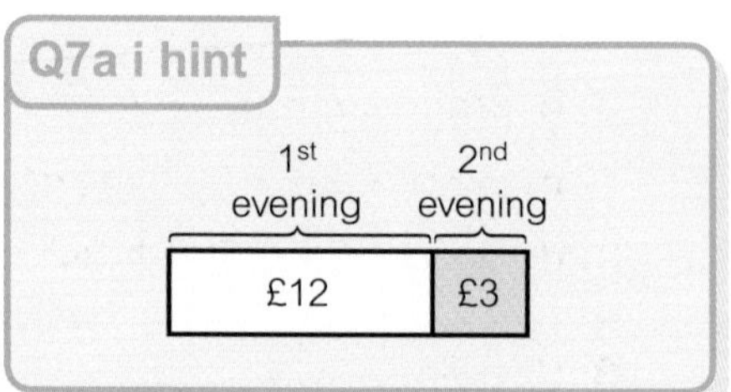

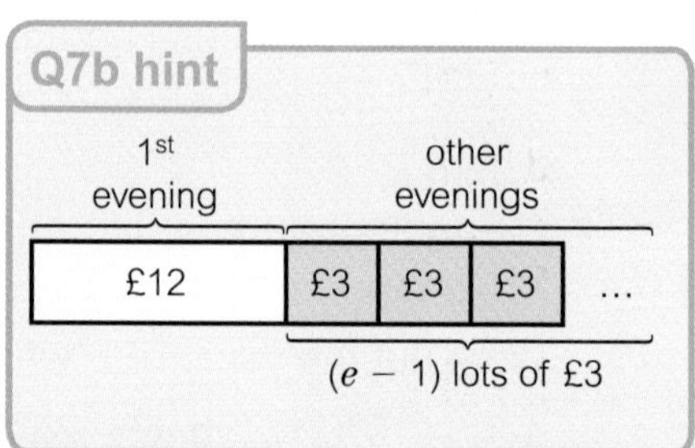

8 Use the formula $X = hr^3$ to work out the value of X when

a $h = 12$ and $r = 3$

b $h = 7$ and $r = 2$

c $h = 100$ and $r = 5$

d $h = 36$ and $r = 4$

9 STEM / Modelling You can use this formula to calculate the energy stored in a stretched string.

$$E = \frac{kx^2}{2l}$$

Work out the value of E when

a $k = 30$, $x = 2$ and $l = 12$

b $k = 60$, $x = 3$ and $l = 18$

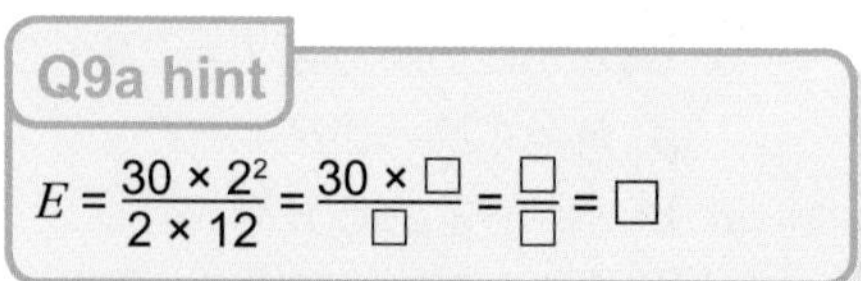

10 Use the formula $R = mu + p$ to work out the value of

a p when $R = 20$, $m = 4$ and $u = 2$

b p when $R = 25$, $m = 2$ and $u = 7$

c m when $R = 23$, $u = 3$ and $p = 14$

d m when $R = 40$, $u = 5$ and $p = 20$

e u when $R = 28$, $m = 6$ and $p = 16$

f u when $R = 79$, $m = 8$ and $p = 7$

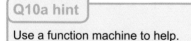

Q10a hint

Use a function machine to help.

Q10c hint

Use a function machine to solve $23 = 3m + 14$

11 Use the formula $A = \frac{(a + b)h}{2}$ to work out the value of b when $A = 24$, $a = 4$ and $h = 3$

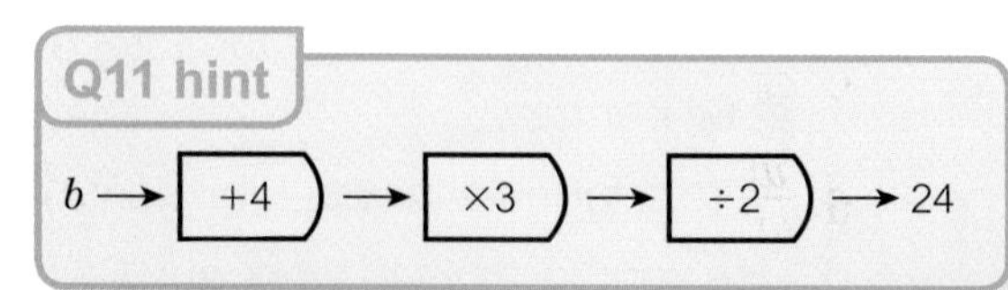

Expanding, factorising and indices

1 You can use a grid method to expand brackets like this:

$a(a^3 - 4a + 3)$

×	a^3	$-4a$	$+3$
a	a^4	$-4a^2$	$+3a$

Answer: $a^4 - 4a^2 + 3a$

Expand

a $d(d^2 + 8d + 6)$

b $a(a^3 + 9a^2 - 2a)$

c $2b(3b^2 + 4b + 8)$

d $c^2(3c^2 - 2c - 1)$

2 Expand and simplify

a $a(a^2 + 4a) + 2a(a^2 + 6a)$

b $y(y^2 + 2y + 8) + y(y^2 + 3y + 5)$

c $a(3a^2 + 6a - 8) + a(2a^2 - a - 4)$

d $5b(b^2 + 3b + 5) - b(3b^2 + b - 2)$

3 Simplify

a $(5a)^3$

b $(3b)^2$

c $(2x)^4$

d $\left(\frac{x}{7}\right)^2$

e $\left(\frac{y}{9}\right)^2$

f $\left(\frac{b}{2}\right)^3$

4 Copy and complete

a $2^{-2} = \frac{1}{2^{\square}}$

b $2^{-3} = \frac{1}{2^{\square}}$

c $x^{-2} = \frac{1}{x^{\square}}$

d $y^{-3} = \frac{1}{y^{\square}}$

5 Simplify these expressions.

a $\frac{x^2}{x^3}$

b $\frac{y^4}{y^6}$

c $\frac{z^3}{z^8}$

d $\frac{w}{w^7}$

Q1a hint

×	d^2	$+8d$	$+6$
d			

Q1d hint

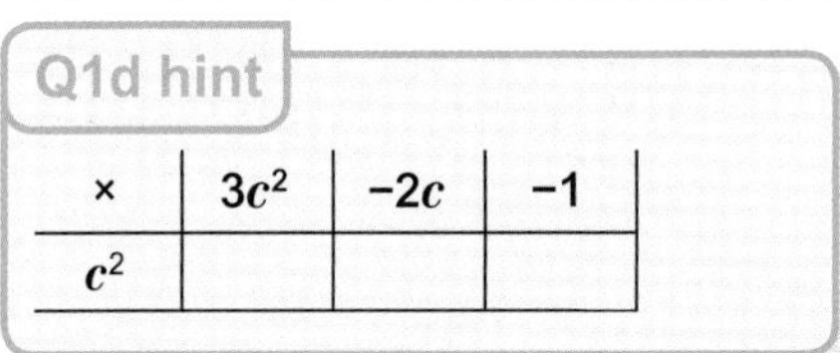

Q2a hint

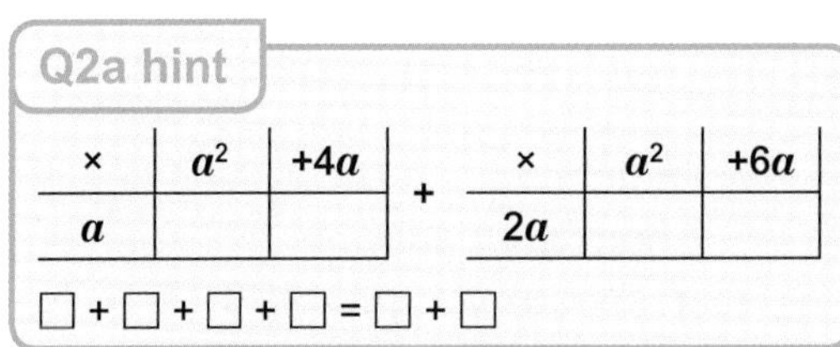

Q2d hint

Watch out for the '$-b$'.

Q3a hint

$(5a)^3 = 5a \times 5a \times 5a$
$= 5 \times a \times 5 \times a \times 5 \times a$
$= 5 \times 5 \times 5 \times a \times a \times a$
$= \square a^3$

Q3d hint

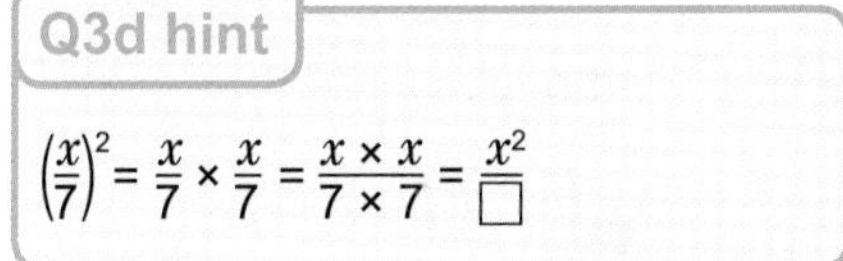

Q4 hint

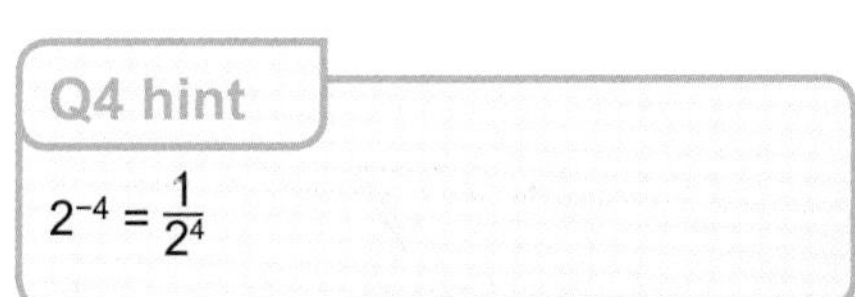

Q5a hint

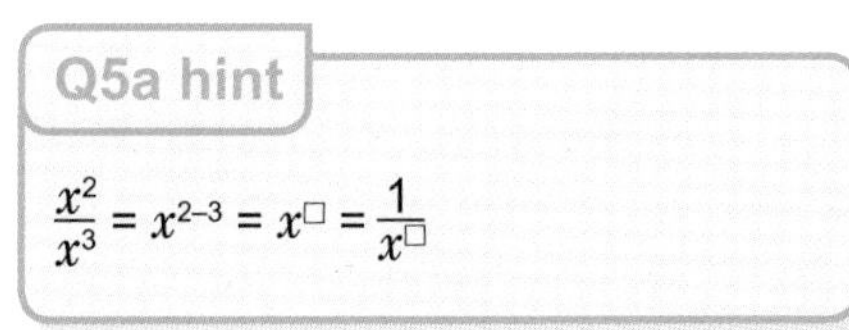

Q5d hint

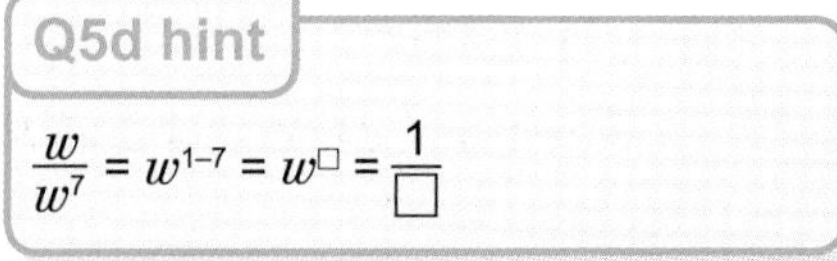

6 a What is the highest common factor of
   i $3x$ and 6 ii $4x^2$ and $12x$ iii $10x^2$ and $15x^3$?
  b Factorise each expression completely.
  Take out the highest common factor and put it in front of the brackets.
  Check your answers by expanding the brackets.
   i $10x + 5 = 5(\square + \square)$
   ii $12x - 9x^2 = 3x(\square - \square)$
   iii $25y^5 + 10y^2 = 5y^2(\square + \square)$
   iv $14a^3 - 10a = \square(\square - \square)$
   v $b^2 + 3b^4 = \square(\square + \square)$
   vi $12c^2 + 18c^3 = \square(\square + \square)$

Q6a ii hint
The HCF of 4 and 12 is 4.
x is also a common factor.
So $4\square$ is the HCF of $4x^2$ and $12x$.

Q6b iv hint
The HCF of 14 and 10 is 2.
a is also a common factor of $14a^3$ and $10a$.
So $2\square$ is the HCF of $14a^3$ and $10a$.

7 Factorise each expression completely.
Check your answers by expanding the brackets.
  a $4x + 14y + 8z = 2(\square + \square + \square)$
  b $x^2 + 3xy + 5xz = x(\square + \square + \square)$
  c $3a^2 + 9ab - 6ac = 3a(\square + \square - \square)$
  d $5mn + 15m^2 + 10m^3 = \square(\square + \square + \square)$
  e $8wx^2 + 4w^2x + 12wx = \square(\square + \square + \square)$
  f $6b + 24ab^3 - 12bc = \square(\square + \square - \square)$

Q7d hint
The HCF of 5, 15 and 10 is 5.
m is also a common factor of $5mn$, $15m^2$ and $10m^3$.
So $5\square$ is the HCF of these terms.

8 Expand and simplify
  a $(a + 2)(a + 5)$ b $(b + 9)(b + 4)$ c $(c + 1)(c + 2)$

9 Expand and simplify
  a $(a + 8)(a - 2)$ b $(b - 5)(b + 4)$ c $(c - 7)(c - 3)$

Q8 hint
To expand $(a + 2)(a + 5)$, use a grid method like this:

×	a	+2
a	$+a^2$	$+2a$
+5	$+5a$	+10

Answer: $a^2 + 2a + 5a + 10$
Simplify: $\square + \square + \square$

Q9a hint

×	a	+8
a		$+8a$
−2	$-2a$	

Enrichment

1 Which of these cards is the odd one out?
Explain how you worked out your answer.

A $3(2x^2 + 4) + 6xy$

B $x(x + 6y) + 6(x^2 + 2)$

C $12(2xy + x^2) - 6(x^2 + 3xy) + 12$

D $6(x^2 + xy + 2)$

2 STEM / Problem-solving These are two formulae that you might use in science.

$$T^2 = \frac{kx}{l} \qquad E = \frac{kx^2}{2l}$$

Use the values $T = 16$, $x = 0.6$ and $l = 3$ to work out the value of E.

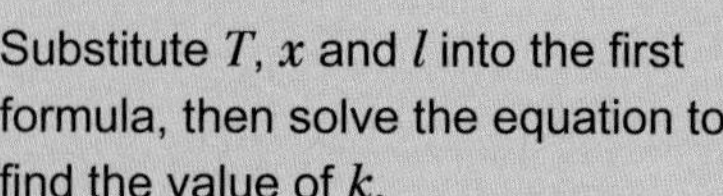

Q2 Strategy hint
Substitute T, x and l into the first formula, then solve the equation to find the value of k.
Use the second formula to find E.

Reflect

3 **Reflect** In Q5 and Q6 in 'Substituting into expressions', you looked at other students' working. Does this help you? How?
Ask someone in your class to show you a question they got wrong.
Try to work out what mistake they made.

2 Extend

You will:

- Extend your understanding with problem solving.

1 Problem-solving

a Match each lettered expression with the correct numbered answer.
Use the value of the letters given in the table.

a	b	c	d	e	f	g	h	i
3	−2	−5	16	25	−27	−4	4	12

A $4a^2 - \sqrt{e}$

B $b(\sqrt{d} + \sqrt{ai})$

C $\sqrt[3]{f} - 8c$

D $\frac{hi}{3} + 3b^2c$

E $\frac{b^2 + g^2}{h}$

F $\sqrt[3]{dh} - 2c^2$

1 −44

2 −20

3 37

4 −46

5 31

6 5

7 12

b One answer card has not been used. Write an expression for this answer card. Use at least three of the letters from the table, and include a power or a root in your expression.

2 STEM / Modelling You can use this formula to calculate the energy, E joules, in a moving object. $E = \frac{1}{2}mv^2$
where
m = mass of object (kg)
v = speed (metres per second, m/s)
Work out the speed, v, of the object when

a $E = 96$ and $m = 12$ **b** $E = 625$ and $m = 8$ **c** $E = 1470$ and $m = 15$

> **Q2a hint**
> When you know v^2, take the square root to find v.

3 Reasoning Carlos is substituting values into the expression $3x^2y + z^3$.
The values he uses for x, y and z are always negative.
Carlos says, 'The value of my expression will never be a positive number.' Is he correct? Explain your answer.

> **Q3 Strategy hint**
> Substitute different negative number values for x, y and z into the expression.

4 Substitute $a = -2$ and $b = -4$ into each expression and simplify the answer.

a $a^4 - b^3$ **b** $\sqrt{a^6}$ **c** $\sqrt[3]{b^2 - 2a^2}$ **d** $ab^2 - a^2b - (ab)^2$

e $\left(\frac{5}{2}b\right)^2$ **f** $\left(\frac{a}{b}\right)^3$ **g** $\frac{a^2b^2}{a^2 + b^2}$ **h** $\frac{\sqrt[3]{ab} + ab}{a^2 - b^2}$

5 STEM / Problem-solving You can use this formula to calculate the elastic potential energy, E joules, stored in a stretched string.

$$E = \frac{kx^2}{2l}$$

where
k = stretch factor
x = distance stretched (m)
l = normal length (m).

a Work out the value of E when

i $k = 40$, $x = 3$ and $l = 15$

ii $k = 32$, $x = 5$ and $l = 20$

You can use this formula to calculate the tension, T newtons, in a stretched string formula.

$$T = \frac{kx}{l}$$

where
k = stretch factor
x = distance stretched (m)
l = normal length (m).

b Work out the value of k when

i $T = 6$, $x = 2$ and $l = 5$

ii $T = 15$, $x = 2.5$ and $l = 8$

c Use both these formulae to work out the value of E when $T = 12$, $x = 1.5$ and $l = 4$

Q5 Literacy hint

Elastic potential energy is the energy stored in a string as a result of stretching it.

Q5c Strategy hint

Substitute T, x and l into the second formula then solve the equation to find the value of k.
Then use the first formula to find the value of E.

6 Modelling The diagram shows a shape made from two rectangles. All measurements are in centimetres.

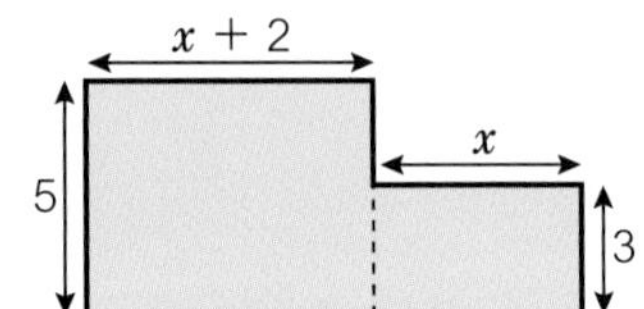

a Write an expression for the total area of the shape.

b The total area of the shape is $30\,cm^2$.
Write an equation in terms of x, then solve it to find the value of x.

c Work out the perimeter of the shape.

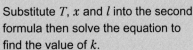

7 You can expand and simplify two sets of double brackets like this:

$$\begin{aligned}(x + 5)(x + 9) - (x + 1)(x + 7) &= [x^2 + 9x + 5x + 45] - [x^2 + 7x + x + 7] \\ &= [x^2 + 14x + 45] - [x^2 + 8x + 7] \\ &= x^2 + 14x + 45 - x^2 - 8x - 7 \\ &= 6x + 38\end{aligned}$$

Expand and simplify

a $(x + 15)(x + 4) - (x + 11)(x + 2)$

b $(x + 6)(x + 5) - (x + 8)(x + 3)$

c $(x + 3)(x + 2) + (x + 13)(x + 1)$

d $(x + 7)(x + 7) + (x + 3)(x + 3)$

e $(x + 9)(x - 2) + (x - 4)(x - 1)$

f $(x - 3)(x + 8) - (x + 7)(x - 6)$

8 Problem-solving / Reasoning

a Show that $(y + 4)(y + 7) - y(y + 8) = (y + 4)(y - 8) - (y - 12)(y + 5)$

b Explain the method that you used.

Topic links: Rounding, Metric and imperial measures, Area; Perimeter, Fractions

Subject links: Science (Q2, Q5, Q11)

9 Emil and Aaron make t the subject of the formula $v = u + at$ like this:

Emil

$v = u + at$

$v - u = at$ Subtract u from both sides.

$\frac{v - u}{a} = t$ Divide both sides by a.

$t = \frac{v - u}{a}$ Rewrite to get t on the left of the equals sign.

Aaron

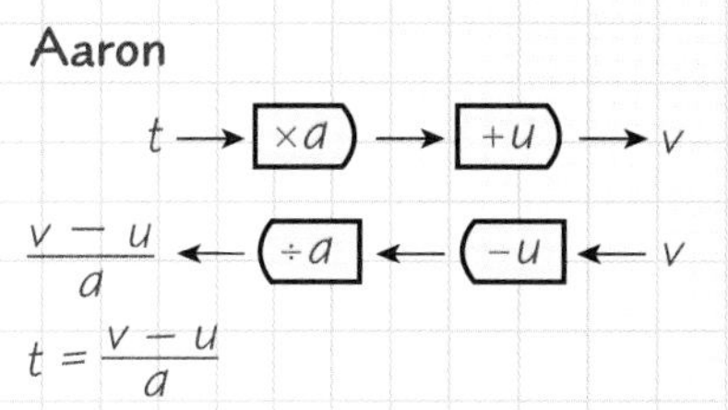

Use either method to make t the subject of each of these formulae.

a $m = 2t + p$ **b** $x = 5t - y$ **c** $A = mt + h$ **d** $N = at - by$

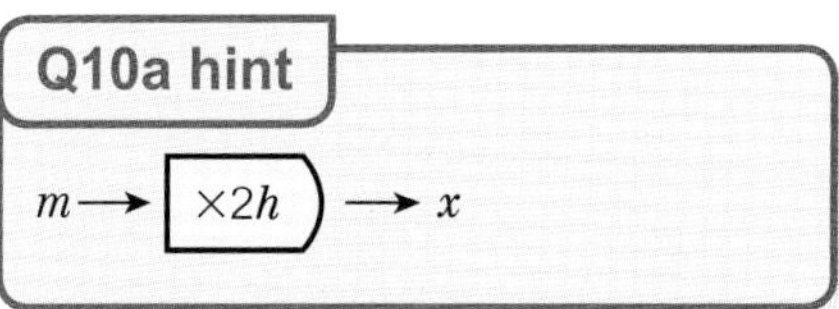

10 Make m the subject of each formula.

a $x = 2hm$ **b** $P = mgh$ **c** $r = \frac{m}{2l}$

d $y = \frac{3m}{4x}$ **e** $y = m^2$ **f** $x = m^2 + 2n$

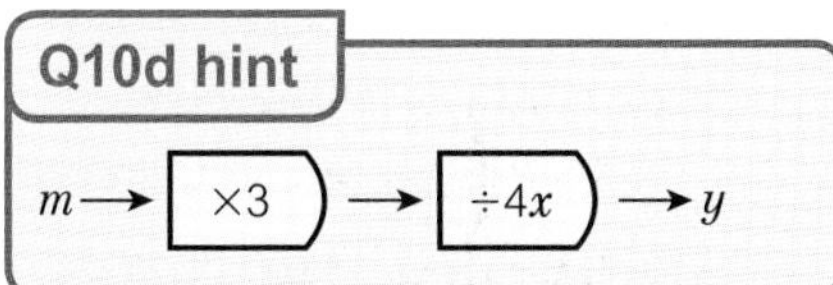

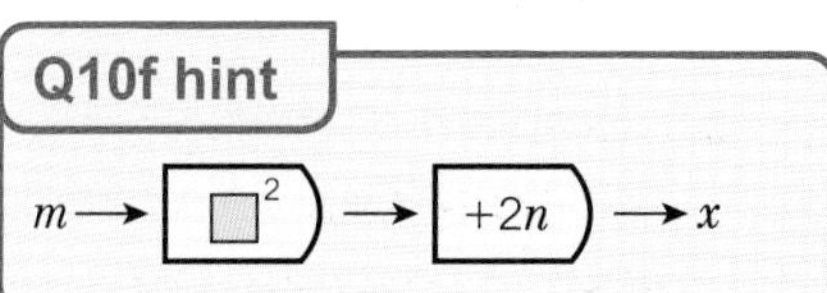

11 STEM You can use this formula to calculate the distance, s, travelled by a body that starts from rest.

$s = \frac{at^2}{2}$

where

a = acceleration (m/s^2)

t = time (s).

a **i** Make a the subject of the formula.

ii Make t the subject of the formula.

b Work out the value of s when $a = 10$ and $t = 3$.

c Use your answer to part **b** and the values given for a and t to check that your rearranged formulae in part **a** are correct.

12 Copy and complete

a $x^4 \times x^5 = x^{\square}$ **b** $x^3 \times x^2 = x^{\square}$ **c** $x^m \times x^n = x^{\square}$

d $\frac{x^7}{x^2} = x^{\square}$ **e** $\frac{x^9}{x^5} = x^{\square}$ **f** $\frac{x^m}{x^n} = x^{\square}$

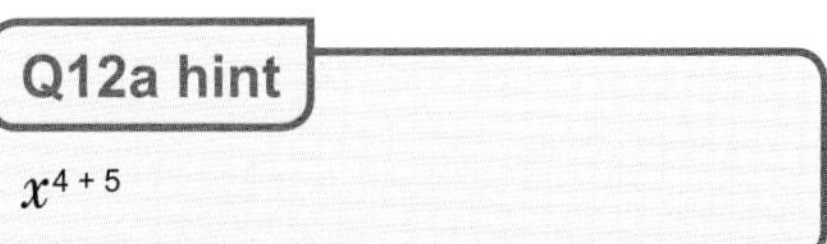

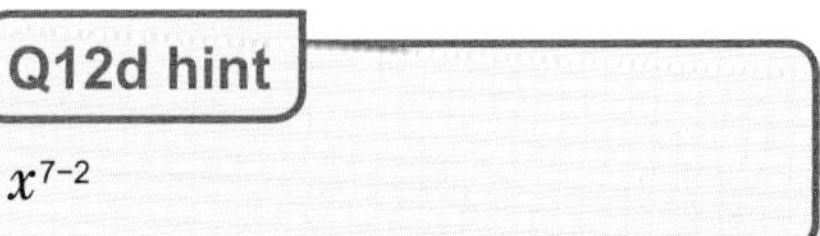

13 When you square a number you multiply it by itself.

For example, $5^2 = 5 \times 5 = 25$

or $16^2 = 16 \times 16 = 256$

or $(x + 2)^2 = (x + 2)(x + 2) = x^2 + 2x + 2x + 4 = x^2 + 4x + 4$

Expand and simplify.

a $(x + 3)^2$ **b** $(x + 5)^2$ **c** $(x - 4)^2$ **d** $(x - 8)^2$

14 Problem-solving / Modelling The diagram shows a red square with a square hole cut out of it.

a Explain how you can work out the red area on the diagram.

b Write an expression for the red area on the diagram. Simplify your expression.

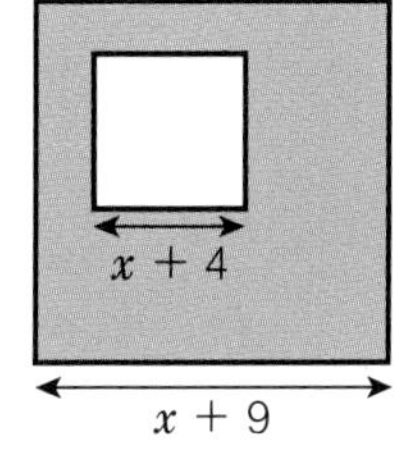

Q14a Strategy hint

How would you work out the red area if the side length of the red square was 20 cm and the side length of the hole was 15 cm?

Q14b hint

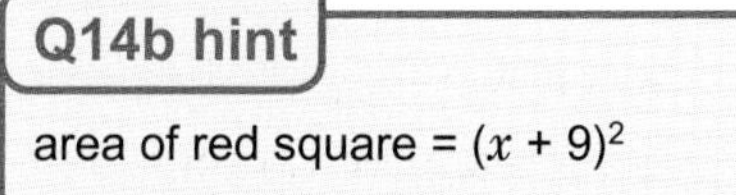

15 You add numerical fractions by using a common denominator like this:

$\frac{1}{6} + \frac{1}{2} = \frac{1}{6} + \frac{3}{6} = \frac{4}{6} = \frac{2}{3}$

You add algebraic fractions in the same way, so

$\frac{x}{6} + \frac{x}{2} = \frac{x}{6} + \frac{3x}{6} = \frac{4x}{6} = \frac{2x}{3}$

Work out these additions and subtractions. Write each answer in its simplest form.

a **i** $\frac{1}{2} + \frac{1}{4}$
ii $\frac{x}{2} + \frac{x}{4}$

b **i** $\frac{3}{10} + \frac{2}{5}$
ii $\frac{3x}{10} + \frac{2x}{5}$

c **i** $\frac{1}{2} - \frac{1}{5}$
ii $\frac{x}{2} - \frac{x}{5}$

d **i** $\frac{3}{4} - \frac{2}{3}$
ii $\frac{3x}{4} - \frac{2x}{3}$

16 **Problem-solving** A piece of wood has length y cm.

Two smaller pieces of wood have a length of $\frac{5y}{12}$ cm and $\frac{2y}{9}$ cm.

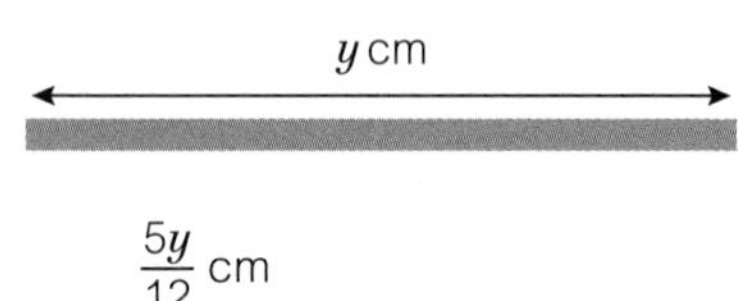

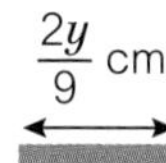

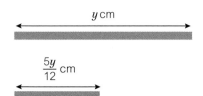

a Work out the total length of the two smaller pieces of wood

b Work out the difference in the lengths of the two smaller pieces of wood

17 Copy and complete

a $(x^2)^3 = x^{\square}$ **b** $(x^5)^4 = x^{\square}$ **c** $(x^m)^n = x^{\square}$

Q17a hint

$(x^2)^3 = x^2 \times x^2 \times x^2 = x^{2\times3} = x^{\square}$

18 **Problem-solving**

a Match each lettered expression with its simplified numbered expression.

A $x^a \times x^b \times x^c$	**E** $\frac{x^a}{(x^b)^c}$	**1** x^{a+b-c}	**5** x^{a-bc}
B $\frac{x^a}{x^b \times x^c}$	**F** $\frac{x^a \times x^b}{x^c}$	**2** x^{a+bc}	**6** x^{ab-c}
C $\frac{(x^a)^b}{x^c}$	**G** $x^a \times (x^b)^c$	**3** x^{ab+c}	**7** x^{a+b+c}
D $(x^a)^b \times x^c$		**4** x^{a-b-c}	**8** x^{ac-b}

b There is one card left over. Write an expression card that goes with it.

19 You can expand three sets of brackets, $(x + 5)(x + 1)(x + 2)$, like this:

First expand and simplify two of the sets of brackets.

$(x + 5)(x + 1) = x^2 + x + 5x + 5 = x^2 + 6x + 5$

Then multiply the expression you get by the remaining brackets.

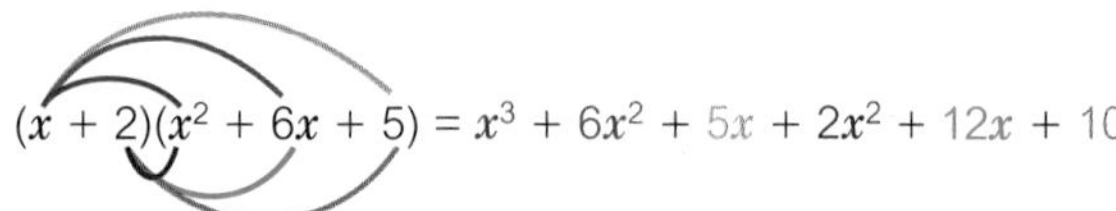

$(x + 2)(x^2 + 6x + 5) = x^3 + 6x^2 + 5x + 2x^2 + 12x + 10$

Then simplify to get the final expression:

$= x^3 + 8x^2 + 17x + 10$

Expand and simplify

a $(x + 1)(x + 2)(x + 3)$ **b** $(x + 4)(x + 9)(x - 1)$ **c** $(x - 3)(x + 4)(x - 2)$

Q19 hint

It doesn't matter which two sets of brackets you expand first.
Be careful with the minus signs.

Investigation

Modelling / Problem-solving

Here is part of a number grid.

1	2	3	4	5	6	7	8
9	10	11	12	13	14	15	16
17	18	19	20	21	22	23	24
25	26	27	28	29	30	31	32
33	34	35	36	37	38	39	40

1 A block of four numbers is shaded green.
You can work out the answer to
top right × bottom left − top left × bottom right
like this: 11 × 18 − 10 × 19 = 198 − 190 = 8

2 Do the same for the block of four numbers shaded
a red
b blue

3 What do you notice about your answers?

4 A block of four squares is shaded yellow on the same number grid.

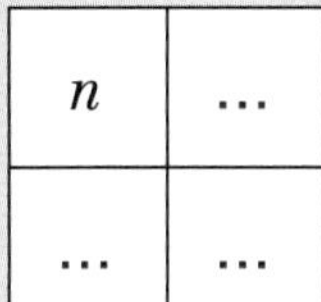

Part 4 hint

Bottom left number is 8 more than top left number, so it will be $n + \square$.

The number in the top left-hand corner is n.
Copy the block of four squares and write an expression for each number in the block in terms of n.

5 For the block of four yellow squares, work out

top right × bottom left − top left × bottom right

Expand and simplify your answer.

6 What do you notice about your answer?

7 Investigate blocks of four squares on different number grids: for example, rows of 6, 9, 12 etc.

8 What do you notice about your answers?

20 Reflect Look back at the questions you answered in these Extend lessons.
Find a question that you could not answer straightaway, or that you really had to think about.
Why couldn't you immediately see what to do?
How did this make you feel?
Did you keep trying or did you give up?
Did you think you would get the answer correct or incorrect?
Write down any strategies you could use when answering tricky algebra questions. Compare your strategies with others in your class.

2 Unit test

Log how you did on your Student Progression Chart.

1 Use the formula $F = pm + r$ to work out the value of F when

a $p = 7$, $m = 6$ and $r = 12$

b $p = 6$, $m = 2.5$ and $r = -8$

2 Use the formula $M = \frac{3r}{t}$ to work out the value of M when $r = 18$ and $t = -6$

3 Work out the value of these expressions.

a $2a + b^2$ when $a = 5$ and $b = 2$

b $40 - (a + b^3)$ when $a = 8$ and $b = 3$

c $(a + b)^2 - 4c$ when $a = 3$, $b = 5$ and $c = 5$

d $\frac{2a^2}{bc}$ when $a = 6$, $b = 4$ and $c = 3$

4 A wedding venue company charges an amount per person for food plus an amount per hour for the room hire.

a Work out the total cost of food for 80 people at £30 per person plus room hire at £50 per hour for 6 hours.

b Write an expression for the cost of food for p people at £x per person plus room hire for h hours at £y per hour.

c Write a formula for the total cost, T, in terms of x, p, y and h.

d Use your formula to work out T when $x = 35$, $p = 100$, $h = 8$ and $y = 30$.

5 Expand and simplify

a $x(x^2 + 15x) + 4x(2x^2 - 3x)$

b $2y(y^2 + 6y + 1) - y(3y^2 + 7y - 4)$

6 Simplify

a $(3x)^3$

b $\left(\frac{y}{4}\right)^2$

7 Find the value of each expression when $x = 4$, $y = -2$ and $z = 3$

a $x^2(3 - y) - 4z$

b $z(8x - z^3) + 2(3x + 2y)$

8 Use the formula $R = \frac{ax^2}{3}$ to work out the value of R when $a = 2$ and $x = 9$

9 Simplify these expressions.

a $\frac{x^3}{x^5}$

b $\frac{y^2}{y^8}$

c $\frac{z}{z^3}$

10 Factorise each expression completely. Check your answers.

a $24x + 8$

b $12x^3 - 9x^5$

c $y^2 + 15xy + 10yz$

d $4x^2 - 14xy - 2xyz$

11 Use the formula $A = bh$ to work out the value of

a h when $A = 35$ and $b = 5$

b b when $A = 20$ and $h = 8$

12 Use the formula $R = mg - T$ to work out the value of m when $R = 40$, $g = 12$ and $T = 8$

13 Expand and simplify $(x + 6)(x + 7)$

14 Expand and simplify

a $(x + 12)(x - 9)$

b $(m - 7)(m - 11)$

15 Make x the subject of these formulae.

a $F = x + p$ **b** $M = xR$ **c** $d = 5x + h$

16 Copy and complete

a $x^a \times x^b = x^{\square}$ **b** $\frac{x^a}{x^b} = x^{\square}$

17 Expand and simplify $(x + 6)^2$.

18 Work out these additions and subtractions.
Write each answer in its simplest form.

a $\frac{x}{3} + \frac{x}{6}$ **b** $\frac{7x}{8} - \frac{3x}{4}$

19 Copy and complete $(x^a)^b = x^{\square}$.

20 Expand and simplify $(x + 3)(x + 2)(x + 4)$.

Challenge

21 **a** Show that $2x(12x + 36) + 3x^2(10x^2 + 12x)$ and $12x(2x + 3x^2 + 6) + 30x^4$ simplify to give the same expression.

b Write three more expressions that all simplify to give the same expression as in part **a**.

22 **Reflect** This may be the first time you have done any algebra for a while.

Choose A, B or C to complete each statement.

In this unit, I did...	**A** well	**B** OK	**C** not very well
I think algebra is...	**A** easy	**B** OK	**C** difficult
When I think about doing algebra, I feel...	**A** confident	**B** OK	**C** unsure

If you answered mostly As and Bs, are you surprised that you feel OK about algebra? Why?

If you answered mostly Cs, look back at the questions in the lessons that you found most difficult. Ask a friend or your teacher to explain them to you. Then complete the statements above again.

Reflect

3 Dealing with data

MASTER

Check P68 | Strengthen P70 | Extend P75 | Test P78

3.1 Planning a survey

You will learn to:

- Identify sources of primary and secondary data
- Choose a suitable sample size and what data to collect
- Identify factors that might affect data collection and plan to reduce bias.

CONFIDENCE

Why learn this?
Shops owners carry out market research to see what products they should stock at different times of year.

Fluency
Work out
- 10% of £60
- 70% of 300 cm
- $\frac{4}{5}$ as a percentage

Explore
Where and when is it best to carry out a survey?

Exercise 3.1

Warm up

1 The table shows the ages of visitors to a library on a Monday.
  a How many visitors were there in total?
  b How many visitors were 18 or under?
  c What percentage of visitors were 61 or over?

Age (years)	Frequency
0–10	23
11–18	5
19–30	9
31–45	34
46–60	87
61+	42

Q2 hint
Which ages have the lowest frequencies?

2 a Where and when do you think the data in Q1 was collected?
  b What question was asked?

3 Henry wants to test if a coin is biased.
Should Henry flip the coin 10, 50 or 100 times?

Q3 Literacy hint
A biased coin is not fair – it lands on either heads or tails more often.

5 4 A town councillor wants to find out information about the ages of the people living in her town.
Which of these sources use **secondary data**?
  A She carries out a survey of the ages of people in the town centre.
  B She looks at the electoral roll.
  C She looks at library records.

Key point
Primary data is data **I** collect myself. **Secondary data** is collected by **s**omeone else.

Q4 Literacy hint
The electoral roll lists all those who are eligible to vote in an area.

Topic links: Percentages, Probability

Subject links: Science (Q8)

5 Reasoning For each survey select the most appropriate **sample** size. Explain your choices.

a A factory producing trainers wants to check the quality of a sample of trainers.
The factory produces 2000 pairs a day.
How many should be checked?
A 2 pairs
B 20 pairs
C 1000 pairs

b Angela thinks that 80% of the customers in her shop are female. She notes down M or F for each customer. How many customers should she do this for?
A 5
B 50
C 500

c A vet thinks that pet rabbits are showing increased levels of disease. How many of the rabbits that are brought into his surgery should he test?
A 20
B 200
C 300

Key point

The more items you test, the more reliable your results. But testing takes time and can be expensive. The group of items you test is called a **sample**.

6 What data would you collect to test each **hypothesis**?

a i 25% of children at a school walk to school.
ii Most households have more than one TV.
iii 40% of people eat at least five portions of fruit or vegetables a day.

b How would you collect the data for each?

Key point

A **hypothesis** is a statement that you can test by collecting data. Different ways of collecting data include **questionnaires**, **surveys**, **modelling** and **data logging**.

Q6b hint

What do you need to find out to test the statement?

7 Real Describe how you would find out information about

a the price of a loaf of bread over the past 10 years
b the average length of life of a UK citizen
c how fast students at your school can run 100 metres
d the population growth in China over the last 50 years
e the most popular magazine read by students at your school.

For each investigation **a–e**, say whether you would use primary or secondary data.

Q7 hint

You must be specific – if you choose the internet suggest what kind of website you would look for.

8 Real / STEM Select an appropriate level of accuracy for these investigations.

a The lengths of worms in a flower bed.
A nearest cm **B** nearest mm **C** nearest 0.1 mm

b The times taken to run 100 m at your school sports day.
A nearest minute **B** nearest second **C** nearest millisecond

c The times taken for athletes to run 100 m in a world record attempt.
A nearest minute **B** nearest second
C nearest hundredth of a second

d The masses of newborn babies.
A nearest kg **B** nearest 0.1 kg **C** nearest gram

Q8 hint

When choosing a level of accuracy, think about what you would measure with.

Q8c hint

At the London 2012 Olympic Games, Usain Bolt ran the 100 m in 9.63 seconds.

9 A school wants to investigate the length of time students spend travelling to school.
There are 1000 students at the school.
- **a** **i** Suggest the number of students that should be sampled.
  ii What level of accuracy should be used to record their times?
- **b** Which of these factors will affect the data?
  - **A** Standing by a bus stop to collect the data.
  - **B** Standing at the gates of the school to collect the data.
  - **C** The gender of the students asked.
  - **D** Asking only students who arrive at school early.
  - **E** Asking only students who travel by train.

Q9a hint

The sample must include enough students to give reliable data, but there must be time to ask them. In many cases, 10% of the total **population** gives a good-sized sample.

10 Four people carry out a survey to find out their town's favourite shop.
Method 1: Amy interviews 100 randomly chosen students at her school.
Method 2: Rudi stands in the centre of town on a Saturday and asks 500 people that he chooses randomly.
Method 3: Helen asks everyone coming out of a particular shop.
Method 4: Paul asks his friends, family and neighbours.
- **a** Which is the best method and why?
- **b** What bias was there in the other methods?
- **c** How could you improve the method you chose in part **a**?

Key point

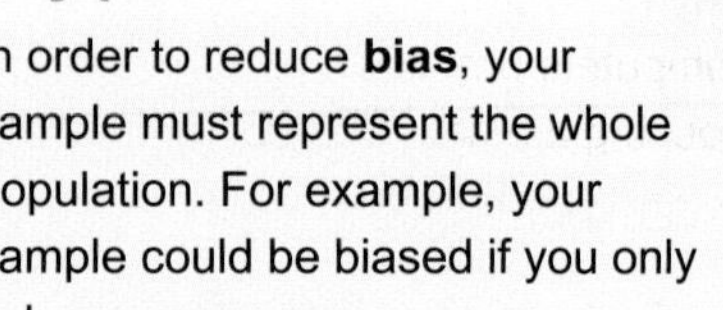

In order to reduce **bias**, your sample must represent the whole population. For example, your sample could be biased if you only ask one age group.

11 A school wants to choose a **random sample** of students to take part in a competition.
Which of these will give a random sample?
- **A** Students whose names begin with 'A'.
- **B** The oldest students.
- **C** Students' names placed into a hat and picked out.
- **D** Every 10th student on the whole school register.

Key point

In a **random sample** everyone must have the same chance of being chosen.

Investigation **Problem-solving**

Choose a topic that you are interested in. It could be sport, music, school activities, where you live – anything you like.

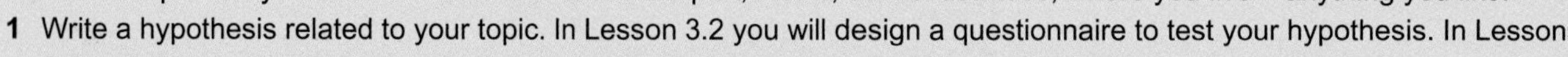

1. Write a hypothesis related to your topic. In Lesson 3.2 you will design a questionnaire to test your hypothesis. In Lessons 3.3 to 3.5 you will calculate averages, draw graphs and write a report of your findings.
2. Plan how you will test your hypothesis.
   - Where and when will you collect your data?
   - What sample size will you use?
   - How will you avoid bias in your sample?

Discussion What type of graph would you use to display the results of your investigation?

Explore

12 **Explore** Where and when is it best to carry out a survey?
Is it easier to explore this question now you have completed the lesson? What further information do you need to be able to answer this?

Reflect

13 **Reflect** How do you use mathematics when you plan a survey?

Q13 hint

Look carefully at some of the questions you answered. What mathematical skills do you need? What mathematical words must you understand?
What measures might you use?

3.2 Collecting data

You will learn to:

- Design a good questionnaire
- Design and use data collection sheets and tables.

CONFIDENCE

Why learn this?
Computers process large amounts of data by grouping the data in order to spot trends.

Fluency
$b = 5$
Which group should it be in?
$0 \leqslant b < 5$
$5 \leqslant b < 10$
$10 \leqslant b < 15$

Explore
What makes a good survey question?

Exercise 3.2

1 Real Here are the ages of 50 users of a leisure centre.
18, 23, 27, 36, 45, 42, 20, 8, 1, 17, 23, 45, 27, 29, 45, 60, 62, 35, 33, 41, 26, 25, 26, 68, 10, 19, 15, 23, 28, 30, 33, 36, 19, 18, 24, 26, 30, 41, 59, 65, 18, 34, 37, 36, 44, 45, 44, 37, 40, 44

a Copy and compete the tally chart for the data.

Age (years)	Tally	Frequency
0–10		
11–20		
21–30		
31–40		
40+		

b What percentage of customers are over 40?

2 In which class does 0.5 cm go for each of these frequency tables?

a

Length, l (cm)	Frequency
$0 \leqslant l < 0.5$	
$0.5 \leqslant l < 1$	
$1 \leqslant l < 1.5$	
$1.5 \leqslant l < 2$	

b

Length, l (cm)	Frequency
$0 < l \leqslant 0.5$	
$0.5 < l \leqslant 1$	
$1 < l \leqslant 1.5$	
$1.5 < l \leqslant 2$	

3 The table shows 50 people's driving test results.

	Men	Women
Pass	11	10
Fail	15	14

a What percentage of the drivers passed their driving test?

b What fraction of the men failed their driving test?

c Work out the pass : fail ratio.

Warm up

Key point
A **grouped frequency table** has 4 or 5 equal width classes. You can add a tally column for recording the data.

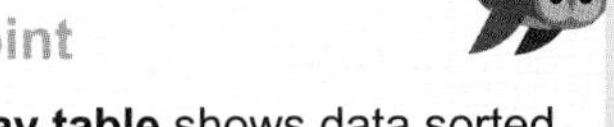

Q2 Strategy hint
For values that are at the limits of a class, check the $\leqslant$ and $<$ symbols carefully.

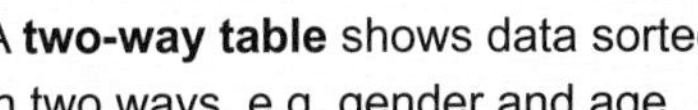

Key point
A **two-way table** shows data sorted in two ways, e.g. gender and age.

4 Here are some records from a hospital database.

a Design a grouped frequency table to record the masses.

b i Copy and complete this two-way table to show the masses and ages of the patients.

		Age (years)		
		10–29	30–49	50+
Mass, m (kg)	$50 \leqslant m < 70$			
	$70 \leqslant m < 90$			
	90+			

ii How many patients who are 50+ have a mass less than 70 kg?

iii What proportion of the patients are aged between 10 and 29 years?

iv What proportion of patients are in the middle mass group?

Name	Age	Mass, m (kg)
Hall	35	63
Field	25	56
Aintree	17	67
Kingley	34	80
Firbrand	56	77
Ruvierra	72	66
Huckelberry	61	70
Tudoristo	43	56
Franklin	45	73
Murphy	81	80
Orringe	34	88
Fruitry	47	93
Smith	65	67
Frankless	32	82
Harrison	45	91
Amberly	63	110
Kingston	45	84
Ocra	35	92
Savile	72	72
Dengel	56	88

5 Participants in a quiz show roll a standard dice and flip a coin. They win if they roll an even number and flip a head. Design a table to record each possible result.

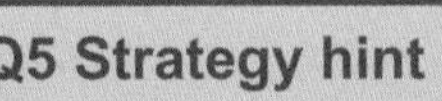

Q5 Strategy hint

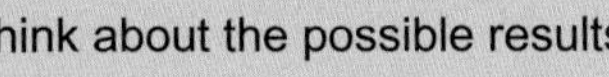

Think about the possible results.

6 The numbers of people using a supermarket each day in one month were
123, 179, 235, 189, 207, 199, 145, 154, 198, 132,
201, 99, 134, 245, 207, 198, 164, 157, 149, 183,
172, 175, 188, 192, 184, 167, 203, 201, 188, 181

a Is the data **discrete** or **continuous**?

b Design a grouped frequency table to record this data.

c Which group has the highest frequency?

7 A post office employee recorded the masses in kilograms of 15 parcels.
2.00, 4.54, 9.75, 8.21, 4.53,
3.45, 6.00, 1.24, 5.22, 3.30,
0.99, 6.12, 5.44, 6.23, 7.12

a Design a grouped frequency table to record this data.

b Which group has the highest frequency?

Key point

Discrete data can only take particular values. For example, dress sizes can only be even numbers. For discrete data you can use groups like 1–10, 11–20, …
Continuous data is measured and can take any value. Length, mass and capacity are continuous. For continuous data there are no gaps between the groups. You must use the $\leqslant$ and $<$ symbols.

Worked example

Here are three questions used in an online survey.
Explain what is wrong with each question and rewrite it.

a How old are you?

☐ 0–10 ☐ 10–20 ☐ 20–30 ☐ 30–50 ☐ 50+

The groups overlap. For example, if you are 20 years old, which box do you tick?

Change to: ☐ 0–10 ☐ 11–20 ☐ 21–30 ☐ 31–50 ☐ 51+

b Do you agree that exercise is enjoyable? ☐ Yes ☐ No

Saying, 'Do you agree?' encourages the answer 'Yes'.

Change to: Do you enjoy exercise?

Topic links: Upper and lower limits, Percentages

c Do you exercise enough?

'Enough' is not precise and means different things to different people.
Change to: How much do you exercise each day?
☐ Less than 1 hour ☐ 1–2 hours ☐ More than 2 hours

8 Anti animal-cruelty campaigners want to find out how people feel about killing animals for fur. They ask, 'It is cruel to kill animals for fur, isn't it?'

a What do you think most people will answer?

~~Discussion Why is this a leading question?~~

b Rewrite the question to find out what people really think about killing animals for fur.

Q8 Literacy hint

A **leading question** encourages people to give a particular answer.

9 a Explain what is wrong with each of these questions and rewrite them.

i How many portions of fruit or vegetables do you eat a day?
☐ 0–2 ☐ 4–6 ☐ 6–8

ii Do you eat a healthy diet?
☐ Yes ☐ No

iii Do you agree that fruit and vegetables are good for you?
☐ Yes ☐ No

b Imagine you are carrying out a survey using your new questions. Design a data collection sheet with tables to collect together all the answers.

10 Design your own questionnaire to test this hypothesis.
'Most people watch at least two hours of television a day.'

Investigation **Problem-solving**

Look at the hypothesis that you wrote in the investigation in lesson 3.1.

1 Design a questionnaire to collect the information you need to test your hypothesis.
2 Test your questionnaire on a friend.
3 Collect data from a suitable sample.
4 Record your findings in a two-way table or spreadsheet.

11 **Explore** What makes a good survey question?
Is it easier to explore this question now you have completed the lesson?
What further information do you need to be able to answer this?

12 **Reflect** You have learned lots of new terminology so far in this unit.
For example

- primary data and secondary data
- hypotheses
- bias
- random samples
- discrete and continuous data

Work with a classmate. Discuss what you think 'primary data' and 'secondary data' are. Now write definitions for 'primary' and 'secondary data'. Try to be as accurate as possible.
Look at the key point for primary and secondary data in lesson 3.1 to see if you got it right. If not, write a definition in your own words to help you remember.
Do the same for the other words in the list.

Q12 Literacy hint

'Terminology' is the special words or 'terms' used in a subject.

Explore

Reflect

3.3 Calculating averages

You will learn to:
- Find the modal class of a set of grouped data
- Estimate the mean from a large set of grouped data.

CONFIDENCE

Why learn this?
Medical researchers need to deal with large amounts of data. They often group it to make it easier to deal with and then calculate averages.

Fluency
Work out the mean of
−5, −4, −3, −2, 3.

Explore
Why might the owner of a large business estimate the mean number of sick days taken by staff?

Exercise 3.3

Warm up

1 The table shows the numbers of goals scored by a football team in matches over one season.
   a What is the modal number of goals scored?
   b How many matches did the team play?
   c Work out the mean number of goals scored.
   d Work out the range of goals scored.

Number of goals	Frequency
0	5
1	6
2	3
3	2
4	3
5	1

2 The grouped frequency table shows the ages of players in the team.

Age (years)	Frequency
10–15	1
16–20	8
21–25	2

   a What is the modal class?
   b Work out an estimate for the range of ages.

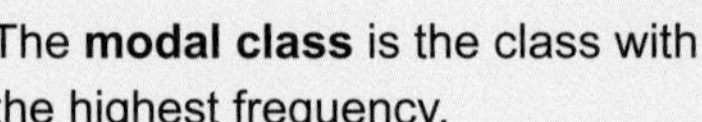

Q2a Literacy hint
The **modal class** is the class with the highest frequency.

3 a Calculate the mean of 30.2, 29.8, 30.04, 31, 30.5.
   b Now calculate the mean using this method.
      i Assume the mean is 30.
        Subtract this assumed mean from each of the values.
      ii Find the mean of your answers to part **b i**.
      iii Add this value to 30.
   Discussion Do you get the same answer in parts **a** and **b**? Which method did you find easier? Which method took less time?

Key point
An **assumed mean** is an estimated value for the mean, close to all the data values.

4 Real / Reasoning The ages of five students are:
10 years 3 months, 10 years 9 months, 10 years 1 month,
9 years 11 months, 10 years 0 months
Work out the mean of their ages.
Discussion Which method did you use? Explain why.

Q4 hint
You could use an assumed mean.

Topic links: Adding negative numbers, Finding midpoints

Subject links: Science (Q10)

5 

12	13	8	11	?

What is the missing number if

a the mode is 11

b the mean is 10

c the range is 10?

6 **Reasoning / Problem-solving** Five whole numbers have mode 10, median 12 and mean 12.
Work out what they are.

Worked example

In a survey, people were asked their age. The table shows the results.

Age, a (years)	Frequency
$0 \leqslant a < 10$	12
$10 \leqslant a < 20$	15
$20 \leqslant a < 30$	2
$30 \leqslant a < 40$	11

a Work out an estimate for the range of ages.

From the frequency table, the smallest possible age is 0 years.
The largest possible age is 40 years.
So an estimate of the range is $40 - 0 = 40$ years.

Add a column to calculate the midpoint of each class. This represents the ages, because you don't know the exact values in each class.

b Calculate an estimate for the mean age.

Age, a (years)	Frequency	Midpoint of class	Midpoint × Frequency
$0 \leqslant a < 10$	12	$\frac{0 + 10}{2} = 5$	$5 \times 12 = 60$
$10 \leqslant a < 20$	15	$\frac{10 + 20}{2} = 15$	$15 \times 15 = 225$
$20 \leqslant a < 30$	2	25	$25 \times 2 = 50$
$30 \leqslant a < 40$	11	35	$35 \times 11 = 385$
Total	40		720

Add a column to calculate an estimate of the total age for each class.

Calculate the total number of people in the survey and the sum of their ages.

mean = sum of ages ÷ total number of people

$= \frac{720}{40}$

$= 18$

7 **a** The table shows the lengths of a sample of grass snakes. Copy and complete the table.

~~**b** What is the modal class?~~

~~**c** Work out an estimate for the range.~~

d Calculate an estimate for the mean length.

~~**Discussion** Why is the mean an estimate?~~

Length, l (cm)	Frequency	Midpoint of class	Midpoint × Frequency
$0 \leqslant l < 6$	8		
$6 \leqslant l < 12$	7		
$12 \leqslant l < 18$	2		
$18 \leqslant l < 24$	3		
Total			

8 Real The table shows the earnings of workers in a factory.

Earnings (per annum), e	Number of employees
$0 < e \leqslant \pounds 10\,000$	3
$\pounds 10\,000 < e \leqslant \pounds 20\,000$	52
$\pounds 20\,000 < e \leqslant \pounds 30\,000$	29
$\pounds 30\,000 < e \leqslant \pounds 40\,000$	27
$\pounds 40\,000 < e \leqslant \pounds 50\,000$	5
$\pounds 50\,000 < e \leqslant \pounds 60\,000$	3

a What is the modal class for this data?

b Work out an estimate for the range.

c Calculate an estimate for the mean earnings. Round your answer to the nearest pound.

9 a What is the modal class for each of these data sets?

i

Class	Frequency
$0 \leqslant a < 2$	3
$2 \leqslant a < 4$	5
$4 \leqslant a < 6$	11
$6 \leqslant a < 8$	1

ii

Class	Frequency
$0 < b \leqslant 0.5$	2
$0.5 < b \leqslant 1$	1
$1 < b \leqslant 1.5$	7
$1.5 < b \leqslant 2$	0

iii

Class	Frequency
$0 \leqslant l < 0.4$	52
$0.4 \leqslant l < 0.8$	13
$0.8 \leqslant l < 1.2$	22
$1.2 \leqslant l < 1.6$	13

b Work out an estimate of the range for each data set.

c Calculate an estimate of the mean for each data set.

10 STEM A scientist is testing the hypothesis that each year tadpoles are bigger. She recorded the lengths of 100 of this year's tadpoles.

a What is the modal class?

b Estimate the range of lengths.

c Calculate an estimate for the mean length.

d Last year the estimate for the mean length was 5.92 mm. Is the scientist's hypothesis correct?

Discussion Should the scientist draw a conclusion based on this data?

Length, l (mm)	Frequency
$3 < l \leqslant 4$	7
$4 < l \leqslant 5$	18
$5 < l \leqslant 6$	27
$6 < l \leqslant 7$	31
$7 < l \leqslant 8$	11
$8 < l \leqslant 9$	6

Investigation — **Problem-solving**

Look at the data that you recorded in the investigation in lesson 3.2.
Work out the modal class, mean and range for your data.

Explore

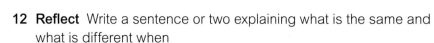

11 Explore Why might the owner of a large business estimate the mean number of sick days taken by staff?
Look back at the maths you have learned in this lesson.
How can you use it to answer this question?

Reflect

12 Reflect Write a sentence or two explaining what is the same and what is different when

- finding the mean of a set of data
- finding the *assumed* mean of a set of data
- finding the *estimated* mean of a set of grouped data.

Q12 hint

How do you define the mean?
What is the first thing you do when you find the mean, assumed mean and estimated mean?

3.4 Display and analyse data

You will learn to:

- Construct and use a line of best fit to estimate missing values
- Identify and explain outliers in data
- Identify further lines of enquiry
- Construct and use frequency polygons.

CONFIDENCE

Why learn this?
A good scientist can spot any outliers in data and suggest what might have caused them.

Fluency
Find the midpoint of each group.

- $2 < e \leqslant 8$
- $0.5 < e \leqslant 1$
- $5 < e \leqslant 12$

Explore
What is a temperature anomaly map?

Exercise 3.4

1 **Real** The table shows the age and number of visits to a doctor's surgery from April to September for 20 people.

Age (years)	25	67	35	92	35	48	72	18	25	63	28	19	26	50	38	78	93	38	1
Number of visits	2	7	4	12	3	6	8	0	2	7	3	1	4	8	5	13	12	4	8

a Draw a pair of axes with the horizontal axis from 0 to 100 labelled 'Age' and the vertical axis from 0 to 15 labelled 'Number of visits'. Plot a scatter graph showing this data.

b What type of correlation does the graph show?

c Draw a line of best fit.

2 **a** **Modelling** Use the line of best fit in Q1 to estimate the number of visits a 40-year-old would make between April and September.

b Use the line of best fit to estimate the age of a patient who visited the doctor 11 times between April and September.

c A doctor suggests this hypothesis.
'The older you are, the more times you visit the doctor per year.'
Does the data collected match the hypothesis?

d Explain what you would need to do to investigate this hypothesis further.

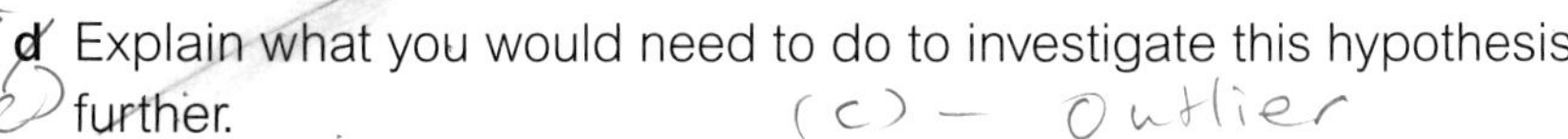

Discussion Did everyone in your class get the same answer to parts **a** and **b**?

3 Identify an outlier in Q1 and suggest what might have caused it.

Q2a hint
Find 40 on the correct axis. Draw a line up to the line of best fit and then across to the other axis.

Q2d Strategy hint
Is the sample size suitable?

Key point
An **outlier** is a value that doesn't follow the trend or pattern.

Warm up

4 Real / Modelling The manager of a shop wants to work out when she needs the most staff in her shop. She records the numbers of customers in a shop at half-hour intervals one Monday.

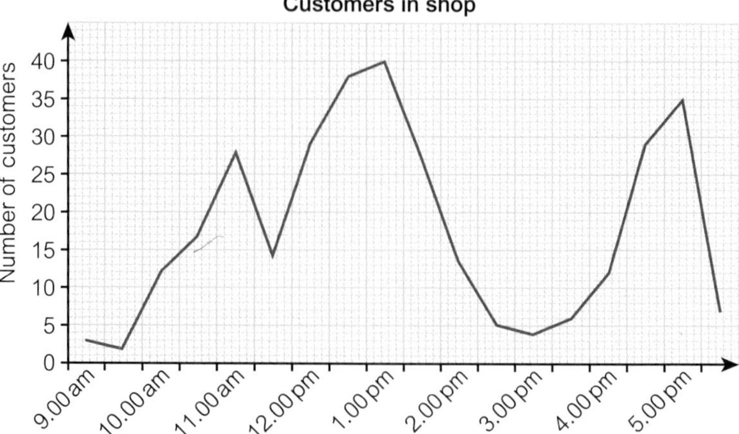

She draws this graph.

a Which times is she most likely to need extra staff?

b Suggest a reason why these times might be the busiest.

c How could she investigate further?

Worked example

Draw a frequency polygon to represent this data.

Age, a	Frequency
$0 \leqslant a < 10$	12
$10 \leqslant a < 20$	15
$20 \leqslant a < 30$	2
$30 \leqslant a < 40$	11

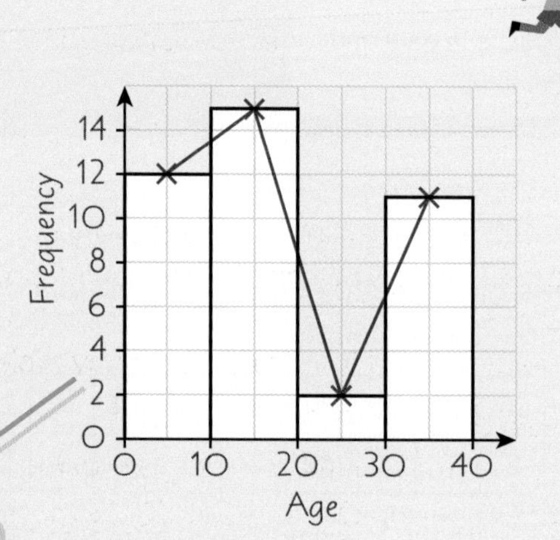

First draw a frequency diagram. Then join the midpoints of the tops of bars.

Key point

You can draw a **frequency polygon** by joining the midpoints of the tops of the bars in a frequency diagram.

5 Samarah constructs a frequency polygon for this data.

Earnings (per year), e	Number of employees
$0 < e \leqslant £10\,000$	3
$£10\,000 < e \leqslant £20\,000$	52
$£20\,000 < e \leqslant £30\,000$	29
$£30\,000 < e \leqslant £40\,000$	27
$£40\,000 < e \leqslant £50\,000$	5
$£50\,000 < e \leqslant £60\,000$	3

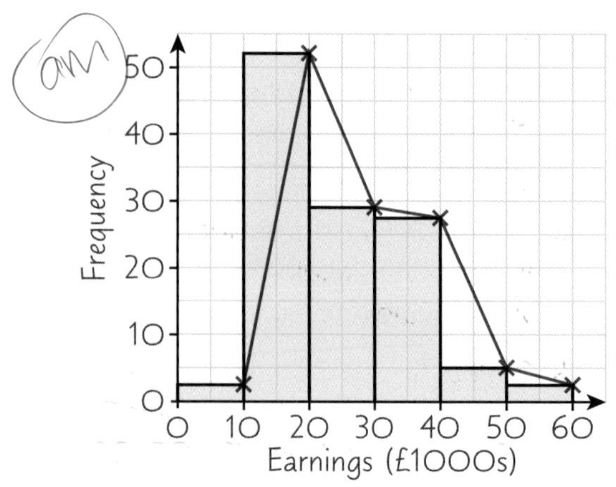

a Explain what she has done wrong.

b Construct an accurate frequency polygon for the data.

Discussion Can you see a shortcut for drawing a frequency polygon?

6 A leisure centre records the number of customers hourly through the day.

Leisure centre A

Time	9–10 am	10–11 am	11–12 pm	12–1 pm	1–2 pm	2–3 pm	3–4 pm	4–5 pm
Number of customers	35	79	182	23	31	245	90	118

a Draw a pair of axes with the horizontal axis showing time from 9 am to 5 pm and the vertical axis from 0 to 250 labelled 'Number of customers'. Construct a frequency polygon for the data.

Another leisure centre records this data.

Leisure centre B

Time	9–10 am	10–11 am	11–12 pm	12–1 pm	1–2 pm	2–3 pm	3–4 pm	4–5 pm
Number of customers	127	23	65	213	189	34	21	17

b Construct a frequency polygon for the second leisure centre on the same axes as part **a**.

c Compare the busiest times for the two leisure centres.

Q6b hint

Do you need to draw a frequency diagram first or can you simply construct a frequency polygon?

7 A teacher recorded the time (in minutes) that Class 2B spent on their maths homework.

34, 29, 3, 55, 16, 23, 30, 39, 59, 45, 35, 48, 33, 56, 29, 51, 23, 41, 31, 45

a Identify any outliers in the data.

b Construct a grouped frequency table, ignoring any outliers.

c Construct a frequency polygon to display the data from your frequency table.

d What is the modal class?

e Work out the range and mean from your frequency table.

Discussion How could the outliers have occurred?

Class 3C spent these lengths of time on their homework.

44, 51, 34, 62, 34, 56, 49, 44, 48, 23, 54, 34, 35, 36, 55, 56, 47, 44, 41, 20

f Construct a frequency polygon of this data on the same axes.

g What is the modal class for Class 3C?

h Work out the range and mean.
Are these accurate values or estimates?

i Compare the times spent on homework by the two classes.

Q7i hint

Use the averages and range, and look at the shape of the frequency polygons.

Investigation — **Problem-solving**

Construct a graph to present your findings from your investigation in lesson 3.2.

You may choose any graph you know how to draw: scatter graph, pie chart, frequency diagram, frequency polygon, bar chart.

Think about what you wish to display and how easy it will be to read the mean, mode, median and range from it.

8 **Explore** What is a temperature anomaly map?
Is it easier to explore this question now you have completed the lesson?
What further information do you need to be able to answer this?

9 **Reflect** In this lesson you used a

- scatter diagram (for Q1 and Q2)
- line graph (for Q4)
- frequency polygon (for Q5, Q6 and Q7)

a Which type of diagram do you find easiest? Why?

b Which type of diagram do you find hardest? Why?

c What could you do to make it easier to work with the diagram you chose in part **b**?

Explore

Reflect

3.5 Writing a report

You will learn to:
- Write a report to show survey results.

CONFIDENCE

Why learn this?
Chemical engineers use ICT to manage experimental data. They might also produce a report that explains how their experiments could lead to improved household products.

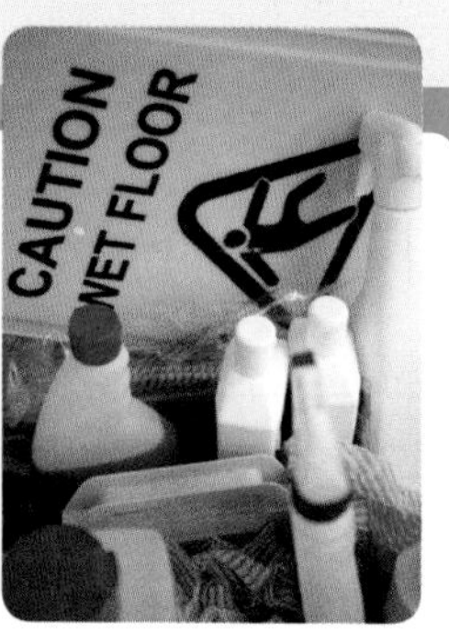

Fluency
Work out the midpoint of these classes.
- 0–5
- 1–5
- 0–4
- 1–6

Explore
What could a company do to find out how the price of a new product might affect demand?

Exercise 3.5

Warm up

1 The table shows the languages studied by students in a Year 9 class. Draw a pie chart to show this data. You could use a spreadsheet.
Which average can you find from the chart?

Language	Number of students
German	18
Spanish	5
French	13

2 **Real** This dual bar chart shows the child population (in millions) by age in the USA for 1950 and 2012.

Child population in the USA

1950
2012

Number of children (millions)
30
25
20
15
10
5
0
0–5
6–11
12–17
Age (years)

Source: www.childstats.gov

a What is the modal age group for
i 1950 ii 2012?

b i Copy and complete the frequency table for 1950.

Age	Midpoint	Frequency
0–5		
6–11		
12–17		

ii Use the frequency table to calculate an estimate of the mean age of a child in 1950. Give your answer to one decimal place.

c Calculate an estimate of the mean age in 2012. Use the method from part **b**.

3 **Real** 'GDP per capita' means 'Gross Domestic Product per person'. This is an average, worked out by calculating how much the country earns as a whole and dividing by the population.
The spreadsheet shows the GDP of nine countries in 2012.

	A	B
1	**Country**	**GDP per capita ($)**
2	Congo	262
3	Burundi	251
4	Central African Republic	483
5	Sierra Leone	635
6	Afghanistan	687
7	Mozambique	565
8	Nepal	690
9	Guinea	492
10	Mali	694

Source: World Bank

a Use a spreadsheet to draw a bar chart.
b Write two sentences about what the bar chart shows.
c Explain whether you think your results are a good representation of the GDP across the world.
d Describe how you might investigate this further.

Topic links: Pie charts, Bar charts, Stem and leaf diagrams

Subject links: Science (Q5), Computing (Q6)

4 Tyler recorded the numbers of words in 20 sentences in two different newspapers.

Paper A 9, 11, 13, 15, 12, 8, 12, 13, 14, 13, 12, 11, 8, 7, 5, 5, 11, 7, 6, 8

Paper B 15, 17, 19, 23, 21, 24, 22, 20, 18, 5, 18, 17, 14, 9, 11, 13, 14, 18, 15, 9

a Draw a back-to-back stem and leaf diagram for this data.

b Find the median, range and mean number of words in a sentence for both papers.

c Write two sentences comparing the two papers.

d Do you think this statement is true? Explain your answer.
'Paper B always uses longer sentences than Paper A.'

e How could you investigate further to confirm or refute this hypothesis.

Q4a hint
To draw a back-to-back stem and leaf diagram, write the 'tens' down the central stem. Paper A data will form the leaves to the left of the stem and Paper B the leaves to the right.

Q4e Literacy hint
'Confirm' means to show it is true.
'Refute' means to show it is false.

5 STEM A scientist suggests this hypothesis.
'Coffee cools faster than tea.'
She measures the temperature of cooling cups of tea and coffee over 30 minutes.

Time (minutes)	0	5	10	15	20	25	30
Temperature of tea (°C)	91	81	72	64	57	51	45
Temperature of coffee (°C)	91	80	74	67	60	59	55

a Plot two line graphs for this data on the same axes.

b Write a report based on her findings.
Make sure your report answers these questions.
- What do the results show?
- How could she improve her results?
- Do her results give a reliable conclusion?

Key point
A report should include
- the hypothesis or what you are investigating
- the data shown in a graph or chart
- averages and range
- a conclusion
- what else you could investigate.

Q5a Strategy hint
Plot time on the horizontal axis.

6 Real A geography student wants to find out how far people are willing to travel to visit the cinema. He asks 100 customers at cinema A, 'How far is this cinema from your home?'
The table shows his results.

Cinema A

Distance, d (miles)	Frequency
$0 < d \leqslant 5$	21
$5 < d \leqslant 10$	32
$10 < d \leqslant 15$	23
$15 < d \leqslant 20$	15
$20 < d \leqslant 25$	7
$25 < d \leqslant 30$	2
$30 < d \leqslant 35$	0
$35 < d \leqslant 40$	0
$40 < d \leqslant 45$	1

a Use ICT to write a report on the data he has collected. Make sure you
- include at least one graph – think carefully about which type to use
- identify any outliers and explain how they might have occurred
- include an estimate of the mean, range and modal class (ignore any outliers)
- explain how you could improve the student's investigation.

NEW
Q5 - interpret B to B S+L diag
Q6 - draw B to B S+L diag

The student completed a second survey at another cinema.
The table shows his results.

Cinema B

Distance, d (miles)	Frequency
$0 < d \leqslant 5$	0
$5 < d \leqslant 10$	8
$10 < d \leqslant 15$	34
$15 < d \leqslant 20$	15
$20 < d \leqslant 25$	7
$25 < d \leqslant 30$	19
$30 < d \leqslant 35$	17
$35 < d \leqslant 40$	0
$40 < d \leqslant 45$	0

b Use a spreadsheet to construct two frequency polygons on the same axes showing the data for both cinemas.

c For cinema B

i calculate an estimate of the mean distance people travel

ii calculate an estimate of the range of distances

iii find the modal class.

d Compare the averages and range for the two cinemas.

Q6b hint

You need two columns in your spreadsheet: midpoint and frequency. To draw the graph, click the insert tab. Click 'scatter' and select graph with straight lines and markers.

Cinema A is a town centre cinema with three screens. Cinema B is in a leisure complex and has ten screens.

e Write a conclusion to explain what the student has found out about the distances people will travel to large and small cinemas.

Investigation **Problem-solving**

Write a report on your findings from the hypothesis you have been investigating throughout this unit.

Explore

7 Explore What could a company do to find out how the price of a new product might affect demand?
Look back at the maths you have learned in this unit. How can you use it to answer this question?

Reflect

8 Reflect Why do you think people use mathematical diagrams or graphs when they write reports? Write down at least two ideas. Compare them with your classmates.

3 Check up

Log how you did on your Student Progression Chart.

Surveys

1 A student wants to find out about the type of food students prefer. She collects two sets of data.

A A survey of students about the food they like.
B A record of food sold in the canteen.

a Are A and B primary data or secondary data?
b There are 1500 students at the school.
What size sample should she use: 20, 200 or 1000?

2 Explain what is wrong with each question.
a What is your shoe size?
☐ 1–3 ☐ 3–5 ☐ 5–7 ☐ 7+
b Do you agree that it is harder to buy shoes for larger feet?

3 Which units, m, cm or mm, should you use to measure these?
a the lengths of the long jump at a school sports day
b the length of a screw
c the length of a swimming pool

4 A farmer logs the mass (in grams) of 20 eggs laid by her chickens.
70.5 61.2 75.3 77.7 79.7 80.0 84.3 69.9 70.5 91.3
90.0 68.9 73.8 80.4 78.4 81.9 70.1 73.3 82.3 79.9
a Design a frequency table to record the data.
b Complete your frequency table.

5 At stage school the head teacher records the gender (male or female) and the course (singing, dancing, acting) of all the students.

M – singing	F – dancing	M – dancing	M – acting	F – acting
F – singing	F – acting	M – singing	M – acting	M – singing
M – singing	M – acting	F – acting	F – acting	F – dancing
M – dancing	M – dancing	M – dancing	M – singing	F – acting

a Put the data into a two-way table.
b Which course do most of the boys do?
c Which course do fewest girls do?

6 You wish to identify the most popular clothing brand. You are going to survey 200 people in a town.
Which is the best sample to reduce bias?
A customers in one shop
B females
C people over 60
D 200 people randomly selected

Calculating averages

7 The table shows the projected population for the UK in 2020. Which is the modal class of this data?

Age (years)	Population (thousands)
0–9	8165
10–19	7521
20–29	8640
30–39	8921
40–49	8265
50–59	9032
60–69	7159
70–79	5797
80–89	2914
90–99	689
100+	23

Source: ONS

8 The table shows the lifespan of a sample of butterflies. Calculate an estimate for the mean lifespan.

Lifespan, w (days)	Frequency
$0 < w \leqslant 5$	3
$5 < w \leqslant 10$	91
$10 < w \leqslant 15$	96
$15 < w \leqslant 20$	80

Display and analyse

9 **a** Draw two frequency polygons on the same axes to show the lifespans of butterflies and moths.

Lifespan, w (days)	Butterflies	Moths
$0 < w \leqslant 5$	3	1
$5 < w \leqslant 10$	88	123
$10 < w \leqslant 15$	76	91
$15 < w \leqslant 20$	83	35

b Describe the main differences.

10 The scatter graph shows the number of driving lessons plotted against the number of driving tests taken before a successful pass.

a Identify an outlier.

b Suggest a reason for this outlier.

c Adil has 36 lessons. Estimate how many tests he would take before passing.

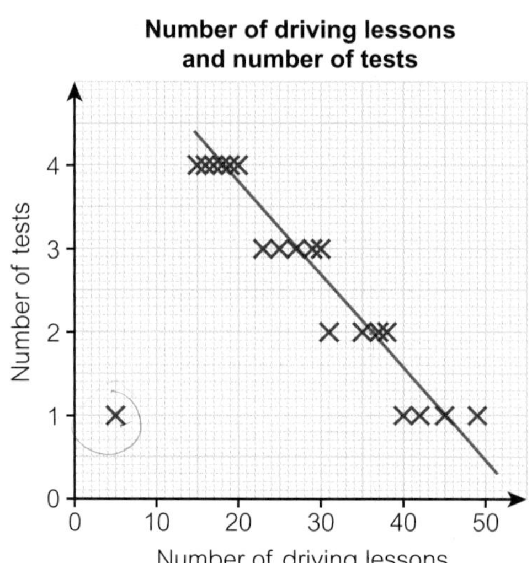

Reflect

11 How sure are you of your answers? Were you mostly

Just guessing **Feeling doubtful** **Confident**

What next? Use your results to decide whether to strengthen or extend your learning.

Challenge

12 **a** What would you choose as an assumed mean for this set of data?
25, 26, 27, 28, 29, 30, 31, 32, 33, 34, 35

b Work out the mean of 55, 56, 57, 58, 59, 60, 61, 62, 63, 64, 65.

13 The mean of a set of five positive whole numbers is 20. The mode, median and range are all 25. Suggest as many possible different whole number values for the numbers as you can.

14 The data in Q7 has been rounded to the nearest thousand.

a What is the largest number of people aged 10 to 19 there could be?

b What is the smallest number of people aged 20 to 29 there could be?

3 Strengthen

You will:

- Strengthen your understanding with practice.

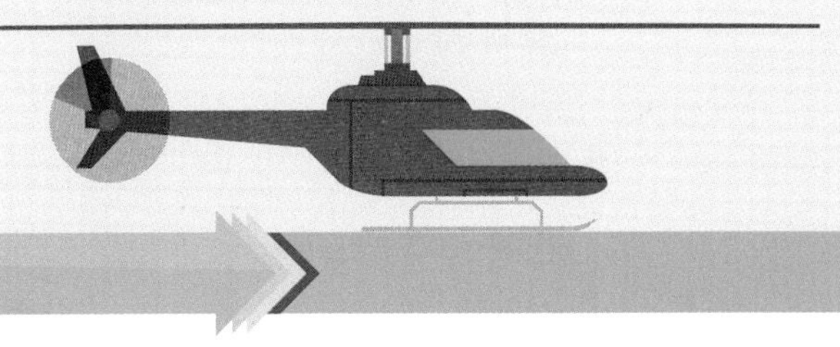

Surveys

1 Rahni is doing a geography investigation on soil types in her area.

a She tests 10 different samples of soil.
Is this primary or secondary data?

b She asks the Environment Agency for data on the soil.
Is this primary or secondary data?

> **Q1 hint**
> I collect primary data for my investigation. Someone else collects secondary data.

2 A large supermarket is planning a survey on the nation's favourite food.
How many people should they interview: 10, 500 or 30 000?

> **Q2 hint**
> The results will be more reliable when more people are surveyed, but you need to think about whether it is practical or not.

3 The head teacher of a school wants to find out how long students spend on their homework. There are 1000 students in the school.

a How many students should he ask: 1, 10 or 100?

b What should he ask pupils to round their answers to?

A the nearest hour
B the nearest 10 minutes
C the nearest minute

c He decides to ask only students from Year 11. Is this a good idea?
Explain your answer.

> **Q3b hint**
> Think about how long you spend on your homework. What would you answer?

4 A researcher measures the lengths of a sample of 100 caterpillars using a ruler.

What level of accuracy should the lengths be measured to?

A the nearest millimetre **B** the nearest centimetre **C** the nearest metre

5 A student wants to record the lengths of pebbles in a stream to the nearest centimetre. He suggests the following groups.

0–10 cm 10–20 cm 20–30 cm

a In which groups could he record a 10 cm long pebble?

b What is the problem with his choice of groups?
He redesigns his groups.
Copy and complete the new groups.
0–9 cm □–19 cm □–29 cm

6 The times (in minutes) that 10 people spent in the gym are 65, 34, 49, 58, 23, 45, 40, 36, 55, 69
Copy and complete the frequency table.
All groups must be the same width.

Time, t (minutes)	Tally	Frequency
$20 < t \leqslant 30$		
$30 < t \leqslant \square$		
$\square < t \leqslant \square$		
$\square < t \leqslant \square$		
$60 < t \leqslant 70$		

7 Design a frequency table to record the times (in minutes) people spend making mobile phone calls.

Q7 hint

Think about the answers you would expect to get to your question.

8 In a canteen you can choose
beef or chicken
chips, jacket potato or mashed potato

a Copy the two-way table and fill in the headings.

	Beef	

b Put this data in your table.

beef and chips	20
beef and jacket potato	15
beef and mashed potato	13
chicken and chips	35
chicken and jacket potato	13
chicken and mashed potato	17

9 At GCSE, students can choose one language (Spanish, German or Mandarin) and one humanities subject (History or Geography).

a Design a two-way table to record students' choices.

b Here are the choices of ten students.

Ella	Spanish and History
Helen	Mandarin and History
Jake	Spanish and History
Katrina	German and Geography
Lee	German and History
Mike	German and History
Peter	German and History
Renata	Spanish and Geography
Steve	Mandarin and History
Vicki	German and Geography

Record these choices in your two-way table.

c Which combination is the most popular choice for these 10 students?

d Is there any combination that none of these students chose?

Q9 hint

Write all the language choices along the top of the table. Write the humanities down the side.

Q9c hint

Look for the table cell with the highest number.

10 A company is carrying out a survey on pet insurance.

a The company surveys everyone who comes to the vet on one day. Why will this give a biased result?

b The survey includes the question, 'Do you want the best possible treatment for your pet if it becomes ill?'
Explain why this question will result in a biased survey.

c Reasoning Which of these questions would you choose for the survey? Explain why.

A Your pet is an important part of your household. Do you have pet insurance?

B Do you love your pet and want the best for him/her?

C Do you currently have pet insurance?

D Do you agree that insurance is a waste of money?

Q10a Literacy hint

Biased means that the results are not fair.

Q10b hint

What are you likely to answer?

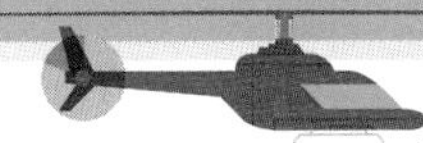

Calculating averages

1 Rebecca records the ages of people in a squash club in a tally chart.

Age (years)	Tally	Frequency
10–19	|||	3
20–29	𝍸 𝍸 ||	
30–39	𝍸 |||	
40–49	|||	

a How many people were in the 40–49 age group?

b What is the modal group?

Q1b hint
The modal group contains the most data values.

2 In a survey, 12 people said they spent 0–20 minutes on the phone each day.
Which of these is the best estimate for the average time?
A 2 minutes **B** 5 minutes **C** 10 minutes **D** 20 minutes
Explain your decision.

Q2 hint
We don't know the exact times so we have to estimate an average time.

3 A phone company recorded the lengths of time some people spent on the phone in a day.

Time, t (minutes)	Midpoint	Frequency	Midpoint × Frequency
$0 < t \leqslant 20$	10	5	$10 \times 5 = 50$
$20 < t \leqslant 40$	30	12	
$40 < t \leqslant 60$	☐	19	
$60 < t \leqslant 80$	☐	8	
$80 < t \leqslant 100$	☐	6	
	Total	☐	☐

a Copy and complete the table.

b Which column shows the total number of people?

c Which column shows the total time?

d Work out an estimate for the mean.

Q3a hint
The midpoint is an estimate for the average of each group.

Q3d hint
It is an estimate because you are using the midpoints to caculate average time.

$$\text{mean} = \frac{\text{total time}}{\text{total number of people}}$$

4 A theatre manager recorded the number of audience members at a theatre over 10 nights.

Number in audience, a	Frequency
$100 < a \leqslant 150$	5
$150 < a \leqslant 200$	2
$200 < a \leqslant 250$	2
$250 < a \leqslant 300$	1

a What columns do you need to add to the table to calculate an estimate of the mean?

b Copy the table and add the extra columns from part **a**.
Complete the table.

c Find an estimate for the mean number of people in the audience.

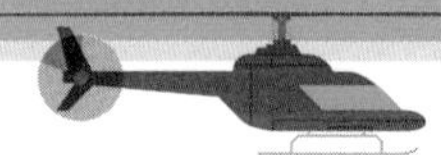

Display and analyse

1 A nurse recorded the heights of 14 children in Year 3.

Height, h (cm)	Frequency
$130 < h \leqslant 135$	3
$135 < h \leqslant 140$	4
$140 < h \leqslant 145$	7

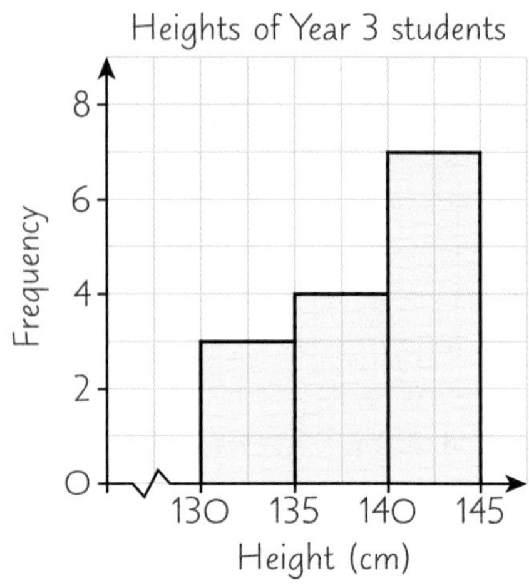

Polly is drawing a frequency polygon for this data.
She starts by drawing the bars.
What does Polly need to do next?

2 A vet recorded the masses of some puppies in a litter.

Mass, m (kg)	Midpoint	Frequency
$0.4 \leqslant m < 0.6$	0.5	1
$0.6 \leqslant m < 0.8$	☐	6
$0.8 \leqslant m < 1$	☐	2

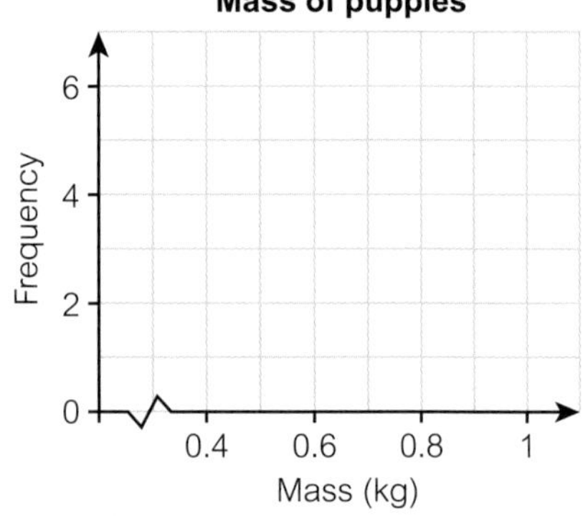

a Copy the axes.

b Draw a frequency polygon for this data.

3 The scatter graph shows the times taken for 20 students to run 200 m plotted against their times taken to run 100 m.

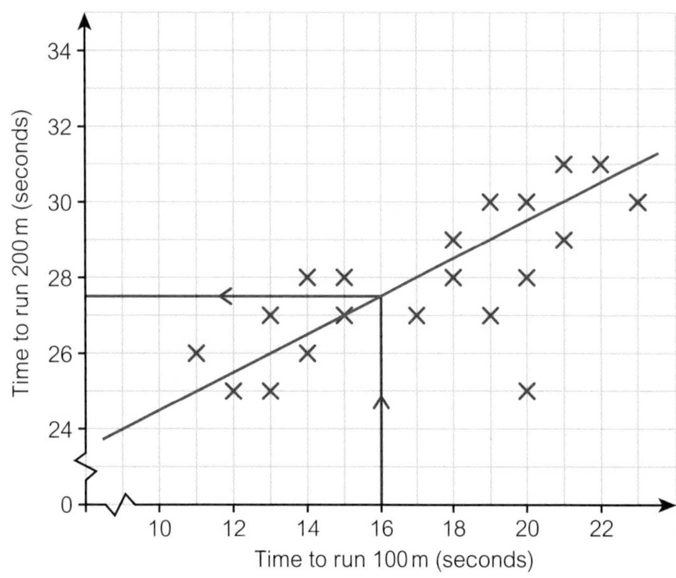

a Describe the type of correlation.

b Modelling Use the line of best fit to predict the 200 m times for a student who ran the 100 metres in

i 16 seconds

ii 19 seconds

iii 17 seconds?

c One point shows an outlier. What were the times for 100 m and 200 m for this point?

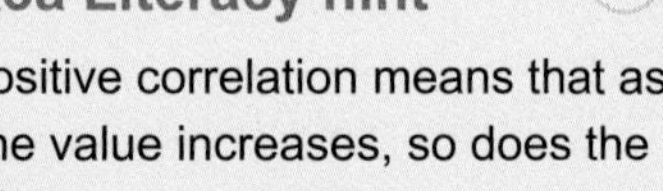

Q3a Literacy hint

Positive correlation means that as one value increases, so does the other.
Negative correlation means that as one value increases, so does the other.

Q3bi hint

Find 100 m in 16 seconds on the correct axis.
Draw a line up to the line of best fit and then across to the other axis.
Read off the value.

Q3b Literacy hint

Outliers are points that don't follow the trend.

4 A school records the exam results of 9 pupils in Mandarin and maths.

Mandarin	75%	81%	45%	24%	57%	91%	89%	93%	63%
Maths	83%	92%	35%	30%	62%	25%	80%	84%	59%

a Draw a scatter diagram for this data.
b Draw a line of best fit.
c Predict the maths score for students whose Mandarin score was
i 30% **ii** 50% **iii** 90%
d Predict the Mandarin score for students whose maths score was
i 60% **ii** 40% **iii** 70%
e Put a ring around the data point that is an outlier.

Q4a hint
Put Mandarin marks on the horizontal axis. What is the highest value you need to plot?

Enrichment

1 A train company records the numbers of passengers on a regular train journey.
a Calculate an estimate of the mean using the first table.

Number of passengers, n	Frequency
$0 < n \leqslant 30$	1
$30 < n \leqslant 60$	3
$60 < n \leqslant 90$	2
$90 < n \leqslant 120$	4

The same data can be recorded in a different way.
b Calculate an estimate of the mean using the second table.
c The train company running the train wants to cancel it. Which average should they use to support their argument?

Number of passengers, n	Frequency
$0 < n \leqslant 40$	4
$40 < n \leqslant 80$	3
$80 < n \leqslant 120$	3

2 These frequency polygons show the amount of petrol used by two drivers.

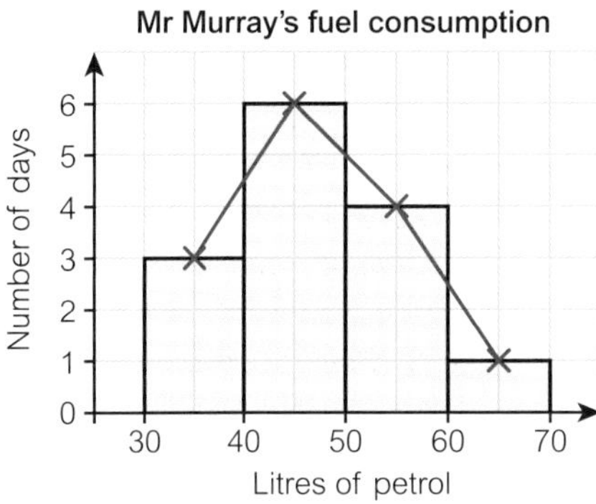

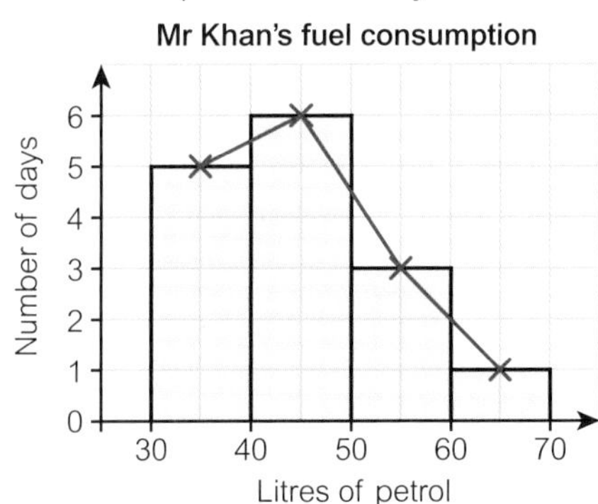

a Write two sentences comparing their fuel consumptions.
b If an estimate of the mean were calculated for both, whose do you think would be higher? Explain your answer.

Q2 Literacy hint
Fuel consumption is how much petrol is used.

3 Reflect Gabby says, 'When I see a question with a table:
- I cover the question with my hand, so I can only see the table
- then I look for a title or a description of the table
- then I read any row or column headings
- finally, I randomly pick a number in the table and ask myself what this number tells me.

It only takes a minute, and stops me panicking about all the information I am being given.'
Look back at any Strengthen question that has a table in it. Use Gabby's method.
Now find an Extend question with a table. Use Gabby's method again.
Is Gabby's method helpful?

Reflect

3 Extend

You will:

- Extend your understanding with problem-solving.

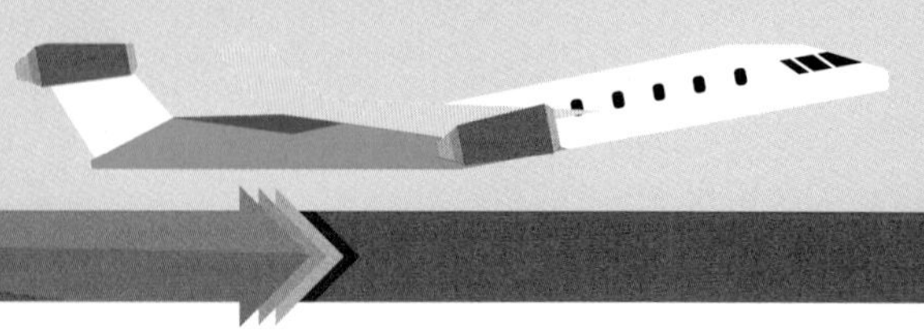

1 **Real** The owner of a beauty salon thinks that the average age of her customers is decreasing.
Suggest ways in which she could collect primary data to support her hypothesis.

2 **Real** A factory produces 1 kg bags of flour. It randomly samples the bags of flour to check that they are the correct weight.
The factory produces 200 000 bags a week.

a Suggest how many bags they should sample.

b What level of accuracy should the bags be weighed to?
A the nearest milligram **B** the nearest gram **C** the nearest 100 grams

3 A company is designing an online survey to find out whether their employees are happy in their work.
Which data should they collect about each employee? Explain why you did or didn't choose each one.

A name
B age
C level of satisfaction with the company
D number of years with the company
E how their working conditions should be improved

4 **Real** Write down the name or URL of a website you might use to investigate

a how house prices have changed over time

b bank savings rates

c changes in pollution levels in UK rivers.

Q4 hint

URL stands for Uniform Resource Locator. It is the web address (e.g. www.pearsonschoolsandfecolleges.co.uk).

5 Which is the most dangerous job?

a What type of data would you need to investigate this?

b List some sources for this data.
State whether they are primary or secondary sources.

c What kind of organisation might need to know this?

6 A driving school wanted to find out whether students who revised were more likely to pass their driving theory test.
120 students were surveyed. 98 of them had passed.
Of the 98 who passed, 75 said they had revised.
Of those who failed, 20 said they had revised.

a Construct a two-way table to show this information.

b What do you think the problem might be with a survey like this?

Topic links: Significant figures, Pie charts, Probability, Stem and leaf diagrams

Subject links: Science (Q14, Q17), Geography (Q15, Q16)

7 This spreadsheet shows the results (in %) that students in a Year 10 class received in their end-of-term exams in English and maths.

a Construct a back-to-back stem and leaf diagram for the data.

b Write two sentences to compare the distributions.

	A	B	C
1	**Student**	**English (%)**	**Maths (%)**
2	Ali	90	47
3	Allan	73	84
4	Anderly	47	57
5	Avery	92	90
6	Blick	47	85
7	Brainchild	83	66
8	Brierly	79	46
9	Brown	78	90
10	Emmery	82	84
11	Mercal	83	55
12	Murphy	72	73
13	Oxbury	68	57
14	Rothchild	41	94
15	Shilpa	46	49
16	Shunnington	73	75
17	Wilson-Smith	50	86

8 **Real** Angie is carrying out a survey to find out how much people spend on clothes each month.
She plans to carry out the survey in a shopping centre.

a Explain why this sample could be biased.

b Suggest a way in which she could carry out the survey.

c Which question should she use in her survey?
Give a reason for your answer.

A How much do you spend on clothes each month?

B How much do you spend on clothing a month?
Tick the most appropriate box.
☐ £0–£20 ☐ £20–£40 ☐ £40–£60 ☐ £60–£80 ☐ £80–£100

C How much do you spend on clothing a month?
Tick the most appropriate box.
☐ £0–£40 ☐ £41–£80 ☐ £81–£120 ☐ £121+

D How much do you spend on clothing a month?
Tick the most appropriate box.
☐ £0–£20 ☐ £21–£40 ☐ £41–£60 ☐ £61–£80 ☐ £81–£100

d What is the problem with carrying out a survey like this?

Q8d hint

How might you feel if you were asked a question like this?

9 For the survey in Q8, Angie wants to compare spending on clothes for different age groups.

a Write a suitable question to find out people's age group.

b Design a two-way table for her to collect the data in.

Discussion A pet food advert claims, '9 out of 10 cats prefer it'.
What questions might you ask about how the survey was carried out?
Think about sample size, how the data was collected, and what might affect the data collection.

10 **Real** A political party uses a phone-in poll to find out what is important to voters.
Why does a phone-in poll usually produce biased results?

Q10 Literacy hint

A 'phone-in poll' is when people are asked to phone in to say what they think.

11 **Real** A council wants to find out what facilities the people living in the town would like to improve.

a Explain what is wrong with the following question.
'Do you agree this town needs more play parks for children?'

b Write some questions you might ask instead.

12 **Problem-solving** Find a possible set of five negative whole numbers that have
mean = −6, median = −6, mode = −6, range = 7

13 **Problem-solving** Calculate the mean, median, mode and range of these numbers.

1 3 5 5 9

Discussion What is the minimum information you could give someone for them to be able to identify these exact numbers?

14 **STEM** A nurse records the mass and height of 18 patients at a clinic.

Mass (kg)	72	78	90	110	67	68	105	82	73
Height (cm)	171	175	188	145	168	167	190	180	174

Mass (kg)	101	76	89	91	90	82	76	79	91
Height (cm)	190	172	189	185	187	181	175	177	188

a Plot a scatter diagram for this information.

b Identify any outliers in the data.

c Draw a line of best fit on the scatter diagram. Use it to estimate

i the mass of a patient who is 175 cm tall

ii the height of a patient who weighs 60 kg.

d How reliable do you think your answers to part **c** are? Explain your answer.

15 **Real / Modelling** This table shows the projected population (in thousands) by age group of the UK up to 2020.

Age (years)	2014	2015	2016	2017	2018	2019	2020
0–14	10970	11131	11305	11476	11623	11744	11854
15–29	12305	12247	12161	12062	11960	11892	11820
30–44	12127	12177	12225	12303	12443	12612	12806
45–59	12514	12652	12783	12865	12881	12849	12790
60–74	9350	9453	9592	9727	9840	9945	10056
75+	5157	5256	5335	5441	5593	5762	5937
All ages	62424	62917	63401	63874	64341	64804	65263

Source: ONS

Give all answers to three significant figures.

a In 2014 what percentage of the population will be

i 60 or over ii under 30?

b In 2020 what percentage of the population will be

i 60 or over ii under 30?

c What do your answers to parts **a** and **b** tell you?

d Draw two frequency polygons on the same axes to compare the populations of 2014 and 2020. (You may use a spreadsheet.)

e Describe any differences or similarities between the two frequency polygons.

f Calculate an estimate for the mean age of the population in 2020.

g i In 2020, what proportion of the population will be 15–29?

ii In 2020, the population of Petersfield is predicted to be 15000. How many of these people would you expect to be between 15 and 29? Assume that Petersfield is representative of the UK.

Q15f hint

For the midpoints of the groups you must use 7.5, 22.5, 37.5 etc. since the group 0–14 will contain all children right up to the age of 15. Use 82.5 as the midpoint of the group 75 and over.

16 Real The tables show the populations (in millions) of Asia and Europe, by age and gender.

Asia

Age, a (years)	Male	Female
$0 \leqslant a < 20$	757	700
$20 \leqslant a < 40$	655	615
$40 \leqslant a < 60$	415	400
$60 \leqslant a < 80$	155	180
$80 \leqslant a < 100$	17	33

Europe

Age, a (years)	Male	Female
$0 \leqslant a < 20$	84	80
$20 \leqslant a < 40$	105	103
$40 \leqslant a < 60$	100	104
$60 \leqslant a < 80$	54	71
$80 \leqslant a < 100$	8	18

a Construct two pie charts to show the age distributions in Asia and in Europe.

b Find the modal age group for each continent.

c Calculate an estimate of the mean for each continent.

d Write three sentences comparing the populations of Asia and Europe.

17 Finance Two investment funds record the percentage increase in the value of their investments over the past 20 years.

Company A

Percentage increase in investment, I	Frequency
$0 \leqslant I < 2$	3
$2 \leqslant I < 4$	11
$4 \leqslant I < 6$	5
$6 \leqslant I < 8$	1

Company B

Percentage increase in investment, I	Frequency
$0 \leqslant I < 2$	0
$2 \leqslant I < 4$	15
$4 \leqslant I < 6$	5
$6 \leqslant I < 8$	0

a Can you use the tables to find out how many percentage increases were exactly 4 per cent?

b Can you use the tables to find out the exact value of the biggest percentage increase?

c By plotting frequency polygons and calculating the estimated mean, explain which investment fund you would use and why.

Q17 hint

You might wish to think about where your money would be safest or where you could invest to make the most profit.

18 These frequency tables are for the same data grouped in two different ways.

Class	Frequency
$0 \leqslant b < 20$	7
$20 \leqslant b < 40$	25
$40 \leqslant b < 60$	15
$60 \leqslant b < 80$	3

Class	Frequency
$0 \leqslant b < 15$	3
$15 \leqslant b < 30$	11
$30 \leqslant b < 45$	21
$45 \leqslant b < 60$	12
$60 \leqslant b < 75$	3

For each set of data

a give the modal class **b** estimate the range **c** estimate the mean.

Reflect

19 Reflect A census is a survey of all the people and households in a country on a particular date.

Who do you think uses census data? What do you think they use it for?

What skills have you learned in this unit to help you plan a census?

3 Unit test

Log how you did on your Student Progression Chart.

1 You are going to investigate this hypothesis.
'Buttered toast always lands butter-side down.'
How many times should you drop a piece of toast?
A 10 times **B** 100 times **C** 1000 times

2 An insurance company suggests, 'Men are better drivers than women.'
It uses these questions in a survey.
A How many accidents have you had in the last 10 years?
☐ 0–2 ☐ 2–4 ☐ 4–6 ☐ 6+
B Would you agree that women have more accidents than men?
a Explain what is wrong with the questions.
b Rewrite the questions.

3 You are investigating the average daily temperature in July.
You collect data by:
A Recording the temperature using a thermometer every morning, midday and evening.
B Getting the average temperature from the Met Office website.
Which is secondary data?

4 'Girls at St Margaret's School score better in Maths exams than in English exams.'
a Describe how you would collect data to test this hypothesis.
There are 400 girls at St Margaret's.
b How large a sample should you use?

5 For a 'Stop Speeding' campaign, Brendan measures the speed that cars travel along his road. The road has a 30 mph limit.
a How accurately should he record the data to state his case to the council?
A nearest 10 mph **B** nearest 1 mph **C** nearest 0.1 mph
b Design a frequency table to record his data.

6 Students at a school can choose one sport from each group.
Group A Tennis, Badminton, Squash
Group B Swimming, Athletics, Gymnastics
Design a two-way table to record the results.

7 A supermarket wants to find out how much its customers spend on ready meals. Which is the most appropriate sample?
A customers who bought a ready meal in the last week
B customers who spend over £100 in the shop
C the next 100 customers through the tills

8 The scatter graphs show the relationship between the maximum daily temperature and the number of ice creams sold in a shop. They show the same data but have different lines of best fit.

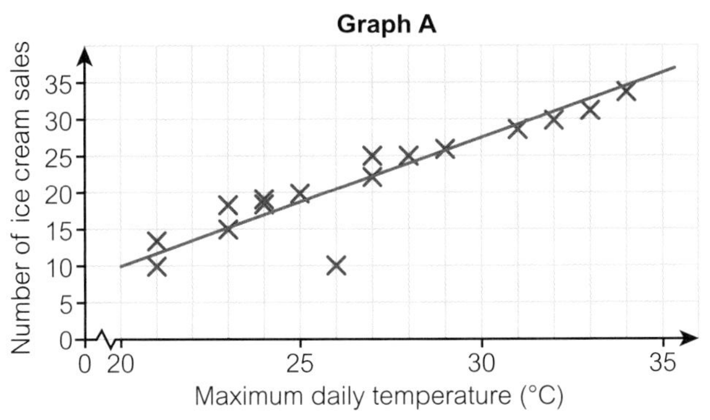

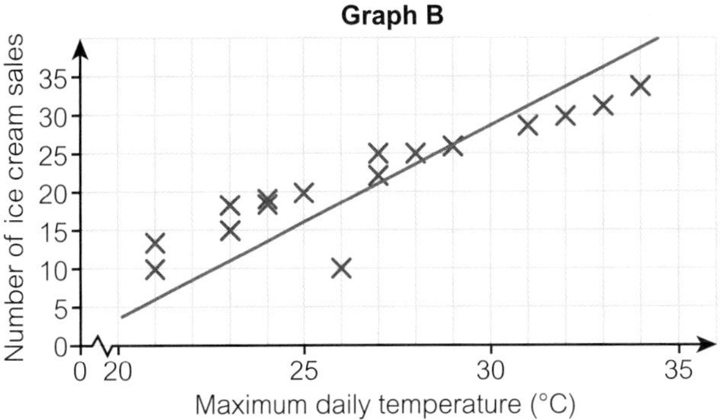

a What type of correlation do the graphs show?
b What is the temperature for the outlier in Graph A?
c Which graph has the most accurate line of best fit?
d Use this line of best fit to estimate
 i the maximum daily temperature when the shop sells 20 ice creams
 ii the number of ice creams the shop will sell when the temperature is 30 °C.

9 Two airline companies record the numbers of people travelling on their Airbus 320s for 200 flights.

Airline A

Number of passengers, p	Frequency
$0 \leqslant p < 40$	20
$40 \leqslant p < 80$	43
$80 \leqslant p < 120$	112
$120 \leqslant p < 160$	25

Airline B

Number of passengers, p	Frequency
$0 \leqslant p < 40$	0
$40 \leqslant p < 80$	44
$80 \leqslant p < 120$	54
$120 \leqslant p < 160$	102

a Which is the modal class of passengers for
 i Airline A ii Airline B?
b Calculate an estimate of the mean number of passengers for each airline.
c Estimate the range for each airline.
d On the same set of axes construct two frequency polygons to show both airlines.
e Write two sentences comparing the data for each airline.

Challenge

10 Plan how you might investigate the hypothesis 'Women are better drivers than men.' Make sure you include
- where you might find your data
- how you might collect your data
- how you will avoid bias
- what sample size you should consider
- how you might display the data.

11 **Reflect**
a Write down three ways it helps to have good numeracy skills when dealing with data.
b Write down three ways it helps to have good literacy skills when dealing with data.
c How does having good literacy skills help you in other ways with your mathematics learning?

Q11 Literacy hint
Good numeracy skills means good at working with numbers.
Good literacy skills means good at reading, writing and communicating.

Reflect

4 Multiplicative reasoning

MASTER | Check P95 | Strengthen P97 | Extend P101 | Test P105

4.1 Enlargement

You will learn to:
- Enlarge 2D shapes using a positive whole number scale factor
- Find the centre of enlargement by drawing lines on a grid.

CONFIDENCE

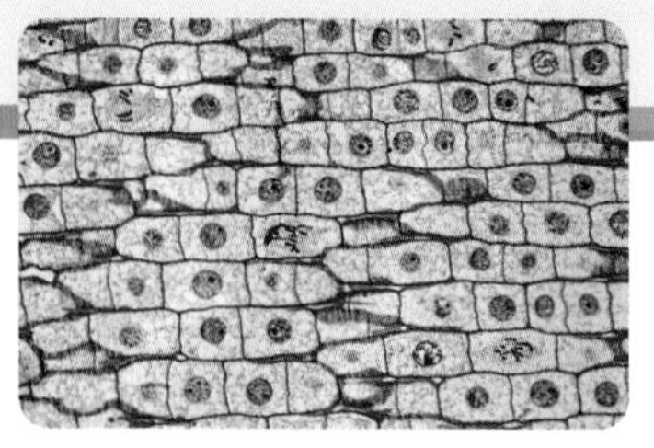

Why learn this?
Scientists use enlargements with very large scale factors to study the microscopic world around us.

Fluency
What scale factor has been used to enlarge the small triangle to make the big triangle?

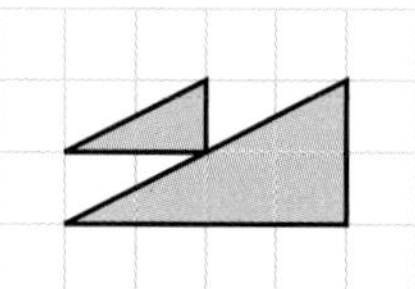

Explore
How can you enlarge a photo using picture tools on a computer?

Exercise 4.1

Warm up

1 Copy each shape onto squared paper and enlarge it by the scale factor shown.

a scale factor 3

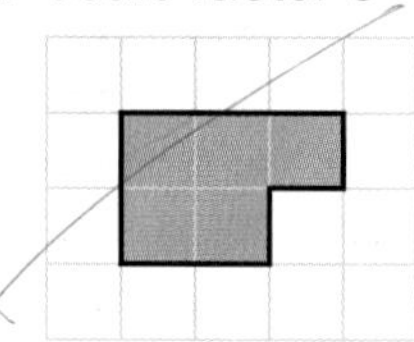

b scale factor 4

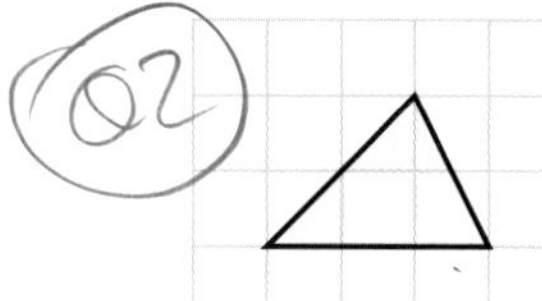

Key point
When you enlarge a shape by a scale factor from a **centre of enlargement**, the distance from the centre to each point on the shape is also multiplied by the scale factor.

2 Shape B is an enlargement of shape A.
What is the scale factor of the enlargement?

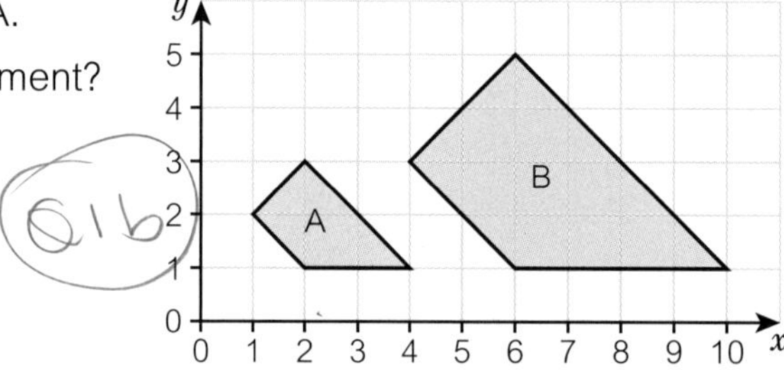

Worked example

Enlarge this triangle using a scale factor 2 and the marked centre of enlargement.

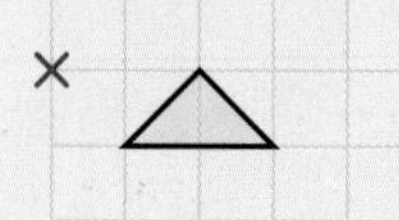

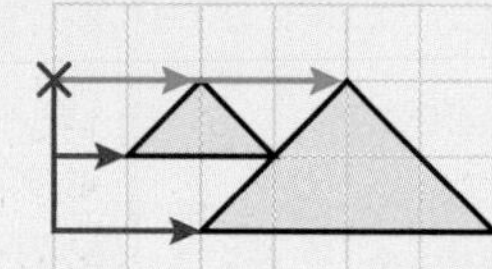

Multiply all the distances from the centre by the scale factor. Count the squares from the centre of enlargement:
- The top vertex of the triangle changes from 2 right to 4 right.
- The bottom left vertex changes from 1 down and 1 right to 2 down and 2 right.

Topic links: Perimeter

Subject links: Computing (Q12)

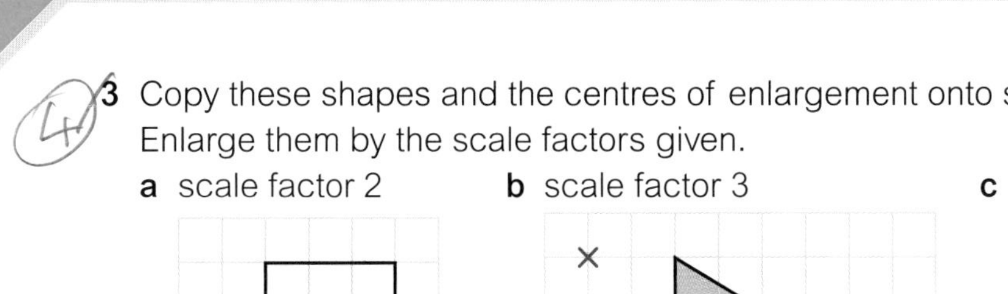

3 Copy these shapes and the centres of enlargement onto squared paper. Enlarge them by the scale factors given.

a scale factor 2   b scale factor 3   c scale factor 3

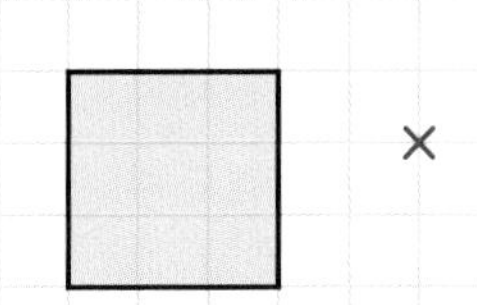

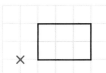

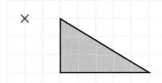

4 Copy this diagram onto squared paper. Enlarge the rectangle by scale factor 2, with centre of enlargement (9, 5).

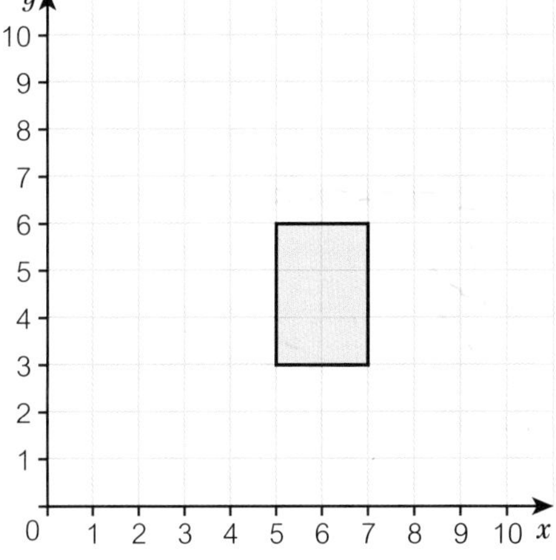

5 **Problem-solving / Reasoning** Draw a pair of axes from 0 to 10.
Draw a triangle A with vertices at (3, 2), (5, 2) and (3, 4).
Draw a triangle B with vertices at (8, 6), (9, 6) and (8, 7).

a Draw an enlargement of triangle A with scale factor 2 and centre of enlargement (1, 1).
b Draw an enlargement of triangle B with scale factor 4 and centre of enlargement (9, 7).
c What do you notice about your answers to parts **a** and **b**?
d Triangle C has vertices at (3, 6), (4, 6) and (3, 7). Draw triangle C on the grid.
e Salim says, 'If I enlarge triangle C by a scale factor of 3 and centre of enlargement (2, 7), it will give exactly the same triangle as my answers to parts **a** and **b**.'
Is Salim correct? Explain your answer.

6 Copy these shapes and the centres of enlargement onto squared paper and then enlarge them, using the scale factors.

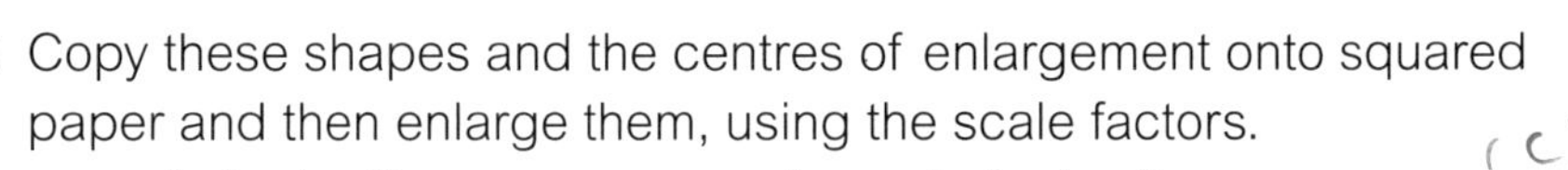

a scale factor 2   b scale factor 3

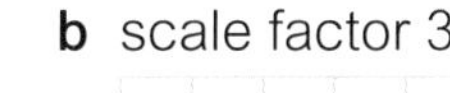

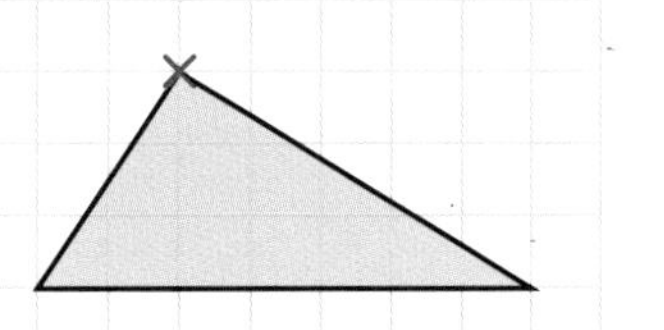

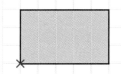

Q6 hint

When the centre of enlargement lies on the edge of the shape, the distance from the centre of enlargement to the shape is 0.
This point is in the same place on the grid in the enlarged shape.
You could use dynamic software to check that your enlargements are correct.

7 a Copy this shape onto a coordinate grid. Enlarge it by scale factor 2, with centre of enlargement (4, 1).
b Measure the angles in the shape and in the enlargement. What do you notice?
c Measure the sides in the shape and in the enlargement. What do you notice?
Discussion Is this true for all enlargements?

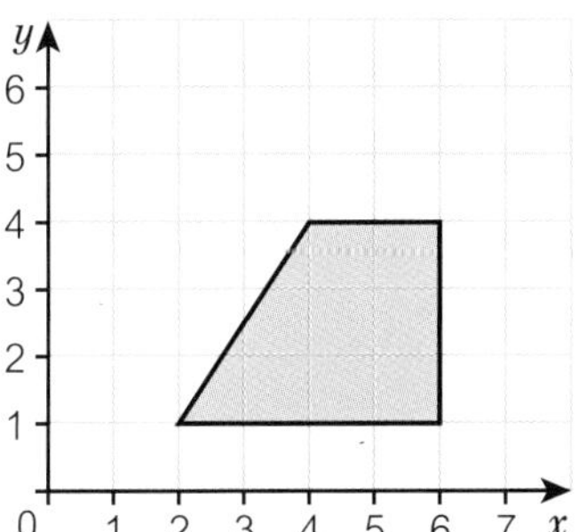

8 Copy these shapes on a coordinate grid and then enlarge them, using the marked centres of enlargement and scale factors.

a scale factor 2   b scale factor 3

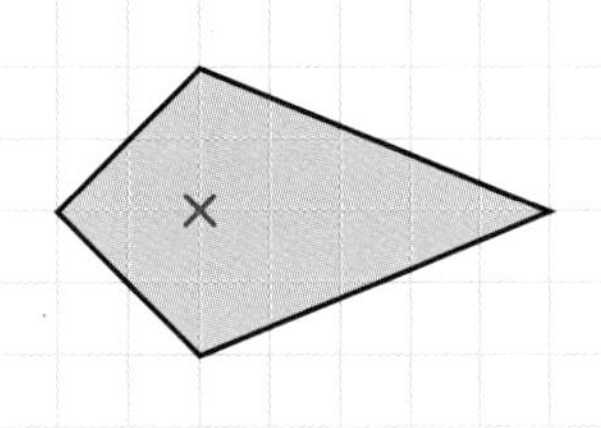

Q8 hint

Follow the same method. Multiply the distance from the centre of enlargement to each vertex by the scale factor.

9 Copy this diagram.
Enlarge the shape by scale factor 4, with centre of enlargement (4, 4).

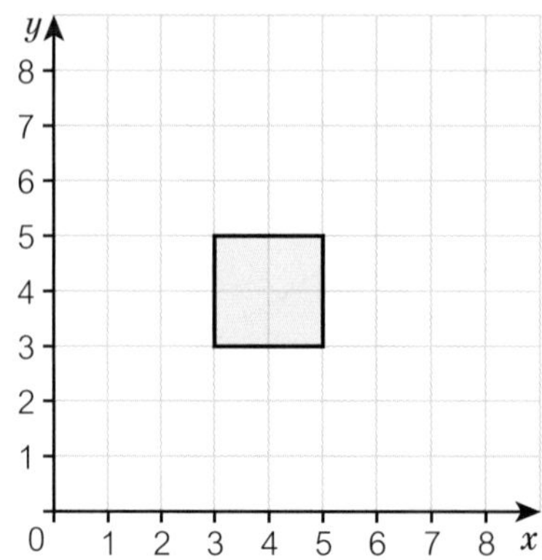

Investigation **Problem-solving \ Reasoning**

Shape A has been enlarged to give shape B.

1 What is the scale factor of the enlargement?

2 What do you think the coordinates of the centre of enlargement are? Try some different values.

3 Copy the diagram and use straight lines to join together corresponding corners of the two shapes. Extend these lines across the whole grid. The first one is shown in red on the diagram. These lines are called **rays**.

4 What are the coordinates of the centre of enlargement? Use the rays you drew in part 3.

5 Draw a shape on a coordinate grid and enlarge it using your own scale factor and centre of enlargement. Don't mark the centre of enlargement on the diagram. Swap with a partner and ask them to work out the scale factor and centre of enlargement, using rays.

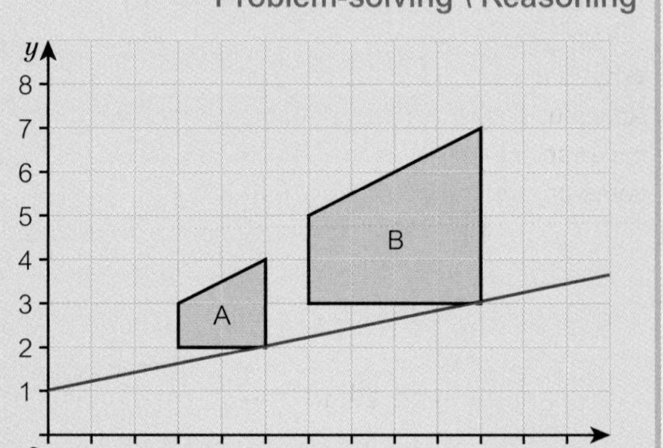

10 Describe the enlargement that takes shape A to shape B in each of these diagrams.

a

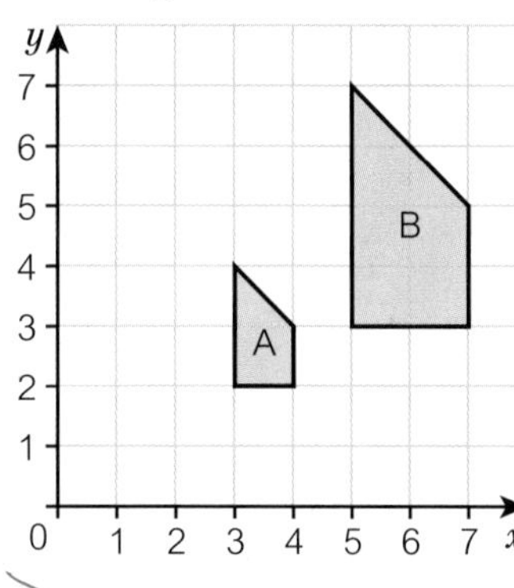

b

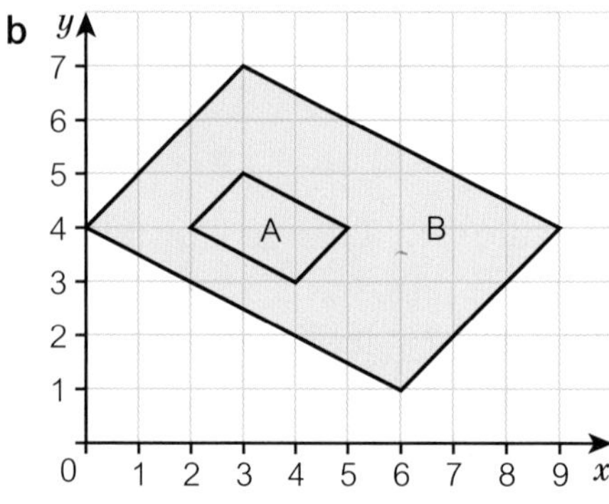

Key point

To describe an enlargement, give the scale factor and the coordinates of the centre of enlargement .

Explore

11 **Explore** How can you enlarge a photo using picture tools on a computer?
Is it easier to explore this question now you have completed the lesson?
What further information do you need, to be able to answer this?

Reflect

12 **Reflect** This unit is called 'Multiplicative reasoning'.
How is enlargement multiplicative?
Why is it good to use reasoning in mathematics?

Q12 Literacy hint

'Multiplicative' means 'involving multiplication and/or division'. Reasoning is being able to explain why you have done some maths a certain way.

4.2 Negative and fractional scale factors

You will learn to:

- Enlarge 2D shapes using a negative whole number scale factor
- Enlarge 2D shapes using a fractional scale factor
- Understand that the scale factor is the ratio of the lengths of corresponding sides.

Why learn this?
Artists use fractional scale factors to produce micro-sculptures of objects that are in the same proportion as the real-life objects.

Fluency
Write these ratios as unit ratios in the form 1 : m.

- 5 : 10
- 2 : 3
- 4 : 5
- 5 : 4

Explore
How high is a table in a doll's house?

Exercise 4.2

1 Copy these shapes and centres of enlargement on a coordinate grid and then enlarge them, using the scale factors given.

a scale factor 3

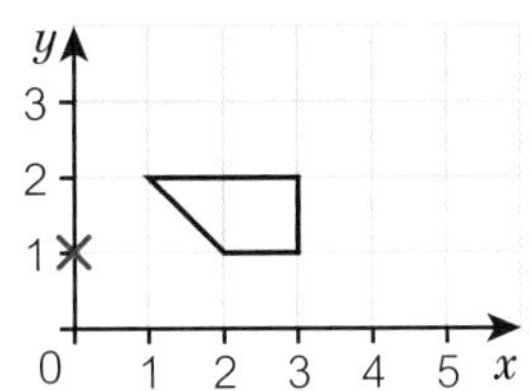

b scale factor 2

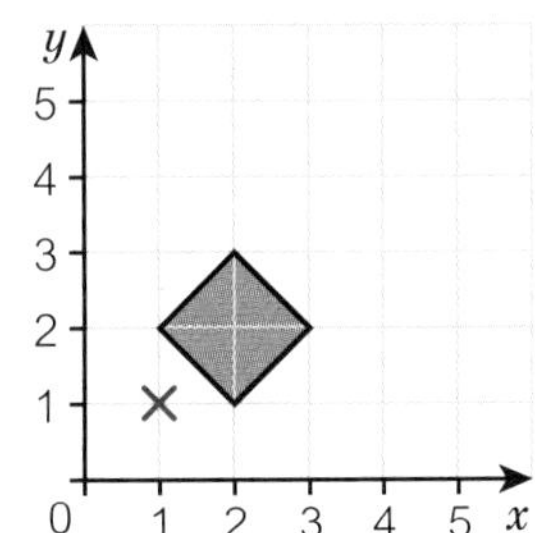

+(c)

Worked example

Enlarge this triangle using scale factor −2 and centre of enlargement (3, 2).

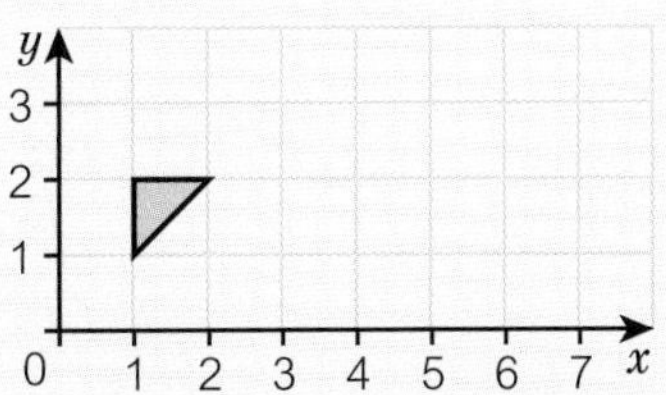

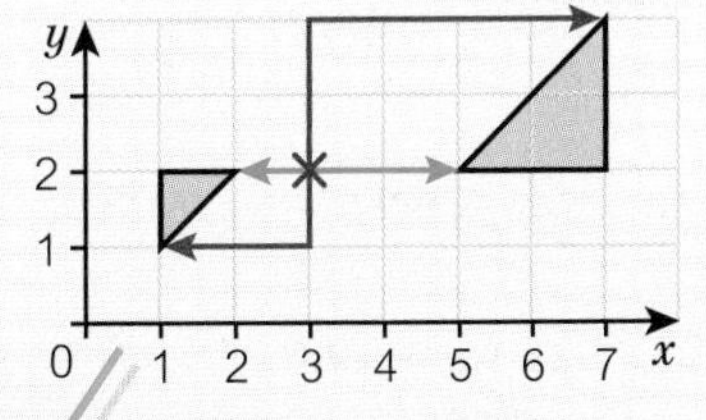

Count the squares from the centre of enlargement:

- The top right vertex of the small triangle changes to the bottom left vertex of the enlarged triangle, from 1 left to 2 right.
- The bottom vertex of the triangle changes to the top vertex of the enlarged triangle, from 1 down and 2 left to 2 up and 4 right.

Key point
A **negative scale factor** has the same effect as a positive scale factor except that it takes the image to the opposite side of the centre of enlargement.

2 Copy these diagrams. Enlarge the shapes using the marked centres of enlargement and **negative scale factors**.

a scale factor −3

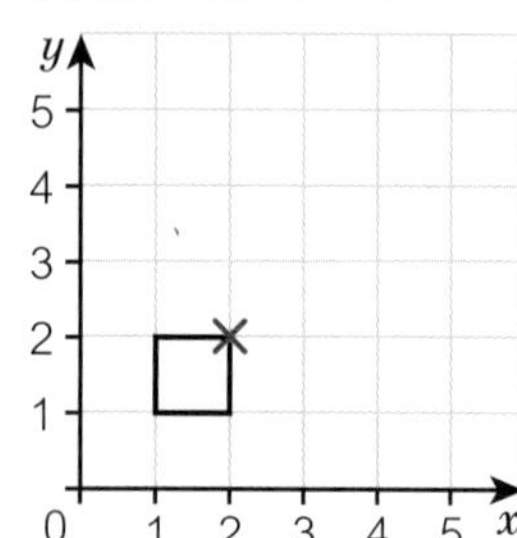

b scale factor −2

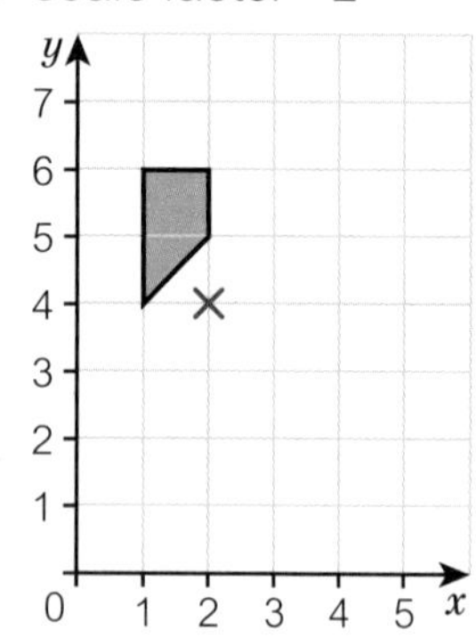

c scale factor −3

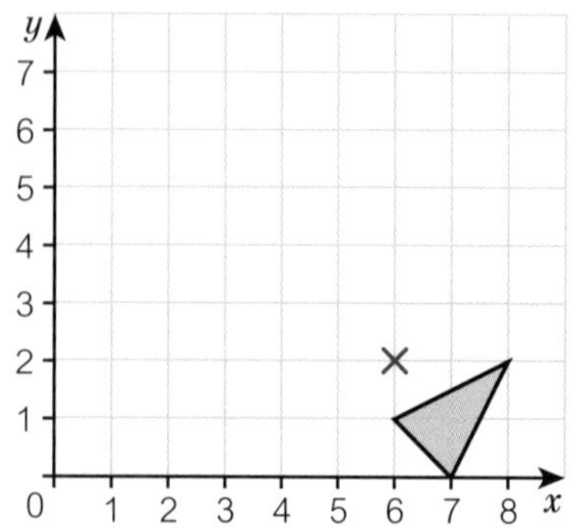

Discussion What is the effect on the side lengths and angles of enlarging a shape by scale factor −1?

Q2 hint

Use dynamic software to check your enlargements are correct.

3 Reasoning Draw a pair of axes from 0 to 12. Draw shape A with vertices at (3, 3), (4, 3), (5, 4), (5, 5) and (3, 5).

a Enlarge shape A using scale factor −2 and centre of enlargement (6, 6).

b Enlarge shape A using scale factor 2 and centre of enlargement (6, 6), then rotate the enlarged shape 180° about the point (6, 6).

c What do you notice about your answers to parts **a** and **b**?

Key point

You can enlarge a shape using a **fractional scale factor**. Use the same method of multiplying the length of each side by the scale factor.

4 Copy each shape onto squared paper.
Enlarge each shape by the scale factor given.

a scale factor $\frac{1}{2}$

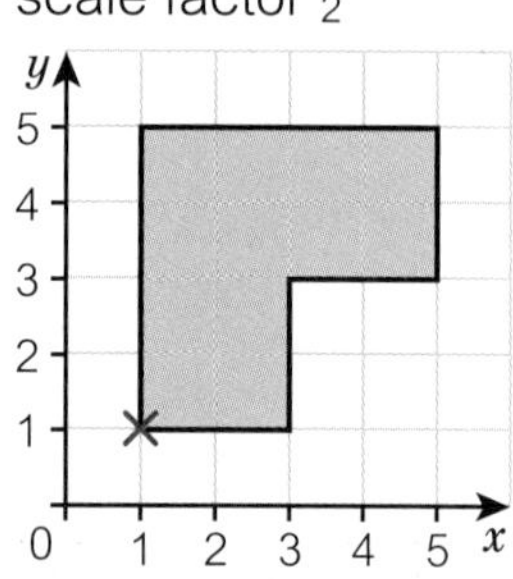

b scale factor $\frac{1}{4}$

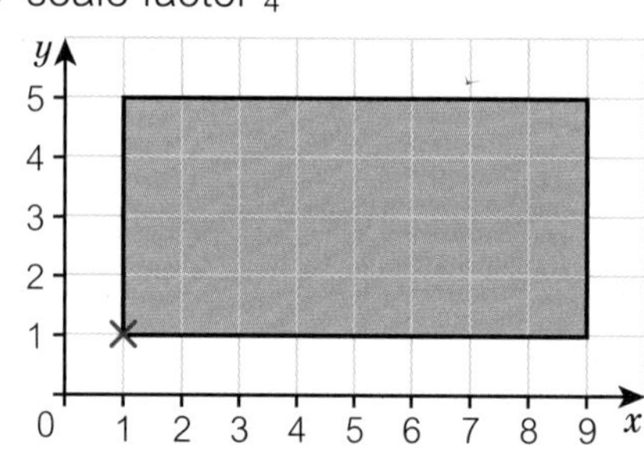

Q4 Literacy hint

We still use 'enlarge' for fractional scale factors, even though they make the shape smaller!

Discussion What happens to the side lengths and angles of a shape when you enlarge it by a positive number less than 1?

5 For each of these diagrams work out the scale factor for

a enlarging shape A to give shape B

b enlarging shape B to give shape A.

i

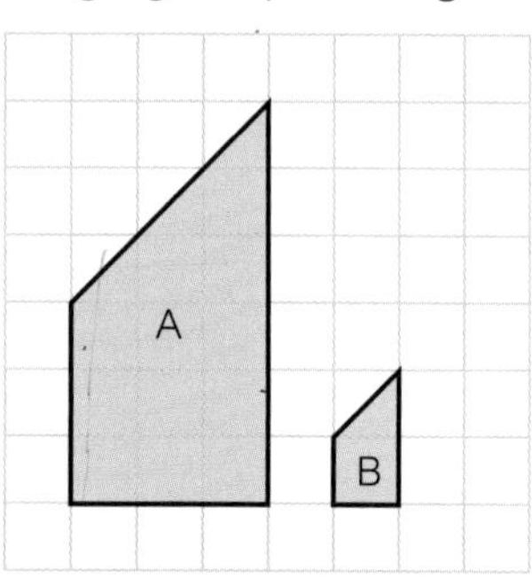

ii

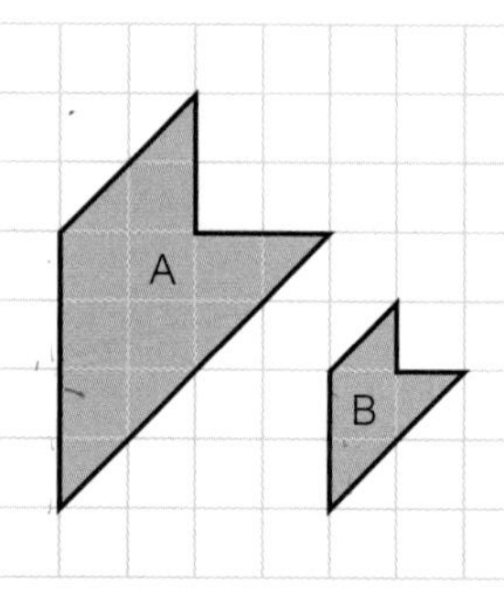

Topic links: Metric units, Rounding

6 **Reasoning** The diagram shows two rectangles.

5 cm
2 cm A
10 cm
4 cm B

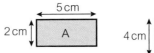

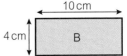

a What is the scale factor for enlarging rectangle A to give rectangle B?

b Write the ratio, in its simplest form, of

  i the height of rectangle A to rectangle B

  ii the length of rectangle A to rectangle B.

c What do you notice about your answers to parts **a** and **b**?

Discussion What is the ratio of corresponding sides in a shape and its image, where the shape has been enlarged by scale factor 3?

7 **Real** A model lifeboat is made using a ratio of 1 : 72.
The length of the model is 236 mm.
What is the length of the real lifeboat?
Give your answer in metres to one decimal place.

Q7 hint

The lifeboat and the model are enlargements of each other.

8 Copy this diagram.

a Enlarge shape A using scale factor $\frac{1}{3}$ and centre of enlargement (7, 1). Label the shape B.

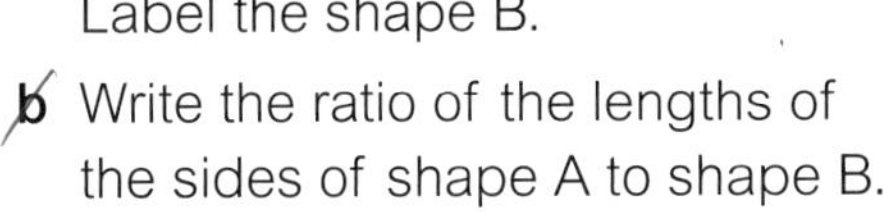

b Write the ratio of the lengths of the sides of shape A to shape B.

c Write the enlargement that will take shape B back to shape A.

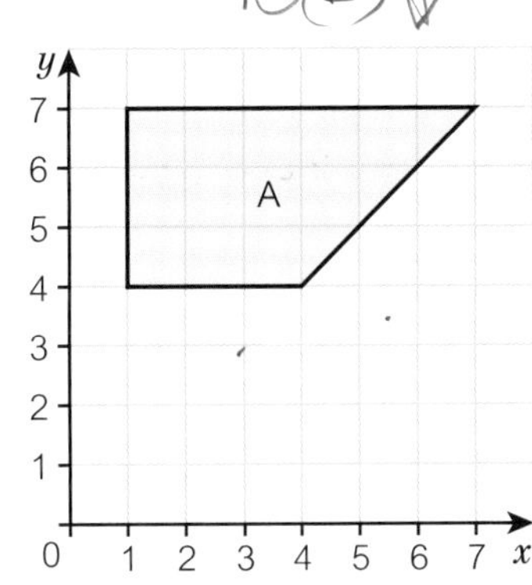

Q8c hint

Remember to include the scale factor and the centre of enlargement.

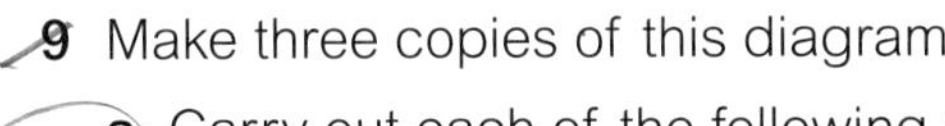

9 Make three copies of this diagram.

a Carry out each of the following combined transformations.

  i Translate the shape 4 squares left and 1 square down, then enlarge it by scale factor 2, centre of enlargement (0, 12).

  ii Rotate the shape 180° about the point (6, 8), then enlarge it by scale factor $\frac{1}{2}$, centre of enlargement (0, 0).

  iii Reflect the shape in the line $x = 9$, then enlarge it by scale factor $\frac{1}{2}$, centre of enlargement (10, 8).

b Describe a combined transformation that will take the image in part **a ii** to the position of the image in part **a iii**.

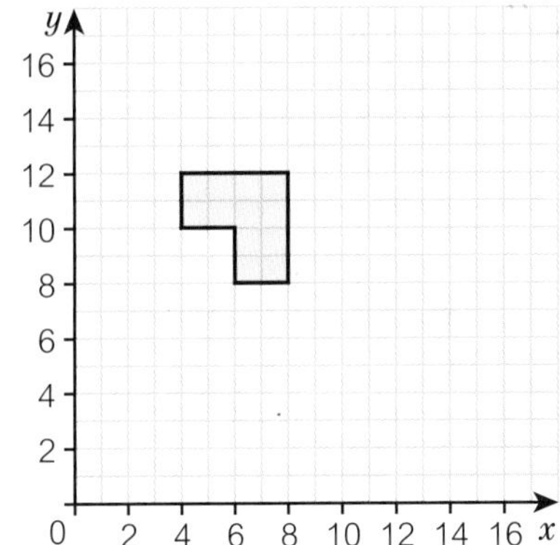

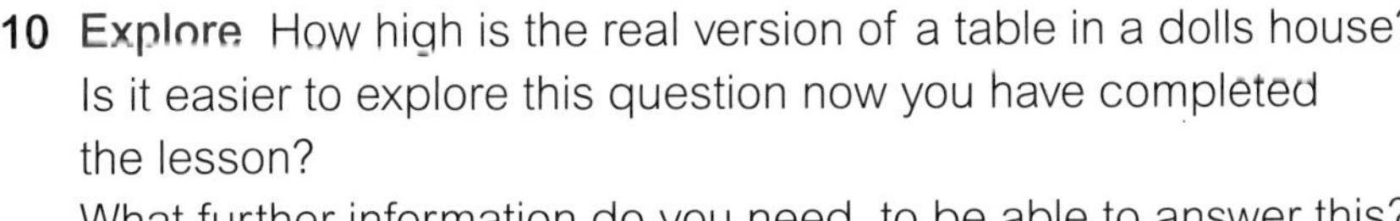

10 **Explore** How high is the real version of a table in a dolls house?
Is it easier to explore this question now you have completed the lesson?
What further information do you need, to be able to answer this?

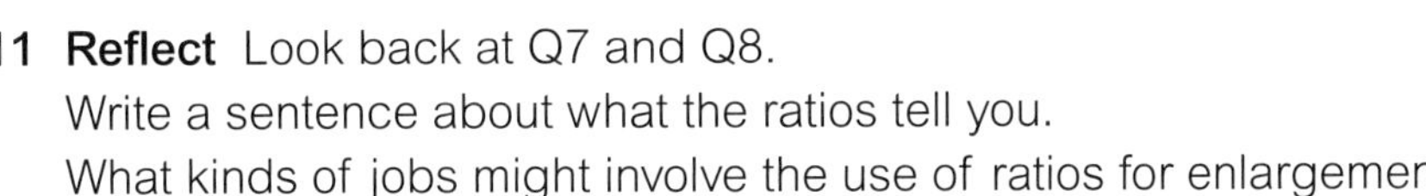

11 **Reflect** Look back at Q7 and Q8.
Write a sentence about what the ratios tell you.
What kinds of jobs might involve the use of ratios for enlargement?

Explore

Reflect

4.3 FINANCE: Percentage change

You will learn to:
- Find an original value using inverse operations
- Calculate percentage change.

Why learn this?
Shop managers calculate percentage change in order to compare the profit or loss they have made on different items.

Fluency
Match each percentage to its equivalent decimal.

70% 35% 7% 3.5% 700% 0.35%

0.035 7 0.7 0.0035 0.07 0.35

Explore
Did the countries within the EU have similar increases in their Gross Domestic Product (GDP) between 2012 and 2013?

Exercise 4.3: Profit and loss

1 Work out the percentage $\frac{A}{B} \times 100$, when

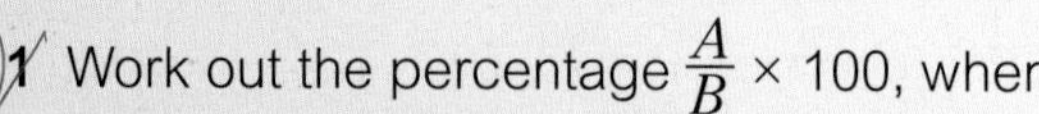

a A = £27 and B = £50 b A = £54.99 and B = £85.99

Q1 hint
Round your answer to the nearest whole number.

2 a Increase £23 by 25%. b Decrease £576 by 35%.

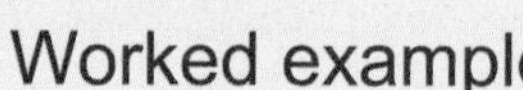

Worked example

In a year the value of a car dropped by 15% to £4760.
How much was the car worth at the start of the year?

100% − 15% = 85% = 0.85

Original number → × 0.85 → 4760

Draw a function machine.

5600 ← ÷ 0.85 ← 4760

The car was worth £5600 at the start of the year.

Key point
You can use **inverse operations** to find the original amount after a percentage increase or decrease.

3 Finance There was a 20% discount in a sale.
A coat had a sale price of £38.
What was the original selling price?

4 Finance A shop has three items on sale.
The table shows the discount for each item and the sale price.

	Original price	Discount	Sale price
Item 1		10%	£63.00
Item 2		35%	£53.30
Item 3		65%	£99.75

Work out the original price for each item.

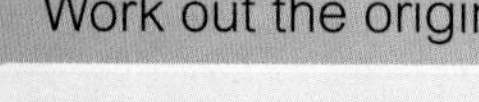

Topic links: Ratio

5 Finance / Problem-solving Jessica bought a computer for £420. It had been reduced by 25%.

a What was the original price of the computer before the reduction?

Sam bought a computer for £483. It had been reduced by 30%.

b Who saved the most money?

6 Finance The value of a house increased by 30% to £156 000. What was the original value of the house?

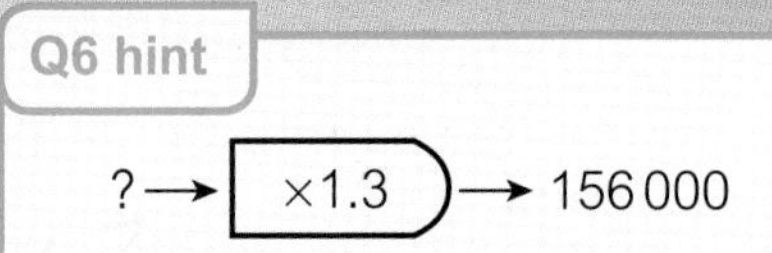

Q6 hint

? → ×1.3 → 156 000

7 Finance / Real Between 2008 and 2012, average weekly earnings in Wales increased by 5% to £522.90. Source: StatsWales

What was the average weekly pay in Wales in 2008?

Key point

You can calculate a **percentage change** using the formula

$$\text{percentage change} = \frac{\text{actual change}}{\text{original amount}} \times 100$$

8 Finance Maya invests £2400. When her investment matures she receives £2592.

Copy and complete the working to calculate the percentage increase in her investment.

actual change = £2592 − £2400 = £□

$$\text{percentage change} = \frac{\text{actual change}}{\text{original amount}} \times 100 = \frac{\square}{2400} \times 100 = \square\%$$

Q8 Literacy hint

An investment 'matures' when the investment period (e.g. 5 years) ends.

9 Finance Sim invests £3500. When his investment matures he receives £3430.
Calculate the percentage decrease in his investment.

Q9 hint

Use the same formula,

$$\text{percentage change} = \frac{\text{actual change}}{\text{original amount}} \times 100$$

10 Finance The table shows the price a shopkeeper pays for some items (cost price) and the price he sells them for (selling price).

Item	Cost price	Selling price	Actual profit	Percentage profit
Hoody	£12	£21		
T-shirt	£5	£8		
Fleece	£30	£45		
Polo shirt	£8	£18		

Q10 Literacy hint

Percentage profit is the percentage change between cost price and selling price.

a Work out the percentage profit (percentage change) on each item he sells.

b Discussion Is the item with the greatest actual profit the item with the greatest percentage profit?

11 Finance Hannah bought a flat for £125 000. She sells it for £110 000. What percentage loss has she made on the flat?

12 Finance / Real The estimated UK cost of the HS2 high speed rail link increased from £32.7 billion to £42.6 billion in June 2013.
What is the percentage increase in the estimated cost?
Give your answer to the nearest whole number.

Q12 hint

You don't need to write the billions.
42.6 − 32.7 = □

13 Problem-solving / Reasoning The table shows information on visitor numbers to a theme park in 2012 and 2013.

Year	Total number of visitors	Ratio of children to adults	Price of child ticket	Price of adult ticket
2012	12460	3 : 2	£8	£15
2013	11220	2 : 1	£10	£18

a Work out the percentage change in the total number of visitors from 2012 to 2013.
Give your answer to one decimal place.

b Does your answer to part **a** show a percentage increase or decrease?

c Work out the percentage change in the amount of money taken in ticket sales from 2012 to 2013.
Give your answer to one decimal place.

Q13c Strategy hint
What information do you need? How can you use the figures in the table?

Explore

14 **Explore** Did the countries within the EU have similar increases in their Gross Domestic Product (GDP) between 2012 and 2013?
Is it easier to explore this question now you have completed the lesson?
What further information do you need, to be able to answer this?

Reflect

15 **Reflect** Marcia says, 'I find it difficult to remember the percentage change formula. Is it actual change divided by original amount or the other way round?'
Andrew says, 'I know that if I invest £2 and get £3 in return, I've made £1, which is 50% of £2 or a 50% change.
That helps me to remember the formula.'
Andrew writes

Try both Marcia's formulae suggestions using Andrew's numbers.
Which is the correct formula?
What do you think of Andrew's strategy? Do you have another way of remembering the formula? If so, what is it?

4.4 Rates of change

You will learn to:
- Solve problems using compound measures
- Solve problems using constant rates and related formulae.

Why learn this?
Engineers use compound measures to work out the mass of the individual parts of a building or structure, such as a bridge.

Fluency
What are the missing values?
- 1 hour = ☐ minutes
- 1 m = ☐ cm
- 1 kg = ☐ g
- 1 km = ☐ m
- 1 mile ≈ ☐ km

Explore
Why do stiletto heels damage wooden floors?

CONFIDENCE

Exercise 4.4

1 Write these times as decimals.
  a 30 minutes b 15 minutes c 12 minutes
  d 36 minutes e 1 hour 15 minutes f $2\frac{1}{2}$ hours

2 Write these times in hours and minutes.
  a 0.75 hours b 0.4 hours c 0.9 hours
  d 1.25 hours e 3.75 hours f 2.2 hours

3 Change
  a 5 cm^2 to m^2 b 25.3 cm^2 to m^2

4 a Jared walks at a speed of 2 m/s. How far does he walk in 20 seconds?
  b Tom cycles at a speed of 5 m/s. How far does he cycle in 60 seconds?

5 Modelling Work out the **average speed** for these journeys.
  a A car travels 180 km in 3 hours.
  b A train travels 150 km in 2 hours.
  c A cyclist rides 24 miles in $1\frac{1}{2}$ hours.

6 Modelling Work out the **distance** travelled for these journeys.
  a A car travels for 4 hours at an average speed of 88 km/h.
  b An aeroplane travels for $2\frac{1}{2}$ hours at an average speed of 600 mph.
  c A motorcycle travels for $\frac{3}{4}$ of an hour at an average speed of 72 km/h.

7 Modelling Work out the **time** taken for these journeys.
  a A car travels 210 km at an average speed of 70 km/h.
  b A cyclist travels 18 miles at an average speed of 12 mph.
  c A train travels 128 km at an average speed of 160 km/h.
  Give your answer in minutes.

Q1 hint
6 minutes = $\frac{6}{60}$ = 0.1 hours

Q3 hint
1 m^2 = ☐ cm^2

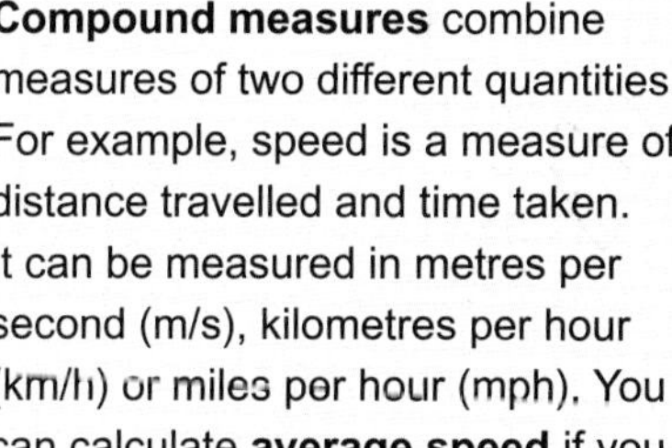

Key point
Compound measures combine measures of two different quantities. For example, speed is a measure of distance travelled and time taken. It can be measured in metres per second (m/s), kilometres per hour (km/h) or miles per hour (mph). You can calculate **average speed** if you know the **distance** and the **time**.

Speed = $\frac{\text{Distance}}{\text{Time}}$ or $S = \frac{D}{T}$

Q6 hint
Rearrange the formula $S = \frac{D}{T}$ to make D the subject.

Q7 hint
How do you need to rearrange the formula?

Warm up

Worked example

Convert 8 m/s into km/h.

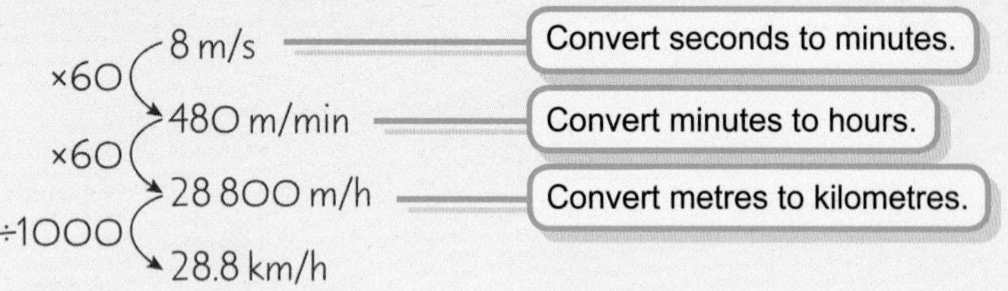

8 Convert these speeds.

a 6 m/s into km/h **b** 25 m/s into km/h **c** 72 km/h into m/s

d 162 km/h into m/s **e** 50 mph into km/h **f** 92 km/h into mph

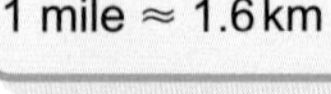

Q8 e and f hint

1 mile ≈ 1.6 km

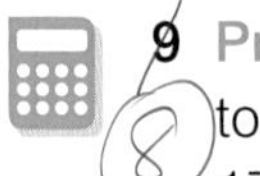

9 Problem-solving / Real The distance by train from Haverfordwest to Swansea is 64 miles. Lynn leaves Haverfordwest train station at 17 23 and arrives at Swansea train station at 18 53.
Calculate the average speed of the train in km/h.

Q9 hint

The distance is in miles, but you are asked for the speed in km/h.

Worked example

A silver pendant has a mass of 31.5 g and a volume of 3 cm³.
Work out the density of the silver.

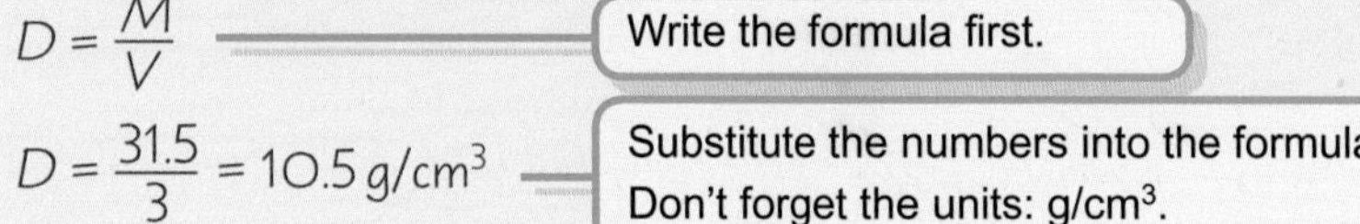

$D = \frac{M}{V}$ Write the formula first.

$D = \frac{31.5}{3} = 10.5\text{ g/cm}^3$ Substitute the numbers into the formula. Don't forget the units: g/cm³.

Key point

Density is a compound measure.
Density is the **mass** of substance contained in a certain **volume**.
To calculate it, you need mass in g and volume in cm³.
density = $\frac{\text{mass}}{\text{volume}}$ or $D = \frac{M}{V}$
Density is usually measured in grams per cubic centimetre (g/cm³).

10 STEM A piece of gold has **mass** 48.5 g and **volume** 2.5 cm³.
Work out the **density** of the gold.

11 STEM / Reasoning 1 cm³ of graphite has mass 2.25 g.
1 cm³ of diamond has mass 3.51 g.

a Write down the density of each.

b Which is more dense?
Explain your answer.

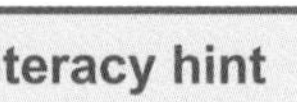

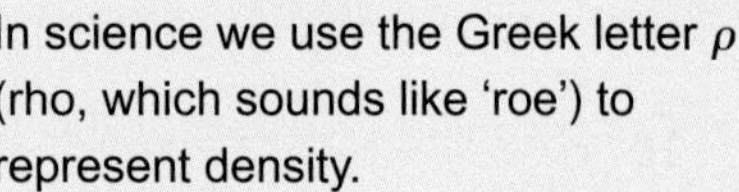

Literacy hint

In science we use the Greek letter ρ (rho, which sounds like 'roe') to represent density.

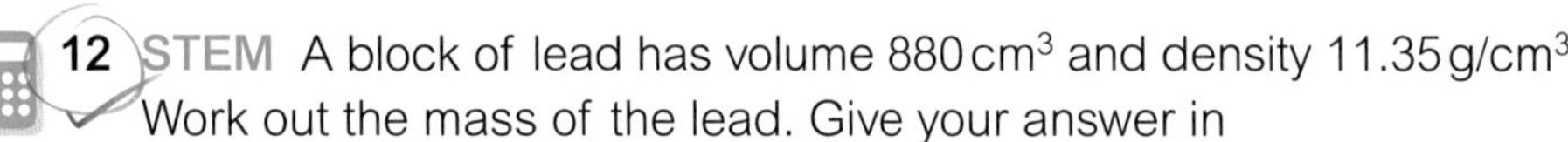

12 STEM A block of lead has volume 880 cm³ and density 11.35 g/cm³.
Work out the mass of the lead. Give your answer in

a grams

b kilograms.

Q12 hint

Rearrange the formula $D = \frac{M}{V}$ to make M the subject.

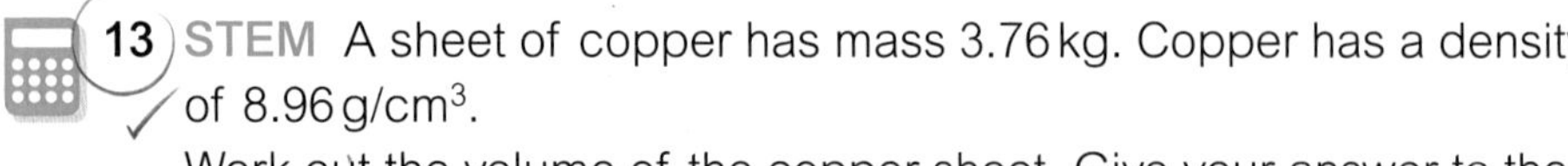

13 STEM A sheet of copper has mass 3.76 kg. Copper has a density of 8.96 g/cm³.
Work out the volume of the copper sheet. Give your answer to the nearest cm³.

Q13 hint

How do you need to rearrange the formula? Be careful about the different units of measurement.

Topic links: Time, Changing the subject of a formula

Subject links: STEM (Q10–15)

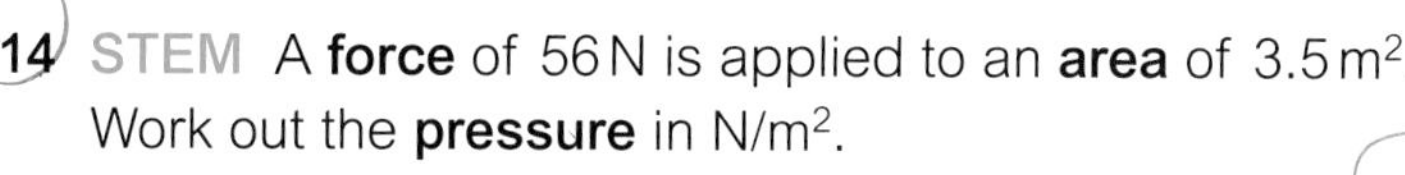

14 STEM A **force** of 56 N is applied to an **area** of 3.5 m². Work out the **pressure** in N/m².

Key point

Pressure is a compound measure. Pressure is the **force** applied over an **area**.

pressure = $\frac{\text{force}}{\text{area}}$ or $P = \frac{F}{A}$

Pressure is usually measured in newtons (N) per square metre.
To calculate it, you need pressure in N and area in m².

15 STEM Copy and complete this table.

Force	Area	Pressure
120 N	1.25 m²	□ N/m²
□ N	3.6 cm²	20 N/m²
40 N	□ m²	16 N/m²

Q15 hint

Rearrange the formula $P = \frac{F}{A}$.

Look carefully at the units of measurement.

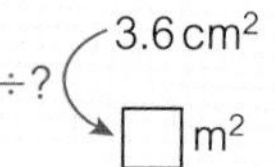

16 Real Here are some multipacks of crisps. Each pack is the same brand and contains the same size smaller packs.

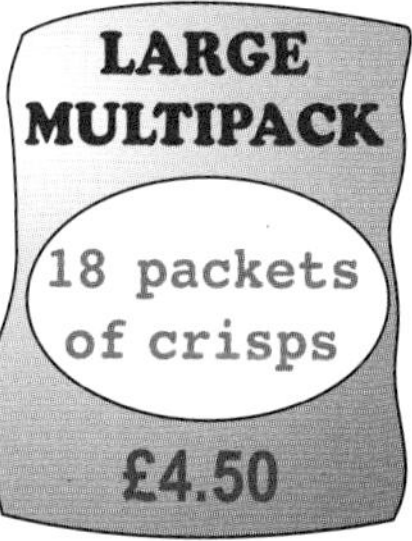

a Work out the price of one packet of crisps from the
- **i** small multipack
- **ii** medium multipack
- **iii** large multipack.

b Which multipack is the best value for money? Explain your answer.

Discussion How else could you compare the prices of these multipacks to work out which is the best value for money?

17 Real / Reasoning Here are some jars of honey at different prices from different producers.

a Work out the cost of 10 g of honey from each jar.

b Which jar of honey is the best value for money? Explain your answer.

18 **Explore** Why do stiletto heels damage wooden floors?
Is it easier to explore this question now you have completed the lesson?
What further information do you need, to be able to answer this?

19 **Reflect** Jesse says, 'A compound measure combines measures of two different quantities. A rate of change describes exactly how one of the quantities changes in relation to another.'
Jesse starts this table to show what he means.

Compound measure	Rate of change (example)
Speed – measure of distance and time	40 miles per hour

Copy the table and add more examples.

Q19 hint

Look back at the compound measures and rates of change you worked with in this lesson.
Can you think of other examples?
Think about subjects like science and geography, or activities outside school.

Explore

Reflect

4.5 Problem-solving

You will learn to:

- Round numbers to a given number of significant figures
- Solve problems using percentage change and rates of change
- Solve problems using ratio and scale factors.

CONFIDENCE

Why learn this?
Students planning an expedition need to work out how far they will walk in one day, and how long it will take them.

Fluency
Complete these formulae.

- speed = $\frac{\square}{\square}$
- density = $\frac{\square}{\square}$
- pressure = $\frac{\square}{\square}$

Explore
How long does it take to walk to the next town?

Exercise 4.5

Warm up

1 Maggie's hourly rate of pay increases from £8.70 to £9.57.
What is her percentage change in pay?

Q1 hint
Use the formula

$$\text{percentage change} = \frac{\text{actual change}}{\text{original amount}} \times 100$$

2 Convert 225 mm² into
a cm² **b** m²

3 Finance In its second year of trading, a company's profits fell by 8% and the company made £1.38 million.
How much did it make in its first year of trading?

4 STEM / Problem-solving A seal pup gains 28% of its birth weight each day for the first 10 days of its life. A one-day-old pup weighs 17.92 kg.
How much will it weigh at the end of the first 10 days of its life?

Q4 hint
Work out how much it weighed at birth, then how much weight it put on each day.

Worked example

Round these numbers to the number of significant figures shown.

a 34.069 (4 s.f.)
34.07 — The 4th significant digit is 6, but the 5th digit is 9, so round the 6 up.

b 0.046 12 (3 s.f.)
0.0461 — The 3rd significant digit is 1, but the 4th digit is 2, so leave the 1 as it is.

c 12 575 (2 s.f.)
13 000 — The 2nd significant digit is 2, but the 3rd digit is 5, so round the 2 up.

Key point
You can round numbers to a certain number of **significant figures (s.f.)**. The first significant figure is the one with the highest place value. It is the first non-zero digit in the number, counting from the left.

Topic links: Metric units, Imperial units

Subject links: STEM (Q4, Q6, Q7)

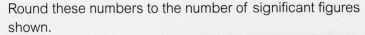

5 Round these numbers to the number of significant figures shown.

a 60.247 (4 s.f.) **b** 0.00572 (1 s.f.) **c** 364295 (2 s.f.)

6 **STEM / Modelling** The diagram shows a wooden block in the shape of a cuboid.
The block has a mass of 20.8 kg.
Work out the density of the wood.
Give your answer in g/cm^3 to two significant figures.

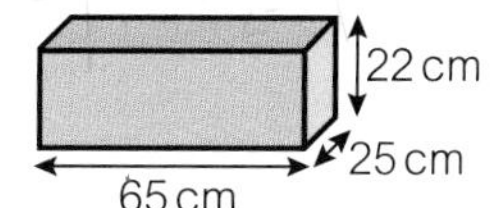

Q6 Strategy hint

Write down the formula you need. What quantities do you need to put into it? In what units of measurement?

7 **STEM / Modelling** The diagram shows the dimensions of a rectangular piece of metal.
A force of 45 N is applied to the piece of metal.
Work out the pressure in N/cm^2 to one significant figure.

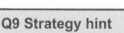

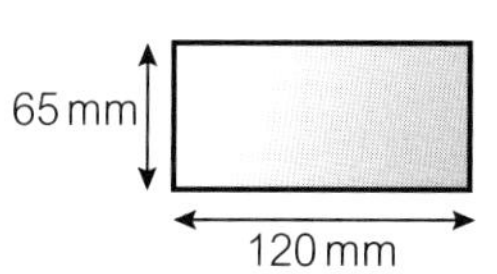
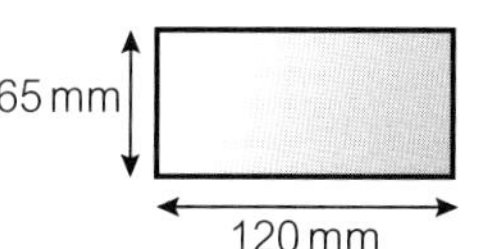

8 **Problem-solving / Reasoning** Hassan makes a model of Buckingham Palace using a scale of 1 : 12. The height of the real palace is 24 m.

a What is the height of the model?
Hassan then makes a doll's house of the palace to go inside his model.
The scale of the doll's house compared with the model is 1 : 10.

b What is the height of the doll's house?
Hassan says, 'The scale of the doll's house to Buckingham Palace is 1 : 22 because 12 + 10 = 22.'
Raj says, 'The scale of the doll's house to Buckingham Palace is 1 : 120 because 12 × 10 = 120.'

c Who is correct? Explain your answer. Check your answer by comparing the real height of Buckingham Palace to your answer in part **b**.

9 **Modelling** Your boss says you can either have a 1% pay rise this year and then a 2% pay rise next year, or a 1.6% pay rise this year.
Which would you prefer?

Q9 Strategy hint

Decide on a salary figure to work with.

10 **Problem-solving** The table shows the number of people at a music festival between 2008 and 2013.

Year	2008	2009	2010	2011	2012	2013
Number of people	33450	38568	33851	37589	44328	41678

a Work out the percentage increase in the number of people between 2008 and 2009. Give your answer to three significant figures.

b **i** Between which two years was the greatest percentage increase in the number of people?

ii What was this percentage increase to three significant figures?

c In 2008 each person paid a £185 entrance fee.
In 2013 each person paid a £210 entrance fee.
What was the percentage increase in total entrance fee takings between 2008 and 2013? Give your answer to two significant figures.

11 **Explore** How long does it take to walk to the next town?
Is it easier to explore this question now you have completed the lesson?
What further information do you need, to be able to answer this?

12 **Reflect** In this lesson there is a strategy hint for solving problems with formulae.
Did the strategy hint help you? Explain.
List at least two other strategies you find helpful when problem-solving.

Q12 hint

Look back at the problems you solved in this lesson. What strategies were useful? Look back at some of the strategy hints in previous lessons too, such as 2.2. How did these strategy hints help you solve problems?

Explore

Reflect

4 Check up

Log how you did on your Student Progression Chart.

Enlargement

1 Copy these shapes and centres of enlargement on coordinate grids and then enlarge them, using the scale factors given.

a scale factor 3

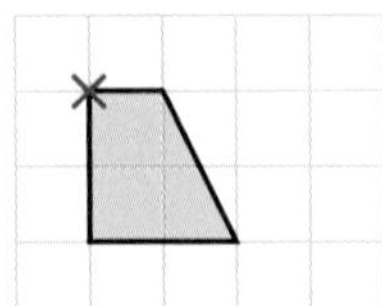

b scale factor −2

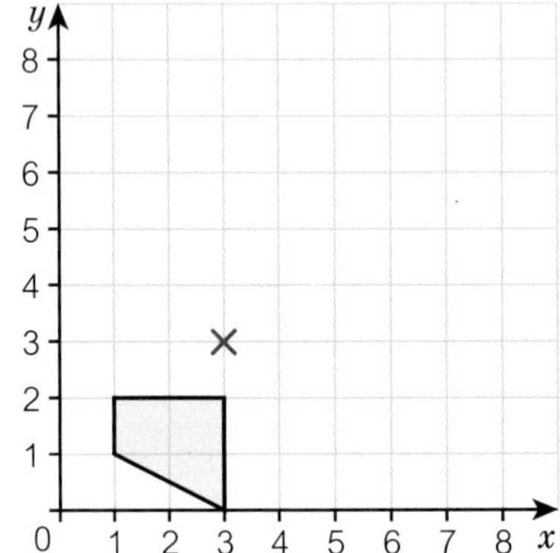

2 Describe the enlargement that takes shape A to shape B.

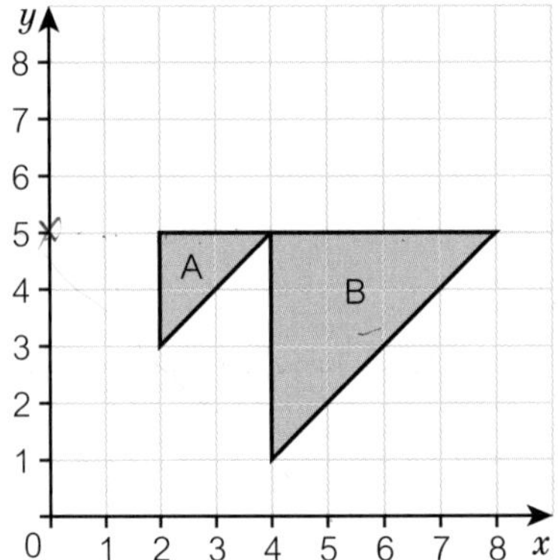

3 Copy the diagram and enlarge the triangle using scale factor $\frac{1}{2}$.

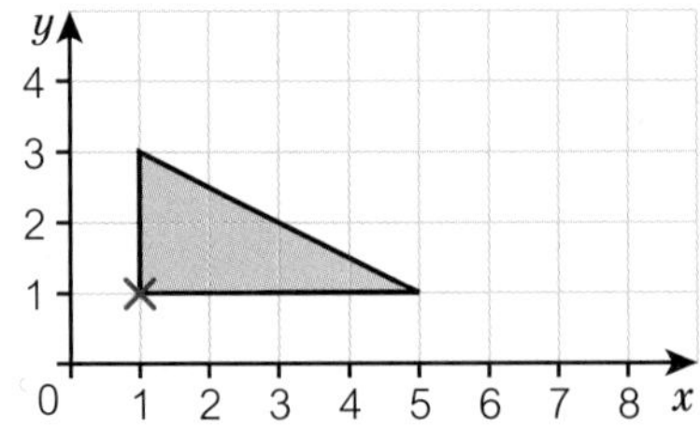

4 A model helicopter is made using a ratio of 1 : 48.
The width of the real helicopter is 18.72 m.
What is the width of the model? Give your answer in millimetres.

Compound measures

5 Round these numbers to the number of significant figures shown.

a 126.328 (4 s.f.) **b** 0.0652 (1 s.f.) **c** 205 694 (3 s.f.)

6 **a** Sol takes 2 hours to drive 114 miles.
Work out the average speed of his journey.

b Mair cycles at an average speed of 12 mph for $1\frac{3}{4}$ hours.
How far does she cycle?

7 Copy and complete this table to show the mass, volume and density of ash.

Tree	Mass (g)	Volume (cm^3)	Density (g/cm^3)
Ash	402	600	

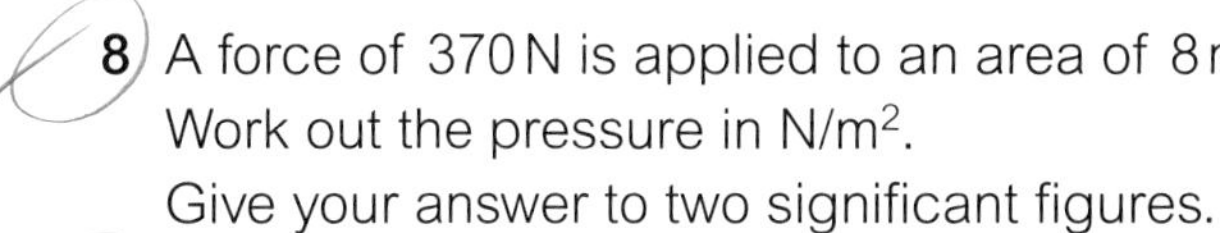

8 A force of 370 N is applied to an area of $8\,m^2$.
Work out the pressure in N/m^2.
Give your answer to two significant figures.

9 Toilet rolls come in three different size packs.
Which pack is the best value for money?
Explain your answer.

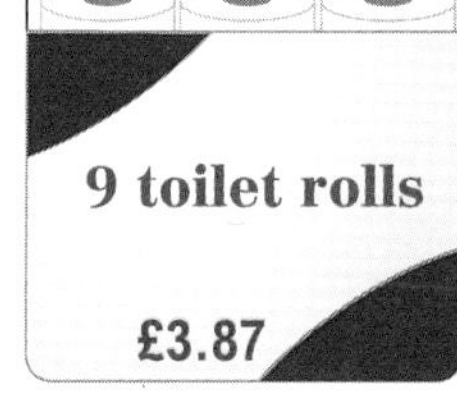

Percentage change

10 There was a 30% discount in a sale. A bag had a sale price of £28.
What was the original selling price?

11 Ellie invests £3200. When her investment matures she receives £3584.
Work out

a the actual increase in her investment

b the percentage increase in her investment.

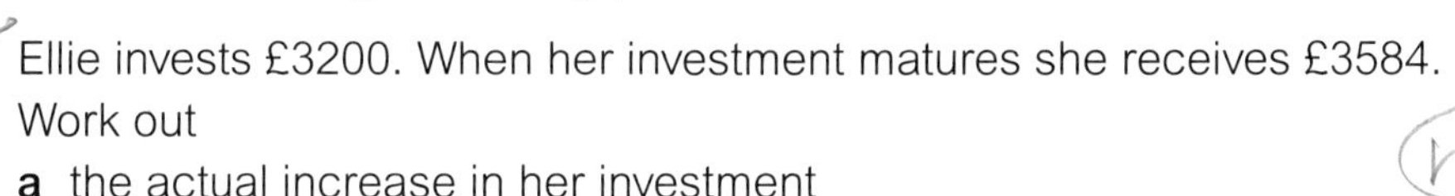

12 **How sure are you of your answers? Were you mostly**
Just guessing **Feeling doubtful** **Confident**
What next? Use your results to decide whether to strengthen or extend your learning.

Reflect

Challenge

13 In this spider diagram, the four calculations give the amount in the middle.
Work out three possible sets of missing values.

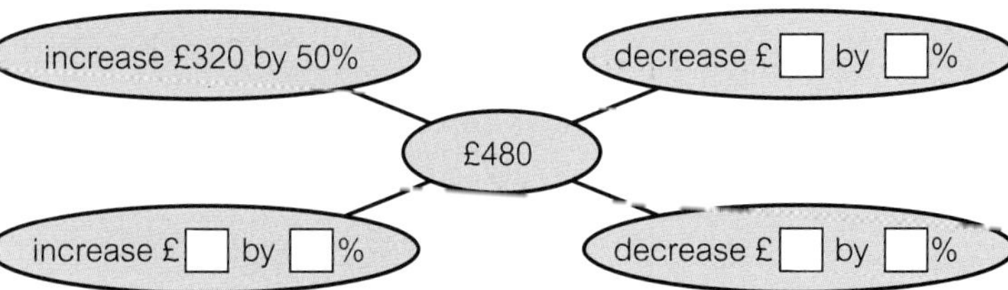

14 Jon has to go to a meeting that starts at 10.30 am. He plans to drive the 150 miles from home to the meeting.
Most of the journey is on the motorway.
The speed limit on the motorway is 70 mph.
Use an average speed measure of your choice to work out how long the journey will take and what time he should leave home when

a there is not much traffic on the roads

b there is a lot of traffic on the roads.

4 Strengthen

You will:

- Strengthen your understanding with practice.

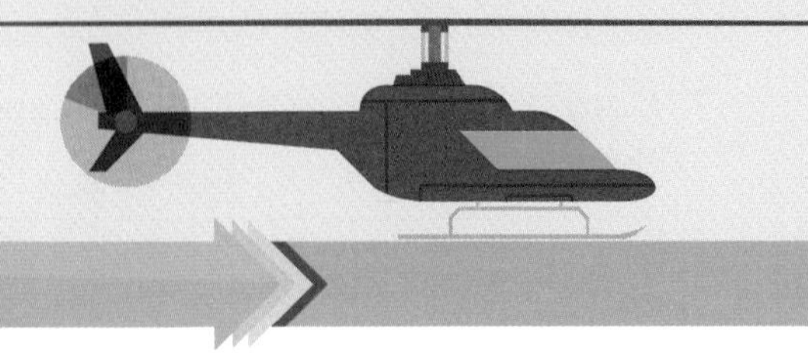

Enlargement

1 Copy these shapes onto coordinate grids. Complete the enlargements using the marked centres and scale factors.

a scale factor 2

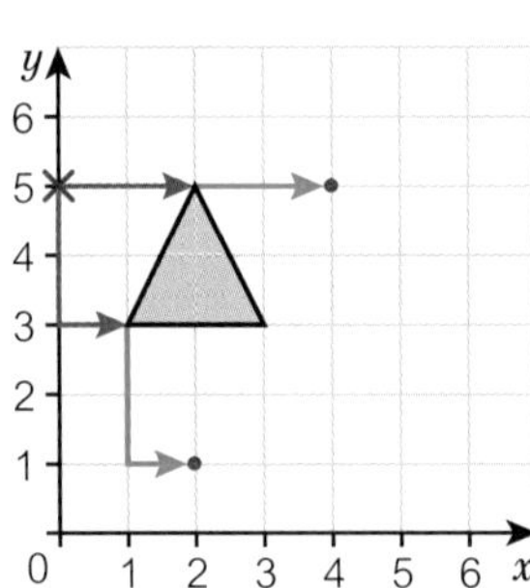

b scale factor 3

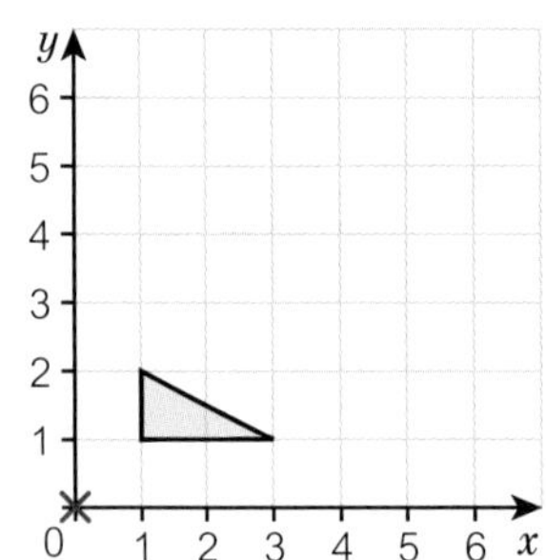

c scale factor 3

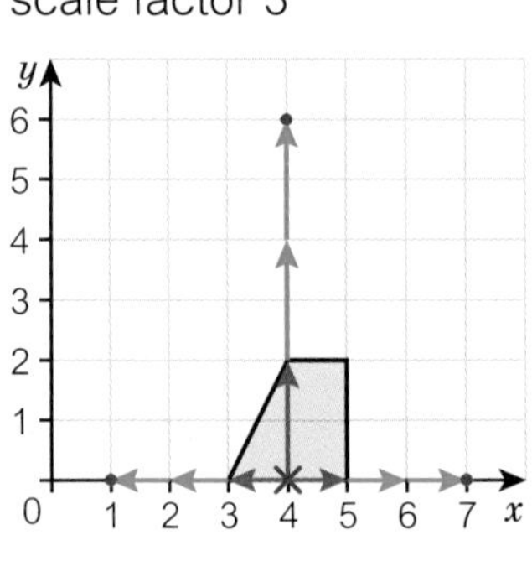

d scale factor 2

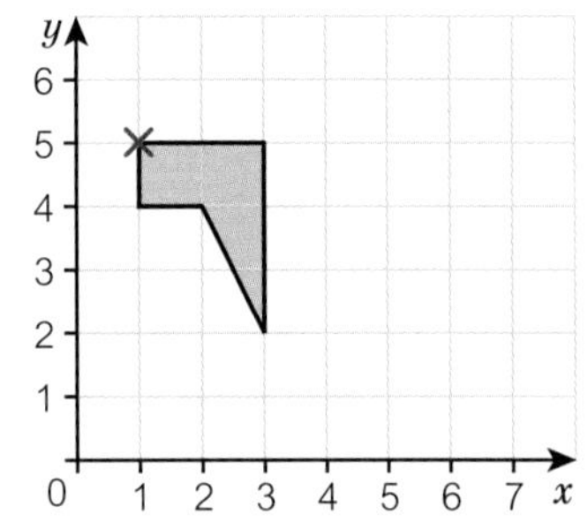

2 In each of these diagrams shape A has been enlarged to shape B. Write down the scale factor and the coordinates of the centre of enlargement.

a

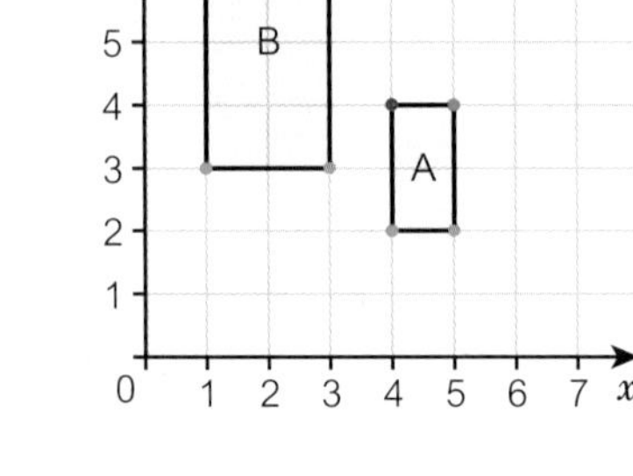

b

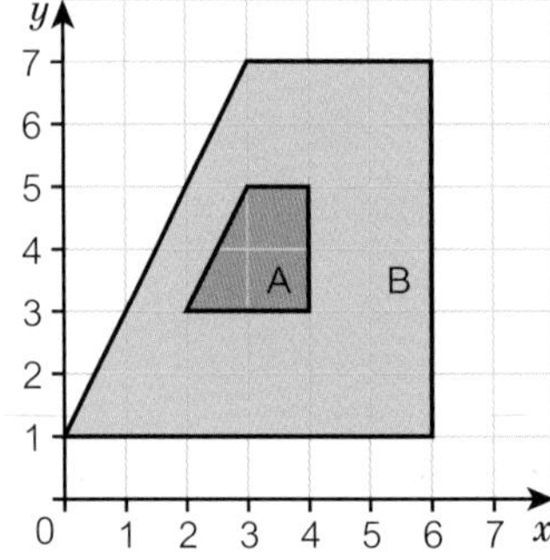

Q1b hint

Draw an arrow from the centre to a vertex. Multiply the arrow length by the scale factor. Repeat for other vertices.

Q2a hint

Join the corresponding corners of the shapes (the coloured dots on the diagram) with straight lines. Make sure the lines are long enough to cross each other.

3 Copy these shapes onto coordinate grids. Complete the enlargements using the marked centres and scale factors.

a scale factor −2

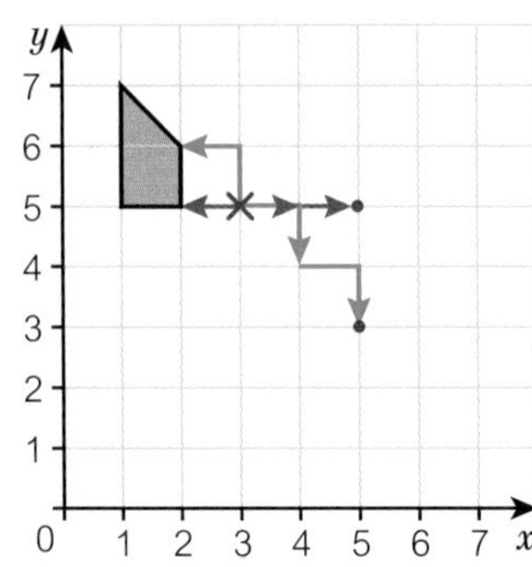

b scale factor −3

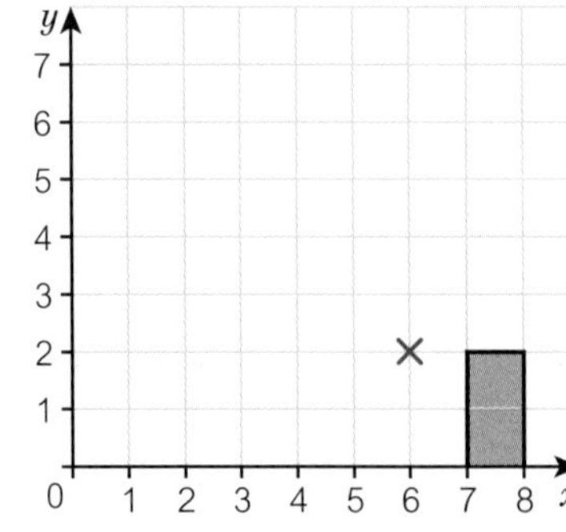

Q3 hint

Draw an arrow from the centre to a vertex. Multiply the arrow length by the scale factor. Draw arrows to the new vertex in the opposite direction. Repeat for other vertices.

4 Copy each shape onto squared paper. Enlarge each shape by the scale factor shown.

a scale factor $\frac{1}{2}$

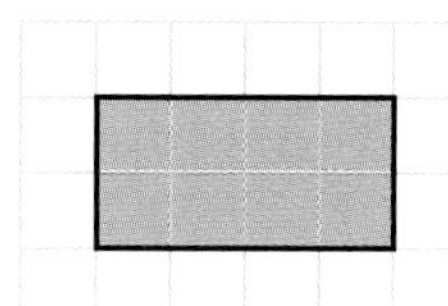

b scale factor $\frac{1}{3}$

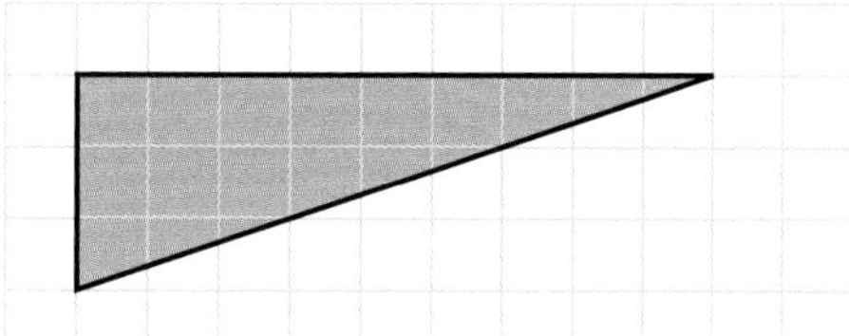

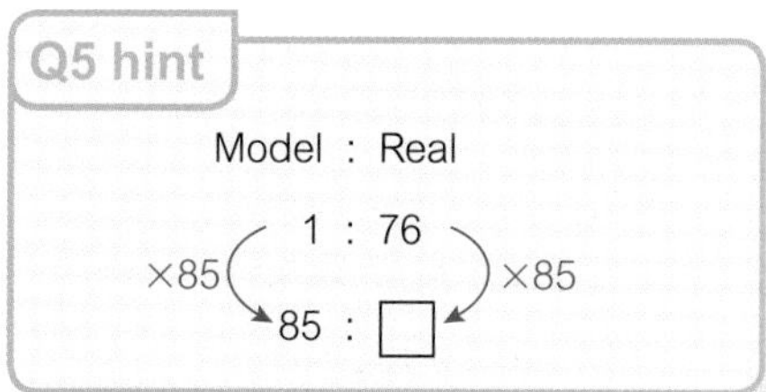

5 Real A model farmhouse is made using a ratio of 1 : 76.
The height of the model is 85 mm.
What is the height of the real farmhouse? Give your answer in

a millimetres

b metres.

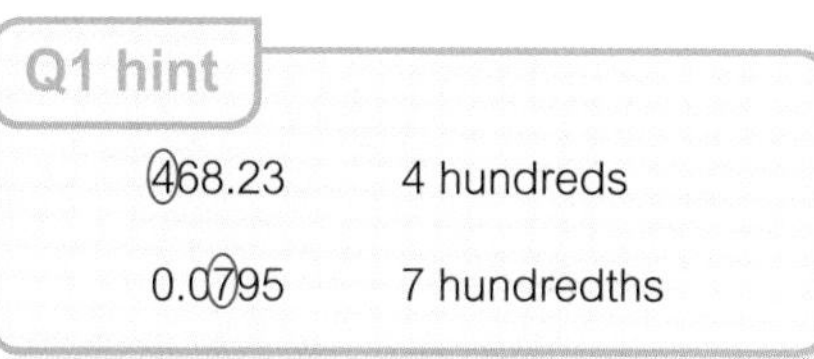

Q5 hint
Model : Real
1 : 76
×85
×85
85 : □

6 Real A model aeroplane is made using a ratio of 1 : 24.
The length of the real aeroplane is 11.28 m.
What is the length of the model? Give your answer in millimetres.

Compound measures

1 Copy these numbers. Circle the first significant figure.
Write its value.

a 56.882 b 0.00456 c 673500 d 0.8834

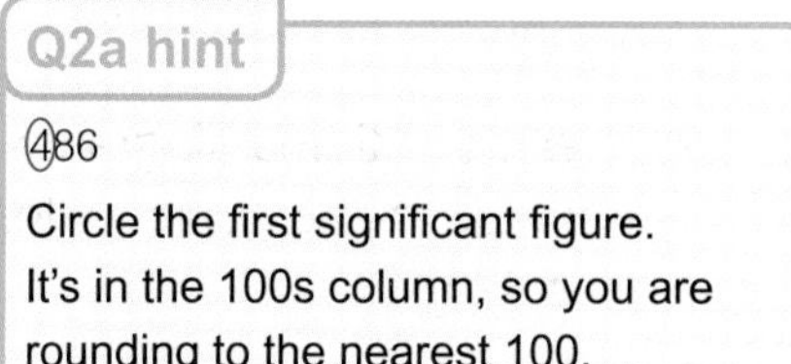

Q1 hint
468.23
4 hundreds
0.0795
7 hundredths

2 Write these numbers to one significant figure.

a 486 b 394.55 c 3495

d 187340 e 0.03394 f 0.000479

Q2a hint

486

Circle the first significant figure.
It's in the 100s column, so you are rounding to the nearest 100.

3 Round these numbers to the number of significant figures shown.

a 568 (2 s.f.) b 63349 (3 s.f.)

c 0.6528 (2 s.f.) d 0.004781 (3 s.f.)

4 Modelling Copy and complete this table of distance, time and speed.

Distance (miles)	Time (hours)	Speed (mph)
	3	55
	$1\frac{1}{2}$	68
120	4	
144	$2\frac{1}{4}$	
70		35
180		48

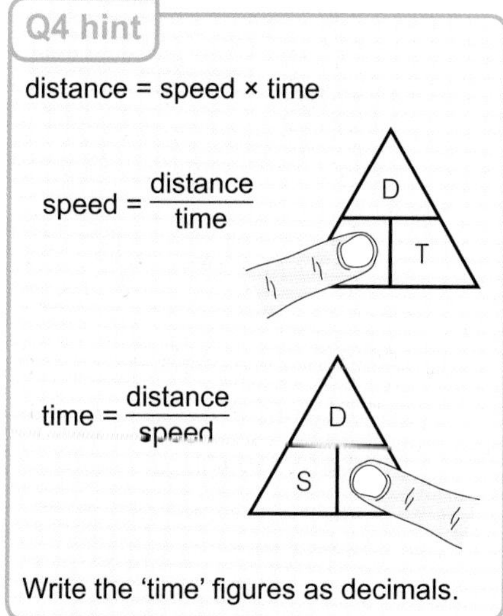

Q4 hint
distance = speed × time
speed = distance / time
D
T
time = distance / speed
D
S
Write the 'time' figures as decimals.

5 STEM / Modelling Copy and complete this table of mass, volume and density.

Metal	Mass (g)	Volume (cm^3)	Density (g/cm^3)
Tin		100	7.31
Iron	472.2		7.87
Nickel	311.5	35	

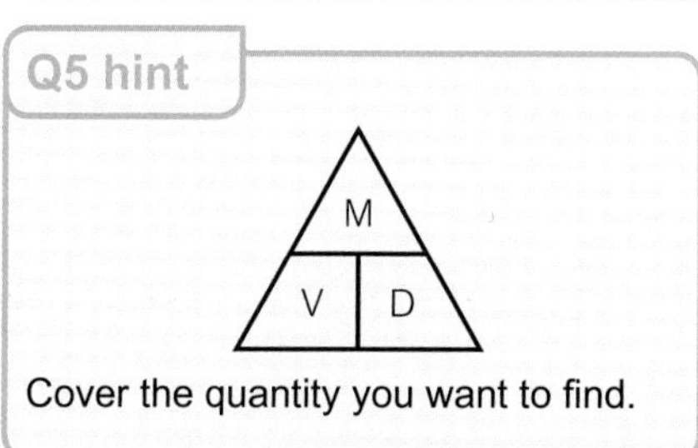

Q5 hint
M
V
D
Cover the quantity you want to find.

6 STEM / Modelling Copy and complete this table showing the force, area and pressure.

Force (N)	Area (cm^2)	Pressure (N/cm^2)
	12	7
45	15	
56		14

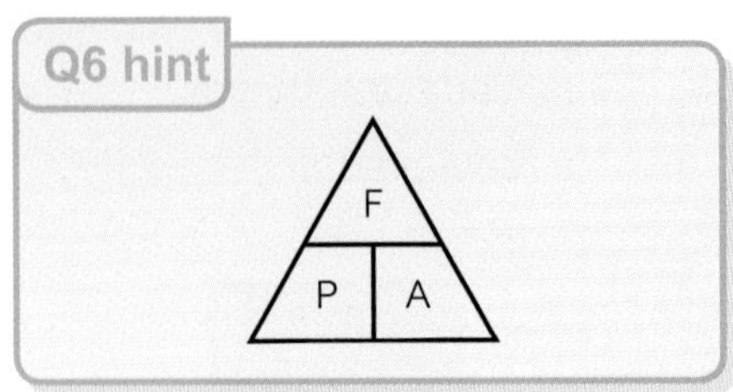

7 Real Pasta is sold in three different size bags.

a Work out the price of 1 kg of pasta based on the 500 g bag and the 3 kg bag.

b Which bag is the best value for money? Explain your answer.

Q7a hint

×2 (500 g = £0.76) ×2
1 kg = £☐

÷☐ (3 kg = £4.26) ÷☐
1 kg = £☐

8 Real The price of a pack of 16 soaps is £4. The price of a pack of 20 soaps is £5.

a Work out the price of one soap from the pack of 16. Then work out the price of 20 of these soaps.

b Which pack is the better value for money?

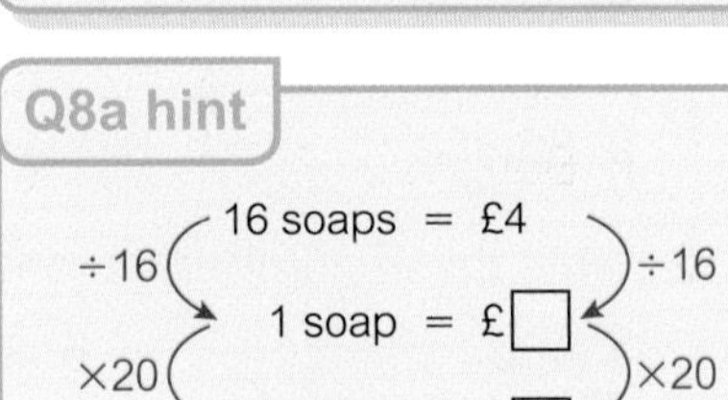

Percentage change

1 There was a 10% discount in a sale. A jacket had a sale price of £36. Complete the working to find the original selling price.

÷90 (90% = £36) ÷90
1% = £0.40
×100 ( ) ×100
100% = ☐

2 Work out the original price for each of these items

a Discount 20%, sale price £48

b Discount 40%, sale price £72

c Discount 15%, sale price £68

Q2a hint

÷? (☐% = £48) ÷?
1% = ☐

3 After a 25% increase in membership, the number of members in a surf club went up to 20.
Complete the working to find the original number of members in the club.

100% + 25% = 125%

÷125 (125% = 20) ÷125
1% = 0.16
×100 ( ) ×100
100% = ☐

4 Work out the original number of members in each of these clubs.

a Increase of 10%, up to 66 members

b Increase of 30%, up to 195 members

c Increase of 45%, up to 174 members

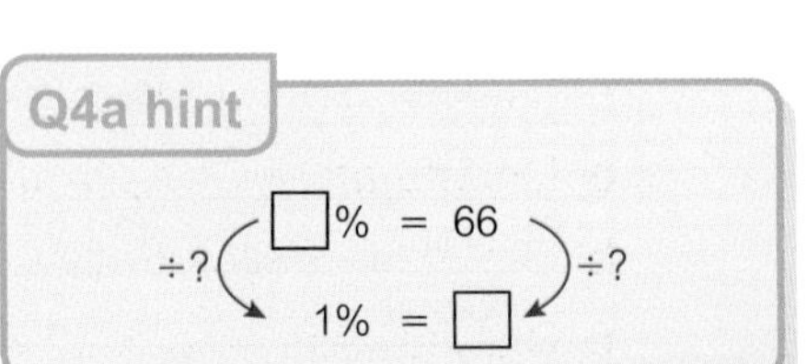

5 Anil invests £6000. When his investment matures he receives £6240.

a Copy and complete the working to calculate his percentage increase.

original amount = 6000
actual change = 6240 − 6000 = 240

percentage change = $\frac{\text{actual change}}{\text{original amount}} \times 100 = \frac{240}{6000} \times 100 = \square\%$

b Check your answer by increasing £6000 by the percentage you calculated. Do you get £6240?

Q5 hint

Draw this information as a bar model.

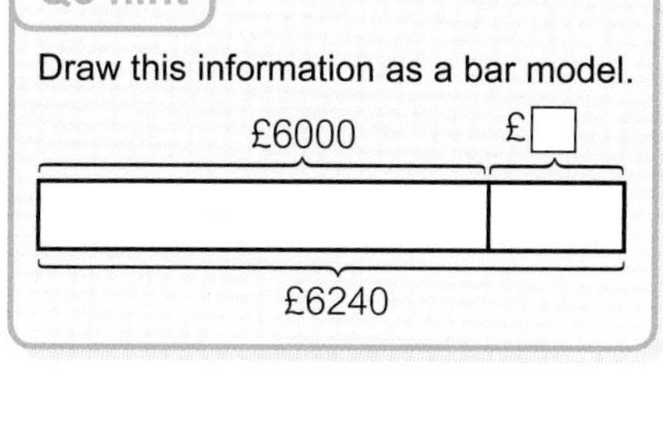

6 Work out the percentage profit made on each of the items. For each part, copy and complete the following working. Check your answers.

original amount = □
actual change = □

percentage profit = $\frac{\text{actual change}}{\text{original amount}} \times 100 = \frac{\square}{\square} \times 100 = \square\%$

a Bought for £6, sold for £7.50

b Bought for £15, sold for £19.50

c Bought for £120, sold for £222

7 Work out the percentage loss made on each of these items. Check your answers.

a Bought for £12, sold for £9

b Bought for £360, sold for £306

c Bought for £42, sold for £26.46

Q7a hint

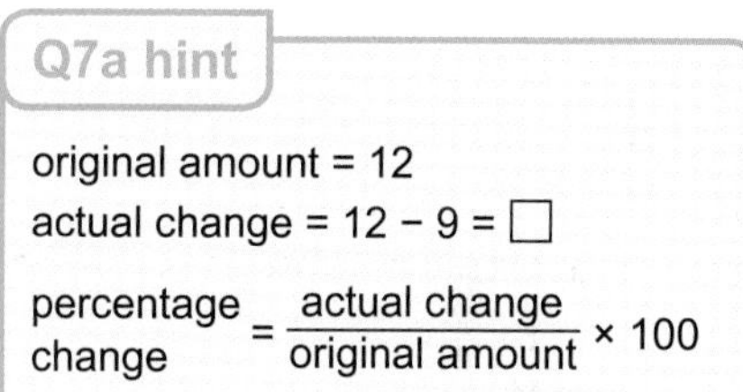

original amount = 12
actual change = 12 − 9 = □

percentage change = $\frac{\text{actual change}}{\text{original amount}} \times 100$

Enrichment

1 Lowri and Tyler take a typing test.
Lowri types 312 words in 8 minutes.
Tyler types 220 words in 5 minutes.
Who types faster?

2 It takes Becky 18 seconds to download a 37.8 MB file onto her computer.
It takes Abir 14 seconds to download a 32.9 MB file onto her computer.
Whose computer is faster?

3 The area of the yellow rectangle is 60% of the area of the blue rectangle.

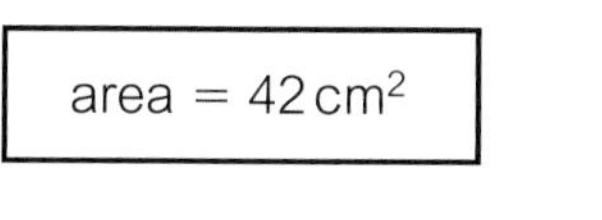

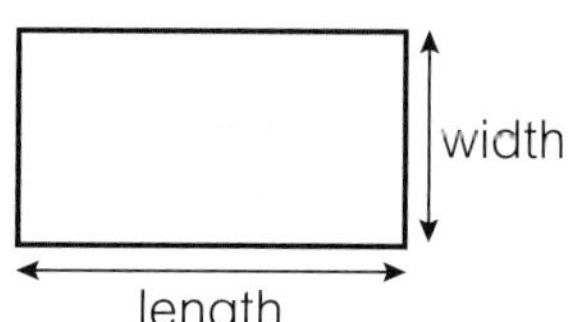

a Work out the area of the blue rectangle.

b Work out a possible length and width of the blue rectangle.

4 **Reflect** These Strengthen lessons suggested using arrows, triangles or bars to help you answer questions.
Look back at the questions where you used arrows, triangles and bars.

a Did the arrows help you? Explain why.

b Did the triangles help you? Explain why.

c Did the bars help you? Explain why.

Reflect

4 Extend

You will:

- Extend your understanding with problem-solving.

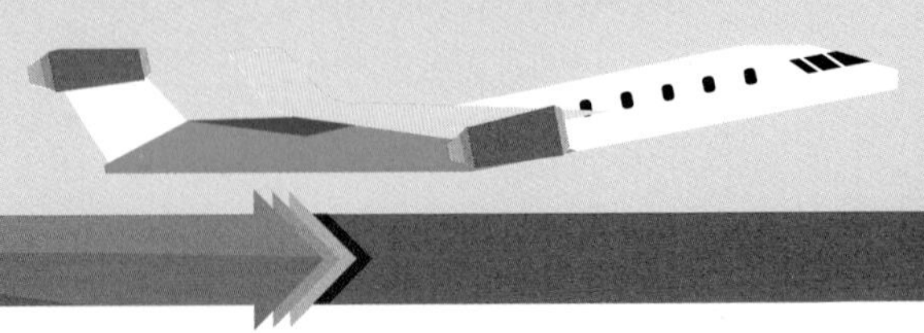

1 Describe the enlargement taking shape A to shape B in these diagrams.

a

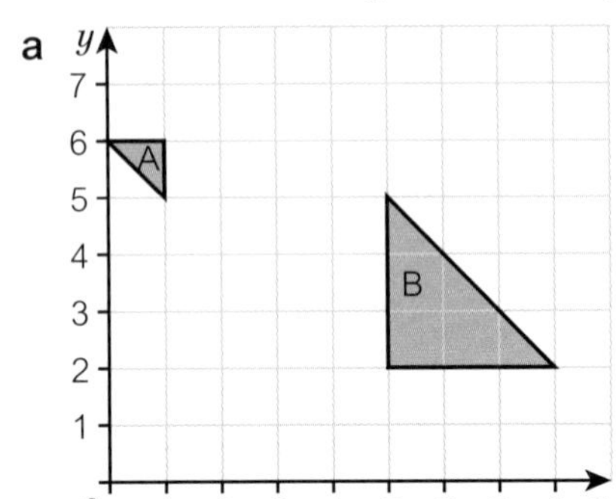

b

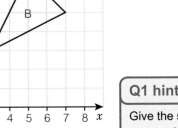

Q1 hint
Give the scale factor and the centre of enlargement.

2 **Problem-solving** The perimeter of the red square is 20% greater than the perimeter of the yellow square.
Work out the side length of the yellow square.

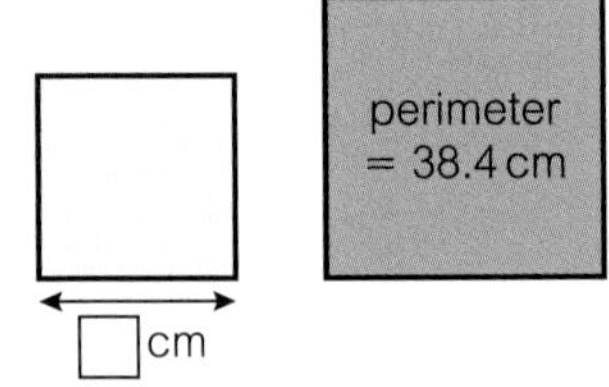

3 **Reasoning** Between the ages of 3 and 5 years old a tree grows at a rate of approximately 10% per year. At 5 years old it is 2 m tall.

a Work out the height of the tree when it is

i 4 years old **ii** 3 years old.

Write each answer to the nearest cm.

b Omar says, 'The tree has grown 10% each year for two years, which makes 20% in total. This means if I divide 2 m by 1.2 I will find the height of the tree when it is 3 years old.'
Is he correct? Explain your answer.

4 **Problem-solving** Between 2011 and 2012 visitor numbers to a zoo increased by 15%.
Between 2012 and 2013 visitor numbers to the zoo decreased by 20%.
In 2013 there were 69 552 visitors.
How many visitors were there in 2011?

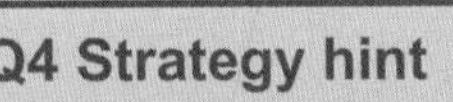

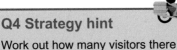

Q4 Strategy hint
Work out how many visitors there were in 2012 first.

5 **Finance** In 2012 the mean value of a residential property in the UK was £179 500.
There were 23.4 million residential properties.

a Work out the total value of all the residential property in the UK in 2012.

b Write your answer as an ordinary number, correct to one significant figure.

c In 2013, the total value of residential property in the UK rose to £5 trillion.
Work out the increase in value since 2012.

6 **Problem-solving** There are 10 teachers in a primary school. One teacher leaves and another teacher arrives. The mean age of the teachers increases by 5% to 42 years old.

a What is the mean age of the teachers before the teacher leaves?

The teacher who leaves is 25 years old.

b What is the age of the teacher who arrives?

Q6b hint

Work out the total age of the teachers before the teacher leaves and after the other teacher arrives.

7 **Problem-solving / Modelling** A car travels at an average speed of 24 m/s. Work out the time it takes to travel 325 km.
Give your answer in hours and minutes, to the nearest minute.

8 **Problem-solving / Modelling** Toby cycled 15 miles in $1\frac{1}{4}$ hours.
He had a 30-minute rest, and then cycled a further 9 miles in 45 minutes.
Work out his average speed for the whole journey.
Give your answer in

a miles per hour

b kilometres per hour

c metres per second.

9 **Real / Modelling** It is 235 miles from London to Manchester by train.
The table shows the top speed and average speed of a high-speed train and an Intercity train.

	Top speed	Average speed
High-speed train	200 mph	185 mph
Intercity train	125 mph	110 mph

a How much quicker is the journey from London to Manchester on a high-speed train than an Intercity train when you use
i the top speeds ii the average speeds?
Give your answers to the nearest minute.

b Which answer is more realistic? Explain why.

10 **Real / Reasoning** The line graph shows the mean household mortgage and rent payments from 2008 to 2010.

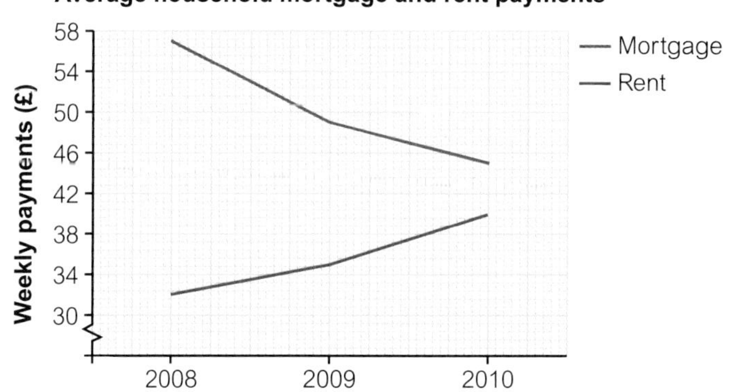

a Work out the percentage increase, to the nearest 1%, in rent payments for the average household between
i 2008 and 2009
ii 2009 and 2010
iii 2008 and 2010.

b Explain why the sum of your answers to parts **i** and **ii** is not the same as your answer to part **iii**.

c Work out the percentage decrease, to the nearest 1%, in mortgage payments for the average household between
i 2008 and 2009
ii 2009 and 2010.

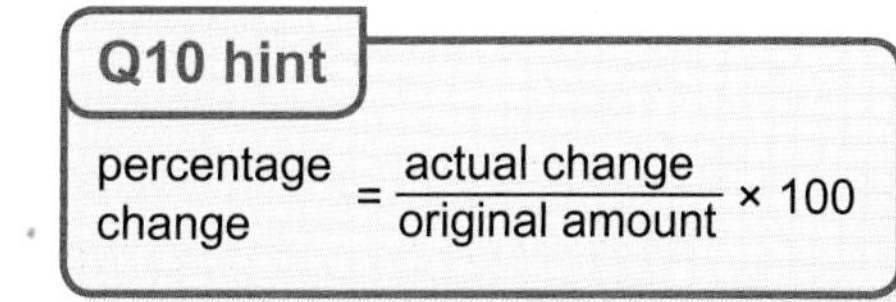

Q10 hint

$$\text{percentage change} = \frac{\text{actual change}}{\text{original amount}} \times 100$$

11 Problem-solving / Modelling The block of wood (A) has a mass of 1.44 kg. The wooden cube (B) is made from wood with a density 50% greater than the block of wood.

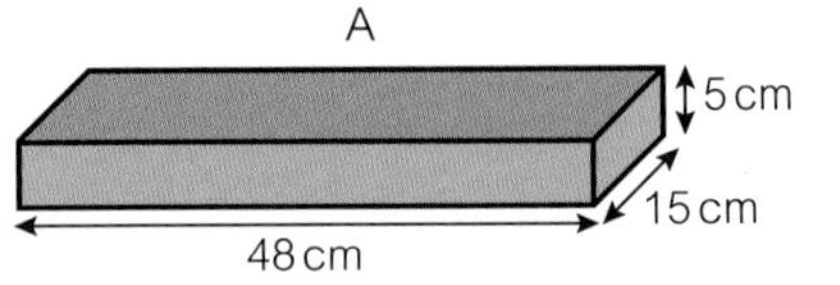

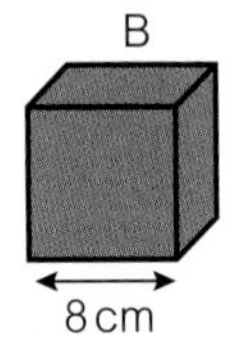

Work out the mass of the wooden cube.
Give your answer in grams to three significant figures.

12 STEM / Problem-solving The diagram shows the dimensions of a piece of metal. A force of 53.8 N is applied to the metal. Work out the pressure in N/cm^2.

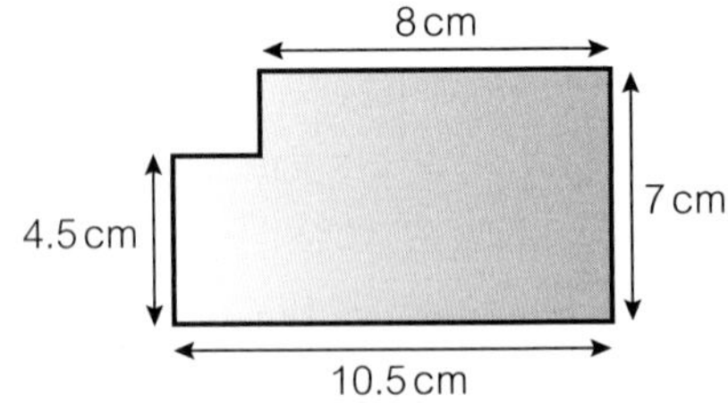

13 STEM / Reasoning Lisa sits on a chair with four identical legs. The foot of each chair leg is a square measuring 3 cm by 3 cm.
The force produced by the mass of Lisa and the chair is 522 N.
Work out

a the total area of the floor covered by the feet of the chair.

b the pressure on the floor when Lisa sits on the chair with all four chair feet flat on the floor.

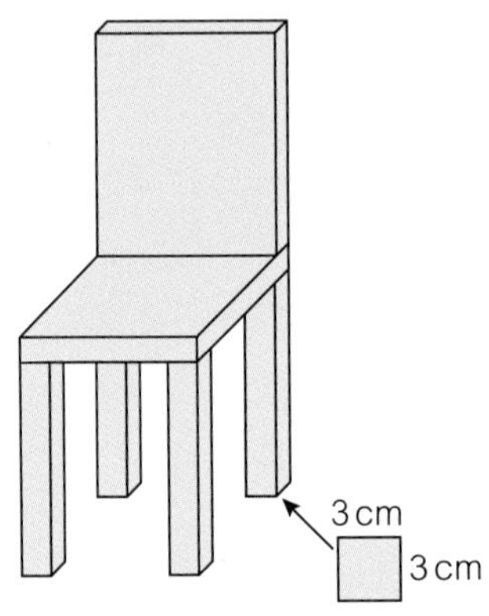

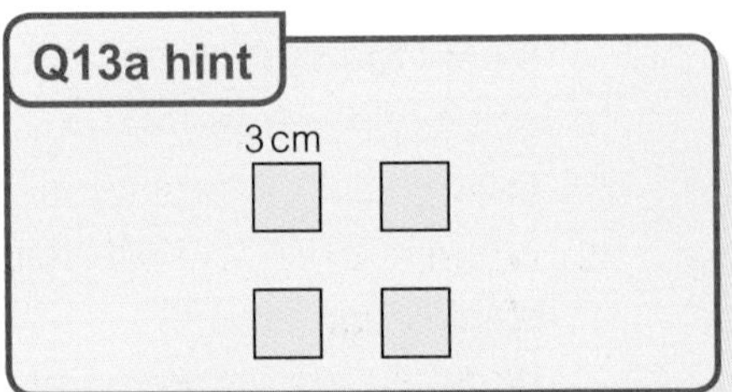

14 Problem-solving Triangles B and C are enlargements of triangle A.

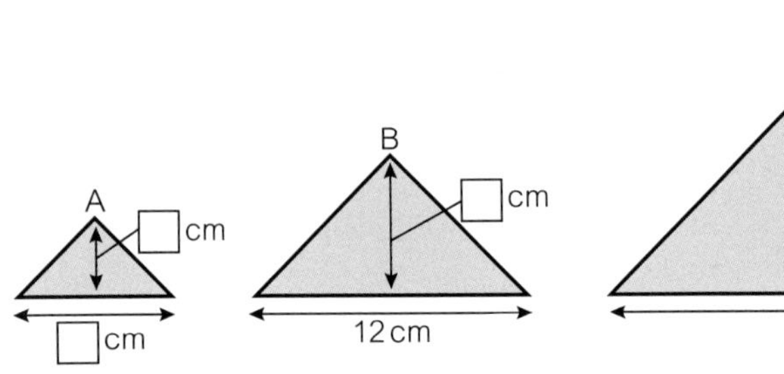

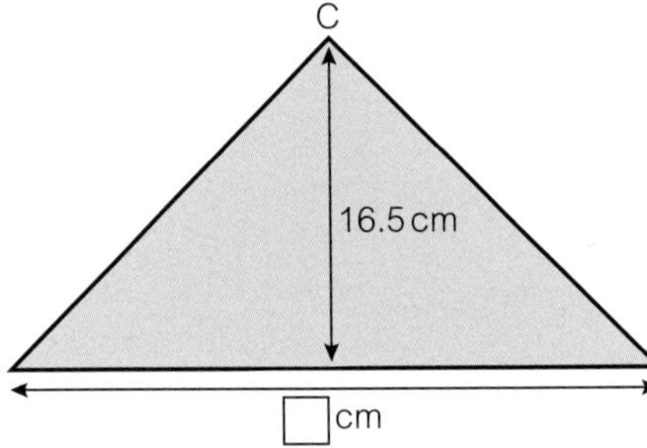

Q14 hint
Work out the height of triangle B first, from its area. Then use the ratio of the lengths.

Triangle B has an area of 54 cm^2.
The scale factor of enlargement of the lengths of triangle A to triangle C is 2 : 11.
Work out the missing lengths.

15 Copy this diagram.

a Work out the perimeter of the shape.

b Transform the shape using an enlargement with scale factor $-\frac{1}{3}$ and centre of enlargement (10, 4). Then reflect the enlargement in the line $x = 7$.

c Use your answer to part **a**, and the scale factor of the enlargement, to work out the perimeter of the final shape. Use the diagram to check that your answer is correct.

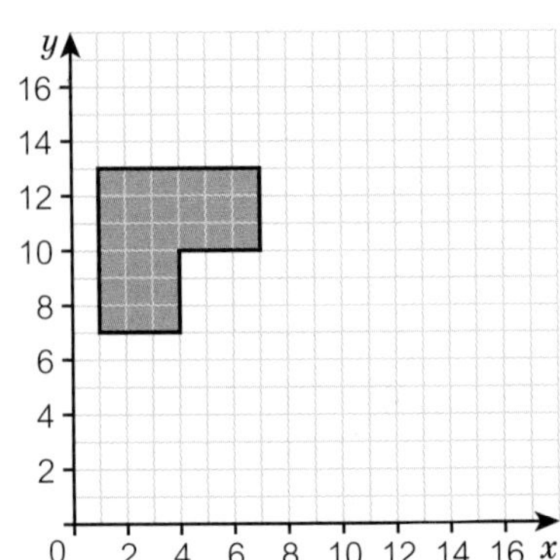

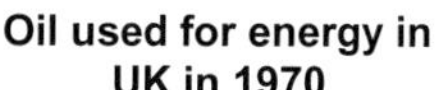

16 Real / Reasoning The pie charts show the proportion of oil used for different energy needs in the UK in 1970 and 2012.

- In 1970 the total amount of oil used for energy in the UK was 146 million tonnes.
- In 2012 the total amount of oil used for energy in the UK was 140 million tonnes.

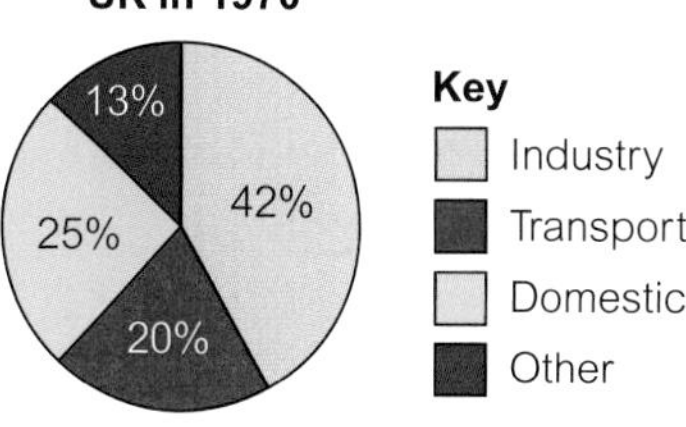

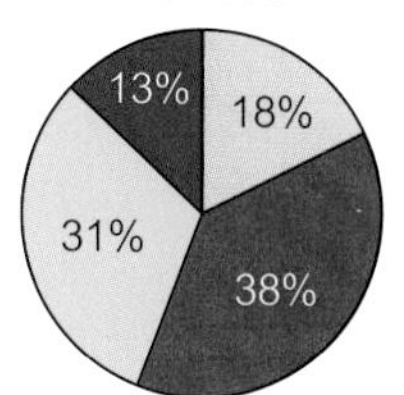

Source: DECC

a How many tonnes of oil were used by transport in 1970?

b How many tonnes of oil were used by transport in 2012?

c Work out the percentage increase in the amount of oil used by transport from 1970 to 2012.

d Work out the percentage decrease in the amount of oil used by industry from 1970 to 2012.

e 'Other' accounted for 13% in both 1970 and 2012. Does this mean that the same amount of oil was used for 'Other' purposes in 1970 and 2012? Explain your answer.

17 STEM / Problem-solving The diagram shows a piece of plastic cut into the shape of a trapezium. Work out the force required to create a pressure of 12 N/cm^2 on the trapezium.

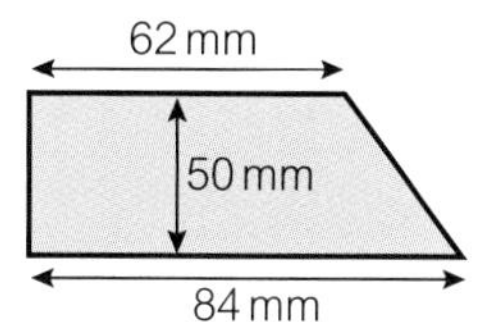

Q17 hint

Work out the area of the trapezium in cm^2 first.

18 STEM / Problem-solving The diagram shows a rectangular piece of metal. When a force of 328 N is applied to the metal, it creates a pressure of 16 N/cm^2. Work out the length, x, of the rectangle.

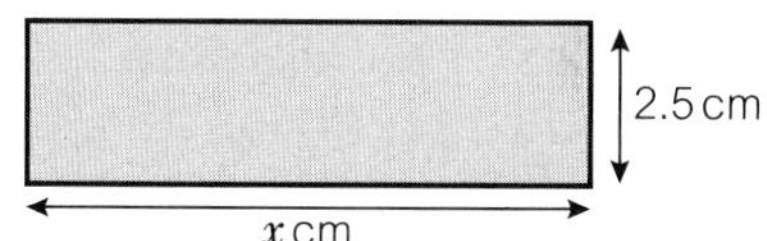

19 Copy this diagram.

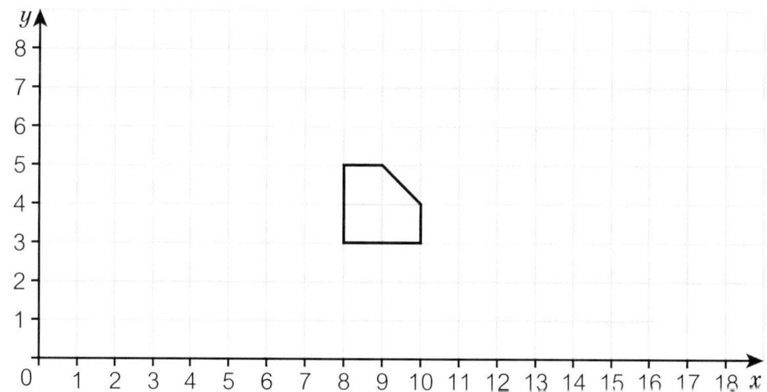

a Transform the shape using a rotation of 180° about (10, 5) then enlarge by scale factor −2 using centre of enlargement at (13, 5).

b Describe the single enlargement that will take the finishing shape back to the starting shape.

Q19b hint

Work out the scale factor.
Use rays to work out where the centre of enlargement is.

20 Reflect Look back at the questions in these Extend lessons.

a Write down the question that you found easiest to answer. What made it easiest?

b Write down the question that you found most difficult to answer. What made it most difficult?

c Look again at the question that you wrote down for part **b**. What could you do to make this type of question easier to answer?

Q20c hint

Ask your classmates how they answered this question. Do they have any hints for you?

Reflect

4 Unit test

Log how you did on your Student Progression Chart.

1 Copy this shape onto squared paper and then enlarge it, using the marked centre of enlargement and scale factor.

scale factor 3

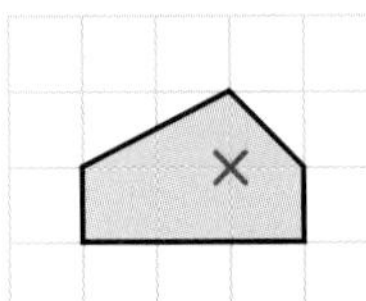

2 In each of these diagrams describe the enlargement from A to B.

a

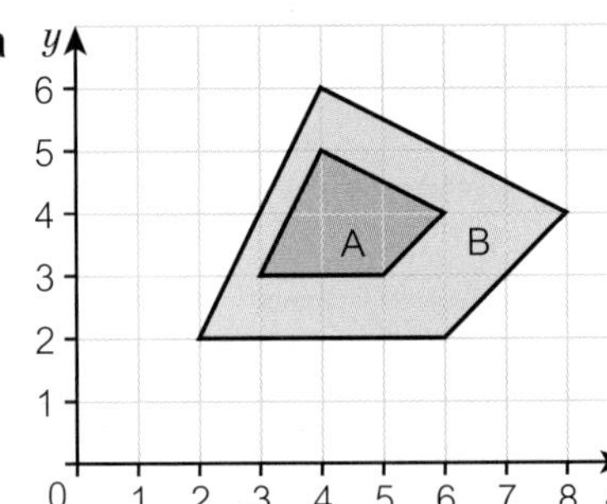

b

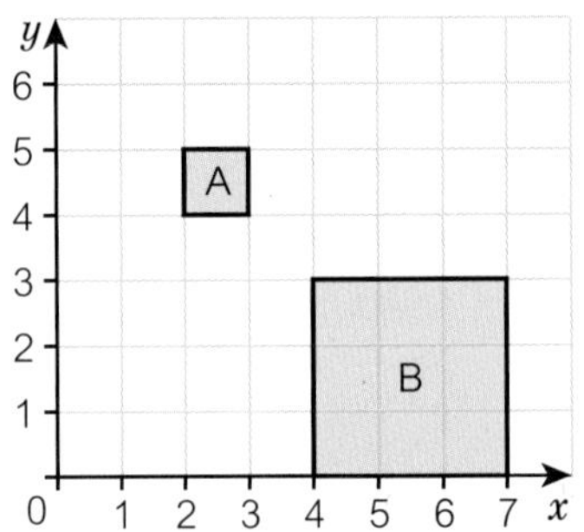

3 Copy this shape onto squared paper and then enlarge it, using the marked centre of enlargement and scale factor.

scale factor −3

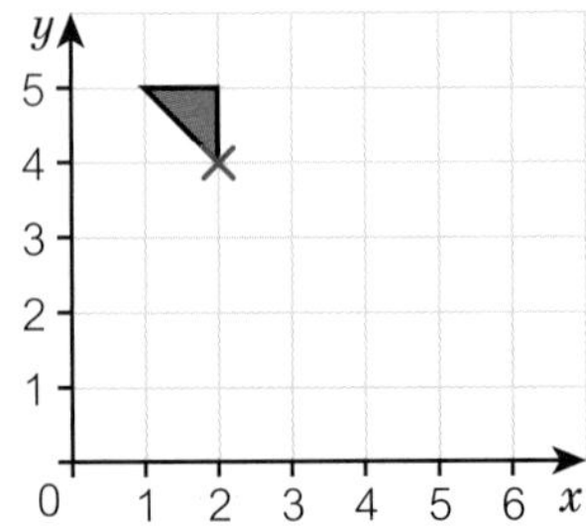

4 Round these numbers to the number of significant figures shown.

a 75 650 (2 s.f.)

b 0.008 72 (1 s.f.)

c 45.669 (3 s.f.)

d 200.925 (4 s.f.)

5 In one year the number of members in a chess club increases by 20%.
At the end of the year there are 30 members.
How many are there at the start of the year?

6 Chan invests £2800. When his investment matures he receives £2968.
Work out

a how much his investment increased by

b the percentage change in his investment.

7 a Joel takes 4 hours to drive 188 miles. Work out his average speed.
  b Ava walks at an average speed of 8 km/h for $3\frac{1}{4}$ hours.
  How far does she walk?
  c Rowan flies a helicopter at an average speed of 115 mph for 92 miles. How long does it take him? Give your answer in minutes.

8 This table shows the mass, volume and density of two pieces of plastic. Work out the missing values in the table.

Mass (g)	Volume (cm^3)	Density (g/cm^3)
	280	1.15
846	450	

9 A force of 84 N is applied to an area of 15 cm^2.
Work out the pressure in N/cm^2.

10 Cartons of fruit juice come in different size multipacks.

Which pack is the best value for money? Explain your answer.

11 Copy this diagram and enlarge the triangle, using scale factor $\frac{1}{3}$ and centre of enlargement (7, 1).

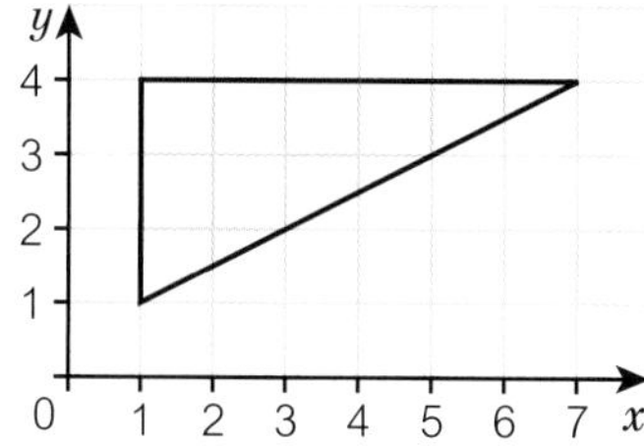

12 A model of a building is 40 cm high. The real building is 6.4 m high.
Work out the scale factor of the model to the building.
Write your answer as
  a a number
  b a ratio, in the form 1 : n.

13 Jan bought a camper van for £28 000. She sells it for £16 800.
Work out her percentage loss.

Challenge

14 The diagram shows a triangle, some scale factor cards and some area cards.

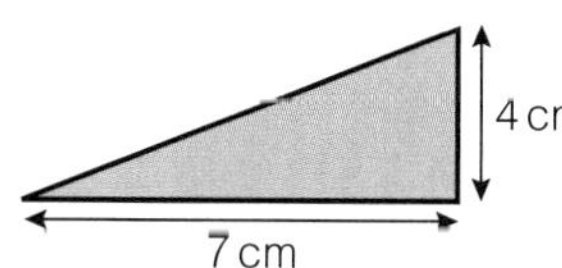

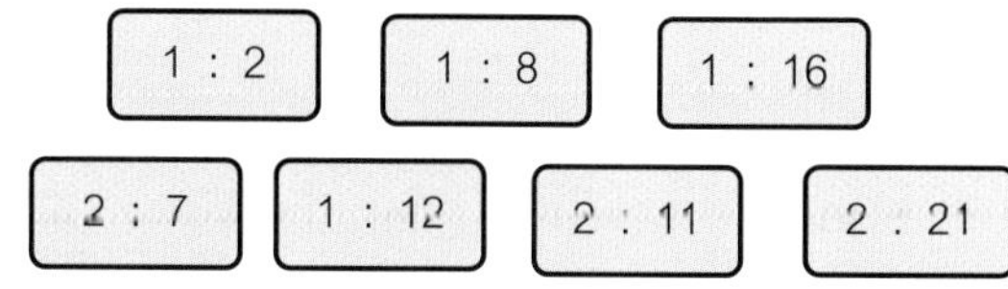

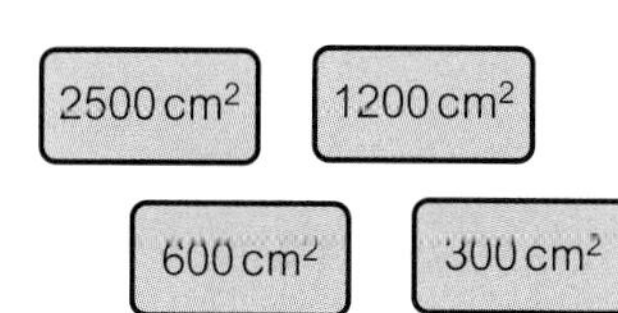

Choose one of the area cards.
Then work out which scale factor card, if used to enlarge the triangle, would give the closest possible area to the one on your card.
Try again with a different card.

15 **Reflect** Make a list of all the topics you have worked on in this unit where you have used multiplicative reasoning.
Look back at other units you have studied in this book.
List some other mathematics topics that use multiplicative reasoning.
Compare your list with those of your classmates.

Q15 hint
Remember that 'multiplicative' means 'involving multiplication or division'. Reasoning is being able to explain why.

Reflect

5 Constructions

5.1 Using scales

You will learn to:
- Use scales on maps and diagrams
- Draw diagrams to scale.

CONFIDENCE

Why learn this?
A map is an enlargement of the real world, but with a fractional scale factor.

Fluency
What is the scale factor of enlargement from the small triangle to the large one?

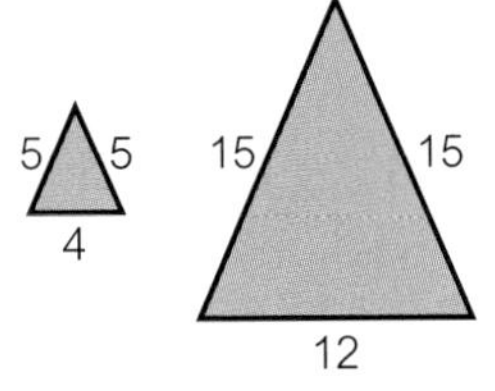

Explore
How big would your school be if it was in a model of your town?

Exercise 5.1

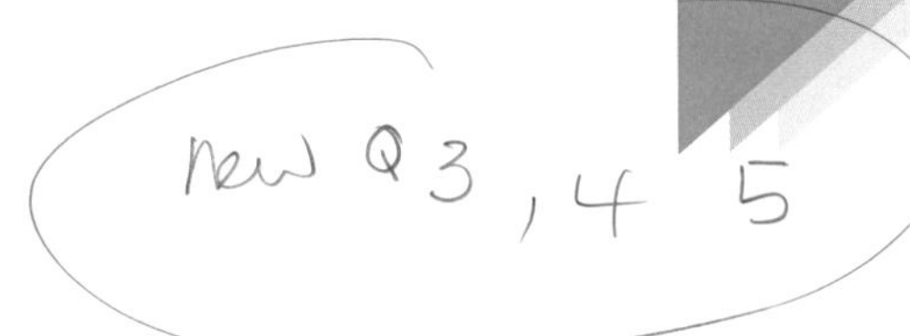

Warm up

1 On a scale drawing 1 cm represents 1 m.
  a What length line represents
    i 4 m   ii 6.5 m?
  b On the same drawing a line is 10.5 cm. How long is the real distance in metres?

2 Write each ratio as 1 : n.
  a 3 : 15   b 5 : 250   c 14 : 7

3 Real This map of Liverpool uses a scale of 1 cm for every 200 m.
Use the map to estimate as accurately as possible the real distance in metres between
  a the Town Hall and the Walker Art Gallery
  b Tate Gallery Liverpool and The Beatles Story
  c the Anglican Cathedral and the Metropolitan Cathedral.

Discussion Why can you only estimate the distances from the map?

Q3 Strategy hint
Measure the distances on the map in centimetres. Then use the scale to work out the real-life distances.

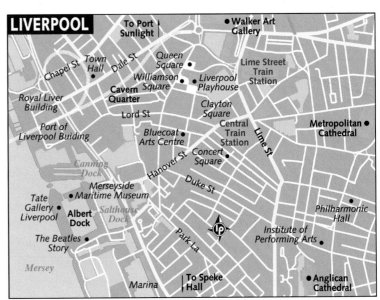

Topic links: Ratio, Measure

Subject links: Geography (Q3, Q8)

4 Neeta has drawn this scale diagram showing a design for her garden.
The length of the fence is 4 m in real life.

a Work out the scale of the diagram.
Write the scale as 1 cm to _______.

b Use this scale to find
   i the length of the pond
   ii the length of the border
   iii the area of the border
   iv the area of the decking.

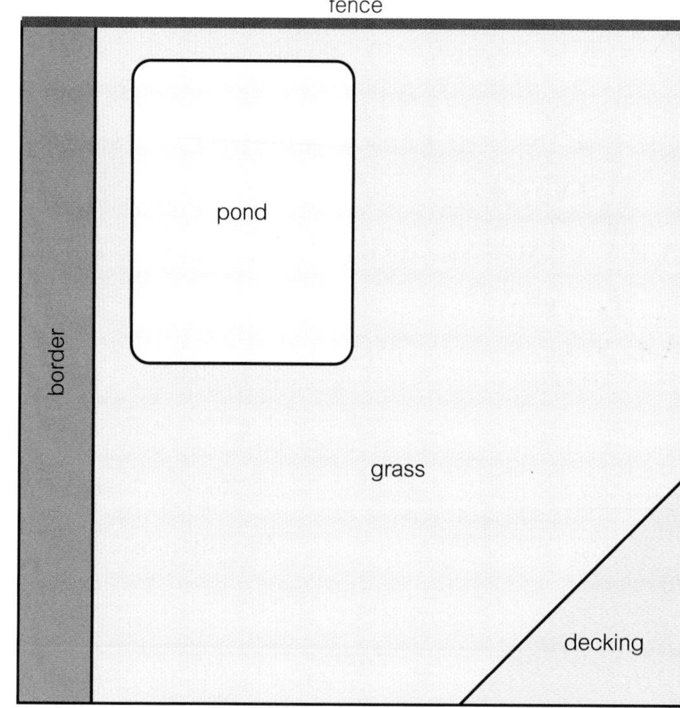

5 Draw a floor plan for the kitchen and utility room of this house.
Use a scale of 1 cm to 0.5 m.

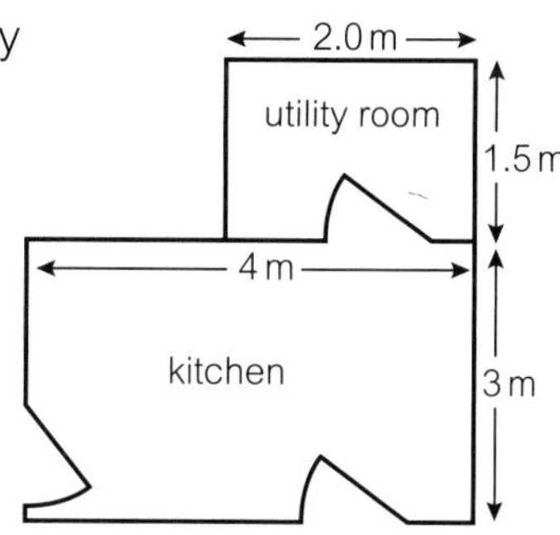

Q5 hint
Draw your plan on cm squared paper.

6 A shop has an access ramp for wheelchairs.
The ramp makes an angle of 15° with the ground and climbs 50 cm.
The wall of the shop is at right angles to the ground.

a Draw a scale diagram to show the side view of the ramp.
Use a ruler and protractor. Use the scale 1 : 10.

b Use your diagram to work out
   i how far the ramp will stick out from the shop
   ii how long the ramp surface will be.

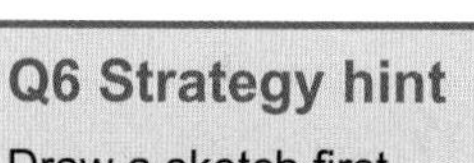

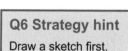

Q6 Strategy hint
Draw a sketch first.

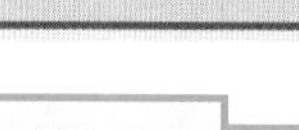

Q6a hint
1 : 10 means 1 cm represents 10 cm.

Worked example

A map has a scale of 1 : 25 000.
What distance in metres does 3 cm on the map represent?

	Map		Real life	
×3	1 cm	is	25 000 cm	×3
	3 cm	is	75 000 cm	

1 cm represents 25 000 cm,
3 cm represents 3 × 25 000 = 75 000 cm. — Work out the real life distance in cm.

75 000 cm ÷ 100 = 750 m — Convert to metres

7 A map has a scale of 1 : 25 000.

a What distance in metres does 5 cm on the map represent?

b What distance in kilometres does 8 cm on the map represent?

8 Real This map is from a road atlas with a scale of 1 : 2 500 000.

Use the map and the scale to estimate these distances in km as accurately as possible.

a the distance between Hay-on-Wye and Aberystwyth

b the distance between Cardiff and Bangor

c the width of Brecon Beacons National Park.

~~Discussion Why do road atlases often use the scale 1 : 250 000?~~

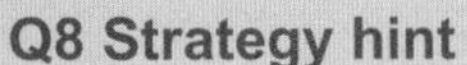

Q8 Strategy hint

Measure each distance on the map with a ruler.

9 A map has a scale of 1 : 30 000.

What distance on this map represents a real distance of

a 600 m

b 9 km

c 5.7 km?

Explore

10 **Explore** How big would your school be if it was in a model of your town? Choose some sensible numbers to help you explore this situation. Then use what you've learned in this lesson to help you answer the question.

Reflect

11 **Reflect** Santiago says, 'When working with scales on maps and diagrams, one of the most important things is multiplying by the correct scale factor.'

a Do you agree with him? Explain.

b What else is important when working with scales on maps and diagrams?

5.2 Basic constructions

You will learn to:

- Make accurate constructions using drawing equipment.

Why learn this?
Before computers, engineers used constructions for making accurate technical drawings.

Fluency

- What does perpendicular mean?
- Can you see examples of perpendicular lines in the classroom?

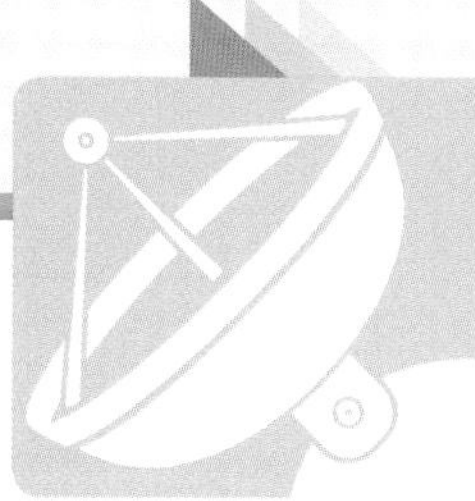

Explore
What are compasses used for?

CONFIDENCE

Exercise 5.2

1 Use a ruler and a sharp pencil to draw these lines.
 a 6.5 cm b 10.6 cm c 27 mm

2 Use compasses to draw accurately
 a a circle of radius 5 cm b a circle of radius 8 cm.

Warm up

Q2a hint

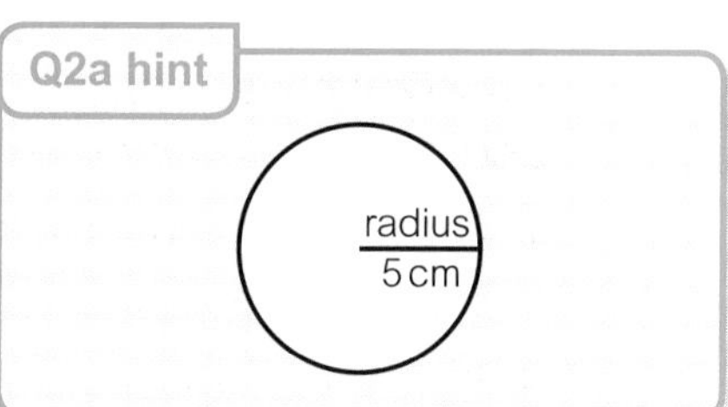

Worked example

Draw a line that is 5 cm long.
Construct its perpendicular bisector.

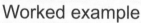

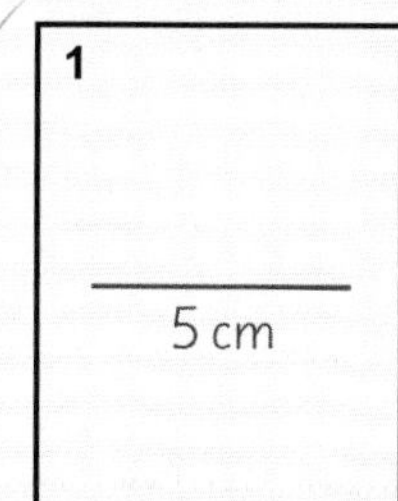

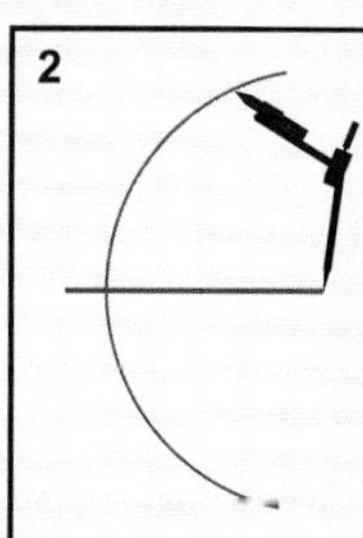

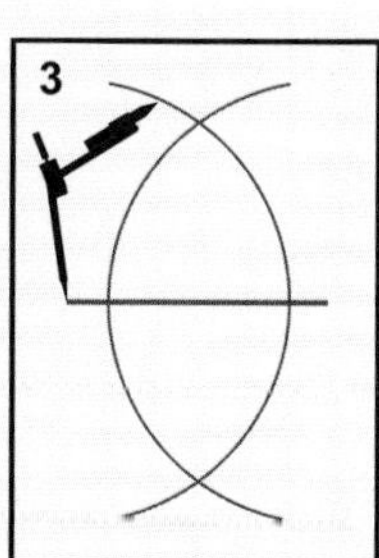

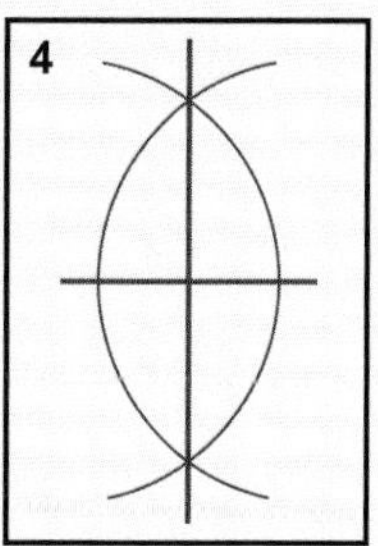

1 Use a ruler to draw the line.
2 Open your compasses greater than half the length of the line. Place the point on one end of the line and draw an arc above and below.
3 Keeping the compasses the same, move them to the other end of the line and draw another arc.
4 Join the points where the arcs intersect. The vertical line divides the horizontal line exactly in half.
Do not rub out the arcs.

Key point

Construct means draw accurately using ruler and compasses.

A **perpendicular bisector** cuts a line in half at right angles.

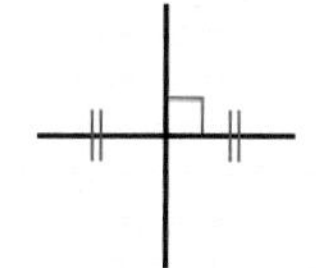

Literacy hint

Bisect means cut in half.

3 a Draw a line 7.5 cm long. Construct its perpendicular bisector.
b Check by measuring that your line cuts the original line in half.
c Check the angle where the lines cross.

Discussion How can you accurately construct the midpoint of a line?

4 Make an accurate scale drawing of this plan.
Use a scale of 1 : 100.

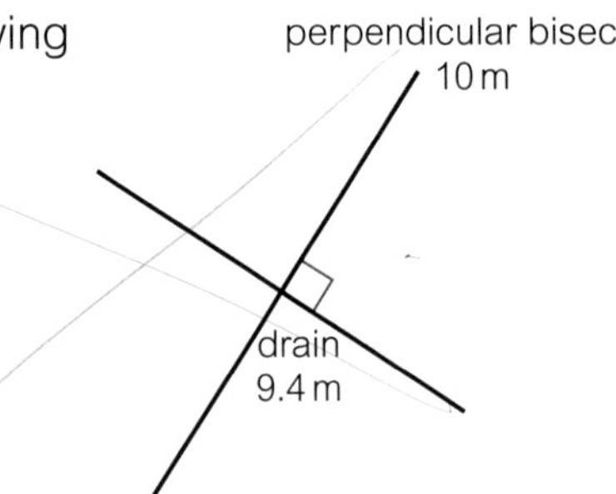

Q4 hint
Use a ruler and a pair of compasses to construct the perpendicular bisector.

Worked example

Draw an angle of 50°. Construct the angle bisector.

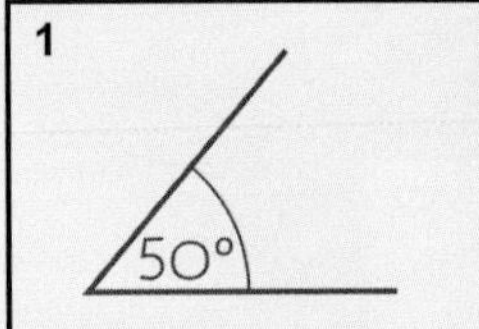

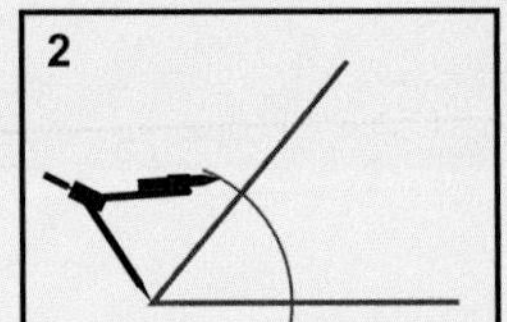

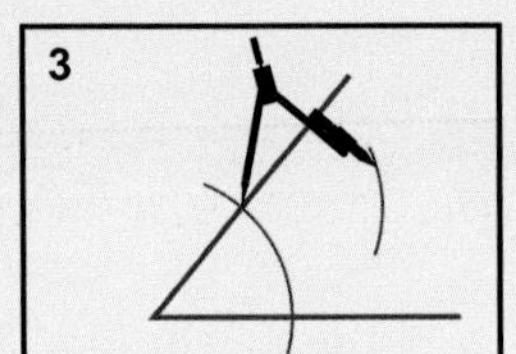

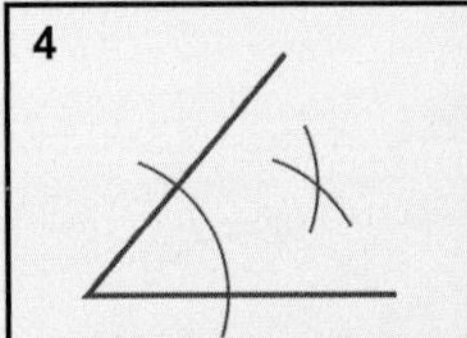

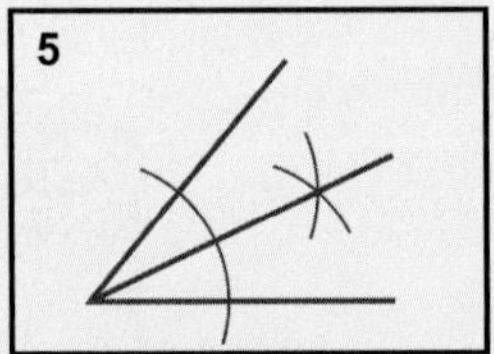

1 Draw the angle using a protractor.
2 Open your compasses and place the point at the vertex of the angle. Draw an arc that cuts both arms of the angle.
3 Keep the compasses the same. Move them to a point where the arc crosses one of the arms. Make an arc in the middle of the angle.
4 Do the same from the point where the arc crosses the other arm.
5 Join the point where the arcs cross to the vertex of the angle.
The line joins the point where the two small arcs intersect to the point of the angle; it divides the angle exactly in half.

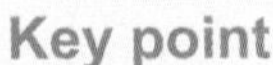

Key point
An **angle bisector** cuts the angle in half.

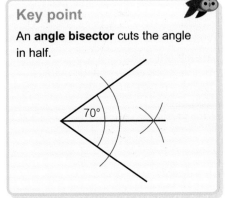

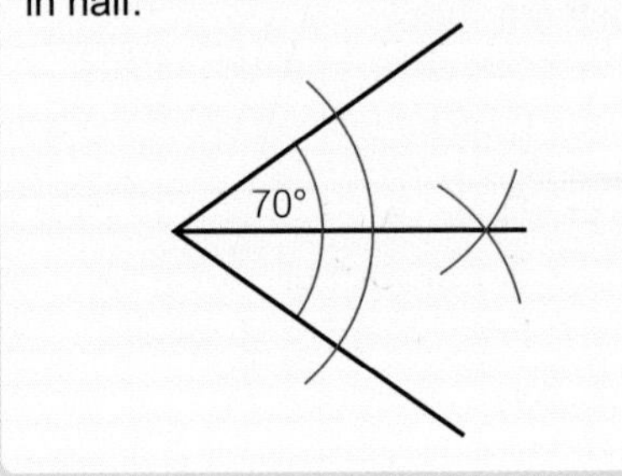

5 a Draw an angle of 60°. Construct the angle bisector.
b Check by measuring that it cuts the angle in half.

6 Draw an angle of 75°. Construct the angle bisector.

Discussion Why is a well-drawn construction an accurate way of bisecting a line or bisecting an angle?

7 Follow these instructions to draw a perpendicular from a point to a line.
a Draw a line segment 12 cm long.
b Mark a point above the line.
c Put your compasses on the point.
Draw an arc that crosses the line segment.
d Construct the perpendicular bisector of the straight line segment between the arcs.

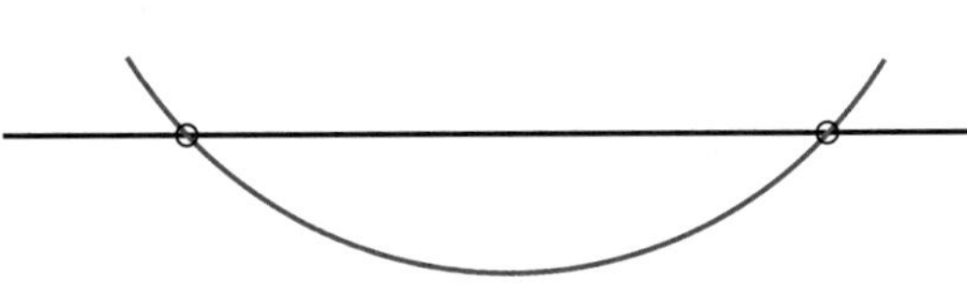

Topic links: Ratio, Measure

8 a Trace this diagram.

P

b Construct a perpendicular line from the point to the line segment.

9 a Trace this diagram.

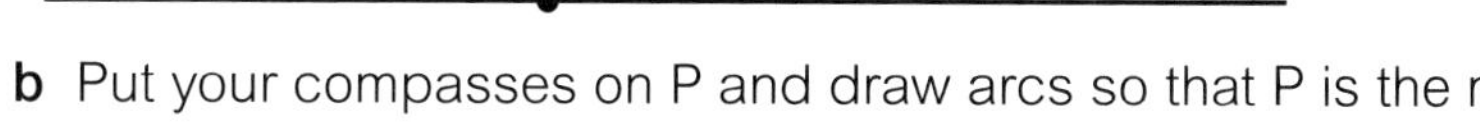

b Put your compasses on P and draw arcs so that P is the midpoint of the segment between the arcs.

c Construct the perpendicular bisector for this new segment.

10 Copy this diagram and then draw a perpendicular from P.

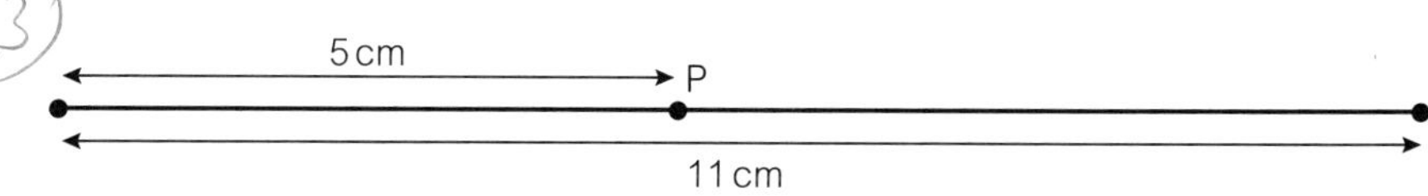

Q10 hint

Use the same method as in Q9.

11 **Real** A new road is to be built at right angles to a dual carriageway. Construct an accurate scale drawing of this sketched plan. Use a scale of 1 cm to 1 km.

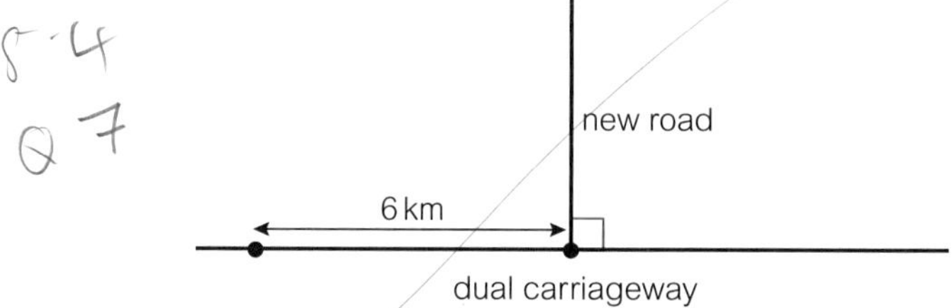

Investigation **Reasoning**

1 Draw a line segment and construct the perpendicular bisector.
2 Choose any point on the bisector. Measure the shortest distance to each end of the line segment.
3 Repeat this for other points on the bisector.

What do you notice? Is this always true? Why?

12 **Explore** What are compasses used for?
Look back at the maths you have learned in this lesson.
How can you use it to answer this question?

13 **Reflect** Miguel says, 'Constructions in maths are all about drawing accurate diagrams with only a pair of compasses and a straight edge or ruler. No measurement of lengths or angles is allowed.'
Look back at the constructions you did in this lesson. Is he correct?
Which do you find easier:

- using compasses and a straight edge to construct, or
- using a ruler and a protractor to measure lengths and angles accurately?

Explain why.

Explore

Reflect

5.3 Constructing triangles

You will learn to:
- Construct accurate triangles
- Construct accurate nets of solids involving triangles.

CONFIDENCE

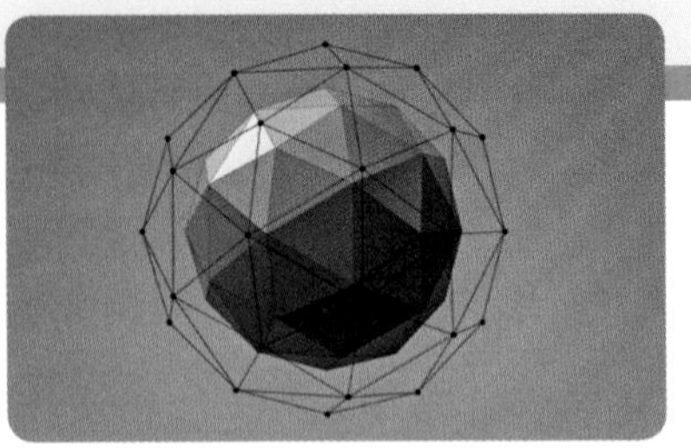

Why learn this?
You need an accurate net to make a 3D shape.

Fluency
- What is special about an isosceles triangle?
- Describe an equilateral triangle.

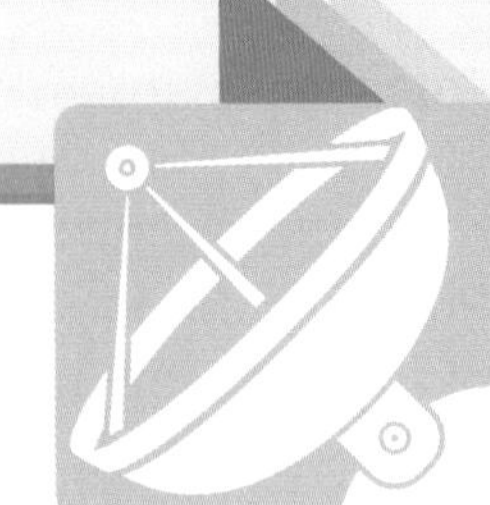

Explore
How could you design and make a four-sided dice for a board game?

Exercise 5.3

Warm up

1 Sketch a possible net for this square-based pyramid.

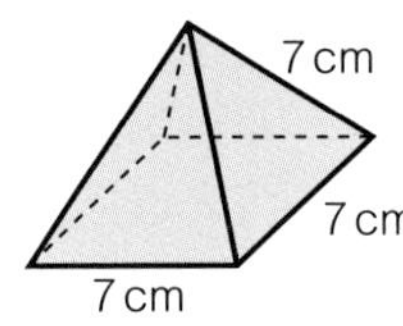

2 Draw a 9 cm line. Construct the perpendicular bisector.

Worked example

Construct a triangle with sides of 8 cm, 6 cm and 9 cm.

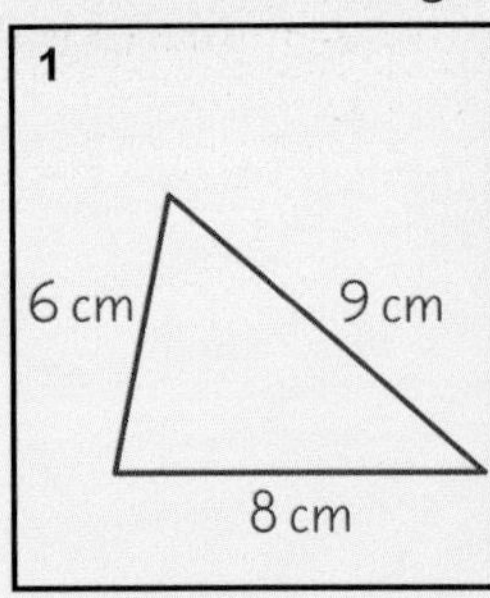

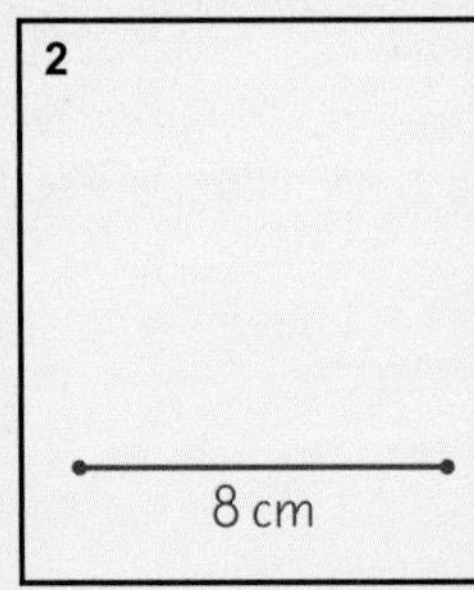

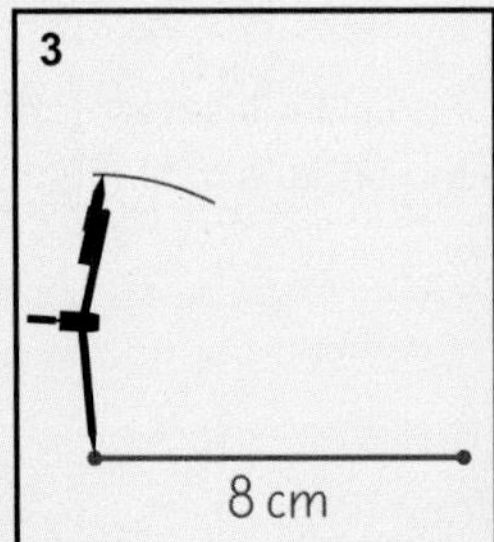

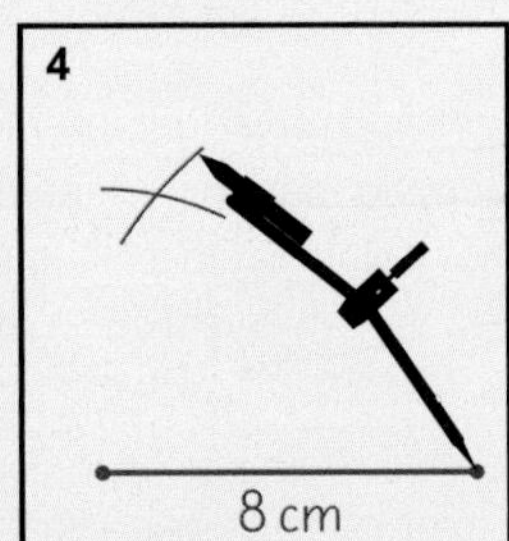

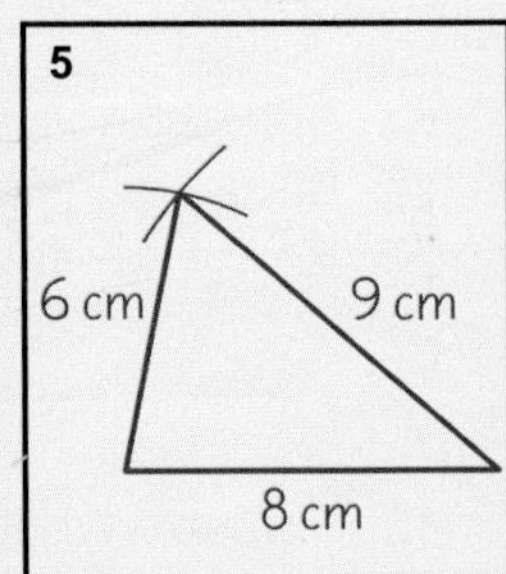

1 Sketch the triangle first.
2 Draw an 8 cm line.
3 Open your compasses to 6 cm. Place the point at one end of the 8 cm line. Draw an arc.
4 Open the compasses to 9 cm. Draw an arc from the other end of the 8 cm line.
5 Join the intersection of the arcs to each end of the 8 cm line.

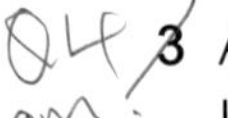

3 A triangle has sides of 5 cm, 6 cm and 7 cm.
Use a ruler and compasses to construct this triangle accurately.

Q3 hint
Always start with a sketch.

4 A triangle has sides of 7 cm, 8.5 cm and 10 cm.
Construct an accurate drawing of the triangle.

Discussion Has everyone drawn the same triangle?
Does it matter which side you draw first?

5 Real A carpenter is drawing plans for a roof truss. The roof truss is an isosceles triangle made from two 10 m lengths and a 15 m length.

a Construct a scale drawing. Use a scale of 1 cm : 1 m.

b Bisect the angle enclosed between the equal sides.

i What angle does the bisector make with the opposite side?

ii Explain why.

6 Follow these instructions to construct this right-angled triangle.

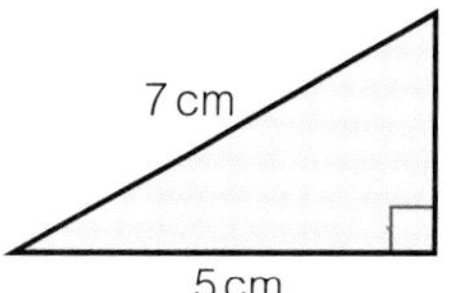

a

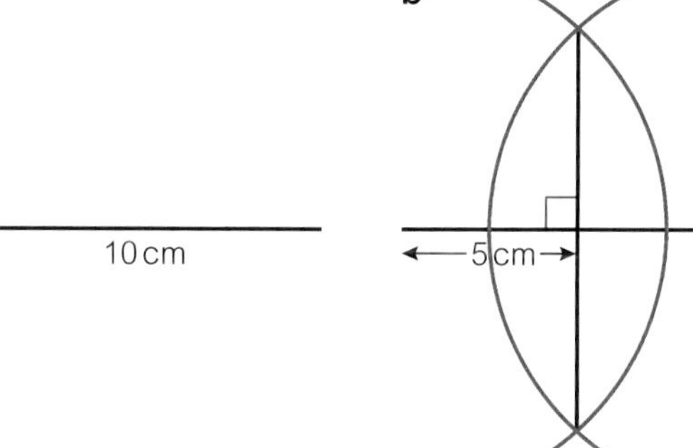

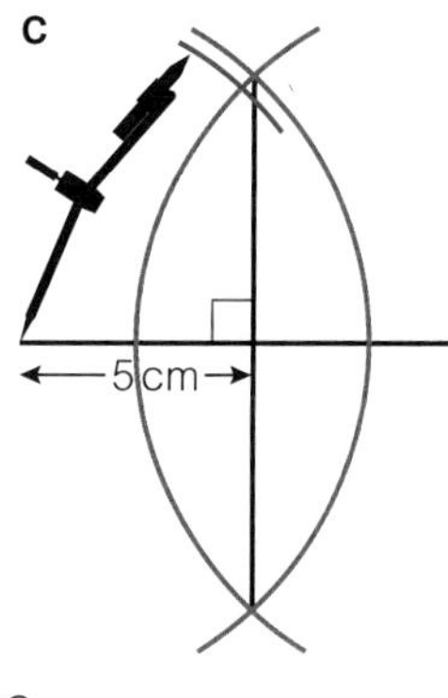

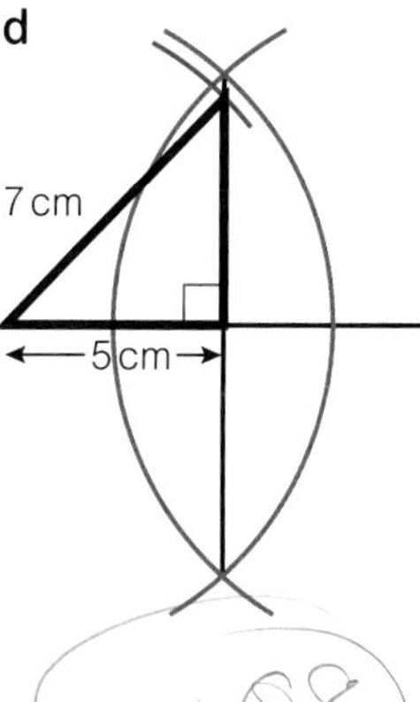

a Draw a straight line twice the length of the base.

b Construct the perpendicular bisector.

c Open your compasses to 7 cm (for the sloping side).
Put the point of your compasses at the end of your base line.
Draw an arc to cut the vertical line.

d Join the points.

7 a Construct this triangle accurately.

b How long is the other side in the triangle?

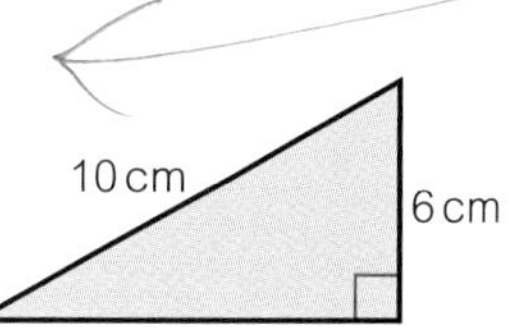

Q7b hint

Turn the triangle around so the 6 cm side is the base.

8 Real The picture below shows sound proofing material.

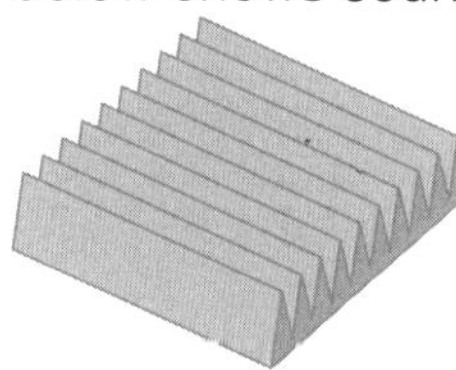

Two pieces are cut by machine from a cuboid of foam like this.

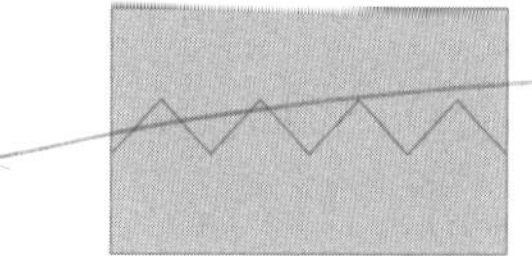

a Construct an accurate diagram of one triangle in the soundproofing.

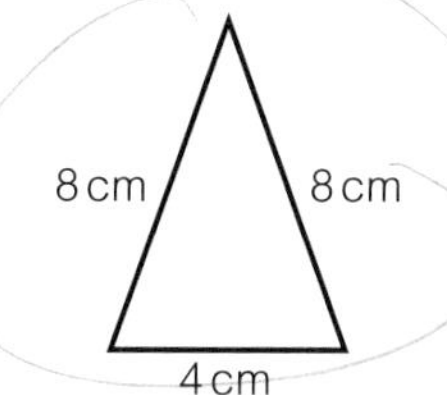

b Measure the angle at the top of the triangle.

9 Draw an accurate net for the square-based pyramid in Q1.

10 The ends of a triangular prism are equilateral triangles of side length 6 cm. The prism is 10 cm long.
Construct an accurate net for this prism.

11 A wedge of cheese is sold in a box like this.

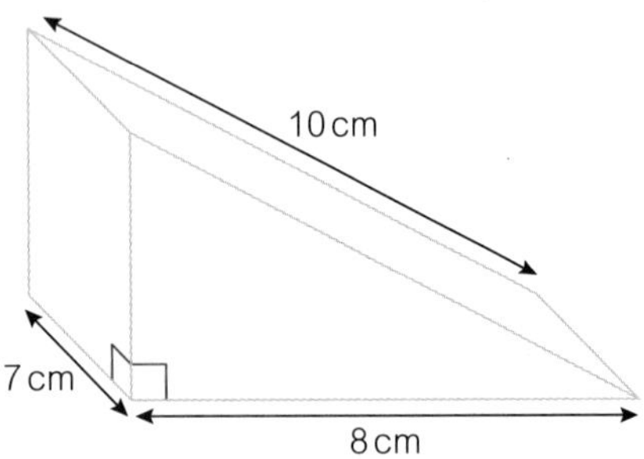

a What is the mathematical name for this 3D shape?
b Draw an accurate net for the box.
c How tall is the box?

Q9 hint
Use a protractor for the right angles.

Q10 hint
Sketch the prism and the net first.

Investigation

Reasoning

The Wheel of Theodorus is a spiral formed by constructing triangles.
The first triangle has a right angle and is isosceles.
The first two triangles have been drawn for you.

1 Start with a right-angled isosceles triangle.
Construct a second triangle on the sloping side of the first one.

2 Repeat several times, and a spiral shape will appear.

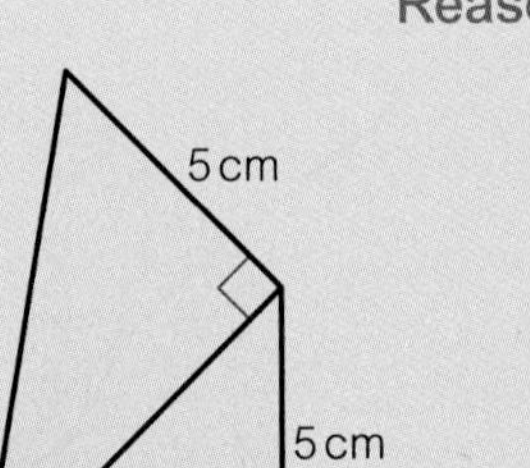

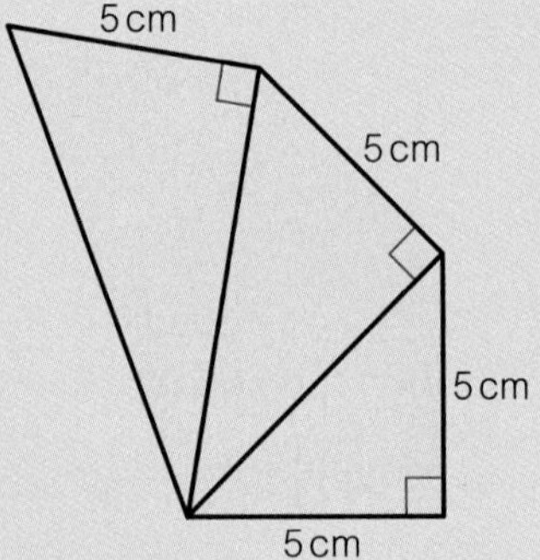

3 Measure the angle formed at the centre of the spiral by each triangle.
What do you notice about the sizes of the angles?

4 Repeat for different starting measurements. Do you get the same results?

Explore

12 **Explore** How could you design and make a four-sided dice for a board game?
Look back at the maths you have learned in this lesson.
How can you use it to answer this question?

Reflect

13 **Reflect** In this lesson you drew constructions and accurate diagrams.
What were you good at?
What were you not so good at?
Write yourself a hint to help you with the constructions or diagrams you are not so good at.
Ask your classmates for ideas for your hint.

5.4 Loci

You will learn to:
- Draw loci for the paths of points.

Why learn this?
Mobile phone companies need to know the area a signal reaches to plan the positions of their transmitters.

Fluency
- The scale of a drawing is 2 cm to 1 m. What distance is represented by 5 cm on the drawing?
- How long on the drawing would a real-life distance of 30 cm be?

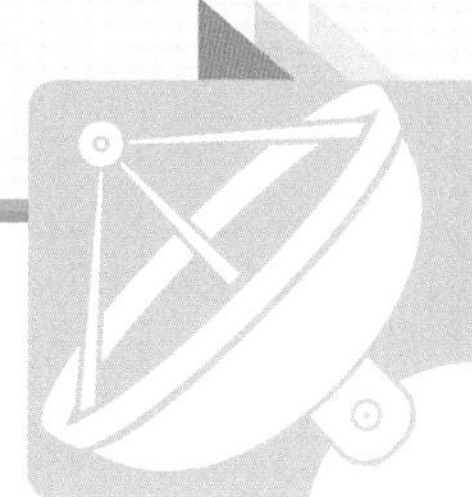

Explore
How can you tie up two guard dogs in a garden so that they can exercise but not fight?

Exercise 5.4

1 Draw a circle with radius 5 cm.
Measure the distance from the centre of the circle to the outside in any direction.
What do you notice?

2 Draw a line of 8.6 cm.
Construct the perpendicular bisector.

3 Draw an angle of 40°.
Construct the angle bisector.

4 A 10 m rope is attached to a metal spike stuck into the ground.
At the other end of the rope is a paintbrush.
The rope is pulled tight and the end moved clockwise.
a Sketch the shape the paintbrush draws on the ground.
b Draw a scale diagram of this.
Use a scale of 1 cm to 1 m.

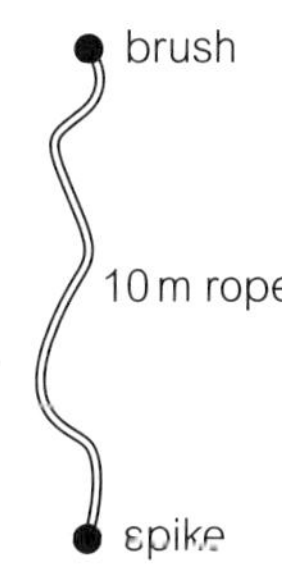

Key point
A **locus** is a set of all points that obey a rule. Often this gives a path. The plural of locus is **loci**.

5 Real On a netball court the goal circle is 8 feet from the goal post.

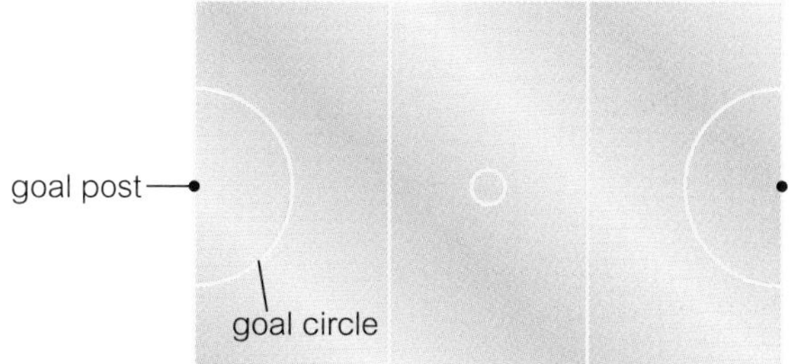

Write instructions so the groundskeeper can mark the goal circles.

6 Mark two points 10 cm apart. Label them A and B.

a Mark a point that is

i 5 cm from point A and from point B

ii 6 cm from point A and from point B

iii 7 cm from point A and from point B.

b Join the points you have drawn with a line. What is this line called?

Discussion How could you draw a line showing all the points equidistant from A and B?

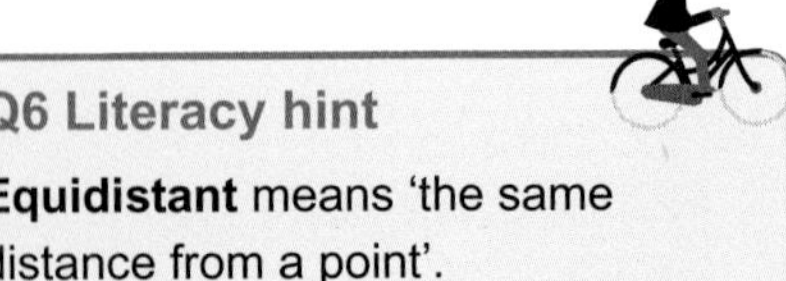

Q6 Literacy hint

Equidistant means 'the same distance from a point'.

7 STEM Two identical magnets are fixed 10 cm apart, with the North poles facing each other.

a Draw a diagram to show this.

b A metal ball moves so it is always equidistant from both magnets. Construct its path.

8 A new TV transmitter is to be built equidistant from two towns that are 5 km apart.
The transmitter has a range of 4 km.
Draw a scale diagram showing all the possible locations of the new transmitter so that both towns are able to receive the transmitted signal. Use a scale of 1 cm : 1 km.

Q8 Strategy hint

First draw dots for the two towns 5 km apart (use the scale).

9 Draw an angle of 80°. Construct the angle bisector.
Measure a distance of 5 cm from the vertex along each arm of the angle and mark a new point.

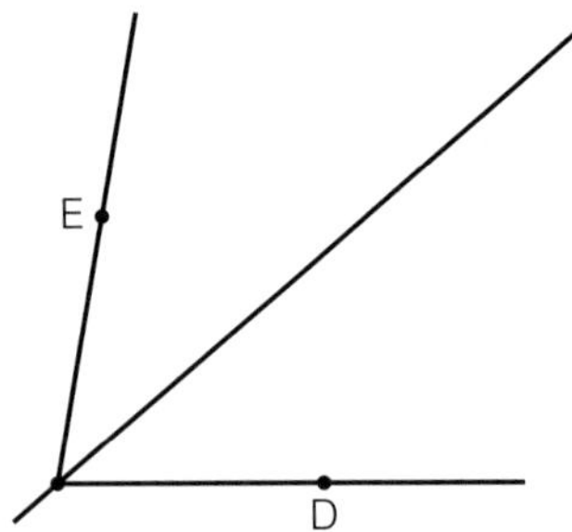

a Measure the shortest distance from each new point to the angle bisector.

b Repeat with two new points 7 cm from the vertex.

Discussion What do you notice? What could you say about any point on the bisector?

10 Two lines meet at an angle of 100°.
Draw the locus of points equidistant from both lines.

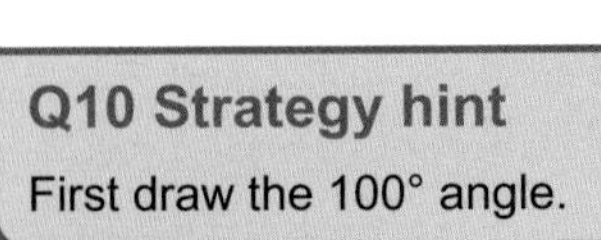

Q10 Strategy hint

First draw the 100° angle.

11 Real Two houses share a garden as shown.
The owners agree to divide the garden between them with a fence equidistant from the two existing fences.

a Draw an accurate diagram showing where the fence will be. Use a scale of 2 cm : 1 m

b How long will the fence be?

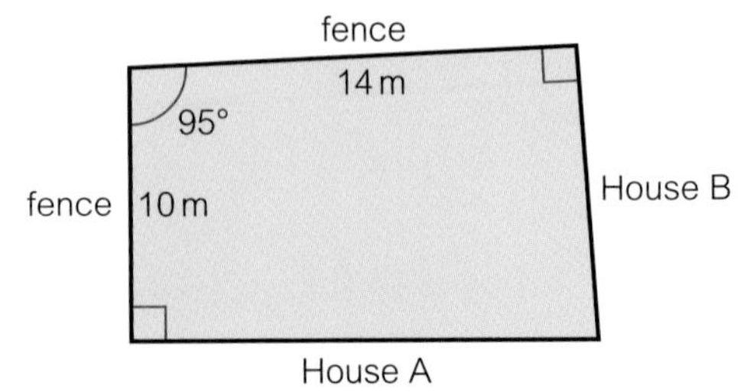

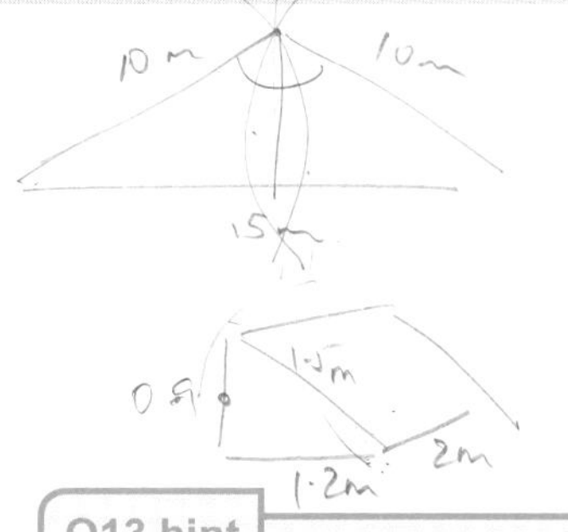

12 Draw a 7 cm line on cm squared paper.
A point moves so it is always exactly 3 cm away from the line.
a Draw points 3 cm from the line.
b Use compasses to draw points 3 cm from the ends.
Discussion What shape is the locus of a point that moves at a fixed distance from a line?

13 Draw a 5 cm by 7 cm rectangle on cm squared paper.
Draw the locus of a point that is 4 cm away from this rectangle.

Q13 hint
Use compasses for the locus at the vertices.

14 Problem-solving Two mobile phone masts are 9 km apart.
Each mast transmits 4 km in any direction.
a Draw a scale diagram to show clearly the range of each mast.
Use a scale of 1 cm : 1 km.
b Is there anywhere between the masts where there is no phone signal?
The mobile phone company want to increase the range of their transmitters.
c What would each transmitter's new range need to be to ensure that everybody living between them will get a phone signal?

Q14a hint
What shape do the points that are 4 km away in any direction make?

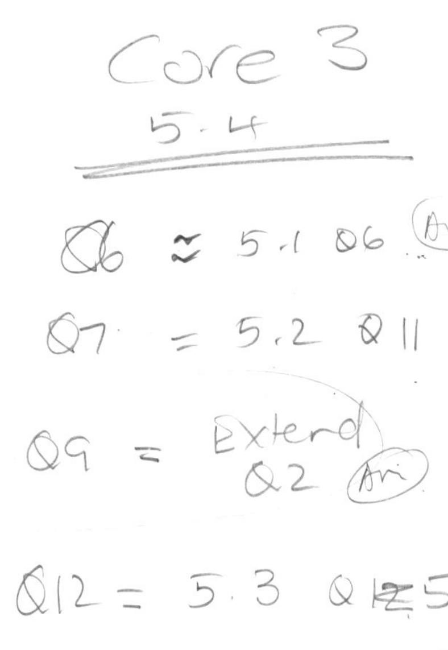

15 A radio transmitter on a space station transmits in all directions.
The signal strength is strong up to a distance of 100 km from the transmitter.
What shape is the region with a strong signal?

16 Explore How can you tie up two guard dogs in a garden so that they can exercise but not fight?
Look back at the maths you have learned in this lesson.
How can you use it to answer this question?

17 Reflect Abbie looks back at this lesson. She says, 'This lesson is about loci, but I have also used lots of other mathematics knowledge and skills.' She begins to make two lists.

Knowledge (what is)	Skills (how to)
radius	draw a circle
measure (e.g. cm, m)	construct a perpendicular bisector
perpendicular	construct an angle bisector

Look back at all the questions in this lesson and make lists of all the knowledge and skills you have used. You might begin in the same way as Abbie.
Read your lists. Put a star beside any of the knowledge or skills that you do not feel confident about.

Explore

Reflect

5 Check up

Log how you did on your Student Progression Chart.

Using scales

1 Huw has a plan of his bedroom, drawn accurately to a scale of 1 cm to 50 cm.

a How wide is Huw's bedroom, from the door to the opposite wall?

b How wide is the door?

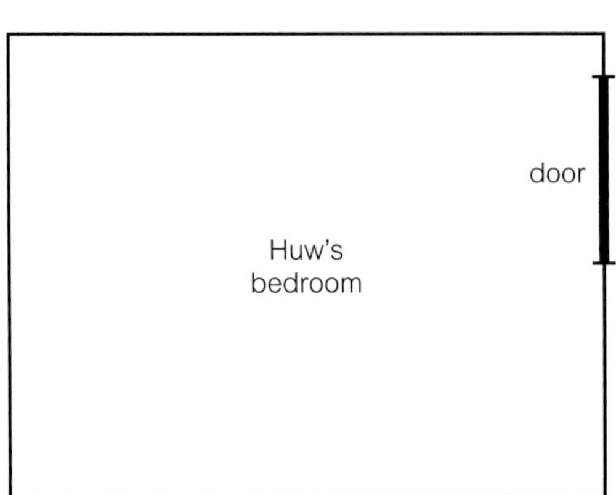

2 The diagram shows a plan of Mary's garden. Make an accurate scale drawing of the garden on cm squared paper. Use a scale of 2 cm to 1 m.

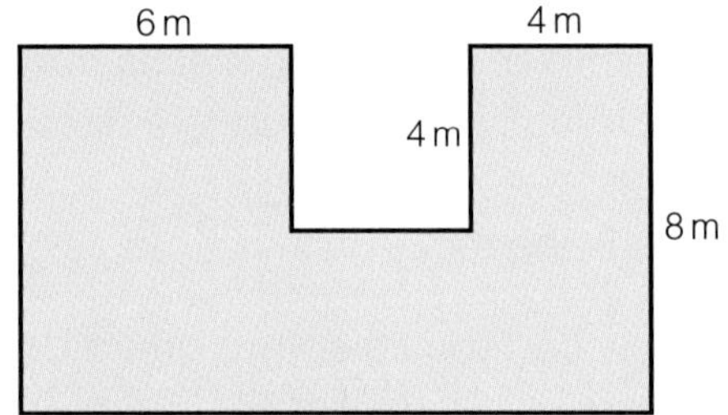

3 The map below has a scale of 1 : 25 000.

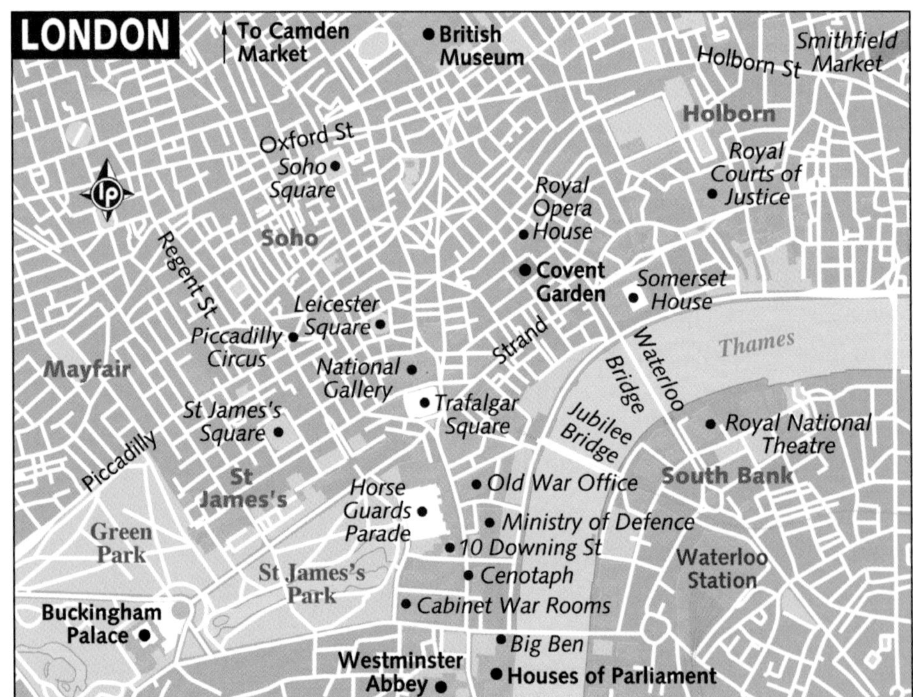

Use the map to find the distances, in metres

a from Covent Garden to Westminster Abbey

b from Buckingham Palace to the National Gallery

c from Trafalgar Square to Big Ben.

Basic constructions

4 Draw a line 11 cm long. Use a ruler and compasses to construct the perpendicular bisector.

5 Draw an angle of 80°.
Construct the bisector of this angle.

6 The diagram shows a line segment with a point marked above it.
Trace this diagram. Construct a perpendicular line from the point to the line segment.

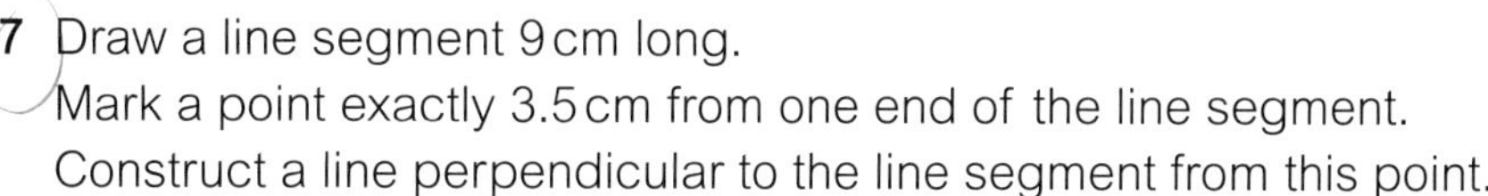

7 Draw a line segment 9 cm long.
Mark a point exactly 3.5 cm from one end of the line segment.
Construct a line perpendicular to the line segment from this point.

Constructing triangles

8 A triangle has sides of length 6.5 cm, 8 cm and 9 cm.
Construct this triangle.

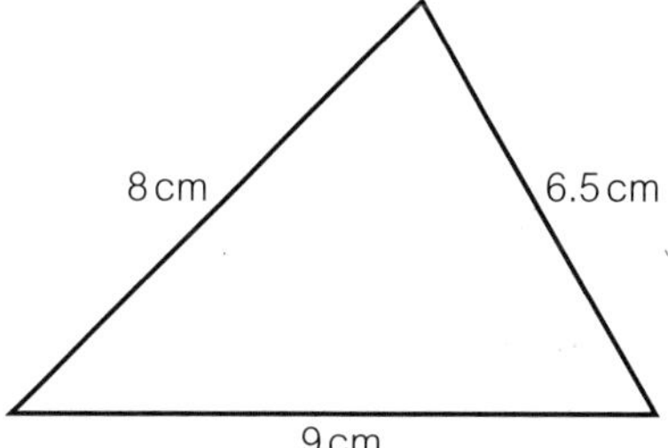

9 **a** Construct this right-angled triangle.
b What is the length of the other side of the triangle?

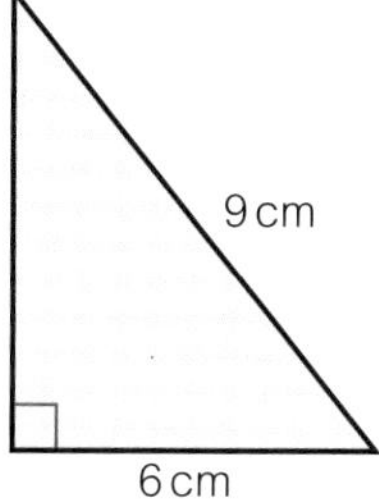

Loci

10 Draw the locus of a point that is 4 cm away from a fixed point.

11 Draw two points that are exactly 7 cm apart.
Construct the locus of the points that are equidistant from these two points.

12 Two lines meet at an angle of 120°.
Draw the locus of the points that are equidistant from the two lines.

Reflect

13 **How sure are you of your answers? Were you mostly**
Just guessing **Feeling doubtful** **Confident**
What next? Use your results to decide whether to strengthen or extend your learning.

Challenge

14 A manufacturer sells a chocolate bar in a box that is an equilateral triangular prism.
Each edge of the triangle is 5 cm long, and the box is 12 cm long overall.
Draw an accurate net for the box.

5 Strengthen

You will:

- Strengthen your understanding with practice.

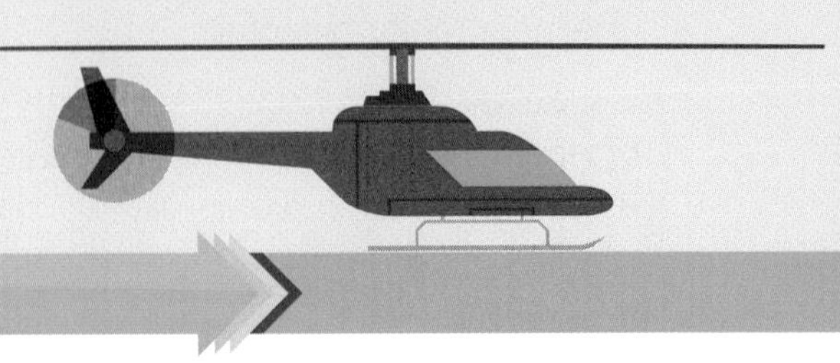

Using scales

1 David has designed this logo for a magazine.
Make an accurate drawing of the logo.
Use a scale of 1 cm to 2 cm.

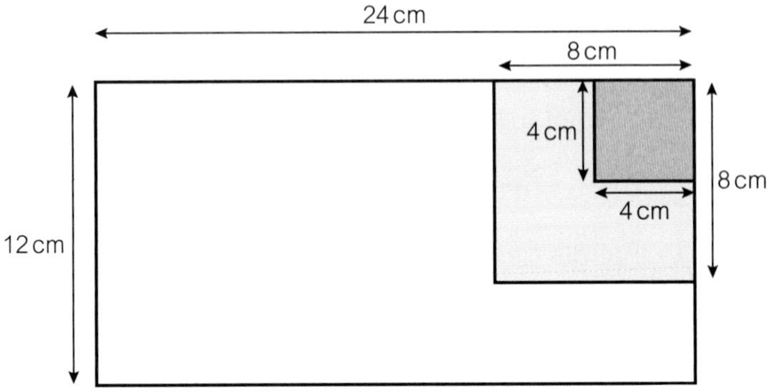

24 cm
8 cm
4 cm
4 cm
8 cm
12 cm

Q1 hint

Use a double number line.

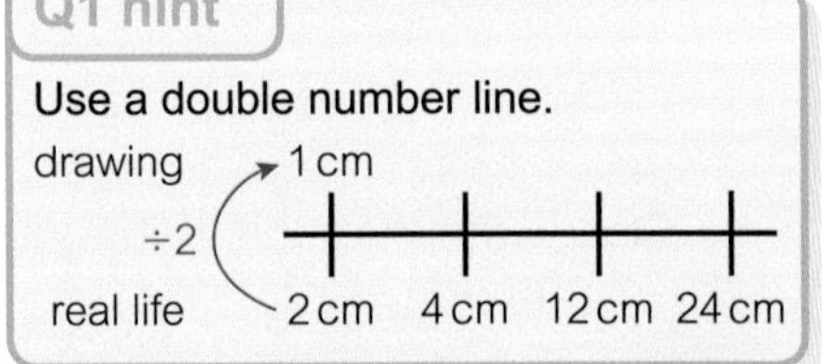

2 Marina is designing a new board game.
She makes a sketch.

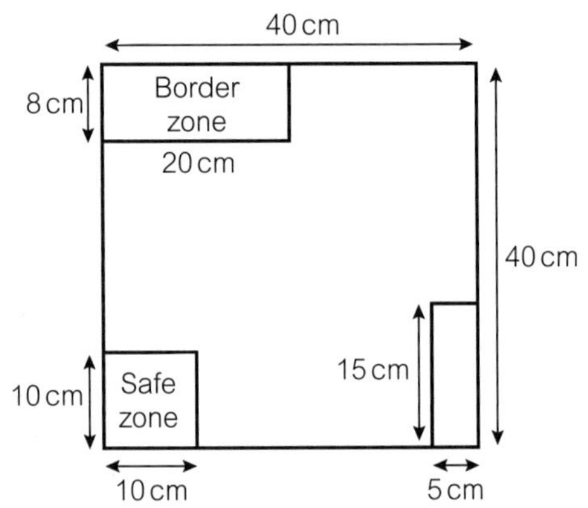

Make an accurate drawing of her board on cm squared paper.
Use a scale of 1 cm to 4 cm.

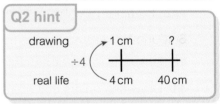

Q2 Strategy hint

Draw the large square first.

Q2 hint

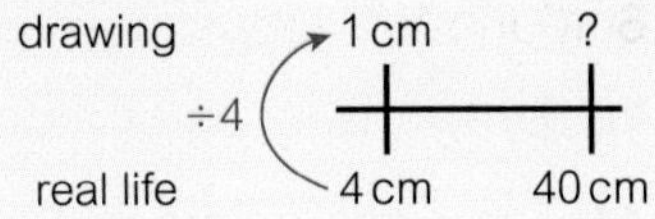

drawing 1 cm ?
÷4
real life 4 cm 40 cm

3 Chan has drawn a scale plan of his new garden.
The scale is 1 cm to 2 m.

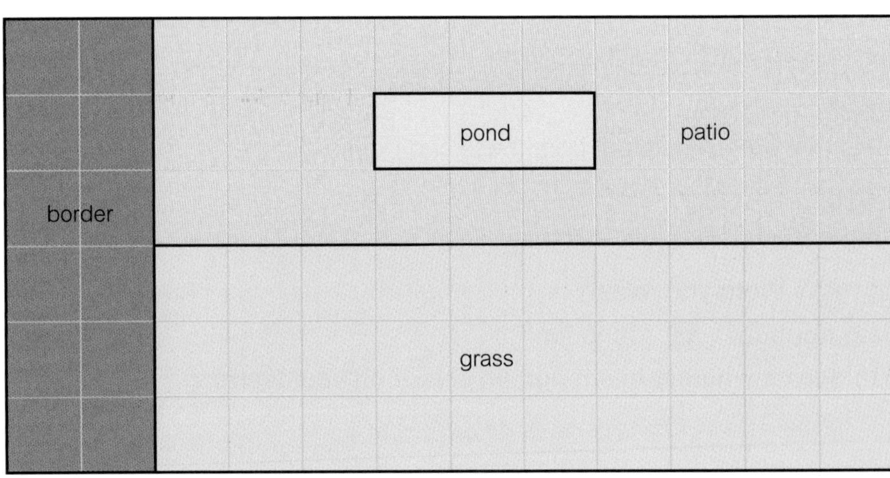

a Work out the length and width of the border.

b Work out the length and width of the pond.

c Work out the length and width of the grass.

d What is the shortest distance between the pond and the border?

Q3 hint

Make a double number line like this to help.

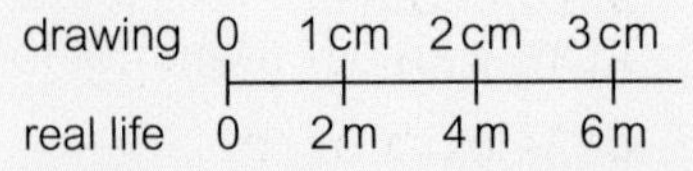

4 Mikel's garden is shown in this plan.
The scale is 1 cm to 3 m.
   a How long is the fence?
   b The decking is a square shape.
   How long is the side of the square?
   c How wide and how long is the vegetable patch?
   d How wide is the grass at its narrowest point?

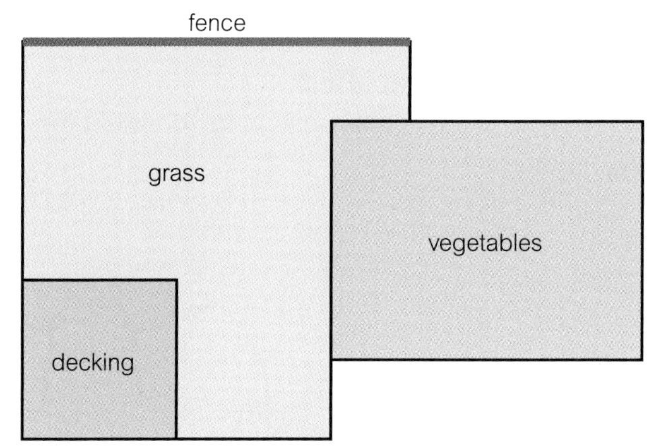

5 On this map of Washington, DC, 1 cm represents 500 m.
Use the scale to find these distances in metres.

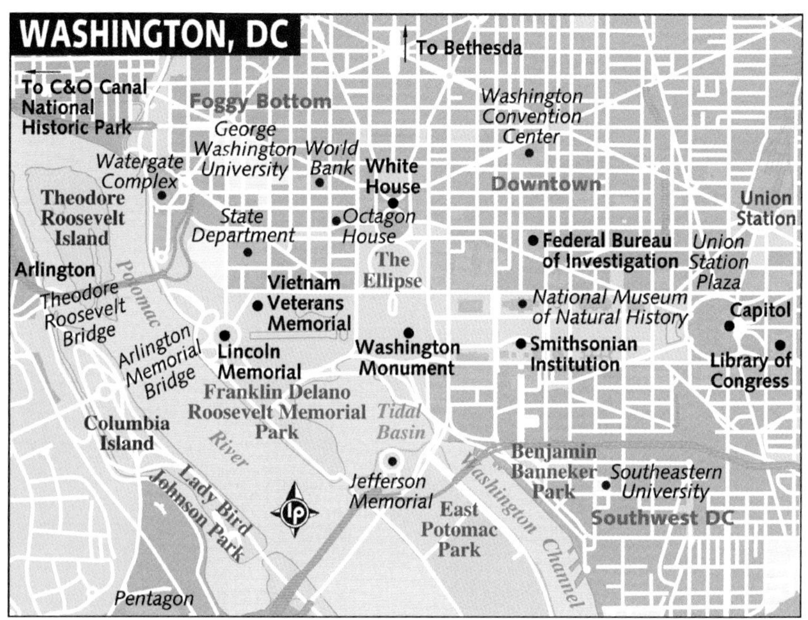

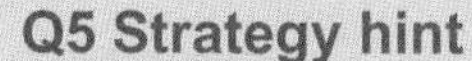

Q5 Strategy hint
Measure the distance on the map. Use the scale to work out the real-life distance.

Q5 hint
Use a double number line to help you.

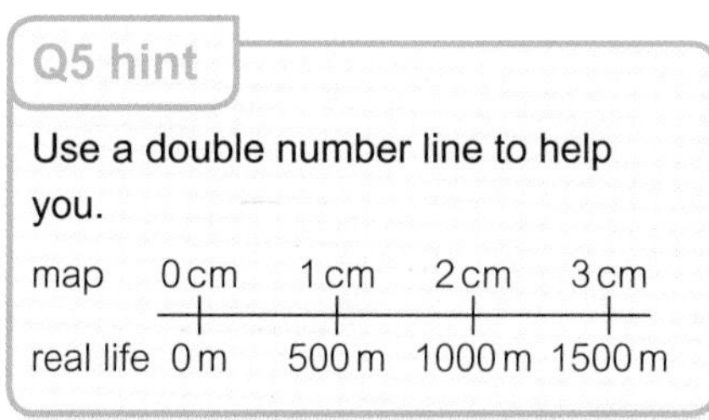

   a from the White House to the Octagon House
   b from the Washington Monument to the National Museum of Natural History
   c from the Lincoln Memorial to the World Bank

6 Maria has sketched a layout for the stages at a festival.

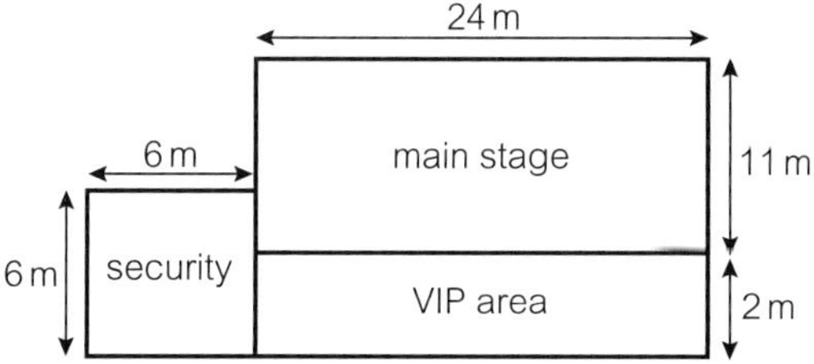

Make an accurate scale drawing of her design on cm squared paper.
Use a scale of 1 cm to 2 m.

Q6 hint
Draw a double number line if you need to.

7 A map has a scale of 1 : 100 000.
A distance is 5 cm on the map. How far is it in real life?

Q7 hint

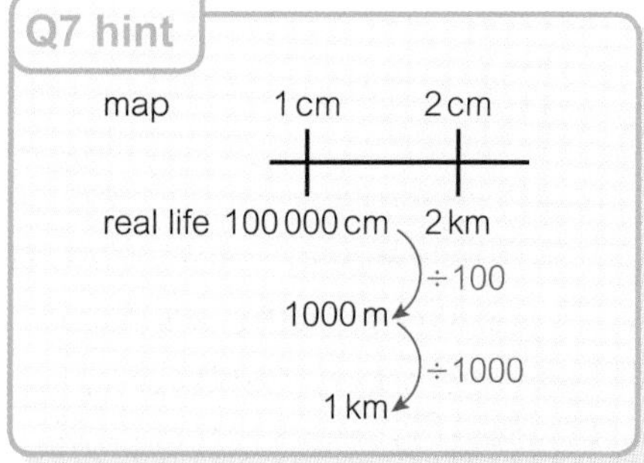

8 A map of the UK has scale 1 : 50 000.
Work out the real-life distance for
   a 8 cm on the map
   b 12.5 cm on the map
   c 14.8 cm on the map.

Basic constructions

1 Draw a line of 16 cm.
Follow these instructions to construct the perpendicular bisector of this line.

a Draw the line. Open your compasses to more than 8 cm.

16 cm

b Draw the first arc.

c Draw the second arc.

d Draw the perpendicular bisector.

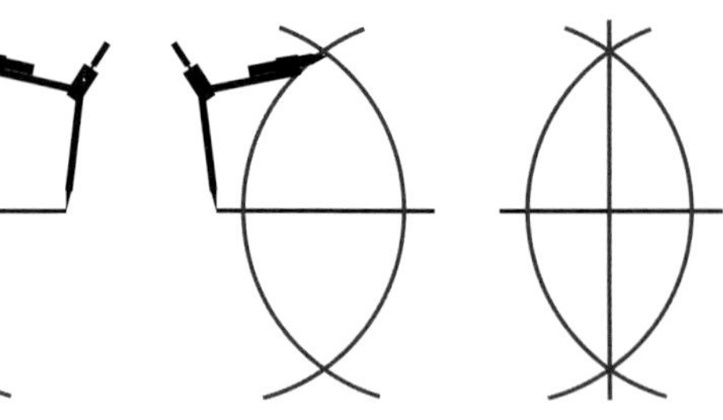

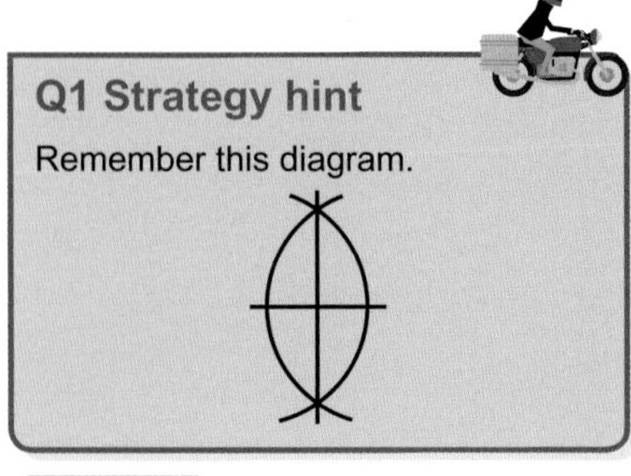

Q1 Strategy hint

Remember this diagram.

Q1 hint

Check by measuring that the angle is 90° and the line is cut in half.

2 Draw a line of 17.5 cm. Construct the perpendicular bisector.

3 Draw an angle of 40°.
Follow these instructions to construct the bisector of this angle.

a Draw the angle.

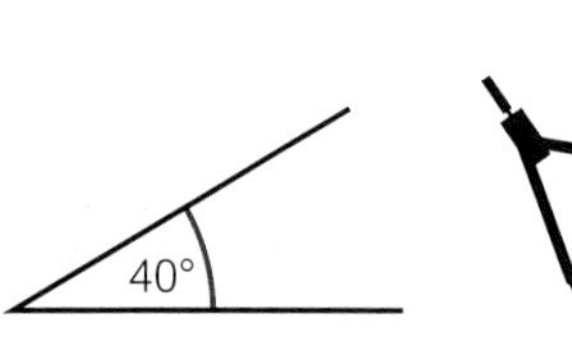

b Draw an arc.

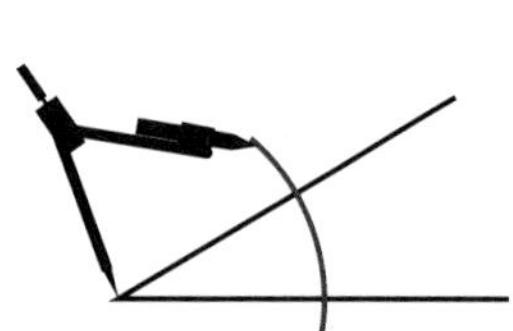

c Draw the first arc between the two sides of the angle.

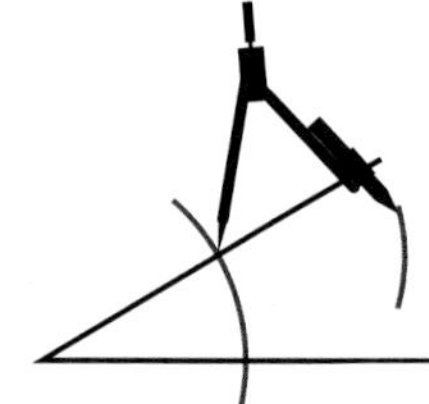

d Draw the second arc.

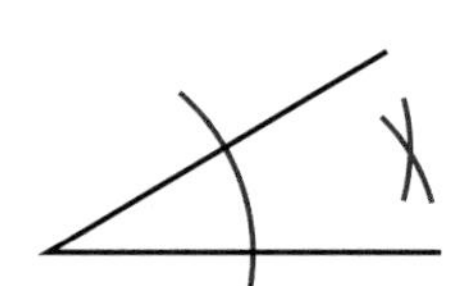

e Draw the angle bisector.

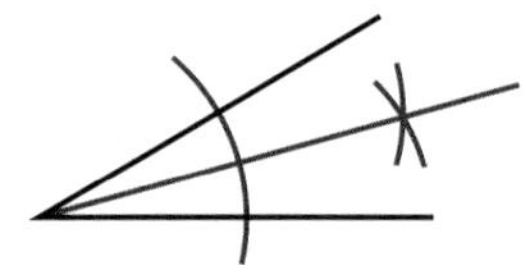

4 Draw an angle of 100°. Construct the bisector of this angle.

Q3 Strategy hint

Sketch what you think it will look like first.

5 Draw a line. Draw point A above the line.

Follow these instructions to construct a perpendicular line from the point A to the line.

a Draw an arc from point A.

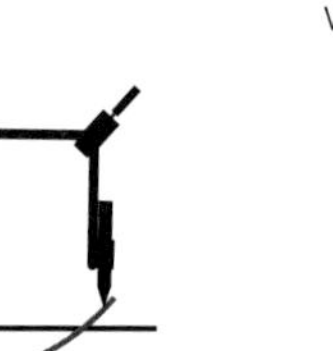

b Keep compasses the same distance apart. Draw an arc from each of the two points where the arc crosses the line.

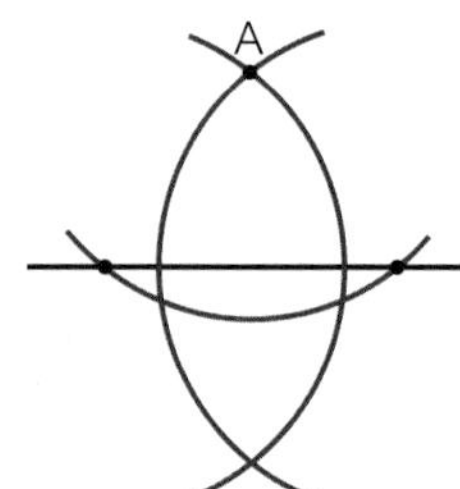

c Join the points where the arcs intersect.

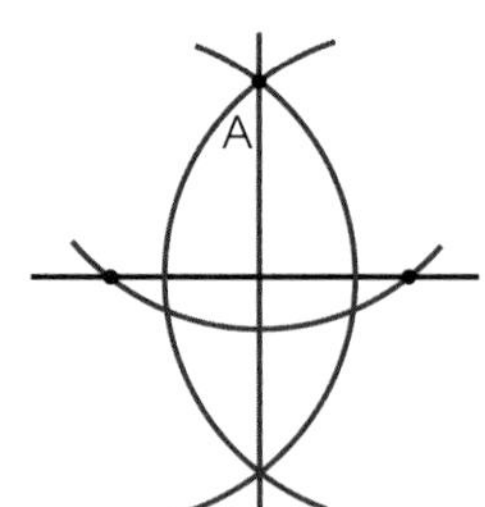

6 The diagram shows a sketch of a garden with a washing line pole. Construct an accurate plan showing the washing line meeting the house at right angles.

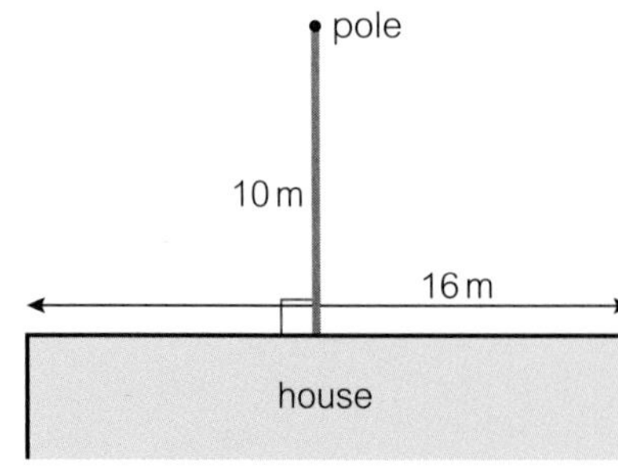

Q6 hint

Use the perpendicular construction you used in Q5.
Start by drawing an arc from the pole.

7 Point P is close to the end of a line.
Follow the instructions to construct a perpendicular to the line at point P.

P

a Mark point A to the right of point P. Point A should be near to, but not on the line. Put your compasses on point A and draw a circle through point P.

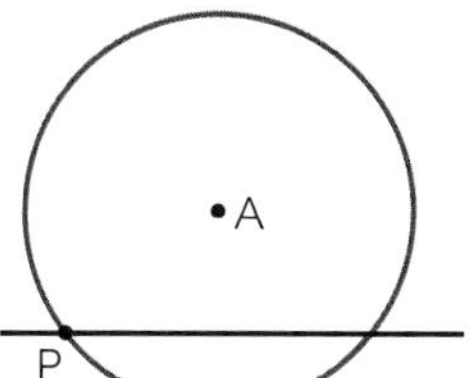

b Mark point B where your circle crosses the line again.

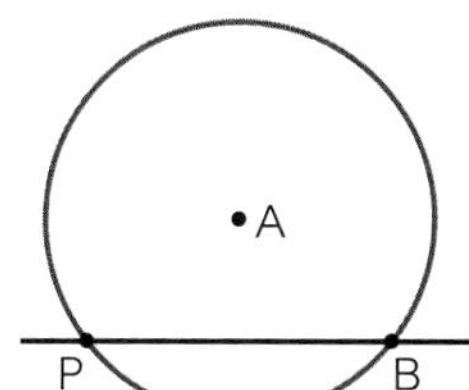

c Draw a line across the circle through point A and point B.

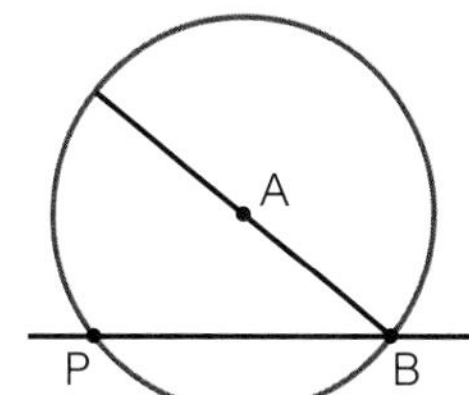

d Join point P to the circle.

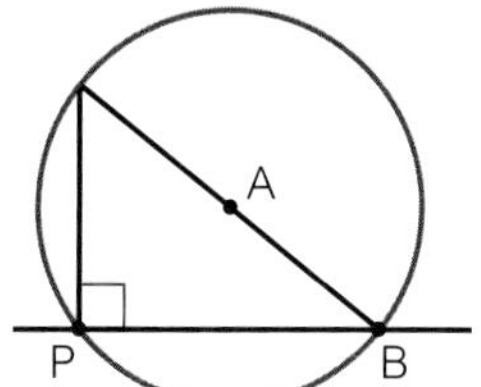

Constructing triangles

1 Follow these instructions to construct accurately a triangle with sides 6 cm, 7 cm and 8 cm.

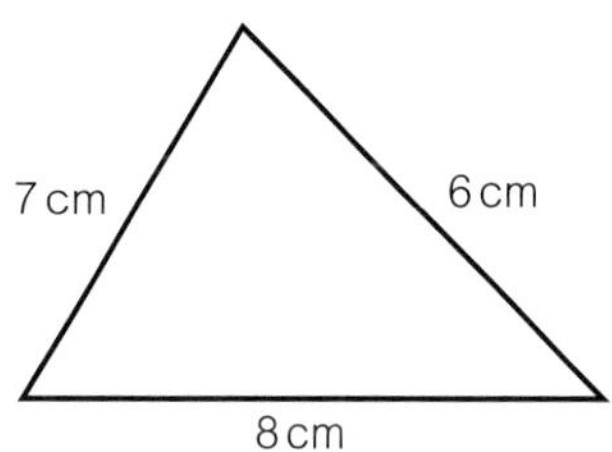

a Use a ruler to draw accurately the first side. The 7 cm side starts at the left-hand end of this line.

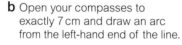

8 cm

b Open your compasses to exactly 7 cm and draw an arc from the left-hand end of the line.

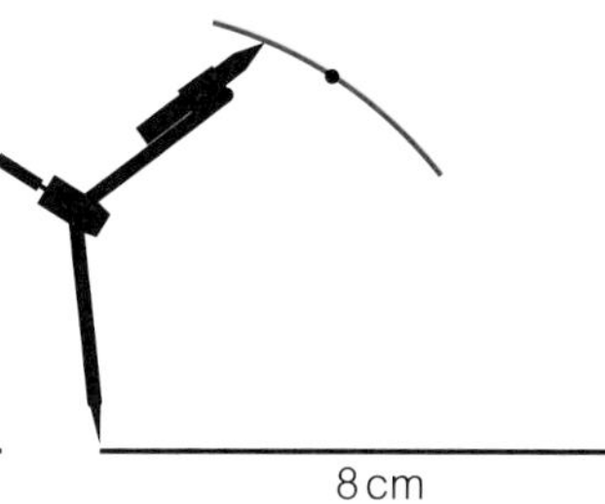

c Open your compasses to exactly 6 cm and draw an arc from the other end.

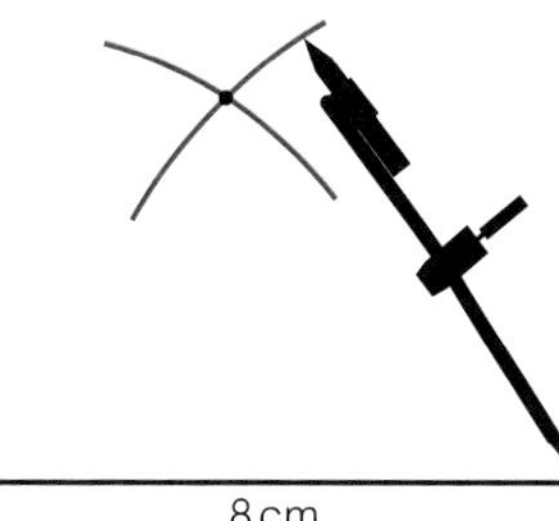

d Use the point where the arcs cross to create the finished triangle.

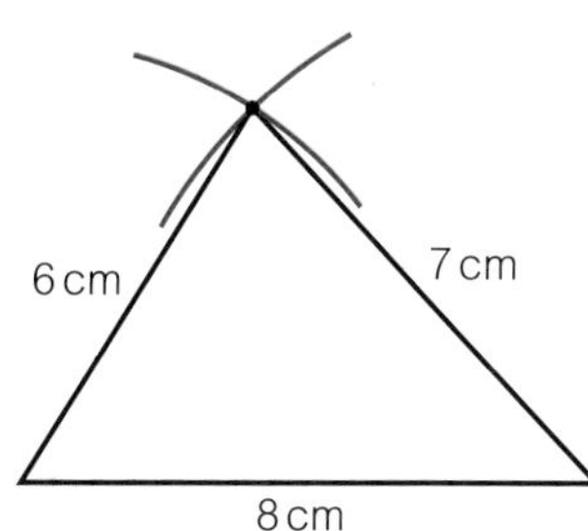

2 Construct accurately a triangle with sides 5 cm, 8 cm and 9 cm.

3 Draw a scale diagram of this triangle.
Use the scale 1 cm to 1 m.

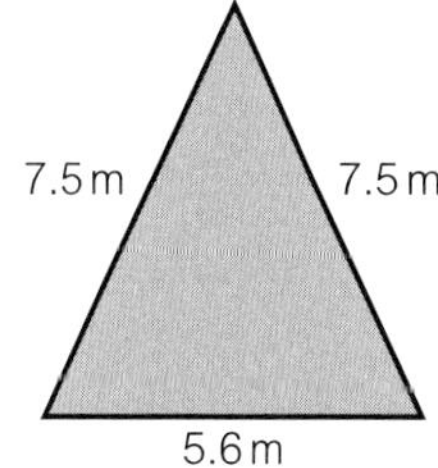

4 Draw an accurate net of this triangular prism.

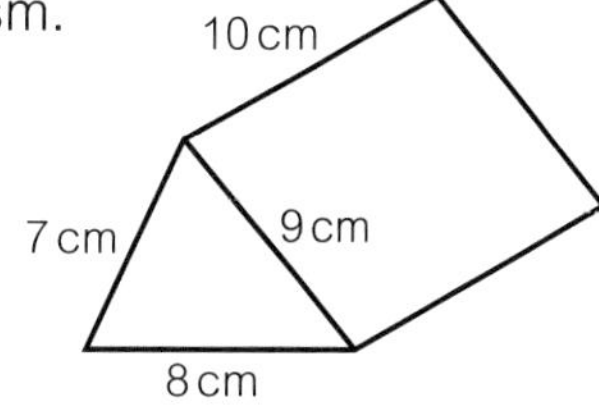

Q4 Strategy hint

1 Sketch the net.
2 Write the measurements on it.
3 Make an accurate drawing of the rectangles using a ruler and protractor.
4 Construct the triangles using compasses.

5 Follow these instructions to construct this right-angled triangle.

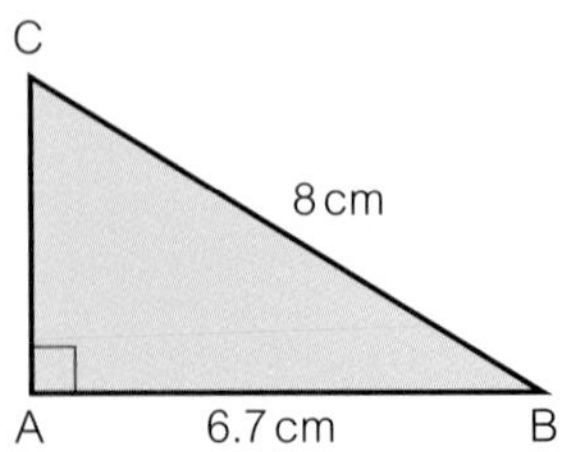

a Use a ruler to draw the short side length (AB).

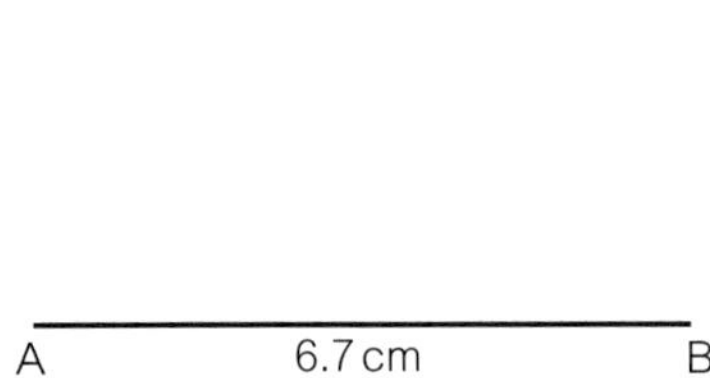

b Construct a perpendicular line at A.

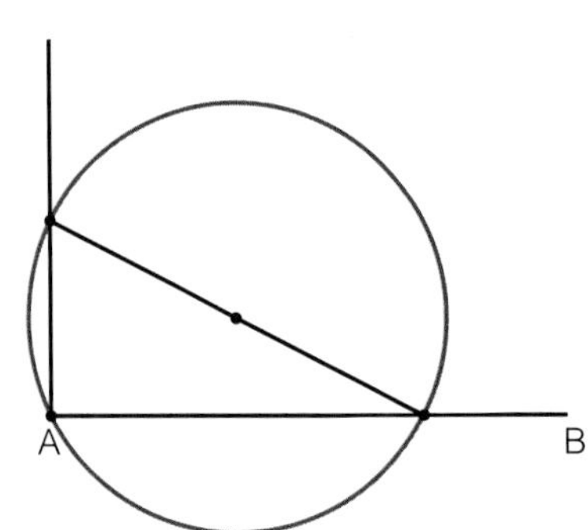

c Open your compasses to 8 cm. Draw an arc from point B.
Join the intersection of the arc and the perpendicular (C) to point B to form the triangle.

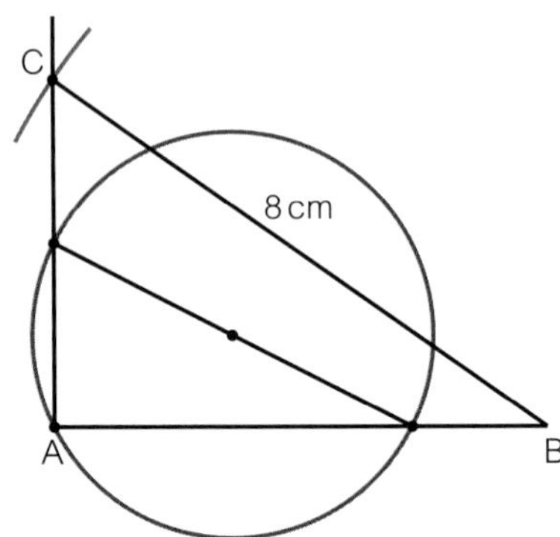

6 Construct this right-angled triangle.

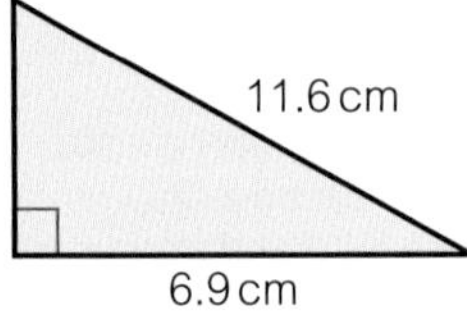

7 A garden storage box is made in the shape of a right-angled triangular prism.
The longest side of the triangle is 1.5 m.
The base of the triangle is 1.2 m.
The length of the box is 2 m.
Draw an accurate net of the storage box. Use a scale of 10 cm to 1 m.

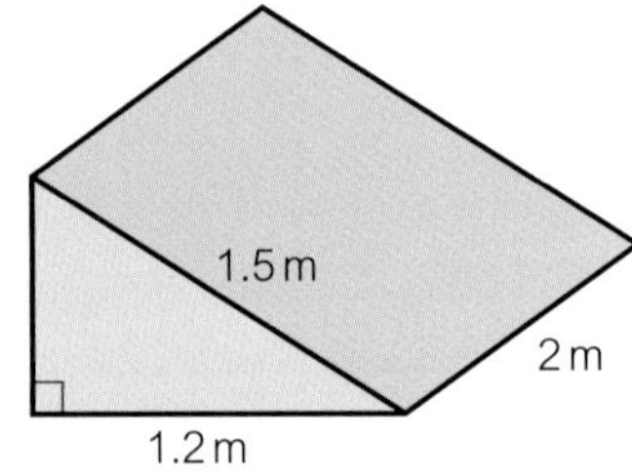

Loci

1 **a** Put a dot somewhere near the middle of a blank sheet of paper.
Draw as many points as you can exactly 3 cm from your dot.

b What shape have you created?

c Write the missing word in this sentence.
Points that are all the same distance from a dot make a _________.

2 **a** Mark an X on a piece of paper.

b Draw an accurate diagram to show all the points 5 cm away from X.

3 **a** Draw the perpendicular bisector of a line AB 9 cm long.

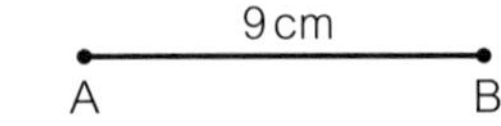

b **i** Choose a point on the perpendicular bisector.

ii Measure its distance from A and from B.

iii Do this again for another point on the perpendicular bisector.
What do you notice?

c Write the missing words in this sentence.
Points that are all the same distance from two dots make the ___________.

4 Hannah and Jerome are standing 3 m apart.
Mica walks between them, the same distance away from each of them.
What path does Mica take?

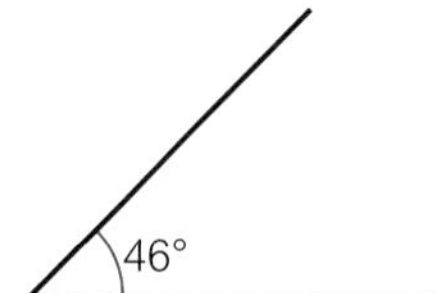

5 a Draw the angle bisector of a 46° angle.
b i Choose a point on the angle bisector.
ii Measure the shortest distance from each of the two lines.
iii Do this again for another point on the angle bisector.
What do you notice?
c Write the missing words in this sentence.
Points that are all the same distance from two lines make the ___________.

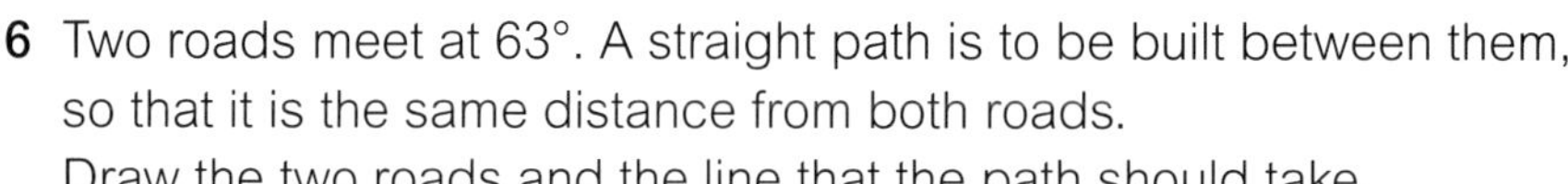

6 Two roads meet at 63°. A straight path is to be built between them, so that it is the same distance from both roads.
Draw the two roads and the line that the path should take.

Q6 hint

Bisecting the angle will keep the path the same distance away from both roads.

Enrichment

1 Problem-solving The diagram shows a crop circle that was found in Wiltshire in May 2011.

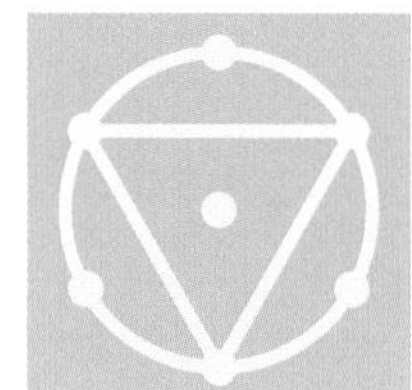

a Using compasses and a ruler, create a plan of the crop circle. Make sure the triangle is equilateral, and the small circles are evenly spaced and all the same size.
b Design your own crop circle design using accurate constructions.

2 Molly the dog has been tied to a railing by a lead.
The diagram shows part of the path that Molly can follow.
Sketch a diagram that shows the area that Molly can move in.

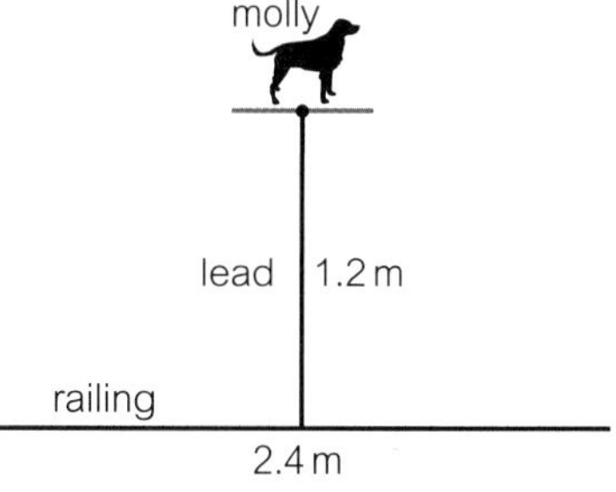

3 **Reflect**
a Look back at the steps in Q1 of Basic constructions.
For each step, answer these questions.
- Do I need compasses?
- If no, what tool(s) do I need?
- If yes, where do I put the point of the compasses? Where do I draw?

b Repeat for the steps in Basic constructions Q3.
c Both of these questions show steps for constructing bisectors.
Compare the steps. What is different and what is the same?
d Do you think you can now construct bisectors without the instructions?
Have a go! Cover the instructions, turn to a new page of your book, and construct
i the perpendicular bisector of an 8 cm line
ii the angle bisector of an 80° angle.

5 Extend

You will:

- Extend your understanding with problem-solving.

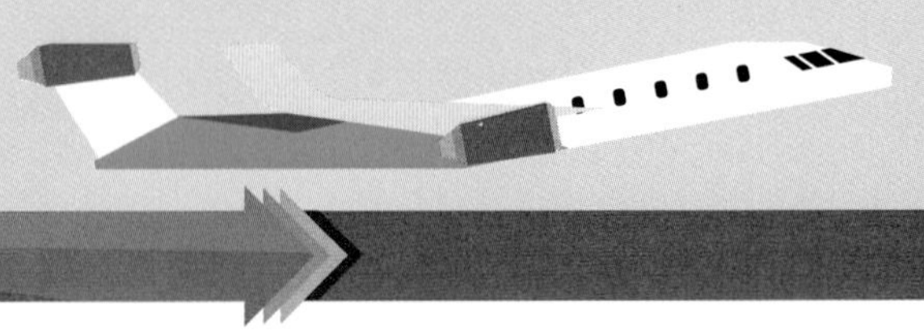

1 The point B is 5 cm away from the line.

• B

Construct a perpendicular line from the point B to the line.

2 The sketched plan shows a new drain that needs to be dug from the manhole to meet the main drain at right angles.

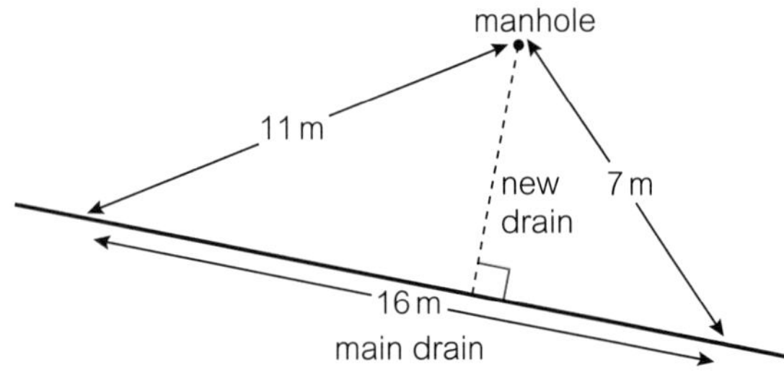

a Construct an accurate plan showing the path of the new drain. Use a scale of 1 cm to 1 m.

b How long will the new drain be?

3 Bill is planning to build a child's swing. he has started by making this sketch. Choose a suitable scale and create an accurate scale drawing of Bill's design.

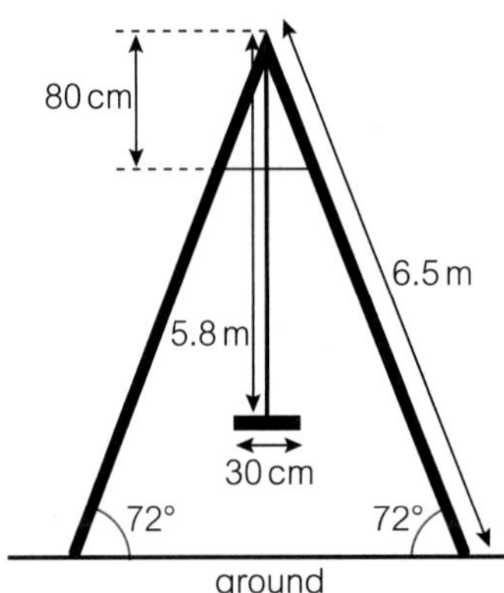

Topic links: Ratio, Geometry

Subject links: Science (Q20)

4 **Real** A tennis court is 24 m long and 11 m wide (for doubles matches).

Choose a suitable scale and draw an accurate diagram showing the net accurately positioned.

The net must be placed exactly at right angles to the court and precisely halfway along its length.

5 A map has a scale of 1 : 25 000.
Seeta says that 4 km is represented by 10 cm.

Is she right? Show your working.

6 How long is a 5 km road on a 1 : 50 000 scale map?

7 **Reasoning** The map shows the route of a 10 km run.

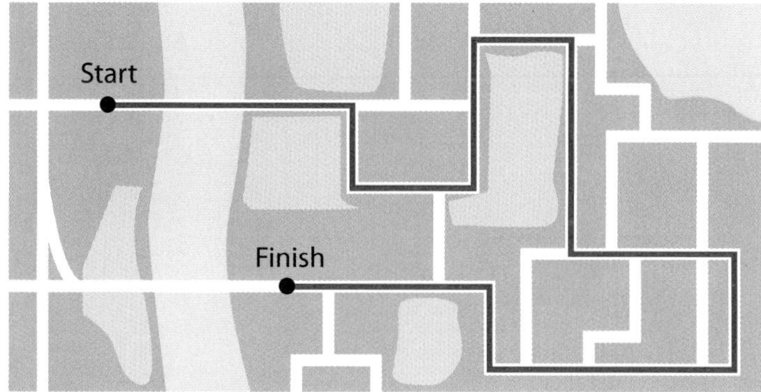

What is the scale of the map?

8 The plan shows Seera's design for a garden.

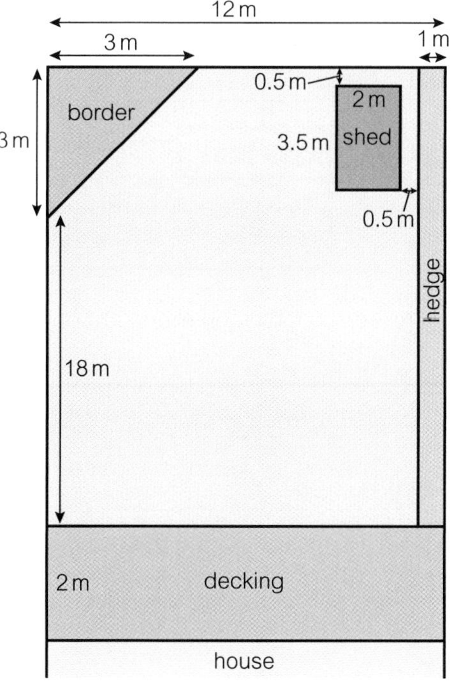

a Construct an accurate scale drawing of her design on cm squared paper.
b How long is the sloping edge of the border?
c What is the area of the border?

The shed will need a concrete pad underneath. It must stick out 20 cm all around the shed.

d What area of concrete will be needed?

9 **Real** The Great Pyramid of Giza is a square-based pyramid with base length 230 m.

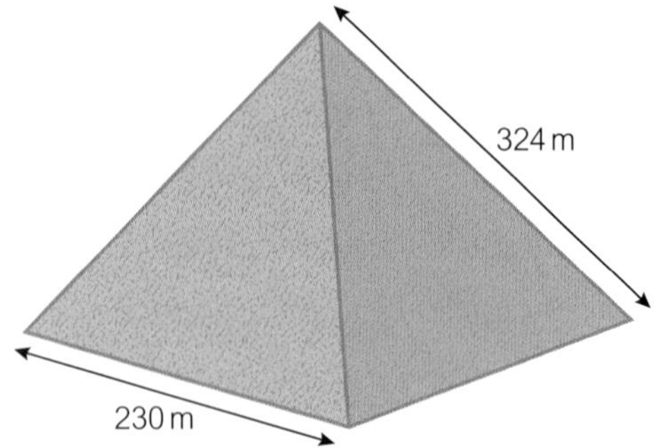

Each triangular face is an isosceles triangle with two sides of 324 m.

a Draw an accurate net of the pyramid. Use a scale of 1 cm to 20 m.

b Measure the angles in each triangular face.

c Add tabs to the edges and glue the net together to make a scale model of the pyramid.

Q9a Strategy hint
Sketch first, then make an accurate drawing.

Q9c Strategy hint
Add tabs like this to join the edges.

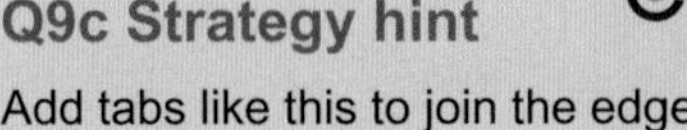

10 A ship leaves a port and sails North for 10 km before turning and sailing East for 15 km.
How far away is the ship from the port?

11 **a** Construct this triangle.

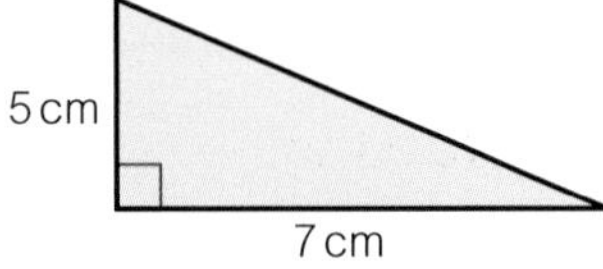

b How long is the unknown side?

Q11 Strategy hint
Construct the right angle first.

12 Construct an angle of precisely 45°.

Q12 hint
Construct a right angle, then bisect it.

13 Construct an angle of exactly 60°.

Q13 hint
An equilateral triangle has angles of 60°.

14 The diagram shows an equilateral triangle with a circle that just fits inside it.
Follow these instructions to construct an accurate copy.

a Construct an equilateral triangle.

b Construct the perpendicular bisector of each side.

c Draw a circle using the point where the bisectors cross as its centre.

15 The diagram shows the loci of two water sprinklers on a cricket pitch.

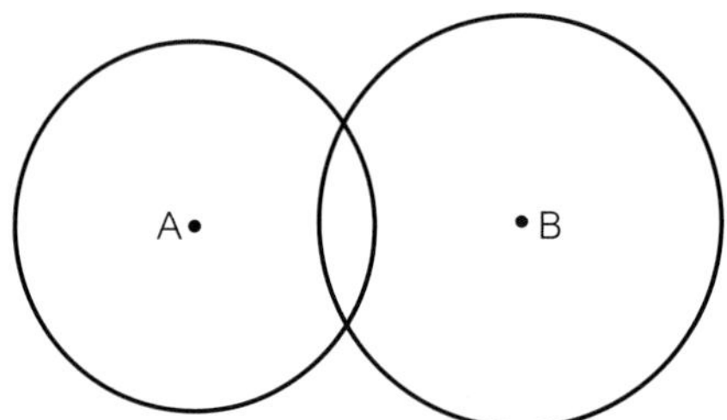

Copy the diagram. Shade in the intersection.
Describe what happens in the shaded area.

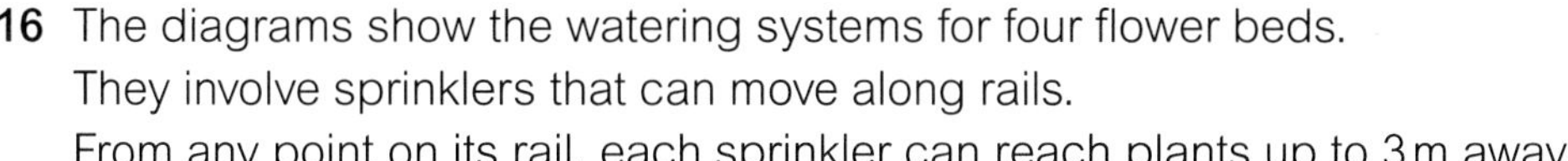

16 The diagrams show the watering systems for four flower beds.
They involve sprinklers that can move along rails.
From any point on its rail, each sprinkler can reach plants up to 3 m away.

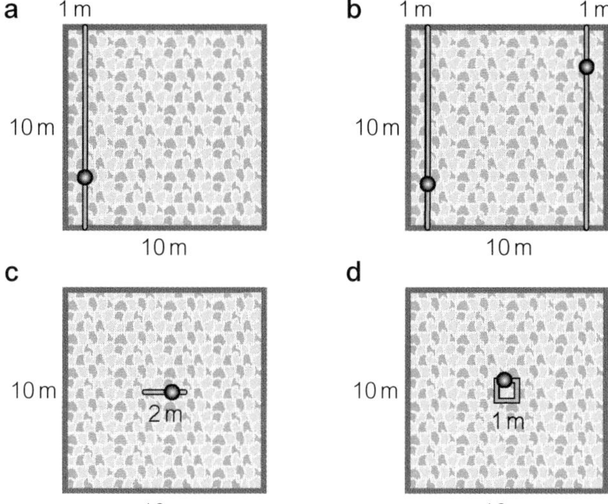

For each flower bed, construct and shade the locus of points the sprinklers can reach.

17 A scale drawing of a car has scale 1 : 32.
The length of the drawing is 109 mm.
What is the length of the real car? Give your answer in metres, correct to one decimal place.

18 Harry is making a scale model of the Angel of the North sculpture using the ratio 1 : 200.
The sculpture is 54 m wide.
How wide is the model? Give your answer in centimetres.

19 **STEM** Three mobile phone masts are at the vertices of an equilateral triangle with side 10 km. They each have an effective range 5 km.
Would your phone get a signal if you were in the middle of this triangle?
Draw a diagram to help you explain.

Investigation **Problem-solving**

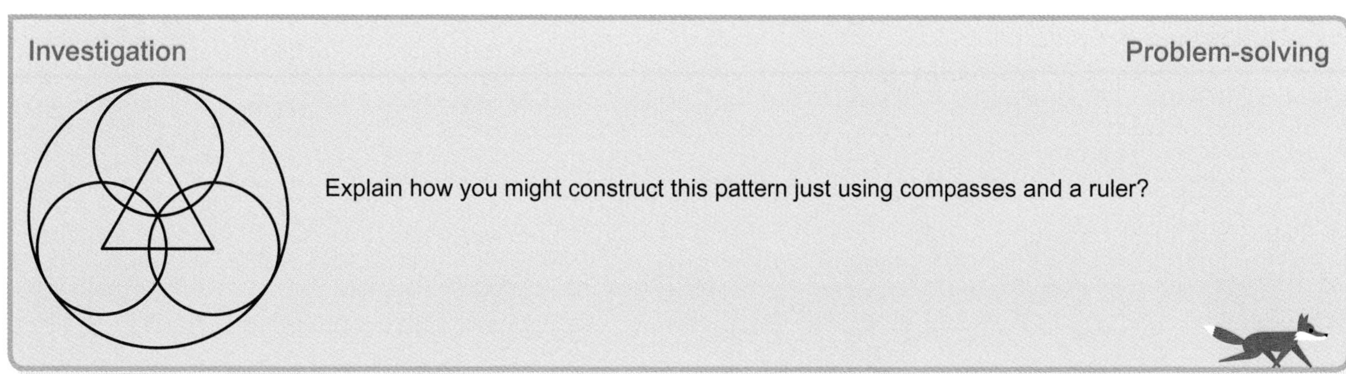

Explain how you might construct this pattern just using compasses and a ruler?

20 **Reflect** Re-read Q10 and Q19.
While you were reading, what were you thinking?
Were you visualising any images? Were you focusing on the numbers?
How did your initial thoughts help you to answer these questions?

Reflect

5 Unit test

Log how you did on your Student Progression Chart.

1 Descheeta has drawn a plan of her desk.
The scale is 1 cm to 5 cm.

a How wide is the desk?

b How long is the desk?

c How long and wide is the in-tray?

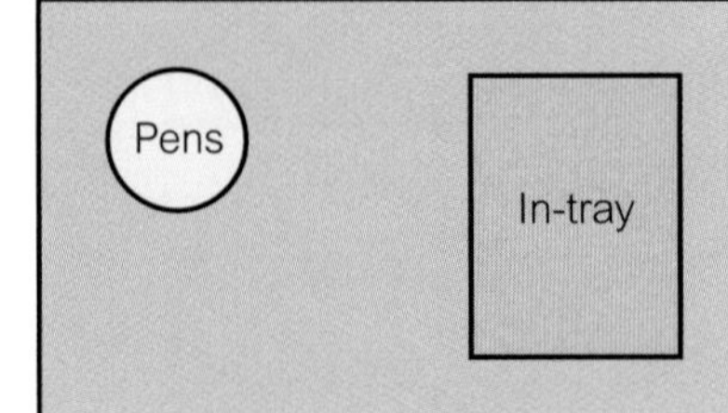

2 In this map of Edinburgh 1 cm represents 200 m.

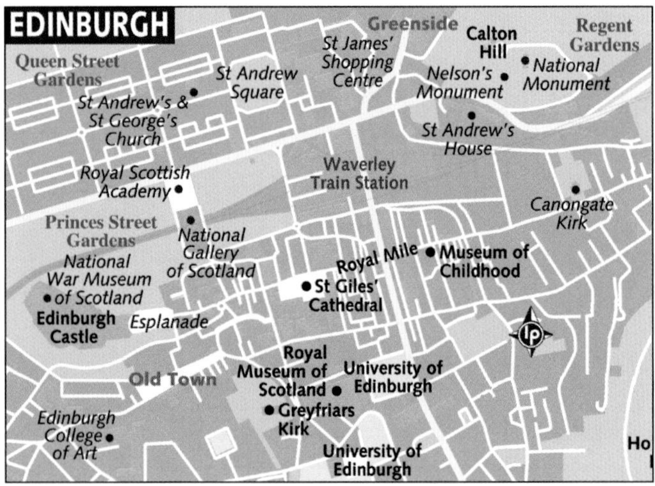

Use the map to estimate the distance between

a the Royal Scottish Academy and Canongate Kirk

b St Andrew's House and the Museum of Childhood.

3 Draw a line segment of 13 cm.
Use a ruler and compasses to construct the perpendicular bisector of the line segment.

4 The diagram shows an angle of 42°.
Make an accurate drawing of this angle. Construct the angle bisector.

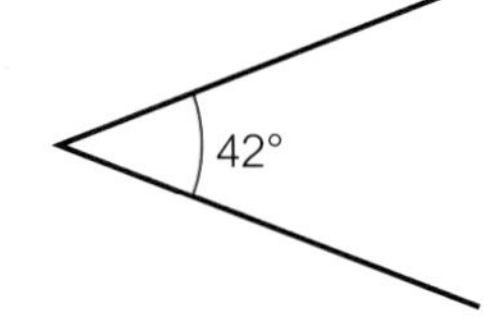

5 A point lies 4 cm away from a straight line.
Construct a perpendicular line from this point to the line.

6 A map has a scale of 1 : 25 000.

a What real distance is represented by a distance of 5.5 cm on the map?

b The distance between two towns is 15 km. How far will this distance be on the map?

7 Use a ruler and compasses to construct a triangle with sides 10 cm, 12 cm and 8 cm.

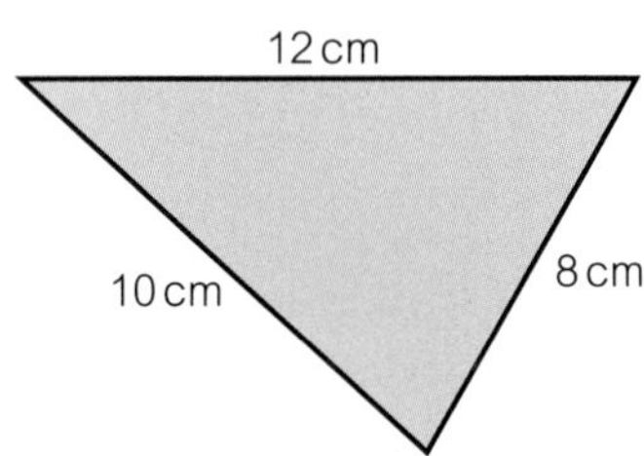

8 The diagram shows a ladder leaning against a wall.

a Construct an accurate scale drawing of the diagram.

b What is the horizontal distance from the foot of the ladder to the wall?

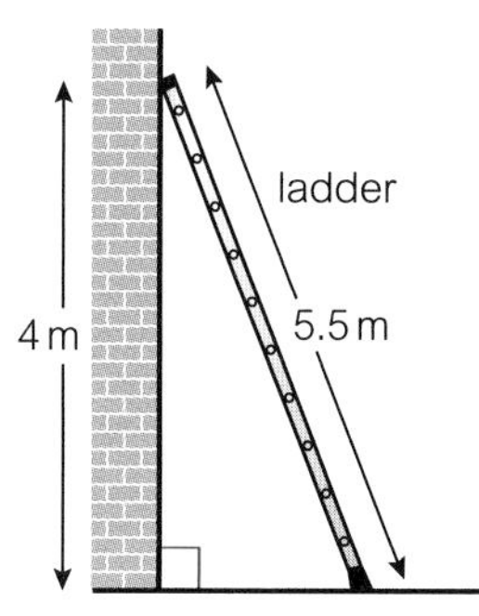

9 A gas pipe must always be the same distance between two towns 10 km apart.
Construct a diagram to show the route of the gas pipe.
Use the scale 1 cm to 1 km.

10 Two water sprinklers are 8 m apart.
One sprinkler has a range of 5 m. The other sprinkler has a range of 4 m.
Sketch the locus of the area that is watered by both sprinklers.

Challenge

11

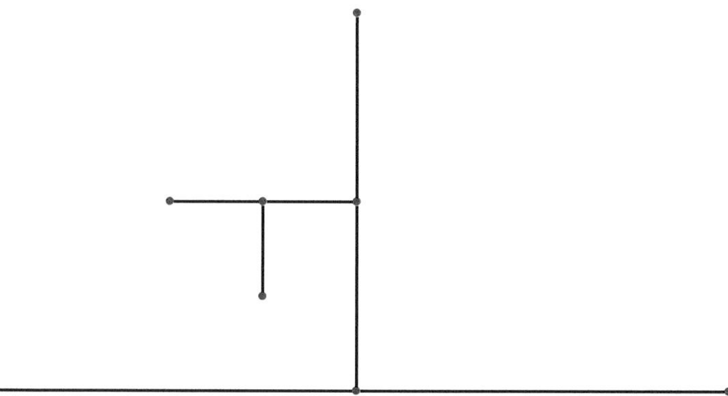

a Draw a straight line which is 16 cm long.

b Draw a perpendicular bisector half the length of the first line and above it.

c Draw a perpendicular bisector half the length of the second line and to its left.

d Keep repeating this process as far as you can, halving the line length each time, and mark the end point of each line segment in red.

e What shape do the red points make?

f What shape do other starting lengths make?

g What shape would be formed if the process was continued and all the red points were joined together?

12 **a** Construct this equilateral triangle.

b Sketch the locus of points that are 2 cm away from this triangle.

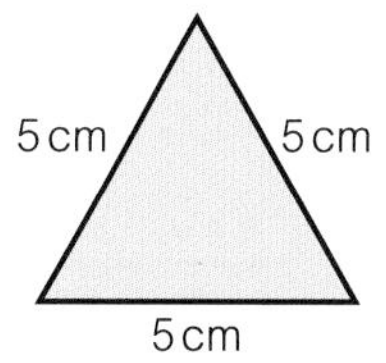

13 **Reflect** For this unit, copy and complete these sentences.

I showed I am good at ____

I found ____ hard.

I got better at ______ by ____

I was surprised by ____

I was happy that ____

I still need help with ____

Reflect

6 Equations, inequalities and proportionality

6.1 Solving equations

You will learn to:

- Construct and solve equations with the unknown on both sides
- Construct and solve equations including brackets, powers and fractions.

CONFIDENCE

Why learn this?
Engineers building bridges have to solve many equations to make sure that the bridge can carry the appropriate weight.

Fluency

- $x^2 = 16$. Give two possible values of x.
- $x^2 = 121$. Give two possible values of x.

Explore
When does an equation like x^2 = 'a number' have only one solution?

Exercise 6.1

Warm up

1 Solve these equations.
a $5x + 8 = 53$ **b** $6 - 2x = -2$ **c** $7 + 5x = 2$ **d** $\frac{x}{5} - 6 = -3$

2 Multiply these expressions by 2
a $4x - 1$ **b** $3x + 6$ **c** $8x + -3$ **d** $6x + 9$

3 Solve these equations.
a $8n + 9 = 6n + 3$ **b** $3(4n - 2) = 10n + 4$
c $3(2x + 1) = 3(x + 2)$ **d** $5(3x + 2) = 7(2x + 1)$

Worked example

Solve the equation $\frac{3x - 2}{2} = 2x - 3$.

$\frac{2(3x - 2)}{2} = 2(2x - 3)$ — This equation has a fraction on one side. Multiply both sides by the denominator.

$\frac{\cancel{2}(3x - 2)}{\cancel{2}} = 2(2x - 3)$ — 'Cancel' the 2 ÷ 2

$3x - 2 = 2(2x - 3)$ — Now you have an equation without fractions.

$3x - 2 = 4x - 6$ — Expand the brackets.

$3x - 4x = -6 + 2$

$-x = -4$

So $x = 4$ — Solve.

LHS: If $x = 4$, $\frac{3x - 2}{2} = \frac{12 - 2}{2} = \frac{10}{2} = 5$

RHS: If $x = 4$, $2x - 3 = 8 - 3 = 5$ — Substitute your solution back into the original equation. If it is correct, both sides of the equation will have the same value.

4 Solve these equations.

a $\frac{2x+7}{3} = x$ **b** $\frac{3a+2}{4} = 2a - 7$

c $\frac{4b-1}{3} = b + 2$ **d** $3y - 16 = \frac{5y-1}{4}$

Key point

You can add the indices only when multiplying powers of the same number.

5 Solve these equations.

a $\frac{3n+4}{2} = 2n + 3$ **b** $\frac{4d+2}{3} = 2d + 2$

c $\frac{2n-4}{3} = 3n + 8$ **d** $2p + 10 = \frac{3p+1}{5}$

6 **Modelling** Shakira and Tal start with the same number. Shakira doubles this number, adds 6 and then divides the result by 2.
Tal multiplies the number by 4, then subtracts 6.
They both get the same answer.
What number did they start with?

Q6 Strategy hint

Use a letter for the number. Write expressions for Shakira and Tal's calculations.

7 Solve these equations.

a $\frac{3y+2}{5} = 4y - 1$ **b** $\frac{2y+3}{4} = 5y - 2$

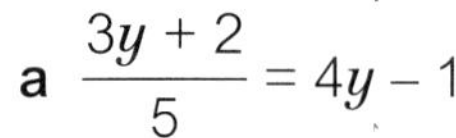

c $4x + 1 = \frac{2x-1}{3}$ **d** $6x + 4 = \frac{4x-1}{3}$

Discussion One of these questions has answer $\frac{7}{17}$. Is this more accurate as a fraction or converted to a decimal?

8 Solve these equations.

a $x^2 + 5 = 21$ **b** $x^2 + 9 = 58$

c $x^2 - 5 = 95$ **d** $\frac{x^2}{2} = 32$

Q8a hint

$x^2 = 21 - \square$

9 **Modelling** Find the missing length in each diagram.

a

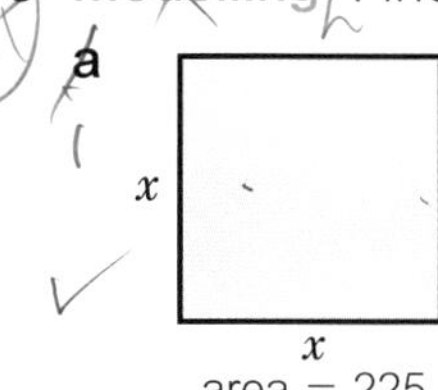

area = 225

b

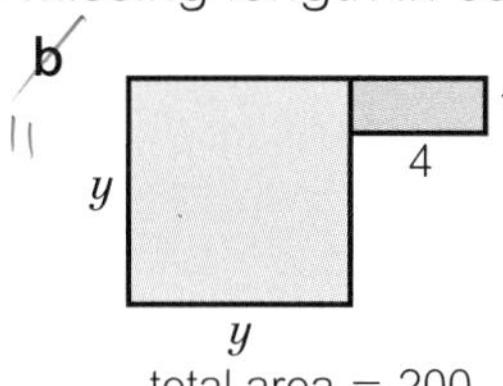

total area = 200

c

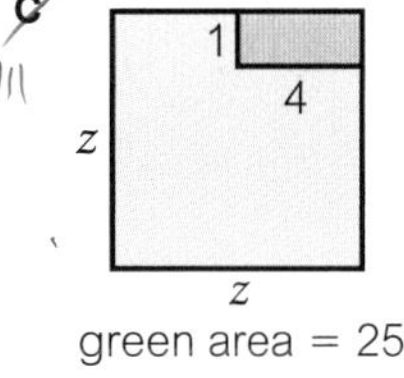

green area = 252

Q9 Strategy hint

Write an equation using the area.

Discussion Are there two possible values of x for each diagram?

10 **Problem-solving / Modelling** Write an equation for each diagram. Solve it to find the missing length.

a

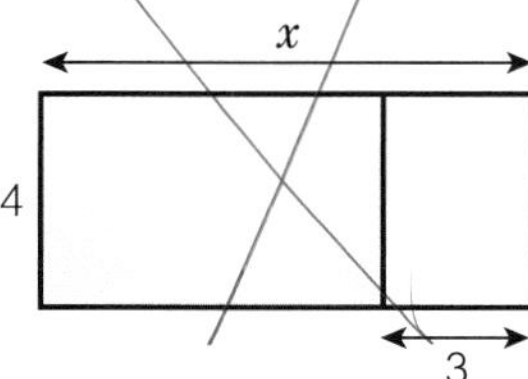

blue area = 32

b

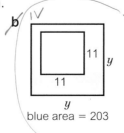

blue area = 203

c

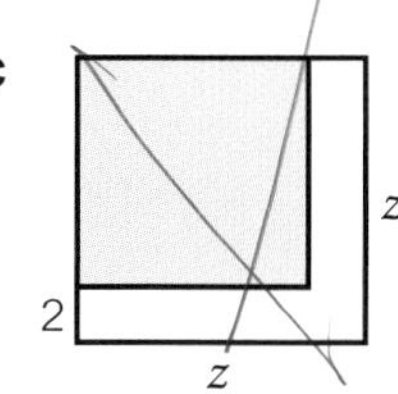

green area = 144

11 Real / STEM Electrical power can be calculated by using the formula $P = \frac{V^2}{R}$, where V is the voltage and R the resistance in a circuit. Use this formula to complete the table below.

Circuit	Power (watts)	Voltage (volts)	Resistance (ohms)
Circuit 1		5	10
Circuit 2	51.2		20
Circuit 3		24	16
Circuit 4	72		8
Circuit 5	31.25		20

12 Solve these equations.

a $-5(x - 3) = 29 + 2x$

b $2(10 - x) = -3x + 50$

c $-3(x - 5) + 2 = 18 - x$

d $4(-2x - 4) - 2x = 62 + 3x$

e $4(-3x + 3) = x - 1$

f $-3(-4x - 2) = -2x - 36$

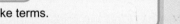

Q12 hint

Collect like terms wherever you can.

13 Solve these equations.

a $4(3a - 6) = 100 - 2(a - 1)$

b $86 - 2(2p + 1) = 9(3p - 1)$

c $-2(6x + 5) = 54 - 2(2x + 12)$

d $40 - 2(t + 6) = -2(4 - 2t)$

Investigation

- I think of a number.
- I add 3 to it.
- I double the result.
- I take 2 away from this.
- I halve the result.
- I take away the number I originally thought of.

1 Write this using algebra.
2 Work out the answer for different starting numbers.
3 Use algebra to show why this happens.
4 Make up similar puzzles where the answer will always be the same.
5 Can you make one where the answer is the number you first thought of?

Part 3 hint

Collect like terms.

Explore

14 Explore When does an equation like x^2 = 'a number' only have one solution?
Look back at the maths you have learned in this lesson.
How can you use it to answer this question?

Reflect

15 Reflect Roshan says, 'When solving equations, I always check that my solution is correct. If it isn't, then first of all I check my check! Then, I cover my original working, and try to solve the equation again.'
Did you check your solutions to the equations in this lesson? If so, how?
What do you think of Roshan's strategy when he gets an incorrect solution?
What is your strategy when you get an incorrect solution?
Compare your strategy with those of others in your class.

6.2 Using equations

You will learn to:
- Convert a recurring decimal to a fraction
- Know the difference between equations and identities.

Why learn this?
You can write and solve equations to change a recurring decimal into a fraction.

Fluency
What do these mean?
- $0.\dot{6}$
- $0.\dot{4}\dot{8}$

Solve
- $5x = 4$
- $3y = 2$
- $100x = 77$
- $99x = 61$

Explore
How would you write 0.999 999 9… as a fraction?

Exercise 6.2

1 Write down
  a a formula for the area of a rectangle
  b an expression for the perimeter of a rectangle
  c an equation stating that an unknown value plus 2 is equal to 3 times the unknown value.

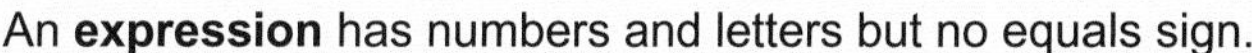

Key point
An **expression** has numbers and letters but no equals sign.
An **equation** has two expressions, or an expression and a number, either side of an equals sign. When there is only one letter, you can solve it to find the unknown value.
A **formula** is a rule that shows a relationship between two or more variables (letters). You can use substitution to find each unknown value.
A **function** is a rule that changes one number into another. $x \to 3x + 4$ is a function.

2 State whether each of these is an expression, equation, function or formula.

a $V = IR$	b $4x - 5$	c $3x + 7 = 14$	d $x \to 3x$
e $3x$	f $E = mc^2$	g $8x + 5 = 7x - 5$	h $x \to 4x - 5$
i $V = \frac{4}{3}\pi r^3$	j $x^2 + x$	k $x \to 2x + 1$	l $2x^2 + x = 10$

3 a Which of these are true for all values of x and which are true for some values of x?

i $x + 5 = 12$	ii $x + 2 = 14 - x$	iii $3x + 2 = 2 + 3x$
iv $4x - 5 = 5 - 4x$	v $3 + 2x = 5x$	vi $5(x + 3) = 5x + 15$
vii $4x + 8 = 4(x + 2)$	viii $x^2 = 5x$	ix $9x^2 = (3x)^2$

  b Rewrite the identities using $\equiv$.

Key point
An **identity** is an equation that is true for all values of the variables.
The $\equiv$ sign shows an identity.
For example, $0.5x \equiv \frac{x}{2}$ and $2x \equiv x + x$ are identities.

4 Copy these statements. Put the correct sign, = or $\equiv$, in each empty box.
  a $x + 3 \,\square\, 7$ b $x + x \,\square\, 2x$
  c $3x + 3 \,\square\, 2 + 4x - x + 1$ d $3x + 1 \,\square\, 4^2$

5 Find the values of a and b such that

a $3(x + 2y) + 4y \equiv ax + by$

b $7(x - 2y) - 3(2x + y) \equiv ax + by$

c $2(3x - 4y) + 6(2y - 5x) \equiv ax + by$

d $-5(x - 3y) - 4(y + x) \equiv ax + by$

Q5 hint

Multiply out the brackets and simplify. Find the number in front of x and the number in front of y.

6 Write an identity for each of these expressions. Use $\equiv$

a $4 + x$ b $0.25x$ c $x + x$

d $\frac{1}{5}x$ e $4(x + 1)$ f $2x \div 3$

Q6 hint

Think how else you could write each expression, e.g. $4 + x \equiv x + 4$.

Key point

All recurring decimals can be written as fractions.

Worked example

Write $0.\dot{3}$ as a fraction.

$0.\dot{3} = 0.333\,333\,333... = n.$ — Call the recurring decimal n.

$n = 0.333\,333\,333...$, so $10n = 3.333\,333\,333...$ — Multiply the recurring decimal by 10.

$10n - n = 3.333\,333\,333... - 0.333\,333\,333...$

$= 3.000\,000\,000...$ — Subtract the value of n from the value of $10n$ so you get all decimal places zero.

$9n = 3$

$n = \frac{3}{9}$ — Solve the equation.

$n = \frac{1}{3}$ — Cancel if possible.

7 Change these recurring decimals into fractions.

a $0.\dot{1}$ b $0.\dot{8}$ c $0.\dot{7}$

Discussion Can you multiply by 10 to write $0.\dot{2}\dot{7}$ as a fraction?
If not, what do you multiply by?
What if you were writing $0.\dot{3}2\dot{6}$ as a fraction?

8 Change these recurring decimals into fractions.

a $0.\dot{3}\dot{6}$ b $0.1\dot{6}$ c $0.\dot{4}\dot{5}$

d $0.8\dot{3}$ e $0.\dot{0}\dot{9}$ f $0.\dot{6}\dot{1}$

Q8 Strategy hint

Multiply by a multiple of 10. Try $10n$ or $100n$ or $1000n$.

9 Change these recurring decimals into fractions.

a $0.24\dot{5}$ b $0.14\dot{5}$ c $0.83\dot{4}$

Investigation

1 When converting fractions to decimals, which denominators always give recurring decimals?

2 Which ones always give terminating decimals?

3 Are there any patterns?

Part 1 hint

Try multiples of 3 to start with.

10 **Explore** How would you write 0.9999999… as a fraction?
Look back at the maths you have learned in this lesson.
How can you use it to answer this question?

11 **Reflect** Look back at the work you did on the investigation.
What denominator did you try first? Why?
What denominator did you try next? Why?
Once you had chosen a denominator, what did you do then?
Could you have used a better approach? Explain your answer.

6.3 Trial and improvement

You will learn to:

- Use trial and improvement methods to find solutions to equations.

Why learn this?
You can use trial and improvement methods to get closer to a solution to a problem.

Fluency
Which two numbers do these roots lie between?

- $\sqrt{48}$
- $\sqrt[3]{39}$

Explore
How did Archimedes work out the value of π over 2000 years ago?

Exercise 6.3

1 Substitute $x = 2$ and $x = 3$ into the expression $5x + 3$
Which value gives an answer closer to 15?

2 a Work out the value of $x^2 + 5$ when
i $x = 3$ ii $x = 2.8$
b Work out the value of x^3 when
i $x = 4$ ii $x = 3.5$
c Work out the value of $x^2 + x$ when
i $x = 3.7$ ii $x = 1.6$

3 Substitute $y = 8$ and $y = 9$ into the expression $\frac{5y}{7}$.
Which value gives an answer closer to 6?

4 Substitute $n = 5$ and $n = 7$ into the expression $8n - 5$
a Which value of n gives an answer closer to 45?
b Would substituting $n = 6$ be closer to 45?

Worked example

Use trial and improvement to find a solution to the equation $x^3 = 31$.

Draw a table. Use a calculator to try values of x.

x	x^3	Comment
3	27	too small
4	64	too big
3.5	42.875	too big
3.1	29.791	too small
3.2	32.768	too big

31 is between the values of 27 (3^3) and 64 (4^3).

x is between 3.1 and 3.2.
3.1^3 (29.791) is closer to 31 than 3.2^3 (32.768).
x is 3.1 (1 d.p.).

Find the two values to 1 d.p. that x is between. Decide which is closer to x.

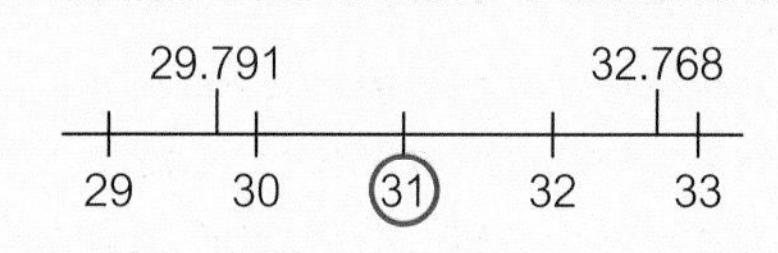

5 Use trial and improvement to find a solution to these equations.
Give your answers to one decimal place.
a $x^3 = 39$ b $x^3 = 95$ c $x^3 + 2 = 49$
d $x^3 - 7 = 87$ e $2x^3 = 145$ f $3x^3 - 1 = 59$

Q5 Strategy hint
Use a table as shown in the worked example.

6 Problem-solving Here is a plan of a square field with an area of trees in it.
a The area of grass in the field is $54\,\text{m}^2$.
Use trial and improvement to find the length of one side of the field to one decimal place.
b How much fence is required to go around the perimeter of the entire field.
Give your answer to one decimal place.

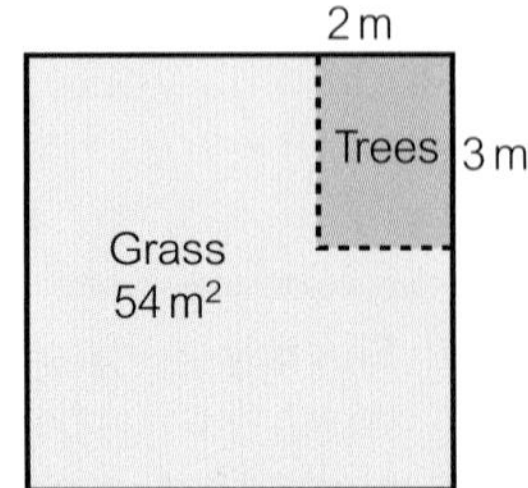

Q6b hint
Use x for the side of the square. Write an equation linking x and the area.

7 Problem-solving / Modelling A packaging company uses the formula $T = x^2 + x$ to calculate how much tape (T), in cm, is needed to wrap a cube-shaped package of side length x cm.
What is the side length of a package that needs
a 45 cm of tape b 65 cm of tape?
Give your answers correct to one decimal place.

8 Use trial and improvement to find the value of y (to one decimal place) in these equations.
a $y^2 + y = 46$ b $y^3 + y = 425$ c $y^3 + 2y = 75$
d $y^3 - y = 94$ e $y^3 - y^2 = 431$ f $y^3 - 4y = 167$

Q8a hint

y^2	$y^2 + y$	Comment

9 
Problem-solving / Modelling
The diagram shows a box made from a cube with an additional cuboid attached.
The area of the cuboid's end face is $7\,\text{cm}^2$.
The entire box has a volume of $140\,\text{cm}^3$.
How long is each side of the cube?
Give your answer to one decimal place.

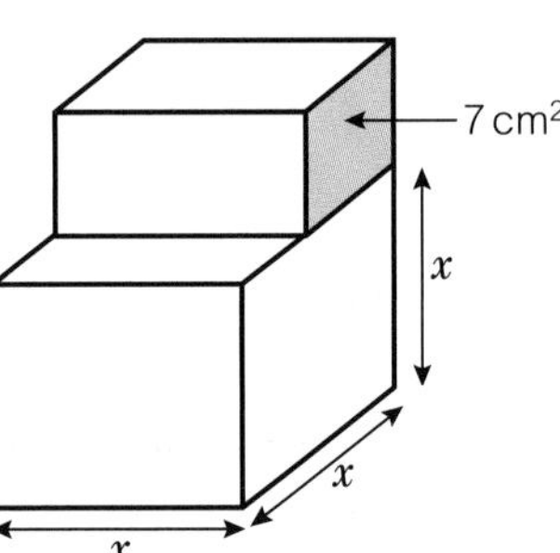

Investigation
A spreadsheet can do trial and improvement calculations quickly.
Use a spreadsheet to find the solution for $x^2 + x = 45$ to two decimal places.

Explore

10 **Explore** How did Archimedes work out the value of π over 2000 years ago?
Look back at the maths you have learned in this lesson.
How can you use it to answer this question?

Reflect

11 **Reflect** This lesson is all about the method of trial and improvement for solving equations.
When do you think this method is useful?
Do you like this method for solving equations?
Explain your answer.

6.4 Using and solving inequalities

You will learn to:
- Solve linear inequalities
- Represent solutions to inequalities on a number line.

Why learn this?
Inequalities allow us to find a range of solutions, for example, comparing costs of two different pricing structures.

Fluency
- What is an integer?
- An integer is < 5. What could it be?
- An integer is $\geqslant 2$. What could it be?

Explore
I need to hire coaches and minibuses for a school trip. How can I make sure I get a seat for everybody?

Exercise 6.5

1 Solve these equations.
a $3x + 5 = 29$ b $5x - 6 = 42$ c $6x + 11 = 32$

2 Which integer values of x satisfy these inequalities?
a $5 < x < 10$ b $6 < x \leqslant 14$ c $-5 \leqslant x < 5$ d $-8 < x < -2$

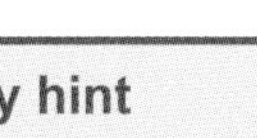

Q2 Literacy hint
'Satisfy' means 'make the statement true'.

Worked example

Use a number line to show the values that satisfy the inequalities

a $x > 4$

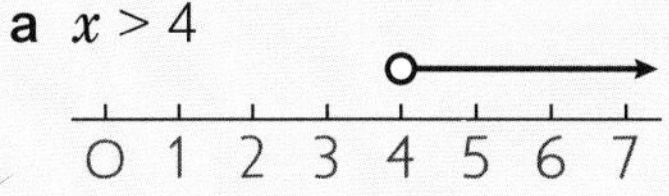

This includes all the numbers greater than 4 (*excluding* 4).

b $2 < x \leqslant 6$

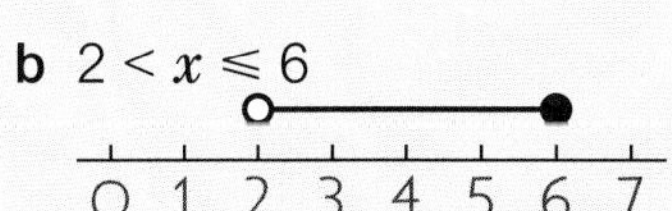

This includes all the numbers greater than 2 (*excluding* 2) and less than or equal to 6 (*including* 6).

Key point
You can also show solutions to inequalities on a number line.
An empty circle shows that the value is not included.

A filled circle shows that the value is included.

An arrow shows that the solution continues towards infinity.

3 Show these inequalities on a number line.
a $x < 3$ b $x \leqslant 8$ c $x > 5$
d $x \geqslant 4$ e $x > -3$ f $x < -2$

4 Write inequalities for each of these sentences and show them on a number line.
a Four is less than n
b n is less than -5
c n is greater than or equal to -6
d Six is more than n
e A number is less than 5 and greater than or equal to -2
f A number is greater than or equal to 0 and less than or equal to 5
g A number is less than or equal to -2 and greater than -7
h A number is greater than or equal to -5 and less than 2

Q4 hint
Choose a letter to represent the number.

5 Write the inequalities shown by each of these number lines.

a 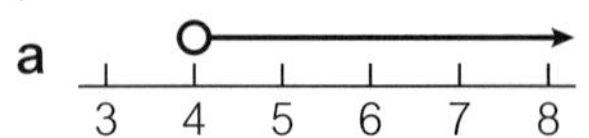

b 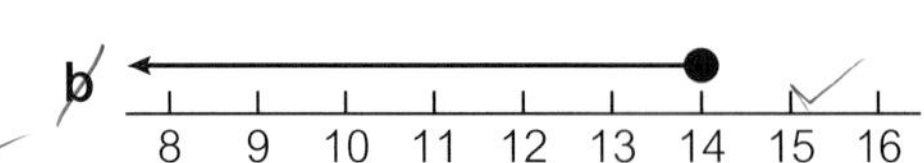

c 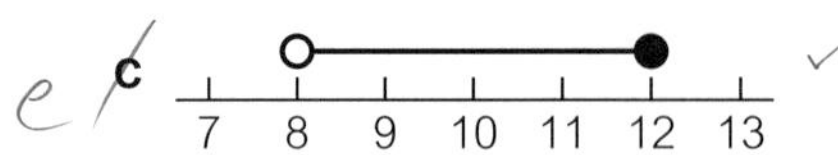

d 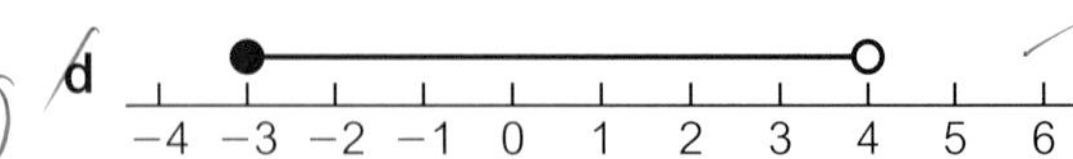

6 Show these inequalities on number lines.
Find the integer values that satisfy each one.

a $2 < x < 7$

b $-3 < x \leqslant 2$

c $-1 < x < 1$

d $-5 \leqslant x < 2$

e $-9 \leqslant x \leqslant -1$

f $-5 < x < -1$

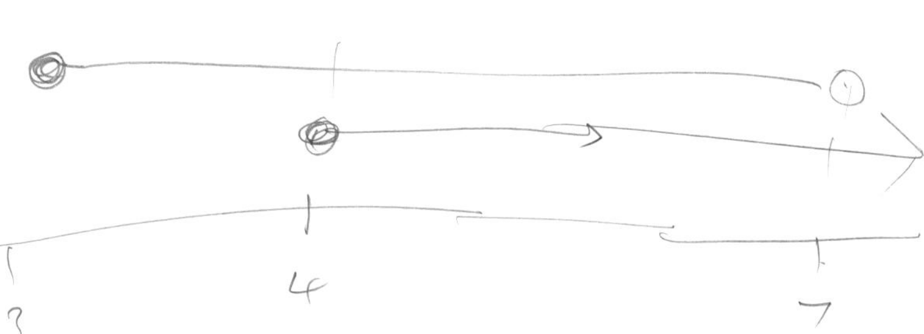

7 $n > 5$

Write an inequality for

a $2n$

b $3n$

c $4n$

d $2n + 1$

Discussion What rules do you use to write these inequalities?

8 I think of a number. My number plus 7 is less than 12.

a Write an inequality to show this.

b What is the largest whole number value for my number?

9 Solve these inequalities.
Show each solution on a number line.

a $x + 3 > 5$

b $x - 6 > 14$

c $2x < 10$

d $\frac{x}{3} > 9$

e $2x + 1 > 13$

f $3x - 2 < 7$

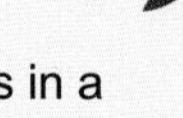

Key point

You can solve inequalities in a similar way to solving equations.

Q9 hint

Use the balancing method of doing the same to both sides of the inequality to solve it.

10 **Modelling** I think of a number, multiply it by 2, and add 7.
My answer is less than 15. Write an inequality.
Find three possible values for my number.

11 **Problem-solving / Modelling** Erica goes to the supermarket with £5.
She buys one melon for £1.50 and spends the rest of the money on bananas. Each banana costs 60p.
Write an inequality. Work out the number of bananas she can buy.

Investigation

On a number line you can see $-5 < -2$

−5 −4 −3 −2 −1

1 Multiply both sides of the inequality $-5 < -2$ by -1

2 Is the statement you wrote as your answer to part **1** true?

3 What does $-x < 8$ mean?

4 What are the solutions to $-x < 8$?

5 Does your answer to part **4** make sense?

Discussion If $x > 2$, what can you say about $-x$?

12 Solve these inequalities.

a $8 - x < 11$

b $-2x > 7$

c $-4x < 12$

d $5 - x > -7$

e $-\frac{x}{2} > 6$

Q12 hint

Check that your answers make sense by substituting your solution into the original inequality.

13 Problem-solving / Modelling John has saved £40 to buy some shirts. It costs £3.50 return on the bus to get to the shops, and shirts are £8.25 each.

a What is the maximum number of shirts that John can buy?

b Could he buy more shirts if he walked instead of taking the bus?

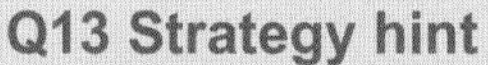

Q13 Strategy hint

Write an inequality using the information you have.

14 Solve these inequalities.
Show each solution on a number line.

a $2(x + 3) < 18$

b $5(x - 3) > 17$

c $6(x + 7) < -3$

d $8 > 8(x - 2)$

15 Reasoning A bus timetable says that buses arrive at quarter past and quarter to each hour.
The buses can be up to 5 minutes early or 7 minutes late.
Noah arrives at the bus stop at 14 35.
Write an inequality that shows how long he will wait for a bus to arrive.

16 **Explore** I need to hire coaches and minibuses for a school trip.
How can I make sure I get a seat for everybody?
Choose some sensible numbers to help you explore this situation.
Then use what you have learned in this lesson to help you answer the question.

Explore

17 **Reflect** Why are pictures like these good for representing inequalities?

Q17 hint

Write down how the circles, lines and arrows help you to understand the inequality.

Reflect

6.5 STEM: Proportion

You will learn to:
- Set up equations to show direct proportion
- Recognise data sets that are proportional
- Use algebra to solve problems involving proportion.

Why learn this?
Knowing simple relationships between quantities can allow us to make predictions.

Fluency
- How many seconds are there in 5 minutes?
- Apples cost £1.25 per kilogram. How much will 3 kg cost?
- 80 km = 50 miles. How far in miles is 20 km?

Explore
Does the price of petrol rise in proportion to the price of oil?

Exercise 6.6: Proportion

Key point
When two or more quantities are in direct proportion, they increase or decrease by the same scale factor.

1 **a** A plumber charges a £30 call-out fee plus £25 per hour. Is the price for a job in direct proportion to the time she spends on it?
b Is the length of an object in cm in direct proportion to the length in inches?
c The exchange rate for £ to € one day is €1.18 per £1. Is this in direct proportion?
d A currency dealer uses the exchange rate in part **c**, but charges 0.5% commission. Is the number of euros you get in direct proportion to the number of pounds you spend?
e A different currency dealer charges a £5 commission for each exchange. Is the number of euros you get in direct proportion to the number of pounds you spend?

2 **Modelling** The graph shows an object moving at a constant speed.
a Is the distance travelled in direct proportion to the time taken?
b If the object continues at the same speed, how long will it take to travel 750 metres?

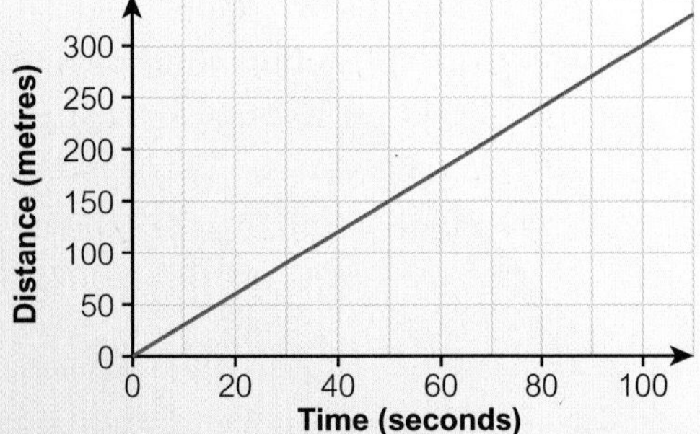

3 **STEM / Modelling** In a science experiment Akmal measures how far a wire extends when he adds different masses to it. The table shows his results.

Mass, m	10 g	20 g	30 g	40 g	50 g
Extension, e	12 cm	24 cm	36 cm	48 cm	60 cm

a Do his results show a proportional relationship between m and e?
b Write a formula that shows this relationship between mass (m) and extension (e).
c Use your formula to predict how far the wire will stretch with a mass of 25 g.

Q3b hint
$e = \square \times m$
What do you do to the value of m to get the value of e?

4 STEM / Modelling
Other students conduct the same experiment but with different wires.
Write a formula that describes the relationship between the mass and extension for each wire.

Wire sample	Mass	Extension
A	10 g	15 cm
	15 g	22.5 cm
B	25 g	20 cm
	45 g	36 cm
C	20 g	25 cm
	32 g	40 cm
D	40 g	30 cm
	60 g	45 cm
E	40 g	70 cm
	75 g	131.25 cm

Key point

When quantities are in proportion, the ratio between them remains the same.

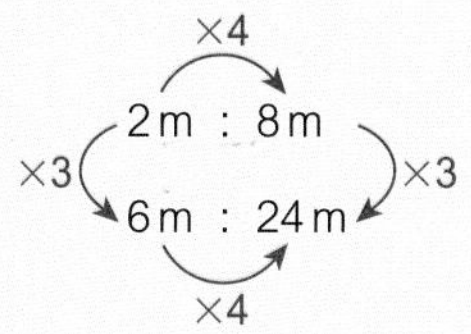

5 Check whether each of these quantities are varying in direct proportion.
- **a** 10 oranges cost £3, 15 cost £4
- **b** 6 game credits cost 48p, 21 cost £1.68
- **c** 5 sacks weigh 15 kg, 12 sacks weigh 35 kg

Q5a hint

Check using ratios. Do the quantity of oranges and the price increase at the same rate?

	Orange	Cost	
×1.5	10	£3	×1.$\dot{3}$
	15	£4	

6 The values of A and B are in direct proportion.
Work out the missing numbers W, X, Y and Z.

Value of A	Value of B
12	21
24	W
30	X
Y	24.5
Z	56

7 STEM A scientist uses the formula $V = IR$, where V is the voltage, I is the current and R is the resistance.
The resistance stays the same. Is the voltage in direct proportion to the current?
Discussion Is the voltage in direct proportion to the current if the resistance changes as the current increases?

Worked example

On a particular day, \$8 will buy 48 Argentinian pesos.
The number of pesos (P) varies in proportion to the number of dollars (D).
How many Argentinian pesos can I buy for \$200?

This means that $P \propto D$, or $P = kD$. — Write the proportional relationship as an equation with a constant of proportionality.

$P = 48$ and $D = 8$, so $48 = k \times 8$. — Substitute the values into the equation.

So $k = 6$ and $P = 6D$. — Solve the equation to find k, and rewrite it using the value of k.

Substitute $D = 200$. — Use your equation to answer the question.

$P = 6 \times 200$
$= 1200$

So \$200 can buy 1200 pesos.

Key point

$y \propto x$ means 'y is proportional to x'.

8 Real Sterling (the UK pound) varies in proportion to the Bulgarian lev.
£15 = 36 Bulgarian lev.
How many Bulgarian lev can I buy with £500?

9 Credits for a computer game cost £2.40 for 16
The cost in pounds is proportional to the number of credits.
How much would 120 credits cost?

10 The price of eggs varies in proportion to the number sold.
The price of 12 eggs is £3.24.

a Write an equation to express this relationship.

b What is the price of 114 eggs?

11 Modelling Argent and Bailey want to find the ratio of their hand spans to their heights to see if there is a relationship.
Argent measures his hand span to be 20 cm and his height to be 1.78 m.

a Write this as a ratio of hand span to height.

b Bailey is 1.65 m tall. If hand spans are in proportion to height, what would you expect her hand span to measure?

c A hand print on a wall has a span of 25 cm. If the quantities are in the same proportion, how tall is the person who left the hand print?

12 STEM / Reasoning Ben reads that bamboo can grow up to 10 cm in a day.
He says, 'This means that after a year a bamboo stem will be 36.5 m long.'

a Is he correct?

According to Ben's theory the same bamboo would be 365 m high after 10 years.

b Do you think Ben's reasoning is good?

13 Real / Problem-solving 5 cm^3 of sand contains 6250 grains.
How many grains of sand are there in 1 m^3?

Investigation

Problem-solving

- Take a piece of A4 paper.
- Measure the dimensions carefully.
- Cut the A4 paper precisely in half by halving the longer side. You now have A5 paper.
- Measure the dimensions carefully.
- Continue this process for different sizes.

1 What do you notice about the relationships between the dimensions?

2 Start again with a different shaped rectangular piece of paper and repeat this experiment.

Do you get the same result?

Explore

14 Explore Does the price of petrol rise in proportion to the price of oil?
Is it easier to explore this question now you have completed the lesson? What further information do you need, to be able to answer this?

Reflect

15 Reflect Tom says, 'Direct proportionality is all about multiplying and dividing.'
What do you think he means?

Q15 hint

Look back at some of the questions you answered in this lesson. How did you use multiplying and dividing?

6.6 Simultaneous equations

You will learn to:

- Solve a pair of simultaneous equations.

Why learn this?
Solving two equations together you can find two unknown values

Fluency
Work out

- 4 − 6
- 7 − 11
- −7 + 5
- −6 + 11

Explore
Which two numbers add together to make 10 and have a difference of 22?

Exercise 6.4

1 Modelling Write an equation for each of these.

a It costs £41 for 2 adults and 3 children to go to the cinema.
Use x for adults and y for children.

b 3 ice lolly sticks and 2 cocktail sticks measure 40 cm in total.
Use x for lolly sticks and y for cocktail sticks.

c 5 LED lightbulbs and 3 halogen bulbs cost £12.
Use x and y, and explain what they represent in your equation.

Key point
You can solve two **simultaneous equations** to find the values of two variables.

Worked example

Solve the simultaneous equations $y = 2x$,
$3x + y = 11$.

$3x + y = 11$ ① — Write one equation above the other with the equals signs lined up. Number them ① and ②.

$y = 2x$ ②

$3x + 2x = 11$ ① — Substitute the value of y in equation ② into equation ①.

$5x = 11$ — Simplify.

$x = 2.2$ — Solve.

Substitute into equation ② — Substitute the value of x into one equation. Choose the simplest one to solve.

$y = 2 \times 2.2$

$y = 4.4$ — Solve to find the value of y.

Check:

$3x + y = 11$ ① — Check the values in the other equation.

$3 \times 2.2 + 4.4 = 11$ ✓

2 Solve these pairs of simultaneous equations.

a $2x + y = 19$
$y = 2x$

b $3x + y = 24$
$y = 3x$

c $3x + y = 13$
$y = 2x$

d $x + 3y = 18$
$\frac{1}{2}x = y$

e $4x + y = 22$
$y = 2x$

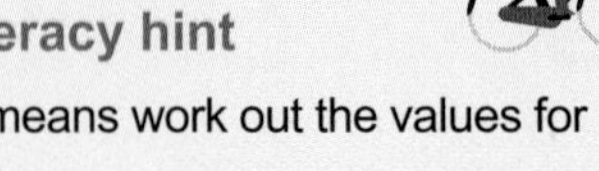

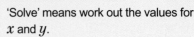

Q2 Literacy hint
'Solve' means work out the values for x and y.

3 **Problem-solving / Modelling** Four identical lorries and a car have a total length of 52 m. One lorry is 3 times as long as a car.
How long is a lorry and how long is a car?

Q3 hint
Write the equations, stating x is ..., y is ...

4 **Problem-solving / Modelling** It costs 4 adults and a child £85.50 to get into a football match.
Child tickets are half the price of adult tickets.

a What is the price of an adult ticket?

b What is the price of a child ticket?

Q4 Strategy hint
Write simultaneous equations and solve them.

5 **Problem-solving** A restaurant can seat 80 people using 8 round tables and 4 square tables.
One round table seats twice as many people as one square table.
How many people can sit at a round table?
How many people can sit at a square table?

Worked example

Solve the simultaneous equations $3x + y = 15$,
$x - y = 1$

$3x + y = 15$ ①
$x - y = 1$ ②

Write one equation above the other with the equals signs lined up. Number them.

$3x + y = 15$ ①
$+ \quad x - y = 1$ ②
$4x + 0 = 16$

Add equations ① and ② together.

$x = 4$

Solve.

Substitute $x = 4$ into equation ②.

Substitute $x = 4$ into one equation.

$4 - y = 1$
$y = 3$

Check:
$3x + y = 15$ ①
$3 \times 4 + 3 = 15$ ✓

Discussion This is called the elimination method.
Why, do you think?

Key point
You can add whole equations together to help solve simultaneous equation problems.

6 Solve these pairs of simultaneous equations.

a $3x + y = 21$
$2x - y = 9$

b $3x + y = 13$
$4x - y = 1$

c $4x - y = 39$
$5x + y = 60$

d $3x - y = 19$
$2x + y = 16$

e $3x + 2y = 24$
$x - 2y = 0$

f $4x - 2y = 20$
$3x + 2y = 29$

7 Modelling In a number puzzle, a and b add together to make 18, and the difference between them is 7.
Write an equation for this.
What are the values of a and b?

8 Bill is using long and short sticks for measuring.
He knows that 3 long sticks and 2 short sticks measure 47 cm, and that 2 long sticks take away 2 short sticks measures 13 cm.
How long is each type of stick?

Q8 hint
Subtract one equation from the other.

9 Solve these pairs of simultaneous equations.

a $2x + y = 14$
$4x + y = 20$

b $3x + 2y = 22$
$2x + 2y = 13$

c $4x + 5y = 39$
$4x + 2y = 30$

d $8x + 2y = 58$
$3x + 2y = 23$

10 Problem-solving Mr and Mrs Singh and their 3 children visit the theatre. The total price of the tickets is £96.
Another party of 5 adults and 3 children pays £163.50.
How much are adult and child tickets?

11 **Explore** Which two numbers add together to make 10 and have a difference of 22?
Choose some sensible numbers to help you explore this situation.
Then use what you have learned in this lesson to help you answer the question.

12 **Reflect** Look back at the pairs of simultaneous equations you solved in this lesson.
Write down a pair of simultaneous equations that was easy to solve.
Write down a pair of simultaneous equations that was more difficult to solve.
What made your first pair of simultaneous equations easier to solve than your second pair?

Explore

Reflect

6 Check up

Log how you did on your Student Progression Chart.

Solving equations and inequalities

1 Solve these equations.

a $\frac{3x + 5}{2} = 4$

b $\frac{4x + 1}{3} = x + 4$

2 Solve these equations. Give both possible values of x.

a $x^2 + 9 = 90$

$x = \square$ or $\square$.

b $\frac{x^2}{2} = 50$

$x = \square$ or $\square$.

3 Solve these.

a $4(x + 2) = 14 + 2x$

b $5(2x - 2) = 3(x - 4)$

4 Find the integers that satisfy these inequalities. Show each solution on a number line.

a $n > 7$

b $-5 < n \leqslant 2$

5 Solve these inequalities.

a $x - 9 > 2$

b $3a < 12$

6 Solve these inequalities.

a $\frac{x}{-2} < 14$

b $2x - 1 \geqslant 7$

7 Convert $0.\dot{4}$ to a fraction.

Trial and improvement

8 Use trial and improvement to find a solution to $x^2 + 3 = 45$. Give your anwer to one decimal place. Show your working.

Proportion

9 Meena weighed different lengths of a wooden plank. Here are her results.

Length	Mass
3 cm	51 g
5 cm	85 g
8 cm	136 g

Is the mass in proportion to the length? Explain your answer.

10 The values of X and Y are in direct proportion.
Work out the missing numbers A, B, C and D.

X	Y
12	20
18	A
B	40
C	10
30	D

11 Distance travelled at a constant speed is in proportion to time taken.
It takes 45 minutes to travel 25 miles.

a How long would it take to travel 40 miles at the same speed?

b How far would you travel in 2 hours?

12 The price of oranges varies in proportion to the number sold.
The price of 15 oranges is £3.90.

a Write an equation to express this relationship.

b What is the price of 98 oranges?

Simultaneous equations

13 Solve this pair of simultaneous equations.

$4x + y = 28$

$y = 3x$

14 Solve this pair of simultaneous equations.

$4x + y = 15$

$5x - y = 3$

15 Write = or ≡ for each box.

a $y + y + y \square 3y$

b $2y + 5 \square 11$

c $4 \times y + 4 \square 15$

d $2y + y - 4 \square 4y - y - 3 - 1$

16 How sure are you of your answers? Were you mostly

☹ Just guessing 😐 Feeling doubtful ☺ Confident

What next? Use your results to decide whether to strengthen or extend your learning.

Reflect

Challenge

17 Start with the expression $4x + 2y$.
Create as many identities as you can.

6 Strengthen

You will:

- Strengthen your understanding with practice.

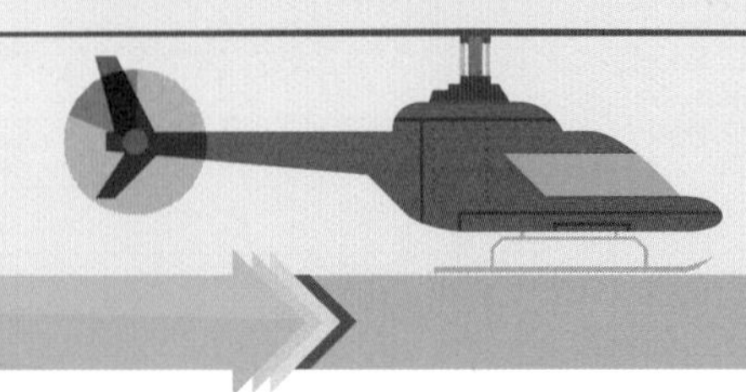

Solving equations and inequalities

1 Solve these equations.

a $2x + 4 = 3x$ **b** $3x + 21 = 5x$

c $3x + 7 = 2x$ **d** $7x + 2 = 10x$

2 Solve these equations.

a $4(x - 1) = 3x$ **b** $3(x + 2) = 2x$

c $4(x - 7) = 2x - 4$ **d** $2(x + 1) - 3x = 5x + 8$

> **Q2 hint**
> Multiply each term inside the bracket by the number outside. Watch out for negatives.

3 Copy and complete the workings to solve these.

a $\frac{x}{3} = 5$

$\frac{\cancel{3} \times x}{\cancel{3}} = 3 \times 5$

$x = \square$

b $\frac{x}{4} = x - 3$

$\frac{\cancel{4} \times x}{\cancel{4}} = 4 \times (x - 3)$

$x = \square - \square$

$x = \square$

c $\frac{4x}{3} = 3x - 6$

$\frac{3 \times 4x}{3} = \square(3x - 6)$

d $\frac{2x + 3}{2} = 4x$

$\frac{2(2x + 3)}{2} = \square \times 4x$

> **Q3 Strategy hint**
> Multiply by a number that cancels with the denominator.

> **Q3b hint**
> Use brackets to multiply all the terms on the right-hand side.

4 Solve these equations.

a $\frac{5x + 1}{4} = x + 2$ **b** $\frac{3x + 1}{4} = 3x$ **c** $\frac{3y + 2}{3} = 2y + 1$

d $4x + 3 = \frac{5x + 6}{4}$ **e** $5a + 6 = \frac{2a + 1}{3}$ **f** $\frac{3x + 3}{4} = 4x + 7$

5 a Work out

i $(-5)^2$ and 5^2 **ii** $(-7)^2$ and 7^2

b Solve these equations. Give both possible values of x.

i $x^2 = 81$ **ii** $x^2 = 16$ **iii** $x^2 + 3 = 67$

iv $x^2 - 17 = 83$ **v** $x^2 - 13 = 12$ **vi** $x^2 + 4 = 40$

> **Q5bi hint**
> What numbers square to give 81?

> **Q5b iii Strategy hint**
> Rearrange to get x^2 on its own.

6 Modelling Write an equation for each diagram. Solve it to find the length x.

a

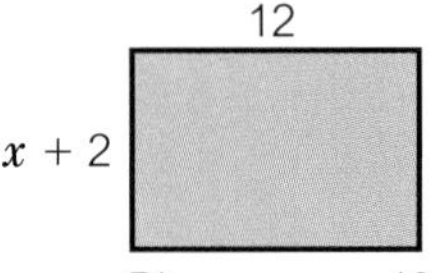

b

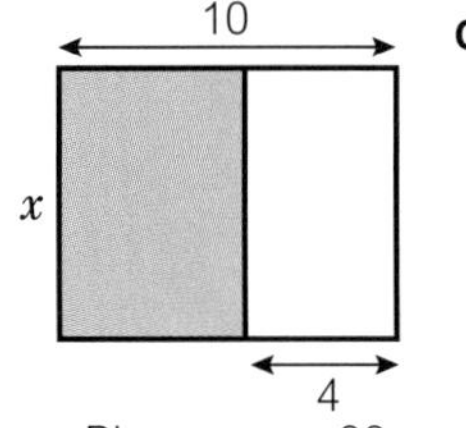

c

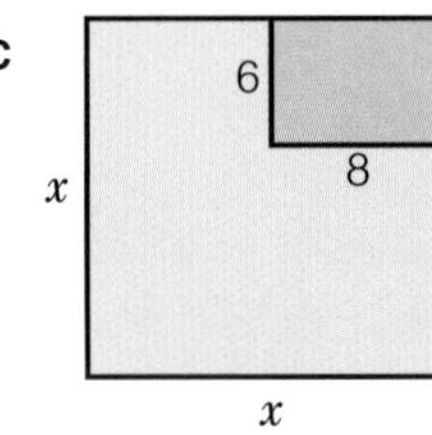

> **Q6a Strategy hint**
> area of a rectangle = length × width

> **Q6b hint**
> area = length of blue rectangle × width of blue rectangle

7 **a** Expand

i $-2(3x + 5)$ **ii** $-3(4x - 2)$

b Solve

i $-2(6x + 5) = 88 - 2(2x + 1)$ **ii** $-3(2x - 2) = 6(2x - 5)$

iii $5(2x - 3) = 47 - 2(x - 5)$ **iv** $-4(5x - 1) = 25 - (6x + 49)$

c Solve

i $-2(-3x + 4) = -2x + 16$ **ii** $-3(4x - 5) = 4x - 9$

iii $-2(-3x - 7) = -5x + 69$ **iv** $-5(2x + 3) = -7x + 6$

8 Show each inequality on a number line.

a $n < 8$ **b** $x \geqslant 5$

c $y > 6$ **d** $x \leqslant 7$

e $4 < x \leqslant 9$ **f** $7 < x < 11$

g $-3 \leqslant x \leqslant 2$ **h** $-6 < n < -1$

i $-4 < y < -1$ **j** $-8 < n < -2$

Q8 hint

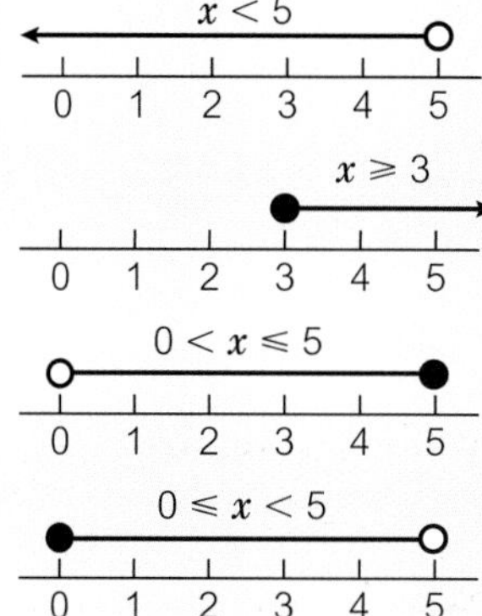

○ shows the value is not included.

● shows the value is included.

9 Solve these inequalities and show each one on a number line.
The first one has been started for you.

a $x + 3 > 8$
$x > \square$ **b** $x - 3 > 11$

c $3x \geqslant 12$ **d** $\frac{x}{4} < 4$

e $3x + 3 > 10$ **f** $2x - 4 \leqslant 9$

Q9 Strategy hint

Use the same method as for solving an equation.

10 Solve these inequalities.

a $3(x + 2) > 15$ **b** $2(x - 2) \geqslant 12$

c $3(x + 4) \leqslant 13$ **d** $2(x - 7) < 14$

Q10 hint

Expand the brackets first.

11 Copy and complete.

a $-2 < 4$ ($\times -1$) → $2 \ \square \ -4$

b $3 < 4$ ($\times -5$) → $-15 \ \square \ -20$

c $2 > 1$ ($\times -3$) → $-6 \ \square \ -3$

d $24 > 16$ ($\div -4$) → $-6 \ \square \ -4$

e $1 < 3$ ($\times -1$) → $-1 \ \square \ -3$

f $30 < 42$ ($\div 6$) → $-5 \ \square \ -7$

12 Solve these inequalities.

a $6 - x < 14$ **b** $-3x > 7$

c $-4x < 15$ **d** $6 - x < -11$

e $\frac{x}{-2} > 5$ **f** $-3x < -4$

g $8 - x > -7$ **h** $\frac{x}{-3} < 12$

Q12a hint

Solve using the same method as for an equation. Watch out though!

$-x < \square$ ($\times -1$) → $x \ \square \ \square$

13 Copy and complete the working to convert $0.\dot{4}$ into a fraction.

$n = 0.444...$

$10n = 4.444...$

$10n - n = 4.444... - 0.444... = \square$

$9n = \square$

$n = \square$

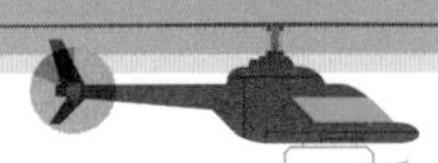

14 Change these recurring decimals into fractions.

a $0.\dot{7}$ **b** $0.\dot{6}$ **c** $0.\dot{5}\dot{4}$

$n = 0.5454...$

$100n = 54.5454...$

$100n - n = 54.5454... - 0.5454... = \square$

$99n = \square$

$n = \square$

Q14a hint

Follow the steps in Q13.

Trial and improvement

1 Use trial and improvement to solve $x^2 = 42$ to one decimal place.

x	x^2	Comment
6.4	40.96	too small
6.5	42.25	too big
6.45	41.6025	too small

Try a value between 6.4 and 6.5

Copy this number line.

40.96 41.6025 42.25

6.4 6.45 6.5

Shade the part of the line where x must be.
What do all the values in this part round to, to one decimal place?

2 Use trial and improvement to solve $x^2 = 73$ to one decimal place.
Copy and complete the table.

x	x^2	Comment
8	64	too small

Start with 8 because you know that 8^2 is close to 73

3 Use trial and improvement to solve these equations to one decimal place.

a $x^2 = 93$ **b** $x^2 = 103$ **c** $x^2 = 131$

4 Use trial and improvement to solve these equations to one decimal place.

a $x^2 + 3 = 36$ **b** $x^2 + 6 = 62$

c $x^2 - 11 = 49$ **d** $x^2 - 8 = 132$

Q4 Strategy hint

You can rearrange the equation if it helps.
$x^2 = \square$

5 Use trial and improvement to solve these equations to one decimal place.

a $x^3 = 85$ **b** $x^3 = 100$ **c** $x^3 + 15 = 98$

Q5 Strategy hint

Learn your cube numbers!
You should know that $1^3 = 1$, $2^3 = 8$, $3^3 = 27$, $4^3 = 64$, $5^3 = 125$, $10^3 = 1000$

Proportion

1 Modelling A gardener charges £60 for four hours' work and £105 for 7 hours' work. Are her charges in proportion to length of time worked?

2 Modelling A plumber charges £45 for 2 hours' work and £55 for 3 hours' work. Are his charges in proportion to the length of time worked?

3 Modelling / Real A garden centre sells Christmas trees for £15 per metre. Is the price of a tree in proportion to its height?

Q1 hint

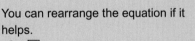

£60

1 hr	1 hr	1 hr	1 hr

How much is this for 1 hour? Multiply it by 7. Is this her charge for 7 hours?

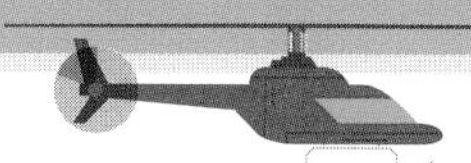

4 Real / Modelling The prices of fertiliser at a garden centre are £2.50 for 5 kg or £8.50 for 20 kg.
Is the price of fertiliser proportional to the weight?

Q4 hint
Find the price for 1 kg.

5 A and B are in direct proportion.

A	B
5	3
10	X
Y	24

Find the missing values X and Y in this table.

Q5 hint

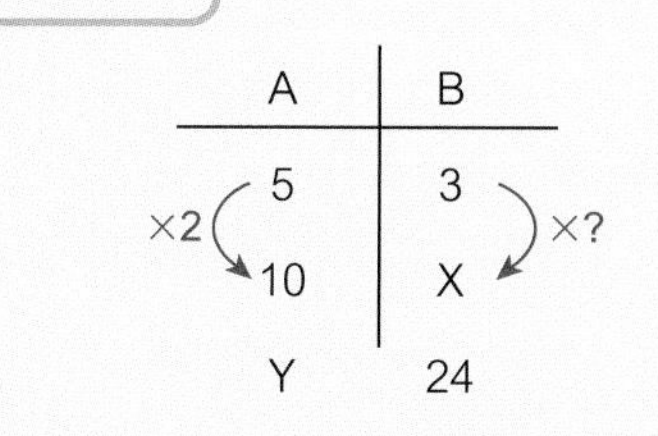

6 P and Q are in direct proportion.

P	Q
3	4
	5

Find the missing value.

Q6 hint
3 : 4
: 1
: 5

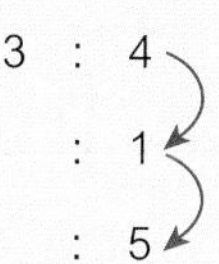

7 The values of A and B are in direct proportion.

A	B
6	9
12	W
X	24
Y	36
30	Z

Find the missing numbers W, X, Y and Z.

Q7 hint
Write pairs of numbers in table as ratios, as in Q5 and Q6.

8 I can exchange £80 for 1040 Hong Kong dollars (HKD).

a How many HKD can I buy with £1?

b Copy and complete this equation relating HKD to £.
h = □*p*, where *h* is HKD and *p* is pounds

c How many HKD can I buy with £150?

9 I can exchange £30 for 5760 Icelandic kroner.
How many kroner can I buy with £75?

Simultaneous equations

1 Find the values of x and y that satisfy these pairs of equations.

a $3x + y = 10$
$y = 2x$

b $2x + y = 20$
$y = 2x$

c $4x + y = 18$
$y = 5x$

d $x + 3y = 15$
$x = 2y$

Q1 hint
The values of x and y that work in the first equation must also work in the second. You need to find x and y.

Q1a hint
$3x + y = 10$
Replace y with $2x$ from the other equation.
Solve for x and use it to find y.

2 Find the values of x and y that satisfy these pairs of equations.

a $3x + y = 9$
$4x - y = 5$

b $5x + y = 21$
$4x - y = 15$

c $2x + y = 11$
$3x - y = 4$

d $6x + y = 20$
$4x - y = 0$

e $3x + 2y = 32$
$3x - 2y = 4$

f $5x + 2y = 43$
$4x - 2y = 2$

Q2 Strategy hint
Adding both equations together will cancel out y in these examples. Remember to add all like terms together.

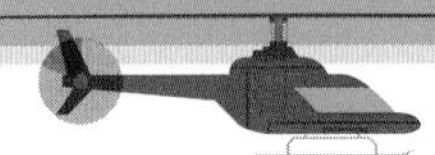

3 Real / Modelling On a trip to a theme park, Graham buys 1 adult and 4 child tickets. This costs him £81.
Adult tickets are twice the price of child tickets.

a Write an equation that shows what Graham paid.

b Copy and compete the equation that shows the relationship between adult and child tickets.

$x = \square y$

c Use your equations to find the cost of adult and child tickets.

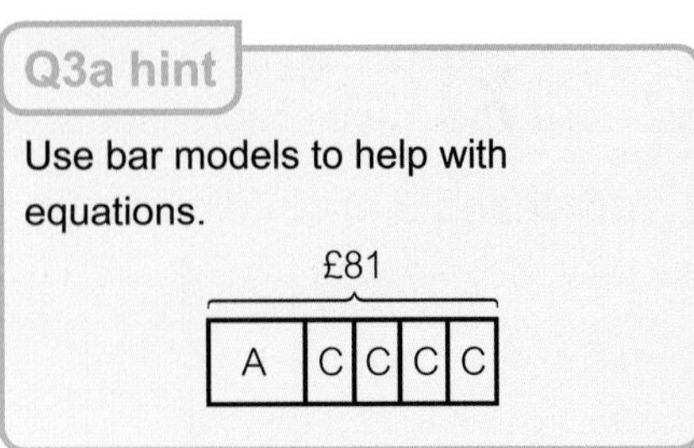

Q3a hint
Use bar models to help with equations.
£81
A
C
C
C
C

4 Real / Modelling On a trip to the circus, Paula spends £98 on tickets for 2 adults and 3 children.
If adult tickets are twice the price of child tickets, how much are adult and child tickets?

Enrichment

1 Two music download websites have different pricing structures.
Website A charges 49p per download with a monthly fee of £1.
If you buy 10 tracks in a month you get the 11th free.
Website B charges 59p per download only.
Three friends discuss which website is better value for money.
Match their statements to the number of tracks they buy per month.

Rachel: 'Website A is better value.'	8 tracks
Anita: 'Website B is better value'	20 tracks
Peter: 'Both websites cost the same.'	10 tracks

2 Decide which of these are identities and which are equations.
Write = or ≡ for each one.

a $x + 5 \square 11$
b $3x \square x + x + x$
c $5x \square 3x + 2x$
d $5x \square 3x + 2$
e $2(x + 1) \square 2x + 2$
f $2(x + 1) \square 14$
g $2 + x \square x + 2$
h $x - 2 \square 2 - x$

Q2 hint
If you can solve to find x, it's an equation (=).
If it is always true, it is an identity (≡).

Reflect

3 **Reflect** For these Strengthen lessons, copy and complete these sentences:

I found questions ______ easiest. They were on _________ (list the topics).

I found questions ________ most difficult. I still need help with ________ (list the topics).

6 Extend

You will:
- Extend your understanding with problem-solving.

1 Problem-solving Shape A is 3 times the area of shape B.

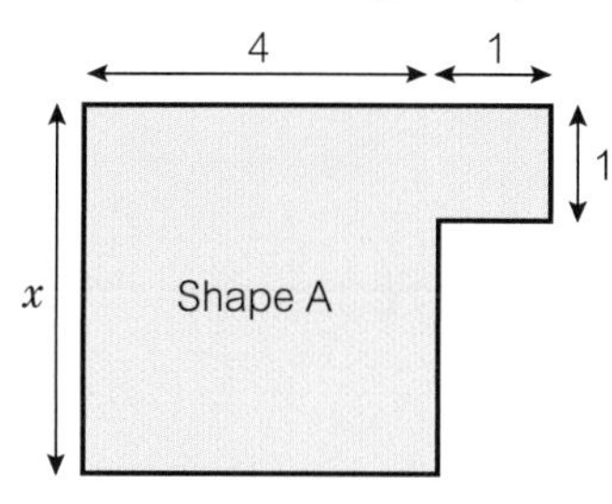

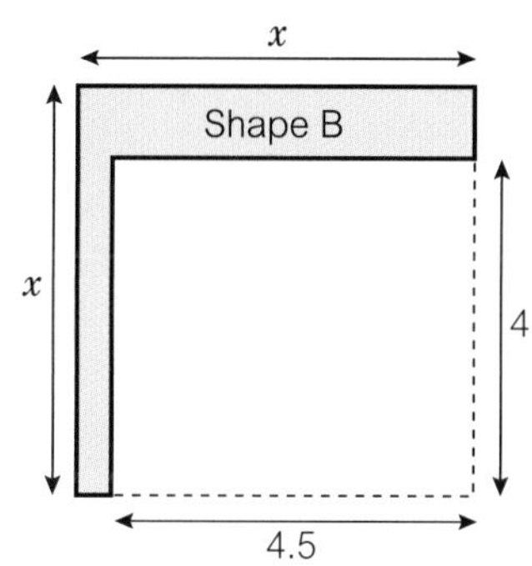

Write an equation using the areas.
Solve it to find length x.

Q1 hint

$\frac{\text{Area A}}{3}$ = Area B

2 Solve these equations.

a $\frac{5x + 1}{3} = -5x + 7$

b $\frac{-3x - 3}{4} = -5x - 22$

c $\frac{8x - 6}{5} = 2x - 4$

d $\frac{-5x + 3}{3} = -3 - 3x$

3 Solve these equations.

a $\frac{3x}{2} = \frac{4}{3}$

b $\frac{3x + 4}{2} = \frac{5x - 3}{3}$

c $\frac{2x + 1}{3} = \frac{6x - 2}{4}$

d $\frac{8x - 2}{5} = \frac{6x + 4}{3}$

e $\frac{3x + 5}{6} = \frac{9x - 4}{4}$

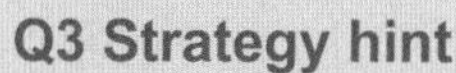

Q3 Strategy hint

Multiply both sides of the equation by the lowest common multiple of the denominators to remove the fractions.

4 Real This table shows distances between cities, in miles and km.

a Calculate the missing distances A, B, C and D.

From	To	Miles	Kilometres
London	Paris	210	336
New York	Los Angeles	A	3932
Birmingham	Wolverhampton	B	20
Berlin	Munich	310	C
Beijing	Shanghai	613	D

b It takes 1 hour 15 minutes to fly from Berlin to Munich.
Work out the average speed in

i miles per hour

ii metres per second.

5 The formula $a = \frac{v - u}{t}$ is used to calculate the acceleration of an object where v is the final velocity, u the initial velocity and t is the time taken.
The acceleration of an object is 2 m/s^2, the final velocity is 20 m/s and the time taken is 6 seconds. What was the initial velocity of the object?

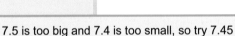

Q5 Literacy hint
Velocity is the speed of an object in a certain direction.
The initial velocity is the starting velocity.

6 **Modelling** Josh thinks of a number. He adds 3 to it and multiplies the result by 4. Then he divides this new number by 5.
He finds that he gets the same result by doubling the same original number, adding 2 to it, trebling this number, then dividing the result by 6.

a Write an equation to express this.
b Solve the equation to find the number that Josh first thought of.

Worked example

Use trial and improvement to solve $x^2 + 3x = 78$ to two decimal places. Copy and complete the table.

x	$x^2 + 3x$	Comment
7.5	78.75	too big
7.4	76.96	too small
7.45	77.8525	too small
7.46	78.0316	too big
7.455	77.942...	too small

7.5 is too big and 7.4 is too small, so try 7.45

The solution is between 7.45 and 7.46. To find the answer to two decimal places, you need to know which is closer, so try 7.455

7.455 is too small. This means that the solution is closer to 7.46 than 7.45

The solution is $x = 7.46$ to two decimal places.

7 For each equation, use trial and improvement to find the value of x to two decimal places.

a $x^3 + 14 = 27$
b $x^3 + 4x = 93$

8 A box is made from a cube of side length x with a cuboid of volume 86 cm^3 attached to it. The volume of the whole box is 1244 cm^3.
Use trial and improvement to find the length of x to one decimal place.

9 A rectangular field has an area of 432 m^2 and sides of length x and $x - 2$
How long is the shorter side, to two decimal places?

10 Variable x is proportional to the square of y.
You can write this as $x = ky^2$
When x is 20, y is 2.

a Work out the value of k.
b Work out the value of x when y is 5.
c Work out the value of y when x is 80.

Topic links: Ratio, Geometry, Compound measures

Subject links: Science (Q10)

11 Shapes B and C are enlargements of Shape A.

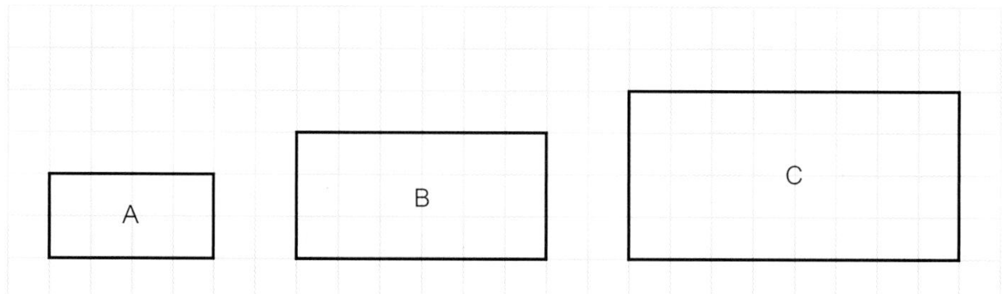

a Copy and complete this table.

Shape	Length (l)	Width (w)	Area (A)
A			
B			
C			

b Write an equation to express the relationship between the length and the width.

c Write an equation to express the relationship between the length and the area.

12 In each of these questions, $y = kx^2$.
Give each value of y to two decimal places.

a When $y = 3$, $x = 18$. What will be the value of y when $x = 45$?

b When $y = 4$, $x = 15$. What will be the value of y when $x = 30$?

c When $y = 8$, $x = 25$. What will be the value of y when x is 49?

13 **STEM / Modelling** A stone is dropped from a tall building.
The distance it falls is proportional to the square of the time it takes to fall.
If the stone falls 19.6 metres after 2 seconds, how far will it fall after 4 seconds?

14 $2x + 3y = 12$ and $4x - 3y = 6$ are a pair of simultaneous equations.

a Add the equations together.

b What happens to the value of y?

c Solve your equation for x.

d Using the value of x, find the value of y.

15 Copy and complete the steps to solve this pair of simultaneous equations.

$3x + 2y = 14$ ①

$x - y = 3$ ②

a Multiply equation ② by 2 to give equation ③.

$2x - 2y = \square$

b Add equations ③ and ① together. Solve to find x.

c Substitute your value for x into one of the equations to find y.

d Check your answers using the other equation.

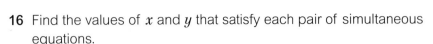

16 Find the values of x and y that satisfy each pair of simultaneous equations.

a $5x + 2y = 26$
$x - y = 1$

b $3x + 4y = 46$
$2x + 2y = 26$

c $3x + 2y = 21$
$5x + 3y = 34$

d $5x + 2y = 21$
$3x - 5y = -37$

Q16 hint

You can multiply whole equations by a number.
You can add whole equations together or subtract one from another to eliminate x or y.

17 **Problem-solving / Modelling** Twice the sum of two numbers is 32 and their difference is 3.
What are the two numbers?

Q17 hint

Create a pair of simultaneous equations that represents this situation.

18 **Real / Modelling** Bob used his mobile phone to make 5 minutes of calls and send 18 texts. This cost him £2.44.
Amie is on the same price plan and made 10 minutes of calls and sent 12 texts. This cost her £2.96.
How much does the phone company charge for

a 1 minute of talk time

b 1 text?

19 **Real / Modelling** Two runners start from the same place at the same time and run at a constant pace.
If they run in the same direction they will be 6 miles apart after 3 hours.
If they run in opposite directions they will be 20 miles apart after 2 hours.
What is the speed, in mph, of each of the two runners?

20 2 men take 3 days to paint a room.

a How long would it take 1 man to paint the same room?

b How long would it take 3 men to paint the same room?

Q20a hint

Will 1 man take more time or less time than 2 men?

21 2 florists take 4 hours to arrange all the flowers for a wedding.
How long would it take 3 florists to arrange the same flowers?

22 A 5-piece band takes 4 minutes to play a song.
How long would a 7-piece band take to play the same song?

Investigation **Problem-solving**

The Fibonacci series is a famous number sequence.
Start with the numbers 0 and 1. Find the next number by adding the previous two numbers together. Continue like this.
0, 1, 1, 2, 3, 5, 8, …

1 Call the 1st number a, and the 2nd number b. Then the 3rd number is $a + b$. Write expressions for all the numbers up to the 10th term.

Anya uses the same rule for generating the sequence but starts with different numbers,. Her 7th number is −1 and her 10th number is −5.

2 What were her two starting numbers?

3 Create similar sequences using different rules, for example, the 3rd number could be twice the 1st number added to the 2nd.

4 Create expressions for each of the first 10 numbers, then create puzzles for other students to solve.

Reflect

23 **Reflect** Look back at Q9. What did you do first to answer this question? Why?
Look back at Q17. What did you do first to answer this question? Why?
Look back at Q19. What did you do first to answer this question? Why?
For each question, what clues helped you decide what to do first?

6 Unit test

Log how you did on your Student Progression Chart.

1 Decide which of these is an expression, equation, function or formula.
A $5x + 4 = 17$ B $A = bh$ C $4x - 6$ D $x \rightarrow 3x$

2 Which sign, = or ≡, will make each statement correct.
a $3x + 2x$ □ $5x$
b $3x + 4$ □ 11
c $2x - 3$ □ 7
d $3(x + 1)$ □ $3x + 3$

3 In an experiment, Emma records the time taken to travel different distances.
a Write a formula to show the relationship. The time and distance are in direct proportion.
b Use your formula to calculate the time it would take to travel 54 m.

Time (t)	Distance(d)
3 seconds	13.5 m
7 seconds	31.5 m
9 seconds	40.5 m

4 Solve these equations.
a $\frac{8x - 3}{2} = 2x + 1$
b $\frac{6x + 3}{4} = 2x - 3$

5 Solve these equations.
a $x^2 + 5 = 21$
b $\frac{x^2}{3} = 12$

6 The values of a and b are in direct proportion.
Use the equality of ratios to find the missing values, X and Y.

a	b
12	60
X	50
65	Y

7 Use trial and improvement to find the value of x to one decimal place.
$x^3 + 7 = 49$

8 Solve $3(x - 4) = -2(x + 11)$

9 Solve this pair of simultaneous equations.
$5x + 2y = 18$
$y = 2x$

10 Solve these inequalities. Show the solutions on a number line.
a $x + 6 > 15$ b $4x + 5 < 12$

11 The formula $a = \frac{v - u}{t}$ is used to calculate acceleration of an object, where $v$is the final velocity, u is the initial velocity and t is the time taken.
The acceleration of an object is 3 m/s^2, the initial velocity is 5 m/s and the time taken is 5 s.
What is the final velocity of the object?

12 Solve this pair of simultaneous equations.
$3x + 2y = 21$
$4x - 2y = 14$

13 Use trial and improvement to find the value of x to one decimal place.
$x^3 + 2x = 24$

14 Solve this inequality.
$3(x + 4) < 13$

15 Convert these recurring decimals to fractions.
a $0.\dot{2}$
b $0.\dot{7}\dot{3}$

16 Solve this pair of simultaneous equations.
$2x + 5y = 24$
$x + 3y = 13$

17 Solve this equation.
$$\frac{3x + 5}{2} = \frac{4x - 3}{3}$$

18 $p = kq^2$
a Use the first pair of values to find k.
b Work out the missing values, A, B and C, in this table.

p	q
704	8
A	6
1859	B
C	9

Challenge

19 In each of these squares, different combinations of the three values $a = 3$, $b = 5$ and $c = 4$ have been used to generate numbers.
Suggest expressions for each number, using a, b and c, that would give the correct value in each of these squares. Use each letter at least once.

A 12	B 15	C 9
D 2	E 125	F 6
G 4	H 20	I 11

For example, this expression would work for square A.
$bc - (a + b) = 5 \times 4 - (3 + 5) = 12$

20 **Reflect** This unit is called ‘Equations, inequalities and proportionality’.
List at least two new things you have learned about each of these three mathematics topics.
Which of these things did you like learning about most? Why?
Which of these things did you like learning about least? Why?

Reflect

7 Circles, Pythagoras and prisms

MASTER

Check P175 | Strengthen P177 | Extend P182 | Test P187

7.1 Circumference of a circle

You will learn to:

- Calculate the circumference of a circle
- Estimate calculations involving pi (π)
- Solve problems involving the circumference of a circle.

CONFIDENCE

Why learn this?
A bicycle speedometer uses the circumference of the wheels to work out the distance travelled, and the journey time to work out the speed.

Fluency

- Round 2.6637 to
  1 d.p.   2 d.p.   3 d.p.
- Round 9.458 m to the nearest cm.
- Round 4758 m to one significant figure.

Explore
How many turns of a can opener are needed to remove the lid?

Exercise 7.1

1 Solve these equations.
Give your answers correct to two significant figures, where necessary.

a $2r = 17.4$ **b** $3.14d = 65$ **c** $\frac{C}{6.28} = 15$ **d** $\frac{2w}{3} = 12$

2 $\boxed{F = 3ab}$

$a = 5.1$ and $b = 7$. Use the formula to find F.

3 Write down the number of significant figures of each measurement.

a 2.7 m **b** 0.04 cm **c** 32 000 km **d** 2.06 km

4 **a** Draw a circle.

b Use this information to mark the points O, A, B and T on your diagram.
O is the **centre**.
OT is a **radius**.
AB is a **diameter**.

c Mark any other point S on the **circumference**.

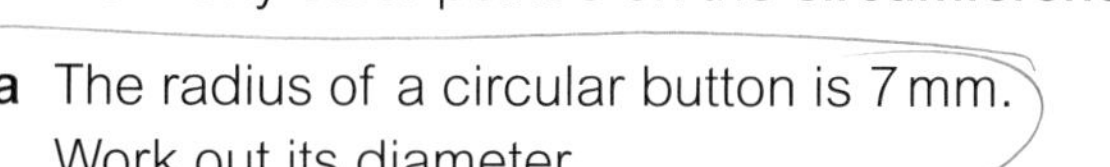

5 **a** The radius of a circular button is 7 mm.
Work out its diameter.

b The diameter of a circular Mexican hat is 42 cm. What is its radius?

c **i** r is the radius of a circle. Write a formula to give its diameter, d.
ii d is the diameter of a circle. Write a formula to give its radius, r.

d The 22 balls of a snooker game are placed along the edge of the table, touching each other. Their total length is 1.115 m.
Work out the radius of a snooker ball, in mm.

Warm up

Key point

The **circumference** (C) is the perimeter of a circle.
The **centre** of a circle is marked using a dot.
The **radius** (r) is the distance from the centre to the circumference.
The plural of radius is **radii**.
The **diameter** (d) is a line from one edge to another through the centre.

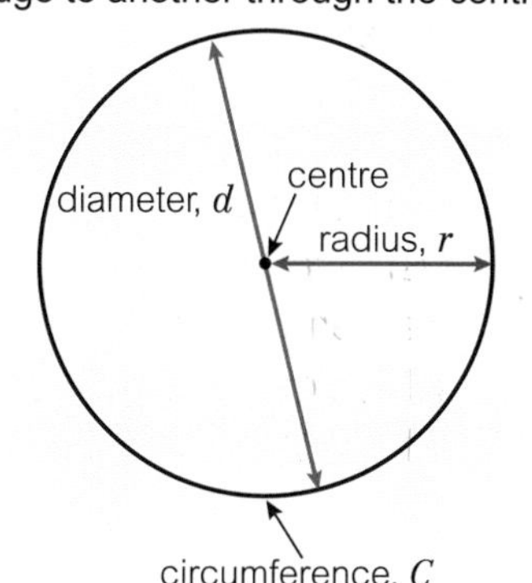

6 Real / Reasoning The table shows the diameters and approximate circumferences of some fishing reels.

Diameter, d (mm)	Circumference, C (mm)	$\frac{C}{d}$
51	160	
57	179	
65	204	
71	223	

a Copy and complete the table.
Round the values of $\frac{C}{d}$ to two decimal places.

b What do you notice about the value of $\frac{C}{d}$? What does this mean?

c Copy and complete the formula $C = \square \times d$.

d Use your formula to estimate the circumference of a fishing reel with diameter 77 mm.

> **Key point**
> The Greek letter π (pronounced pi) is a special number 3.141 592 653 5…
> To find the circumference C of a circle with diameter d, use the formula $C = \pi d$.
> If you know the radius r you can use the equivalent formula $C = 2\pi r$.
> Use the π key on your calculator.

7 Work out the circumference of each circle. Round your answers to an appropriate degree of accuracy.

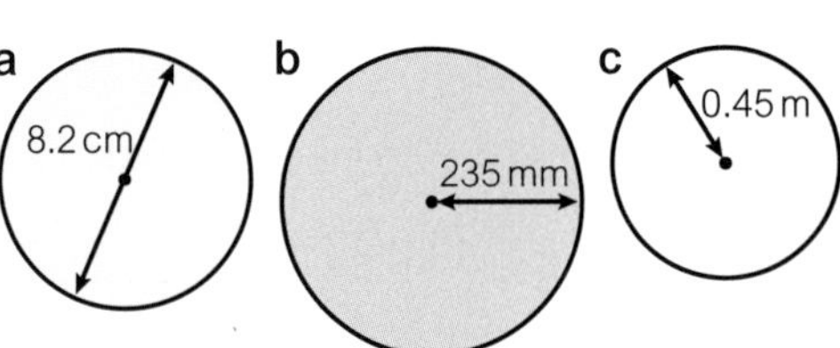

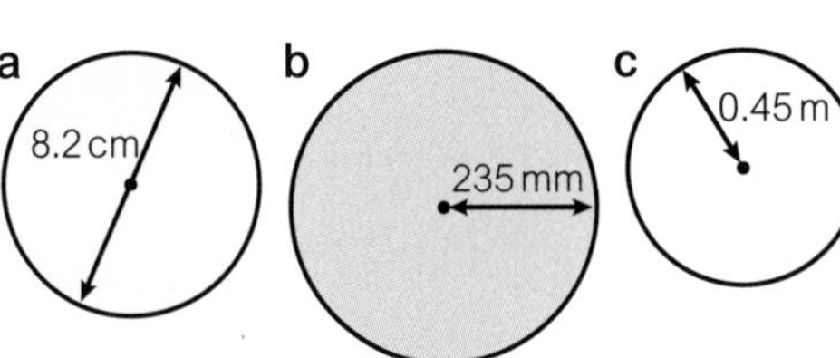

Discussion Do you need two formulae: one for the radius and one for the diameter?

> **Q7a hint**
> 8.2 cm is measured to the nearest mm (or one decimal place) so your answer should have the same degree of accuracy. Use a sensible approximation for π.

8 STEM Calculate the circumference of each circular object. Round your answers to an appropriate degree of accuracy.

a The lens of a mobile phone camera with a diameter of 3.85 mm.

b A bass drum with a diameter of 56 cm.

c A GPS satellite's circular orbit with a diameter of 53 156 km.

9 Reasoning / Modelling Monty has to estimate the length of edging needed for a circular lawn with a diameter of 9.4 m.
He forgot to bring his calculator to the store.

a Calculate an estimate by rounding the numbers to one significant figure.

b Is your answer an underestimate or an overestimate? Explain why.

c Estimate how much edging Monty should buy.

10 Modelling Europe's largest stone circle is at Avebury in Wiltshire. It has a radius of 210 m.

a Estimate the circumference of the circle.

b Write the circumference in terms of π.

c Calculate the circumference to the nearest metre.

Discussion Which is the most accurate answer?

> **Q10a hint**
> Round the numbers to one significant figure.

> **Q10b hint**
> Your answer should look like $\square\pi$ m.

Investigation Reasoning

1 a Mark a dot on the edge of a 2p coin and align it with the zero mark on a ruler.
b Roll the coin along the ruler to find the circumference of the coin.
c Use the circumference to estimate the diameter of the coin.

2 Make a better estimate by rolling the coin further.

3 Check your estimate using a ruler

4 Explain how you can estimate the diameter of a football or other spherical shape.

Topic links: Direct proportion, Formulae

Subject links: STEM (Q8c)

11 Modelling The string of a yo-yo is wound around a spool of diameter d. When fully wound, the yo-yo rotates 25 times before it reaches the end of the string.

a Write a formula for the length L mm of the string in terms of π.

b Work out the length of the string for a spool of diameter 13 mm. Give your answer in terms of π.

c Is your formula a good model for the length of string? Explain your answer.

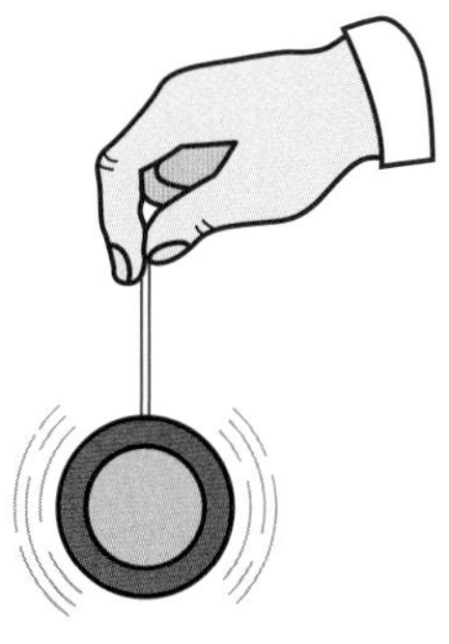

12 Work out the perimeter of this **semicircle**, correct to the nearest cm.

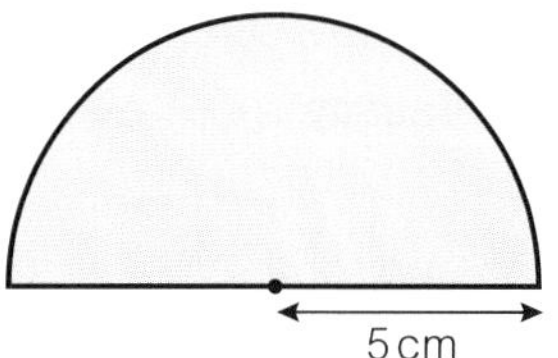

Q12 Literacy hint

Half a circle is called a **semicircle**.

Q12 hint

Find the circumference of half a circle. Add the diameter.

13 a Work out, to two significant figures, the diameter of a circle with circumference

i 20 cm ii 2.5 m

b Work out, to two significant figures, the radius of a circle with circumference

i 150 mm ii 4000 km

Q13a hint

Start by writing the value you know in the formula $C = \pi d$.

14 a i How far does a wheel of radius 48 cm travel in one revolution?

ii How many times will it rotate when travelling a distance of 15 m?

b A tractor wheel travels 4 m in 1 revolution. What is its radius? Round your answer to an appropriate degree of accuracy.

Discussion What is an appropriate degree of accuracy?

15 Problem-solving / Modelling A daredevil motorcyclist drives around a circular wall of death of radius 9 m.
The wheels of her motorcycle have a diameter of 0.85 m.
How many times will each wheel rotate for each trip around the wall?

Discussion Is a calculator necessary for this question?

Q15 Strategy hint

Work out each part of the problem separately.

16 Problem-solving The diagram shows a semicircular Victorian door window frame. Work out the total length of the frame, including all of the radii.

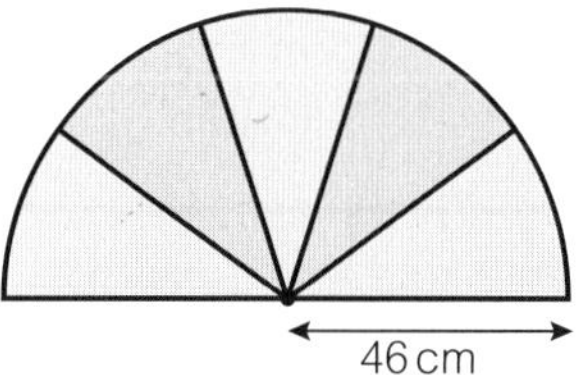

17 **Explore** How many turns of a can opener are needed to remove the lid?
Is it easier to explore this question now you have completed the lesson?
What further information do you need to be able to answer this?

18 **Reflect** Close your book and write down as many facts about circles as you can.
Make sure you include all the facts you remember from this lesson.
Then open your book again and look back at the lesson.
Did you miss any facts? If so, add them to your list.
Did you make any spelling mistakes? If so, correct them.

Explore

Reflect

7.2 Area of a circle

You will learn to:
- Calculate the area of a circle
- Solve problems involving the area of a circle.

CONFIDENCE

Why learn this?
You need to know the area of a floor to refloor it.

Fluency
Work out
- 8^2
- 30^2
- 0.4^2
- $\sqrt{36}$
- $\sqrt{400}$

How can you find the diameter if you know the radius?

Explore
How much does it cost to lay a circular wood floor for a gazebo?

Exercise 7.2

Warm up

1 Substitute into each formula to work out the unknown quantity. Give your answers to two significant figures, where necessary.

a $A = 3r^2$, where $r = 4$
b $s = 9.81t^2$, where $t = 12$
c $r = \sqrt{A}$, where $A = 14$
d $d = \sqrt{2A}$, where $A = 0.75$

2 A radio transmitter transmits up to 10 miles distance. Sketch a diagram to show the area covered.

Key point
The formula for the area A of a circle with radius r is $A = \pi r^2$.

3 Work out the area of each circle.
Round your answers to an appropriate degree of accuracy.

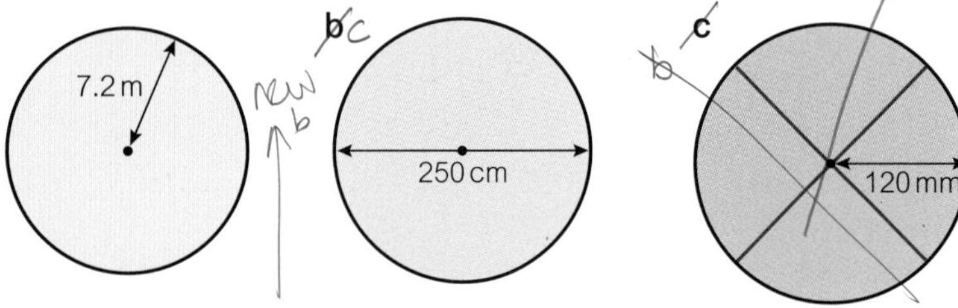

Q3 hint
Use the π key on your calculator.

Q3a hint
Round your answer to the nearest $0.1\,m^2$.

4 **a** Estimate the area of each circular object.
- **i** The head of a screw with a radius of 2.8 mm.
- **ii** A pizza plate with a diameter of 32 cm.
- **iii** The Mach crater on the Moon with a diameter of 180 km.

b Calculate the areas in part **a** using the π key of your calculator. Round your answers to two significant figures.

c Work out the area of the Mach crater in m^2. Give your answer in standard form, correct to two significant figures.

Q4a hint
What is an easy estimate for π?

Q4c hint
$\square \times 10^{\square}$

Topic links: Standard form, Loci, Direct proportion, Measures

Subject links: STEM (Q10)

5 Problem-solving / Modelling The diagram shows a plastic tray with holes for holding paper cups.
Work out the area of plastic in the tray.

Q5 Strategy hint
First calculate the area of one hole.

6 The diagram shows a semicircle.
Work out its area in terms of π.

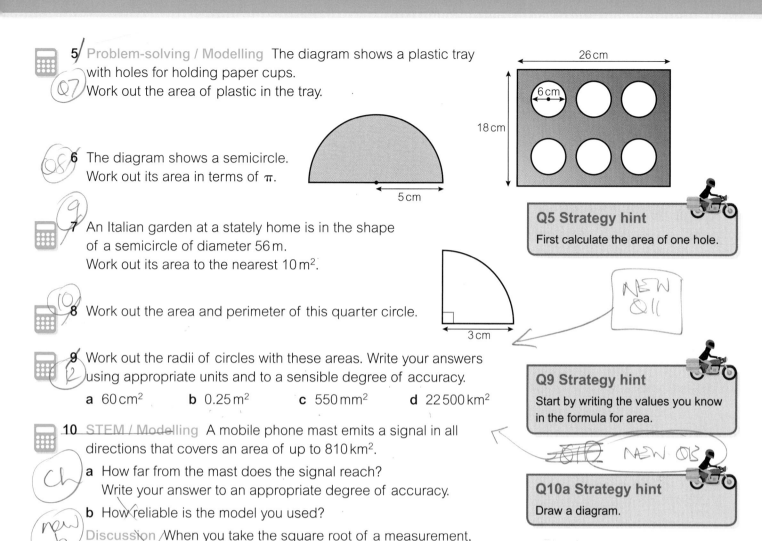

7 An Italian garden at a stately home is in the shape of a semicircle of diameter 56 m.
Work out its area to the nearest $10\,m^2$.

8 Work out the area and perimeter of this quarter circle.

9 Work out the radii of circles with these areas. Write your answers using appropriate units and to a sensible degree of accuracy.

a $60\,cm^2$ **b** $0.25\,m^2$ **c** $550\,mm^2$ **d** $22\,500\,km^2$

Q9 Strategy hint
Start by writing the values you know in the formula for area.

10 STEM / Modelling A mobile phone mast emits a signal in all directions that covers an area of up to $810\,km^2$.

a How far from the mast does the signal reach?
Write your answer to an appropriate degree of accuracy.

b How reliable is the model you used?

Discussion When you take the square root of a measurement, why should you write the answer more accurately than the measurement itself?

Q10a Strategy hint
Draw a diagram.

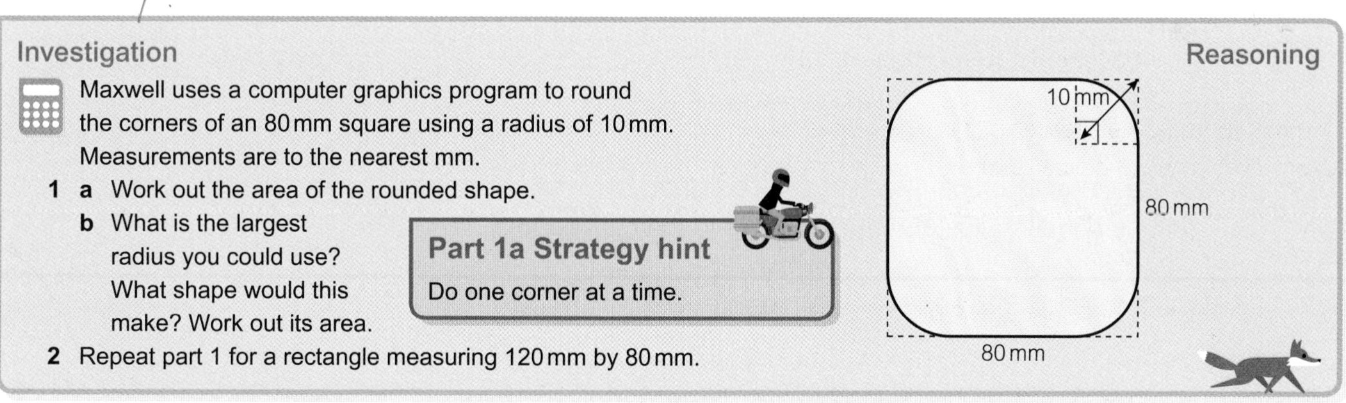

Investigation Reasoning

Maxwell uses a computer graphics program to round the corners of an 80 mm square using a radius of 10 mm. Measurements are to the nearest mm.

1 **a** Work out the area of the rounded shape.
b What is the largest radius you could use? What shape would this make? Work out its area.

2 Repeat part 1 for a rectangle measuring 120 mm by 80 mm.

Part 1a Strategy hint
Do one corner at a time.

11 **Explore** How much does it cost to lay a circular wood floor for a gazebo? Is it easier to explore this question now you have completed the lesson? What further information do you need to be able to answer this?

12 **Reflect** Look back at the investigation. Write down the steps you took to answer it. Explain why you did each one.

Imagine you had to do the investigation again with different measurements. Would you follow the same steps? If not, what would you change? Why?

Q12 hint
You could start, 'I copied the diagram so that I could write new information on it, as I found it'.

Explore

Reflect

7.3 Pythagoras' theorem

You will learn to:
- Find the length of an unknown side of a right-angled triangle
- Solve problems involving right-angled triangles.

CONFIDENCE

Why learn this? Yacht riggers use Pythagoras' theorem to work out the length of wire to hold up the mast.

Fluency
Work out
- $3^2 + 4^2$
- $5^2 - 4^2$

Explore
How long is the rigging on the world's largest single-masted yacht, Mirabella V?

Exercise 7.3

Warm up

1 Work out these.
Give your answers correct to three significant figures where necessary.
a $7^2 + 14^2$
b $2.5^2 + 4.2^2$
c $120^2 - 72^2$
d $\sqrt{5^2 + 8^2}$
e $\sqrt{3.2^2 - 1.8^2}$

2 Find the positive solution of each equation.
Give your answers correct to three significant figures where necessary.
a $a^2 = 45$
b $a^2 = 324 + 841$
c $a^2 = 6^2 + 5^2$
d $6.25 = b^2 + 2.25$
e $13^2 = b^2 + 12^2$

Key point
The longest side of a right-angled triangle is called the **hypotenuse**.

3 a Draw this triangle on centimetre squared paper.
b i Measure the lengths of the three sides to the nearest mm.
ii What is the length of the **hypotenuse**?
c i Measure the three angles of the triangle.
ii Look at each angle and the length of its opposite side.
What do you notice?

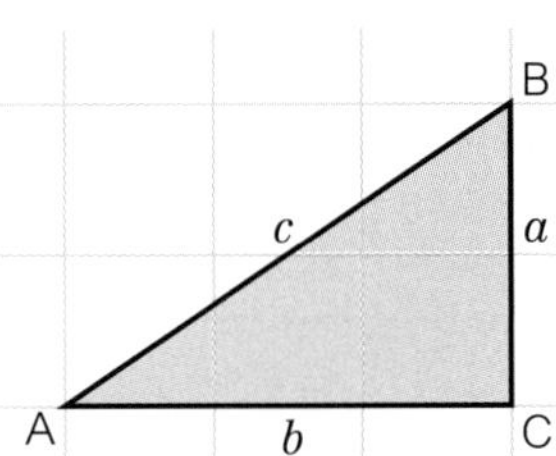

Discussion Will the largest angle in a right-angled triangle always be the right angle?

4 Write down the length of the hypotenuse for each of these triangles.

a 13 cm, 5 cm, 12 cm

b 44 mm, 100 mm, 90 mm

c 2 cm, 7 cm, 7.3 cm

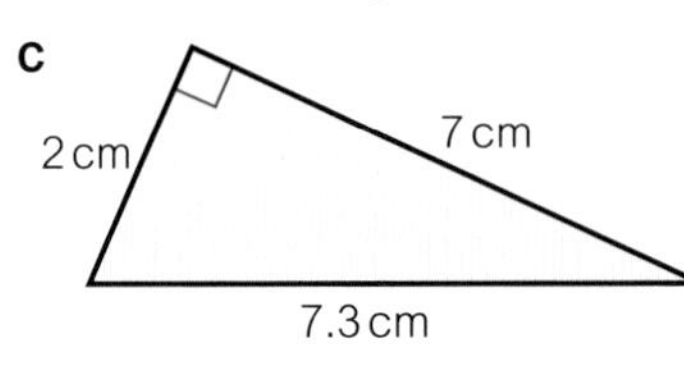

d 1.8 cm, 2.2 cm, 1.3 cm

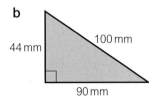

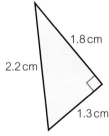

Topic links: Quadratic equations, Formulae, Powers and roots

Subject links: PE (Investigation)

Worked example

Work out the length of the hypotenuse of this right-angled triangle, correct to the nearest mm.

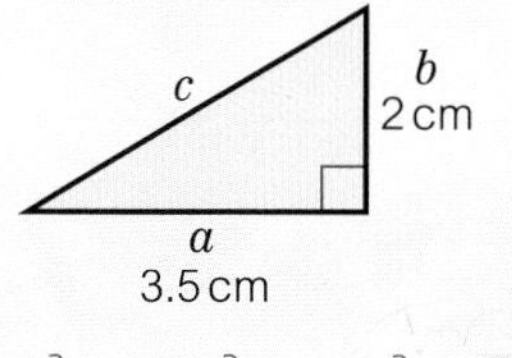

> Sketch the triangle. Label the hypotenuse c and the other sides a and b.
> Substitute $a = 3.5$ and $b = 2$ into the formula for Pythagoras' theorem, $c^2 = a^2 + b^2$.

$$c^2 = a^2 + b^2$$
$$= 3.5^2 + 2^2$$
$$= 12.25 + 4 = 16.25$$
$$c = \sqrt{16.25} = 4.031128874...$$

> Use a calculator to find the square root of c^2.

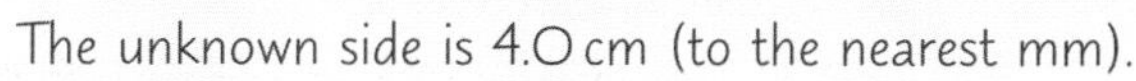

The unknown side is 4.0 cm (to the nearest mm).

> Round to the nearest mm.

Key point

Pythagoras' theorem shows the relationship between the lengths of the three sides of a right-angled triangle.

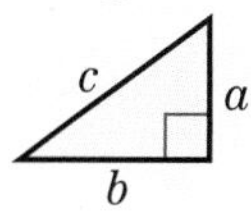

$c^2 = a^2 + b^2$

Discussion Does it matter which way around you label the sides a and b?

5 Work out the length of the hypotenuse in each of these right-angled triangles, correct to the nearest mm.

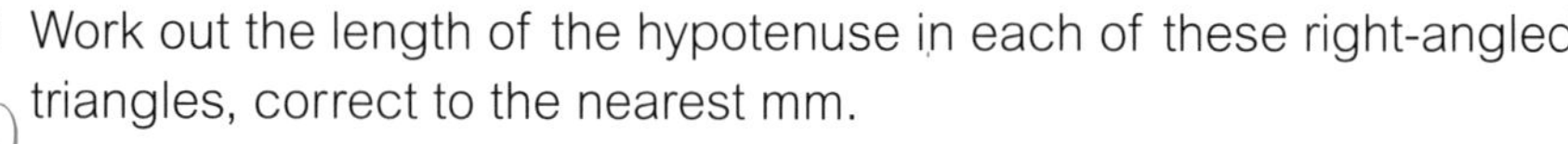

a

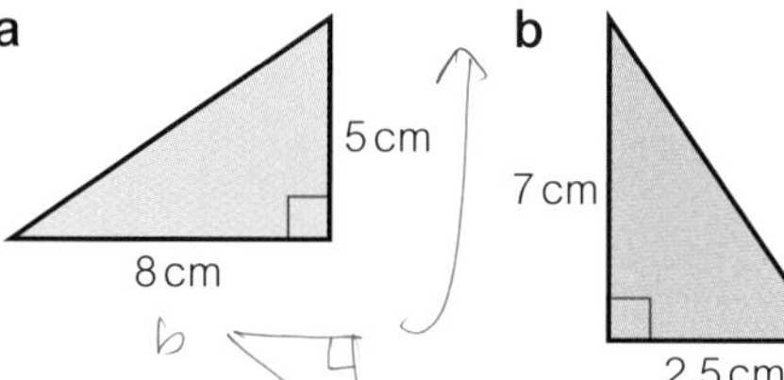

b

c

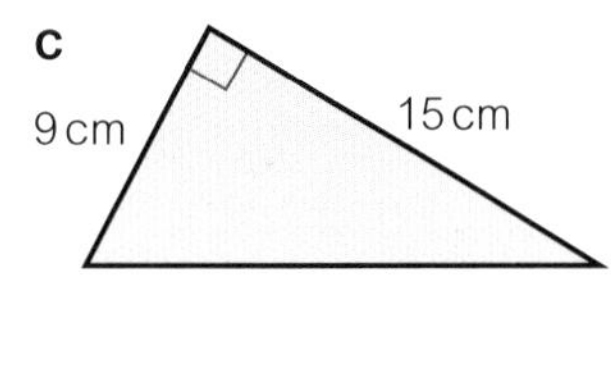

d

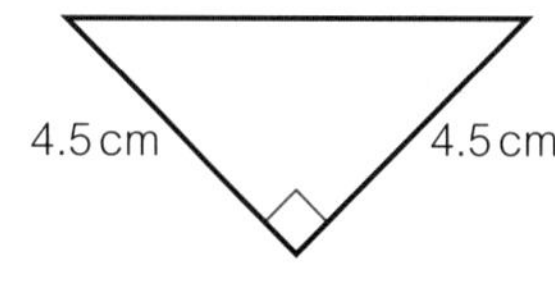

Discussion Do you need to give the negative square root of c?

6 Work out the length of the unknown side of each right-angled triangle. Give your answers to an appropriate degree of accuracy. Part **a** has been started for you.

a

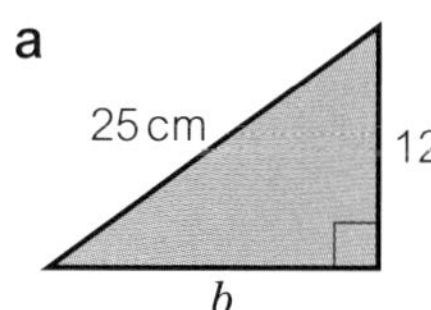

$$25^2 = 12^2 + b^2$$
$$25^2 - \square = b^2$$
$$b = \sqrt{\square}$$

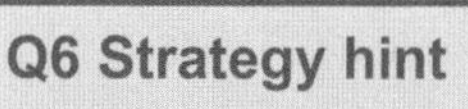

Q6 Strategy hint

Label the sides a, b, c.
Substitute into Pythagoras' theorem $c^2 = a^2 + b^2$. Solve the equation.

b

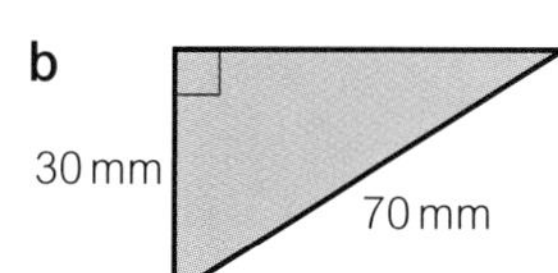

c

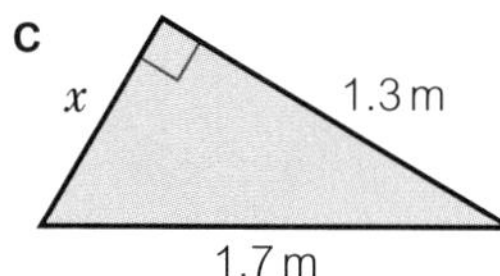

d

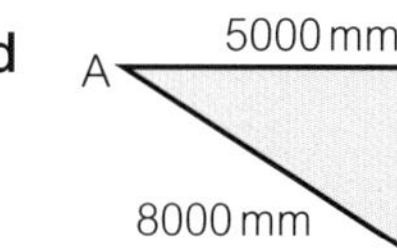

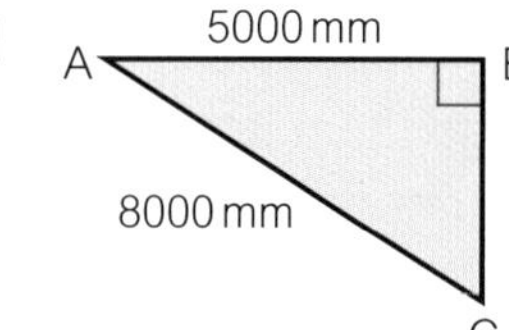

7 **Real / Modelling** The diagram shows a ladder leaning against the wall of a house.

a Sketch the triangle.

b Work out the length of the ladder, to the nearest cm.

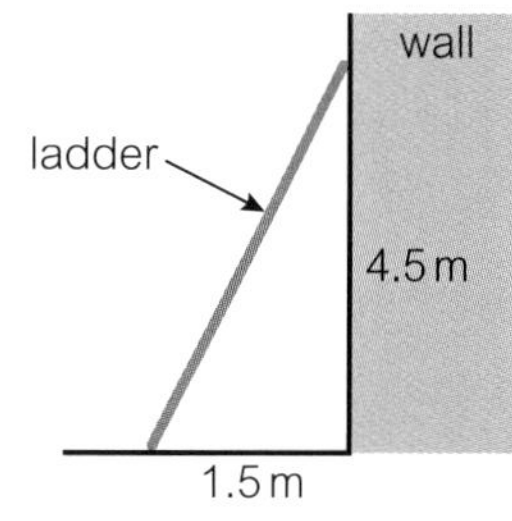

Q7a hint

Label the lengths a, b and c, and the right angle.

8 **Modelling** A person at point A is flying a kite B.
The length of string is 75 m and the kite is 48 m above the ground.

a The kite falls vertically to point C on the ground.
How far is it from point A?

b Is the diagram a good model for flying a kite?
Explain your answer.

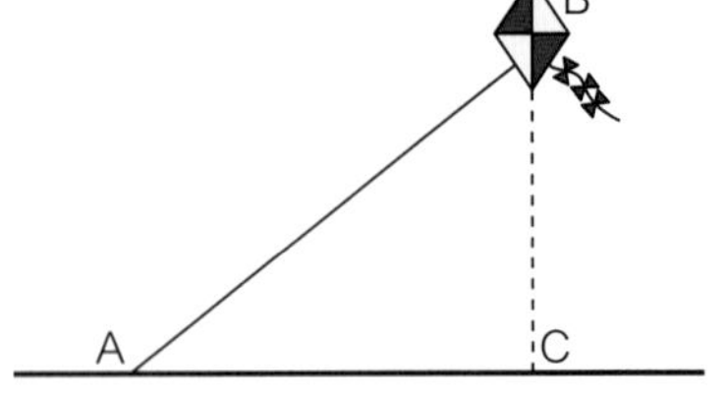

9 The diagram shows a trapezium.
The measurements are correct to the nearest cm.

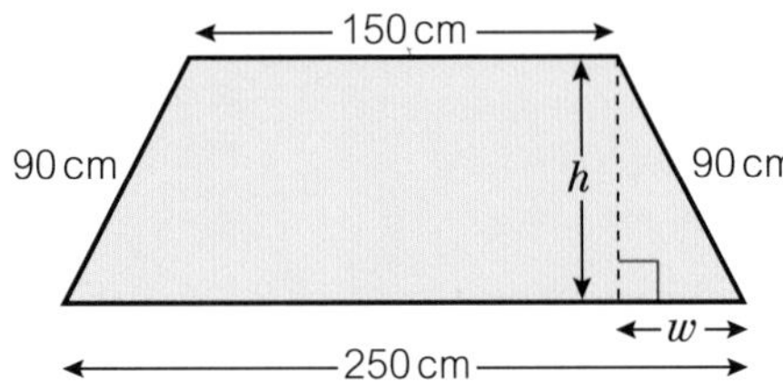

Work out

a the length w

b the height of the trapezium, h

c the area of the trapezium in m^2.

Investigation

Modelling / Problem-solving

1 A football club plans to build a rectangular pitch of length 105 m and width 68 m.
The lengths of the diagonals can be used to check if the rectangle has been marked out accurately.
Work out the length of the diagonal joining two corners, writing your answer

a as a **surd**

b to the nearest m

c to the nearest 10 cm

d to the nearest cm

e correct to five decimal places.

2 **a** Which of your answers is the most accurate? Explain why.

b Which of your answers is the most useful? Explain why.

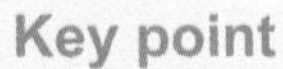

Key point

A **surd** is a square root that cannot be simplified any further.

Explore

10 **Explore** How long is the rigging on the world's largest single-masted yacht, Mirabella V?
Is it easier to explore this question now you have completed the lesson?
What further information do you need to be able to answer this?

Reflect

11 **Reflect** Look at the worked example.
In your own words, list the steps to solve the problem. Use pencil in case you wish to change them later. Also, leave some space between them in case you need to add more steps later.
Look back at Q5. Do your steps work to solve these problems?
If not, change them.
Look back at Q6 and do the same, and then look back at Q8.
Now compare your steps for solving these problems with others in your class. Have you missed out any steps?

Q11 hint

You could write, 'Step 1: label the sides of the triangle a, b and c (hypotenuse)'.

7.4 Prisms and cylinders

You will learn to:
- Calculate the volume and surface area of a right prism
- Calculate the volume and surface area of a cylinder.

CONFIDENCE

Why learn this?
The ice in an ice rink has the shape of a right prism.

Fluency
- What is the formula for the volume of a cuboid?
- How can you find the surface area of a cuboid?
- What is the formula for the area of a circle?

Explore
How much water is frozen to make a circular ice rink?

Exercise 7.4

Warm up

1 Convert
a $4\,m^3$ to cm^3 b $5000\,mm^3$ to cm^3 c $1200\,cm^3$ to litres

Q1a hint
$1\,cm^3 = 1\,ml$

2 Use area formulae to find the area of these shapes.

a
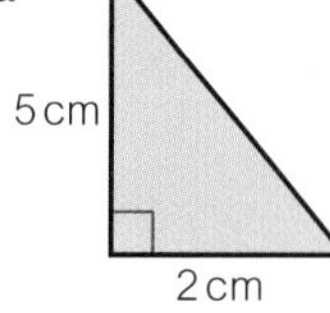

b
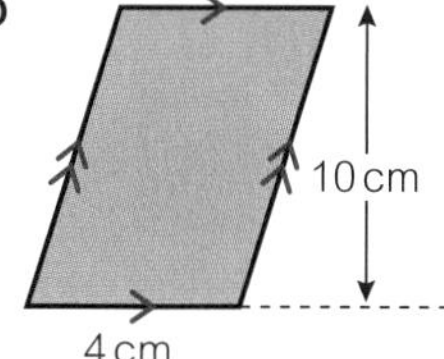

c
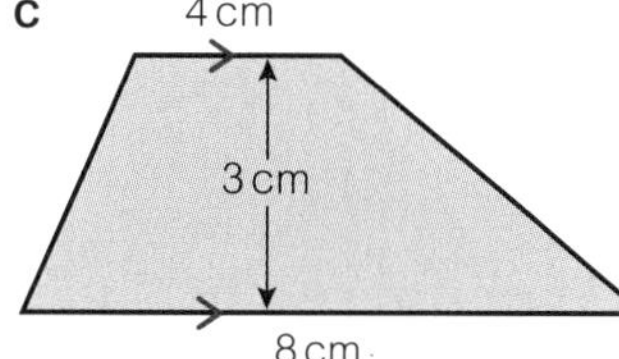

3 a Calculate the volume of each shape.

i
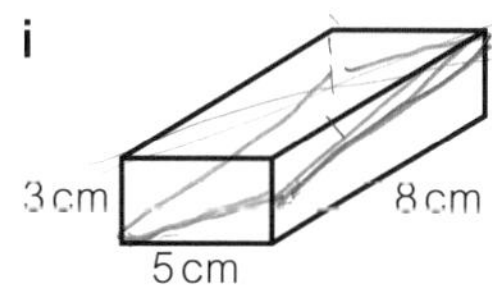

ii

iii
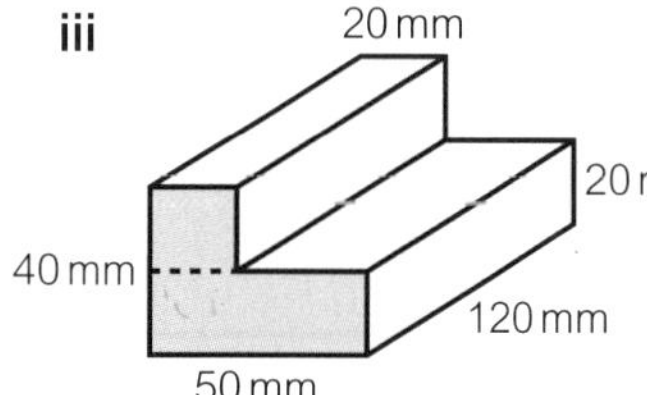

b Calculate the total surface area of shapes **i** and **ii**.

4 Which of these shapes are **right prisms**?
What shapes are their **cross-sections**?

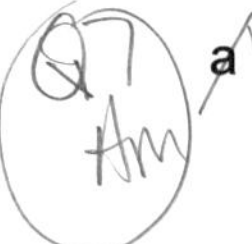

a
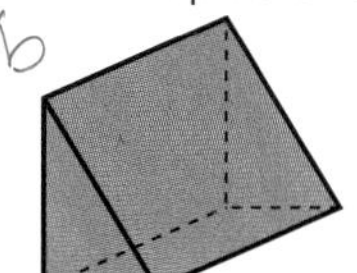

b
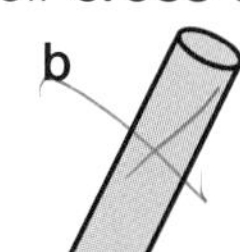

c
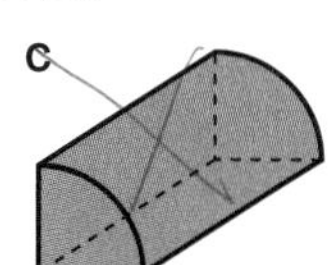

d
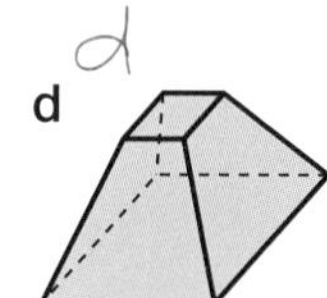

e

f
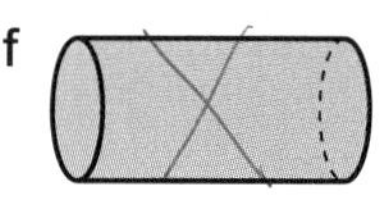

g
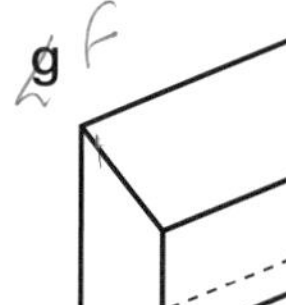
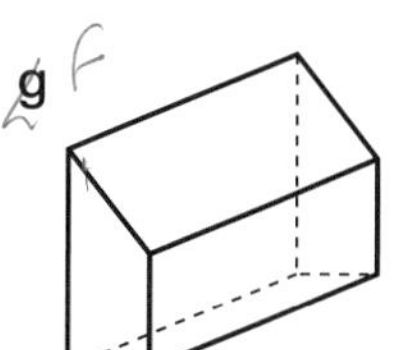

Discussion If you cut a right prism in half, do you get two prisms?

Key point
A **right prism** is a solid shape that has the same **cross-section** throughout its length.

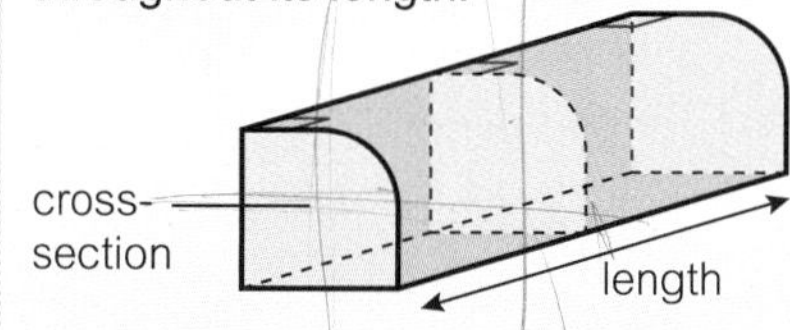

The cross-section can be any flat shape. It is at right angles to the length of the solid.

5 For each shape in Q3
a work out the area of the darker shaded cross-section
b multiply the area of the cross-section by the length of the solid
c compare the result with the volume found in Q3. What do you notice?

Q5c hint
$V = l \times w \times h$
Which part of the formula gives the area of the cross-section?

Worked example

The diagram shows a triangular prism.

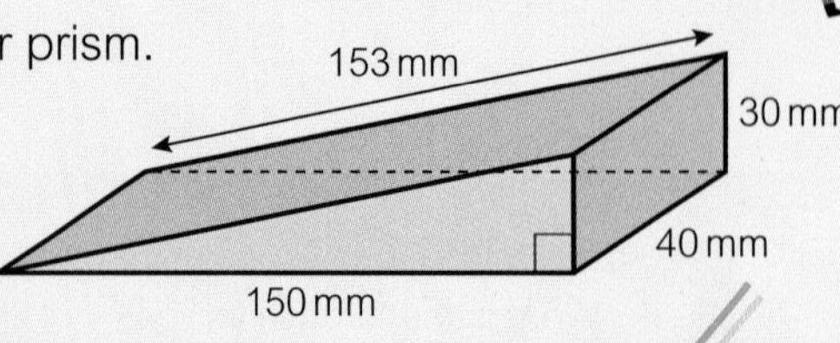

Cross-section is a right-angled triangle.

Length of prism

Sketch the cross-section.

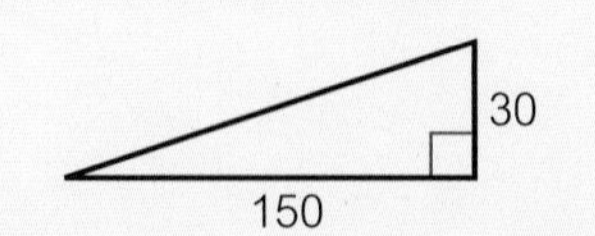

Work out

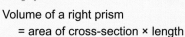

a its volume

area of cross-section = $\frac{1}{2}$ × base × height = 0.5 × 150 mm × 30 mm
= 2250 mm²

volume of prism = area of cross-section × length
= 2250 mm² × 40 mm = 90 000 mm³

90 000 mm³ ÷ 1000 = 90 cm³

Key point
Volume of a right prism
= area of cross-section × length

90 000 has too many figures, so mm is not a sensible unit to use. Convert to cm³ instead.

b its total surface area

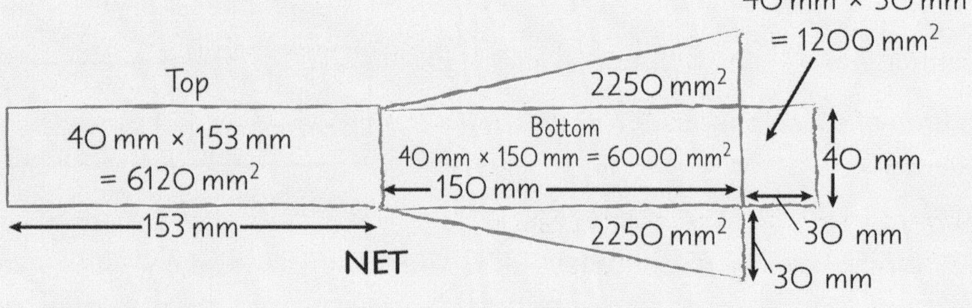

total surface area
= area of top + area of bottom + area of end + area of triangular side × 2
= 6120 mm² + 6000 mm² + 1200 mm² + 2 × 2250 mm²
= 17 820 mm²

17 820 mm² ÷ 100 = 178.2 cm²

Key point
To find the surface area, sketch the net and work out the area of all the faces.

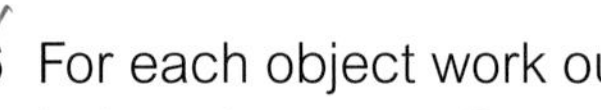

6 For each object work out
i its volume ii total surface area.
Give your answers to an appropriate degree of accuracy.

Q6b hint
Convert your answers to cm².

a

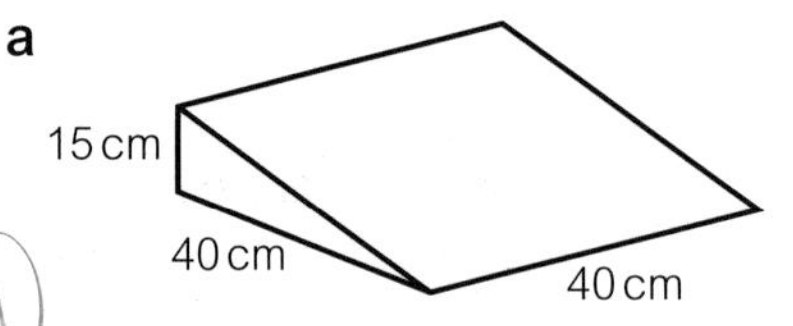

b

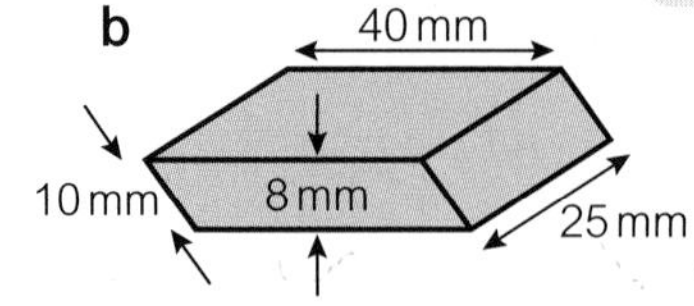

7 **Modelling** The diagram shows the cross-section of water in a pool.
The pool is 8 m wide.

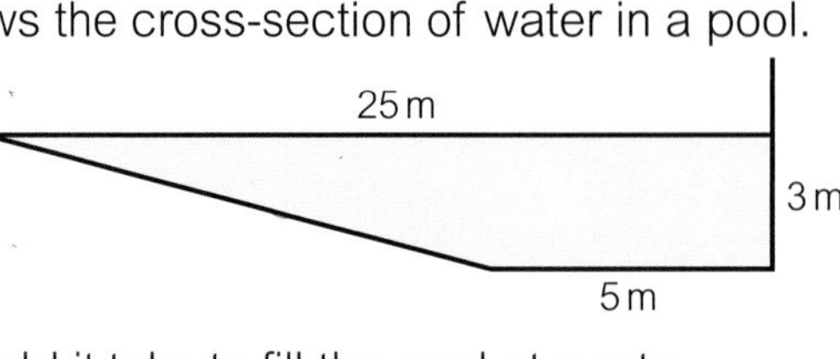

a Work out the volume of water in the pool in
i m³ ii litres

Q7a ii hint
1 m³ = 1000 litres

b **Real** How many hours would it take to fill the pool at a rate of 5 litres per second?

Topic links: Geometry, Measures

Subject links: STEM Q10, Q11

8 **a** Write an expression for the area of the circular cross-section of the cylinder.

b Write an **expression** for the volume of the cylinder.

c Write a **formula** for the volume of a cylinder, $V =$

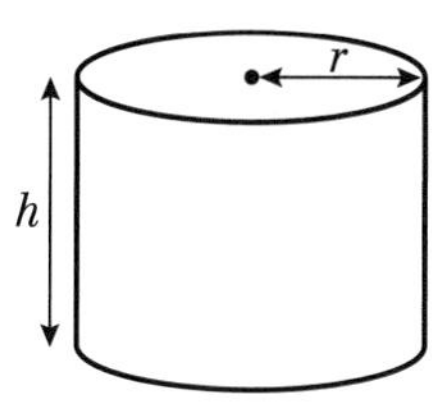

Q8 Literacy hint

A **cylinder** is a right prism with a circular cross-section.

9 Work out the volume of these cylinders.
Give your answers to an appropriate degree of accuracy.

a

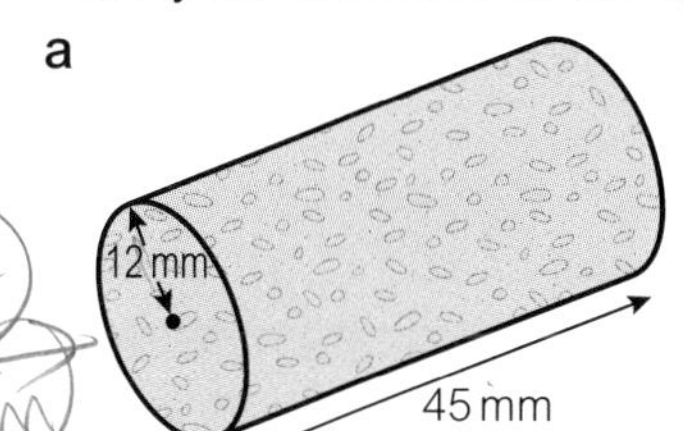

b

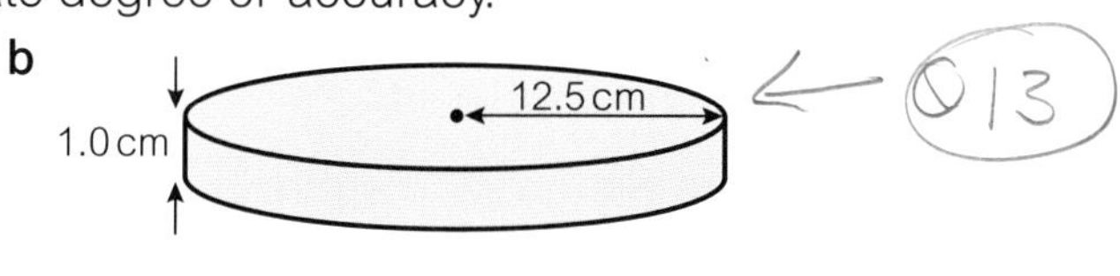

Worked example

Work out the area of the label on this tin of tuna to the nearest cm^2.

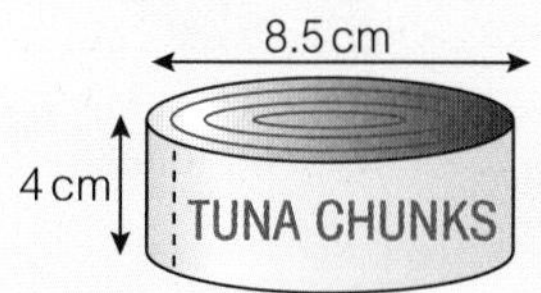

length of label = circumference of tin
$= \pi \times 8.5\text{ cm}$

area of rectangular label = base × height
$= \pi \times 8.5\text{ cm} \times 4\text{ cm}$
$= 107\text{ cm}^2$ (3 s.f.)

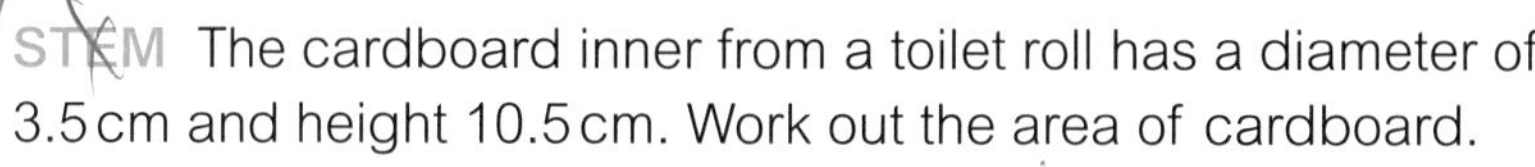

10 STEM The cardboard inner from a toilet roll has a diameter of 3.5 cm and height 10.5 cm. Work out the area of cardboard.

11 STEM The diagram shows a closed cardboard poster tube.

a Sketch the net of this cylinder. Mark the dimensions on your diagram.

b Work out the circumference of the tube to the nearest mm.

c Work out the area of cardboard needed to make the tube, to the nearest 100 cm^2.

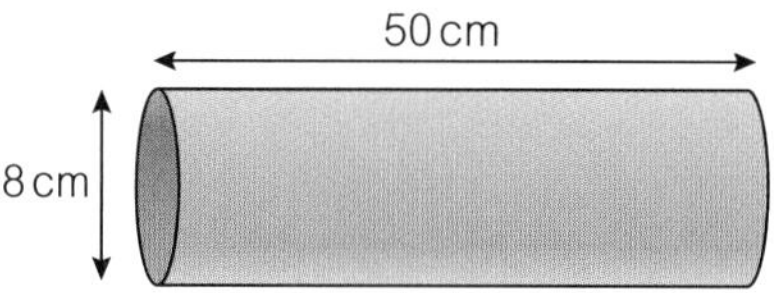

12 **Explore** How much water is frozen to make a circular ice rink?
Is it easier to explore this question now you have completed the lesson?
What further information do you need to be able to answer this?

13 **Reflect** Toby says, 'A right prism always has two end faces that are exactly the same.'
Ed says, 'The faces that are not at the ends are always rectangles.'
Issy says, 'It is called a *right* prism because the end faces and other faces are always at *right* angles to each other.'
Mel says, 'The shapes of the end faces give the prism its name.'
Are they all correct?

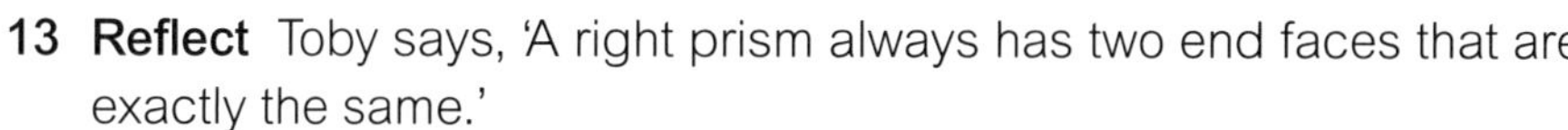

Q13 hint

Look carefully at the pictures of the right prisms you identified in Q4.

Explore

Reflect

7.5 STEM: Errors and bounds

You will learn to:

- Find the lower and upper bounds for a measurement
- Calculate percentage error intervals.

CONFIDENCE

Why learn this?
The amount of food in a can will be within a minimum and maximum value.

Fluency

- What is 19.3 cm to the nearest cm   10 cm?
- What is 328 g to the nearest 10 g   5 g   100 g?
- What is 10% of 80 g?

Explore
What is the total area of plastic wrapping needed for a pack of four tins of tomatoes?

Exercise 7.5: Packaging

Warm up

1 a Increase 40 cm^2 by
  i 10%   ii 5%   iii 1%
 b Decrease 1800 g by
  i 10%   ii 2%   iii 0.5%

2 A circle has a diameter of 8.0 cm. Work out
 a its circumference   b its area.

3 a What is the smallest value that can be rounded up
  i to 5 ml, to the nearest ml ii to 120 cm, to the nearest cm?
 b Which values round down
  i to 5 ml, to the nearest ml ii to 120 cm, to the nearest cm?

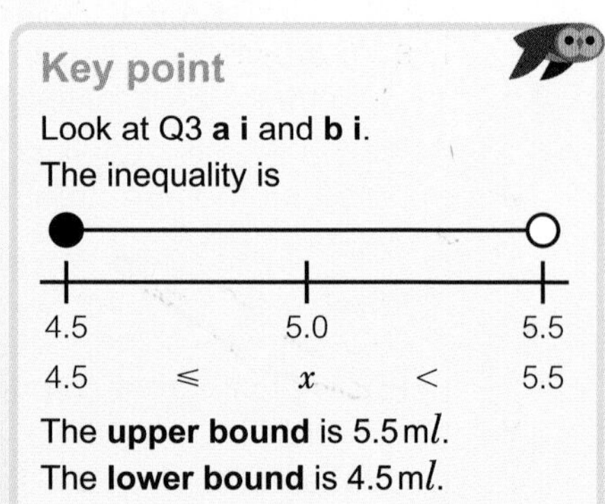

Key point

Look at Q3 **a i** and **b i**.
The inequality is

$4.5 \leqslant x < 5.5$

The **upper bound** is 5.5 ml.
The **lower bound** is 4.5 ml.

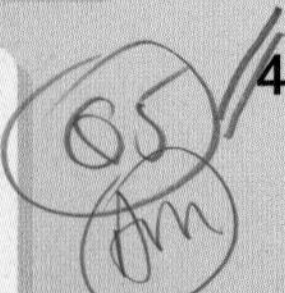

4 Draw an inequality to show the **lower** and **upper bounds** for each measurement.
 a A length l is 15 cm, to the nearest cm.
 b A mass m is 4 kg, to the nearest kg.
 c A length x is 60 cm, to the nearest 10 cm.
 d A mass m is 400 g, to the nearest 50 g.
 e A length l is 3 cm, to the nearest 1 mm.
 f A number n is 120, to the nearest 20.

5 STEM / Problem-solving An online bookseller wraps a novel in a rectangular sheet of brown paper.
 a The width of the sheet is 30 cm, to the nearest cm.
  What are the lower and upper bounds?
 b The length of the sheet is 90 cm, to the nearest 2 cm.
  What are the lower and upper bounds?
 c Work out the lower and upper bounds for the area A of the paper.
  Write your answer as an inequality, using three significant figures.

Q5c hint
Sketch and label the smallest and largest possible rectangles.

Topic links: Percentages, Inequalities, Area of a rectangle, Measures

Subject links: Design and technology (Investigation)

Worked example

The mass m of a 500 g pack of sausages has a 2% error interval.
Work out the minimum and maximum values for m.

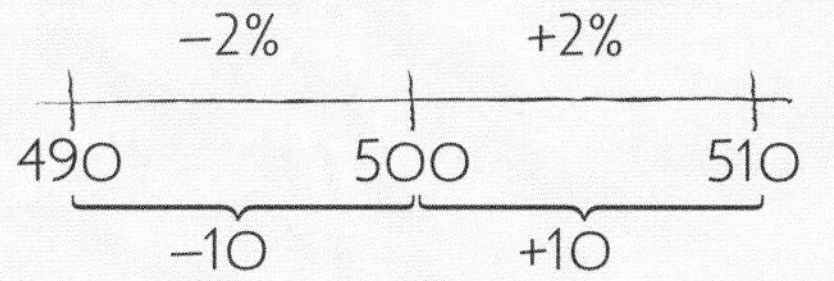

Work out 2% of 500.

Minimum mass = 500 − 10 = 490 g

Maximum mass = 500 + 10 = 510 g

$490 \leqslant m < 510$

Write your answer as an inequality.

Key point

An **error interval** tells you the minimum and maximum possible measurement.

6 a The mass m of 200 g block of cheese has a 5% **error interval**. Work out the minimum and maximum possible mass of the cheese. Write your answer as an inequality.

b The number n of a box of 300 matches has an 8% error interval. Work out the minimum and maximum possible values for n. Write your answer as an inequality.

7 STEM A machine fills 500 g cereal boxes with a ±2% error. One day it fills 20 000 boxes with the maximum error possible. How much extra cereal (in grams) does it use than if it had been filling at the minimum?

8 STEM / Reasoning The diagram shows a circular rice cake. The measurements are to the nearest mm. A tube contains 20 rice cakes stacked on top of each other. A 10 mm deep metal top is pushed into the tube. The bottom of the tube is cardboard. Work out the total area of cardboard needed to make the tube. Give your answer to an appropriate degree of accuracy.

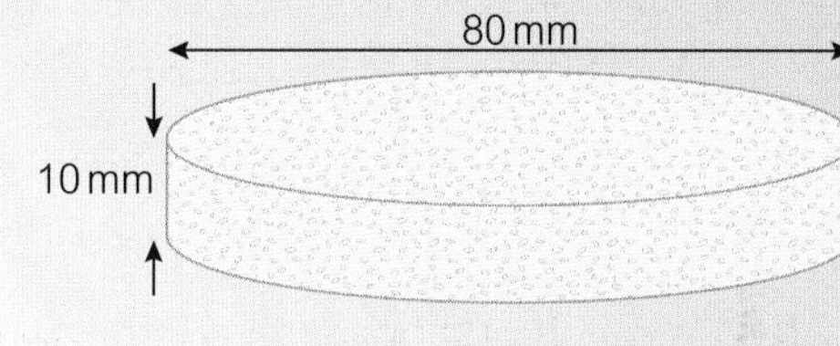

Investigation STEM / Problem-solving

The diagram shows a cereal biscuit with semicircular ends. Each biscuit is 22 mm thick. Ten biscuits are stacked together in plastic and placed inside a cuboid cardboard box.

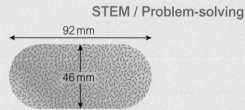

1 Work out
  a the area of plastic, assuming no overlaps
  b the area of cardboard, assuming no overlaps.

2 The dimensions of the biscuit have an error interval of ±5%. What size of box should be used?

3 Design your own cereal biscuit. Decide how many to wrap in plastic. Design a cuboid box to contain them. Work out the answers to part **1** for your box of cereal.

9 **Explore** What is the total area of plastic wrapping needed for a pack of four tins of tomatoes? Is it easier to explore this question now you have completed the lesson? What further information do you need to be able to answer this?

10 **Reflect** Look back at Q6a. Imagine your friend is stuck on this question. How would you explain it to them? You may begin with, 'I would explain that the ±5% error interval means …'

7 Check up

Log how you did on your Student Progression Chart.

Circles

1 The diagram shows a circle with a diameter of 7.5 cm.
Calculate the circumference of the circle, correct to one decimal place.

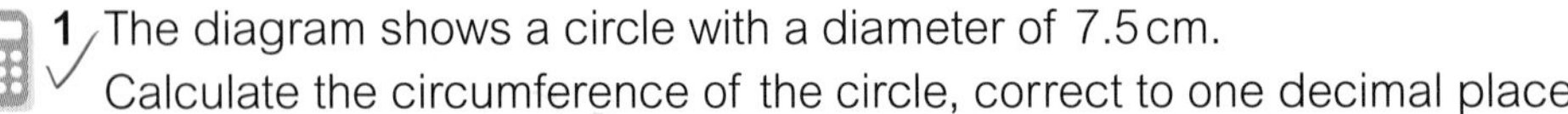

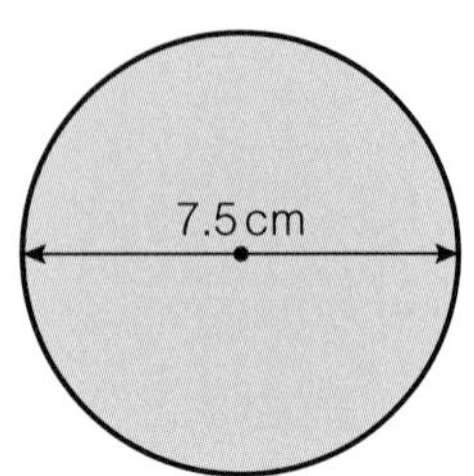

2 A circular steering wheel has a radius of 20 cm.
Work out the circumference of the wheel.
Give your answer in terms of π.

3 The diagram shows a circular disc with a diameter of 15 mm.
Work out the area of the disc.
Give your answer to the nearest mm^2.

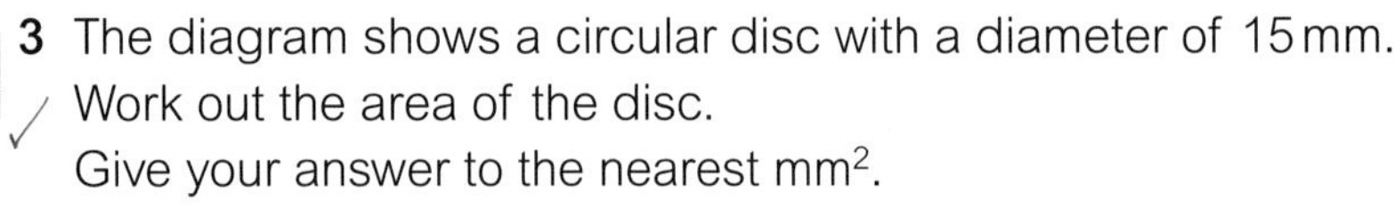

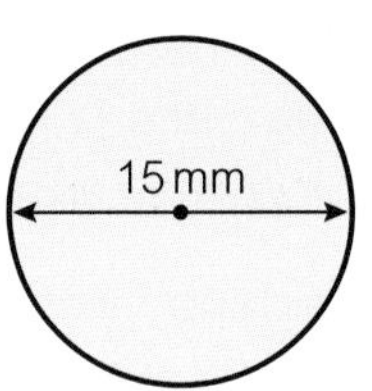

4 The diagram shows a semicircle.

a Work out the area to the nearest cm^2.

b Work out the perimeter, correct to one decimal place.

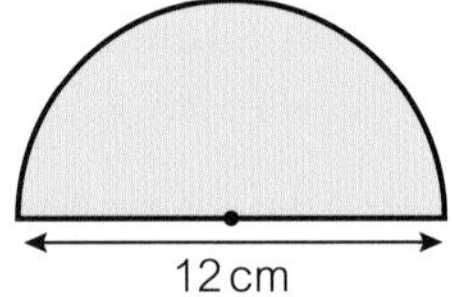

5 A circle has a diameter d and circumference 30 cm.
Work out the value of d, correct to the nearest mm.

6 A circle has a radius r and an area of 200 m^2.
Work out the value of r, correct to the nearest cm.

Pythagoras' theorem

7 Work out the length d, correct to the nearest mm.

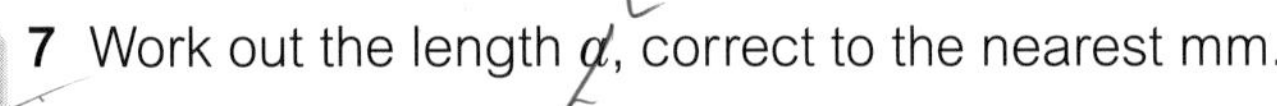

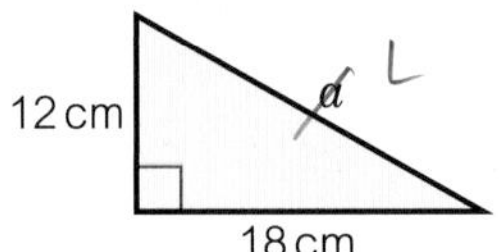

8 **a** Work out the length of the unknown side in this triangle.
Give your answer to a sensible degree of accuracy.

b Write down the length of the hypotenuse.

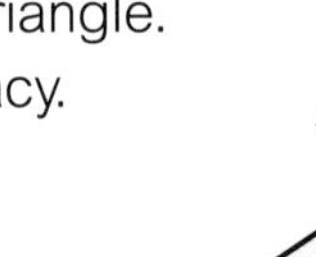

Prisms

9 The diagram shows a triangular prism.

a Work out the volume.

b Work out the surface area.

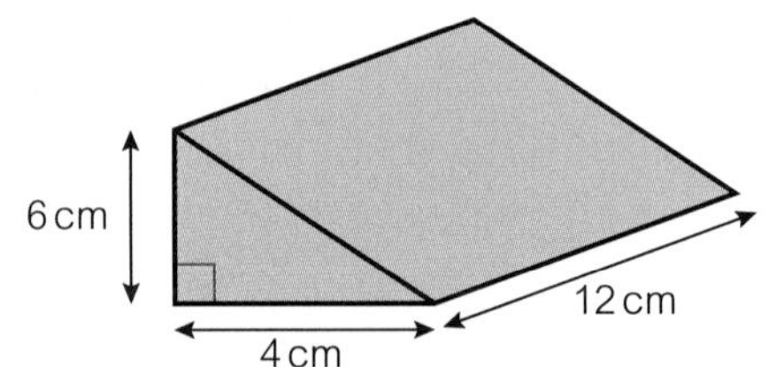

10 Work out the volume of this cylinder.

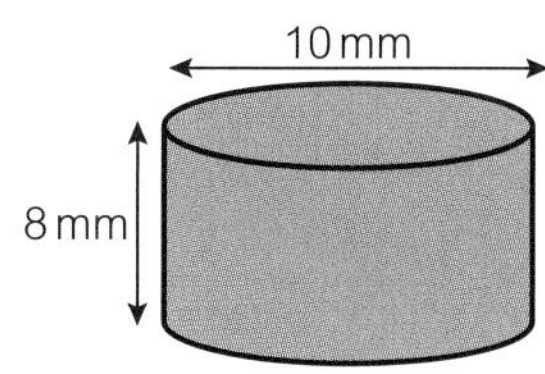

11 The diagram shows a packet of biscuits wrapped in plastic.
Work out the total surface area of plastic.

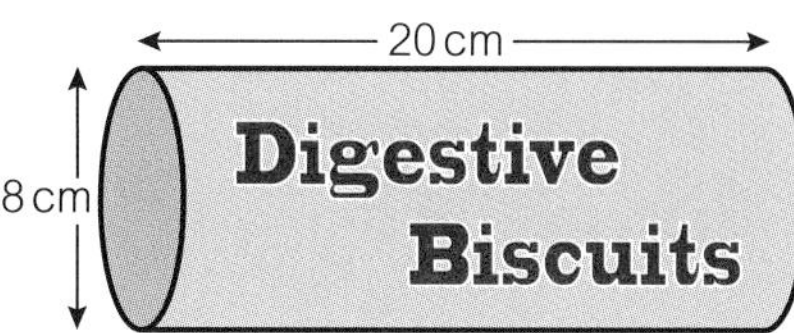

12 The diagram shows a metal drinking trough on a farm.
How many litre of water can the trough hold?

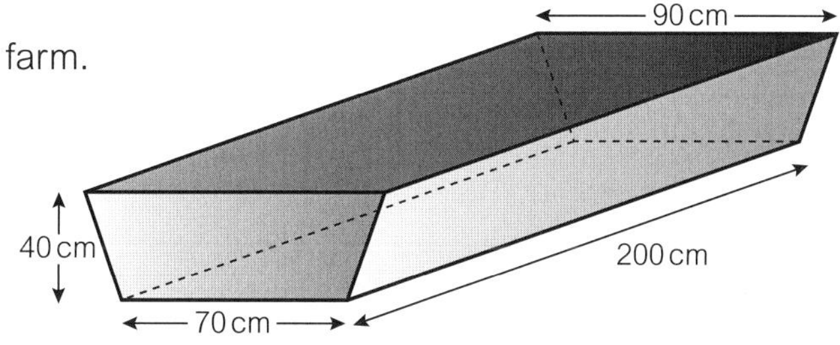

Measurements

13 A square has sides of length 20 cm, to the nearest cm.

a Work out the lower and upper bounds for the length d of the side of the square.

b Work out the lower and upper bounds for the area A of the square.

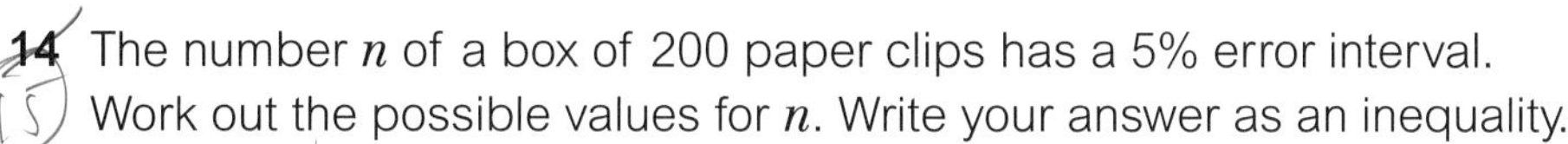

14 The number n of a box of 200 paper clips has a 5% error interval.
Work out the possible values for n. Write your answer as an inequality.

15 How sure are you of your answers? Were you mostly

Just guessing **Feeling doubtful** **Confident**

What next? Use your results to decide whether to strengthen or extend your learning.

Reflect

Challenge

16 a i Draw a triangle by joining grid line intersections on centimetre squared paper. Here is one possibility.

ii Calculate the perimeter of the triangle.

iii Use a pair of compasses to draw a circle with the same perimeter.

b i Calculate the area of the triangle.

ii Use a pair of compasses to draw a circle with the same area.

c Repeat parts **a** and **b** with a different shape.
Try starting with a rectangle, parallelogram or trapezium.

17 The diagram shows a wheelchair ramp and wheelchair.
The ramp length is 3 m.

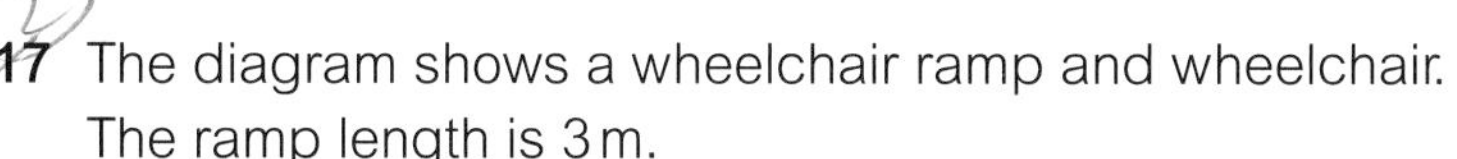

The wheelchair moves from the top of the ramp to the bottom.

a Work out the number of complete wheel revolutions.

b The small wheel at the front rotates 8 times.
Work out its diameter.

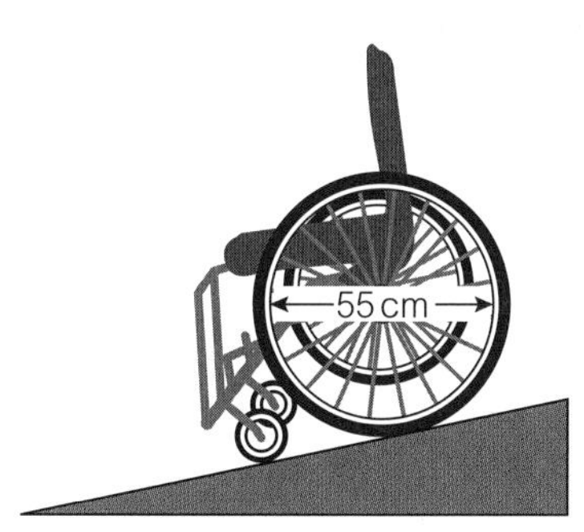

7 Strengthen

You will:

- Strengthen your understanding with practice.

Circles

1 Use your calculator to work out
  a π b $2 \times \pi$ c $\pi \times 5^2$ d 4π e $\pi 2^2$

Q1a hint
Find the π key on your calculator.

2 Circumference C, $= \pi \times$ diameter
  a What is the diameter of this circle?
  b Copy and complete.
  $C = \pi \times \square$
  c Work out the circumference.
  Give your answer to one decimal place.

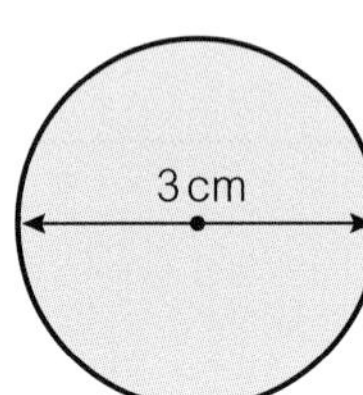

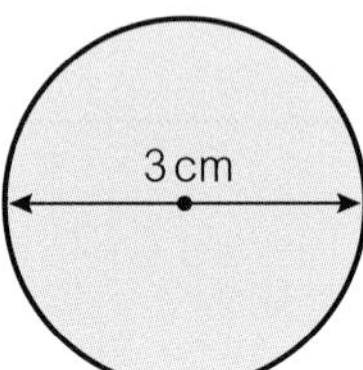

Q2b hint
Write down the calculation before you use your calculator.

3 Work out the circumference of these circles using the formula $C = \pi \times d$.
  Give your answers to one decimal place.

a 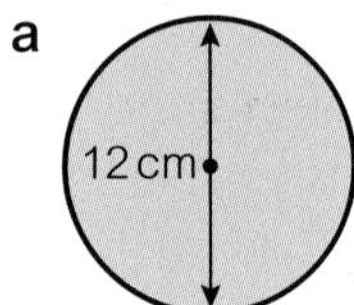

b 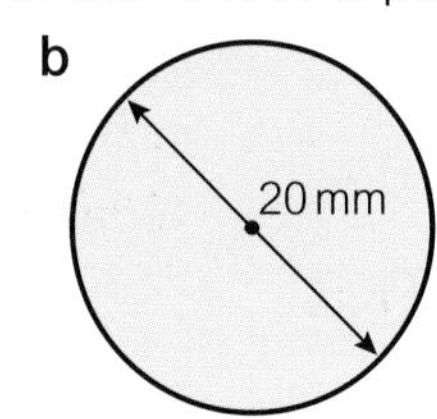

c 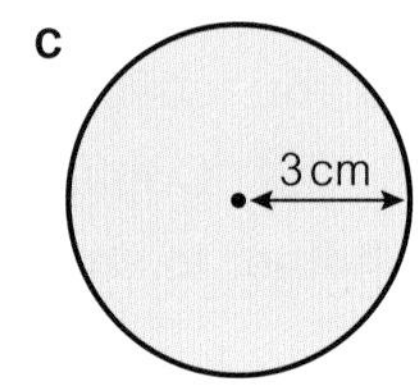

Q3c hint
Work out the diameter first.

4 A circle has a diameter of 5 cm.
  Write down its circumference in terms of π.

Q4 hint
Substitute the value of $d = 5$ into $C = \pi \times d$.
Rearrange to $C = \square\pi$.

5 Work out the circumference of these objects.
  Give your answers to one decimal place.
  a A circular button with diameter 8 mm.
  b A circular tin lid with diameter 12.5 cm.
  c A round table mat with radius 9.5 cm.

Q5 Strategy hint
Draw a sketch. Label the measurements you know.

6 Area $= \pi \times \text{radius}^2$
  a What is the radius of this circle?
  b Copy and complete.
  $A = \pi \times \square^2$
  c Work out the area. Give your answer to one decimal place.

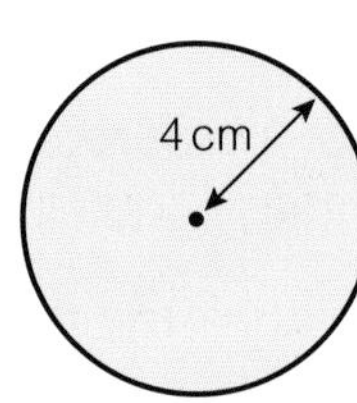

7 Work out the area of each circle.

a 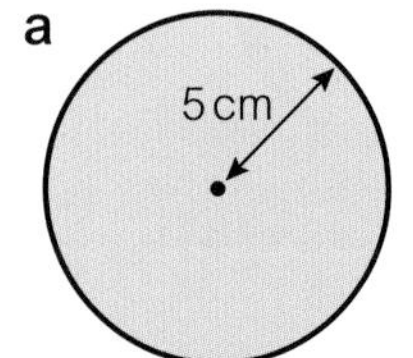

b 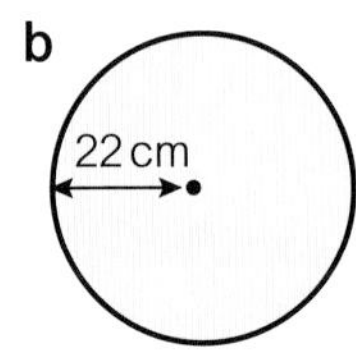

c 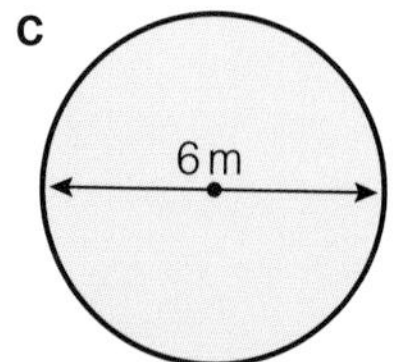

d 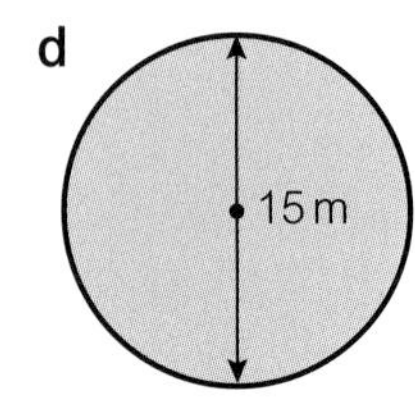

Q7c hint
Work out the radius first.

Topic links: Inequalities, Percentages

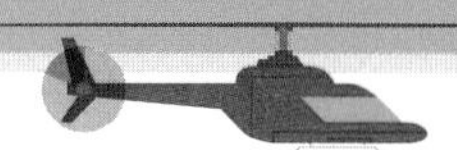

8 A circle has a radius of 11 cm.
Write down its area in terms of π.

9 Work out the diameter d of the circles with these circumferences.
Give your answers to one decimal place.

a 12 mm b 8 cm c 25 m
d 1.8 m e 300 km f 0.05 mm

10 Work out the radius of each circle from its area.
Give your answers to one decimal place.

a 31 cm^2 b 12 cm^2 c 100 cm^2
d 2.5 m^2 e 500 mm^2 f 0.6 m^2

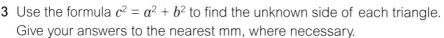

Q8 hint

Substitute $r = 11$ into $A = \pi \times r^2$.

Q10a hint

Use an inverse function machine.
$A = \pi r^2$, so divide the area by π and take the square root to find the radius.

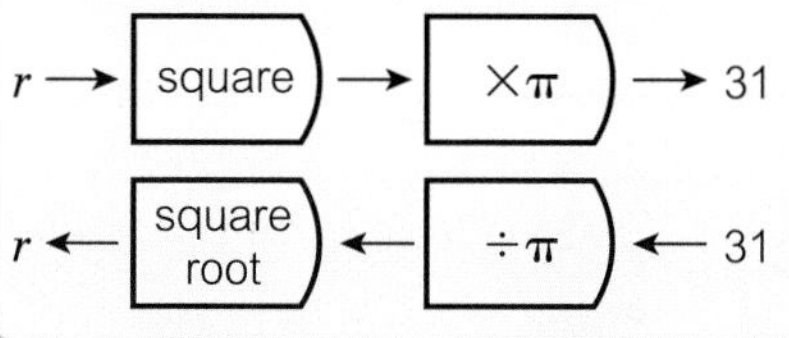

Pythagoras' theorem

1 a Copy these right-angled triangles.

i
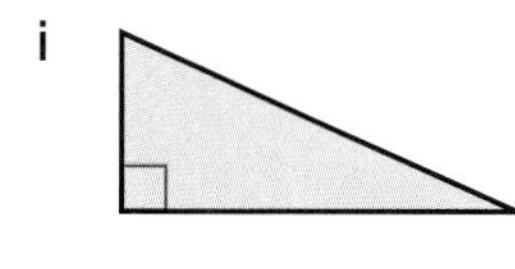
ii
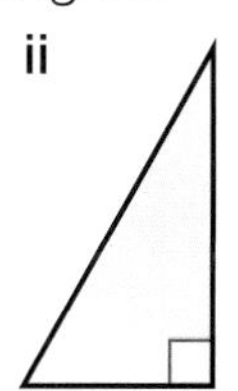
iii
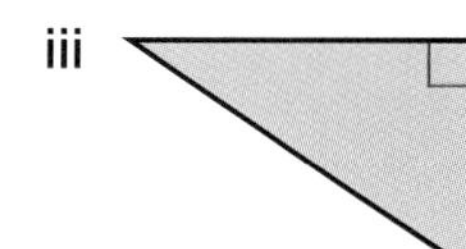
iv
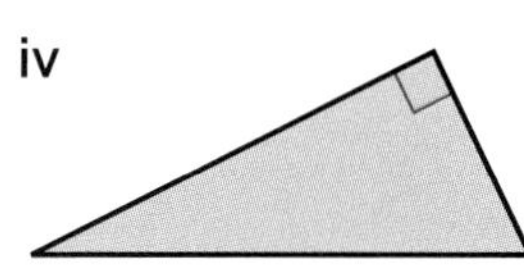

b Label the hypotenuse of each triangle c.

c Label the two shorter sides a and b.

Q1b hint

The hypotenuse is the longest side and is opposite the right angle.

Q1c hint

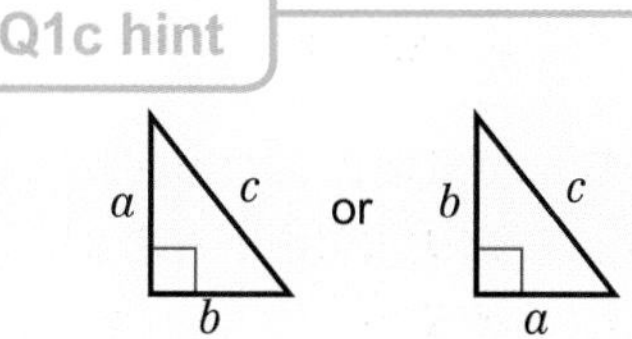

It doesn't matter which side length is a and which is b.

2 Use the formula $c^2 = a^2 + b^2$ to find the hypotenuse c of each triangle.
Give your answers to the nearest mm.
The first one has been started for you.

a

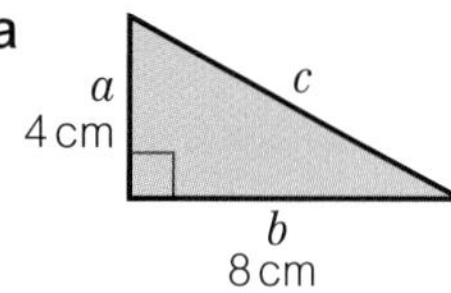

$a = 4$, $b = 8$

$c^2 = a^2 + b^2$

$c^2 = \square^2 + \square^2 = \square$

$c = \sqrt{\square} = \square$ (1 d.p.)

b

2 cm

5 cm

c
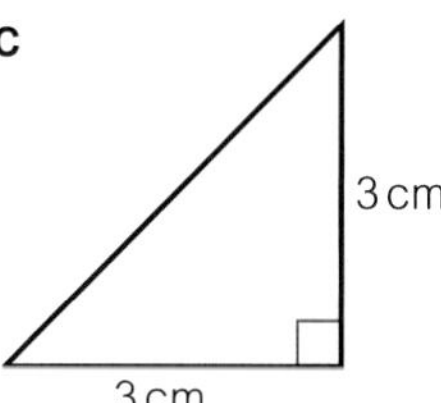

Q2 hint

Follow the same steps for the other two triangles.

3 Use the formula $c^2 = a^2 + b^2$ to find the unknown side of each triangle.
Give your answers to the nearest mm, where necessary.

a
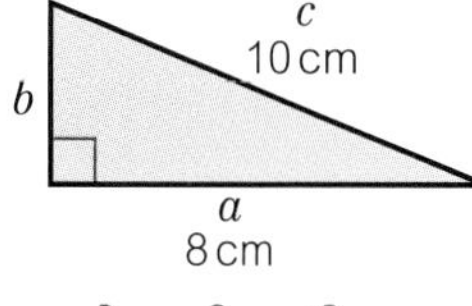

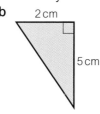

$c^2 = a^2 + b^2$

$10^2 = 8^2 + b^2$

$\square = \square + b^2$

$\square - \square = b^2$

$b^2 = \square$

$b = \sqrt{\square} = \square$ cm

b
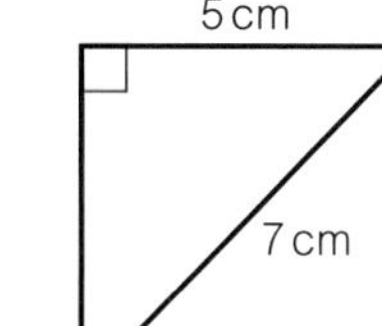

c
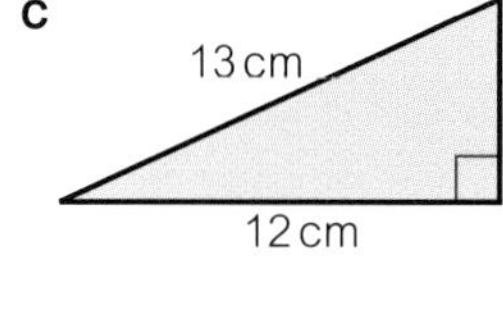

4 Problem-solving Work out the area of each shape, correct to one decimal place.

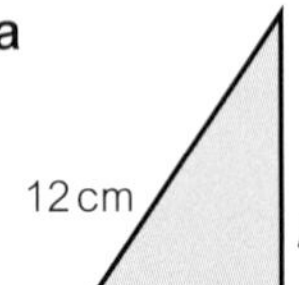

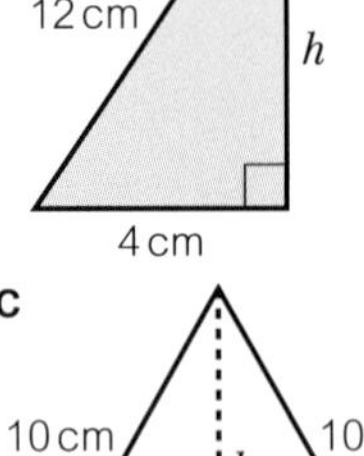

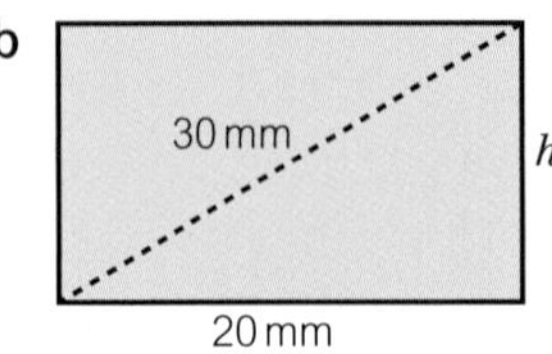

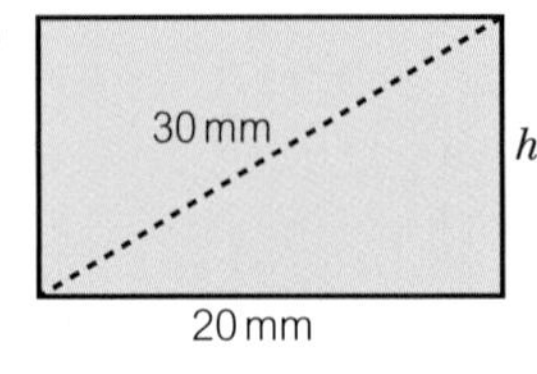

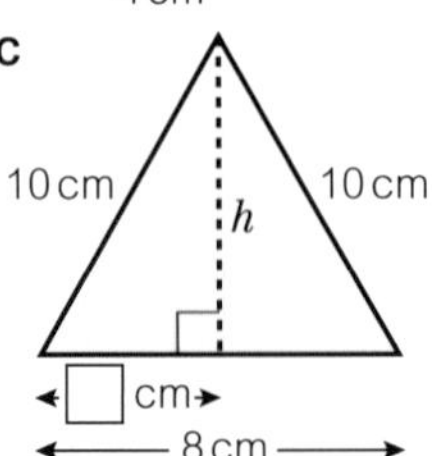

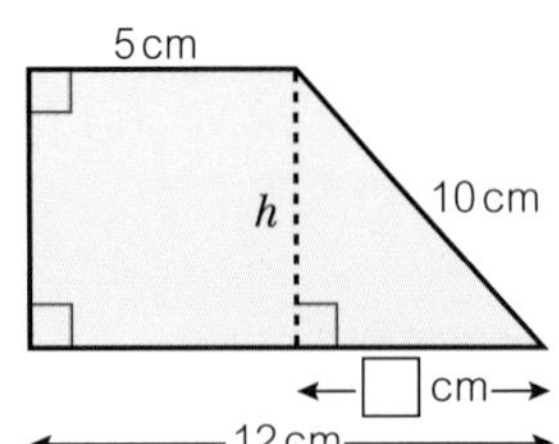

Q4 hint

Use Pythagoras' theorem to work out the height first.

Prisms

1 a These prisms are made using centimetre cubes. For each prism find the area of the darker shaded surface and the volume.

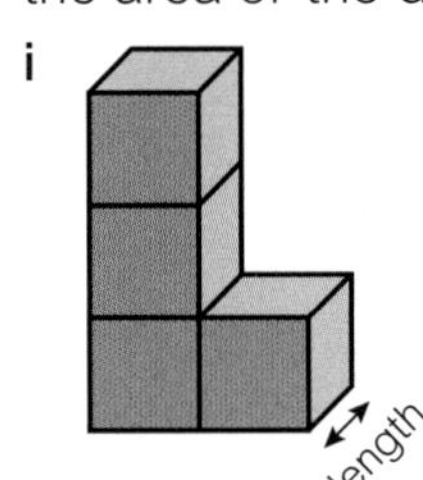

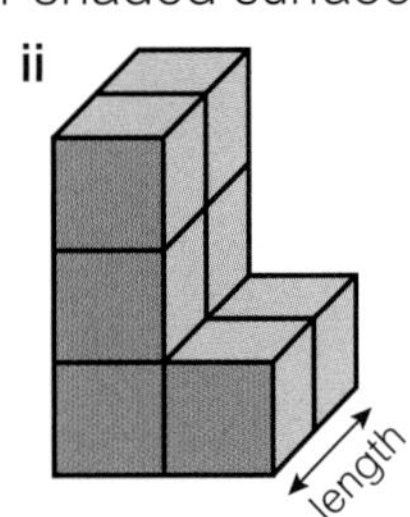

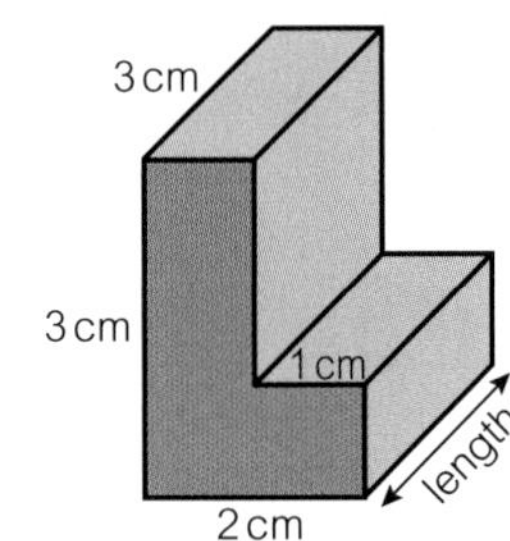

b Copy and complete.
Volume of prism = ... × ....

2 a Sketch the cross-section of each prism.

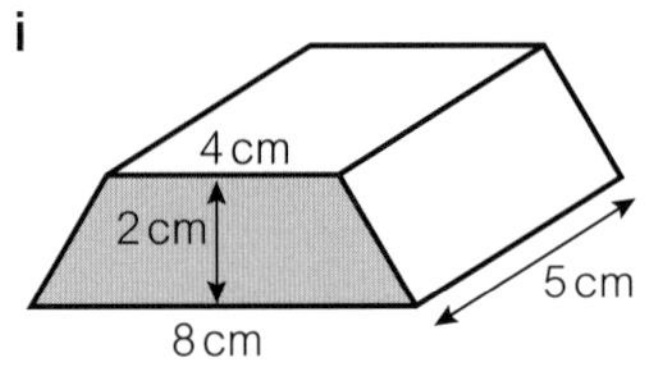

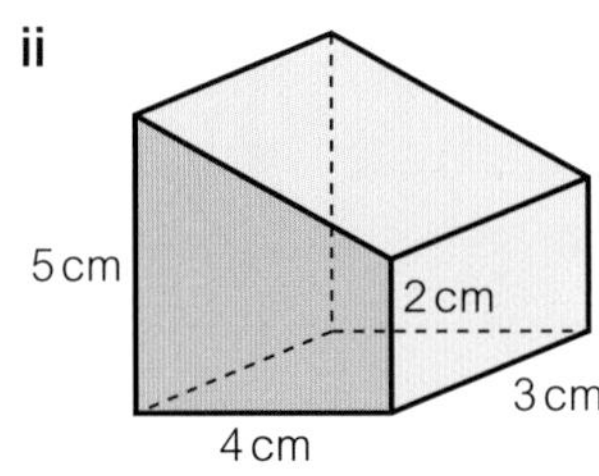

b Work out the area of the cross-section for each prism.
c Work out the volume of each prism.

Q2 hint

The cross-sections are trapezia.

Q2 hint

The darker area is the area of cross-section.

3 a How many faces does this prism have?

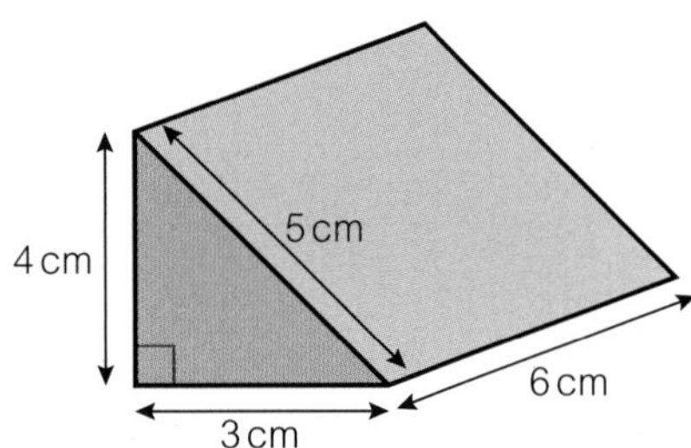

b Sketch all the faces. Label the measurements.
c Work out the area of each face.
d Work out the surface area of the prism.

Q3d hint

The surface area is the total area of all the faces.

4 Work out the surface area of each prism.

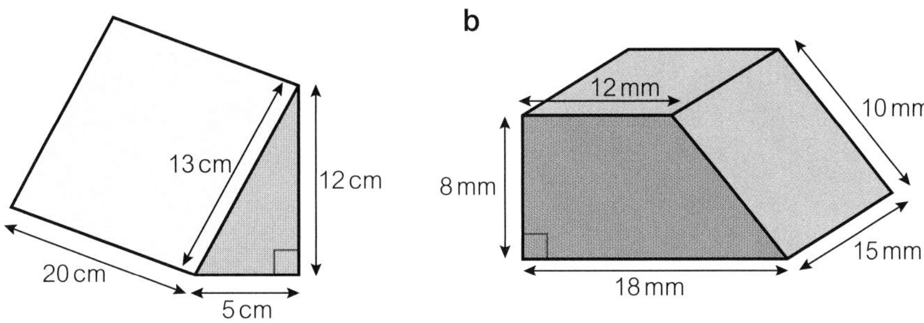

Q4 hint

Follow the same steps as in Q3d.

5 For each cylinder

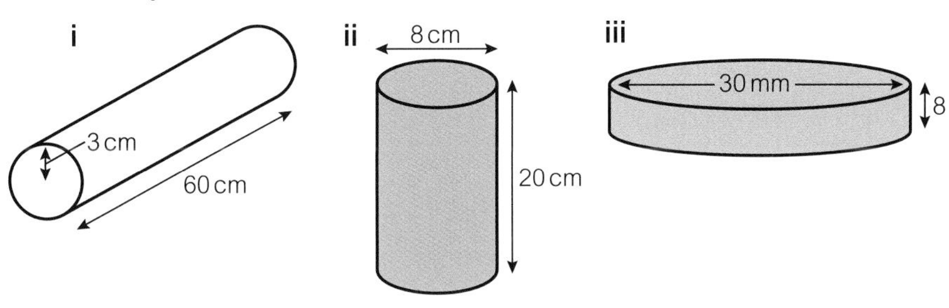

a sketch the cross-section and label the radius

b work out the area of the cross-section

c work out the volume of the cylinder, correct to one decimal place.

Q5b and c hint

radius = half of diameter = □

area of circular cross-section

= $\pi \times \square^2$ = □

volume

= area of cross-section × height

= □ × □ = □

6 Modelling The diagram shows a tin of baked beans. The top and bottom lids were removed using a tin opener. The wall was then cut along the dotted line and pressed flat.

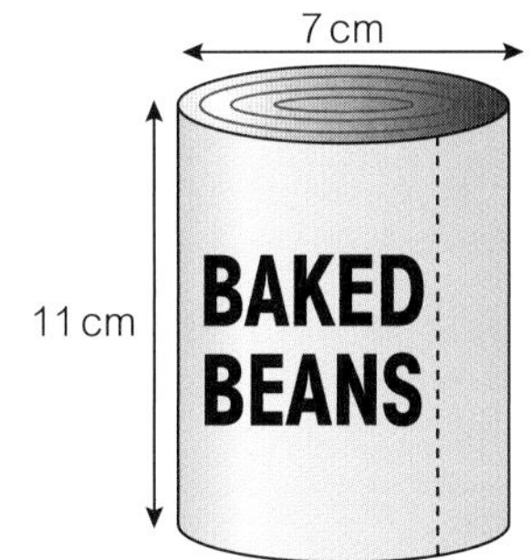

a Sketch the ends and wall of the tin. Label the lengths you are given.

b Using an appropriate degree of accuracy, work out

i the total area of the top and bottom lids

ii the circumference of the tin lid

iii the area of the flattened wall of the tin

iv the total surface area of the tin.

Measurements

1 Which of these measurements round to 9 cm, to the nearest cm?

A 8.1 cm	B 5.2 cm	C 8.4 cm	D 9.6 cm
E 8.6 cm	F 8.8 cm	G 9.1 cm	H 9.4 cm

Q1 hint

Look at a ruler to help you.

2 a Copy this number line.

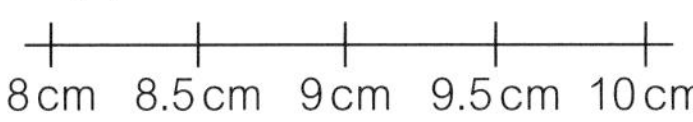

Shade the part where all the values round to 9 cm, to the nearest cm.

b Write down the lower and upper bounds for the measurement.

Q2b hint

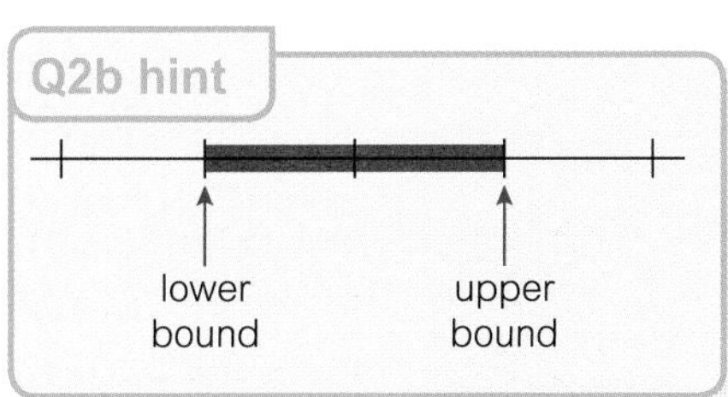

3 Write the lower and upper bounds for each measurement.

a 8 cm, correct to the nearest 1 cm

b 80 g, correct to the nearest 10 g

c 60 cm, correct to the nearest 5 cm

d 300 cm^2, correct to the nearest 100 cm^2

e 1000, correct to the nearest 50

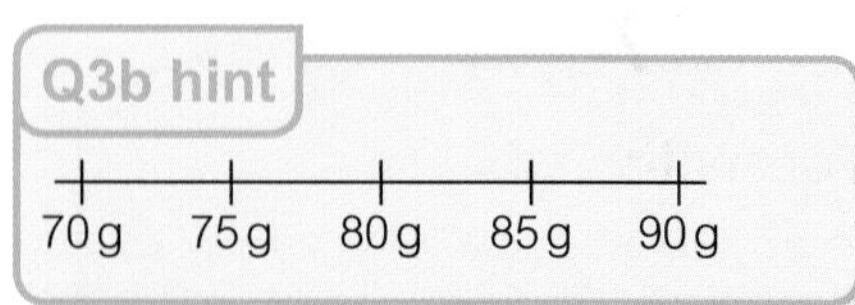

4 The table shows the lower and upper bounds for the value x.

Lower bound	Upper bound	Inequality
10 cm	20 cm	10 cm $\leqslant x <$ □
6.5 g	7.5 g	□ $\leqslant x <$ □
30 km	34 km	

Copy and complete the table.

Q4 hint
The upper bound is not included, so the 'less than' symbol is used.

5 A rectangle measures 15 cm by 10 cm, to the nearest 2 cm.

a Write the lower and upper bounds for the length and the width.

b Draw the smallest and biggest possible rectangles on centimetre squared paper.

c Work out the area of each of your two rectangles.

d Copy and complete the inequality for the area A.
□cm^2 $\leqslant A <$ □cm^2

Q5b hint
The smallest height and width will give the smallest rectangle.

6 Use an inequality to describe the range of possible values.

a The length x is 30 cm, to within a ±10% error interval.

b The length x is 100 cm, to within a ±5% error interval.

c The weight w is 200 g, to within a ±2% error interval.

d The number n is 500, to within a ±1% error interval.

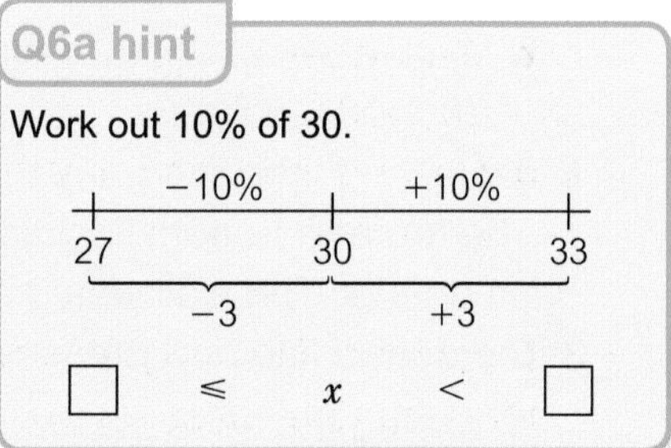

Enrichment

1 a How many different ways can you make this statement true?
square number = square number + square number

b Write your answers to part **a** in the form of Pythagoras' theorem:
$c^2 = a^2 + b^2$.

c Sketch and label right-angled triangles with these sides.

Q1a hint
Make a list of square numbers to help you.

Reflect

2 **Reflect** In these lessons you used these formulae:

- circumference = π × diameter (in Circles Q1–Q5 and Q9)
- area of a circle = π × radius^2 (in Circles Q6–Q8 and Q10)
- Pythagoras' theorem: $c^2 = a^2 + b^2$ (in Pythagoras' theorem Q2–Q4)
- volume of a prism = area of cross-section × length (in Prisms Q1–Q2 and Q5)

Which formula was easiest to use? Explain why.
Which formula was most difficult to use? Explain why.
Discuss the formula you found most difficult with a classmate.
Ask them to explain questions they answered using this formula.

7 Extend

You will:
- Extend your understanding with problem-solving.

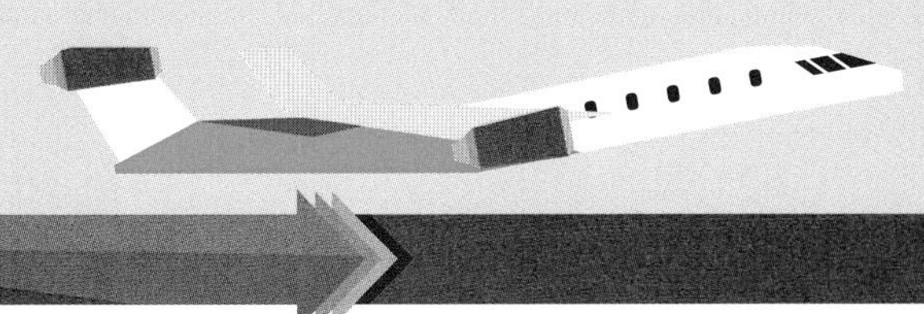

1 Work out the area and perimeter of this shape.

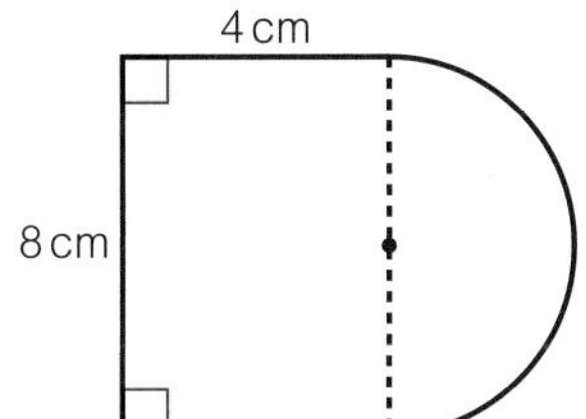

2 **Modelling** The diagram shows a bicycle wheel with an **odometer** sensor fitted.

a Work out the circumference of the wheel to the nearest cm.

b What does the odometer show after 100 000 revolutions of the wheel?

c How many times does the wheel turn in 12 km?

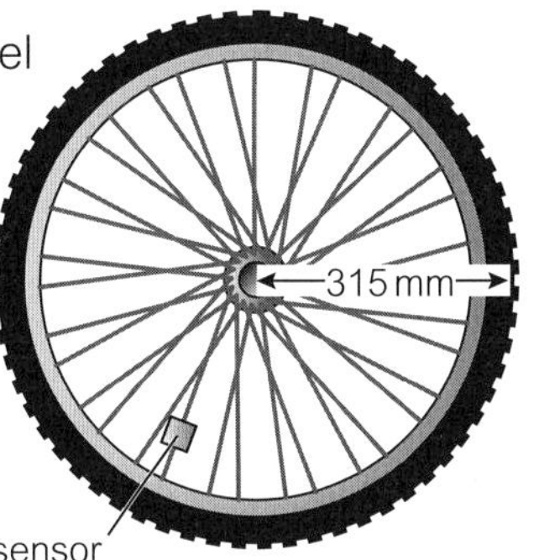

Q2 Literacy hint
An **odometer** measures distance travelled.

3 **Modelling** The diagram shows a donkey tethered to a rail using a 5 m rope.

a Work out the area that the donkey can graze.

b The donkey walks around the edge of the grazing area five times. How far has it walked?

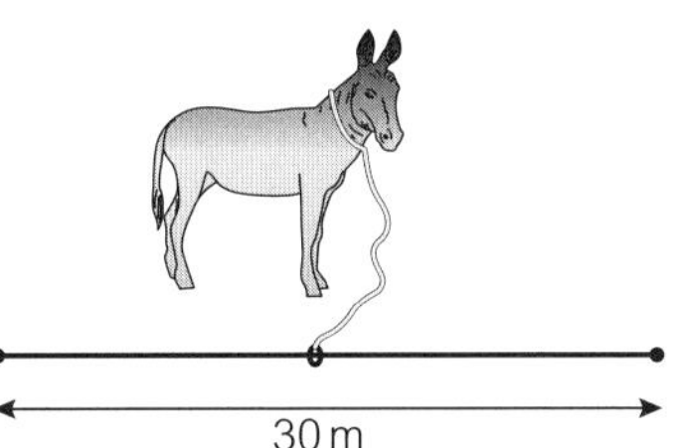

Q3 Strategy hint
Draw a diagram to show the area it can graze.

4 **Problem-solving / Modelling**
The diagram shows how three rows of four equally-spaced biscuits have been cut from a rectangular sheet of dough.
The rows and columns are 1 cm apart.
The top and bottom rows are 1 cm from the edge and so are the first and last columns.
Work out the area of dough left over.

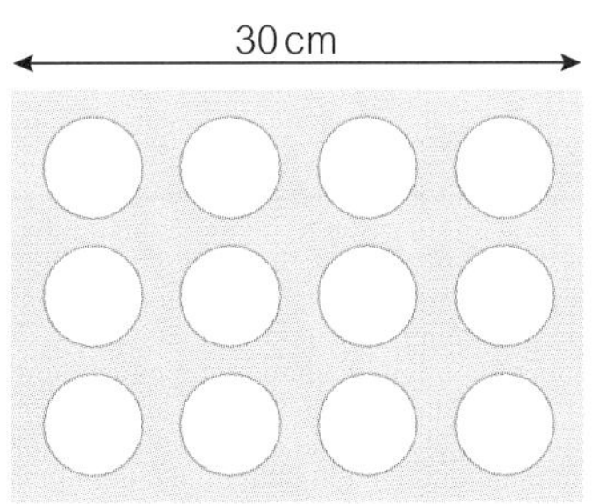

Q4 Strategy hint
Work out the diameter of a biscuit first.

5 **Modelling** A cylindrical electromagnet core is rotated 165 times to wind 17.5 m of copper wire onto it.

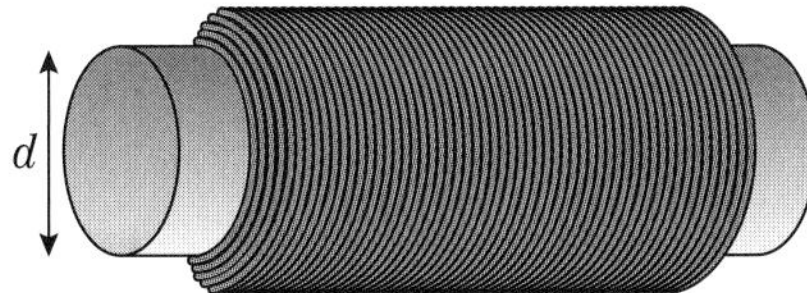

a Work out the diameter d of the core.

b Explain why the method you used is not an accurate model.

6 **Real / Problem-solving** A hedge trimmer runs on a mixture of petrol and oil in the ratio 40 : 1.
The fuel tank has the shape of a right-angled triangular prism.

a Work out the capacity of the tank.

b **i** How much oil is used to fill the tank?

ii How much petrol is used to fill the tank?

c After 10 minutes of use, the tank had 100 ml of fuel left in it.
Work out the depth d of fuel.

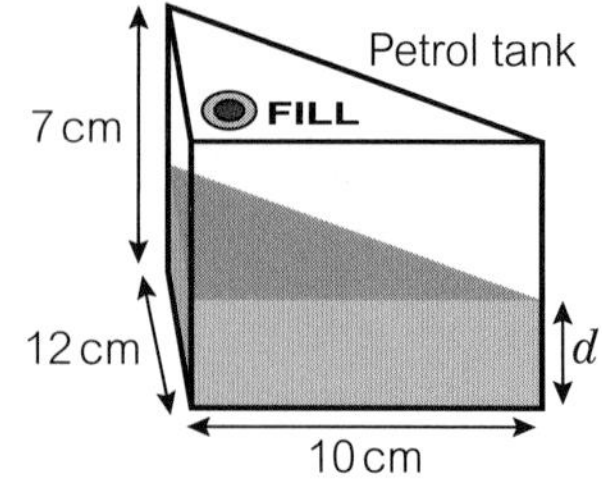

7 **Real / Problem-solving** The diagram shows the inner and outer lanes of a circular race track.
The tracks are 5 m apart.
The finish line is shown in red.

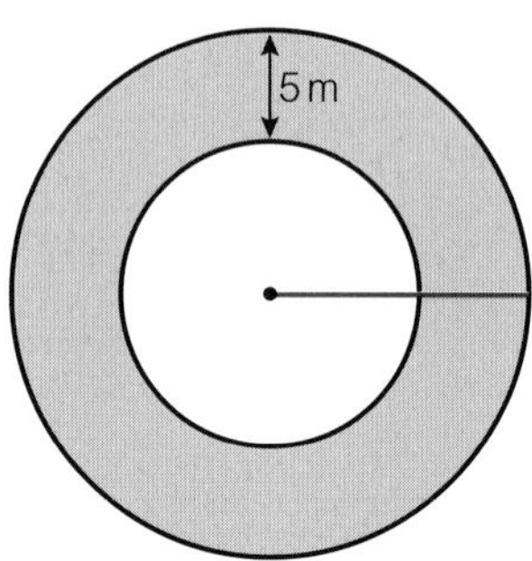

a The length of the inner track is 400 m.
Work out its radius.

b In a 400 m race, the runner on the inner track starts from the red line. How far in front of the red line should the runner on the outer track start?

8 **Problem-solving / Real** This diagram shows the values of two football clubs in 2013.

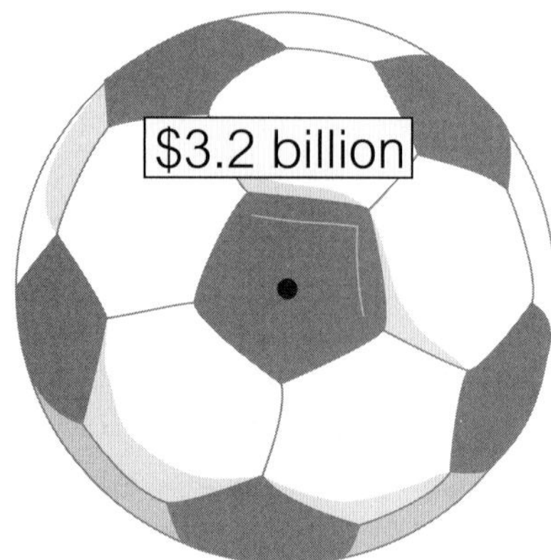

Manchester United

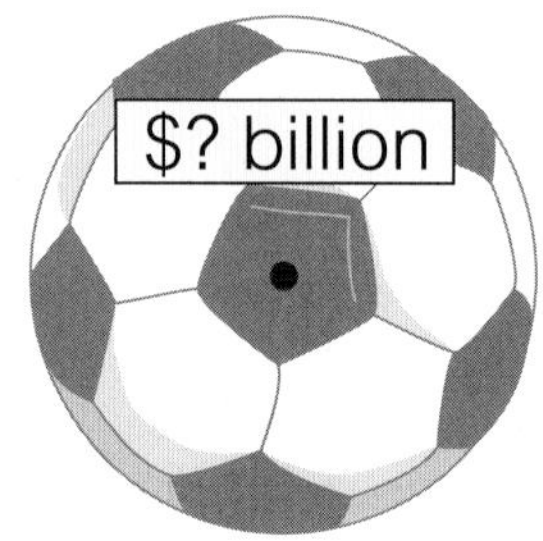

Arsenal

a Measure the radius of each circle.

b Estimate the value of Arsenal.

9 **STEM / Problem-solving** A 3D printer prints layers of plastic particles to build solid objects like this hexagonal prism dice.
Each layer is 50 μm thick.

8.7 mm

5 mm

a Work out the area of the cross-section.

b The prism has a volume of 2 cm^3. Work out the length of the prism.

c Work out the number of layers needed to make the prism.

d Each layer takes 2 seconds to print.
How long does it take to print the prism?

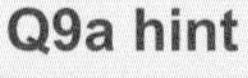

Q9a hint
Split the hexagon into two trapeziums or six equilateral triangles.

10 A natural mineral deodorant stone has a mass of 120 g with an error interval of ±5%.
A shipment contains 10 000 stones to the nearest 50. Work out the range of possible values for shipment mass, M.
Write your answer as an inequality.

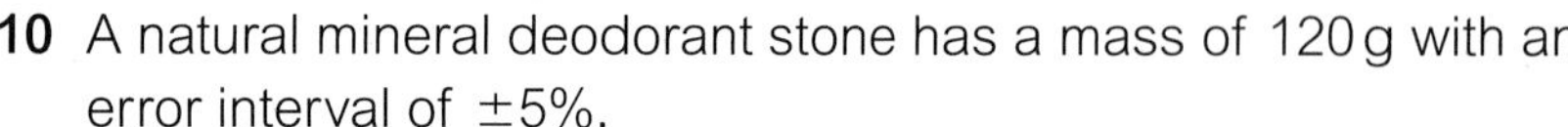

Topic links: Loci, Representing data, Percentages, Probability, Coordinates, Graphs

Subject links: STEM (Q9, Q18, Q23, Q29)

11 Problem-solving The diagram shows a dartboard.
Its dimensions are in the table.

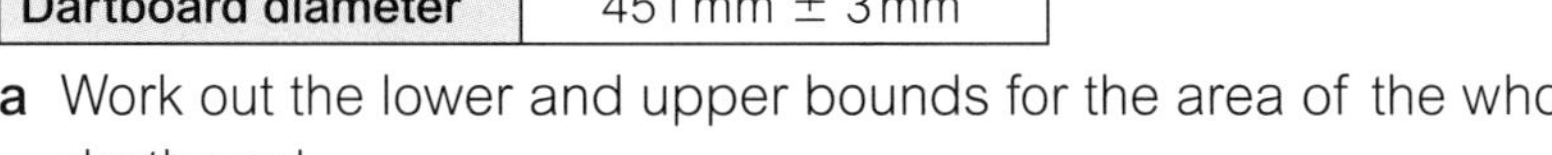
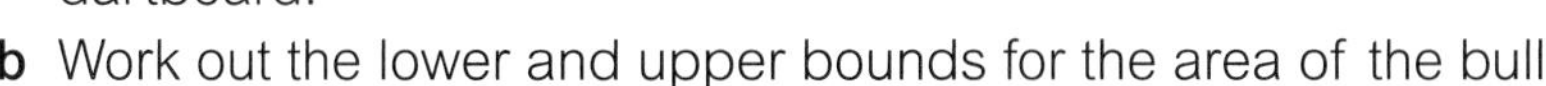

Bull diameter	12.7 mm ± 0.2 mm
Dartboard diameter	451 mm ± 3 mm

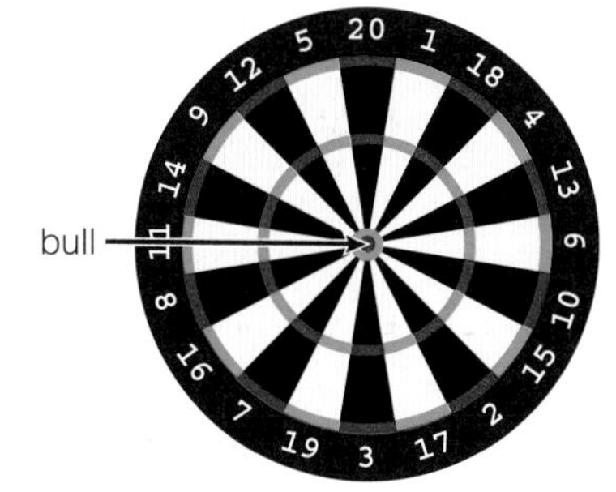

a Work out the lower and upper bounds for the area of the whole dartboard.

b Work out the lower and upper bounds for the area of the bull.

c A dart thrown at random hits the dartboard.
Work out the lower and upper bounds for the percentage probability P that the dart hits the bull.

12 Real / Problem-solving The diagram shows a wooden gate, where AC = 2.4 m and AD = 1 m.
Work out the total length of wood needed to make the gate.

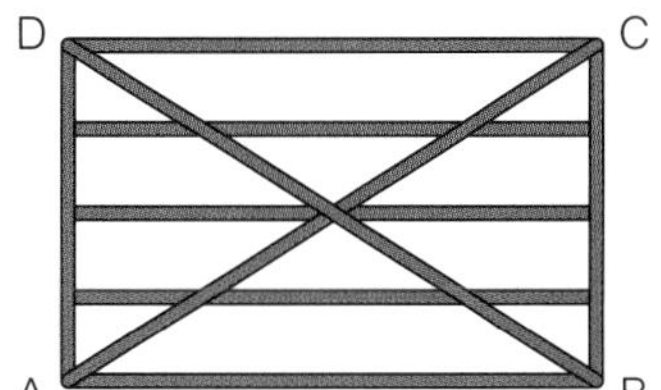

13 Problem-solving
The diagram shows a bow being stretched to release an arrow.

a Write down length CD.

b Work out the length AB before the bow was stretched.

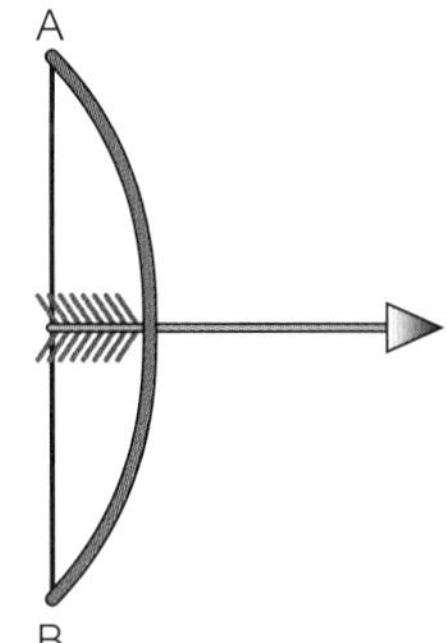

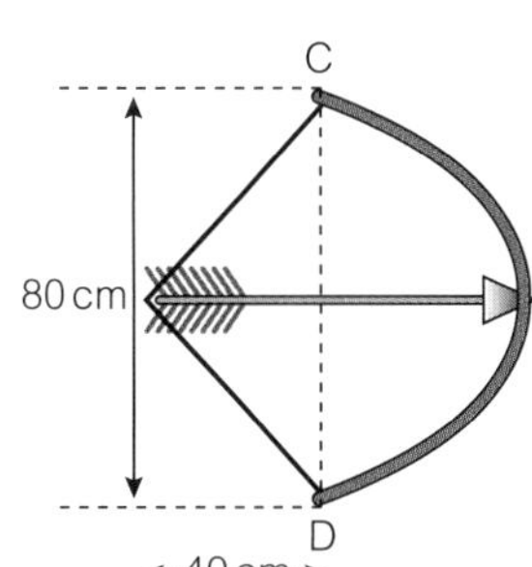

Q13 hint
Assume that the string does not stretch.

14 Problem-solving / Modelling
The diagram shows a swing in two different positions.
Work out the height h (in metres) of the swing seat at B.

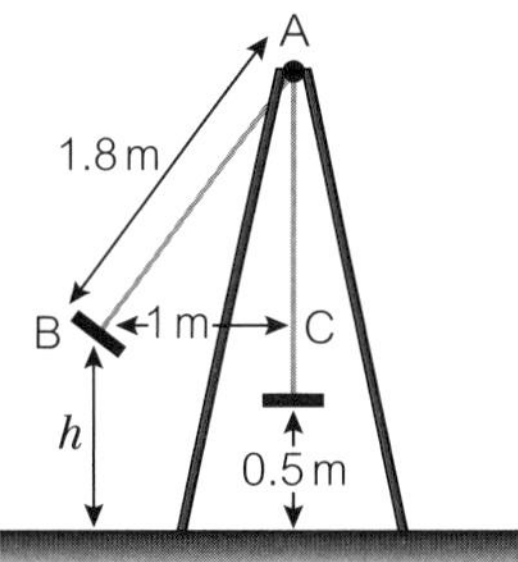

Q14 hint
Work out the length AC first.

15 These lines were drawn on centimetre squared paper.
Work out the length of each line, correct to one decimal place.

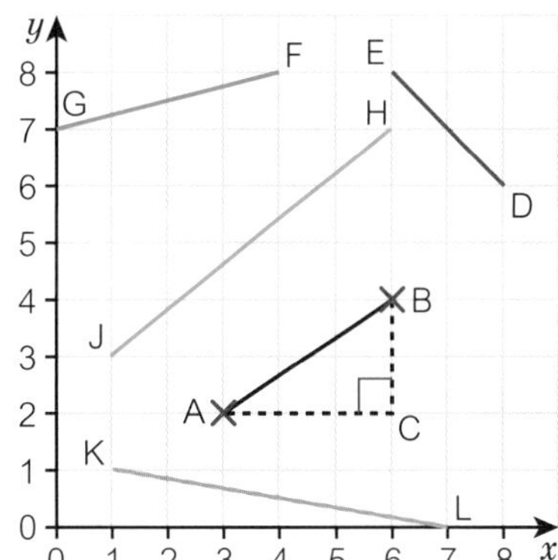

Q15 hint
For the line AB, use the coordinates of A and B to find lengths AC and BC.

16 Work out the distance between each pair of points, correct to one decimal place.

a (2, 3) and (7, 5)
b (0, 6) and (8, 4)
c (−2, 3) and (4, 6)
d (5, 2) and (3, −1)
e (−3, −2) and (1, 6)
f (−4, 3) and (2, −5)

Q16 Strategy hint
Draw a diagram.

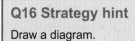

17 The sailfish is the world's fastest fish and can swim at a speed of 30 m/s.

a How far can it travel in

i 10 seconds **ii** 1 minute **iii** 1 hour?

b Convert 30 m/s to km/h.

Q17b hint

Convert your answer from part **a iii** to km.

18 STEM / Modelling The tip of the blade of a wind turbine travels at 320 km/h.

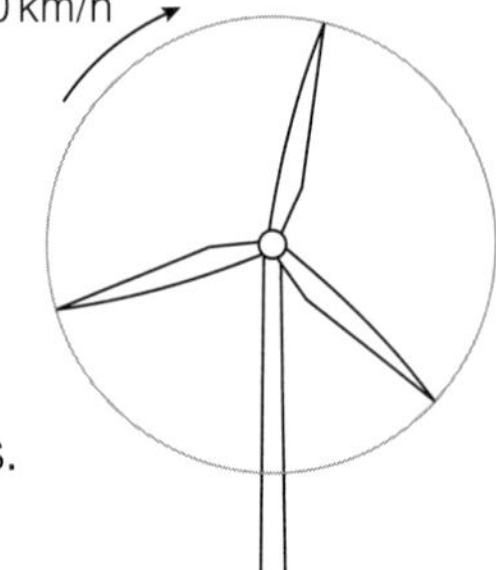

a Convert this speed to m/s.

b The blade has a length of 50 m.
How long does it take for the blade to rotate 360°? Give your answer to two decimal places.

Key point

Compound measures like km/h are used to show how one quantity changes with another. Examples are

- a speed of 25 km/h means 'every hour, you travel 25 km'
- the density of gold is 19.3 g/cm³ means '1 cm³ of gold has a mass of 19.3 g'
- a rate of flow of 5 l/min means 'every 1 minute, 5 l of liquid flows'.

19 Modelling The density of gold is 19.3 g/cm³.

a Work out the mass of

i 15 cm³ **ii** 0.1 cm³ **iii** 1 mm³

b Convert 19.3 g/cm³ to mg/mm³.

20 Finance / Modelling The diagram shows a standard bar of silver in the shape of a prism.

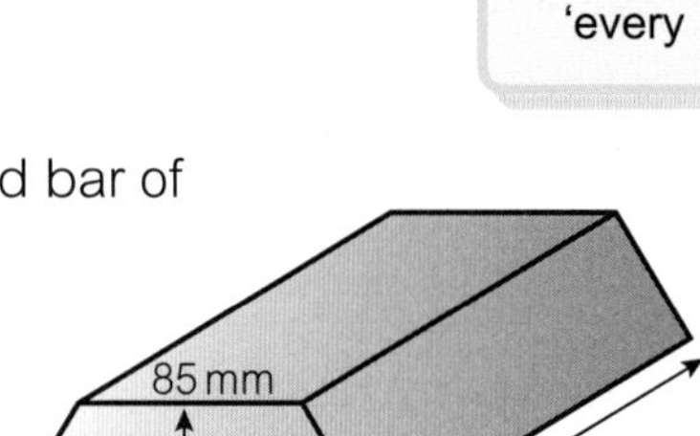

a Work out the volume of silver in the bar.

b The density of silver is 10.5 g/cm³.
Work out the mass of the bar, to the nearest 1 g.

c The price of silver is 35p/g.
Work out the value of the bar.

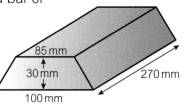

21 A car uses fuel at the rate of 90 ml/min.

a How much petrol will it use in

i 10 minutes **ii** 1 hour **iii** 1 second?

b Convert 90 ml/min to l/h.

22 Real / Finance / Modelling The interior of a toilet cistern measures 15 cm by 30 cm by 15 cm.

a The cistern takes 1 minute to refill after flushing.
Work out the rate of flow in ml/s.

b A cuboid brick measuring 215 mm by 102.5 mm by 65 mm is placed in the bottom of the cistern to save water.

i Work out the new volume of water in the cistern.

ii How long will it take to fill the cistern now?

c The price of water is 0.34375p per litre. If the cistern is flushed 2000 times in a year, work out the amount of money saved by using the brick.

Discussion Is this a good model for a toilet cistern?

23 STEM / Reasoning A 250 g bag contains approximately 120 sweets. There is a ±10% error interval in the weight of the bag and a ±5% error interval in the number of sweets.

a Work out the lower and upper bounds for the mass m of a sweet.

b Explain why your answers might not be accurate.

24 Modelling A $1 coin has a diameter of 26.5 mm and is 2 mm thick.

a Work out the volume of the coin. Give your answer in cm³.

b The coin has a mass of 8.1 g.
Work out the density of the coin.

25 Modelling The diagram shows a square nut and square-headed bolt.
Work out the total volume of metal.
Discussion What assumptions did you make?

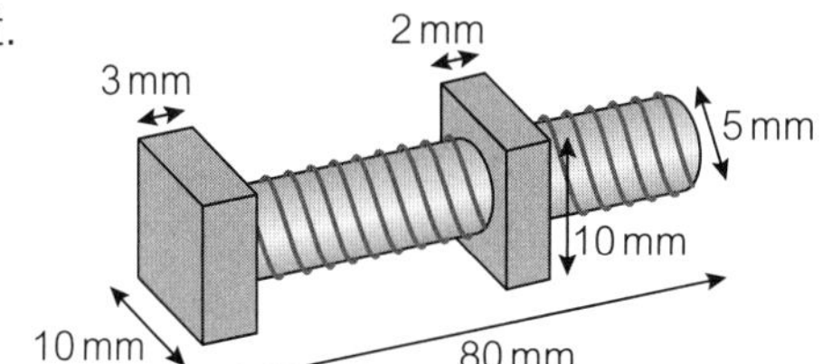

26 Problem-solving / Modelling A cylindrical paint roller has a diameter of 10 cm and length of 30 cm.
The roller has to be refilled with paint every 20 complete revolutions.

a Work out the number of times a painter will need to refill the roller when painting a ceiling measuring 1 m by 5 m.

b Explain why your answer will not be accurate.

27 Problem-solving The diagram shows a Nissen hut built by the army during the First World War.
The hut has a semicircular cross-section and is 12 m long.
The area of the metal roof is 175 m^2.
Make a scale drawing of the front end.

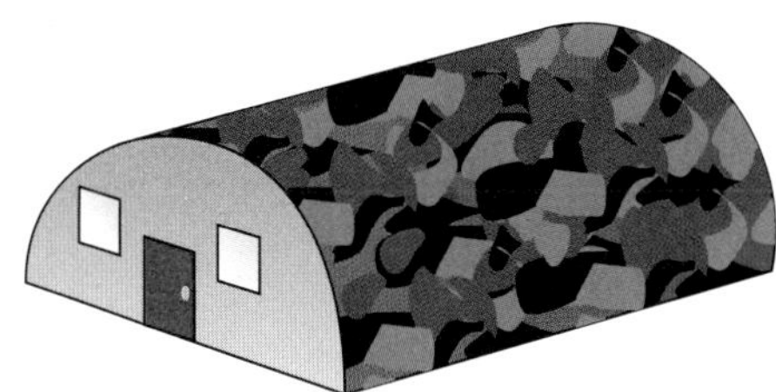

28 Problem-solving A quarter-circle has a perimeter of 50 cm.
Work out its radius, r cm.

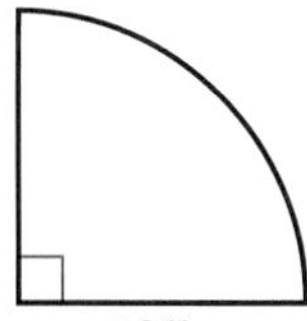
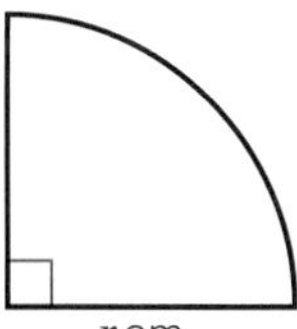

Q28 hint
Write an equation involving π and r.

29 STEM / Problem-solving A hospital patient receives drops of saline solution at a rate of 2 ml/min from a cylindrical container with diameter 5 cm and height 20 cm.

a How long does it take to empty a full container?

b There are 15 drops per ml. How many drops are in a full container?

c Draw a graph to show the height of the saline solution in the container during the first hour.

30 Problem-solving / Reasoning A python is tightly coiled on the ground in four full turns.

a Estimate the length of the python.

b How do you think the length of the python depends upon its thickness? Would it be half as long if it was half as thick?
Try out a calculation and see.

c Modelling Do you think this a good model for the length of a python?

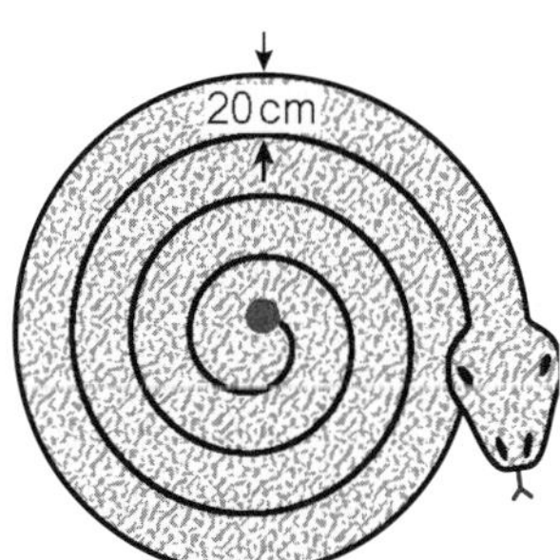

Investigation **Problem-solving**

The diameter of a circular patio is 3.6 m

1 Work out its circumference and area.

2 The diameter is doubled. What happens to **a** the circumference **b** the area?

3 Work out a rule to describe how the circumference and area change for different diameters of patio.

31 Reflect In problem-solving in mathematics and other sciences, you are not always told the steps to follow or the formula to use.
You have to think of them for yourself.
Look back at Q15.
Why do you think the hint suggests that your first step is to work out the length of AC?
What formula did you use? Why?

Q31 hint
If you find AC, then you can ___.
Then, this means you can ___.

Reflect

7 Unit test

Log how you did on your Student Progression Chart.

1 A circle has a radius of 4.2 cm.

a Work out the diameter of the circle.

b Work out the circumference of the circle.
Use a sensible degree of accuracy for your answer.

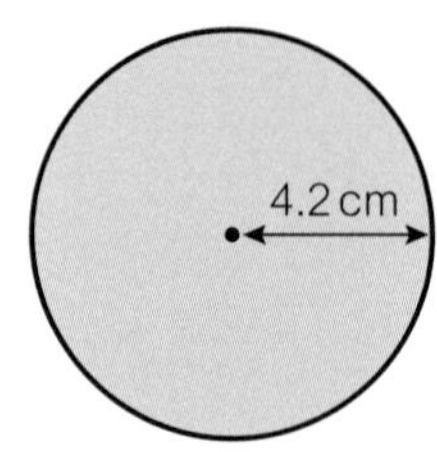

2 A circle has a circumference of 45 m.
Give your answers to an appropriate degree of accuracy.
Work out

a the diameter b the radius c the area.

3 Calculate the length of the unknown side of each triangle.

a

3 cm, x, 5 cm

b

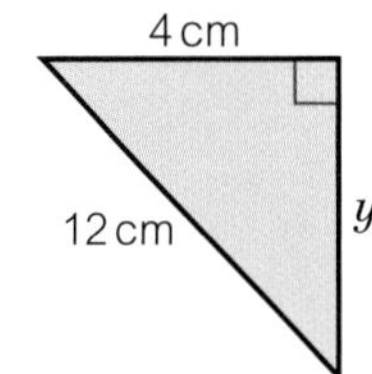

Give your answers to the nearest mm.

4 A circle has an area of $2\,\text{m}^2$.

a Work out the radius of the circle, correct to two decimal places.

b Work out the circumference, correct to the nearest cm.

5 Work out the volume of this prism.

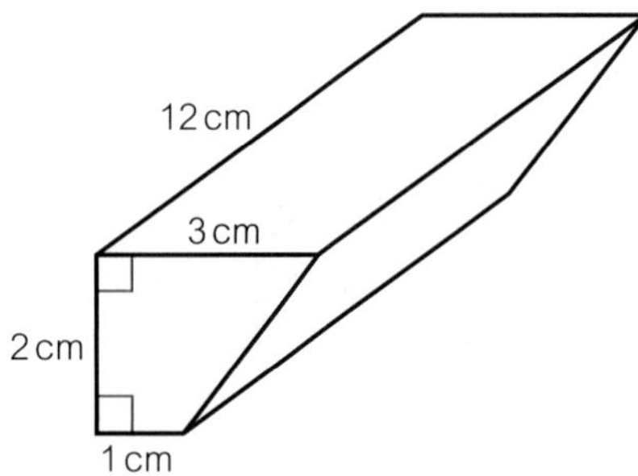

6 A wheel has a diameter of 35 cm, to the nearest 10 cm.

a Write an inequality to show

i the lower and upper bounds for the diameter d of the wheel

ii the lower and upper bounds for the circumference C of the wheel.

b In one day the wheel revolves 1200 times, to the nearest 100.
Work out the lower and upper bounds for the total distance travelled.
Give your answers in km.

7 A rectangle has length 5 m and height 3 m, measured to the nearest 1 m.
Work out the lower and upper bounds for the area A of the rectangle.
Write your answer using an inequality.

8 A pack of mixed flower bulbs contains 20 bulbs, to within a $\pm 10\%$ error interval.

a Work out the minimum and maximum possible number of bulbs in a pack.

b Write the number of bulbs n in a pack using an inequality.

9 a Work out the area of the cross-section of this prism.

b Work out the length of the sloping side, l.

c Work out the total surface area of the prism.

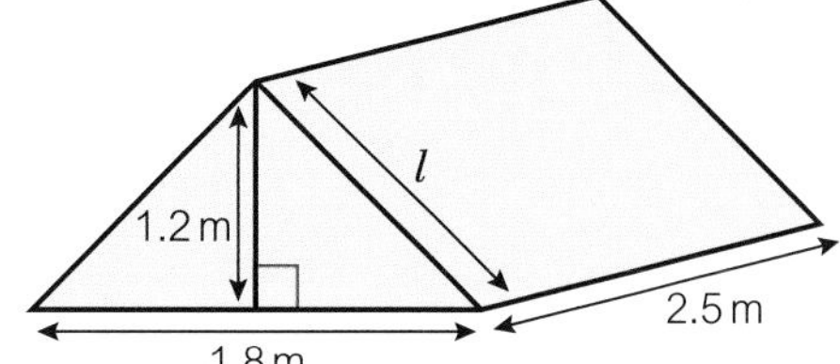

10 A cylinder has a radius of 5 cm and height of 12 cm.

a Work out the volume of the cylinder, correct to the nearest cm^3.

b Work out the total surface area of the cylinder, correct to the nearest cm^2.

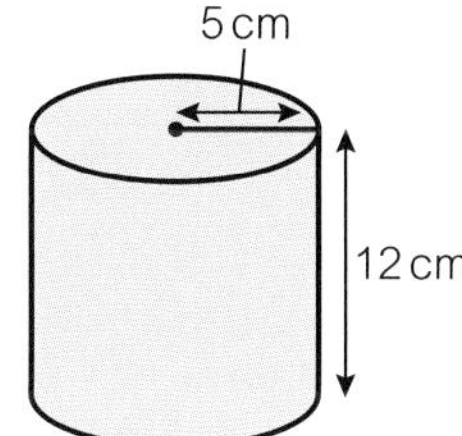

11 The world's biggest coin is an Australian $1 million pure gold coin. It has a diameter of 80 cm and a thickness of 12 cm.

a Work out the volume of the coin, to the nearest cm^3.

b The density of gold is 19.3 g/cm^3.
Work out the mass of the coin, to the nearest kg.

c The price of pure gold is $44.50 per gram.
Is the coin worth $1 million?
Explain your answer.

Challenge

12 A garden centre sells bird food in cylindrical tubs.
Which tub provides the best value for money?
Which is the worst value?

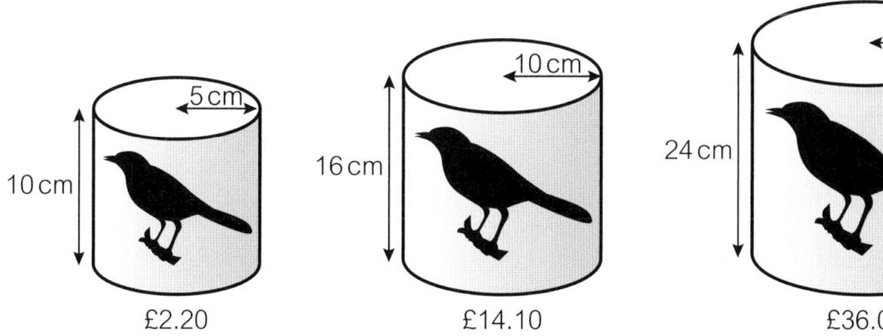

13 **Reflect** This unit is called, 'Circles, Pythagoras and prisms'.
Which of these topics did you like best? Why?
Which of these topics did you like least? Why?

Reflect

8 Sequences and graphs

MASTER

Check P212 | Strengthen P214 | Extend P219 | Test P223

8.1 nth term of arithmetic sequences

You will learn to:

- Use the nth term to generate a sequence
- Find the nth term of a sequence.

CONFIDENCE

Why learn this?
Position-to-term rules can help you find the 100th term in a sequence without finding the first 99.

Fluency
Which of these are arithmetic sequences? Find the common differences of the ones that are.

- 1, 5, 9, 13, …
- 2, 4, 8, 18, …
- 10, 8, 6, 4, …
- 0.7, 1.2, 1.7, 2.2, …

Explore
Will you be an expert by the time you are 18?

Exercise 8.1

Warm up

1 Write down the first four multiples of
a 6 b −2 c −10

2 Work out the value of
a $2x$, when $x = 4$
b $3x$, when $x = 2$
c $4x + 1$, when $x = 3$
d $5x - 1$, when $x = 7$
e $50 - 4x$, when $x = 5$
f $-2x + 4$, when $x = 3$

3 a Find the **position-to-term** rule for each sequence.

i

Position	1	2	3	4	5
Term	3	4	5	6	7

ii

Position	1	2	3	4	5
Term	8	16	24	32	40

b Write your answers to part **a** using algebra to give the ***n*th term** of each sequence.

4 Copy and complete to generate the first five terms of the sequence $3n$.
When $n = 1$, $3n = \square$
When $n = 2$, $3n = \square$
When $n = 3$, $3n = \square$
When $n = 4$, $3n = \square$
When $n = 5$, $3n = \square$
First five terms: $\square, \square, \square, \square, \square$

new Q4
new Q5

Key point
The ***n*th term** of a sequence is its **position-to-term** rule. It tells you how to work out the term at position n. The nth term is sometimes called the **general term** of the sequence.

Q3a hint
Work out what you do to the position number to get the term.

Q4 Literacy hint
'To **generate**' means 'to create' or 'to produce'.

Q4 Strategy hint
To generate the 1st term, substitute $n = 1$ in the nth term.
To generate the 2nd term, substitute $n = 2$ in the nth term, and so on.
Write the terms in a list, separated by commas.

Topic links: Plotting graphs

5 Write the first five terms of the sequence with nth term

a $4n$ b $2n + 1$ c $3n - 2$

d $\frac{1}{2}n + 1$ e $20 - 5n$ f $-2n + 3$

Discussion Look at the common difference for each sequence and its nth term. What do you notice?

6 **Problem-solving** Match each sequence to its nth term.

6, 12, 18, 24, 30, …

2, 4, 6, 8, 10, …

$-2n$

$-3n$

$6n$

4, 8, 12, 16, 20, …

−2, −4, −6, −8, −10, …

−3, −6, −9, −12, −15, …

$5n$

$2n$

$4n$

5, 10, 15, 20, 25, …

Discussion What is the name for the sequence generated by $2n$? … by $5n$?

7 Write true or false for each of these. Show your working.

a The 3rd term of the sequence $4n + 2$ is 14.

b The 5th term of the sequence $3n - 8$ is 6.

c The 10th term of the sequence $2 - n$ is 8.

d The 7th term of the sequence $6 - 2n$ is -8.

Worked example

Find the nth term of the sequence 3, 7, 11, 15, 19, …

$4n$ 4, 8, 12, 16, 20, …) −1

3, 7, 11, 15, 19, …

The nth term is $4n - 1$.

The common difference is 4. Write out the first five terms of the sequence for $4n$, the multiples of 4. Compare the two sequences.

Work out how to get from each term in $4n$ to the term in the sequence.

Key point

To find the nth term of an arithmetic sequence:

1 Find the common difference.

2 If the common difference is 3, compare with the sequence for $3n$.

3 If the common difference is 4, compare with the sequence for $4n$.

And so on.

8 Find the nth term of each sequence.

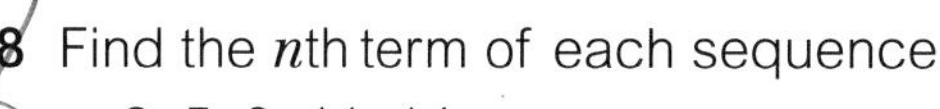

a 2, 5, 8, 11, 14, …

b 5, 7, 9, 11, 13, …

c 1, 5, 9, 13, 17, …

d 12, 17, 22, 27, 32, …

e 21, 16, 11, 6, 1, …

f −4, −7, −10, −13, −16, …

Q8e hint

When the common difference is negative, compare with the multiples of a negative number.

9 Work out the 10th term and 100th term of each sequence in Q8.

Q9 Strategy hint

To find the 10th term, substitute $n = 10$.

10 Here is a sequence of patterns made from dots.

a Draw the next pattern in the sequence.

b Copy and complete this table for the sequence of numbers of dots.

Pattern number	1	2	3	4	5
Number of dots	4	7			

c **Modelling** Work out the nth term of this sequence.

d How many dots will there be in the 40th pattern?

Q10d hint

Use the nth term.

Investigation — **Reasoning / Modelling**

1 Copy and complete the table for the first five terms of the sequence $2n + 5$.

n	1	2	3	4	5
$2n + 5$	7				

2 Draw a pair of axes with the x-axis from 0 to 6 and the y-axis from 0 to 20.
Plot the values from your table on your axes.
For example, for the first term plot (1, 7). Join the points.

3 In the same way, plot the first five points of the sequences with nth term

a $3n + 3$

b $5n - 6$

c $10 - 2n$

Part 3 hint

Use different colours for the points in **a**, **b** and **c**.

4 Why do you think arithmetic sequences are also called linear sequences?
Test your idea with some of the other sequences from this lesson.

11 Here is a sequence of fractions.

$\frac{2}{7}, \frac{3}{10}, \frac{4}{13}, \frac{5}{16}, \frac{6}{19}, \ldots$

a Work out the nth term.

b What do you look for in the terms of a sequence to help you find the nth term?

Q11a hint

Work out the nth term of the numerator and the nth term of the denominator.

Explore

12 **Explore** Will you be an expert by the time you are 18?
Look back at the maths you have learned in this lesson.
How can you use it to answer this question?

Reflect

13 **Reflect** Look back at Q3 and Q8.
What was the same and what was different about finding the nth terms for the sequences in Q3 and the sequences in Q8?

8.2 Non-linear sequences

You will learn to:

- Recognise and continue geometric sequences
- Recognise and continue quadratic sequences.

Why learn this?
When a ball bounces, the heights of the bounces form a sequence.

Fluency
What is the next term?

- 1, 2, 4, 8, …
- 1, 3, 9, 27, …
- 50, 25, 12.5, …

Explore
How long will it take for an object dropped from the top of The Shard to hit the ground?

CONFIDENCE

Exercise 8.2

Warm up

1 Complete these statements.

a Multiplying by $\frac{1}{2}$ is the same as dividing by □.

b Multiplying by $\frac{1}{10}$ is the same as dividing by □.

2 Generate the first five terms of the sequence with nth term

a $4n - 5$ b $\frac{1}{2}n + 3$

3 Work out the value of

a $2x^2$, when $x = 5$

b $3x^2$, when $x = -2$

c $-4x^2$, when $x = 3$

d $\frac{1}{2}x^2$, when $x = 6$

4 All these sequences are **geometric sequences**.

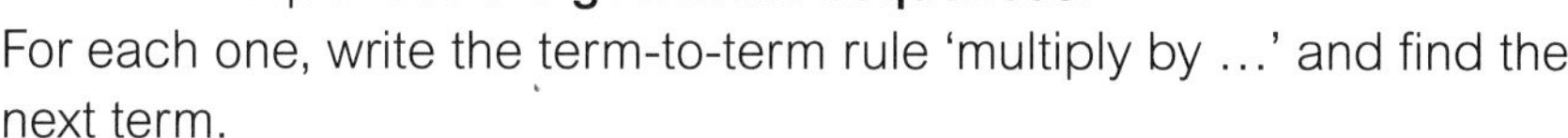

For each one, write the term-to-term rule 'multiply by …' and find the next term.

a 1, 4, 16, 64, …

b −2, −6, −18, −54, …

c 120, 60, 30, 15, …

d 2, 3, 4.5, 6.75, …

e 600, 200, $66\frac{2}{3}$, $22\frac{2}{9}$, …

f 1000, 100, 10, 1, …

Key point

In a **geometric sequence**, the term-to-term rule is 'multiply by a number'.

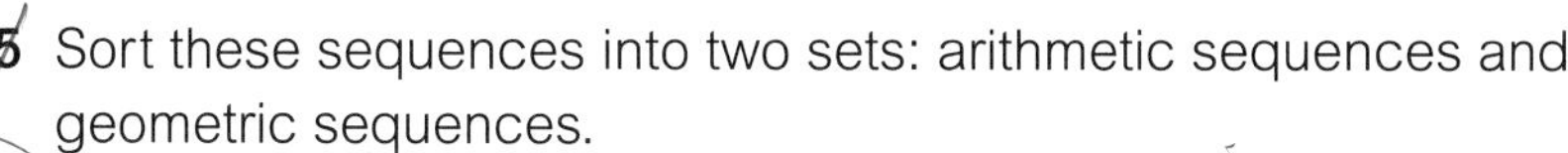

5 Sort these sequences into two sets: arithmetic sequences and geometric sequences.

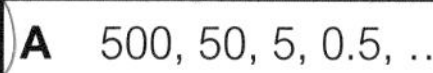

A 500, 50, 5, 0.5, …	B 1.8, 3.6, 5.4, 7.2, …	C 1, 5, 9, 13, …
D 2, 4, 8, 16, …	E 0.3, 1.2, 4.8, 19.2, …	F 10, 25, 62.5, 156.25, …

6 **Problem-solving** For each geometric sequence, find the first term that is less than 1.

a 3296, 329.6, 32.96, …

b 1000, 500, 250, …

c 30, 10, $3\frac{1}{3}$, …

d 10^5, 10^4, 10^3, …

Discussion Will there be negative terms in these sequences?

7 Work out the term-to-term rule for each sequence and write down the next two terms.

a −5, −25, 125, −625, …

b 3, −6, 12, −36, …

Investigation **Problem-solving**

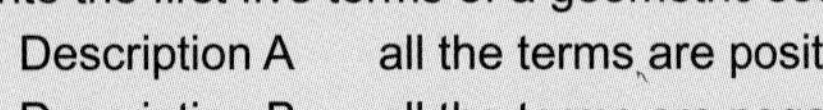

1 Write the first five terms of a geometric sequence and the term-to-term rule to match each description.

Description A	all the terms are positive
Description B	all the terms are negative
Description C	the first term is negative, second is positive, third is negative and so on
Description D	all the terms are less than 1

Strategy hint

Choose an easy starting number.
Try out different term-to-term rules.

2 Which of your sequences are increasing? Write decreasing sequences that match the same descriptions.

3 Which of your sequences are decreasing? Write increasing sequences that match the same descriptions.

8 **Real / Modelling** A ball is dropped on to a hard surface from a height of 300 cm. It bounces back up to half the previous height each time.

a Copy and complete the table.

Bounce number	1	2	3	4	5
Height of bounce (cm)	150	75			

b Which is the first bounce less than 1 cm?

c Will the bouncing ever stop?

Discussion Is this a good model for a bouncing ball?

Q8b hint

Continue the table. You could use a spreadsheet.

Q8c hint

The bouncing stops when the bounce height is zero.

9 **Modelling / Problem-solving** Each day, a GP recorded the number of patients with a throat infection that he saw.

Day	Mon	Tue	Wed
Number of patients	5	15	45

He said, 'If the number of cases continues to grow in the same way, there will be over 1000 cases by the end of the week.'
Is he correct? Explain.

10 Write down the first five terms of the sequence with nth term

a n^2

b $2n^2$

c $n^2 + 3$

d $\frac{1}{2}n^2$

Key point

An nth term that includes n^2 (and no higher power of n) generates a **quadratic sequence**.

11 Here is the sequence $n^2 + 1$.

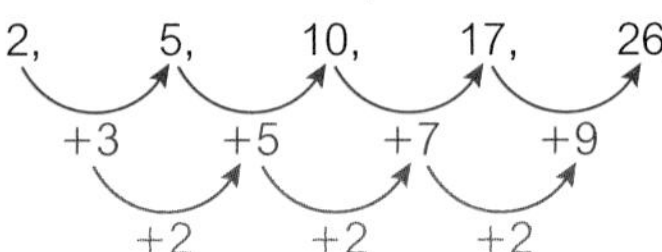

1st differences: the differences between terms

2nd differences: the differences between differences

a What is the pattern in the 1st differences?

b Use the pattern to work out the next term.

Topic links: Expanding double brackets

12 Real / Modelling Some baked bean tins in a supermarket are stacked like this.

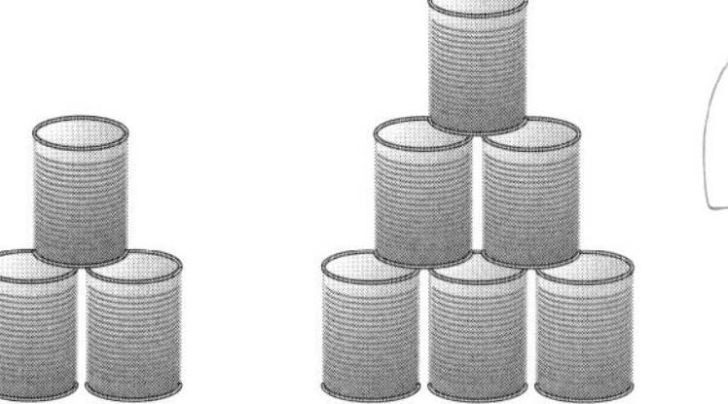

a Copy and complete this table.

Number of rows	1	2	3	4
Number of tins	1	3		

+ □

b Pete wants to make a display of baked bean tins 8 rows high. How many tins does he need?

13 All these nth terms generate quadratic sequences.

A $n^2 + 2$

B $n^2 + 5$

C $n^2 - 4$

a For each one

i write down the first five terms

ii write down the 1st differences

iii write down the 2nd differences.

Q13a hint

Set the sequences out in the same way as in Q11.

b What do you notice about the 2nd differences of sequences with n^2 in the nth term?

c Work out the 1st and 2nd differences of these sequences.

i $2n^2 + 1$

ii $3n^2$

iii $4n^2 - 1$

d What do you notice about the 2nd differences of sequences with a multiple of n^2 in the nth term?

e Reasoning Explain how you can tell if a sequence is quadratic by looking at its 2nd differences.

14 Reasoning

a Write down the first five terms of the sequence with nth term $(n + 4)(n - 1)$.

b What type of sequence is it?

c Jenny says, 'This sequence is not quadratic because the nth term does not include n^2.'

Explain why she is incorrect.

Q14c hint

Can you write $(n + 4)(n - 1)$ in another way?

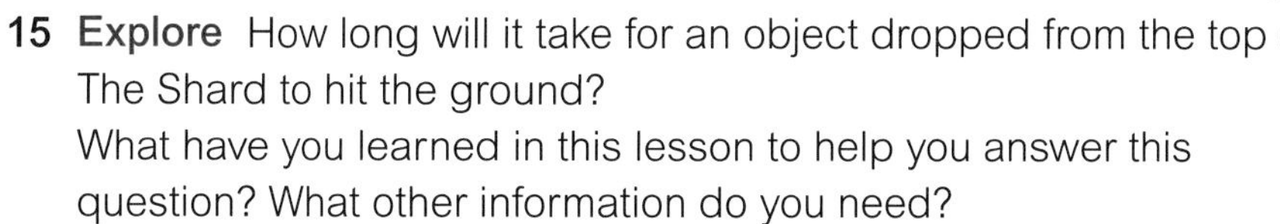

15 **Explore** How long will it take for an object dropped from the top of The Shard to hit the ground?
What have you learned in this lesson to help you answer this question? What other information do you need?

16 **Reflect** Copy and complete this sentence.

I know when a sequence is linear because ______________

Write sentences like this for a geometric sequence and a quadratic sequence.

Explore

Reflect

8.3 Graphing rates of change

You will learn to:

- Use distance–time graphs to solve problems
- Recognise graphs showing constant rates of change
- Interpret graphs showing rates of change.

CONFIDENCE

Why learn this?
Scientists identify when an object is travelling fastest from its distance–time graph.

Fluency
A car travels at a constant speed of 50 km/h.

- What does 'constant speed' mean?
- How far does it go in
  a 1 hour
  b 2 hours
  c 1.5 hours?

Explore
Does a cup of tea cool at a constant rate?

Exercise 8.3

Warm up

1 This distance–time graph shows Chon's car journey.

a What time did he stop for a break?

b How long did he stop for?

c How long did his journey take in total?

d How far did he travel in total?

e How long did it take him to travel the first 150 km?

f What was his average speed for the first part of the journey?
Give your answer in km/h.

g How far did he travel at 100 km/h?

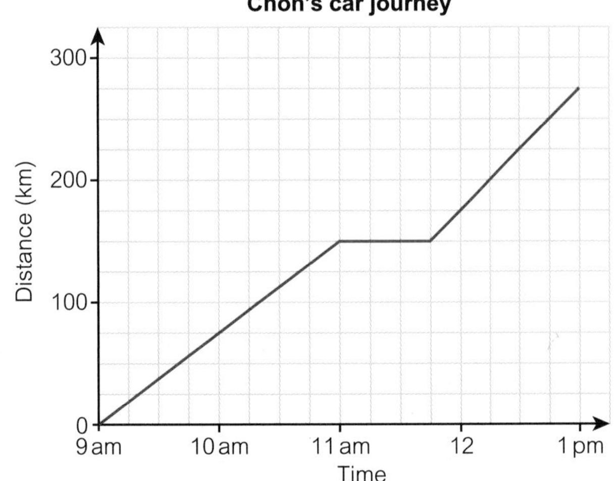

2 Problem-solving Mrs Smith walks 500 m to the shops.
This takes her 10 minutes.
She spends half an hour shopping, then walks home.
It takes her 20 minutes to walk home.

a Minnie and Dan sketch graphs to show Mrs Smith's journey.

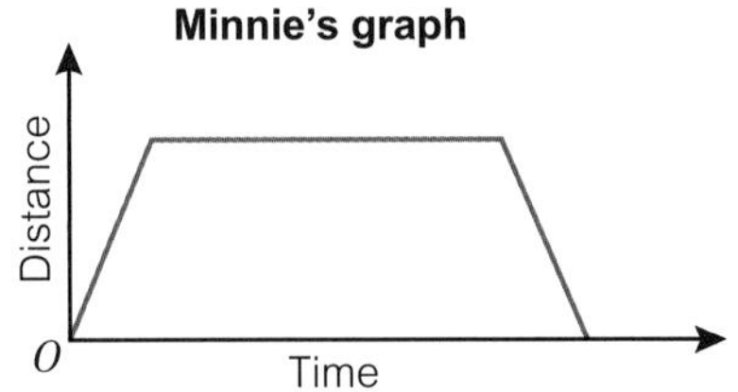

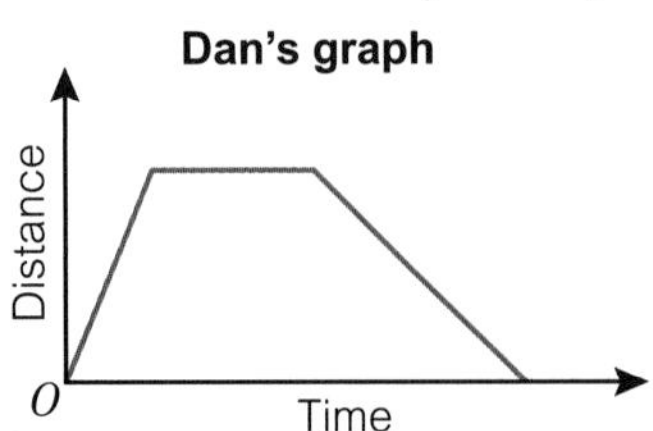

They are both incorrect. Explain what is wrong with each graph.

b Sketch a more accurate graph for Mrs Smith's journey.

c How far does Mrs Smith walk in total?
Give your answer in kilometres.

Q2a hint
Look at the times for the different sections of the journey.

Q2b hint
Use axes like Minnie and Dan's.

Topic links: Sequences, Straight-line graphs

3 Ellie left her house at 10 am. She walked 6 km in $1\frac{1}{2}$ hours. Then she rested for half an hour before she walked back. She arrived home at 3 pm.

a Draw a graph to show this information.

b What speed was she walking on her walk back?

4 Reasoning Look at the graph in Q1 and the graphs you drew in Q2 and Q3.

a How is the steepness of the line linked to speed in a distance–time graph?

b Write a sentence to explain how you can identify from a distance–time graph when an object is travelling fastest.

Worked example

The distance–time graph shows a train journey. What was the **average speed** for the whole journey?

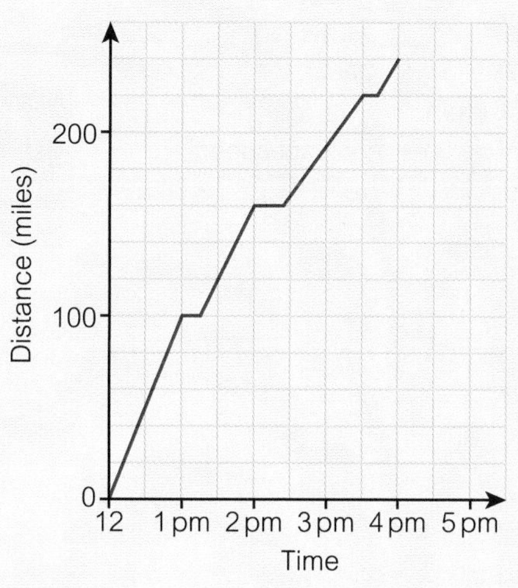

total distance = 240 miles — Read the total distance and total time from the graph.

total time = 4 hours

average speed = $\frac{240}{4}$ = 60 miles per hour — 'Share' the total distance equally between the 4 hours (total time).

Key point

average speed = $\frac{\text{total distance}}{\text{total time}}$

Key point

A **rate of change graph** shows how a quantity changes over time.

A distance–time graph is a rate of change graph because it shows how the distance travelled changes over time.

5 Work out the average speeds for the journeys in Q1, Q2 and Q3. Give your answers in km/h.

6 Real / Modelling Train A travels from York to London. Train B travels from London to York.

a Use the graph to estimate how far they are from London when they pass each other.

b Which train travelled faster on average?

Discussion Are these distance–time graphs good models for train journeys?

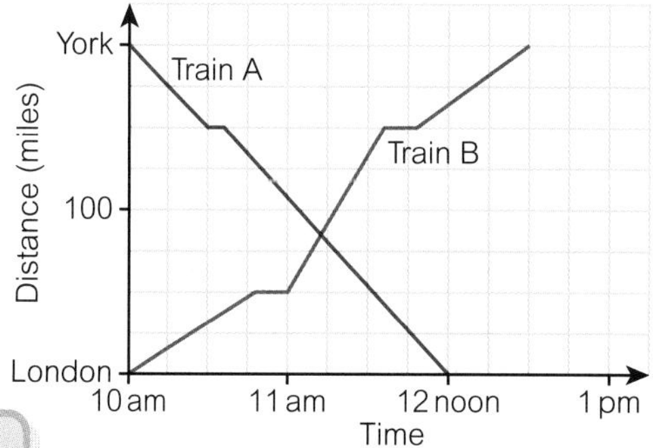

Investigation — Modelling / Reasoning

This table shows the depth of water as a paddling pool fills up.

Time (minutes)	0	1	2
Depth (cm)	0	20	30

1 How much does the depth increase in

a the first minute **b** the second minute?

2 When is the depth increasing faster?

3 Sketch a **rate of change graph** for filling the pool.

4 Draw an accurate graph to check your prediction.

5 Complete this sentence about your graph.

The steeper the graph, the ______ the depth is increasing.

7 Real / Modelling John throws a ball straight up into the air.
The table shows the ball's height above the ground on its way up.

Time, t (seconds)	1	2	3	4	5
Height, h (m)	2	3.12	4.08	4.88	5.52

a Draw a graph to show this information.

b Is the ball travelling at constant speed? How can you tell?

Discussion When is the ball travelling fastest?

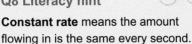

Q7a hint

Put 'Time' on the horizontal axis and 'Height' on the vertical axis.
Plot the points and join them with a smooth curve.

8 Real / Reasoning Water runs into these three containers at a constant rate.

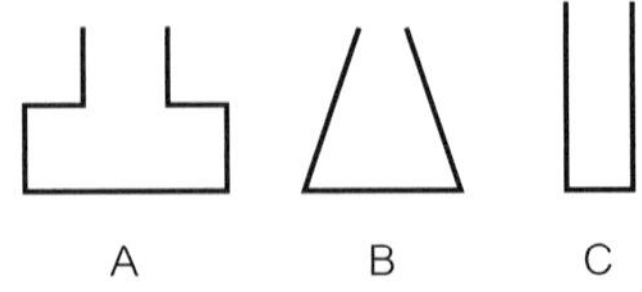

a Which container do you think will fill up the fastest? Why?

The tables show the depth of water in the three different containers for the first 6 seconds.

Time, t (s)	1	2	3	4	5	6
Water depth, h (cm)	2	4	5.5	6.5	7	7.25

Time, t (s)	1	2	3	4	5	6
Water depth, h (cm)	2	4	6	8	10	12

Time, t (s)	1	2	3	4	5	6
Water depth, h (cm)	2	3	4	6	8	10

b Draw the graph of depth of water against time for each container.

c Which graph is for which container? Label your graphs A, B and C.

d What type of graph shows a constant rate of change?

Q8 Literacy hint

Constant rate means the amount flowing in is the same every second.

Q8b hint

Put 'Time' on the horizontal axis.

Q8d hint

In which container does the depth of water increase by the same amount every second?

9 Real The graph shows the depth of water in a bath. Match each statement to a section, A to E, on the graph.

a person gets out of the bath

b water running in at steady rate

c water running out at steady rate

d person gets into the bath

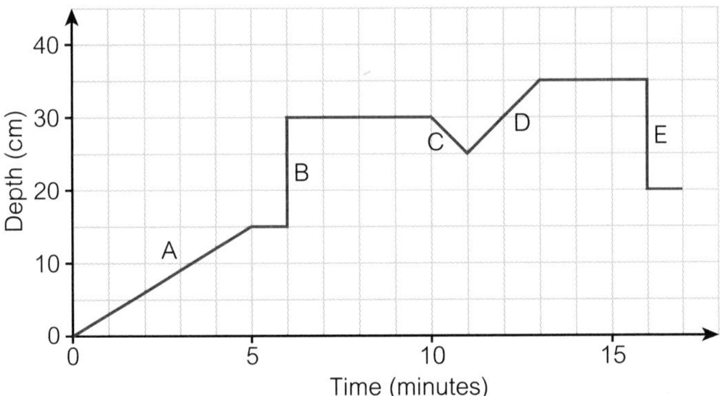

10 Explore Does a cup of tea cool at a constant rate?
Is it easier to explore this question now you have completed the lesson?
What further information do you need to be able to answer this?

11 Reflect Geraldine says, 'You can describe rates like ratios. A ratio is one blue bead *for every* red bead. Speed is the distance you travel *for every* hour.'
Look back at the questions you answered about rates. Is Geraldine correct?
Larry says, 'Ratios compare similar things, like red beads to blue beads, or male people to female people. Rates compare different quantities, like distance to time, or heart beat to time.'
Look back at the questions you answered about rates.
Is Larry correct?
Write down your own example of a ratio and a rate.

Explore

Reflect

8.4 Using $y = mx + c$

You will learn to:
- Draw a graph from its equation, without working out points
- Write the equation of a line parallel to another line
- Compare graph lines using their equations.

CONFIDENCE

Why learn this?
Computer games designers specify how a character moves across the screen by giving the equations of the lines they follow.

Fluency
- Which graph has positive gradient? Which has negative?
- What are the x- and y-intercepts of each graph?

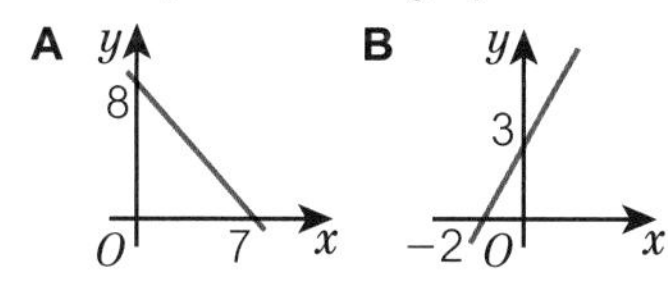

Explore
How can a video game character move around an obstacle?

Exercise 8.4

1 For each line
  a work out the gradient
  b write down the y-intercept
  c write down the equation.

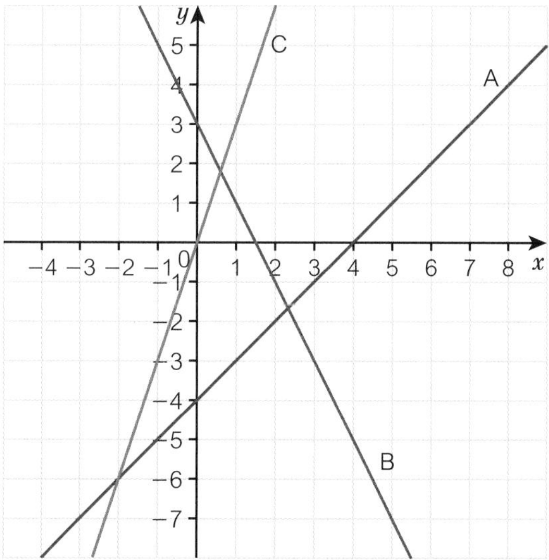

2 **Reasoning** a Look at the graph in Q1. Which line is steepest?
  b How can you tell which graph is steepest just by looking at the equations?

3 Here are the equations of some lines.
Write them in ascending order of steepness.

A $y = 4x$	**B** $y = 2x$
C $y = -x$	**D** $y = \frac{1}{2}x$
E $y = 5x$	**F** $y = 1.5x$

Warm up

Worked example

On the same grid, draw these graphs from their equations.

a $y = 2x - 1$

b $y = -x + 4$

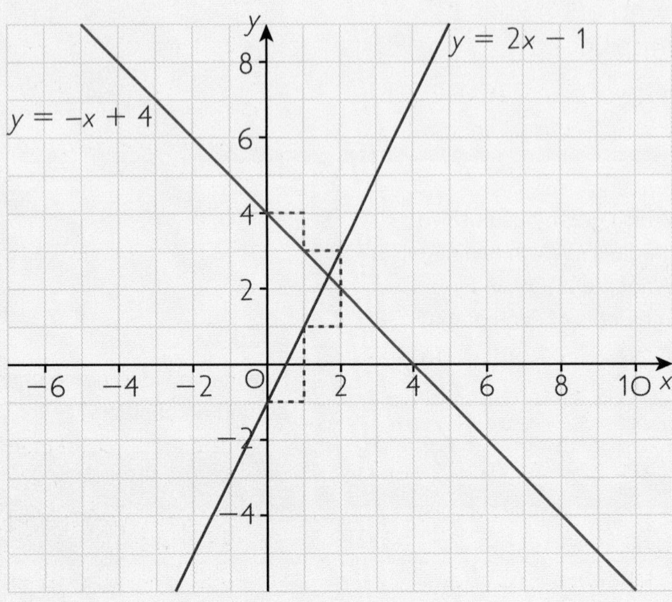

Plot the y-intercept.
Decide if the gradient is positive or negative.
Draw a line with this gradient, starting from the y-intercept.
Extend your line right across the grid.
Label the line with its equation.

4 Draw these graphs from their equations.
Use a coordinate grid from −10 to +10 on both axes.

a $y = 2x + 3$ **b** $y = 2x - 2$

c $y = 3x$ **d** $y = \frac{1}{2}x + 1$

e $y = -2x + 1$ **f** $y = -3x + 4$

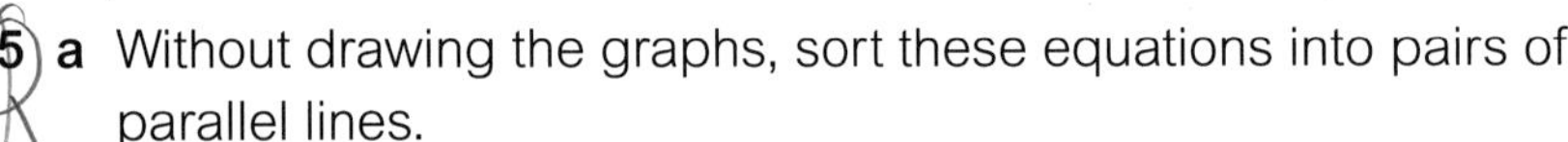

5 a Without drawing the graphs, sort these equations into pairs of parallel lines.

A $y = -2x + 3$ **B** $y = \frac{1}{2}x + 3$

C $y = 2x - 3$ **D** $y = -2x - 23$

E $y = 2x + 3$ **F** $y = 0.5x - 3$

b Which of the equations in part **a** give lines that intercept the y-axis in the same place?

Discussion What is the same in the equations of two lines that are parallel? What is different?

Q5a hint
What do you know about the gradients of parallel lines?

6 Write the equation of a line parallel to

a $y = 3x + 4$

b $y = -2x + 6$

Q6 hint
What has to be the same in the equation? What has to be different?

7 **Real / Problem-solving** A games designer has an alien moving on the line $y = 3x - 1$, a spaceship on the line $y = 2x + 3$ and a stormtrooper on the line $y = 3x + 2$.

a Can the alien get back to the spaceship?

b Can the stormtrooper catch the alien? Explain.

Topic links: 2D shapes

Subject link: Computing (Q7, Q10, Q12, Q14)

8 Write the equation of the line

a parallel to $y = 3x + 5$ with y-intercept $(0, -2)$

b parallel to $y = -4x + 6$ that passes through $(0, 3)$

c parallel to $y = 2x - 3$ that passes through the origin.

9 a What is the x-coordinate of every point on the line $x = 4$?

b Where does the line $y = 2x + 1$ cross the line $x = 4$?

Q9b Strategy hint

Substitute your x-value from part **a** into the equation of the line to get the y-value. Write the x- and y-values as coordinates.

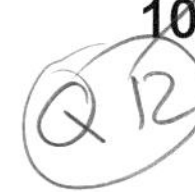

10 **Problem-solving** In a video game, a hungry caterpillar moves along the line $y = 3x + 2$. An apple moves along the line $x = 3$. Where will the caterpillar eat the apple?

11 **Problem-solving** Find the coordinates of the point

a where the line $y = x + 4$ crosses the line $y = 5$

b where the line $y = 2x + 5$ crosses the line $y = -3$.

12 **Problem-solving** In a video game, a character moves along on the line $y = 2x + 5$. A pot of gold is at the point $(3, 8)$.

a Will the character get to the pot of gold?

The character continues to move along the same line in search of other rewards.

b Which of these rewards will it get to?

axe at $(-1, 3)$ crown at $(-2, -1)$ shield at $(-2.5, 0)$

Q12a hint

What is the x-coordinate at the point $(3, 8)$? Substitute this into the equation of the line. Does it give the correct y-value?

13 **Real / Modelling** A sales team boss uses a graph of this equation to work out the monthly pay for his staff.

$$y = 25x + 1500$$

where x is the number of items sold and y is the total monthly pay (£).

a Draw the graph of this equation.

The pay includes a basic payment (£), and then an amount (£) for every item they sell.

b What is the basic payment?

c How much do they get for every item they sell?

Investigation **Problem-solving**

1 Draw a coordinate grid with axes from −10 to +10.

2 On the grid, draw a parallelogram with two sides of gradient 3 and two sides of gradient −2.

3 Write down the equations of the lines that make the parallelogram.

4 What shapes can you make using lines with these gradients?

1, 4, −1, 0

5 Can you make a square? Explain.

Part 4 hint

Draw the lines on squared paper first. Then try them in different positions on a coordinate grid.

14 **Explore** How can a video game character move around an obstacle?

Look back at the maths you have learned in this lesson.

How can you use it to answer the question?

15 **Reflect** Write down, in your own words, as many facts about gradients of straight lines as you can.

Compare your facts with your classmates'.

Q15 hint

Think about what 'gradient' means. Also think about the different types of gradients and how to find a gradient.

8.5 More straight-line graphs

You will learn to:

- Plot graphs with equations like $ax + by = c$
- Rearrange equations of graphs into $y = mx + c$
- Find inverse functions and plot their graphs.

CONFIDENCE

Why learn this?
Equations of graphs are not always written as $y = mx + c$. Reorganising them lets you compare them.

Fluency

- What is the value of y, when x is 0, for these equations?
  - **a** $y = 3x$
  - **b** $y = 3x + 1$
  - **c** $y = 7x - 2$
- What are the inverse operations for
  - **a** ×5
  - **b** −8
  - **c** ×2 + 1?

Explore
What size shoes should you wear?

Exercise 8.5

Warm up

1 Draw the graph of $y = 2x + 5$.

2 Solve

- **a** $5x + 4 = 34$
- **b** $4x + 7 = -5$
- **c** $18 - 2x = 13$

3 Make x the subject of

- **a** $y = x + 4$
- **b** $y = 3x$
- **c** $y = x - 6$
- **d** $y = \frac{1}{2}x$

4

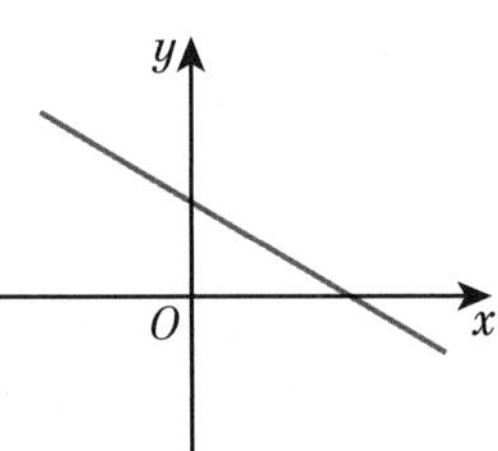

- **a** What is the value of x at any point on the y-axis?
- **b** What is the value of y at any point on the x-axis?
- **c** Copy and complete.
  - **i** The y-intercept of a graph has x-coordinate □.
  - **ii** The x-intercept of a graph has y-coordinate □.

Topic links: Transformations, Changing the subject of a formula

Worked example

Plot the graph of $3x + 4y = 6$.

When $x = 0$,

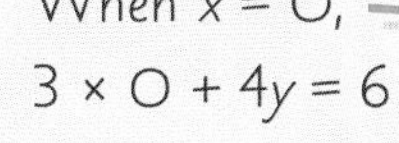

$3 \times 0 + 4y = 6$

$4y = 6$

$y = \frac{6}{4}$

$= \frac{3}{2}$

$= 1\frac{1}{2}$

To find the y-intercept, substitute $x = 0$ into the equation. Solve to find the value of y.

When $y = 0$,

$3x + 4 \times 0 = 6$

$3x = 6$

$x = 2$

To find the x-intercept, substitute $y = 0$ into the equation. Solve to find the value of x.

Draw a table of values with $x = 0$ and $y = 0$.

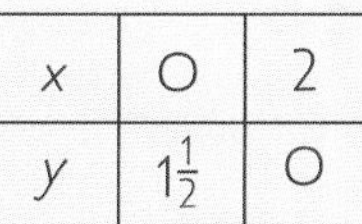

x	0	2
y	$1\frac{1}{2}$	0

Plot the points and join them with a straight line. Label the line with its equation.

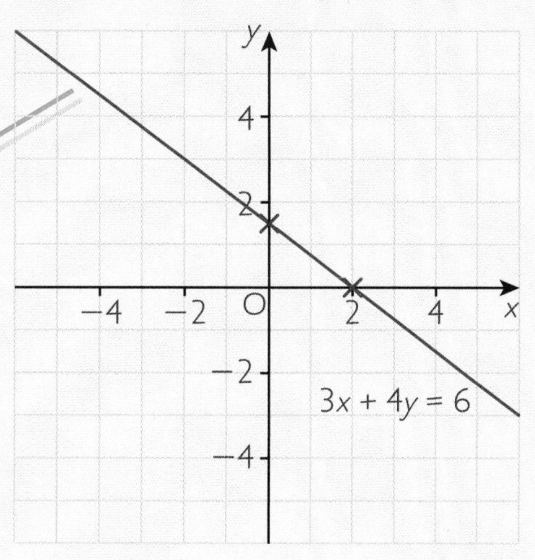

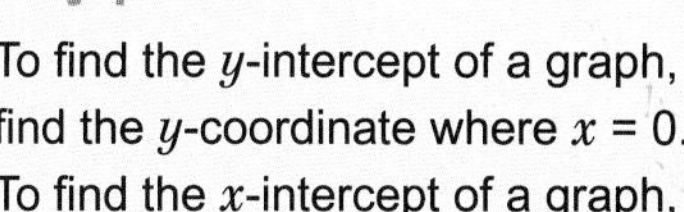

Key point

To find the y-intercept of a graph, find the y-coordinate where $x = 0$.
To find the x-intercept of a graph, find the x-coordinate where $y = 0$.

5 Plot the graph of

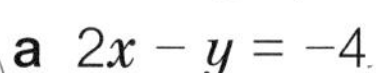

a $2x - y = -4$ **b** $3x - y = 2$ **c** $y + 3x = 1$
d $2y - x = 2$ **e** $x - y = 3$ **f** $x + y = 5$

Discussion Look at the equation and graph in part **f**. Where do you think the graph of $x + y = 7$ will cross the axes? … $x + y = -2$?

Q5 hint

You could use a graph plotting package to plot the graphs.

6 **Real / Modelling** The equation $36y - 5x = 160$ links the temperature in degrees Celsius (y) with the number of times a cricket chirps in 1 minute (x).

a Draw a graph for this equation.
Draw your x-axis from −40 to +120 and your y-axis from 0 to +20.

b Do crickets chirp more or less as it gets hotter?

c Use your graph to estimate
  i the temperature when a cricket chirps 80 times per minute
  ii the number of times a cricket chirps when the temperature is 20°C.

Discussion Crickets live in warm countries. Do you think the graph is a useful model for estimating temperature from the number of cricket chirps?

Q6a hint

Round your values for x and y to the nearest whole number if necessary.

7 Which is the steepest line?

A $y = 2x + 3$ **B** $3x + 2y = 5$

C $y = \frac{1}{4}x - 5$ **D** $10x + 5y = 7$

E $2y - 7x = 8$

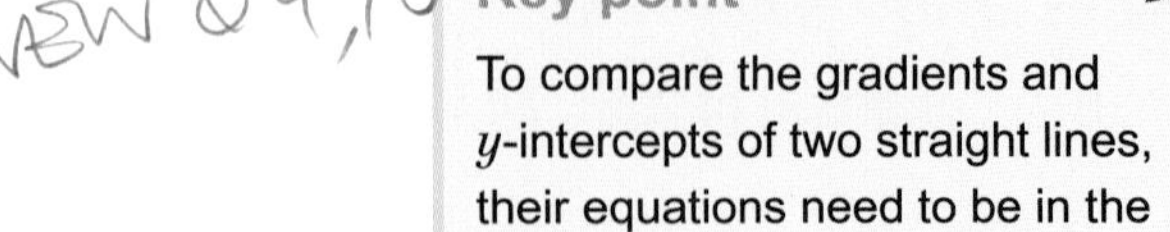

Key point

To compare the gradients and y-intercepts of two straight lines, their equations need to be in the form $y = mx + c$.

8 Which of these lines pass through $(0, -2)$?
Show how you worked it out.

A $y = -2x + 2$ **B** $2y - 3x = -4$

C $3x + 2y = 4$ **D** $5x + y = -10$

E $y = 3x - 2$

Q7 hint

Make y the subject. Write the x-term first on the right-hand side.

Investigation

Reasoning

You can write the equation of a line as a function machine.

$y = 3x + 2$

$x \rightarrow$ ×3 $\rightarrow$ +2 $\rightarrow y$

The function gives an output value y for every input value x.

You can reverse the function machines to find the **inverse function**.

$y \leftarrow$ ÷3 $\leftarrow$ −2 $\leftarrow x$

$y = \frac{x - 2}{3} = \frac{x}{3} - \frac{2}{3}$

1 Find the inverse function of

a $y = 2x$ **b** $y = 3x$ **c** $y = x$

2 Plot the graphs of $y = 2x$ and its inverse function on the same axes.

3 Do the same for $y = 3x$ and its inverse function, and $y = x$ and its inverse function.

a What do you notice about the graph of a function and its inverse function?

b Write a rule connecting the graph of a function and its inverse function.

c Test your rule for a more complex function.

d Plot the graph of $y = 3x + 2$ and its inverse function on the same axes.

e Does this graph obey your rule?

4 a Draw the graph of $y = 4x - 1$.

b Use your rule to draw the graph of the inverse function.

c Work out the equation of this line.

d Check your graph is correct by finding the inverse function of $y = 4x - 1$.

Part 2 hint

You could use a graph plotting package.

Part 3 hint

What transformation takes the graph on to the graph of its inverse function?

Explore

9 Explore What size shoes should you wear?
Is it easier to explore this question now you have completed this lesson?
What further information do you need to be able to answer this?

Reflect

10 Reflect Here are two ways to draw graphs of linear equations.

- The worked example in lesson 8.4 suggested you plot the y-intercept, and then draw a line from the y-intercept with the correct gradient.
- The worked example in lesson 8.5 suggested you draw and complete a table, like this

x	0	
y		0

and then plot the points and join them with a straight line.
Which method is better for each of these equations?

a $y = 4x + 1$ **b** $2x + 3y = 5$

Explain why.

8.6 More simultaneous equations

You will learn to:

- Solve simultaneous equations by drawing graphs
- Find the equation of a line through two points.

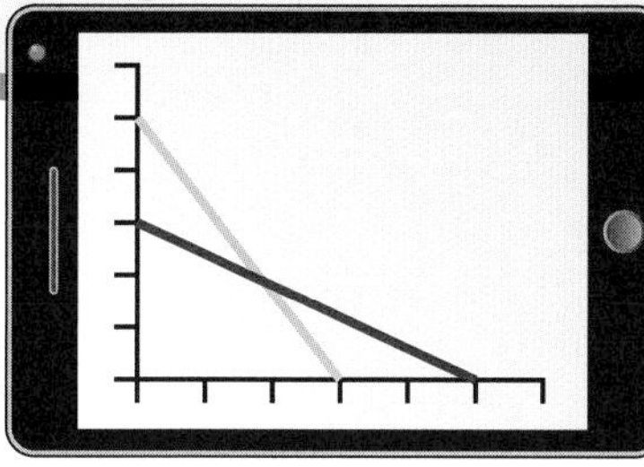

Why learn this?
You can represent and solve equations by drawing graphs instead of using algebra.

Fluency
What is the equation of a straight line? What do m and c represent?

Explore
How can you find the cheapest ski hire?

CONFIDENCE

Exercise 8.6

1 a Plot the graphs of $y = 5$ and $2x + y = 8$.
  b Write down the coordinates of the point where they cross.

2 Which of these points lie on the line $y = 3x - 4$?
A(1, −1) B(4, 1) C(−2, −8) D(3, 5)

3 Solve these pairs of simultaneous equations using algebra.
  a $2x + y = 10$
  $3x - y = 5$
  b $2x + 3y = 16$
  $4x - 3y = 14$

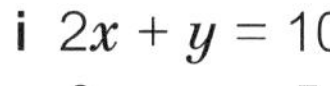

4 a Plot each pair of graphs on the same coordinate grid.
  i $2x + y = 10$
  $3x - y = 5$
  ii $2x + 3y = 16$
  $4x - 3y = 14$
  b Write down the coordinates of their **point of intersection**.

Discussion What do you notice about your answers to Q3 and Q4?

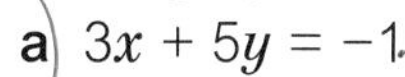

5 Draw graphs to solve these simultaneous equations.
  a $3x + 5y = -1$
  $4x - 2y = 10$
  b $5y + 2x = -20$
  $2y - 4x = 4$

6 Real / Finance A school secretary has this information about ticket costs for a theatre trip.
Mr Smith's group: 2 adults and 12 children, total cost £230.
Mrs Patel's group: 6 adults and 20 children, total cost £450.
The secretary wants to work out how much each child ticket costs and how much each adult ticket costs.
She writes this equation for Mr Smith's group.
$2x + 12y = 230$
  a What do x and y stand for in this equation?
  b Write an equation for Mrs Patel's group.
  c Draw a graph to solve the simultaneous equations from parts **a** and **b**.
  d Write down the cost of a child's ticket and the cost of an adult's ticket.

Discussion How accurate are your prices?

Warm up

Key point
The point where two (or more) lines cross is called the **point of intersection**.

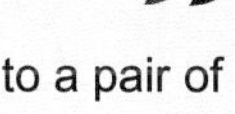

Key point
You can find the solution to a pair of simultaneous equations by
1 drawing the lines on a coordinate grid
2 finding the point of intersection.

Q6 hint
Round any decimal values to the nearest whole number.

7 Real / Modelling Year 8 uses 1 minibus and 3 coaches for a school trip for 122 children. Year 9 uses 2 minibuses and 2 coaches for a school trip for 96 children.

a Write equations for Year 8 and Year 9.

b Solve your simultaneous equations graphically.

c Write down the number of children in a minibus and the number of children in a coach.

Discussion The equations you wrote model the numbers of children in the minibuses and coaches. What assumptions did you make?

Q7a hint

Use x for the number of children in a minibus. How many children will there be in 2 minibuses?

Worked example

Find the equation of the line that passes through the points A(1, 4) and B(3, 10).

At A, $x = 1$ and $y = 4$.

Substituting into $y = mx + c$:

$4 = m \times 1 + c$

$4 = m + c$

The points lie on the line, so their coordinates 'fit' the equation for the line. Use the x- and y-values from each coordinate pair to write an equation for the line using $y = mx + c$.

At B, $x = 3$ and $y = 10$.

Substituting into $y = mx + c$:

$10 = m \times 3 + c$

$10 = 3m + c$

$4 = m + c$ ①

$10 = 3m + c$ ②

Solve the simultaneous equations to find m and c.

$6 = 2m$

$3 = m$

To get an equation without c, subtract equation ① from equation ②.

Substitute $m = 3$ into equation ①.

$4 = 3 + c$

$c = 1$

Equation of line is $y = 3x + 1$.

Substitute the values of m and c into $y = mx + c$.

8 Find the equation of the line that passes through the points C(4, 4) and D(6, 8).

9 Find the equation of the line that passes through the points E(−6, −3) and F(2, 5).

10 **Explore** How can you find the cheapest ski hire?
What have you learned in this lesson to help you answer this question?
What other information do you need?

11 **Reflect** Look back at Unit 6, lesson 6.4. In that lesson you solved simultaneous equations algebraically.
In this lesson you solved simultaneous equations graphically.
Which method is quicker? Explain your answer.
Which method is easier? Explain your answer.
Which method is more accurate? Explain your answer.

NEW Q10, 11 ↓ solving sim eq algebraically (not graphs)

Explore

Reflect

8.7 Graphs of quadratic functions

You will learn to:

- Draw graphs with quadratic equations like $y = x^2$
- Interpret graphs of quadratic functions.

Why learn this?
Engineers use quadratic functions to design bridges – the Golden Gate Bridge in San Francisco is like a 3D quadratic graph.

Fluency
Which of these are quadratic expressions?

A $2x + 3$
B $x^2 + 4$
C $x^3 + x^2 + 1$
D $3x^2 - x - 2$

Explore
How long will a car take to stop if a dog runs into the road?

CONFIDENCE

Exercise 8.7

Warm up

1 Copy and complete this table of values for $y = x^2$.

x	−4	−3	−2	−1	0	1	2	3	4
y									

2 Work out the value of $3x^2$ when

a $x = 1$
b $x = 4$
c $x = -1$

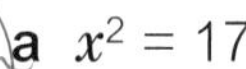

3 Solve

a $x^2 = 17$
b $3x^2 = 29$
c $x^2 + 4 = 7$

Q3 hint
Round your answers to two decimal places.

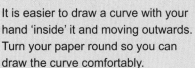

4 Plot the graph of $y = x^2$ using your table of values from Q1.
Draw an x-axis from −5 to +5 and a y-axis from 0 to +20.
Plot the coordinates from your table of values.
Join the points with a smooth curve.
Label your graph $y = x^2$.

Q4 Strategy hint
It is easier to draw a curve with your hand 'inside' it and moving outwards. Turn your paper round so you can draw the curve comfortably.

Key point
A **quadratic equation** contains a term in x^2 but no higher power of x. The graph of a quadratic equation is a curved shape called a **parabola**.

5 a Copy and complete this table of values for $y = 4x^2$.

x	−2	−1	0	1	2
y					

b Plot the graph of $y = 4x^2$. Label your graph with its equation.

Q5b hint
Use axes like the ones in Q4.

6 **Reasoning** Look at your graphs from Q4 and Q5.

a What is the same about them?
b Describe the symmetry of each graph by giving the equation of its mirror line.

7 **Modelling** The graph shows the area of squares of different side lengths.

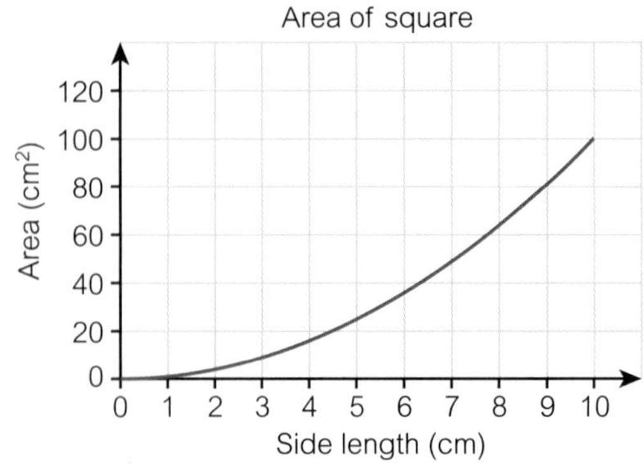

a What is the equation of the curve?

b Use the graph to estimate

i the area of a square of side length 3.2 cm

ii the side length of a square of area 10 cm^2.

c **Reasoning** How accurate are your answers to part **b**? How could you calculate these answers accurately without using the graph?

Discussion Why is the graph only plotted for positive values of x?

Investigation

Reasoning

1 Draw a table of values for $y = -x^2$.

2 **a** Plot the graphs of $y = x^2$ and $y = -x^2$ on the same pair of axes. You could use a graph plotting package to draw the graphs.

b What do you notice?

3 Look at your graph of $y = 4x^2$ that you drew in Q5.

a Predict what the graph of $y = -4x^2$ will look like.

b Draw a table of values for $y = -4x^2$ and plot the graph to check your prediction.

4 If you are given the graph of $y = 2x^2$, how can you draw the graph of $y = -2x^2$? Write an explanation.

Part 1 hint

You could use a table like the one in Q1.

Part 4 hint

Use the correct language to describe a transformation.

8 **a** Copy and complete this table of values for $y = x^2 - 1$.

x	−3	−2	−1	0	1	2	3
x^2							
−1	−1	−1	−1	−1	−1	−1	−1
y							

Q8a hint

For quadratic functions with more than one step, you can include a row for each step in the table.

b Plot the graph of $y = x^2 - 1$.

Discussion Compare your graph to your graph of $y = x^2$. How do you think you could draw the graph of $y = x^2 + 2$?

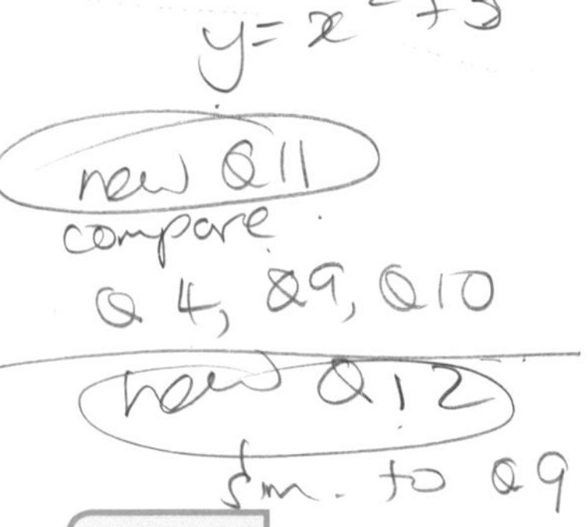

9 Draw the graph of $y = x^2 + 7$ using a graph plotting package or this table of values.

x	−3	−2	−1	0	1	2	3
x^2							
+7	+7	+7	+7	+7	+7	+7	+7
y							

a Draw the line $y = 15$ on your graph.

b Read off the coordinates where the line crosses the **parabola**. These are the solutions to the equation $x^2 + 7 = 15$.

c Use your graph to estimate two solutions to the equation $x^2 + 7 = 10$.

d Use algebra to solve the equation $x^2 + 7 = 15$. How close was your estimate from your graph?

e **Reasoning** Are there any solutions to the equation $x^2 + 7 = 3$? Explain.

Q9c hint

Draw the line $y = \square$

Q9e hint

Look at your graph where $y = 3$.

Topic links: Quadratic sequences, Solving equations, Symmetry, Area, Transformations

Subject links: PE (Q10), Science (Q11)

10 Real / Modelling A sports coach videos players kicking a ball. He uses a program to plot the paths of the ball for kicks at different angles.

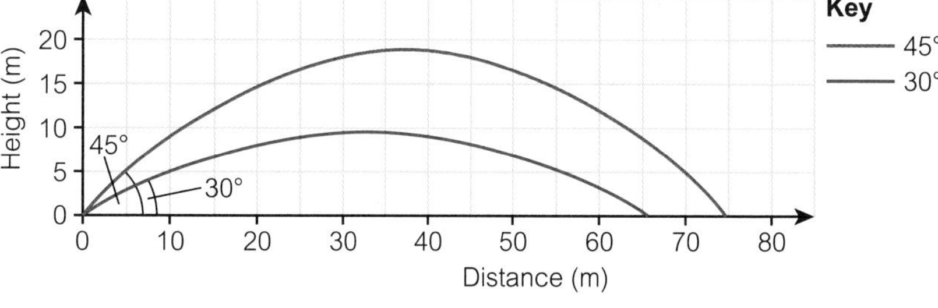

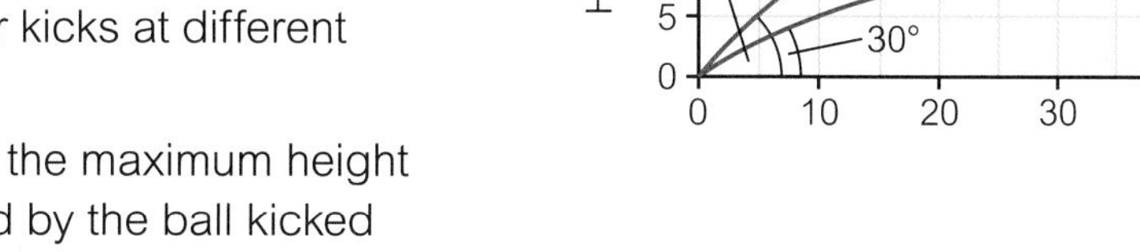

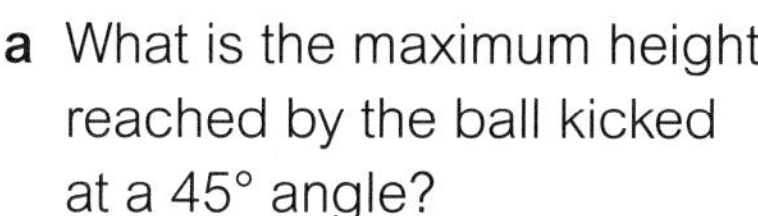

a What is the maximum height reached by the ball kicked at a 45° angle?

b How far does the ball kicked at 30° travel?

c Rugby goal posts have a cross bar 3 m above the ground. Write some tips for rugby players on how to kick the ball to clear the cross bar.

d Football goal posts have a cross bar 2.44 m above the ground. Would your tips on kicking the ball in rugby apply to football? If not, write some new ones for football players.

Q10c hint

Think about the angle of kick and the distance from the posts.

11 Modelling / STEM A scientist studying the effect of gravity measures the distance fallen each second by an object dropped from the top of a tall building.

Time (s)	1	2	3	4	5	6	7
Distance (m)	5	20	45	80	125	180	245

a Plot a graph for this data.

b What type of graph do you think this is?

c When is the object falling fastest?

d A bungee jumper uses a bungee that stretches to 200 m. Use the graph to estimate how many seconds the bungee jumper will fall before they bounce back up again.

e **Reasoning** What is the link between the sequence of values and the type of graph?

12 Explore How long will a car take to stop if a dog runs into the road? What have you learned in this lesson to help you answer this question? What other information do you need?

13 Reflect Use what you have learned so far in this unit to write an equation that could fit each of these graphs.

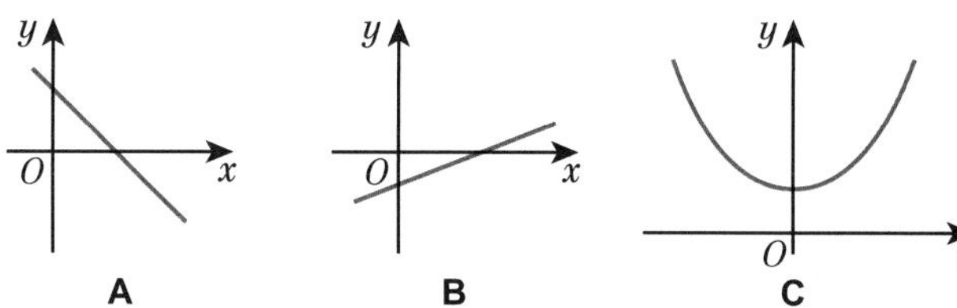

How did you decide on an equation for each of the graphs? Compare your equations with a classmate. In what ways are your equations the same? In what ways are they different?

Q13 hint

What did you look at first? What did you look at next?

Explore

Reflect

8.8 Non-linear graphs

You will learn to:
- Draw graphs of cubic equations like $y = x^3$
- Interpret non-linear graphs.

CONFIDENCE

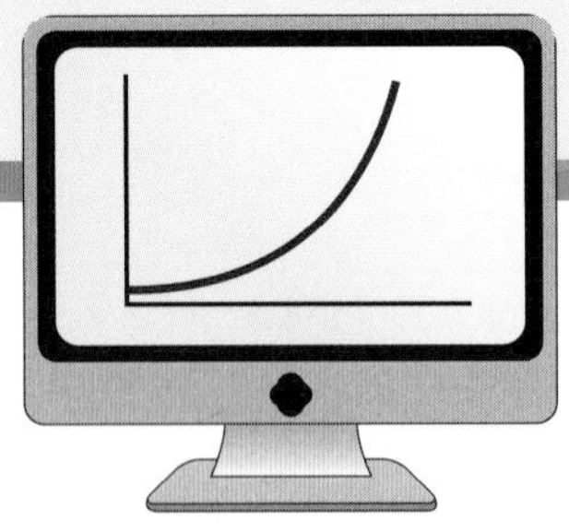

Why learn this?
Scientists need to recognise shapes of curved graphs to recognise relationships between quantities.

Fluency
Work out
- 3^3
- 5^3
- $(-2)^3$
- $(-1)^3$

Explore
How much memory will a laptop have in 2023?

Exercise 8.8

Warm up

1 Work out the volume of this cylinder.
Give your answer to the nearest cm^3.

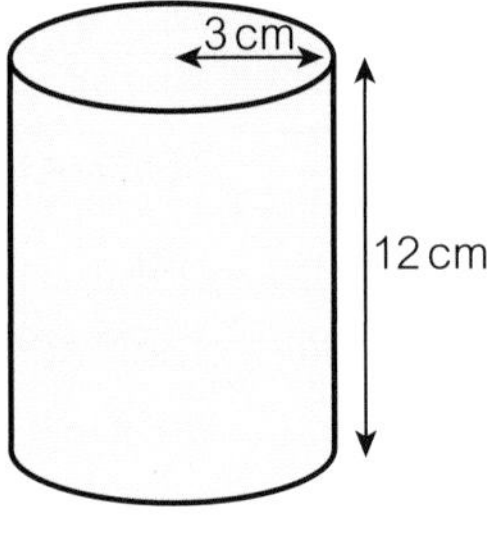

2 Copy and complete this table of values for $y = x^3$.

x	−3	−2	−1	0	1	2	3
y							

3 **a** Plot the points from your table of values for $y = x^3$ (in Q2) on a coordinate grid.
Join the points with a smooth curve.
Label your graph with its equation.

b What type of symmetry does the graph of $y = x^3$ have?

Key point
A **cubic equation** contains a term in x^3 but no higher power of x.

4 **a** Use your graph from Q3 to estimate

i 1.8^3

ii $\sqrt[3]{7}$

b Use a calculator to work out parts **a i** and **ii**.

c Which of your answers are most accurate? Explain.

5 **a** Draw a table of values for $y = 2x^3$.

b Draw a table of values for $y = 5x^3$.

c Plot the graphs of $y = 2x^3$ and $y = 5x^3$ on the same axes.

d What is the same about your two graphs, and your graph of $y = x^3$?
What is different?

Discussion What do you think the graph of $y = 3x^3$ would look like?
What about $y = \frac{1}{2}x^3$?

Q5a hint
Use a copy of the table from Q2.

Q5c hint
You could use a graph plotting package.

Topic links: Sequences, Symmetry, Prefixes, Inequalities, Volumes, Transformations

Subject links: Science (Q6, Q9, Q10), Computing (Q11)

6 Real / STEM The table gives the volumes of cylinders with height 15 cm and radius r, for different values of r.

Radius, r (cm)	0	1	2	3	4	5
Volume of cylinder with radius r and height 15 cm (cm^3)	0	47	188	424		

The volumes are rounded to the nearest cm^3.

a Copy and complete the table.

b Plot a graph for these values. Put radius on the horizontal axis and volume on the vertical axis.

c A cylinder 15 cm high has radius 2.5 cm. Estimate its volume from your graph.

d 250 cm^3 of stainless steel is melted down and made into a cylinder with height 15 cm. Estimate the radius of the cylinder using your graph.

7 a Draw a table of values for $y = -x^3$.

b Plot the graph of $y = -x^3$.

c Describe the transformation that takes the graph of $y = x^3$ on to $y = -x^3$.

d i What do you think the graph of $y = -2x^3$ will look like?

ii Plot the graph of $y = -2x^3$ to test your prediction.

> **Q7 hint**
> You could use a graph plotting package to plot the graphs.

> **Q7c hint**
> Look at the graph of $y = x^3$ you drew in Q3.

8 Real / Modelling A phone contract includes 1 GB of free data each month. The graph shows how much you pay if you go over the 1 GB limit.

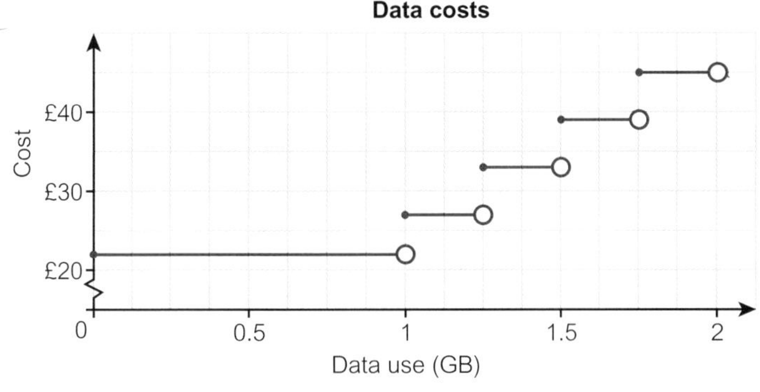

> **Q8 hint**
> The open circles show that the upper value of each graph line is not included in the interval.

a How much do you pay if you use 1.4 GB of data in a month?

b After the first gigabyte, how much does each extra 250 MB of data cost?

c Saleem paid £39. How much data had he used?

d Discussion Can you tell exactly how much data Saleem used?

> **Q8b hint**
> 1 GB ≈ 1000 MB

9 Modelling / STEM The graph shows the count rate against time for iodine-128, which is a radioactive material.
The count rate is the number of radioactive emissions per second.

a What is the count rate after 50 minutes?

b After how many minutes is the count rate 50?

c The half-life of a radioactive material is the time it takes for the count rate to halve. What is the half-life of iodine-128?

d Discussion Does the count rate ever reach zero?

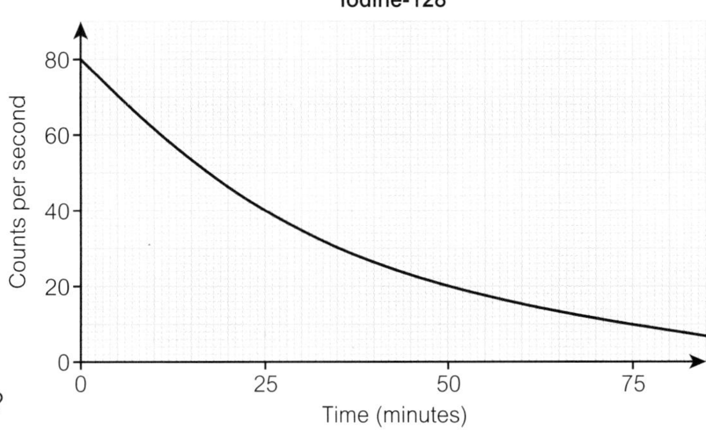

10 Modelling / STEM A scientist counts the number of bacteria in a culture every 4 hours.
The table shows her results.

Time (hours)	0	1	2	3	4	5
Number of bacteria	2	4	7	14	27	53

a Draw a graph to show these results.

b How many bacteria are there after $2\frac{1}{2}$ hours?

c The scientist says, 'A model for the growth of these bacteria is 'double every hour'.'
On the same axes, draw a graph starting with 2 bacteria at time 0 hours, and doubling every hour.

d How good is the scientist's model?

Investigation

Reasoning

1 Work out some values for $\frac{1}{x}$ for positive values of x greater than 1.
Write your values in a table like this.

x	5	250			15 000	
$\frac{1}{x}$						

2 What happens to $\frac{1}{x}$ as you increase the value of x?
Will it ever reach zero?

3 Now try positive values of x less than 1. Write your values in a table.
What happens to $\frac{1}{x}$ as you decrease the value of x?

4 Draw the graph of $y = \frac{1}{x}$ using a graph plotting package.

5 Zoom in to your graph to read the values of x when $\frac{1}{x}$ is very small and very large.
Does the graph ever touch the x-axis or the y-axis?

Explore

11 **Explore** How much memory will a laptop have in 2023?
Is it easier to explore this question now you have completed the lesson?
What further information do you need to be able to answer this?

Reflect

12 **Reflect** Look back at the lessons in this unit on sequences and graphs.
Which of these topics did you find hardest?

- sequences (lessons 8.1 and 8.2)
- graphs (lessons 8.3 to 8.8)

If you chose sequences, then which sequences are hardest?

- arithmetic sequences (lesson 8.1)
- geometric sequences (lesson 8.2)
- quadratic sequences (lesson 8.2)

Look back at the sequences you found hardest. Write two hints or tips about them, in your own words.

If you chose graphs, then which graphs are hardest?

- rates of change graphs (lesson 8.3)
- $y = mx + c$ (lessons 8.4 and 8.5)
- simultaneous equations (lesson 8.6)
- quadratic and other graphs (lessons 8.7 and 8.8)

Look back at the graphs you found hardest. Write two hints or tips about them, in your own words.

8 Check up

Log how you did on your Student Progression Chart.

Sequences

1 Generate the first three terms of the sequences with these nth terms.

a $4n$ b $3n + 1$ c $10 - 3n$
d $n^2 + 2$ e $3n^2$ f $n^2 - 2$

2 Find the 100th term of the sequence with nth term

a $5n + 6$ b $3 - 2n$

3 Find the nth term of each sequence.

a 6, 12, 18, 24, … b −5, −10, −15, −20, …
c 8, 9, 10, 11, … d 2, 6, 10, 14, …
e 11, 9, 7, 5, … f 3.9, 4.8, 5.7, 6.6, …

4 Work out the next two terms of each sequence.

a 4, 9, 14, 19, … b 7, 14, 28, 56, …
c 4, 5, 7, 10, … d 800, 400, 200, 100, …
e 1, 2, 5, 10, … g 0.1, 0.3, 0.9, 2.7, …

5 Look at the sequences in Q4.

a Which ones are arithmetic sequences?
b Which ones are geometric sequences?

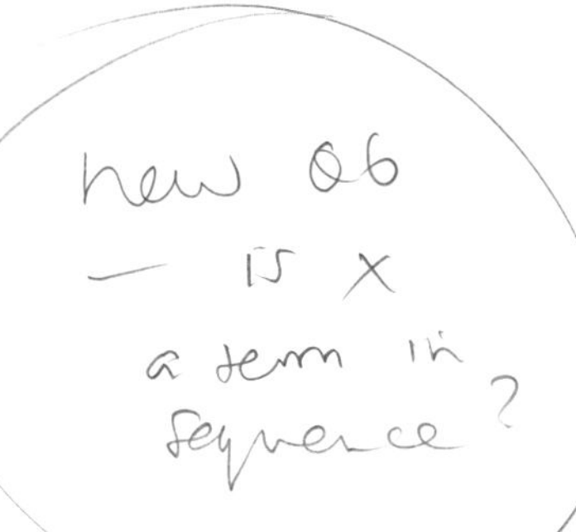

Straight-line graphs

6 Match each equation to one of the graphs below.

i $y = -2x + 5$
ii $y = 2x - 2$
iii $y = 4x + 5$
iv $y = 2x + 5$

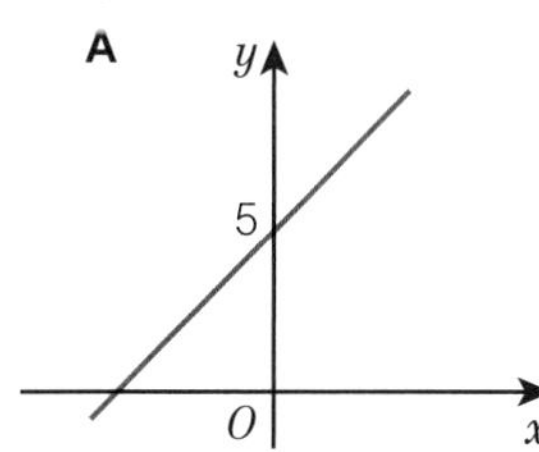

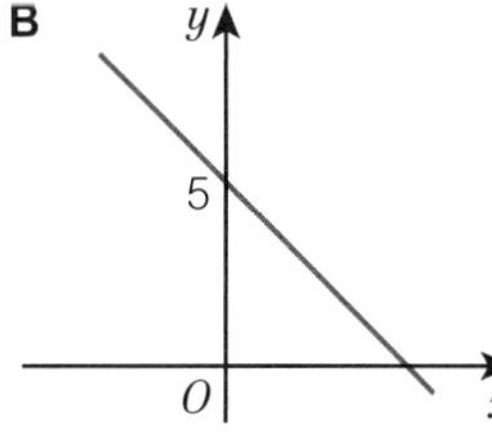

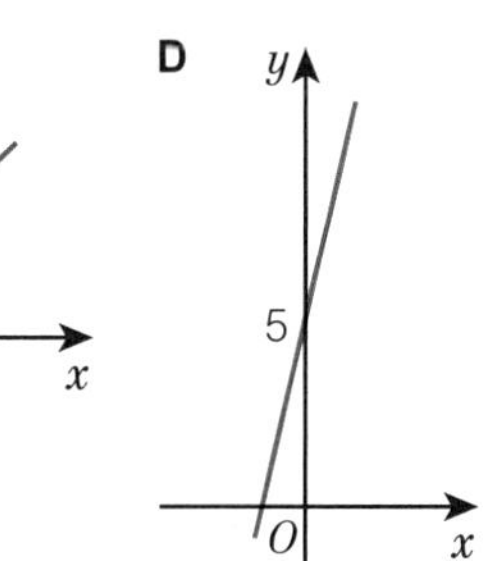

7 Which of these lines are parallel?

A $2x + 3y = 10$ B $y = 2x + 3$
C $2x + y = -6$ D $3y = 6x + 18$

8 Write the equation of the line parallel to $y = -2x + 5$ with y-intercept (0, 3).

9 Solve these simultaneous equations graphically.

$2y + x = 8$
$2y + 6x = 18$

Non-linear graphs

10 The graph shows a car journey.

a Write down

i the total distance travelled

ii the total time taken for the journey.

b Work out the average speed for the journey.

c **i** Between what times was the car travelling fastest?

ii Work out the speed for that part of the journey.

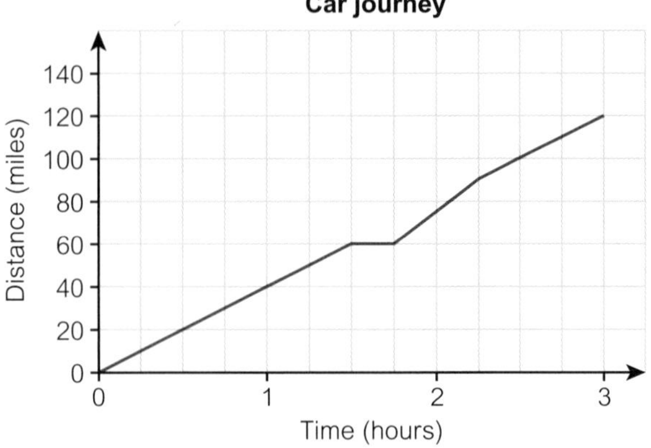

11 Copy and complete the table of values for $y = 3x^2$.

x	−3	−2	−1	0	1	2	3
y							

12 **a** From the graph, work out

i the value of y when $x = 1.5$

ii the value of x when $y = 17$.

b Sam says, 'This is a graph of a cubic function.'
Claire says, 'It is a graph of a quadratic function.'
Who is correct? How do you know?

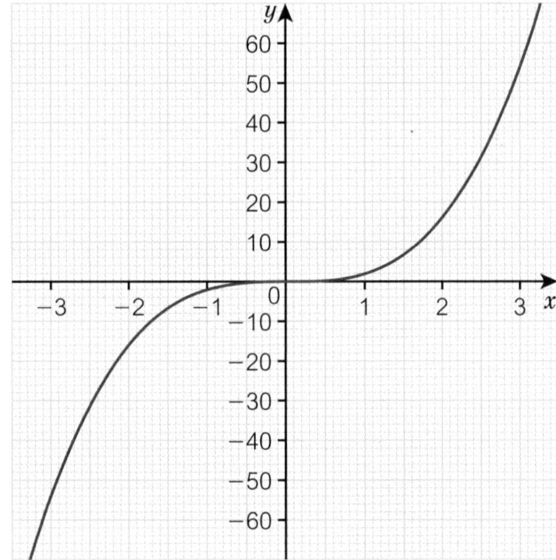

Reflect

13 How sure are you of your answers? Were you mostly

Just guessing **Feeling doubtful** **Confident**

What next? Use your results to decide whether to strengthen or extend your learning.

Challenge

14 The diagrams show the numbers of lines that can join different numbers of dots.

1 dot	2 dots	3 dots	4 dots

0 lines	1 line	3 lines	6 lines

a Look at the sequence of the numbers of lines: 0, 1, 3, 6, …
Predict the next term in the sequence.

b Draw 5 dots and the lines joining them, to test your prediction.

c Work out the next three terms in the sequence.

8 Strengthen

You will:

- Strengthen your understanding with practice.

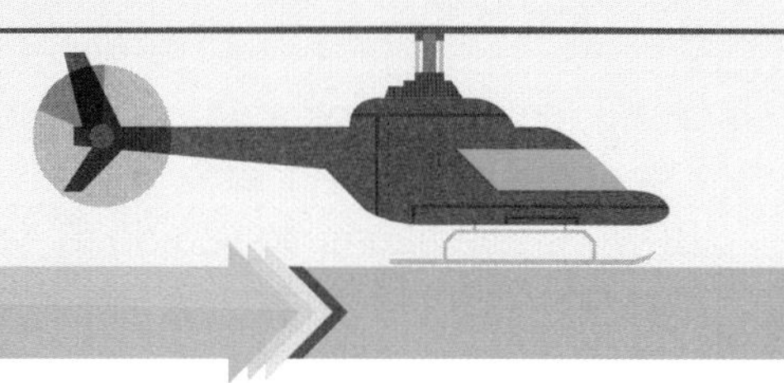

Sequences

1 In this table, n gives the number of the term.

n	1	2	3	4	5
$5n$					
$5n - 1$					

a Copy and complete the table of values for the sequence with nth term $5n$.

b Write down the first five terms of the sequence $5n - 1$.

Q1b hint

The n-value gives the position: $n = 1$ is the 1st term, $n = 2$ is the 2nd term, and so on.
Substitute

- $n = 1$ to find the 1st term: $5 \times 1 - 1$
- $n = 2$ to find the 2nd term: $5 \times 2 - 1$
- and so on.

2 Work out the first five terms of the sequences with these nth terms.

a $n + 4$ b $2n - 3$ c $4n + 5$
d $8 - 2n$ e $25 - 4n$ f $\frac{1}{2}n + 2$

Q2 hint

Draw a table of values like the one in Q1.

3 Copy and complete this table to work out the nth term of the sequence 7, 11, 15, 19, …

Sequence	7	11	15	19
Differences		+□	+□	+□
Multiples of □ (□n)		8		

Q3 hint

1 Work out the differences between terms. Write the differences in □.
2 Write out the first four multiples of this number.
How do you get from the multiples to the terms in the sequence?
3 Check your nth term. Substitute $n = 1$. Do you get 7 (the first term)?

4 Copy and complete this table to work out the nth term of the sequence 2, 8, 14, 20, …

Sequence	2	8	14	20
Differences		+□	+□	+□
Multiples of □ (□n)				

5 Work out the nth term of each sequence.

a 11, 14, 17, 20, … b 8, 13, 18, 23, … c 4, 6, 8, 10, …
d 1, 7, 13, 19, … e −3, −1, 1, 3, … f 8, 6, 4, 2, ..
g 5, 2, −1, −4, …

Q5 Strategy hint

Draw a table for each sequence, like the ones in Q3 and Q4.

Q5f hint

The difference is −□. Write the multiples of −□ in your table.

6 a Write down the first four terms in each sequence.

i 1st term 1; multiply the term by 4 to get the next term.
ii 1st term 10; subtract 3 to get the next term.
iii 1st term 6; add the even numbers starting at 2 (add 2, then 4, then 6, …).
iv 1st term 200; divide by 2 to get the next term.

b Reasoning Which operations (+, ×, − , ÷) give

i ascending sequences
ii descending sequences?

Q6b hint

In ascending sequences the terms get bigger.

7 Work out the next two terms in each sequence.

a 25, 31, 37, 43, …
b 7, 8, 10, 13, 17, …
c 5, 10, 20, 40, …
d 19, 16, 13, 10, …
e 1, 3, 9, 27, …
f 6, 8, 12, 18, …

Q7 Strategy hint
What do you add/subtract to get from one term to the next?

8 a Reasoning Look at the sequences in Q7. Which ones are arithmetic sequences?

b What operations do you do to get from one term to the next in a geometric sequence?

Q8 hint
In an arithmetic sequence you add or subtract the same amount to get from one term to the next.

Straight-line graphs

1 a Copy and complete the table.

$y = mx + c$	Gradient m	y-intercept $(0, c)$
$y = 3x - 4$		
$y = 5x + 4$		
$y = -2x + 1$		
$y = \frac{1}{2}x - 4$		
$y = 3x - 3$		

b Write down the equations of the lines that are parallel.

c Write down the equations of the lines that have the same y-intercept.

d Which line slopes in the opposite direction to the others?

Q1b hint
Parallel lines have the same ________.

Q1d hint
Positive gradients slope uphill left to right. ／
Negative gradients slope downhill left to right. ＼

2 a Problem-solving Sort these equations of lines into two sets: one set with y-intercept (0, 1) and the other set with y-intercept (0, −1).

A $y = \frac{1}{2}x + 1$ B $y = 2x - 1$ C $y = 2x + 1$ D $y = -x - 1$

b By each equation write the gradient and its direction: ／ or ＼

c Match each graph to an equation from part **a**.

i 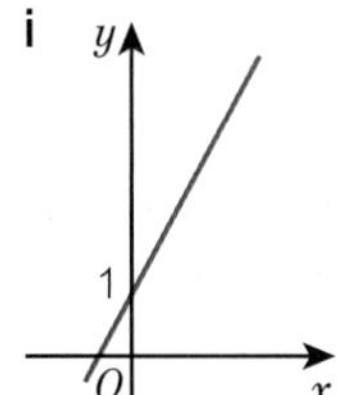

ii 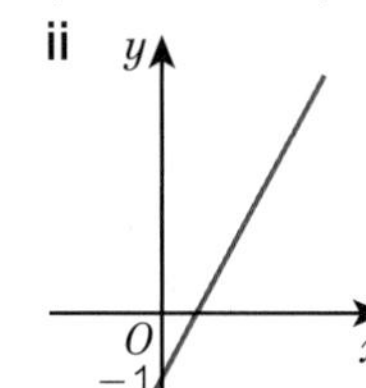

iii 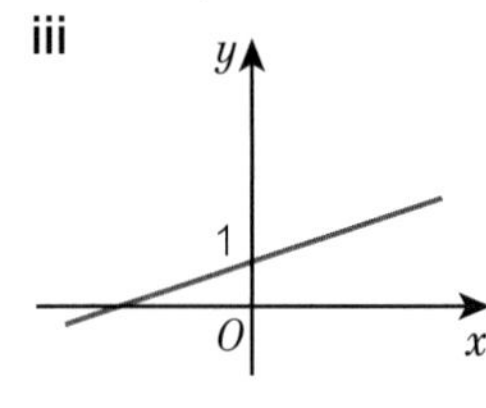

iv 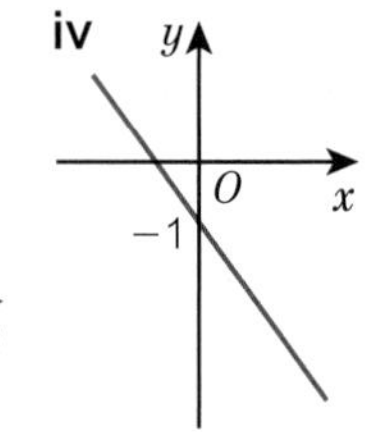

Q2a hint
You could draw a table for the equations, like the one in Q1.

Q2b hint
$-x = -1 \times x$

3 a i Reasoning What is the same about these lines?

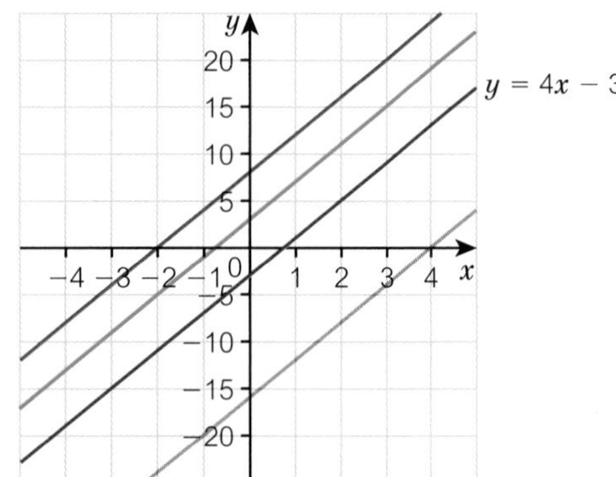

ii What is different about them?

b Which of these equations give lines parallel to $y = 4x - 3$?

A $y = 4x - 0.1$ B $y = 2x + 4$
C $y = 4x + 1002$ D $y = 10x - 4$

c Write the equations of three more lines parallel to $y = 4x - 3$.

Q3a hint
Use these words: gradient, y-intercept.

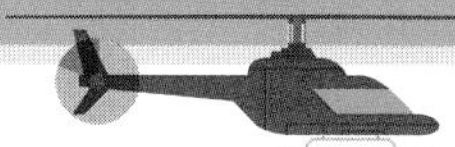

4 Write the equation of a line parallel to

a $y = 2x + 10$ b $y = -\frac{1}{2}x + 3$

c $y = 6x + 5$ d $y = 7x - 12$

5 a Copy and complete these function machines to rearrange $4y + 8x = 16$ into the form $y = mx + c$.

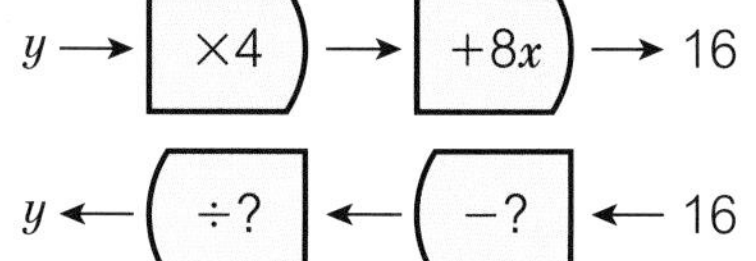

b Use the similar steps to write each equation in the form $y = mx + c$.

i $3x + 6y = 18$

ii $-2x + 4y = -6$

c Which equation has a graph with gradient $\frac{1}{2}$?

d Which equation has a graph which passes through $(0, -\frac{3}{2})$?

6 a Find the point where the line $5x + 2y = 6$

i crosses the y-axis

ii crosses the x-axis.

b Plot the points you found in part **a**, and join them with a straight line.

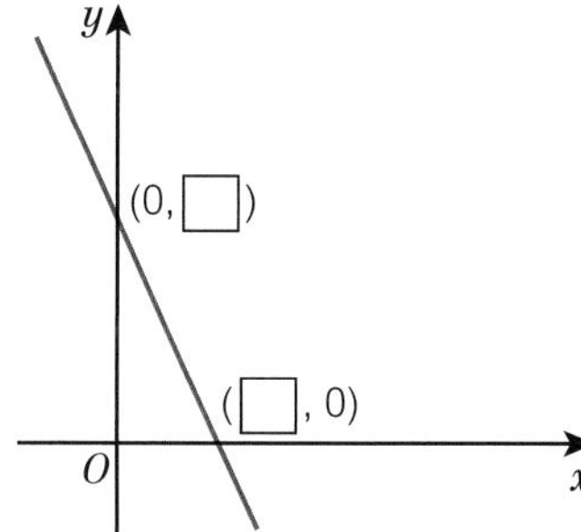

7 a Plot these two graphs on the same axes.

i $2x + 3y = 6$

ii $4x + 2y = -8$

b Write down the coordinates of the point where the two graphs cross.

Q5a hint

Start with y.
What do you do to y to get the number on the right-hand side?
Then go back the other way, starting with 16.

$y = \frac{16 - \square}{4}$

$y = \frac{16}{4} - \frac{\square}{4}$

$= \square - \square$

For the last step, write in the x term first, then the number term, in the form $y = mx + c$.

Q6a Strategy hint

For each point, substitute the value you know into the equation.

Q7a hint

Find the points where the lines cross the x-axis and the y-axis.

Non-linear graphs

1 Modelling The graph shows the amount of water flowing into a swimming pool.

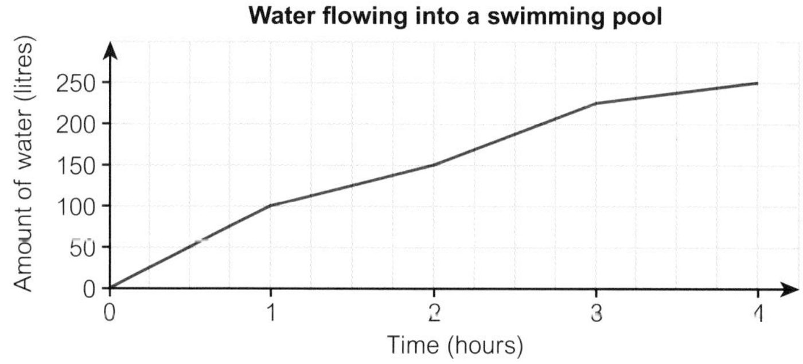

Q1 Literacy hint

The rate of flow is the amount of water flowing per hour.

a Copy and complete the table to show the rate of flow of the water over the 4 hours. Remember to include the units.

Time	Amount of water flowing into the pool	Rate of flow
1st hour	100 litres	100 litres per hour
2nd hour		
3rd hour		
4th hour		

b Where is the steepest part of the graph?

c Reasoning From your table, when was the rate of flow greatest? What do you notice?

d What was the average rate of flow over the 4 hours?

Q1a hint

The 2nd hour is from 1 to 2 hours on the graph.

Q1b hint

In the ____ hour.

Q1d hint

Finding the average rate of flow is like sharing out the total amount of water evenly over the 4 hours.

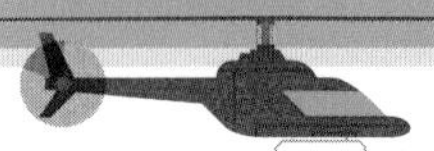

2 **Problem-solving** Match each equation to one of the graphs below.

i $y = x^2 + 2$

ii $y = 2x + 1$

iii $y = -x^2 - 1$

A

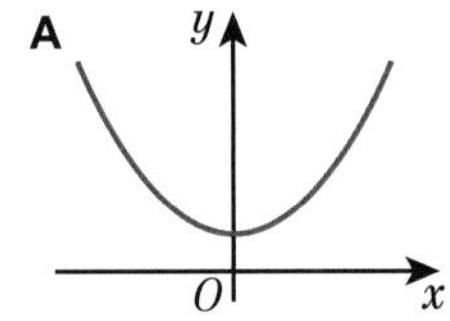

B

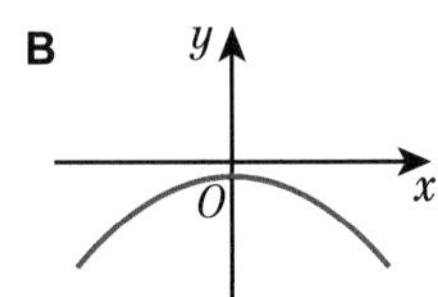

C

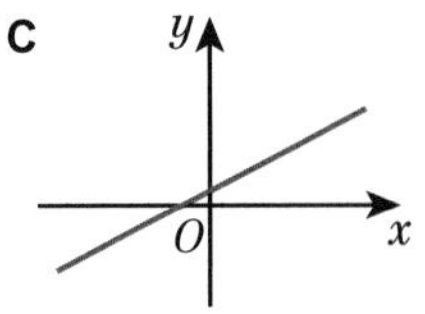

Q2 hint

Look back at the graphs in lessons 8.4, 8.7 and 8.8 to help you.

3 Copy and complete these tables of values.

a $y = -x^2$

x	−3	−2	−1	0	1	2	3
x^2							
$-x^2$							

b $y = 2x^2$

x	−3	−2	−1	0	1	2	3
x^2							
$2x^2$							

c $y = -4x^2$

x	−3	−2	−1	0	1	2	3
x^2							
$-4x^2$							

d $y = 3x^2 + 2$

x	−3	−2	−1	0	1	2	3
x^2							
$3x^2$							
+2	+2	+2					
$3x^2 + 2$							

e $y = 2x^3$

x	−3	−2	−1	0	1	2	3
x^3							
$2x^3$							

Q3 hint

Make a row for each stage in the calculation.

Q3a hint

$-x^2 = -(x^2)$

4 **a** Sketch the rough shape of the graph you expect for each of the equations in Q3.

b Plot the graphs for these equations, using the tables of values from Q3.

Q4a hint

Use your answers to Q2 to help you.

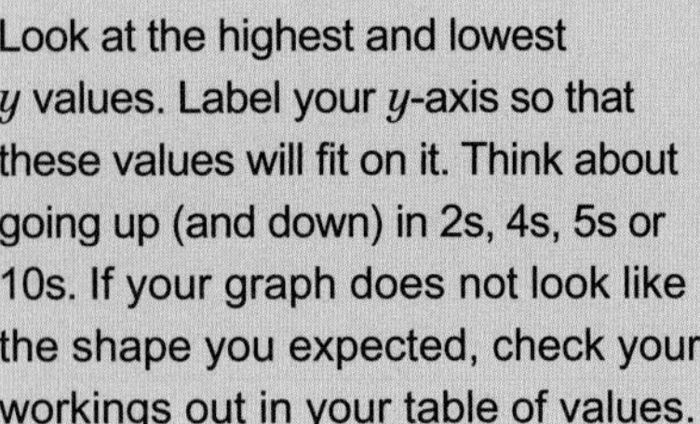

Q4b Strategy hint

Look at the highest and lowest y values. Label your y-axis so that these values will fit on it. Think about going up (and down) in 2s, 4s, 5s or 10s. If your graph does not look like the shape you expected, check your workings out in your table of values.

5 **a** Write down the values marked on these scales.

0 1 2 3 (arrows i, ii)

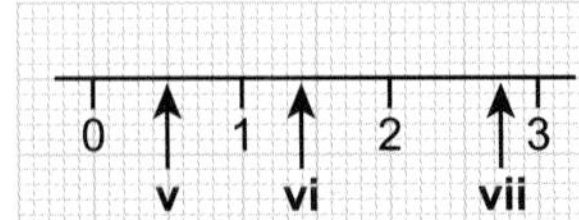

0 1 2 3 (arrows v, vi, vii)

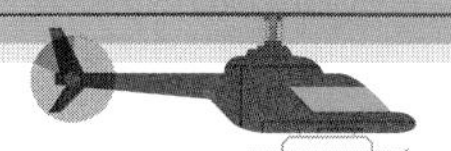

b For each graph

i find the value of y when $x = 1.5$

ii find the value of x when $y = 7$.

> **Q5b hint**
> Look carefully at the scales before you read off the values.

A

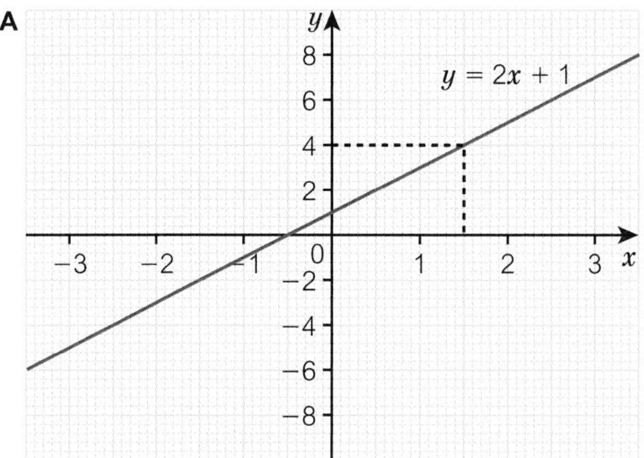

B

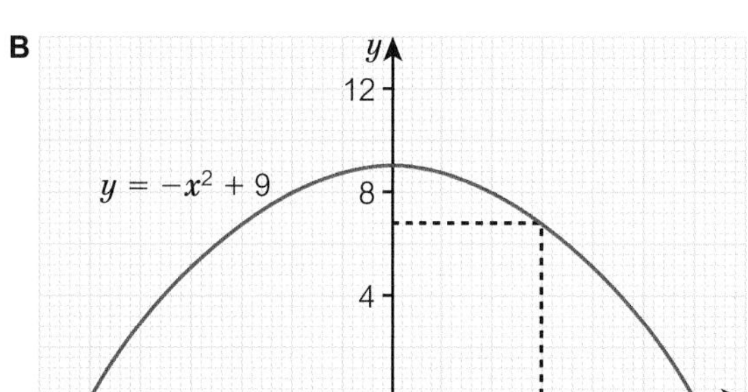

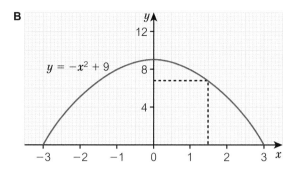

> **Q5b ii hint**
> Look both ways on graph B.

Enrichment

1 Problem-solving / Modelling Here is a pattern sequence made with tiles.

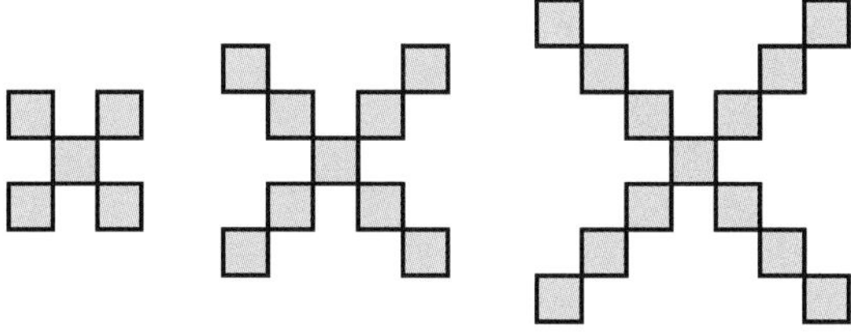

a Draw the next pattern in the sequence.

b Doug is copying the sequence. He has 50 tiles. Has he got enough to make

i the 10th pattern

ii the 15th pattern?

c Work out the number of the biggest pattern he can make.

> **Q1b hint**
> Work out the nth term of the sequence.

2 a Draw graphs of $y = 2x$ and $y = -2x$ on the same axes.

b What transformation takes $y = 2x$ on to $y = -2x$?

c Repeat for $y = x + 1$ and $y = -x + 1$.

> **Q2a hint**
> You could use a graph plotting package.

> **Q2b hint**
> There are four types of transformation: translation, reflection, rotation and enlargement.

3 Reflect Sholly describes what she does when she sees a question with a graph.

- I cover the question with my hand, so I can only see the graph.
- I read the graph title.
- I read the titles of the axes.
- I make sure I know what one square on each axis represents.
- Finally, I randomly pick a point on the graph and ask myself, 'What does this point tell me?'

It is really quick and always helps me to understand and answer the question.

Look at the graph in the Extend lesson, Q14.
Use Sholly's method to help you understand the graph.
Does this help you answer Q14a?
Is Sholly's method helpful? Explain why.

Reflect

8 Extend

You will:

- Extend your understanding with problem-solving.

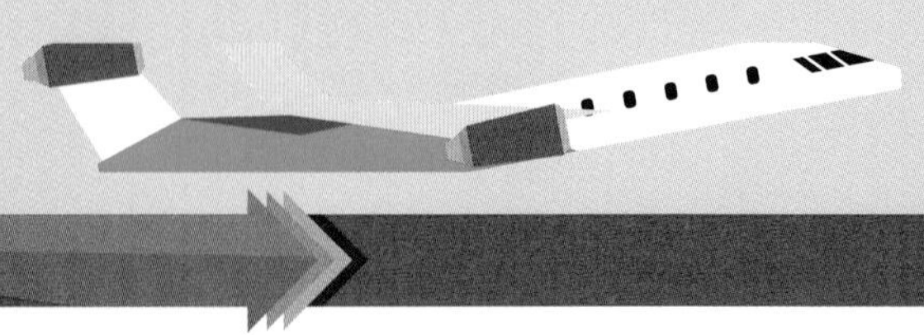

1 Real / Problem-solving One hundred and twenty-eight women play in the Wimbledon Women's Singles Tennis Tournament each year. They each play one first-round match.

a How many matches are there in the first round?

b The winning players from the first round go through to the second round.

i How many players go through to the second round?

ii How many matches are there in the second round?

c After every round, the winning players go through to the next round. How many rounds will there be?

d How many matches does the overall winner play?

e How many matches are there in the tournament?

Q1a hint

How many women play in each singles match?

Q1c hint

Continue the sequence for the number of matches in each round.

2 Problem-solving Write the next three terms in this sequence.
10, 11, 9, 12, 8, 13, 7, …

3 Problem-solving The general term of a sequence is $2n + 4$.

a Work out the first five terms.

b Solve the equation $2n + 4 = 22$ to find the value of n.

c What number term in the sequence is 22?

d What number term in the sequence is 34?

Q3c hint

What is the value of n for the term 22?

Q3d hint

Put $2n + 4$ equal to 34 and solve.

4 Problem-solving The general term of a sequence is $3n - 1$.

a Is 44 a term in this sequence?
Show your working to explain how you know.

b Is 25 a term in this sequence?
Show your working to explain how you know.

5 Problem-solving / Modelling Here is a pattern of black and white tiles.

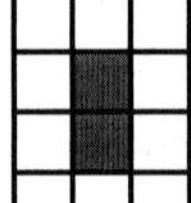

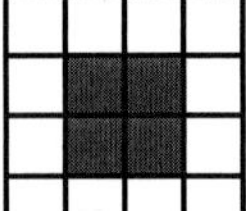

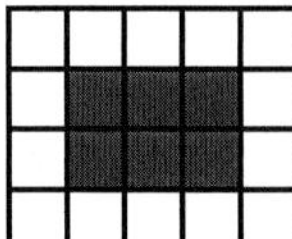

a Copy and complete this table for the sequences of the numbers of white tiles and the numbers of black tiles.

Pattern number	1	2	3	4	5
Number of white tiles	10	12			
Number of black tiles	2	4			

b Write down the nth term for the sequence of black tiles.

c Write down the nth term for the sequence of white tiles.

d How many black tiles will there be in the 15th pattern?

e How many white tiles will there be in the 20th pattern?

f Josh has 75 white tiles and 67 black tiles.
Which is the largest complete pattern he can make?

Q5d hint

Use the nth term.

Worked example

On a coordinate grid, show the region given by $x > 2$, $y \geqslant 3$.
Show clearly the region that satisfies both these inequalities.

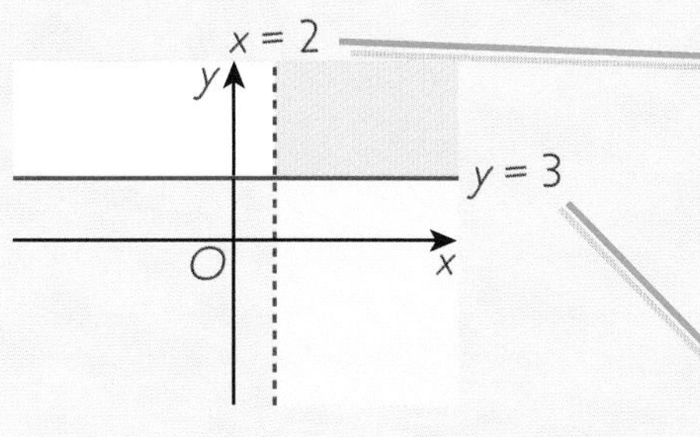

Draw the line $x = 2$.
$x > 2$ does not include points where $x = 2$, so use a dashed line.
Shade the part of the grid where all x-values are greater than 2.

Draw the line $y = 3$.
$y \geqslant 3$ includes points where $y = 3$, so use a solid line.
Shade the part of the grid where all y-values are greater than 3.

x = 2
y
y = 3
O
x

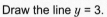

The region that satisfies both inequalities is where all points have x-coordinate > 2 and y-coordinate $\geqslant$ 3. This is where the regions for the two inequalities overlap.

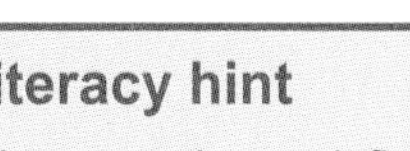

Literacy hint

When a region satisfies an inequality, all the points in it 'fit' the inequality.

6 On a coordinate grid, show the region given by $x \leqslant 3$, $y > -1$.
Show clearly the region that satisfies both these inequalities.

7 Draw the line $x + y = 2$.
Pick any point on one side of your line.
For the coordinates of this point, is $x + y \leqslant 2$?
Shade the region of your graph that satisfies the inequality $x + y \leqslant 2$.

8 Problem-solving

a Draw graphs to show the regions satisfied by $x > 1$, $y \leqslant 2x + 4$.

b Show clearly the region satisfied by both inequalities.

c Choose any point in the region that satisfies both inequalities. Write down the x and y values at that point.

Q8c hint

This pair of x and y values satisfy both inequalities simultaneously.

9 Problem-solving

a Draw graphs to show the region that satisfies both these inequalities: $x + y > 5$, $y \leqslant 2x$.

b Write down a pair of positive x and y values that satisfy both inequalities simultaneously.

c Write down a pair of negative x and y values that satisfy both inequalities simultaneously.

Q9b hint

Choose any point in the region that satisfies both inequalities.
Write down the x and y values at that point.

10 Problem-solving Here are the first four terms of some sequences.

n^2	1, 4, 9, 16
$n^2 + 1$	2, 5, 10, 17
$n^2 - 3$	−2, 1, 6, 13
$2n^2$	2, 8, 18, 32
$2n^2 - 1$	1, 7, 17, 31
$2n^2 + 2$	4, 10, 20, 34

a What are the 2nd differences of the sequences with n^2 in the nth term?

b What are the 2nd differences of the sequences with $2n^2$ in the nth term?

c Work out the 2nd differences of this sequence: 7, 13, 23, 37, …

d Write down the term involving n^2 for the sequence in part **c**.

e Work out the general term for the sequence 7, 13, 23, 37, …

Q10a hint

Find the 2nd differences of all the sequences.

Q10d hint

Use your answers to parts **a** and **b**. Is it n^2 or $2n^2$?

11 Real / Problem-solving A teacher making a worksheet on symmetry draws two sides of a shape using a graph plotting package. Work out the equations of the two lines she needs to draw to make a shape symmetrical about the line $y = x$.

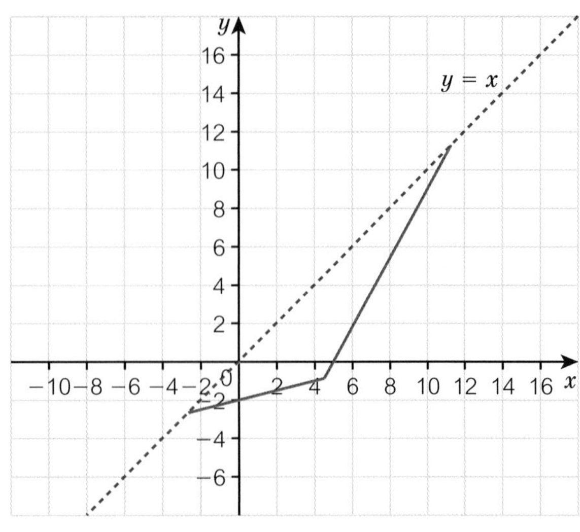

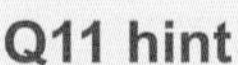

Q11 hint

You could start by finding the equations of the two lines already drawn and using inverse operations, or by drawing your own diagram.

12 Reasoning

a Draw the graph of $y = 2x$ for x values from −3 to +3.

b Use compasses and a ruler to construct the perpendicular bisector of the line $y = 2x$.

c What is the gradient of the perpendicular bisector?

d Predict the gradient of a line perpendicular to the line $y = 3x$. Draw the graph of $y = 3x$ for x values from −3 to +3 and construct its perpendicular bisector to check.

e Predict the gradient of a line perpendicular to the line $y = -4x$. Explain your reasoning. Draw lines to check.

f The gradient of line A is m. What is the gradient of any line perpendicular to line A?

13 Reasoning Use a graph plotting package to plot the graphs of $y = x^3 + 1$, $y = x^3 + 2$ and $y = x^3 - 4$.
What do you think the graph of $y = x^3 - 2$ will look like?
Check by drawing the graph.

14 Real / Modelling The tap on this water butt is opened and the water drains out.
The graph shows the depth of water in the water butt over 10 minutes.

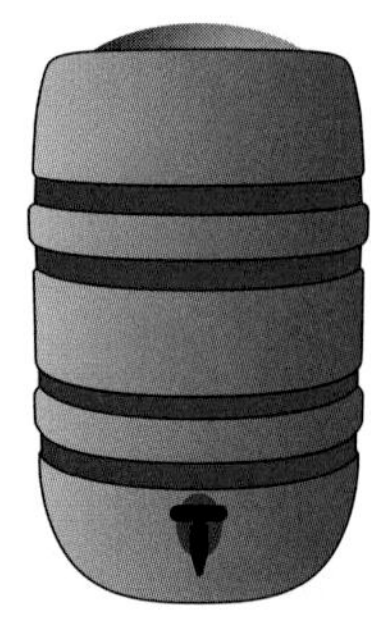

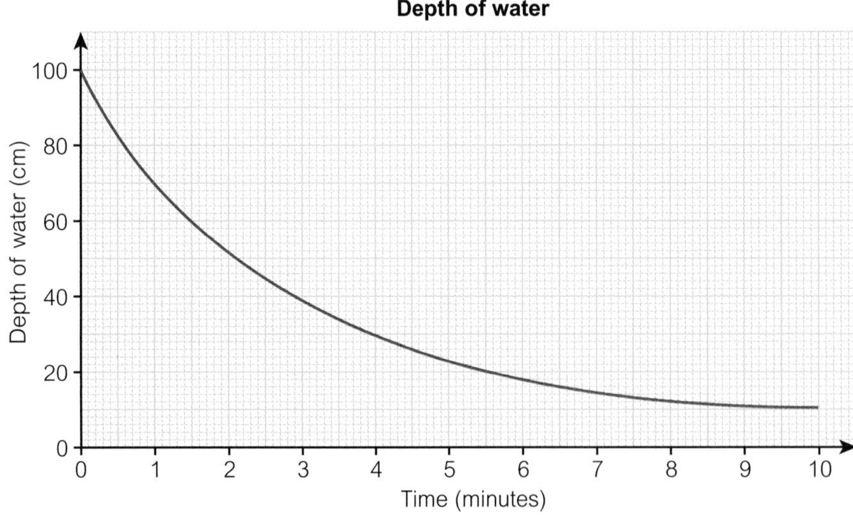

a Compare the change in the depth of water in the 1st minute with the 5th minute.

b When is the water flowing fastest? Explain how you can tell from the graph.

c How high is the tap above the bottom of the water butt?

Q14a hint

The 1st minute is from 0 to 1 minute, the 5th minute is from 4 to 5 minutes.

Q14c hint

What is the depth when the water stops flowing?

Topic links: Symmetry, Percentages, Perpendicular bisectors, Inequalities

Subject links: Sport (Q1)

15 Reasoning Match each equation to one of the graphs below.

i $y = x^2$

ii $y = -x^2$

iii $y = x^3$

iv $y = x^2 + 2$

v $y = x^3 - 3$

A

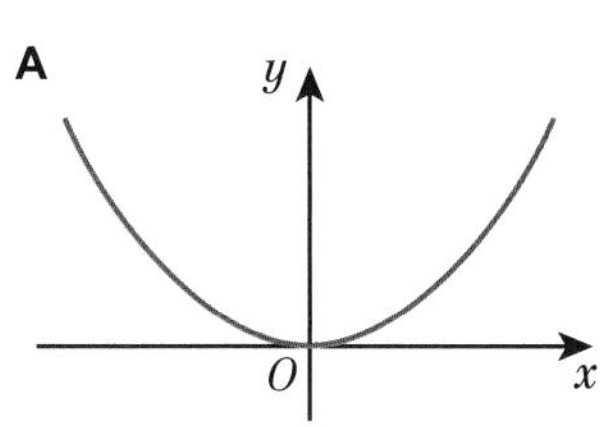

B

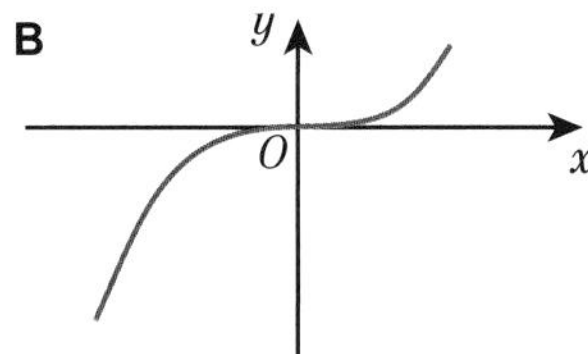

C

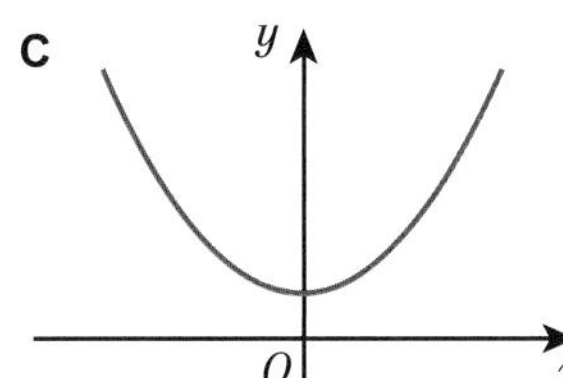

D

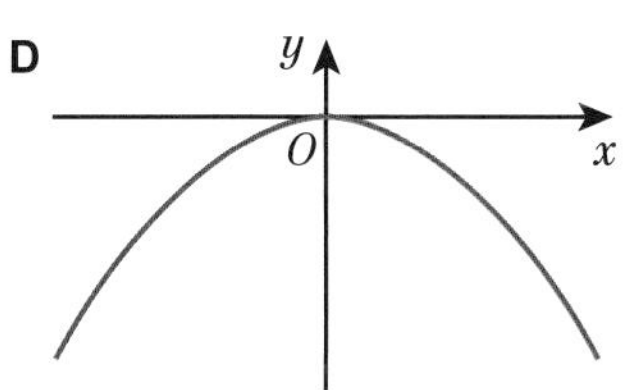

E

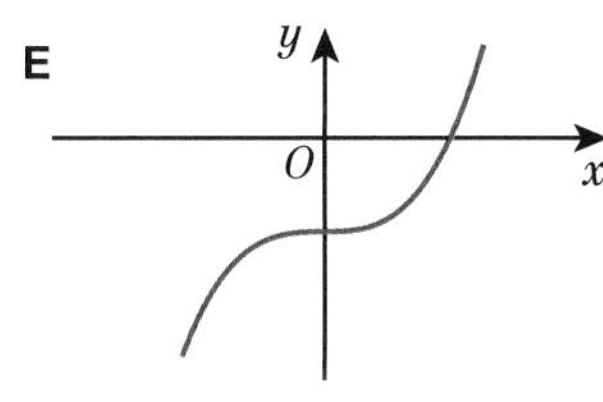

16 Finance / Modelling Jenni invests some money in a savings bond with a fixed rate of interest.

This graph shows how her investment will grow.

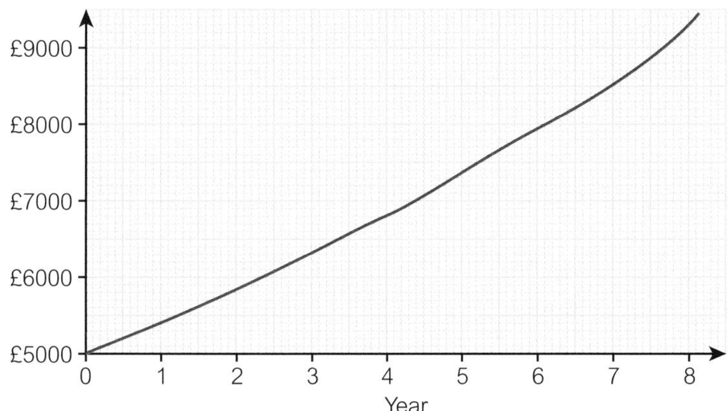

a How much money will she have after 3 years?

b When will she have £8000?
How accurate do you think your answer is?

c How much money did Jenni invest?

d How much money did she have after 1 year?

e Use your answers to parts **c** and **d** to work out the annual interest rate as a percentage.

Q16e hint

Work out the percentage change from 0 years to 1 year.

17 Reflect Look back at the graphs in Q15.

a What steps did you take to match the graphs to the equations?
You could begin with, 'Step 1: I looked for the U-shaped graphs, because …'

b How would you change your steps if Q15 also included the equations $y = 2x + 3$ and $2x + y = 3$ and their graphs?

Q17b hint

What is the shape of these graphs?

Reflect

8 Unit test

Log how you did on your Student Progression Chart.

1 Work out the nth term of the sequence 5, 11, 17, 23, …

2 Write down the first three terms of the sequences with nth term

a $8n - 3$ b $6 - 2n$ c $n^2 + 5$ d $n^2 + 2n + 1$

3 Which of these equations give parallel lines?

A $y = 3x + 2$ B $4y - 12x = 3$ C $5y + 15x = 1$ D $y = 3x + 5$

4 Here is a sketch graph of Jacki's morning jog.

a When was she running fastest?

b Work out her average speed.

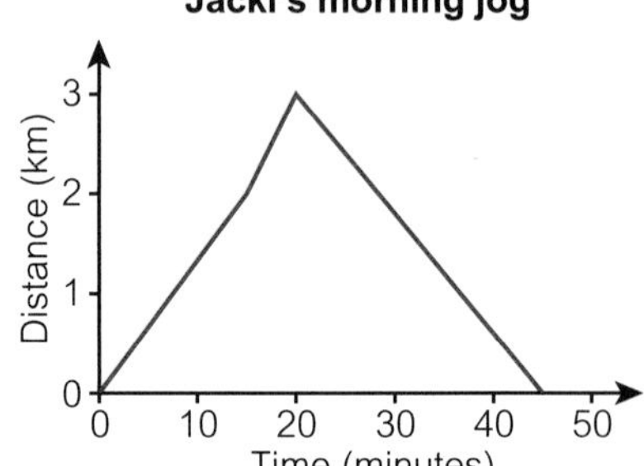

5 Draw the graph of $y = 4x - 1$.

6 These patterns are made from black and white counters.

a Copy and complete the table.

Pattern number	1	2	3	4	5
White counters					
Black counters					

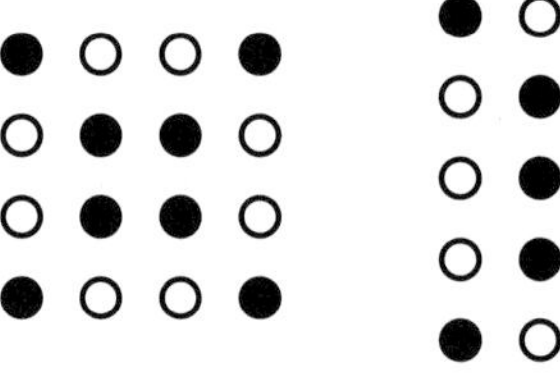

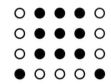

b Work out the nth term for the sequence of white counters.

c Is the sequence of white counters an arithmetic sequence or a geometric sequence?
Explain how you know.

d How many white counters will there be in the 10th pattern?

e Is there a pattern with 68 white counters?
Show your working out to explain.

f What type of sequence is the sequence of black counters?

g Find the nth term of the sequence of black counters.

7 The graph shows the price of a second-hand car.

a Estimate the price of the car when it is 5 years old.

b Between which two years does the price change the most?

c When is the car worth 50% of its original value?

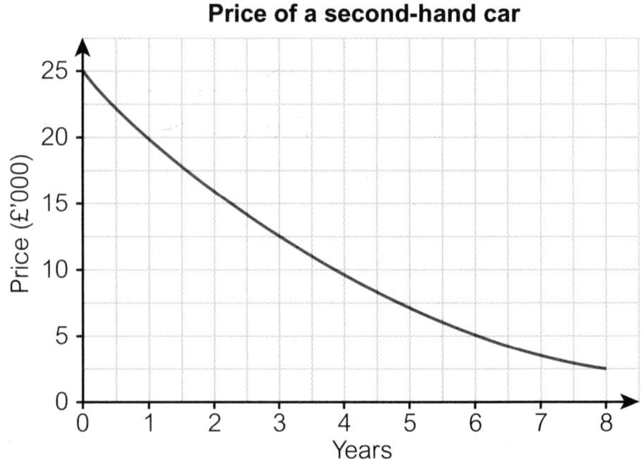

8 Which of these equations

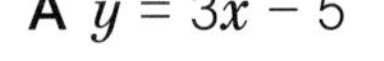

A $y = 3x - 5$ B $2y - 4x = 5$

C $3y + 2x = -4$ D $y = 2x + 5$

a gives the steepest graph

b is a line that passes through (0, 5)

c are lines that pass through (1, −2)?

9 a On the same axes you used for Q5, draw the graph of $2x - y = -3$.
b Use your graphs to solve the simultaneous equations $4x - y = 1$ and $2x - y = -3$.

Q9b hint

$y = 4x - 1$ can be rearranged as $4x - y = 1$.

10 Write down the two inequalities that describe the shaded region.

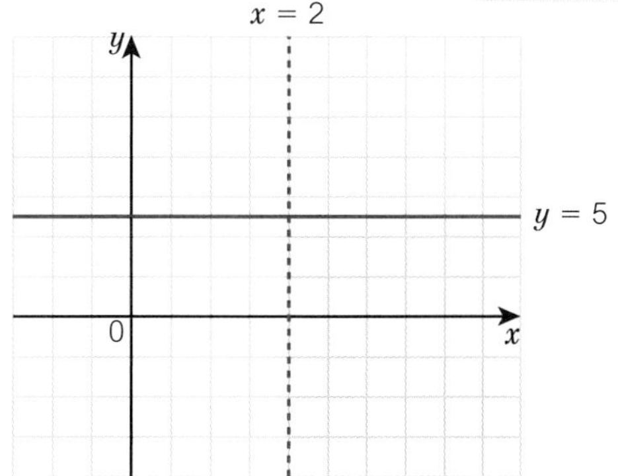

11 Match each equation to one of the graphs below.

i $y = x^3$ ii $y = -x^3$ iii $y = x^2 + 4$ iv $y = 2x + 4$

A
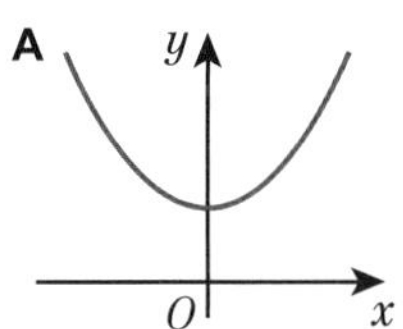

B

C
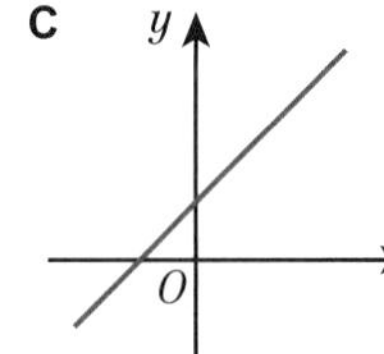

D
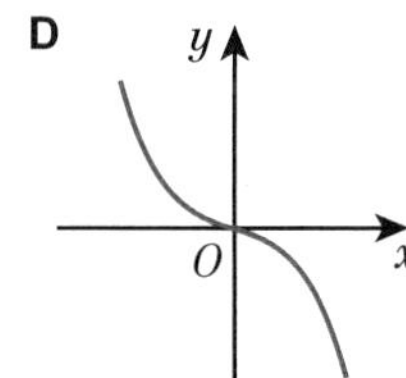

12 The graph shows a company's share price over 5 years.
a How much were the shares worth at the beginning of the 5-year period?
b How much were they worth after 1 year?
c What was the percentage increase in their value during the first year? Give your answer to the nearest whole number.
d Which year had the smallest percentage increase?
e Calculate the mean percentage increase per year.

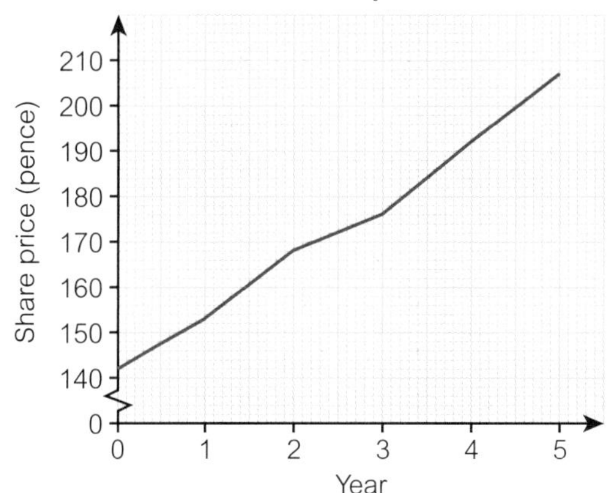

Challenge

13 a Copy the table and write in the first five square numbers.

Term	1st	2nd	3rd	4th	5th
Square numbers	1	4			
Triangle numbers	1	3			

b Write the first five triangle numbers in your table. Use the diagrams to help you.

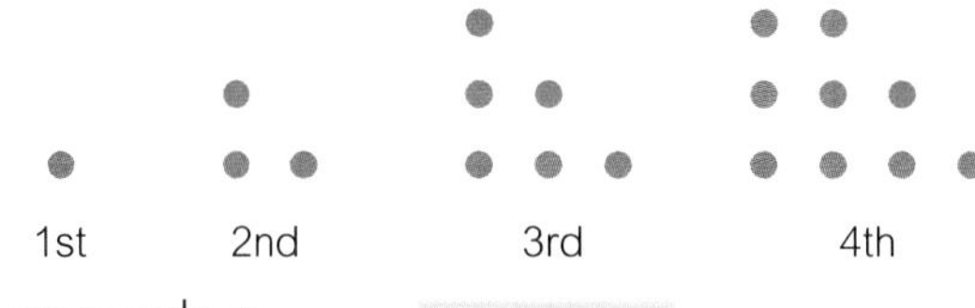

c Add together the 1st and 2nd triangle numbers. Is your answer a square number?
d Find other pairs of triangle numbers that add to make a square number.
e Split these square numbers into two triangle numbers.

i 36 ii 49 iii 81

14 **Reflect** Look back at the questions you answered in this unit test.
- Which took the shortest time to answer? Why?
- Which took the longest time to answer? Why?
- Which took the most thought to answer? Why?

Reflect

9 Probability

9.1 Calculating probabilities

You will learn to:

- Calculate probabilities from tables
- Compare probabilities.

CONFIDENCE

Why learn this?
Insurance companies use data to decide where cars are most likely to be stolen and then charge more for car insurance in those areas.

Fluency
Which is bigger?

- $\frac{2}{7}$ or $\frac{2}{5}$
- $\frac{7}{10}$ or $\frac{3}{5}$
- $\frac{5}{8}$ or $\frac{13}{24}$?

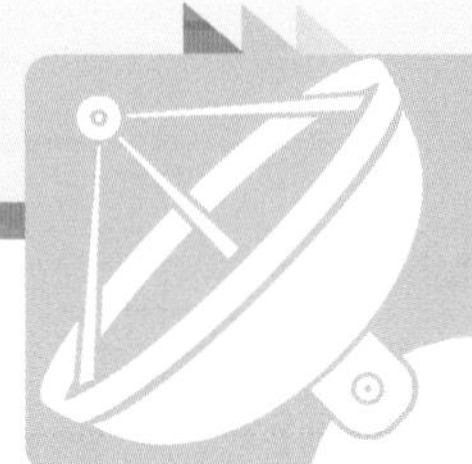

Explore
Why are young drivers charged more for their car insurance?

Exercise 9.1

Warm up

1 Here is a spinner.
What is the probability of it landing on

a red **b** blue **c** red or blue
d white **e** not yellow **f** not red?

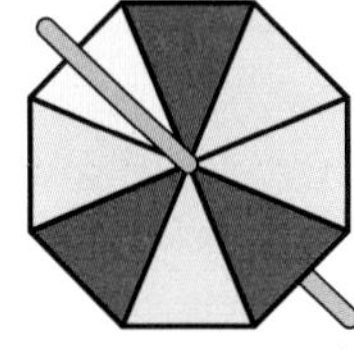

2 Tina spins the spinner in Q1 40 times.
How many times would you expect it to land on

a blue **b** yellow **c** red or yellow?

3 The table shows how Year 9 students at two different schools travel to school.

	Bus	Car	Walk	Cycle	Other
School A	17	13	28	19	5
School B	31	19	13	6	8

a Which school has the most Year 9 students who walk to school?
b How many Year 9 students are there in each school?
c How many students in School B walk or cycle?
d How many students in school A go by car or bus?
e What fraction of the total number of students use the bus?

4 The table shows some information about Year 9 students.

	Age 13	Age 14	Total
Male	48	56	104
Female	49	47	96
Total	97	103	200

A student is picked at random.
What is the probability that this student is

a female **b** male **c** aged 14
d aged 13 **e** a girl aged 14 **f** a 13-year-old boy?

Q4 Literacy hint
'Picked at random' means that each student is equally likely to be picked.

Q4a hint
$\frac{\text{total number of girls}}{\text{total number of students}}$

Q4e hint
$\frac{\text{total number of girls aged 14}}{\text{total number of students}}$

Topic links: Two-way tables, Fractions

5 Modelling Tom carries out a survey on the languages students are learning. Here are his results.
Tom picks one of these students at random.

	French	German
Year 8	76	52
Year 9	59	68

a What is the probability that he picks a Year 8 student who learns French?
b Which is he more likely to pick: a Year 8 student who learns German or a Year 9 student who learns French? Show your working.

Q5b hint
Work out the totals and compare the probabilities.

6 The table shows students' choices for an extended learning day.

	Drama	Science	Art	Totals
Y7	10	41	36	87
Y8	30	33	32	95
Y9	12	28	38	78
Totals	52	102	106	260

A student is picked at random to write an article for the school website about the extended learning day.
a What is the probability that the student is
  i a Year 7 student who chose Drama
  ii a Year 9 student who chose Science?
The headteacher picked a student from Year 9 at random.
b What is the probability that this student chose Art?

7 Real / Modelling The table shows the numbers of car thefts in 2011–12.

	Number of car thefts	Population
Northamptonshire	1202	687 300
Suffolk	746	719 500

Source: ONS

Where is a car more likely to be stolen, Northamptonshire or Suffolk? Show your working.

Key point
Events are **mutually exclusive** if one or other can happen, but not both at the same time.

8 Reasoning Decide whether these possible events from rolling a dice are **mutually exclusive**.
a rolling a 1 and rolling a 2
b rolling a 3 and rolling a prime number
c rolling an odd number and rolling an even number
d rolling a 1 or 6 and rolling a prime number
e rolling an even number and rolling a square number

Q8 hint
List the possible outcomes for each event. Can they both happen at the same time?

Investigation Real / Reasoning

You need a handful of counters of different colours, for a game of 'pick a counter'.
1 Write all your colours (the possible outcomes) in a table like this.

Colour					
Probability					

2 Are all the possible outcomes mutually exclusive? Explain your answer.
3 Count the total number of counters in your handful.
For your set of counters, work out the probability of picking each colour. Write the probabilities in your table.
4 Work out the total of the probabilities in your table.
5 Repeat for another handful of coloured counters.
6 Compare your total probabilities with someone else's. What do you notice?

Discussion Imagine you have only red, white and blue counters. You pick one at random. What is the probability that the counter is either red or white or blue?

Worked example

A bag contains red, blue, yellow and green balls.
A ball is picked at random.
The table shows the probabilities for each colour.

Colour	red	blue	yellow	green
Probability	0.4	0.2	0.1	

a Work out the probability that a green ball is picked.

$0.4 + 0.2 + 0.1 = 0.7$

$1 - 0.7 = 0.3$

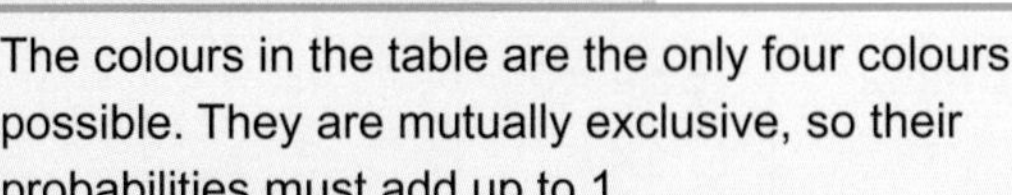

The colours in the table are the only four colours possible. They are mutually exclusive, so their probabilities must add up to 1.

b There are 20 balls in the bag.
How many are red?

$0.4 \times 20 = 8$

0.4 (or $\frac{4}{10}$) of the 20 balls in the bag are red.

> **Key point**
> The probabilities of all the mutually exclusive outcomes of an event add to 1.

9 **Modelling** A spinner has sections labelled 'win', 'lose' and 'try again'.
The table shows the probability of it landing on each section.

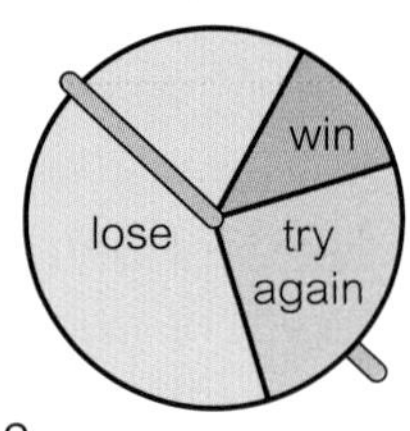

Section	win	lose	try again
Probability	$\frac{1}{8}$	$\frac{5}{8}$	

a Are the three outcomes 'win', 'lose' and 'try again' mutually exclusive?
b What is the probability that it lands on 'try again'?
c The spinner is spun 40 times. How many 'wins' would you expect?

10 A biscuit tin contains three different types of biscuit.
The table gives the probability of choosing different types.

Biscuit	Probability
shortbread	$\frac{1}{4}$
chocolate	$\frac{2}{5}$
jam	

a Work out the probability of picking a jam biscuit.
b Which type of biscuit are there most of?
c There are 60 biscuits in the tin. How many are chocolate?

> **Q10a hint**
> To add and subtract fractions, write them over a common denominator.

> **Literacy hint**
> 'P(event A)' is a useful short way of saying 'the probability of event A happening'.

11 **Reasoning** In the game of 20s each player throws three darts at a dartboard and counts the number of 20s that they hit.
George has eight attempts. He hits three 20s on four occasions, and $P(1) = \frac{1}{4}$.
Fred has eight attempts. $P(0) = P(1) = P(2) = P(3) = \frac{1}{4}$
Bert has six attempts: $P(0) = \frac{1}{3}$, $P(1) = \frac{2}{3}$.
Taking all attempts by the three men, $P(0) = \frac{2}{11}$.
Copy and complete the table. Add a column for the totals.

	Number of 20s hit			
	0	1	2	3
George				
Fred				
Bert				

> **Q11 hint**
> 'P(1)' is short for 'the probability of that player hitting one 20'.

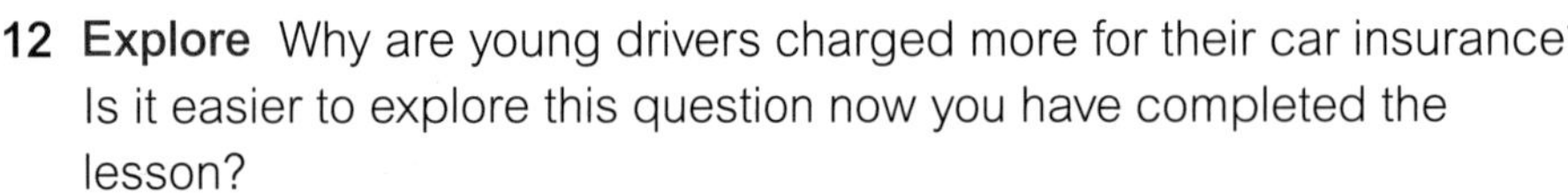

12 **Explore** Why are young drivers charged more for their car insurance?
Is it easier to explore this question now you have completed the lesson?
What further information do you need to be able to answer this?

13 **Reflect** Look back at Q6 in this lesson.
How do you know which total to choose for calculating probabilities from tables?
Write a hint for calculating probabilities from tables.

> **Q13 hint**
> Compare the totals you used for Q6a and Q6b.

Explore

Reflect

9.2 Experimental probability

You will learn to:
- Calculate estimates of probability from experiments or survey results
- Use experimental probabilities to predict outcomes.

CONFIDENCE

Why learn this?
Shop managers can use experimental probability to help them plan staff rotas.

Fluency
Ben is testing whether a dice is fair. How many times should he roll it to get a good estimate of the probability of each score?
- 10
- 50
- 1000

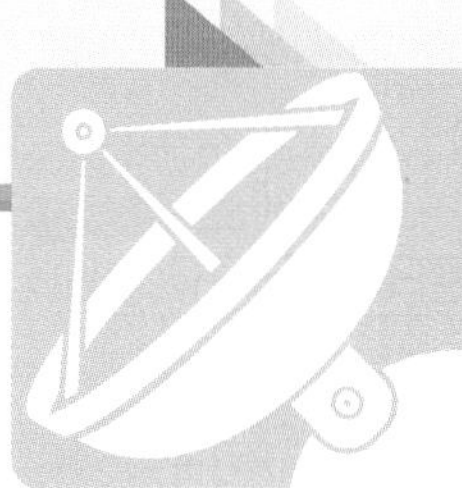

Explore
How many times would you expect a drawing pin to land point up?

Exercise 9.2

Warm up

1 Mike recorded the colour and make of cars passing his school. Here are his results.

	Red	Black	Silver
Ford	5	20	7
Vauxhall	5	9	2
Toyota	5	0	3
Skoda	0	2	2
Jaguar	0	0	2

a Which make of car is most likely to be
  i silver
  ii red?

b Which is most likely to pass the school: a black Ford or a red Toyota?

c Which make of car is least likely to be silver?

2 Modelling The table shows the results of an experiment rolling a 4-sided dice.

Score	Frequency
1	13
2	12
3	11
4	14

a How many times in total was the dice rolled?

b From these results, what is the **estimated probability** of rolling a 3?

c How many 4s would you expect in 200 throws?

Key point

You can estimate the probability of an event from the results of an experiment or survey.

$$\text{estimated probability} = \frac{\text{frequency of event}}{\text{total frequency}}$$

This **estimated probability** is also known as **experimental probability**.

3 Darryl rolled two 4-sided dice and calculated the difference each time between the numbers on the dice. He did this many times and recorded his results in a frequency table.

Difference	0	1	2	3
Tally	卌 卌 卌 卌 卌	卌 卌 卌 卌 卌 卌 卌 |	卌 卌 卌 卌 卌 ||	卌 卌 ||
Frequency	25	36	27	12

a How many times did the difference equal 2?
b How many times did Darryl roll the dice?
c Which outcome is most likely?
d Estimate the probability of getting a difference of 2. Give your answer as a fraction.

4 a Modelling Look again at Darryl's game in Q3. How many times would he expect to get a difference of 0 if he rolled the dice 1000 times?
b Imagine a set of results showing that a difference of 3 occurs 30 times. Roughly how many times might Darryl have rolled the dice?

5 Modelling Phil rolled two 6-sided dice 80 times and added up the numbers each time. He got a total of 7 on 13 occasions.
a Use a calculator to decide whether $\frac{1}{4}$, $\frac{1}{5}$ or $\frac{1}{6}$ is the best estimate for the probability of rolling a total of 7.
b Imagine he rolled the dice 360 times.
Use your estimate to predict how many times he would get a total of 7.

Investigation — Real / Reasoning

1 Roll two dice and add their scores.
Repeat this at least 50 times.
Record your results in a table like this.

Score			
Tally			
Frequency			

Part 1 hint
What scores are possible? Make sure you include them all.

2 Which score did you get most? What is the estimated probability?
3 Which score did you get least? How many times would you expect to get this score in 200 throws?
4 Combine your results with someone else's. Which is the least frequent score now? What is its estimated probability?
In a game, Player 1 wins if they score 2 or 3. Player 2 wins if they score 7.
5 Which player is most likely to win? Use the results of your experiment to explain.
Discussion Why do you think some scores are more likely than others?

6 Reasoning A teacher has a set of red, blue and black pens.
He says, 'There are three colours, so the probability of picking each colour is $\frac{1}{3}$.'
a Use these sets of pens to explain why this might not be true.
b Explain how to design a set of pens so the probability of picking each colour is $\frac{1}{3}$.
c Design a set of pens where the probability of picking black is twice the probability of picking red.

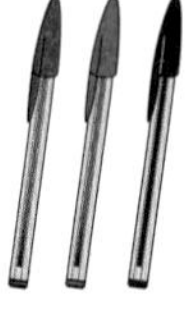
Set 1

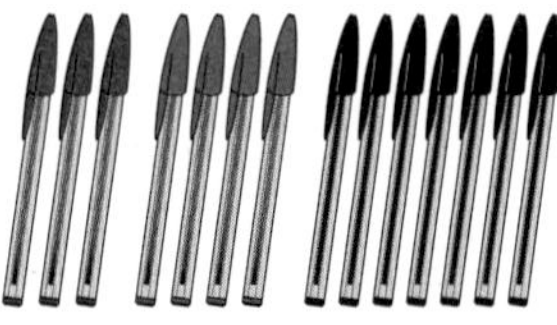
Set 2

Topic links: Mean

7 The school canteen has to serve one vegetable with every main meal choice.

P(sweetcorn) = 0.15 P(tomatoes) = 0.1

P(green beans) = 0.2 P(peas) = 0.3

P(cabbage) = 0.1 P(carrots) = 0.15

What is the probability that these are served with any one meal:

a tomatoes or cabbage

b any vegetable other than tomatoes or cabbage

c a vegetable that is not green

d a vegetable that doesn't begin with the letter 'c'?

Key point

For two mutually exclusive events, you work out the probability that one or the other happens by adding together their probabilities.

Q7a hint

Tomatoes and cabbage are mutually exclusive.
So P(tomatoes or cabbage) = P(tomatoes) + P(cabbage)

8 **Real / Modelling** Researchers recorded the day of the week and the time of birth for over 6000 babies in a hospital, over a six-month period.

	2000–0159	0200–0759	0800–1359	1400–1959
Weekday	994	1239	1284	1109
Weekend	381	501	506	453

a Copy the table and add an extra column and row for totals. Work out the totals.

b Use the data to work out the mean number of babies born

i each day at the weekend

ii each weekday.

c Are babies more likely to be born at the weekend or on a weekday?
Explain your answer.

d Estimate the probability that a baby is born between 8 pm and 1.59 am. Give your answer to three decimal places.

e In this hospital, an average of 1000 babies are born each month. How many would you expect to be born between

i 8 pm and 1.59 am each month

ii 8 am and 1.59 pm each day?

f A midwife uses this information to plan how many staff she needs for the four shifts, 2000–0159, 0200–0759, 0800–1359, 1400–1959.

i Which shift needs the most staff?

ii Which needs the least?

Discussion Another hospital uses data like this from a two-month survey. Which is likely to be the better model for predicting births?

Q8b i hint

mean number of babies born each day at the weekend

$= \frac{\text{total number of babies born at weekend}}{\text{number of days in a weekend}}$

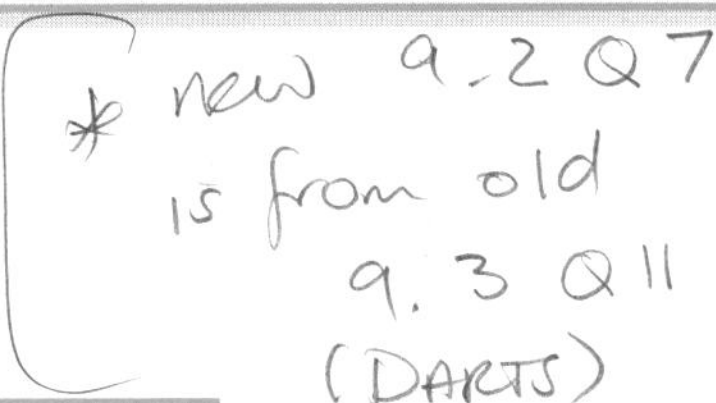

Q8e i hint

Assume that there are an average of 30 days in a month.

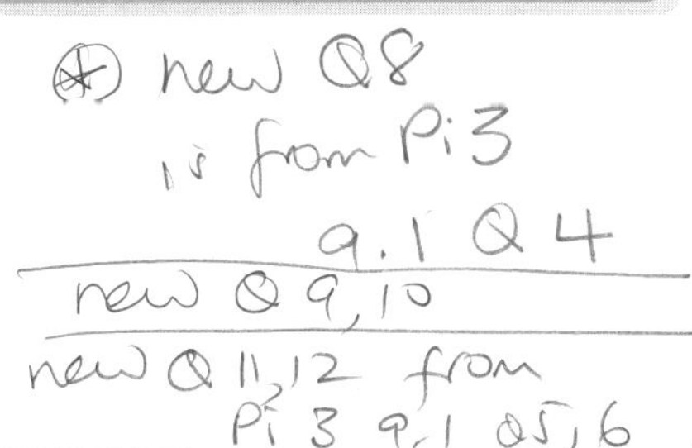

9 **Explore** How many times would you expect a drawing pin to land point up?
Look back at the maths you have learned in this lesson.
How can you use it to answer this question?

10 **Reflect** Clare says, 'Finding an average of a set of data is the same thing as calculating the most likely outcome.' Is Clare correct? Explain your answer.

Q10 hint

Find the mean and mode from the table of data in Q3.
Compare these with your answers for Q3c.
Is finding the average always, sometimes, or never the same as finding the most likely outcome?

Explore

Reflect

9.3 Probability diagrams

You will learn to:
- List all the possible outcomes of one or two events in Venn diagrams, tables and sample space diagrams
- Compare experimental and theoretical probabilities
- Decide if a game is fair.

CONFIDENCE

Why learn this?
Calculating probabilities can help you work out if a game is fair.

Fluency
What are the possible outcomes for
- rolling a dice
- flipping a coin
- picking a playing card?

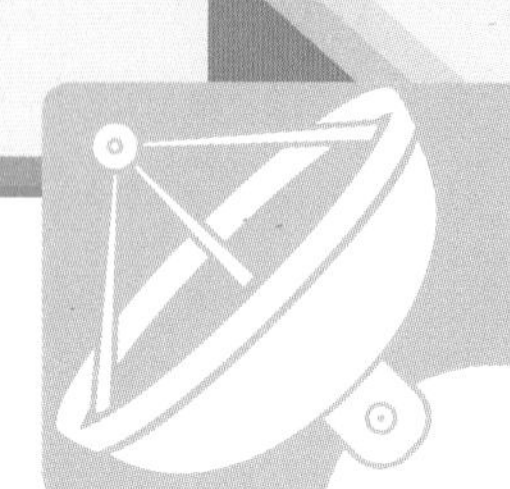

Explore
In Monopoly®, what are the chances of going straight to jail from the Free Parking space?

Exercise 9.3

Warm up

1 From a pack of playing cards (no jokers) what is the probability of picking
 a a red card **b** a spade
 c a picture card **d** a king?

2 On a dice, what is the probability of rolling
 a an even number **b** a prime number **c** a square number
 d a multiple of 3 **e** a factor of 10 **f** an odd number?

Worked example

20 students study French, 30 study German and 5 of them study both French and German.

a Show this information in a Venn diagram.

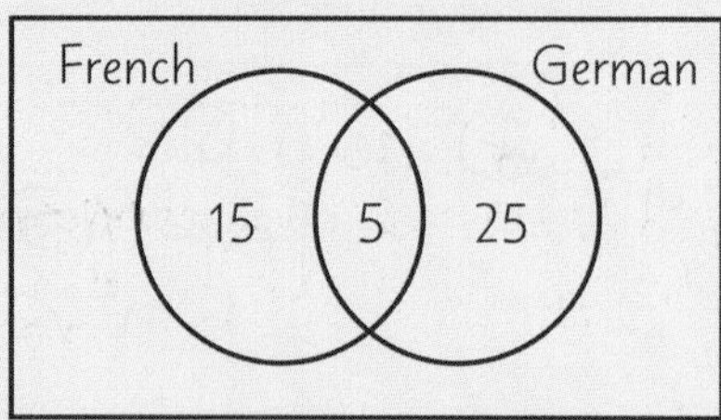

Draw two overlapping circles, one for each set of data.
5 students study French and German, so put 5 in the overlap.

$20 - 5 = 15$
$30 - 5 = 25$

Work out how many are left in the rest of each set and write the values in.
20 students study French, but 5 of these also study German. So 15 study only French.

b What is the probability that a student picked at random
 i studies French and not German
 ii only studies one language?

Total number of students = $15 + 5 + 25 = 45$

To work out the probabilities, you need to know the total number of students.

P(French and not German) = $\frac{15}{45} = \frac{1}{3}$

You don't need to simplify the fraction for probability, but you can if you want to.

$15 + 25 = 40$

P(only one language) = $\frac{40}{45} = \frac{8}{9}$

40 study only one language

Key point
A **Venn diagram** shows sets of data in circles inside a rectangle. You write data that is in both sets in the part where the circles overlap.

3 45 students study Art and 30 study Drama. 10 students study both.

a Show this information in a **Venn diagram**.

b What is the probability that a student picked at random

i studies Art and Drama ii studies Drama but not Art?

Discussion 45 study Art and 30 study Drama. Why aren't there 75 students?

4 a Real Draw a Venn diagram to show the number of hearts in a pack of cards and the number of jacks.

b What is the probability that a card picked at random from a pack is

i a heart ii the jack of hearts iii a heart or a jack?

> **Q4a hint**
> How many cards in a pack are jacks and how many are hearts?

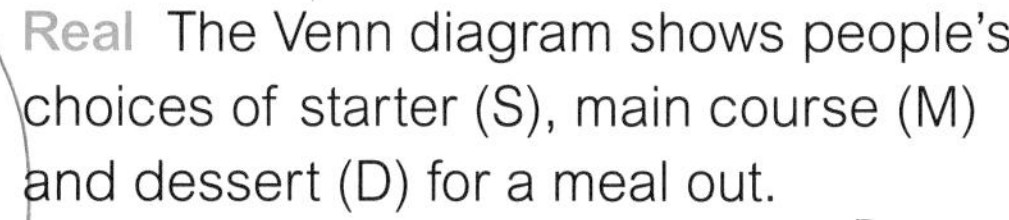

5 Real The Venn diagram shows people's choices of starter (S), main course (M) and dessert (D) for a meal out.

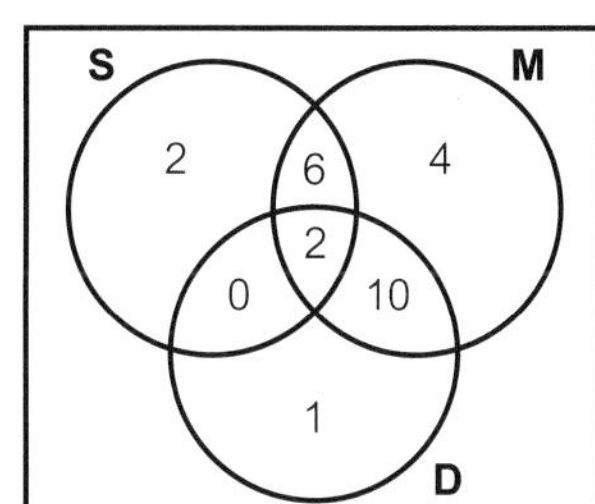

a How many people had

i three courses

ii only one course?

b How many people went out for the meal?

c What is the probability that one of these people, picked at random, had two courses?

6 Modelling A 12-sided dice has a month of the year on each side. Greg challenges Amy to play a game he's invented called JAM FONDS. If he rolls two of these dice and both land with months beginning J, A or M on top he gets a point. If they both start with F, O, N, D or S, Amy gets a point. Amy refuses, saying the game isn't fair.

a Explain why it isn't fair.

b Is it possible for Amy to [illegible]

c How could the rules be [illegible]

> **Q6a hint**
> List all the possible outcomes. How many does Amy get a point for?

> **Key point**
> A **sample space diagram** shows all the possible outcomes of two events.

7 Two dice are rolled and the [illegible] are added.

a Copy and complete this [illegible] **space diagram** to show [illegible] possible outcomes.

b There are 36 possible ou[illegible]

i How many of these o[illegible] are 5?

ii What is the probability [illegible] 5 with two dice?

c What is the probability o[illegible]

i 2 ii 3 iii 7?

d The two dice are rolled 180 times. How many scores of 6 would you expect?

> **Q7a hint**
> 4 + 3 = 7 and 5 + 6 = 11

> **Q7b hint**
> Find all the 5s in your sample space diagram.

> **Key point**
> **Theoretical probability** is the probability you *calculate*. It shows what is likely to happen 'in theory'.

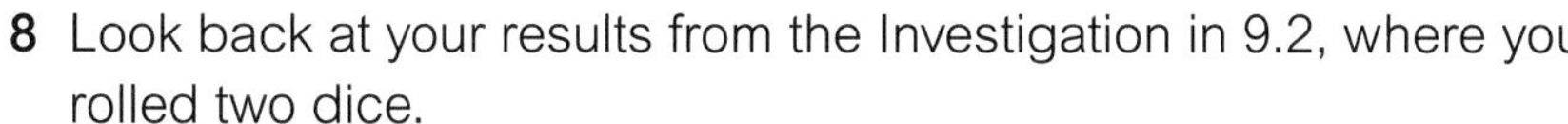

8 Look back at your results from the Investigation in 9.2, where you rolled two dice.

a What were the experimental probabilities of scoring 2, 3 and 7?

b Compare these with the **theoretical probabilities** you calculated in Q7.

Discussion When experimental probabilities are not close to the theoretical probabilities, what could this mean?

> **Q8b hint**
> Are the theoretical and experimental probabilities close to each other or very different?

Investigation

Reasoning / Real

Play this game with a partner. Decide who will be Player 1 and Player 2.
Roll two dice. Find the difference between the two numbers.
Player 1 scores 1 point if the difference is a prime number.
Player 2 scores 1 point if the difference is a square.
The first player to 10 points wins.
Play a few times.

Hint
1 is not a prime number.

1. Does the same person win every time/more often?
2. Do you think the game is fair?
3. Draw a sample space diagram to show all the possible scores from rolling two dice and finding the difference.
4. Calculate the probability of winning for each player.
5. Is the game fair? Explain your answer.

9 **Modelling** Two dice are rolled together 100 times. The number of doubles is recorded. Here are the results.

Doubles	Not doubles
33	67

a What is the experimental probability of rolling a double?
b Work out the theoretical probability of rolling a double.
c How many doubles would you expect from 100 rolls of two dice?
d Do you think the dice are fair? Explain your answer.

Q9 hint
A double means 1, 1 or 2, 2 etc.

Q9b hint
You could use your sample space diagram from Q7.

10 **Real / Modelling** In a game at a charity fête, players pay 50p to roll a dice and flip a coin. They win £1 if they roll an even number and flip a head.

a Copy and complete this sample space diagram to show all the possible outcomes.
b How many equally likely outcomes are there?
c What is the probability of winning?
d How much money can the stall expect to make for charity when the game is played 200 times?

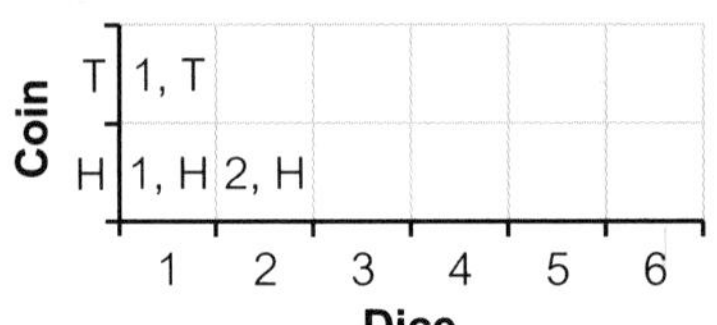

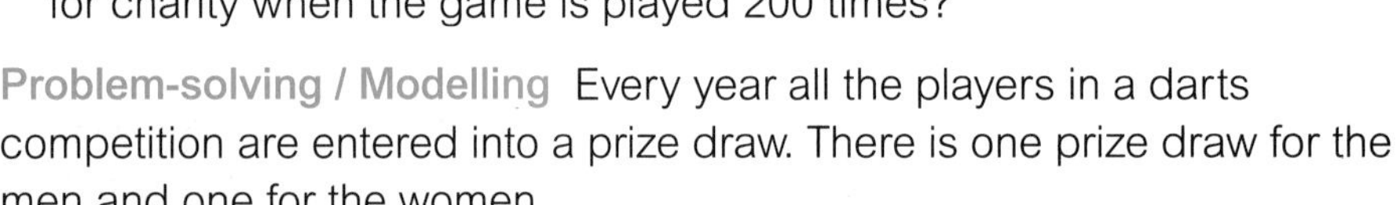

11 **Problem-solving / Modelling** Every year all the players in a darts competition are entered into a prize draw. There is one prize draw for the men and one for the women.
Explain why this might not give everyone a fair chance of winning.

12 **Explore** In Monopoly®, what are the chances of going straight to jail from the Free Parking space?
Look back at the maths you have learned in this lesson.
How can you use it to answer this question?

13 **Reflect** Marlene is asked to complete these sentences.

1. Theoretical probability is _______. An example of this is _______________.
2. Experimental probability is _________. An example of this is _______________.

These are her answers.
A found from actual results
B the chances of two people in a class having the same birthday
C the chances of catching a cold by kissing someone with a cold
D found from a sample space diagram
Match A to D to the correct spaces in the sentences.
Then copy and complete each sentence in your own words.

Explore

Reflect

9.4 Independent events

You will learn to:
- Calculate the probability of two independent events
- Use tree diagrams.

Why learn this?
Fundraisers design lotteries so that the chances of getting five winning balls are very low.

Fluency
Work out
- $\frac{1}{2} \times \frac{1}{2}$
- $\frac{1}{4} \times \frac{1}{3}$
- 0.1×0.4
- 0.3×0.3
- $\frac{3}{8} + \frac{2}{8}$
- $\frac{1}{25} + \frac{11}{25}$

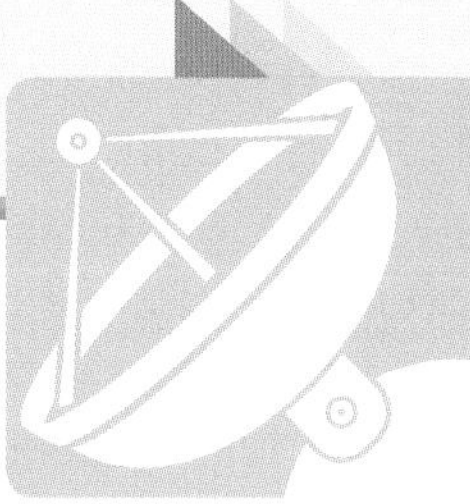

Explore
What is the probability of throwing five 4s on a dice?

Exercise 9.4

1 Copy and complete this sample space table for flipping two coins.

	Head (H)	Tail (T)
Head (H)	H, H	
Tail (T)		

What is the theoretical probability of flipping

a two heads b two heads or two tails

c a head and a tail (in any order)?

new Q4 from P13 9.3 Q3 (Zach)
new Q8 from P13 9.3 Q4

Q2a hint
P(R) is short for P(red).

2 For this spinner, write down

a P(R) b P(B) c P(W)

d P(W or B) e P(R or B) f P(not B)

g Does P(R or B) = P(R) + P(B)?
Use the diagram to explain your answer.

Key point
Two events are **independent** if the results of one do not affect the results of another.

Warm up

Investigation — Reasoning

These three balls are put in a bag and one is taken out at random.

1 Work out P(R), P(Y) and P(B).

Joe takes out two balls, one at a time, like this:
take out a ball at random … put it back in the bag … take out a ball at random.
One possible outcome is R, B. This means he takes a red ball, then a blue one.

2 Are the two events (take one ball, take the next ball) **independent**?

3 Draw a sample space diagram to show all the possible outcomes for taking two balls, one at a time.

4 Work out a P(B, B) b P(B) × P(B) c What do you notice?

5 Work out a P(R, Y) b P(R) × P(Y)

6 Use P(R) and P(B) to work out the probability of P(R, B). Check your answer using your sample space diagram.

7 For a coin, how could you use P(head) to calculate P(head, head)?
Check your answer, using the sample space table in Q1.

Discussion What is the rule for finding the probability of two independent events?

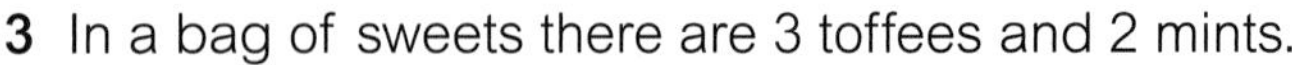

3 In a bag of sweets there are 3 toffees and 2 mints.

a What is the probability of picking a toffee?

Dan picks a sweet at random. It is a toffee, and he eats it.

b Dan picks another sweet at random. What is the probability that he picks a toffee this time?

Discussion Are the two events, picking a toffee first time, and picking a toffee second time, independent?

> **Key point**
> The probability of two independent events is P(event 1) × P(event 2)

4 Which of these pairs of events are independent?

A flipping a coin, then flipping it again

B picking a black sock from a drawer, putting it on, then picking another sock

C rolling a 6 on a dice, then rolling another 6

D getting full marks in a maths test, then getting full marks in the next maths test

5 Alix picks a card from a pack. She replaces it and shuffles the pack, then picks another card.
What is the probability that both cards are hearts?

6 Dante records the colours of cars passing the school.
Use his results to estimate the probability that

a the next car to pass the school is silver

b that the next two cars to pass the school are silver.

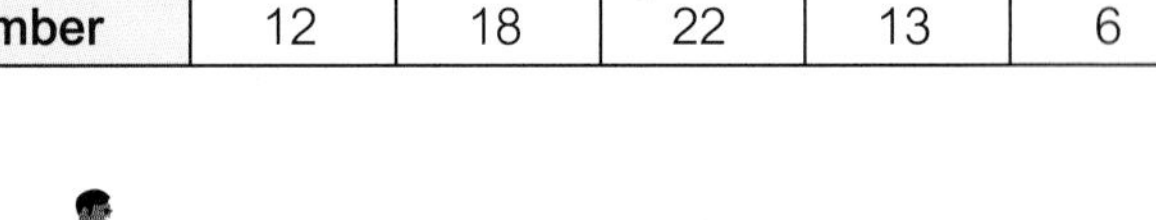

Colour	red	black	silver	blue	other
Number	12	18	22	13	6

Worked example

There are 3 red and 2 blue counters in a bag.
Steff picks a counter, replaces it, and picks again.

a Draw a tree diagram to show this.

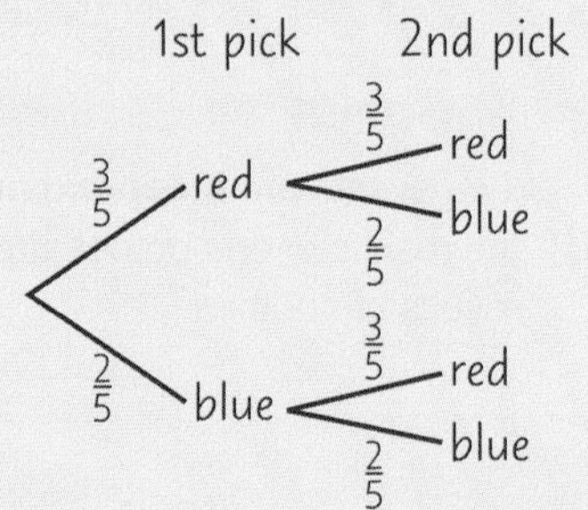

> At each pick the choice is red or blue. Draw a branch for red and one for blue each time. Write the P(B) value on each branch for blue and the P(R) value on each branch for red.

b Work out the probability that she picks 2 red counters.

$P(R, R) = \frac{3}{5} \times \frac{3}{5} = \frac{9}{25}$

> Read along the branches for red, red.
> Multiply the probabilities P(R) × P(R) = P(R, R)

c Work out the probability that she picks 1 red and 1 blue counter.

1 red and 1 blue could be P(R, B) or P(B, R)

$P(R, B) = \frac{3}{5} \times \frac{2}{5} = \frac{6}{25}$

> Find all the paths through the diagram that give 1 red and 1 blue.

$P(B, R) = \frac{2}{5} \times \frac{3}{5} = \frac{6}{25}$

> Multiply along the branches to calculate the probability of each path.

$P(B, R) + P(R, B) = \frac{6}{25} + \frac{6}{25} = \frac{12}{25}$

> Add them together.

> **Key point**
> A **tree diagram** helps you work out the combined probabilities of more than one event.

7 This **tree diagram** shows the possible outcomes of flipping two coins.
Use it to work out the probability of flipping

a two tails

b a head and a tail in any order.

Check your answers using your sample space table from Q1.

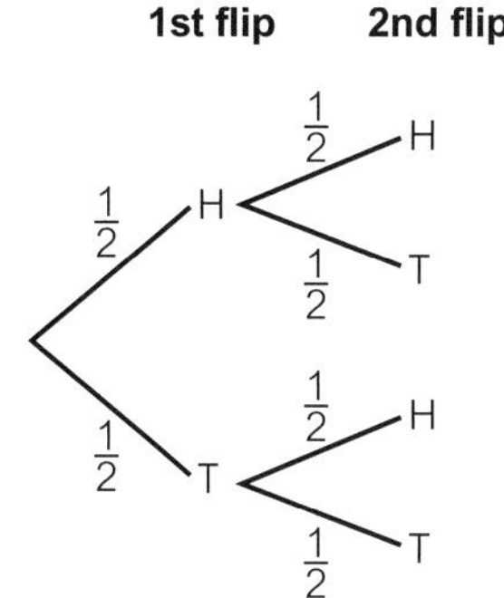

8 Real / Modelling A weather forecaster predicts that the chance of sunshine is 0.7 on Saturday and 0.6 on Sunday.
Draw a tree diagram for the two days, showing the two possible outcomes, 'sunny' and 'not sunny'.
What is the probability that there is sunshine on both days?

Discussion What did you assume to work out this probability? Is it a fair assumption?

9 Real / Modelling A factory makes mugs. The factory owners have found that the usual probability that a mug is damaged at some point during production is 0.05.

a What is the probability that a mug is not damaged?

b Copy and complete this tree diagram to show the possible outcomes of picking two mugs from the production line.

c Two mugs are picked.
What is the probability that they are both damaged?

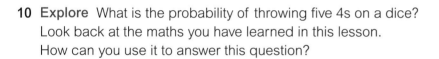

Discussion How can the factory use this probability model to check that the mugs are being made properly day to day?

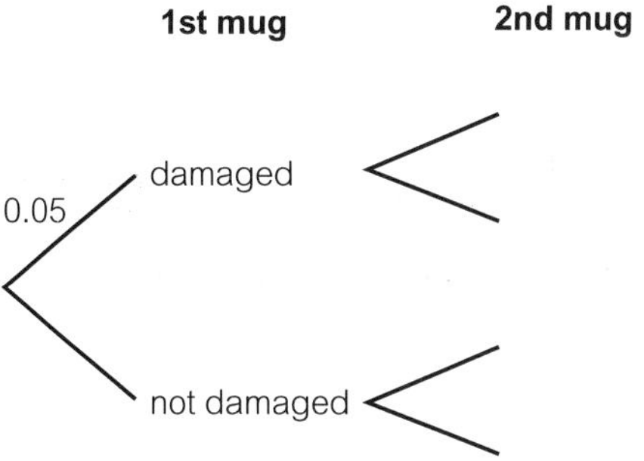

10 **Explore** What is the probability of throwing five 4s on a dice?
Look back at the maths you have learned in this lesson.
How can you use it to answer this question?

11 **Reflect** In lesson 9.1 you learned about mutually exclusive events.
In this lesson you learned about independent events.

a Write a definition, in your own words, for each of these types of events.

b Write a mutually exclusive event and an independent event that involve

i a coin

ii a dice.

c Describe how mutually exclusive events and independent events are different.

d Write mutually exclusive events and independent events that involve a pack of cards.
Compare your events with those of others in your class.

Q11c hint
Look at your examples in part **b**.

Explore

Reflect

9 Check up

Log how you did on your Student Progression Chart.

Probability from tables and diagrams

1 The two-way table shows the membership of a swimming club.

	Under 16	16–25	26–40	over 40	Totals
Male	9	23	5	7	44
Female	11	13	6	10	36
Totals	20	36	11	17	80

A member of the club is picked at random.

a What is the probability that this member is

   i male   **ii** aged 26–40

   iii a girl aged under 16   **iv** a man aged 16–40?

b Which type of member is more likely to be picked: a man aged over 25 or a woman aged 25 or under?

c All the female members' names are put into a hat and one is picked. What is the probability that the one picked is over 40?

2 **a** Copy and complete the Venn diagram to show the numbers of black cards (clubs or spades) and picture cards (jack, queen, king) in a normal pack of 52 cards.

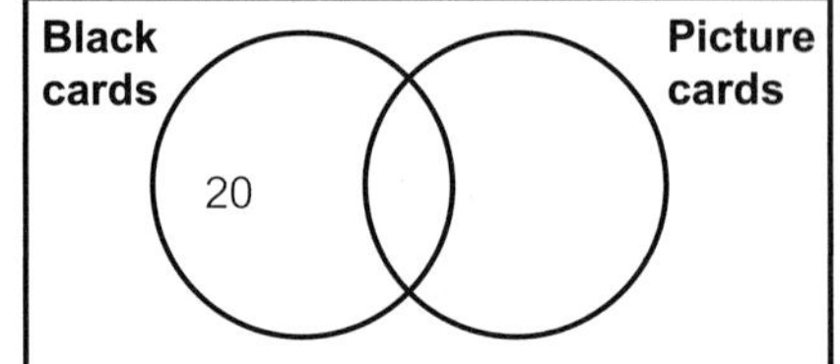

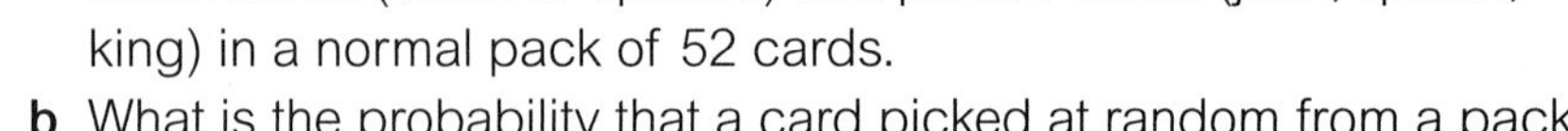

b What is the probability that a card picked at random from a pack is

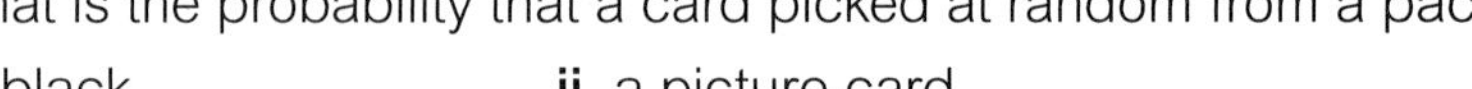

   i black   **ii** a picture card

   iii a picture card from a black suit?

3 Abi and Barry have a set of these number cards.

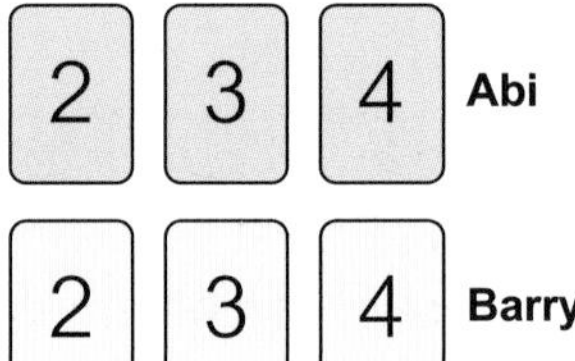

Chloë picks, at random, one of Abi's cards and one of Barry's cards.

a Draw a sample space diagram to show all the possible outcomes.

b What is the probability that Chloë picks

   i two 4s   **ii** at least one 3?

Mutually exclusive events

4 Jim has two bags.
Bag A contains 18 balls. 15 of them are red.
Bag B contains 40 balls. 32 of them are red.
He picks a ball at random from each bag.
From which bag is he most likely to pick a red ball?

5 The table shows the probabilities that trains arriving at a station are either early or late.

Arrival	early	late	on time
Probability	3%	9%	

a Work out the probability that a train is on time.

b 400 trains a week arrive at the station.
How many of these trains would you expect to be late?

c One week 12 out of 450 trains are early. Does this mean that the probability of a train arriving early has changed?

Independent events and experimental probability

6 This 5-colour spinner and a coin are used in an experiment. Alice spins the spinner 200 times, and flips the coin each time. Here are the results.

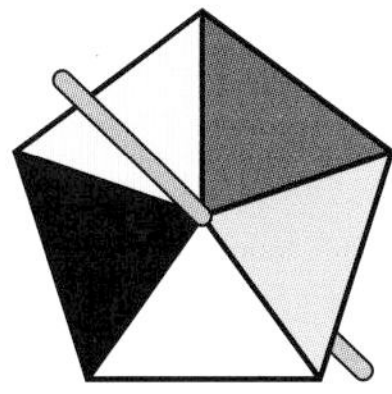

	Red	Blue	Yellow	White	Black
Head	19	22	18	21	17
Tail	21	23	20	17	22

a Use the results to estimate the experimental probability of getting blue and a head.
b Do you think the coin is fair? Explain your answer.

7 Use the results for the spinner and the coin in Q6 to answer these questions.
a Calculate the theoretical probability of getting blue and a head.
b Using this theoretical probability, how many times would you expect to get blue and a head after 200 trials?
c Do you think a game played with this spinner and coin would be fair? Explain your answer.

8 A bag contains lettered tiles. Players pick a letter at random and then replace it. They then pick another letter.
The tree diagram shows the probabilities of picking vowels (V) and consonants (C).
a Are the '1st letter' and '2nd letter' events independent? Explain your answer.
b Calculate the probability of picking
i two vowels ii no vowels iii one vowel and one consonant.

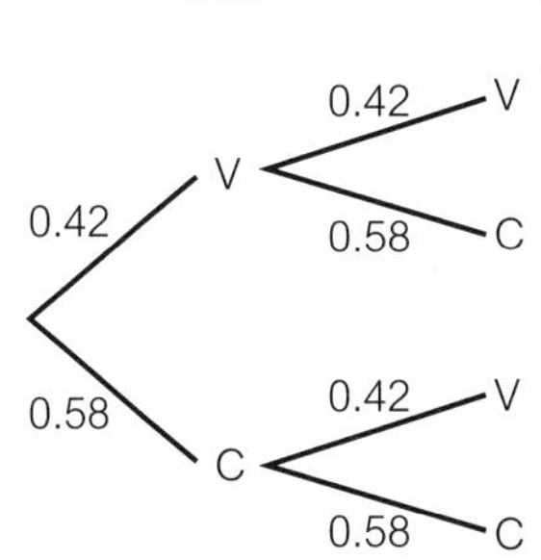

9 **How sure are you of your answers? Were you mostly**
Just guessing **Feeling doubtful** **Confident**
What next? Use your results to decide whether to strengthen or extend your learning.

Reflect

Challenge

10 In a game you roll two dice and add them to get the total.
You win if the total is the same as the number of letters in your name.
Write down some names that are different lengths.
Work out the probability of each one winning.
a Is this game fair? Explain your answer.
b If you multiply the numbers instead of adding them, is the game fair?

11 A Scrabble® set has 100 letter tiles. 42 are vowels, 56 are consonants and 2 are blanks.
At the start of a game you pick 7 letters.
a Copy and complete the diagram to show the probabilities of picking a vowel every time.

$\frac{\square}{100}$	$\frac{\square}{99}$	$\frac{\square}{98}$				

b Convert the fractions to decimals. Are you more or less likely to pick a vowel on your first pick or your seventh pick, if all the letters picked already are vowels?
c Multiply the probabilities to work out the probability of picking 7 vowels.

Q11a hint
You pick the first vowel from 100 tiles. When you have picked a vowel the first time, for the second pick there are 41 vowels left and 99 to pick from, and so on.

9 Strengthen

You will:

- Strengthen your understanding with practice.

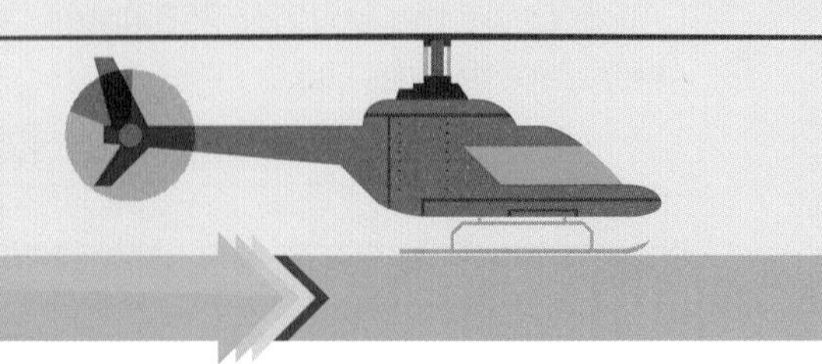

Probability from tables and diagrams

1 Real The table shows data on the birth month of newborn babies.

	Jan–Mar	Apr–Jun	Jul–Sep	Oct–Dec	Totals
Female	36	25	41	29	131
Male	28	38	32	35	133
Totals	64	63	73	64	264

a How many males were born in the months April to September?

b What is the probability that a baby chosen at random is

  i a male born in the months April to September

  ii a female born in the months October to December?

c A male baby is chosen.
What is the probability that he was born in July, August or September?

d A female baby is chosen.
What is the probability that she was born in the first half of the year?

> **Q1b i hint**
> Use your answer to part **a** and the total number of babies born.

> **Q1c hint**
> Use only the values for male babies.

2 Real Here are the results of a football tournament.

Round	0–0	Score draw	Win
1	2	9	5
2	2	3	3
Quarter-finals	2	0	2
Semi-finals	0	0	2
Final	0	0	1

a **i** How many matches were played in Round 1?

  ii Work out the probability of a 0–0 result in Round 1.

b **i** Work out the total number of matches in each round.
Write your results in a table like this.

Round	Number of matches	P(0–0)
1		

  ii Work out the probability of a 0–0 result in each round.
Write these probabilities in your table.

  iii In which round was a 0–0 result most likely?

c **i** Add a column for P(Win) to your table.
Work out the probability of a win in each round.

  ii Was a win more likely in the quarter-finals or the semi-finals?

> **Q2a ii hint**
> $\frac{\text{number of 0–0 results}}{\text{total number of matches in Round 1}}$

> **Q2b hint**
> P(0–0) means the probability of a 0–0 result.

3 Use the tables and your answers to Q2 to answer these questions.

a Work out the probability of a score draw in Round 2.

b Was a win in Round 1 more likely than a score draw in Round 2?

c In which round was a win least likely?

d In which rounds was a win certain?

e In which round was a score draw most likely?

> **Q3a hint**
> What information do you need from the tables to work this out?

Topic links: Place value, Fractions, Decimals

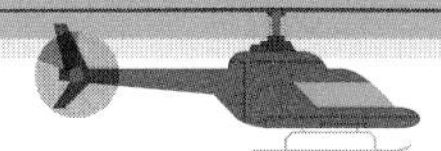

4 In Level 5 and Level 6 of a computer game you randomly get one of these things to help you win.

code-breaker £1000 a banana

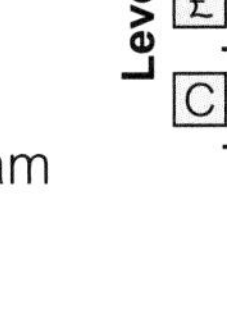

a Copy and complete this sample space diagram to show all the possible outcomes for Levels 5 and 6.
b How many possible outcomes are there?
c What is the probability that you get a banana in both levels?
d Write down the outcomes that give you at least one banana.
e What is the probability of getting at least one banana in both?

5 Modelling Ben spins these two spinners.
One possible outcome is 1, 4.
a Draw a sample space diagram to show all the possible outcomes.
b How many possible outcomes are there?
c Work out the probability of
i a 1 ii one number being double the other
iii both numbers being at least 2.
d Which is more likely: two even numbers or two odd numbers?
e Mia spins the two spinners and adds the two numbers together. Draw a new sample space diagram to show the scores.
f Which score is most likely?
g What is the probability of scoring at least 5?

Spinner 1

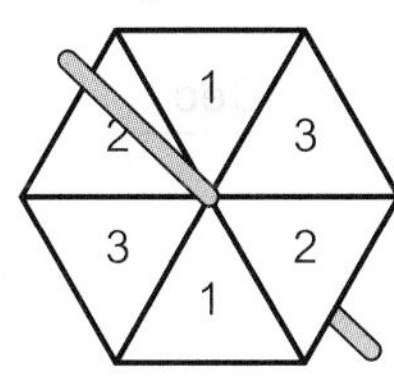

Spinner 2

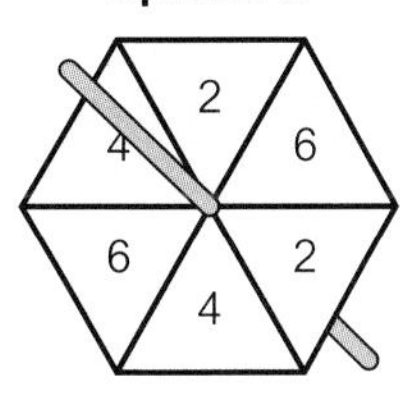

6 In an athletics club
15 members train on Wednesdays
12 members train on Fridays
10 members train on Wednesdays and Fridays.
a Copy the Venn diagram.
i Write the number for Wednesdays and Fridays in the section where the circles overlap.
ii How many people need to go in the rest of the Wednesday circle, so the total in the whole Wednesday circle is 15?
iii How many people train on Fridays? Write in the number of people in the rest of the Friday circle.
b How many members are there altogether?
c What is the probability that a member chosen at random trains on
i Wednesdays and Fridays ii Wednesdays only?

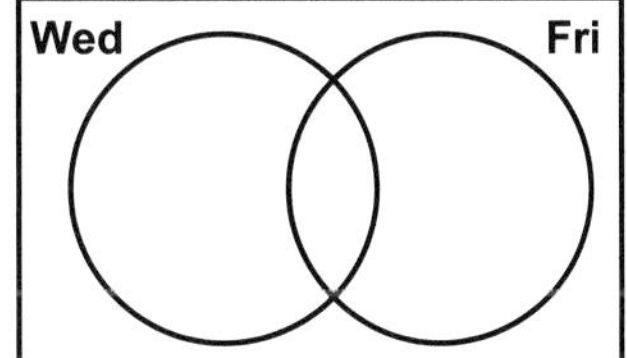

7 a In an ordinary pack of 52 cards, how many are
i red cards ii picture cards iii red picture cards?
b Draw a Venn diagram with circles for picture cards and red cards. Write in
i the number of red picture cards
ii the remaining numbers of picture cards and red cards.
c From a whole pack, what is the probability of picking
i a red picture card ii a red card that is not a picture card?

Q4a hint

What do C, £ and B stand for? And what could you get in Level 6?

Q4b Strategy hint 

Look carefully at what each cell in the sample space diagram tells you.

Q4d Literacy hint 

'At least one banana' means one or more bananas.

Q5a hint

Put spinner 1 on the horizontal axis and spinner 2 on the vertical axis.

Q5e hint

Use the same axes. For the result 1, 2, the score is 1 + 2 = 3

Q6a hint

i 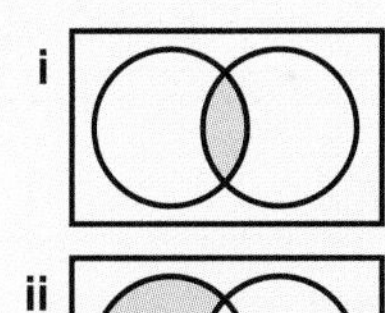

ii 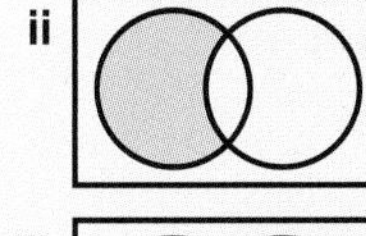

iii 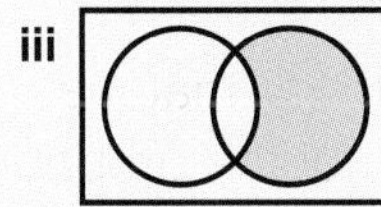

Q6b hint

Add the numbers from every section.

Q7a hint

How many picture cards (J, Q, K) are there in one suit?

Q7b i hint

These belong in both circles. Where will you put them?

Mutually exclusive events

1 Reasoning Here is a set of cards.

1 2 3 4 5 6 7 8 9 10

Which of these pairs of events are mutually exclusive?

a picking a red card and picking a 6
b picking an odd number and picking an orange card
c picking a square number and picking a blue card
d picking a factor of 10 and picking a red card

Q1 hint
Could you pick a card that fits both descriptions at once?

2 A bag contains red, yellow and pink balls. One ball is picked at random.

a Write down all the possible outcomes.
b Are all the possible outcomes mutually exclusive?
c P(yellow) = 0.2 and P(red) = 0.5.
Work out P(pink).

Q2c hint
What must the probabilities of all these outcomes add up to?

3 A game board has squares coloured red, white and black.
The probability of landing on

- a red square is $\frac{2}{9}$
- a black square is $\frac{4}{9}$.

What is the probability of landing on a white square?

4 There are 4 red, 3 yellow, 1 black and 2 orange sweets in a tin.
A sweet is picked at random.

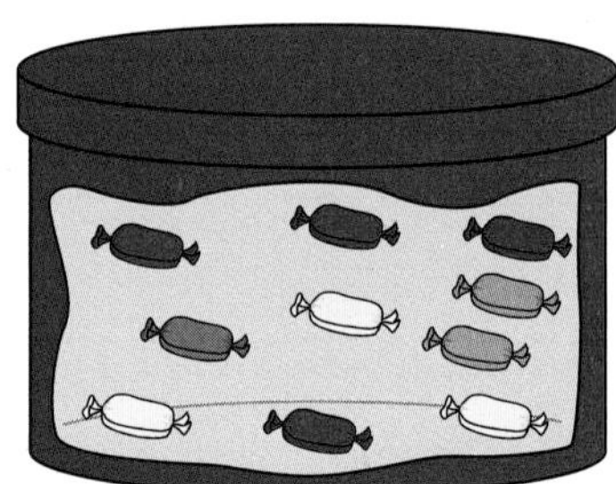

a Which colour is most likely to be picked?
b Copy and complete the table to show the probability of each possible outcome.

Colour		
Probability		

c What is the total of the probabilities in the table?
Explain why.
d A sweet is picked at random.
What is the probability that it is
i red or yellow or orange
ii not red, orange or yellow
iii black?
e Why is the probability of picking a black sweet the same as the probability of picking a sweet that is not red, orange or yellow?

Q4c hint
All the outcomes are __________ __________, so their probabilities add up to ____.

5 The table shows the probabilities that a bus is on time or late.

Arrival	on time	late	early
Probability	76%	9%	

What is the probability that a bus is early?

Q5 hint
What percentage must the probabilities of all these outcomes add up to?

6 A spinner has sections labelled 1 to 5.

Number	1	2	3	4	5
Probability	$\frac{1}{12}$	$\frac{1}{4}$	$\frac{1}{6}$	$\frac{1}{3}$	

What is the probability that it lands on 5?

Q6 hint
Write all the fractions with a common denominator.

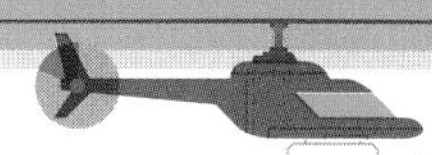

Independent events and experimental probability

1 Modelling Anna drops a piece of buttered toast 40 times.
It falls 'butter side down' 18 times.

a From her results, estimate the probability of it falling butter side down.
Sophie drops the same piece of buttered toast 60 times.
It falls 'butter side down' 31 times.

b How many times did Anna and Sophie drop the toast in total?

c Work out the best estimate for the probability of the toast falling butter side down.

2 Reasoning / Modelling In an experiment, Eric spins these two spinners 90 times.

	Blue	Yellow	White
1	13	10	6
2	13	12	8
3	12	9	7

Spinner 1

Spinner 2

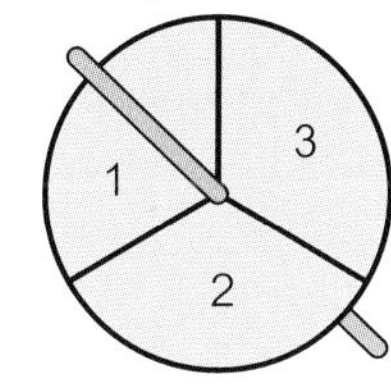

a From these results, estimate the experimental probability of

i yellow and 3 **ii** blue and 2 **iii** white and 1.

b Do you think you could play a fair game with these spinners? Explain your answer.

3 Reasoning / Modelling Bella, Connie and Deepak all use the same dice in their experiments.

	Bella	Connie	Deepak
Number of rolls	30	120	240
Number of 6s	4	22	37

a What is the theoretical probability of rolling a 6? Give your answer as a percentage, to the nearest whole number.

b Work out the number of 6s Bella, Connie and Deepak should expect.

c For each experiment, work out the actual proportion of 6s as a percentage, to the nearest whole number.

d Do you think the dice is fair? Explain your answer.

4 **a** Write down the probability of

i rolling a 2 on a dice

ii flipping a head on a coin.

b Use your probabilities from part **a** to work out the probability of

i rolling a 2 and flipping a head

ii rolling a 4 and flipping a head

iii rolling a 6 and flipping a tail

iv rolling a 3 or a 5 and flipping a head

v rolling a 1 or a 2 and flipping a head or a tail.

5 Reasoning The probability of picking a red card from a pack is $\frac{1}{2}$.
The probability of picking an ace is $\frac{4}{52}$.

a Which calculation gives the probability of picking a card that is red and an ace?

A $\frac{1}{2} + \frac{4}{52}$ **B** $\frac{1}{2} \times \frac{4}{52}$

b Work out the probability of picking a card that is red and an ace.

Q1a hint

'Estimate' in maths means 'do a rough calculation', not just guess.
In this case work out the probability $\frac{18}{\square}$.

Q1c hint

For the best estimate, use the results from the largest number of trials.

Q2a hint

Calculate $\frac{\square}{90}$.

Q2b hint

Compare the experimental probabilities to the theoretical probability, as percentages.

Q3c hint

Bella: $\frac{4}{30}$ = 0.133 … = 13%

Q3d hint

If the dice is fair, all the experiments will have roughly the same proportion of 6s.

Q4a hint

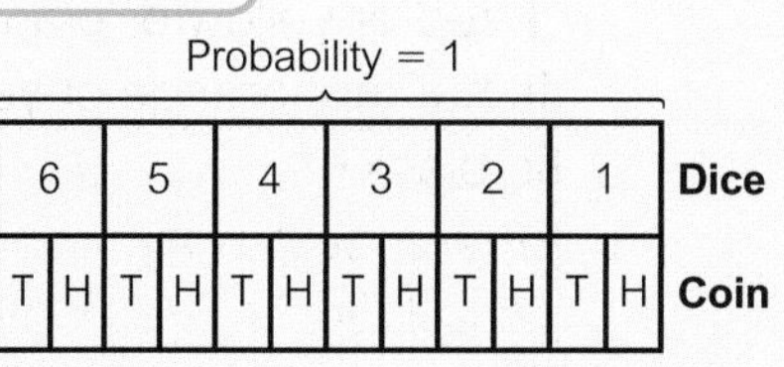

Q5a hint

Is P(red ace) greater or less than P(red)?

Q5b hint

You could draw a Venn diagram to check your answer. Remember to include all the cards in the pack.

6 The tree diagram shows the probabilities of picking red and white counters from a bag.

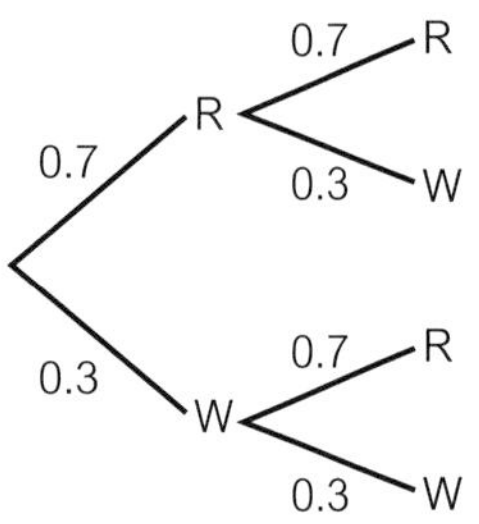

a Work out the probability of picking two reds.

b Work out the probability of picking

i red then white (R, W)

ii white then red (W, R)

iii red or white in any order.

Q6a hint

Move your finger along the branches for red, then red.
Are two reds more or less likely than one red?
Do you add or multiply?

Q6b iii hint

This means (R, W) or (W, R)
Is the probability of these two outcomes greater than the probability of just one of them? Do you add or multiply?

Enrichment

1 Real / Modelling The table shows the numbers of recorded offences in different cities and towns in 2011–12.

Town or city	Population (thousands)	Violence against the person	Robbery offences
Bristol	441.3	10 149	866
Hartlepool	91.3	1545	33
Carlisle and Penrith	156.4	2274	25
Derby	248.7	7280	412
Plymouth	258.7	5548	195

Source: ONS

a Where is the risk of violence against the person greatest?

b Where is the risk of robbery least?

2 a Design a fair game for two people, with

i one dice

ii one dice and a coin

iii one dice and a spinner like this.

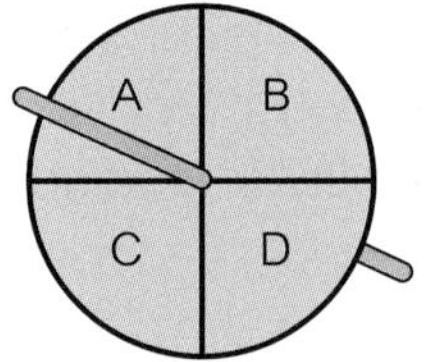

b Design an unfair game using any combinations of dice, coin or spinner.

Q2b hint

In an unfair game, one person is always more likely to win than the other.

Reflect

3 **Reflect** In these Strengthen lessons you have answered probability questions that use

- tables
- Venn diagrams
- sample space diagrams
- tree diagrams.

Which types of question were easiest? Why?
Which types of question were hardest? Why?
Write down one thing about probability you think you need more practice on.

9 Extend

You will:
- Extend your understanding with problem-solving.

1 Problem-solving Ted puts these black and white balls in a bag.
He picks one at random.

a What is the probability of picking a black ball?

He adds more black balls to the bag.
Ted says, 'The probability of picking black is now $\frac{2}{3}$.'

b How many black balls has he added?

2 Problem-solving Lily spins these two spinners and then adds the scores together.
Is the total score more likely to be over 5 or under 5?
Explain how you found your answer.

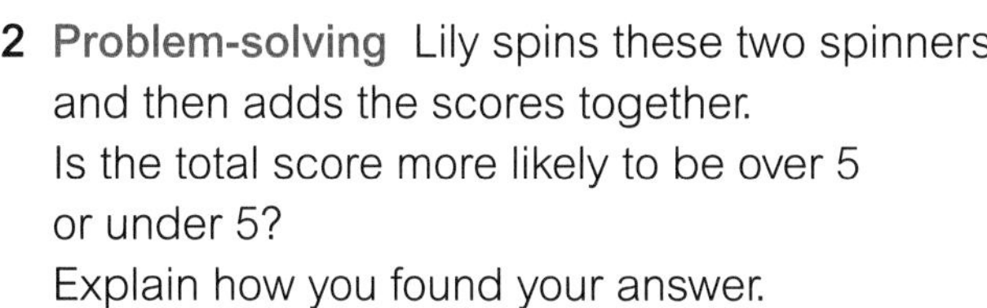

Spinner 1

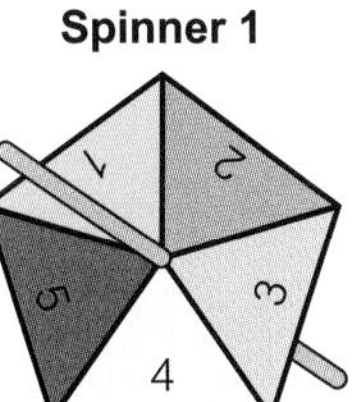

Spinner 2

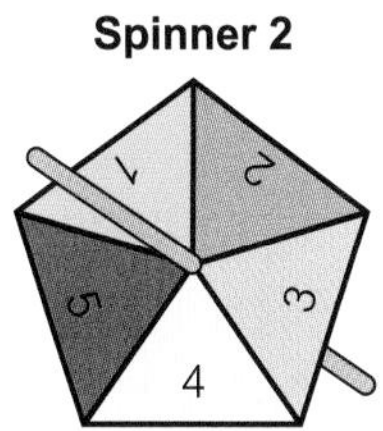

3 Reasoning Imagine you roll a 4-sided dice (numbered 1 to 4) and a 6-sided dice (numbered 1 to 6) and add the scores together.
Are you more likely to get a score less than 6, or 6 or more?
Explain how you found your answer.

4 Modelling A coin and a 4-sided dice are used in an experiment.
The coin is flipped and the dice is rolled at the same time.
This is done 200 times. Here are the results of the experiment.

	1	2	3	4
H	26	20	19	27
T	28	25	28	27

a Calculate the experimental probability of getting a 3 and a tails from these results. Give your answer as a percentage.

b Calculate the theoretical probability of getting a 3 and a tails.
Give your answer as a percentage.

c How many times would you expect to get a 3 and a tails from 200 trials?

d Do you think that either the coin or the dice were biased?
Explain your answer.

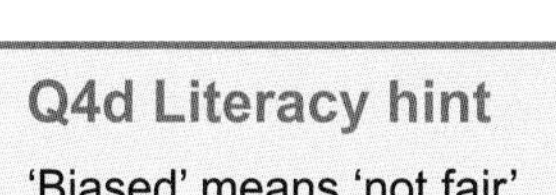

Q4d Literacy hint
'Biased' means 'not fair'.

5 Modelling Two 4-sided dice (numbered 1 to 4) are rolled and the numbers are multiplied to give the score. Jay challenges Mitra to a game. If the score is even, Jay gets a point. If the score is odd, Mitra gets two points.

a Explain why the game is not fair.

b Who is more likely to win?

c How could the rules be changed to make the game fair?

6 Real All students who complete a work experience placement with a travel agency are entered into a prize draw. They always give four prizes – one to a boy and another to a girl from each of the two local schools.
Explain why this might not give everybody a fair chance of winning.

7 Modelling Three friends compare how many MP3 tracks they have by the band 'Wow!' and how many tracks they have in total.
Marlon has 34 tracks by 'Wow!' out of 914 tracks in total.
Tariq has 29 out of 833.
Kay has 18 out of 547.
They each play a track at random.

a Who is most likely to play a track by 'Wow!'?

b Kay adds another 'Wow!' track to her MP3 player.
Will she now be more likely than Tariq to play a track by 'Wow!'?
Explain your answer.

8 Real Here is a summary table for a week's weather predictions last winter.

	Mon	Tue	Wed	Thu	Fri	Sat	Sun
Dry	45%	60%	80%		10%		60%
Rain		40%	20%	80%	80%	65%	
Snow/sleet/hail	0%		0%	5%		10%	30%

Work out the missing percentages.

9 Problem-solving 400 customers were randomly telephoned in a follow-up satisfaction survey. Based on previous surveys, the probability of calling

- someone aged 20–39 is $\frac{2}{5}$
- a 'completely satisfied' customer aged over 60 is $\frac{1}{4}$
- a 'dissatisfied' customer aged 40–59 is the same as that of calling a 'mostly satisfied' customer aged 60 or over.

Copy and complete this table using the information given above.

	Completely satisfied	Mostly satisfied	Dissatisfied
20–39	80	40	
40–59	60		12
60 or over			28

10 Problem-solving A bag contains red, white, green and purple counters.
The probabilities of picking each colour are

Colour	red	white	green	purple
Probability	0.05	0.4	0.35	0.2

a Explain why there must be more than 10 counters in the bag.

b What is the smallest possible number of counters in the bag?

Q10a hint
Calculate the expected results for 10 counters.

11 Problem-solving A bag contains euro coins and £ coins.
Bhavna takes out a coin, records it and replaces it.
She records her results for 100 trials in total.

Number of trials	10	50	80	100
Number of £ coins	4	15	25	34

a Work out the best estimate of the probability of picking a £ coin from the bag.

b Bhavna weighs the bag and works out that there are 60 coins in it.
How many are likely to be £ coins?

Topic links: Mean, Median, Pace value

12 **Real / Reasoning** The table shows the number of recorded burglaries and thefts from vehicles in different areas in 2012.

Area	Population (thousands)	Burglary (from dwelling)	Theft (from vehicle)
Chesterfield	395.5	1170	1356
Middlesbrough	142.4	1018	943
Durham	611.6	1654	2728
Pembrokeshire	117.1	147	228
Rochdale	205.2	1349	1107
Southampton	239.7	1229	1322
East Kent	285.4	1103	1007
Leicester	306.6	2143	2395
Lewisham	266.5	2218	2193
Newcastle	292.2	1228	1375

Source: ONS

Which area had

a the lowest risk of burglary

b the highest risk of theft from a vehicle?

c A newspaper headline says, 'Pembrokeshire, the safest place in the UK!'

  i Does the data support this claim?

  ii Explain why the statement might not be true.

d Sam lives in Newcastle. In 2012 his house was burgled and his laptop was stolen from his car.
He said, 'The chances of that were 1 in a million.'
Was he right? Explain your answer.

Q12 hint

You could input the data into a spreadsheet to do the calculations.

13 Work out the probability of getting three heads when you flip a coin three times.

Q13 hint

Are the outcomes independent?

14 **Real / Reasoning** The table shows the earnings of a company's employees.

Earnings, e (per annum)	Number of employees
$0 < e \leqslant £10\,000$	5
$£10\,000 < e \leqslant £20\,000$	21
$£20\,000 < e \leqslant £30\,000$	30
$£30\,000 < e \leqslant £40\,000$	22
$£40\,000 < e \leqslant £50\,000$	3

a What is the probability that an employee picked at random earns

  i less than the median earnings

  ii more than the mean?

b Explain why the probability you calculated in part **a ii** is an estimate.

Q14a i hint

Where is the median of a set of data?

Q14a ii hint

Calculate an estimate of the mean, to the nearest 100. Estimate how many of the employees earn more than that, using the figures in the table.

15 **a** **Reasoning** Draw a tree diagram to show the possible outcomes of flipping a fair coin twice.

b What is the probability of getting at least one head?

c What is the probability of getting no heads?

d How could you use your answer to part **c** to help you work out the probability of 'at least one head' more quickly?

16 **Modelling** Jayne has 150 pop songs and 100 jazz songs on her MP3 player.

a Draw a tree diagram to show all the possible outcomes and probabilities for selecting two songs at random.

b Jayne says, 'I have more pop than jazz, so I will definitely get at least one pop song when I select two at random.'
Is she right? Explain your answer.

17 This tree diagram shows the possible outcomes when a 6-sided dice is rolled three times.

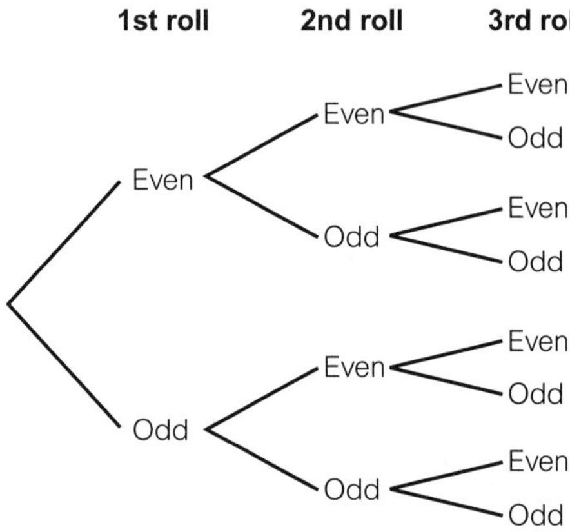

What is the probability of getting an even number

a every time

b in none of the rolls

c in both the first and last rolls

d in at least one of the three rolls?

18 **Modelling** The arrow on this spinner is spun twice. Each time, Sasha records whether the number is a square number or not.

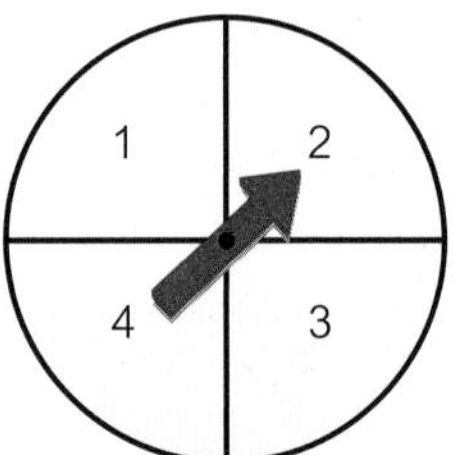

a Draw a tree diagram to show all the possible outcomes and their probabilities.

b Sasha says there is a 50–50 chance of it landing on a square number both times.
Is she right? Explain your answer.

19 Draw a tree diagram to show the possible outcomes and probabilities of picking a ball from this bag, replacing it, and picking another ball. Work out the probability of

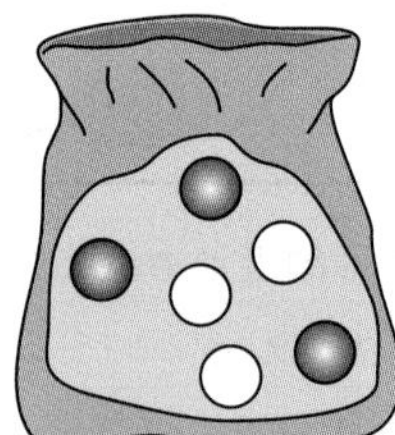

a two blue balls

b at least one white ball.

Reflect

20 **Reflect** Write three probability questions about a sports match, which each give the answer 0.4, for:

- mutually exclusive events
- independent events
- experimental probability.

Compare your three questions with those of others in your class.

Q20 hint

Look back at the lessons where you learned about these types of probability.

9 Unit test

Log how you did on your Student Progression Chart.

1 The table shows the numbers of students choosing different team-building activities.

	Year 7	Year 8	Year 9	Totals
Rafting	32	33	38	103
Orienteering	35	33	29	97
Totals	67	66	67	200

A student is picked at random. What is the probability that it is

a a Year 9 student

b a Year 7 student who chose orienteering?

A student from each activity is picked at random.

c Is a Year 8 student more likely to be selected from the rafting group or the orienteering group?

2 a Draw a sample space diagram to show all the possible outcomes of picking one ball from each of these bags.

b What is the probability of picking two balls the same colour?

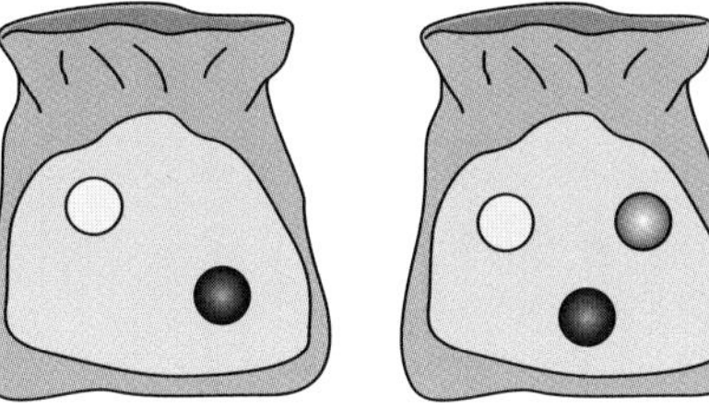

3 The Venn diagram shows the numbers of cat and dog owners at a pet show.

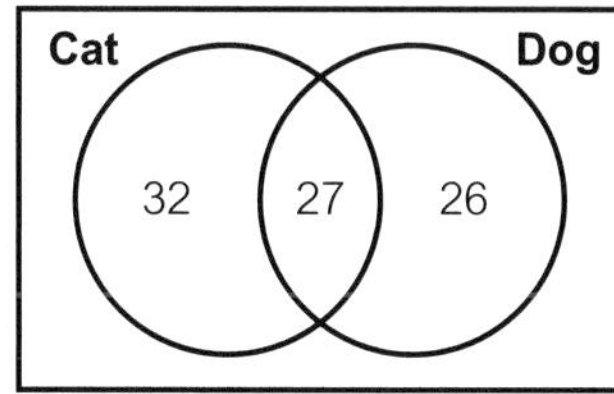

a Write down the missing words.

i 53 people own ______________.

ii 27 people own ______________.

A pet food company chooses one of the people at the show at random to win a lifetime supply of pet food.

b What is the probability that the winner owns a cat?
Write your answer as a percentage to the nearest whole number.

4 Jayden catches two buses to school.
The probability that the first one is on time is 0.8.
The probability that the second one is on time is 0.9.
Work out the probability that

a both buses are on time

b the first one is on time but the second one is not.

5 A random sample of 17-year-olds were asked what they would like to do after they left school. The table shows the results.

Higher education	Apprenticeship	Employment
27	31	17

a How many people were asked?

b What percentage chose higher education?

Another random sample of teenagers gave these results.

Higher education	Apprenticeship	Employment
78	65	57

c Which sample gives the best estimate for the probability that a teenager picked at random chooses an apprenticeship? Explain why.

d There are roughly 740 000 17-year-olds in the UK. Estimate how many apprenticeship places will be needed.

6 A bag contains a total of 24 red (R), yellow (Y) and green (G) marbles.
$P(R) = \frac{3}{8}$ and $P(Y) = \frac{1}{4}$
Work out

a the probability of picking a green marble

b the number of yellow marbles in the bag.

7 These two spinners are spun and the two numbers added together to give the score.
What is the probability that the total is

a less than 7 b more than 7 c exactly 7?

Show your working to explain your answers.
Jenn and Kane spin both spinners.
Jenn wins if the score is more than 8.
Kane wins if the score is less than 8.

d Is the game fair? Explain your answer.

8 The tree diagram shows the probabilities of winning or losing a game.
Work out the probability of

a losing both games b winning at least one game.

9 Joe throws two darts.
The probability that he gets a bull's-eye is 0.4 for each throw.

a Draw a tree diagram to show the probabilities.

b Work out the probability that he gets exactly one bull's-eye.

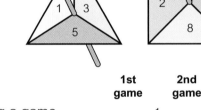

Challenge

10 Draw a sample space diagram for the possible outcomes of spinning the two spinners in Q7 and multiplying the scores.
Design a game using these two spinners.
Your game could be fair or one player could be more likely to win.
Ask someone to play your game with you.
Can they work out if the game is fair or not?

Reflect

11 **Reflect** Look back at the questions you answered in this test.

a Which one are you most confident that you have answered correctly? What makes you feel confident?

b Which one are you least confident that you have answered correctly? What makes you least confident?

c Discuss the question you feel least confident about with a classmate. How does discussing it make you feel?

Q11c hint

Comment on your understanding of the question and your confidence.

10 Comparing shapes

MASTER

Check P264 | Strengthen P266 | Extend P270 | Test P274

10.1 Congruent and similar shapes

You will learn to:

- Use congruent shapes to solve problems about triangles and quadrilaterals
- Work out whether shapes are similar, congruent or neither.

Why learn this?
It is useful to know when shapes are congruent to be able to tell if shapes are reflected, translated or rotated accurately.

Fluency
Which of these triangles are congruent?

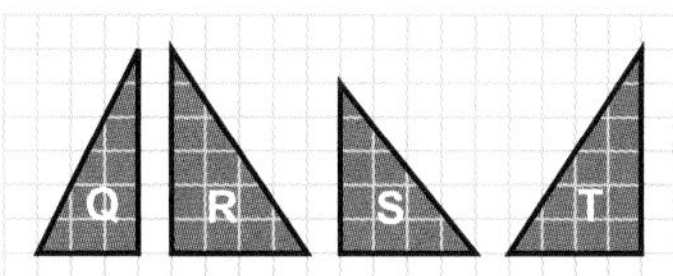

Explore
How do artists use congruent and similar shapes in their work?

Exercise 10.1

1 Copy this shape onto squared paper. Enlarge it using the marked centres of enlargement and scale factor 3.

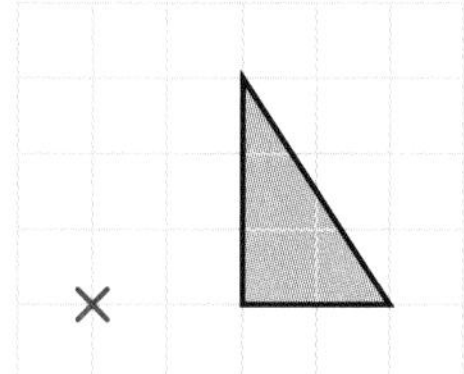

2 Work out the missing angles.

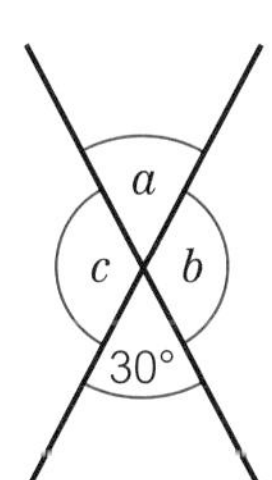

3 This is a drawing of a tennis court.

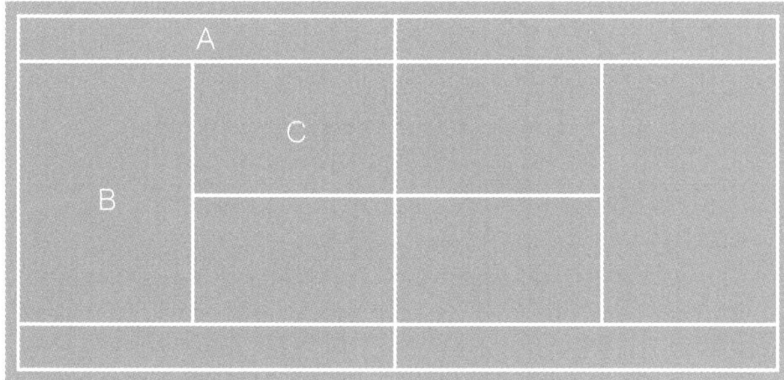

Make a rough sketch of the diagram.
Write A, B or C in each rectangle so that rectangles with the same letter are congruent.

Q3 hint
Two shapes are **congruent** if they are identical.

Warm up

4 **Reasoning** The diagram shows four congruent scalene triangles.

a Draw a sketch of the diagram. Mark equal angles with the same letter. Mark every angle.

b Use your sketch to show that the angles in a triangle add up to 180°.

Discussion Could an enlargement ever give a congruent image?

> **Key point**
> If all lengths and angles on shape A are equal to the **corresponding** lengths and angles on shape B, then shapes A and B are congruent. Shape B can be a reflection or rotation of shape A.

5 Which shapes are similar to each other?

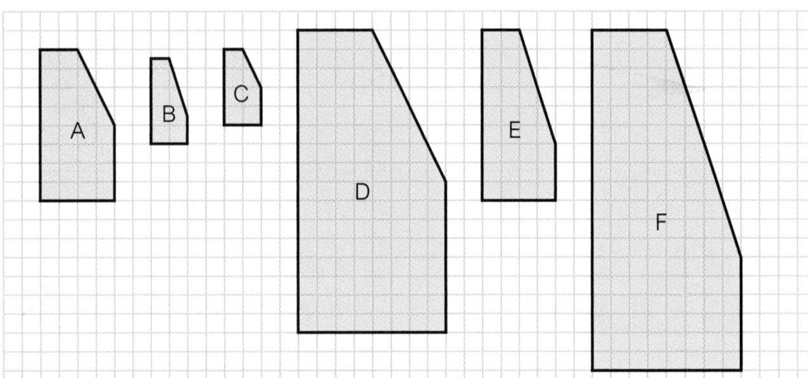

> **Key point**
> Shapes A and D are **similar** if one is an enlargement of the other.

6 **Reasoning** For each shape, decide whether it is
- congruent to shape A
- similar to shape A
- neither of these.

Explain how you know.

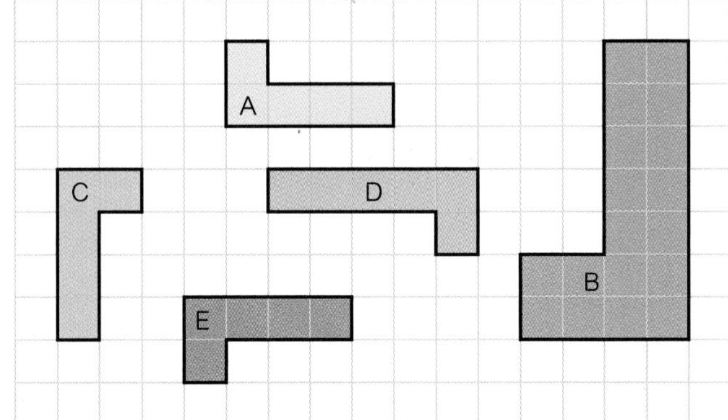

7 Copy the diagram onto squared paper. Carry out the transformations. For each transformation, state whether the image is congruent with or similar to the object.

a Rotate triangle T 270° clockwise about P. Draw the image. Label the image T1.

b Reflect triangle T1 in the line AB. Draw the image. Label the new image T2.

c Translate triangle T2 5 units up parallel to AB. Draw the image. Label this image T3.

d Enlarge triangle T3 with scale factor 2 and centre of enlargement at P. Label this image T4.

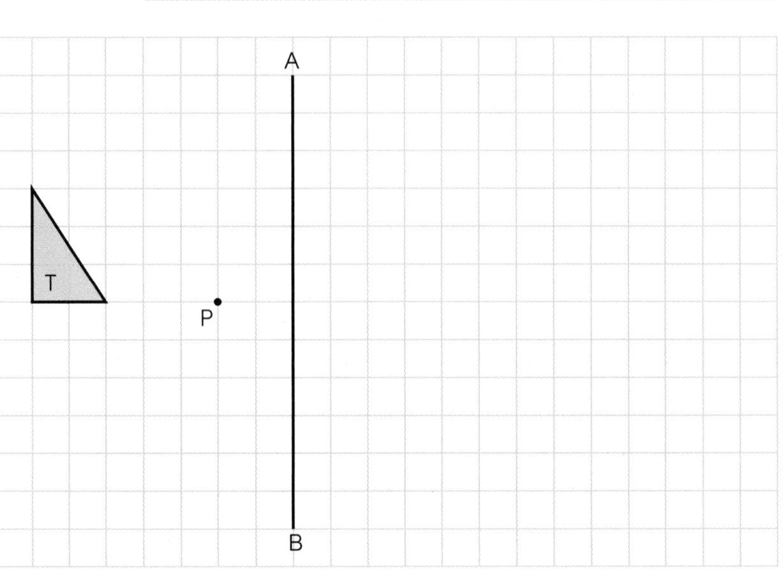

Investigation

Problem-solving

1 Trace these triangles.
Sort them into congruent pairs.

2 Which triangles are left over?
Which ones can you sort into similar pairs?

3 Look at your pairs. What can you say about

a triangles with three sides the same

b triangles with two sides and the angle between them the same

c triangles with two angles and one side the same

d triangles with all angles the same?

4 Does having two sides and an angle the same always give congruent triangles?

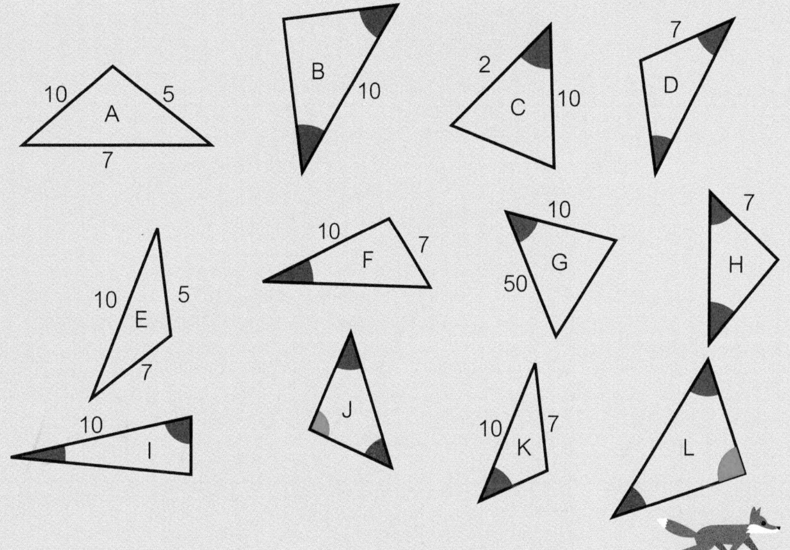

8 Reasoning In this diagram, equal sides and angles are marked.

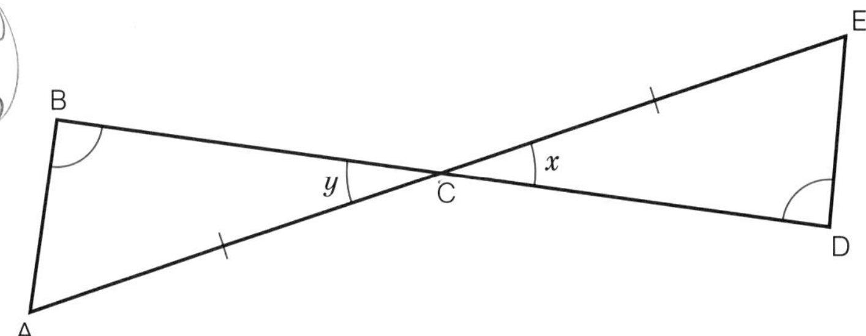

a What can you say about angles x and y?

b Show that triangles ABC and EDC are congruent.
Give the reason for congruency (SSS, SAS, ASA or AAS).

Key point

Triangles are congruent if they have equivalent

- SSS (all three sides)
- SAS (two sides and the included angle)
- ASA (two angles and the included side)
- AAS (two angles and another side)

Triangles where all angles are the same (AAA) are similar, but might not be congruent.

Q8 hint

Draw the two triangles separately to compare them.

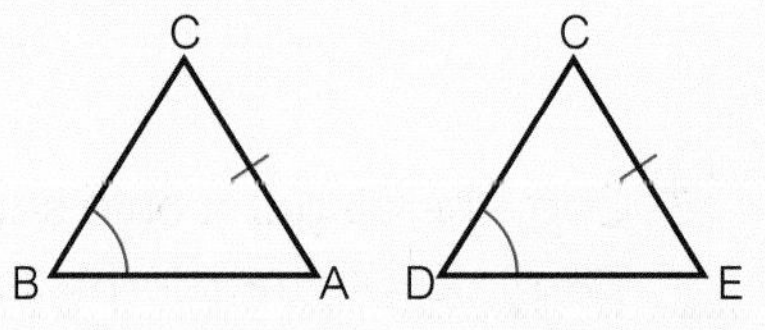

9 Reasoning Are all right-angled triangles with one side 5 cm and hypotenuse 10 cm congruent?

10 Reasoning These triangles are all congruent.
Work out the missing sides and angles.

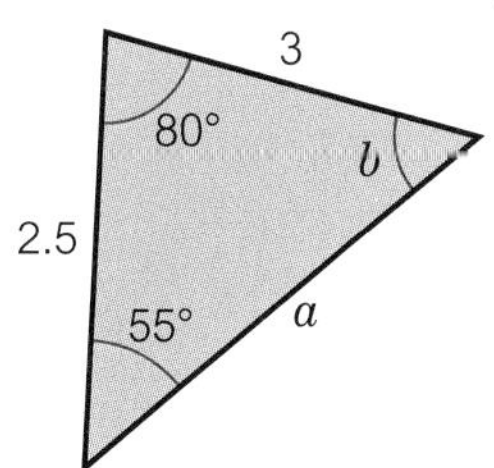

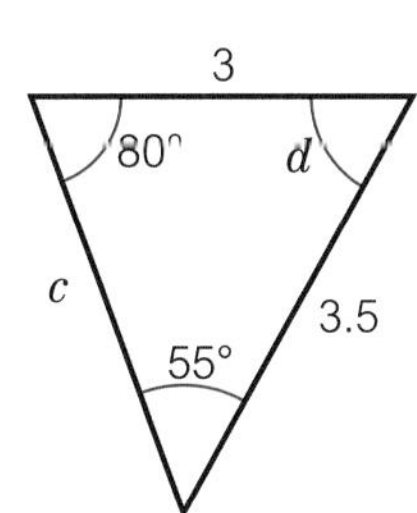

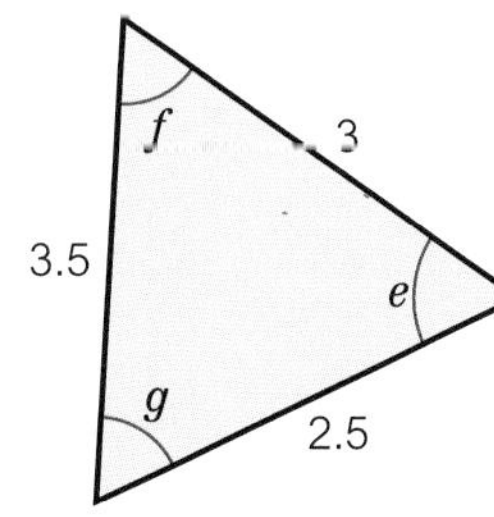

Q9 Strategy hint

Sketch at least two triangles to check.

11 Explore How do artists use congruent and similar shapes in their work?
Is it easier to explore this question now you have completed the lesson?
What further information do you need to be able to answer this?

12 Reflect Write one fact that is always true about

- congruent shapes *and* similar shapes
- congruent shapes but *not* similar shapes
- similar shapes but *not* congruent shapes.

Compare your facts with others in your class.

Q12 hint

Write down mathematical definitions, in your own words, for congruent and similar.
Use your definitions to help you write these facts.

Explore

Reflect

10.2 Ratios in triangles

You will learn to:
- Solve problems involving similar triangles.

CONFIDENCE

Why learn this?
Architects calculate the ratio of 'rise' to 'tread' in staircases to make sure that they aren't too steep.

Fluency
What are the missing numbers?
- 1 : 5 = 2 : □ = 3 : □
- 2 : 3 = 4 : □ = □ : 18
- 4 : 9 = 12 : □ = □ : 63
- 1 : $\frac{2}{3}$ = 6 : □ = □ : 6

Explore
Why do towers often have spiral staircases rather than straight staircases?

Exercise 10.2

Warm up

1 Are these triangles similar?

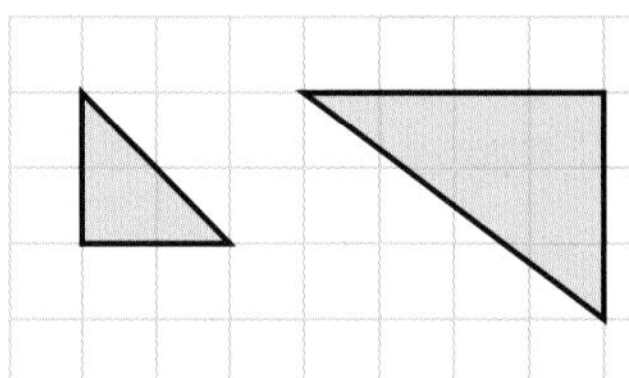

2 Triangle A has been enlarged to make triangle B. What is the scale factor for the enlargement?

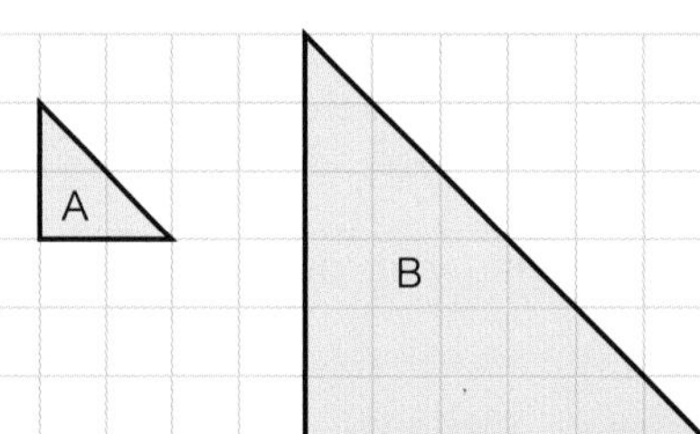

Worked example

Triangles A and B are similar. Work out the height of triangle B.

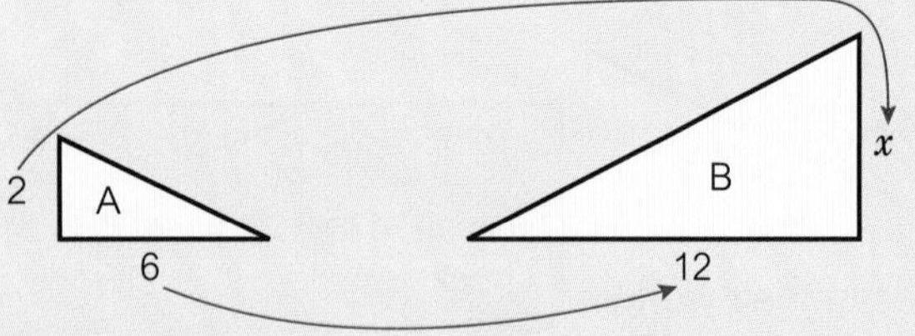

The arrows show the corresponding sides.

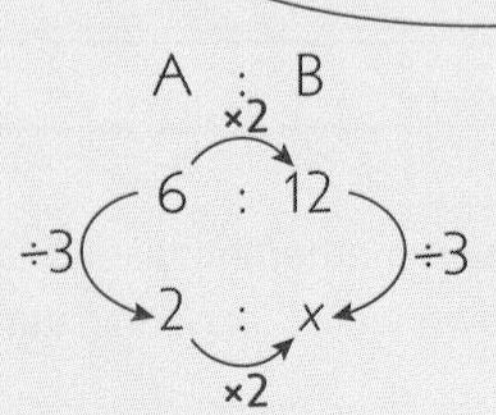

Write down the ratios of corresponding sides.

$x = \frac{12}{3} = 4$

Key point
When two shapes are similar, one is an enlargement of the other.
This means
- pairs of **corresponding** sides are in the same ratio
- their angles are the same (AAA).

Topic links: Ratio

3 In each part, all the right-angled triangles are similar.
Work out the lengths labelled with letters.

a 7, 14 | 5, x | 2, y | 4, z

b

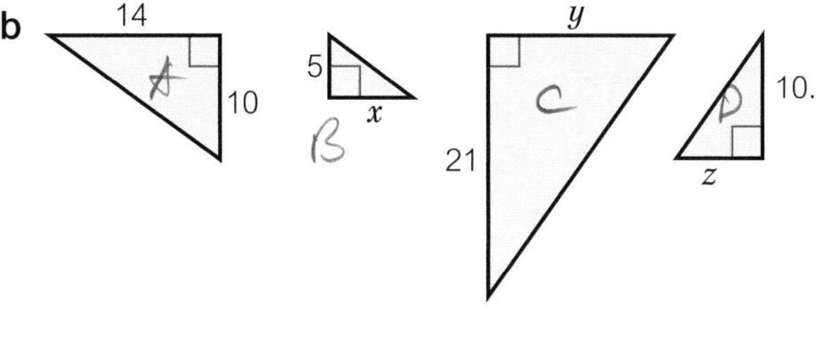

4 Are these triangles similar?

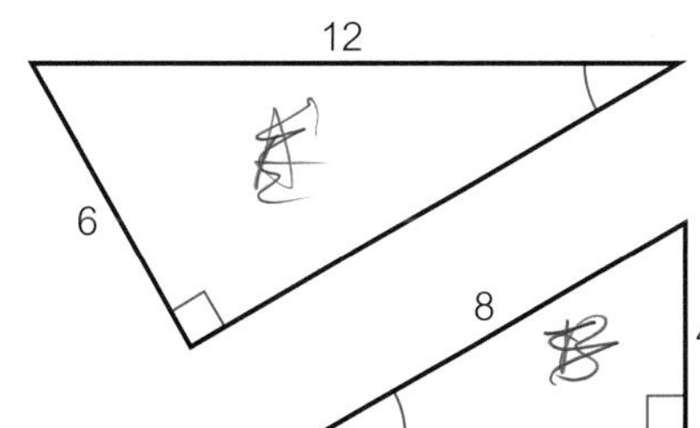

> **Q4 hint**
> Write down the ratios of corresponding sides.

Worked example

a Explain why triangles ABE and ACD are similar.

Triangle ABE	Triangle ACD
∠A	∠A
∠E = 90°	∠D = 90°

∠B = ∠C (corresponding angles)
The triangles have the same angles (AAA).

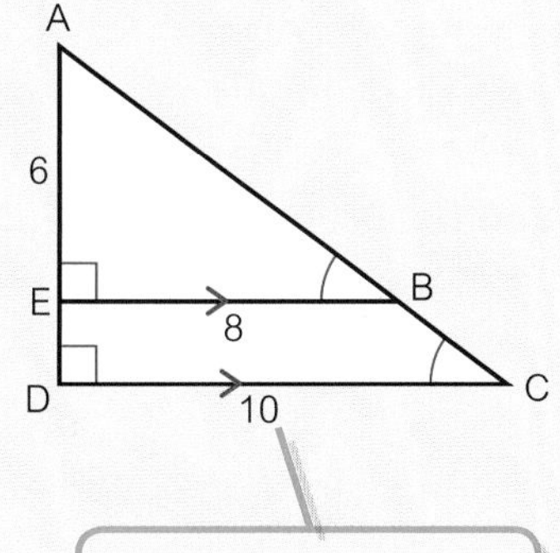

> Write down the ratio of corresponding sides.

b Work out length ED.

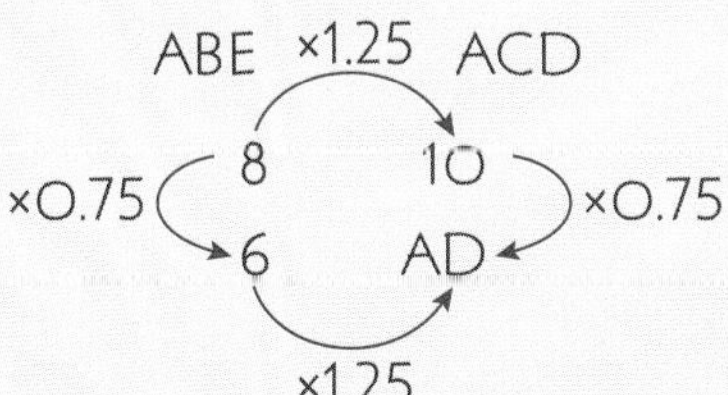

AD = 10 × 0.75 = 7.5 cm ← Work out AD.
ED = AD − 6 = 1.5 cm ← Work out ED.

5 **a** Show that triangles EFI and EGH are similar.
b Work out lengths EG and FG.

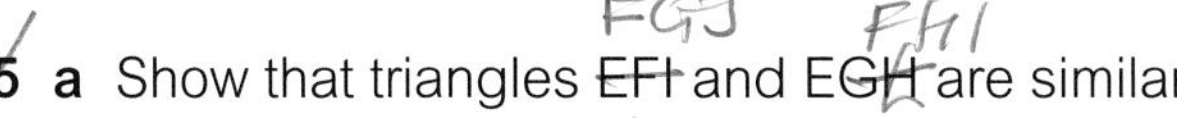

E, G, 5, F, H, 10

6 **Reasoning** **a** Sketch a copy of the diagram. Mark equal angles with the same letters.
Give reasons why they are equal.
b Are the triangles similar? Explain.
c Sketch the triangles the same way up. Label the sides you know and the equal angles.

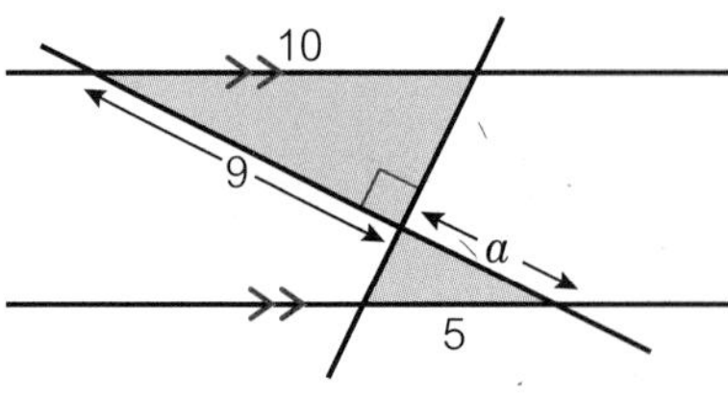

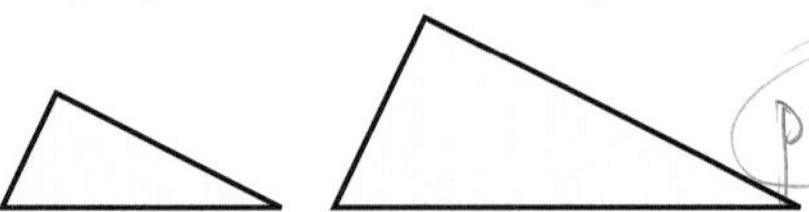

d Work out the length of a.

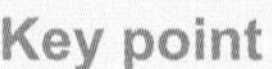

Key point

When two triangles are similar, their corresponding angles are equal.

Q6a hint

Use angles in parallel lines.

7 **Reasoning** Work out the lengths labelled with letters.

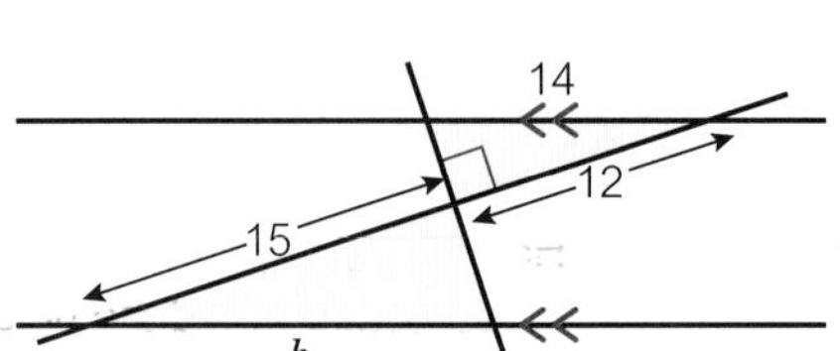

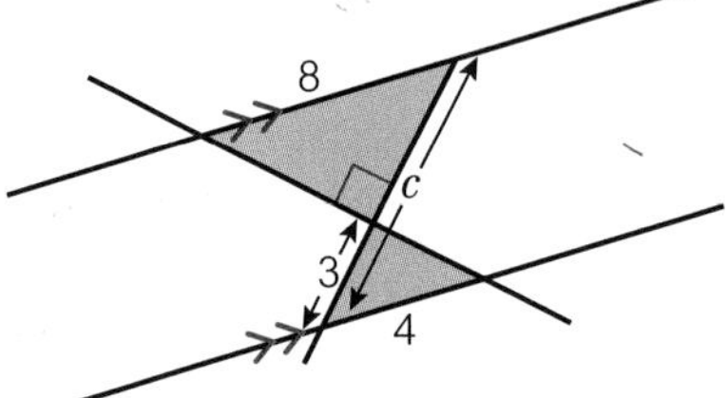

Q7 hint

Use the method in Q6.

8 **Real / Modelling** A street lamp shines light on a circular patch of ground.
When the top of the street lamp is 3 metres above the ground the diameter of the circle of light is 4 metres.
a How far above the ground must the top of the lamp be to throw light on a circle of diameter 10 metres?
b A street is being fitted with lamp posts that are 4.5 metres high. The street is 120 metres long.
How many lamp posts will be needed to light the length of the street?

Discussion Would it be better if the circles of light overlapped?
Why will the lamp post in part **a** not be suitable?

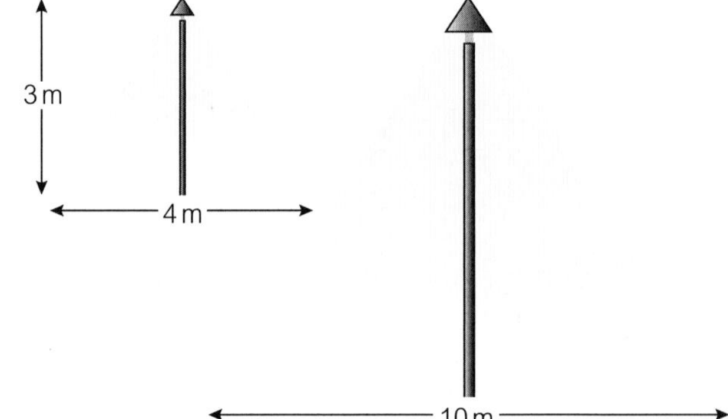

Q8a hint

The light shines at the same angles, so the two triangles are similar.

9 **Problem-solving** Work out the lengths labelled with letters.

a 3, p, 4

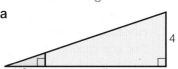

b q, 4, 4.5, 1.5

c 1, 4, r, 6

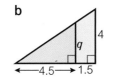

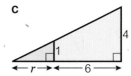

Q9 hint

First show that the triangles are similar.

10 **Explore** Why do towers often have spiral staircases rather than straight staircases?
Is it easier to explore this question now you have completed the lesson? What further information do you need to be able to answer this?

11 **Reflect** Look back at Q9. To answer this question you had to
- show that triangles are similar
- identify corresponding lengths
- solve equations.

Which of these tasks was easiest? Explain why.
Which of these tasks was hardest? Explain why.

10.3 The tangent ratio

You will learn to:
- Use conventions for naming sides of a right-angled triangle
- Work out the tangent of any angle
- Use the tangent to work out an unknown side of a triangle.

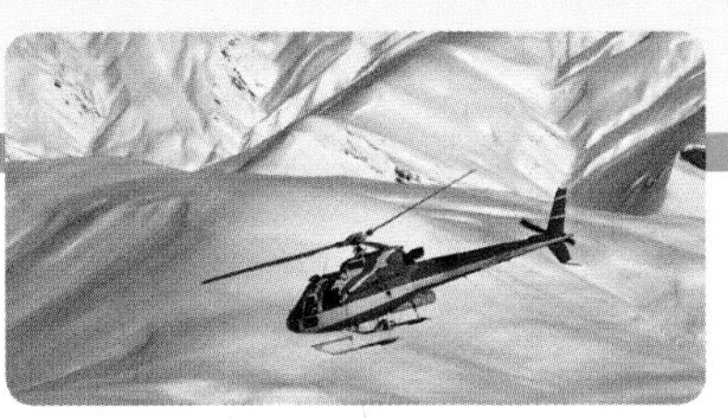

Why learn this?
Trigonometry is the mathematics involving sides and angles in triangles. Air-sea rescue helicopter pilots use trigonometry to help them navigate in dangerous conditions.

Fluency
In each right-angled triangle, which side is the hypotenuse?

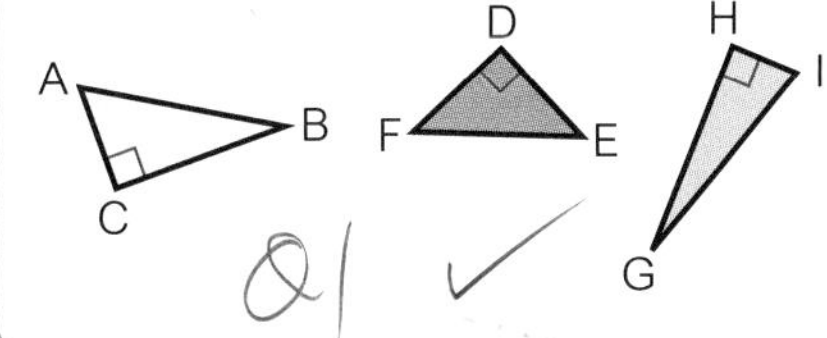

Explore
How do surveyors use the tangent ratio to find the heights of skyscrapers?

Exercise 10.3

1. Use your calculator to convert each fraction to a decimal. Give your answers to one decimal place.
   a $\frac{3}{11}$ **b** $\frac{7}{9}$ **c** $\frac{5}{6}$ **d** $\frac{2}{13}$ **e** $\frac{1}{17}$

2. Rearrange each formula to make S the subject.
   a $3 = \frac{S}{P}$ **b** $A = \frac{S}{3}$

3. In each triangle which side is
   a the opposite side to angle θ **b** the adjacent side to angle θ
   c the hypotenuse?

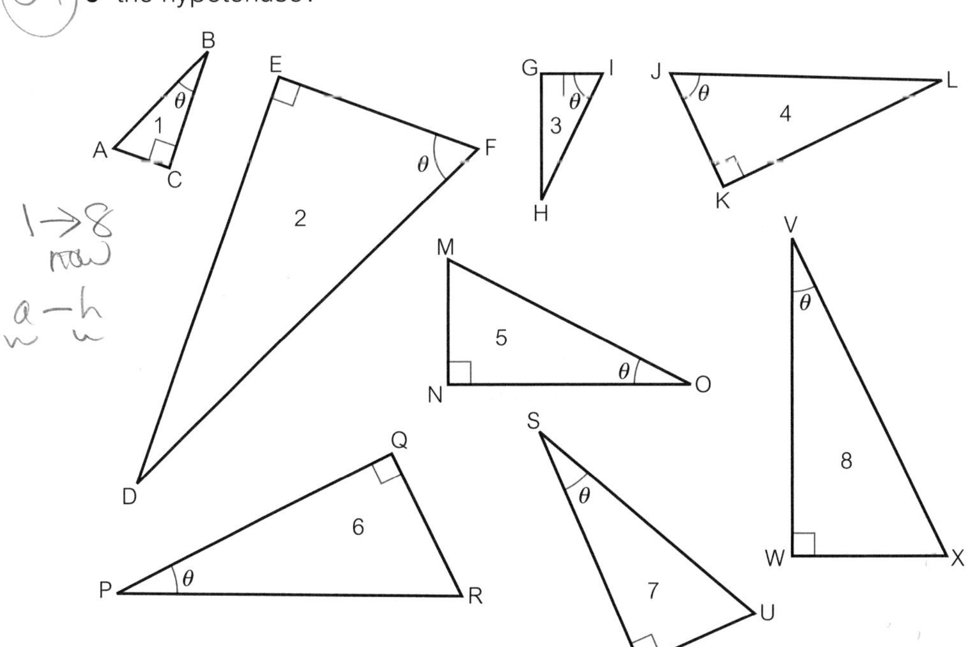

Key point
The side opposite to the chosen angle (angle θ in this diagram) is called the **opposite** side.
The side that runs between the chosen angle and the right angle is called the **adjacent** side.
The side opposite to the right angle is called the **hypotenuse**.

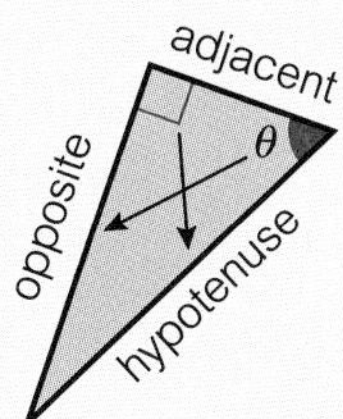

Q3 hint
The Greek letter θ (pronounced theta) is often used for angles.

Investigation **Reasoning**

1 Draw these triangles accurately using ruler and protractor.

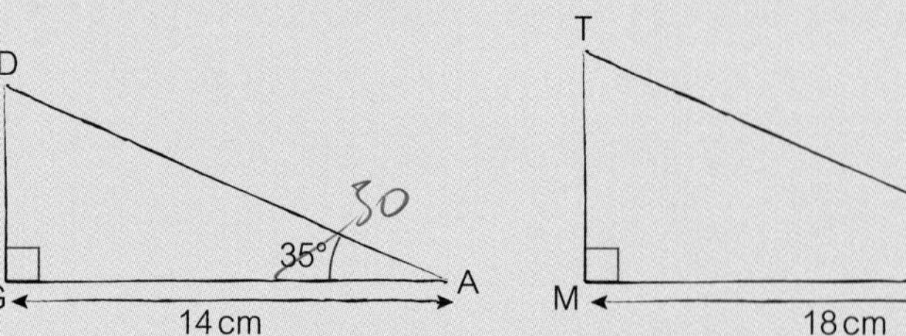

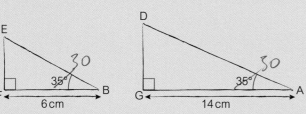

2 Label the opposite side to 35° 'opp' and the adjacent side 'adj'.

3 Measure the adjacent sides.

4 a Write the fraction, $\frac{\text{opposite}}{\text{adjacent}}$, for each triangle and convert it to a decimal (correct to 1 d.p.).

b What do you notice?

c What do you think will happen with other right-angled triangles with an angle of 35°?

d Test your hypothesis by drawing some more right-angled triangles with an angle of 35°.

5 Repeat with an angle of 60° instead of 35°.

Discussion Why are the fractions for the same angle the same? What does this tell you about the ratio of the sides?

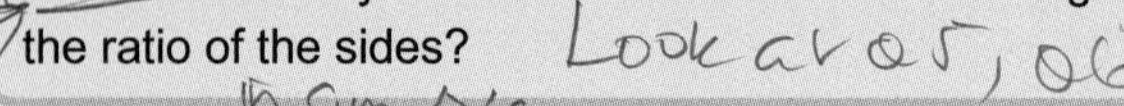

4 Use your calculator to find, correct to one decimal place.

a tan 32° b tan 58° c tan 60° d tan 10°

Q4a hint

On your calculator, enter

=

5 Write $\tan\theta$ as $\frac{\text{opposite}}{\text{adjacent}}$ for each triangle

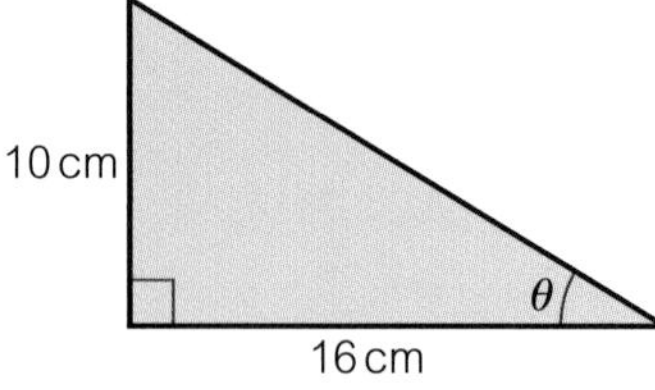

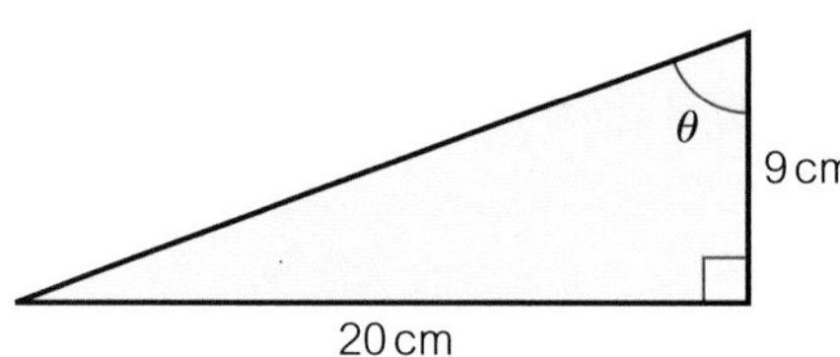

Key point

The ratio of the opposite side to the adjacent side is called the **tangent** of the angle.

The tangent of angle θ is written as $\tan\theta$.

$\tan\theta = \frac{\text{opposite}}{\text{adjacent}}$

6 **Reasoning** a Sketch a right-angled triangle with two angles of 45°.

b Mark any sides that are equal.

c What is the tangent of 45°?

Worked example

Use the tangent ratio to work out x, correct to one decimcal place.

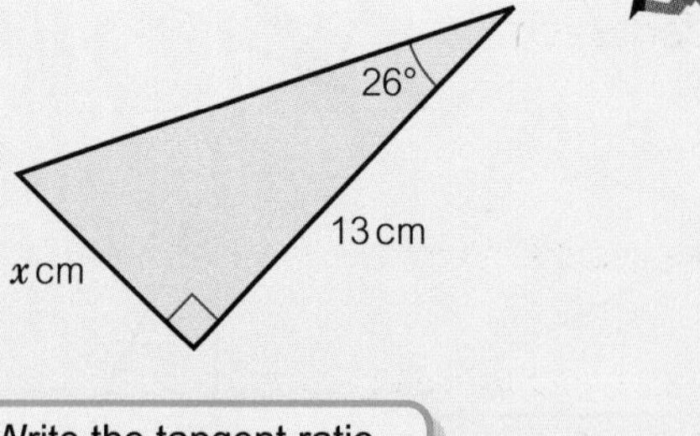

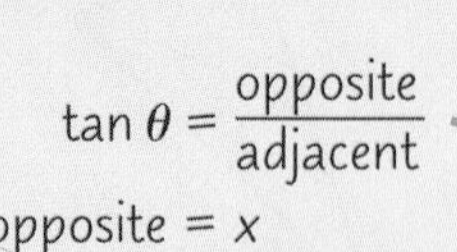

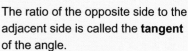

$\tan\theta = \frac{\text{opposite}}{\text{adjacent}}$ — Write the tangent ratio.

opposite $= x$

adjacent $= 13$ — Identify the opposite and adjacent sides.

$\theta = 26°$

$\tan 26° = \frac{x}{13}$ — Substitute the sides and angle into the tangent ratio.

$13 \times \tan 26° = x$ — Multiply both sides by 13. Use your calculator to work out 13 × tan 26°.

$x = 6.3$ cm (to 1 d.p.)

Key point

You can use the tangent ratio to find the length of one of the shorter sides of a right-angled triangle.

Topic links: Using formulae, Conversions

7 Work out x for each triangle, correct to one decimal place.

a

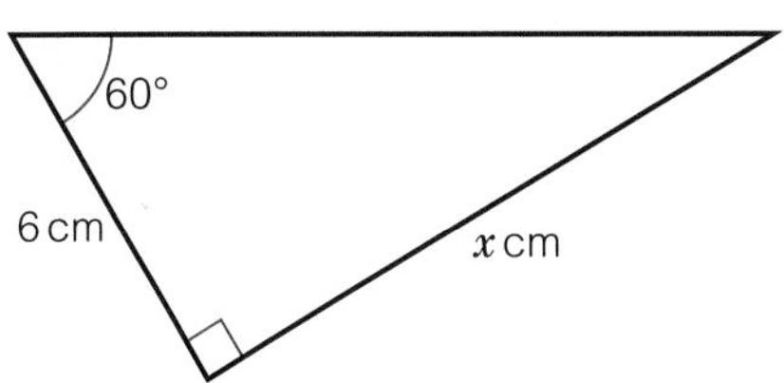

b

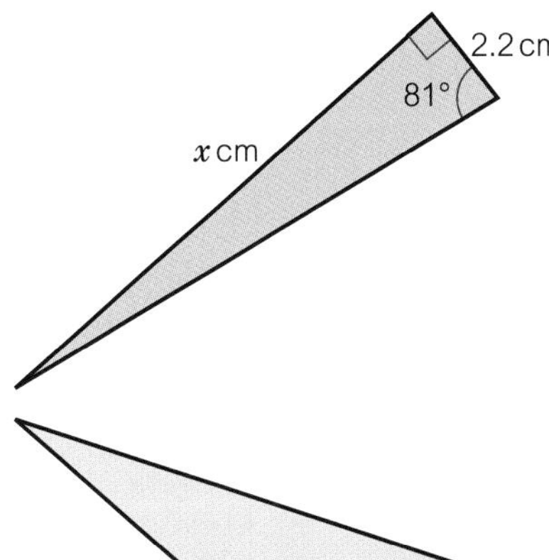

c

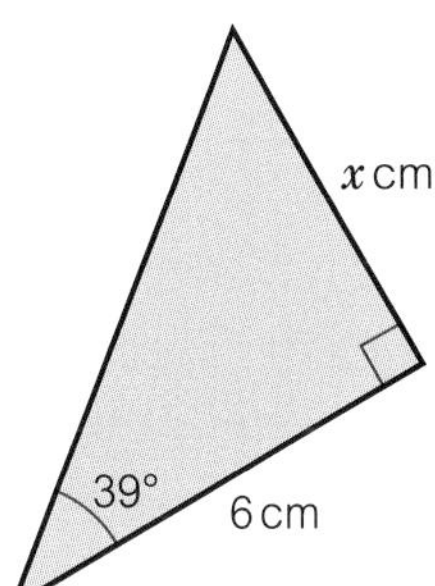

d

x cm, 66°, 5 cm

8 Real / Modelling A gardener needs to know the height of a tree.
The gardener measures 20 metres from the bottom of the tree to a point on the ground.
The angle to the top of the tree is 21°.
What is the height of the tree? Give your answer to the nearest centimetre.

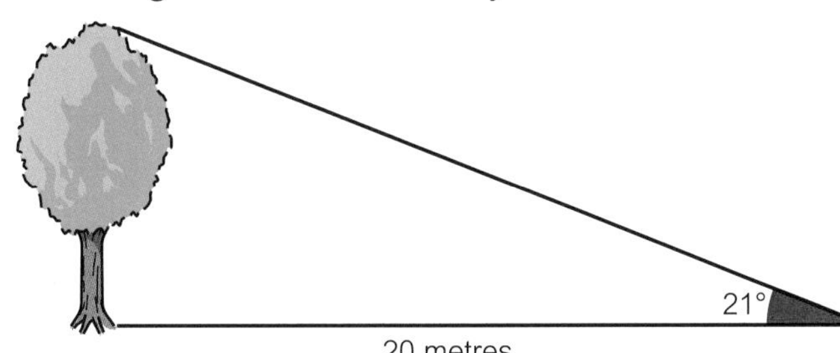

9 Real / Modelling A ladder rests against a wall.
The bottom of the ladder is 2 metres from the bottom of the wall.
The ladder makes an angle of 40° with the horizontal ground.
How far up the wall does the ladder reach?

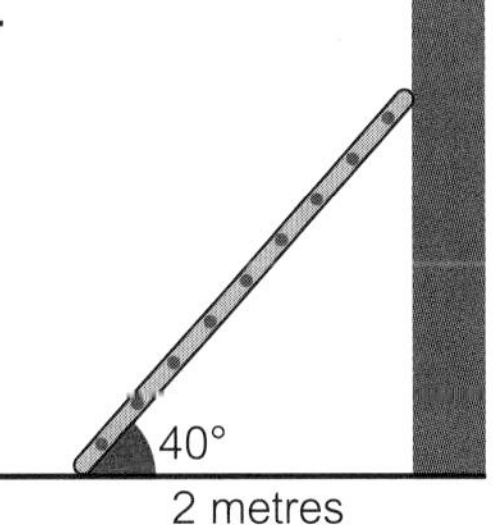

10 Explore How do surveyors use the tangent ratio to find the heights of skyscrapers?
Look back at the maths you have learned in this lesson.
How can you use it to answer this question?

11 Reflect Look back at Q6. This question is tagged 'Reasoning'.
Why?

Q11 hint

How was answering Q6 different to answering Q5 (which is not tagged 'Reasoning')?

10.4 The sine ratio

You will learn to:
- Work out the sine ratio of any angle
- Use sine to work out the opposite side in a right-angled triangle.

CONFIDENCE

Why learn this?
Engineers use ratios in triangles to work out angles and lengths.

Fluency
Make n the subject.
- $4 = \frac{n}{a}$
- $g = \frac{n}{6}$
- $19 = \frac{n}{2d}$

Explore
What heights do the Hastings funicular railways climb to?

Exercise 10.4

Warm up

1 Sketch a triangle and mark one angle θ. On your sketch, label the hypotenuse and the opposite and adjacent sides to angle θ.

Investigation — Reasoning

1 Draw these triangles accurately using protractor and ruler.
2 Label the opposite side to 40° 'opp' and the adjacent side 'adj'.
3 Measure the adjacent sides.
4 a Write the fraction, $\frac{\text{opposite}}{\text{hypotenuse}}$, for each triangle and convert it to a decimal (correct to 1 d.p.).
b What do you notice?
c What do you think will happen with other right-angled triangles with an angle of 40°?
d Test your hypothesis by drawing some more right-angled triangles with an angle of 40°.
5 Repeat with an angle of 80° instead of 40°.

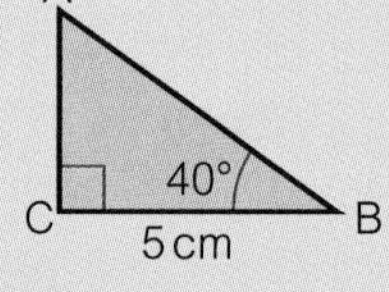

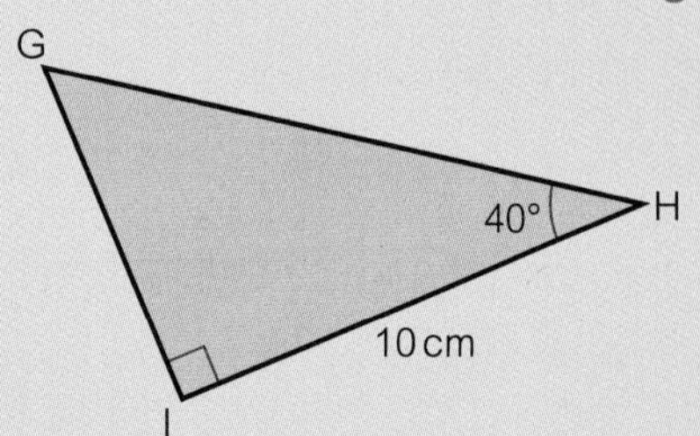

Discussion Why are the fractions for the same angle the same? What does this tell you about the ratio of the sides?

2 Use your calculator to find, correct to one decimal place
a sin 45° b sin 75° c sin 60° d sin 15°

Key point
The ratio of the opposite side to the hypotenuse is called the **sine** of the angle.
The sine of angle θ is written as sin θ.

$$\sin\theta = \frac{\text{opposite}}{\text{hypotenuse}}$$

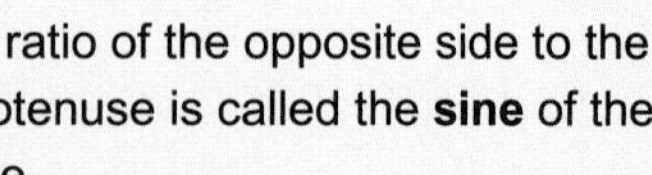

3 Write sin θ as a fraction for each triangle.

a
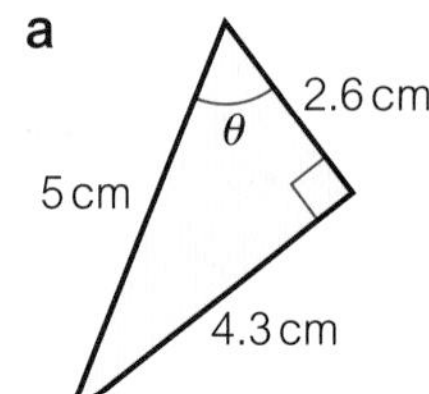

b
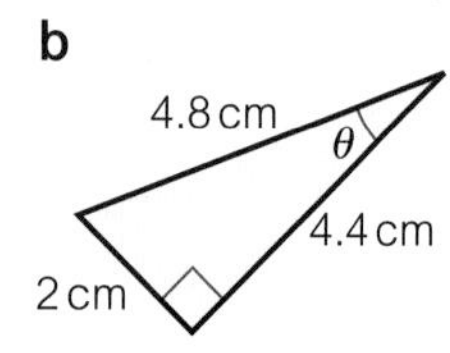

c
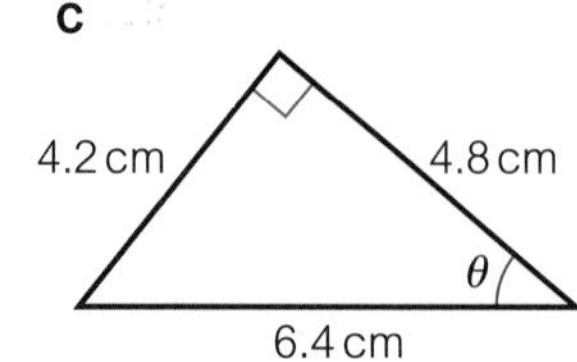

Discussion What is the highest value that sin θ can be?

Topic links: Fractions, Ratio

Worked example

Use the sine ratio to work out x, correct to 1 d.p.

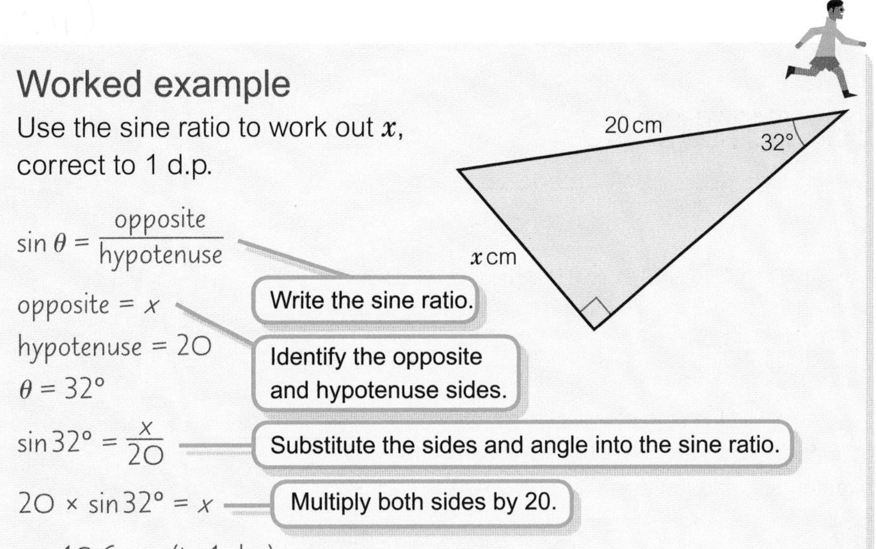

$\sin\theta = \dfrac{\text{opposite}}{\text{hypotenuse}}$ — Write the sine ratio.

opposite $= x$
hypotenuse $= 20$
$\theta = 32°$ — Identify the opposite and hypotenuse sides.

$\sin 32° = \dfrac{x}{20}$ — Substitute the sides and angle into the sine ratio.

$20 \times \sin 32° = x$ — Multiply both sides by 20.

$x = 10.6$ cm (to 1 d.p.)

Key point

You can use the sine ratio to find the length of sides of a right-angled triangle.

4 Use the sine ratio to work out x for each triangle, correct to 1 d.p.

a

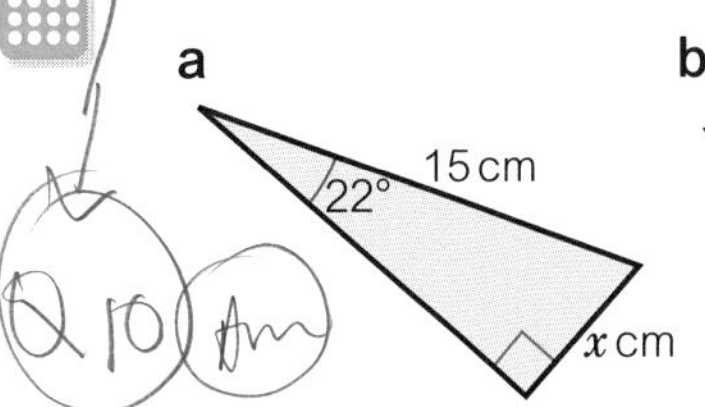

b

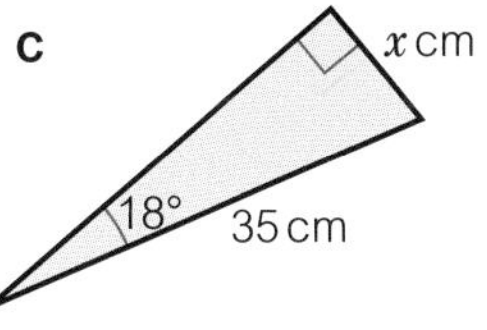

c

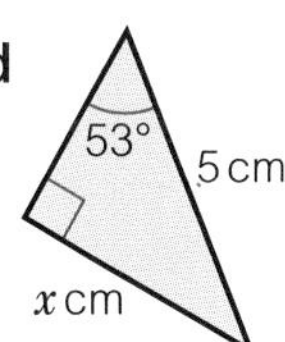

d

53°
5 cm
x cm

5 **Modelling** A kite flies on the end of a string that is tied to a stone on the ground.
The string is 100 metres long and makes an angle of 45° with the ground.
Use the sine ratio to work out how high the kite is flying. Give your answer to the nearest centimetre.

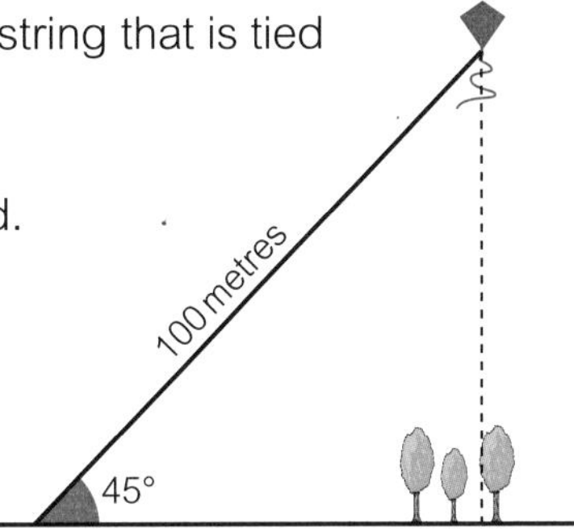

6 **Reasoning / Modelling** A 10-metre ladder rests against the side of a house at an angle of 75° to the ground.
Use the sine ratio to decide whether it will reach a window sill that is 8 metres above the ground.

Q6 hint

Draw a sketch. Use the sine ratio to work out how high the ladder reaches.

7 **Explore** What heights do the Hastings funicular railways climb to?
Is it easier to explore this question now you have completed the lesson? What further information do you need to be able to answer this?

8 **Reflect** Look back at Q6.
What steps did you take to answer this question involving the sine ratio?
You may begin with, 'Step 1: Sketch the right-angled triangle.'

Q8 hint

Use pencil and space out your steps. This will help if you wish to change or add to your steps later.

Explore

Reflect

10.5 The cosine ratio

You will learn to:

- Work out the cosine ratio of any angle
- Use the cosine ratio to work out the adjacent side in a right-angled triangle.

CONFIDENCE

Why learn this?
The theories of how the planets move were developed using trigonometry.

Fluency
In these right-angled triangles, identify the hypotenuse, and the adjacent and opposite sides for the marked angle.

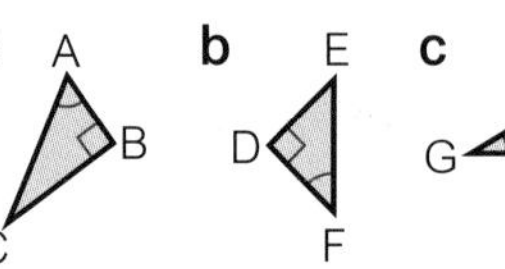

Explore
Some simple tents are triangular prisms. Is there a 'best' ratio of the width to the slant height of a simple tent?

Exercise 10.5

Warm up

1 Copy and complete.

a $\tan\theta = \frac{\square}{\square}$ b $\sin\theta = \frac{\square}{\square}$

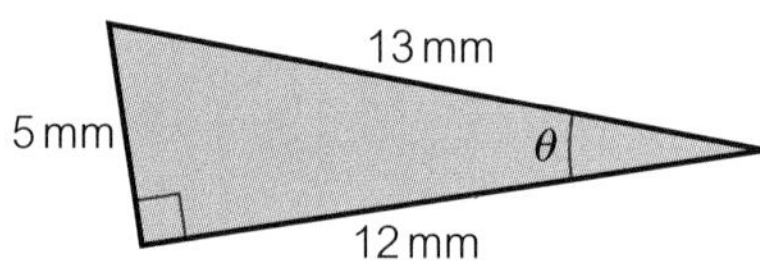

2 Use your calculator to find

a tan 45° b sin 90° c tan 0° d sin 0°

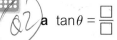

Investigation Reasoning

1 Look at the triangles you drew in the Investigation in lesson 10.4.

2 a Write the fraction, $\frac{\text{adjacent}}{\text{hypotenuse}}$, for each triangle and convert it to a decimal (correct to 1 d.p.).

b What do you notice?

3 Repeat for the triangles with an 80° angle.

4 Find the same ratio for the 80° triangles.

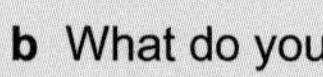

Discussion Why are the fractions for the same angles the same? What does this tell you about the ratio of the sides?

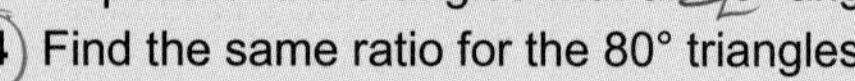

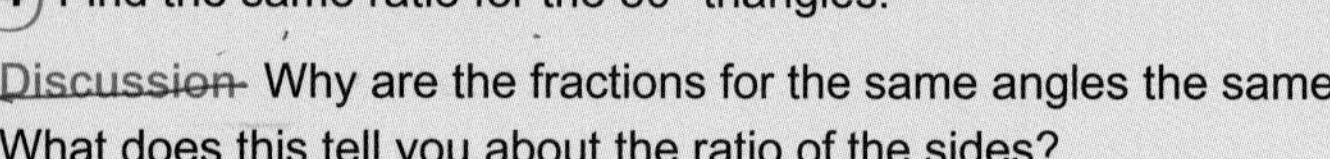

3 Use your calculator to find these, correct to one decimal place.

a cos 45° b cos 65° c cos 30° d cos 25°

4 **Problem-solving** Four different right-angled triangles have hypotenuses of the same length. They fit in a circle with radius 16 cm, like this.

a How long are the hypotenuses?

b Write as a fraction

i $\cos p$ ii $\cos q$

iii $\cos r$ iv $\cos s$

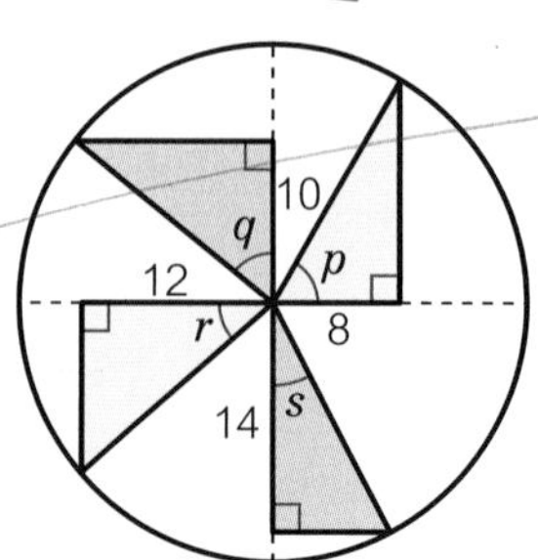

Key point

The ratio of the adjacent side to the hypotenuse is called the **cosine** of the angle.

The cosine of θ is written as $\cos\theta$.

$$\cos\theta = \frac{\text{adjacent}}{\text{hypotenuse}}$$

Topic links: Fractions, Ratio

Worked example

Use the cosine ratio to work out x, correct to 1 d.p.

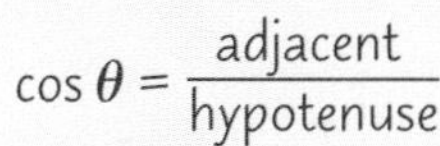

$\cos\theta = \dfrac{\text{adjacent}}{\text{hypotenuse}}$ — Write the cosine ratio.

adjacent = x
hypotenuse = 30
$\theta = 49°$ — Identify the adjacent and hypotenuse sides.

$\cos 49° = \dfrac{x}{30}$ — Substitute the sides and angle into the cosine ratio.

$30 \times \cos 49° = x$ — Multiply both sides by 30.

$x = 19.7$ cm (to 1 d.p.)

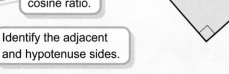

Key point

You can use the cosine ratio to find the unknown lengths of a right-angled triangle.

5 Use the cosine ratio to work out x for each triangle, correct to 1 d.p.

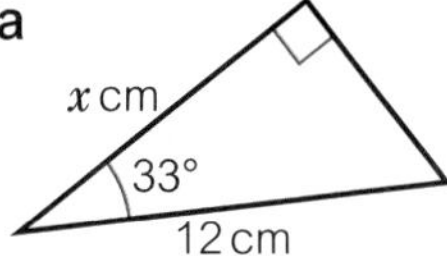

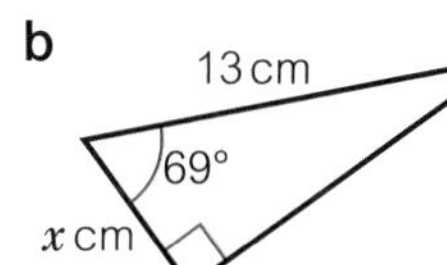

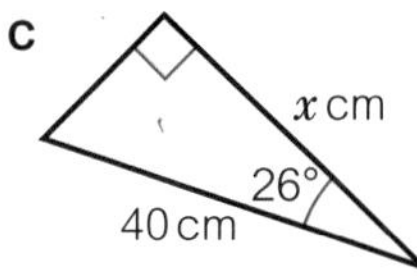

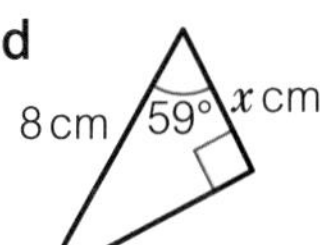

6 **Problem-solving** A tent is an isosceles triangular prism, and the sloping side length is 150 cm.
The side makes an angle of 50° with the horizontal.
Use the cosine ratio to find the width of the tent.
Give your answer to the nearest centimetre.

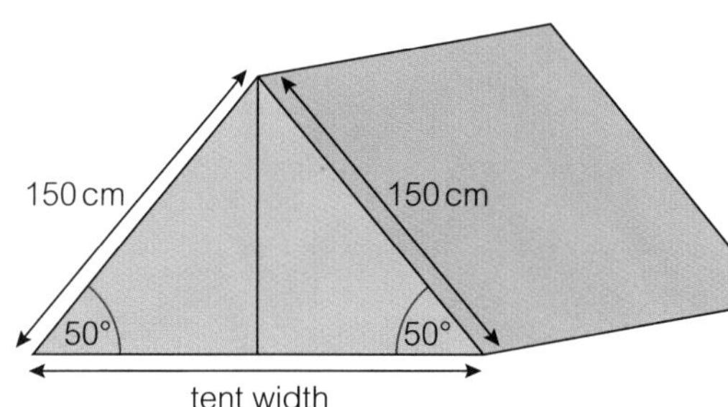

Q6 hint

Divide into two right-angled triangles.

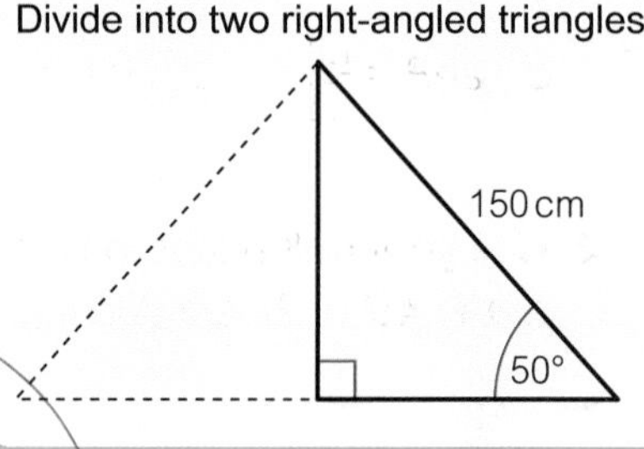

7 **Real** The diagram shows the path of a ship that sails 20 km from P.

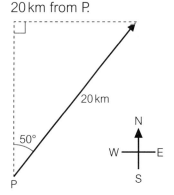

20 km

50°

P

N

W E

S

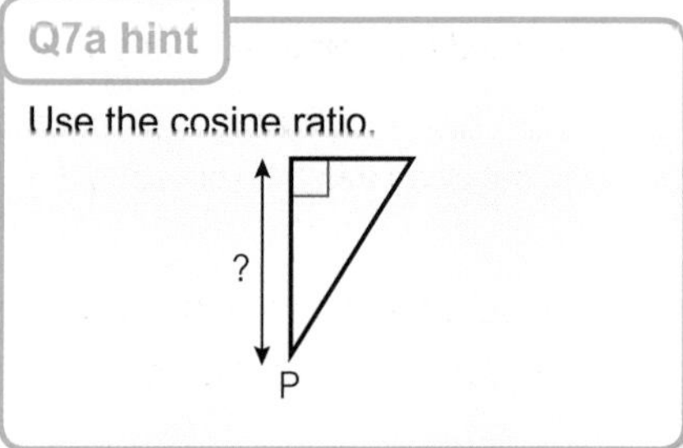

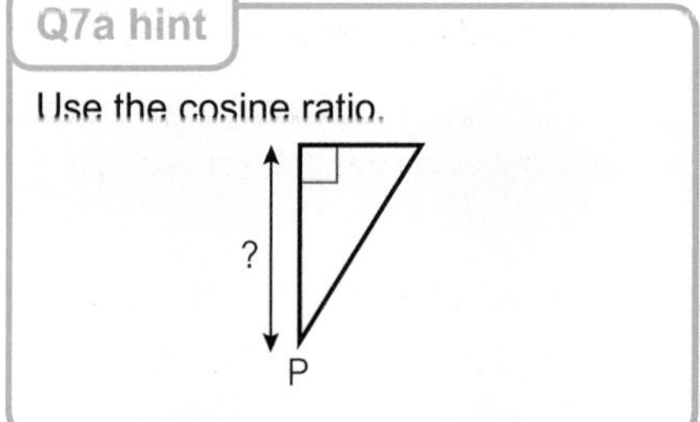

Q7a hint

Use the cosine ratio.

?

P

a How far North has the ship moved? Give you answer to the nearest metre.

b How far East has it moved?

Q7b hint

Use the sine ratio.

Discussion When would you use the tangent ratio? When would you use the cosine ratio?

8 Problem-solving The length of the diagonal of this rectangle is 15 cm.

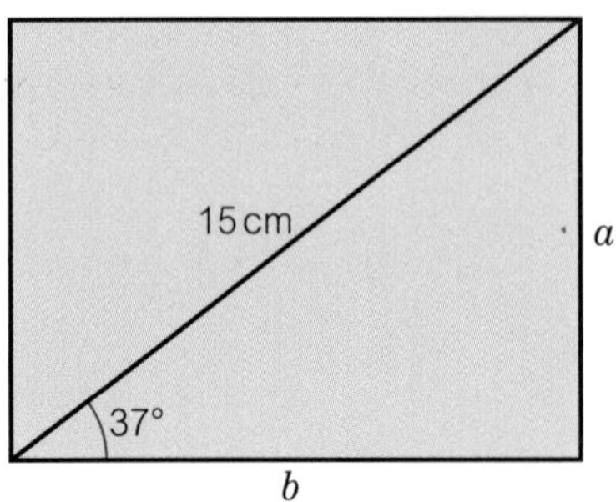

a Use the sine ratio to work out a.

b Use the cosine ratio to work out b.

9 Real A crane lifts a container onto a ship. The crane arm is 40 metres long and makes an angle of 20° with the vertical. The bottom of the container is level with the bottom of the crane arm.
Use the cosine ratio to find the vertical distance, to the nearest cm, from the top of the crane arm to the bottom of the container.

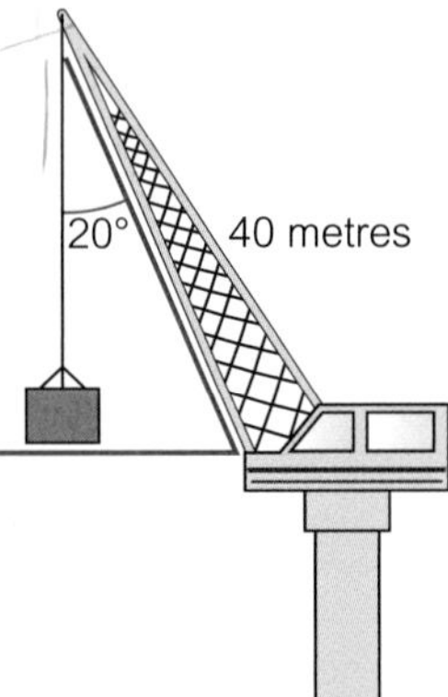

10 Explore Some simple tents are triangular prisms. Is there a 'best' ratio of the width to the slant height of a simple tent?
Is it easier to explore this question now you have completed the lesson?
What further information do you need to be able to answer this?

11 Reflect Look back at your answer to the Reflect question in lesson 10.4. You wrote steps for answering questions involving the sine ratio.

a Do these steps work for problems involving the cosine ratio?
If not, change them, so they work for both sine and cosine ratios.

b Do your steps work for problems involving the tangent ratio too?
If not, change them, so they work for sine, cosine and tangent ratios.

c Now you should have your own steps for working out the sine, cosine or tangent ratio in any right-angled triangle. Compare your steps with others in your class.

10 Check up

Log how you did on your Student Progression Chart.

Congruence and similarity

1 Which rectangles are similar to rectangle A?

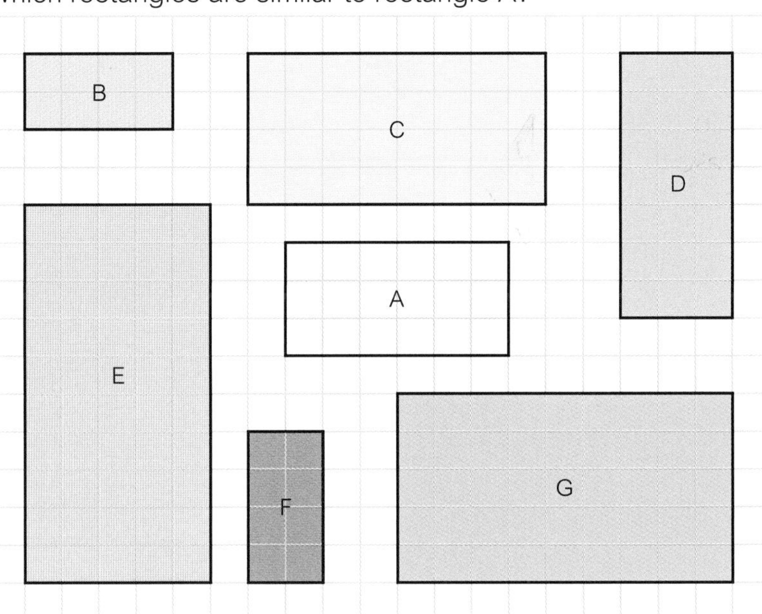

2 The right-angled triangles are similar. Find the value of x.

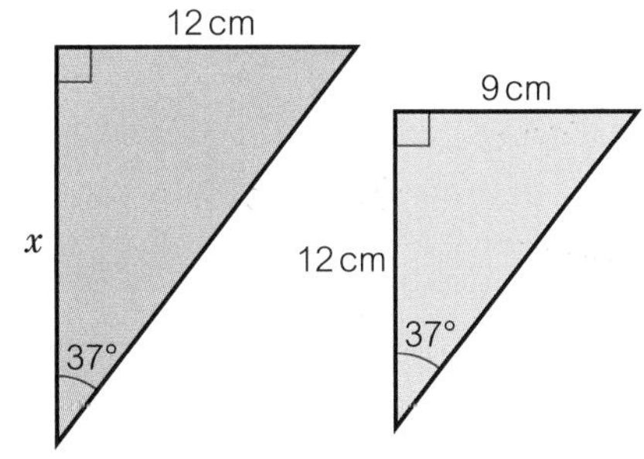

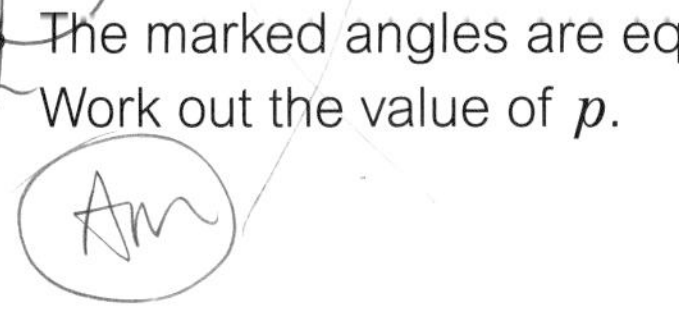

3 The marked angles are equal. Work out the value of p.

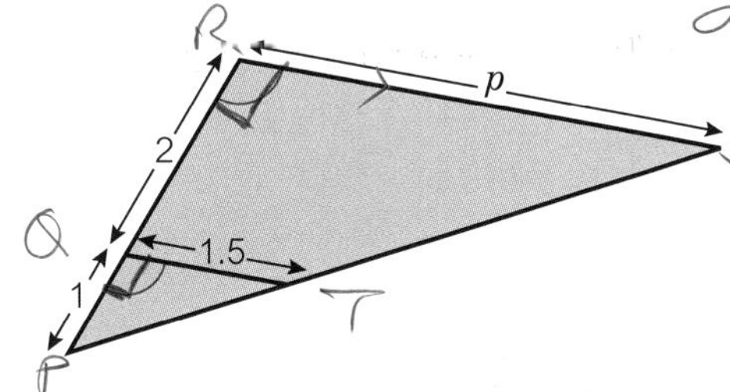

4 Decide whether these pairs of triangles are congruent. Give a reason for each answer.

a

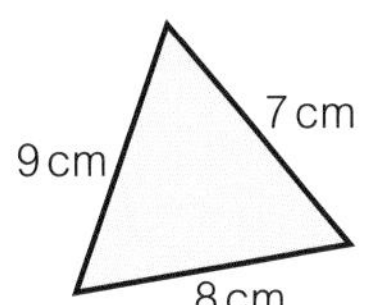

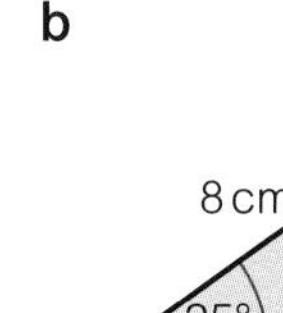

b

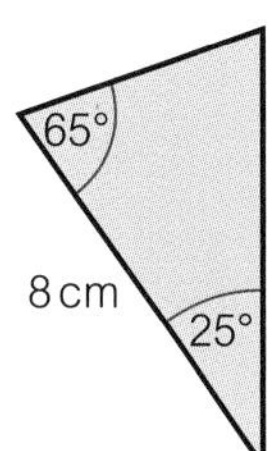

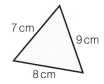

Sine, cosine and tangent

5 In each triangle what is

a the opposite side to angle θ

b the adjacent side to angle θ

c the hypotenuse?

Triangle 1: A, B, C, θ at C, right angle at A
Triangle 2: F, D, E, θ at F, right angle at E
Triangle 3: G, I, H, θ at G, right angle at I

6 Use the sine ratio to work out x, correct to 1 d.p.

10 cm, 46°, x cm

7 Use the tangent ratio to work out x, correct to 1 d.p.

30 cm, 20°, x cm

8 Use the cosine ratio to work out x, correct to 1 d.p.

12 cm, 30°, x cm

Reflect

9 **How sure are you of your answers? Were you mostly**

Just guessing **Feeling doubtful** **Confident**

What next? Use your results to decide whether to strengthen or extend your learning.

Challenge

10 Eight points, labelled A to H, are spaced equally round a circle.
You can make different designs by joining different pairs of those points.
Here are three examples.

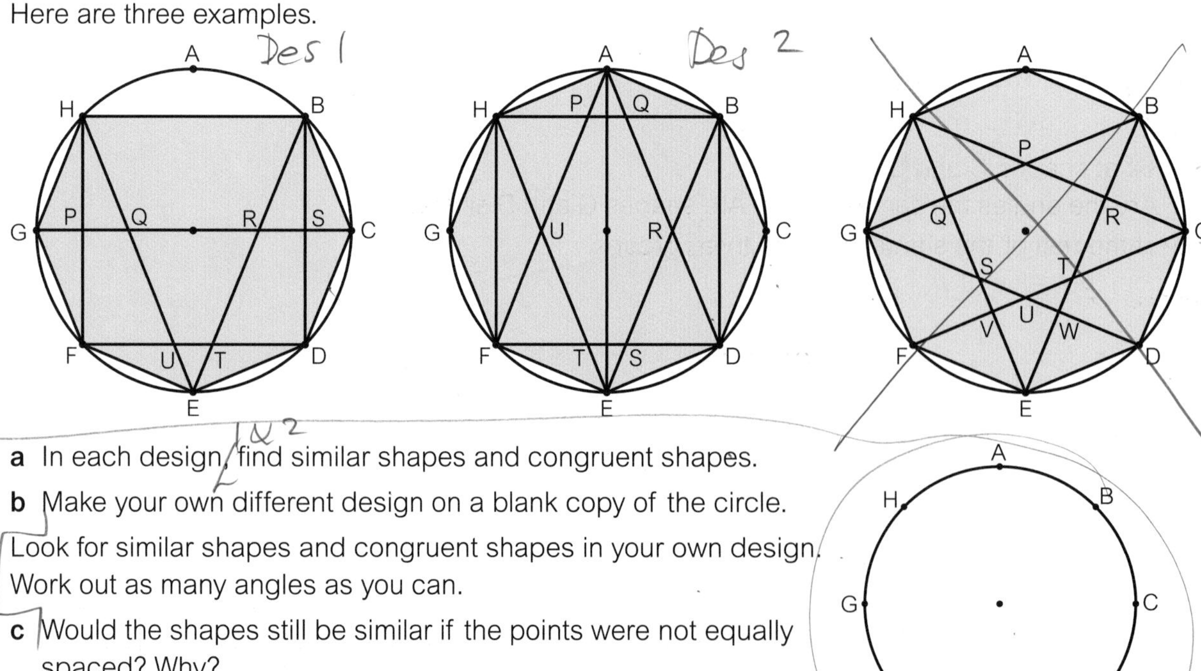

a In each design, find similar shapes and congruent shapes.

b Make your own different design on a blank copy of the circle.
Look for similar shapes and congruent shapes in your own design.
Work out as many angles as you can.

c Would the shapes still be similar if the points were not equally spaced? Why?

10 Strengthen

You will:

- Strengthen your understanding with practice.

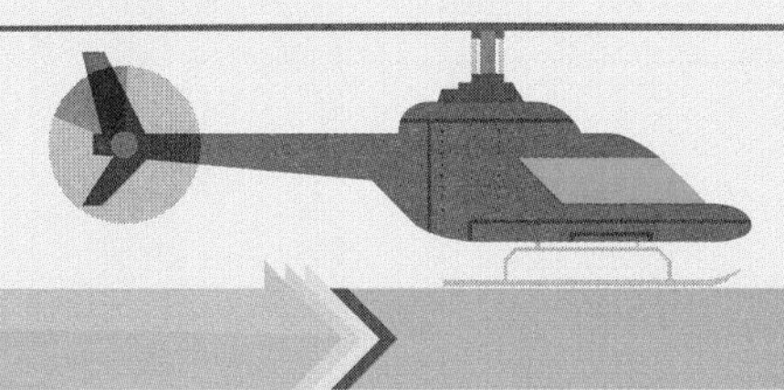

Congruence and similarity

1 Reasoning Six congruent triangles are arranged like this.

a Draw a sketch of the diagram.

b Label all the angles a, b or c so that equal angles have the same letter.

a A b c

Q1 hint

Trace triangle A. Place it over the other triangles to help you find the equal angles.
You will need to rotate your tracing for the yellow triangles.

2 Three groups of similar shapes have been mixed up.

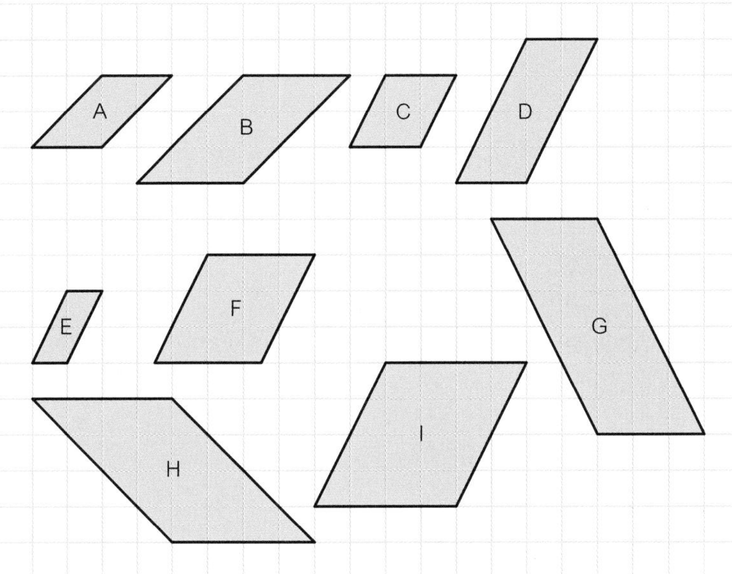

Q2 hint

You could use tracing paper to check whether the angles are the same.

a Look at shapes A and B.

i Are the angles the same? **ii** Are shapes A and B similar?

b Look at shapes C and D.

i Are the angles the same? **ii** Are shapes C and D similar?

c Sort the rest of the shapes into the three groups.

3 Triangles P and Q are similar.

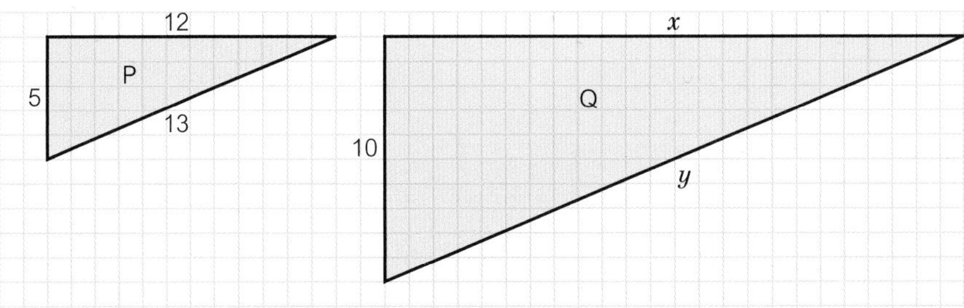

a Copy and complete the table. Show the pairs of corresponding sides.

b Use a pair of corresponding sides to work out the scale factor from P to Q.

c Use the scale factor to work out x and y.

Q3b hint

5 × □ = 10

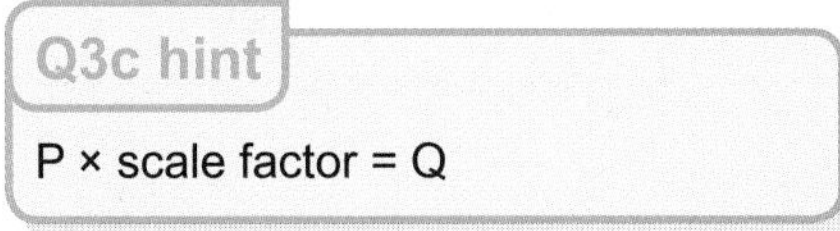

Q3c hint

P × scale factor = Q

Shape	P	Q
Height	5	10
Width		x
Hypotenuse	13	

4 For each pair of similar shapes, work out x and y.

a

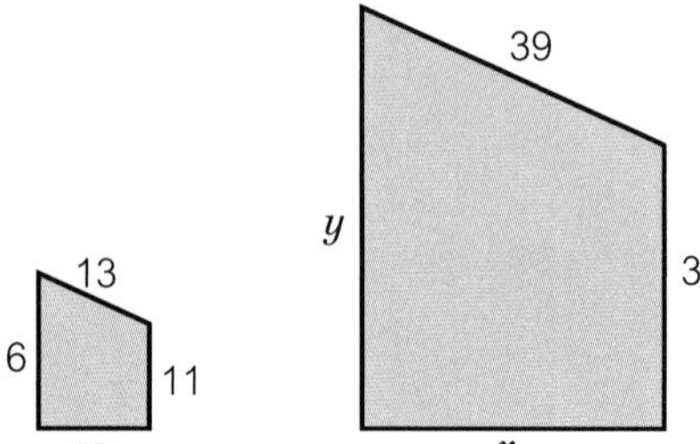

b

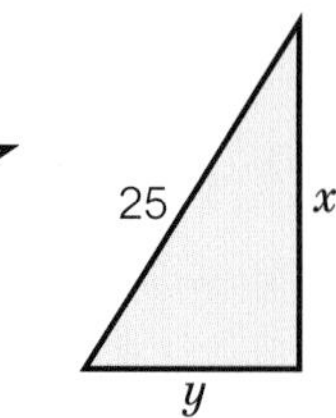

Q4 hint

Use the method in Q3.

5 Which of these triangles are similar to triangle A?

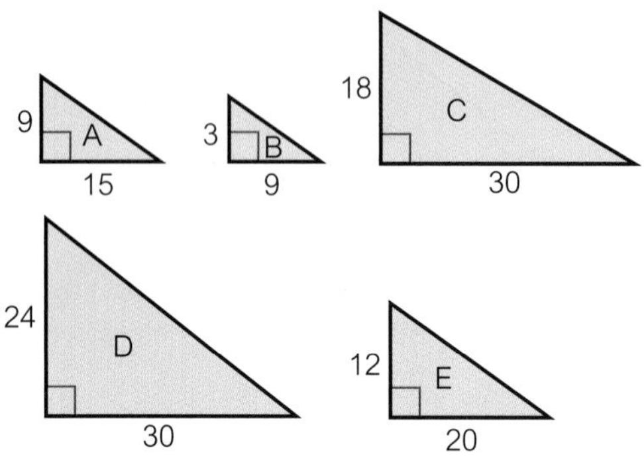

Q5 hint

Write the values in a table, as in Q3.

6 Reasoning The diagram shows two triangles.

a Explain why

i $a = b$ **ii** $c = d$ **iii** $e = f$

b The three pairs of angles are equal.
What does this tell you about the two triangles?

c **i** Trace the triangles and then sketch them the same way up.

ii Label the measurements you know.

iii Find the missing lengths.

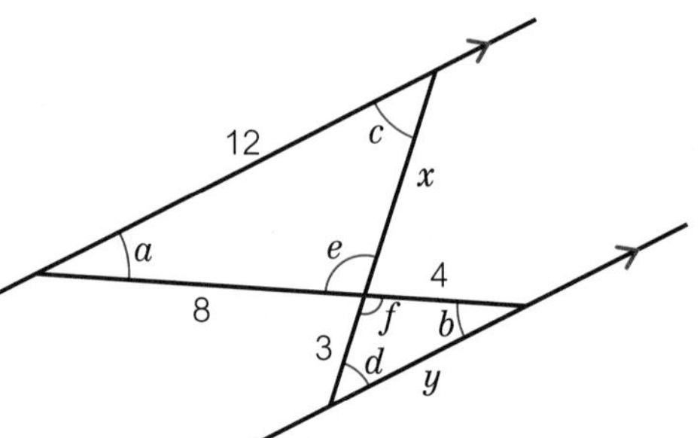

Q6c iii hint

Use the method in Q3.

7 Reasoning **a** Copy each pair of diagrams accurately.
Then draw, or continue, the lines to make two triangles.

i

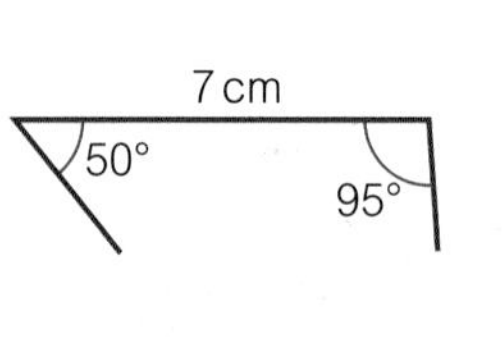

ii

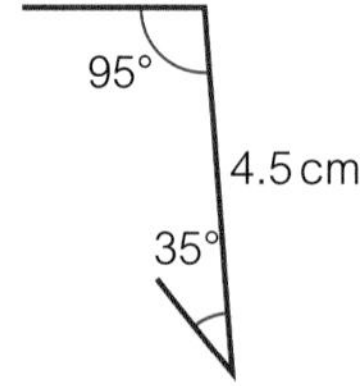

b Use the diagrams to help you decide whether two triangles are congruent if

i two corresponding angles and the length of the side between them are equal (ASA)

ii three angles are equal (AAA)

iii the lengths of two corresponding sides and the angle between them are equal (SAS).

Topic links: Enlargement, Construction, Multiplying by fractions, Angles in parallel lines

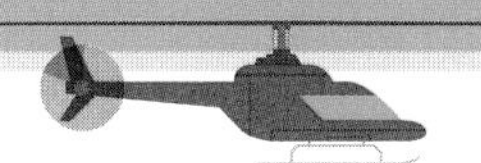

8 Reasoning

a What can you say about BC and DE? Explain how you know.

b Which angle in the diagram is equal to ∠ABC? Explain why.

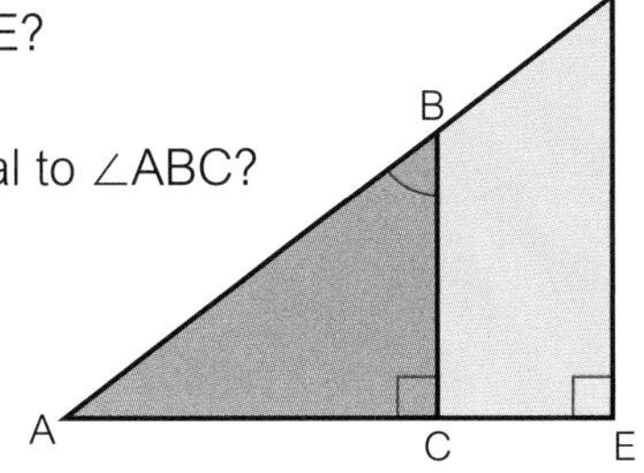

Q8d hint

$77 \times \square = 110$

Q8e hint

BC × □ = DE

c Explain why triangles ABC and ADE are similar.

d What is the scale factor of the enlargement from triangle ABC to triangle ADE?

e Work out the length of DE.

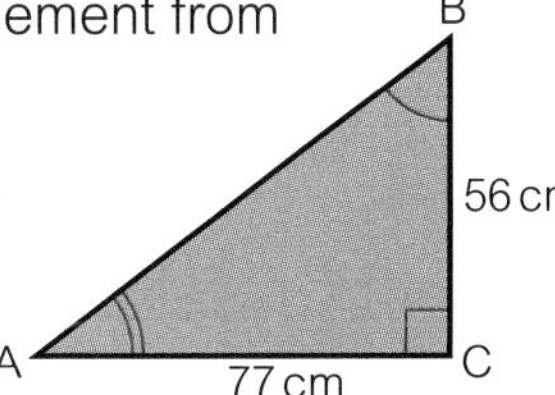

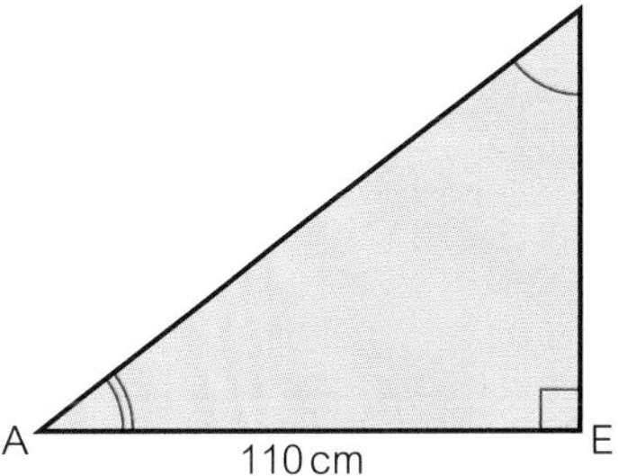

Sine, cosine and tangent

1 Sketch each triangle and label

a 'opp' on the side opposite to $\angle\theta$

b 'adj' on the adjacent side

c 'hyp' on the hypotenuse.

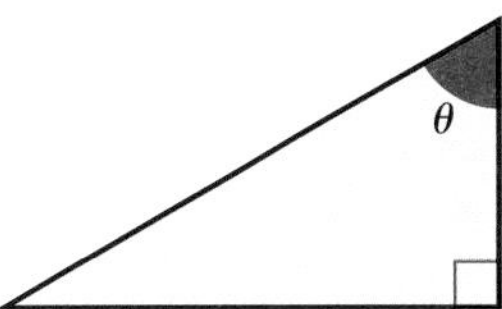

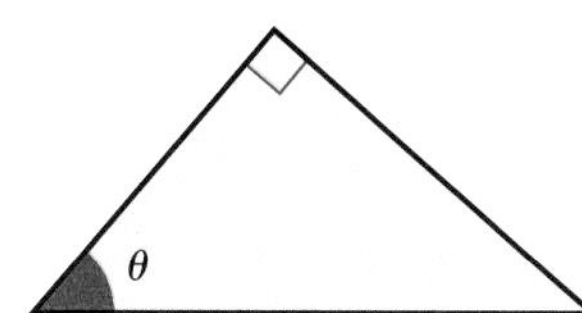

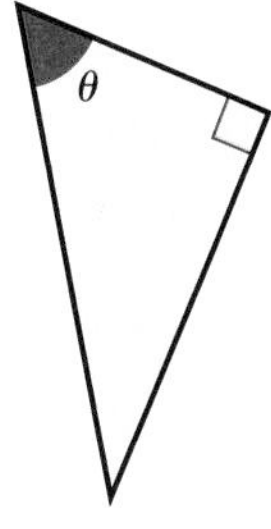

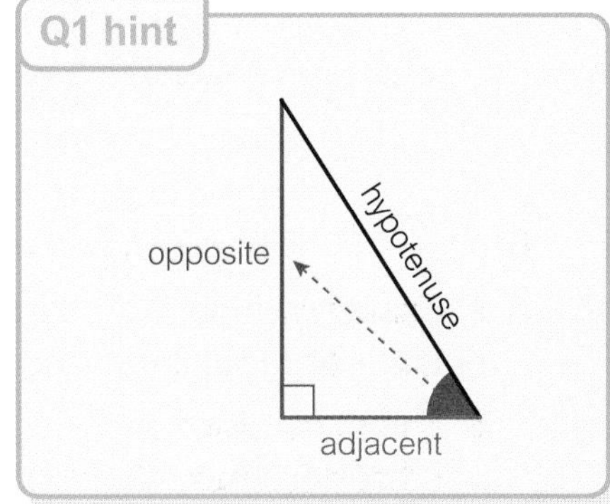
Q1 hint

2 Write the tangent ratio for each triangle.

a

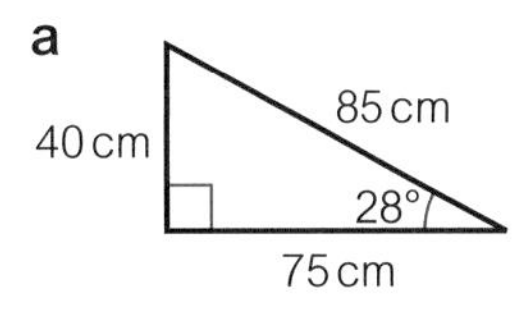

b

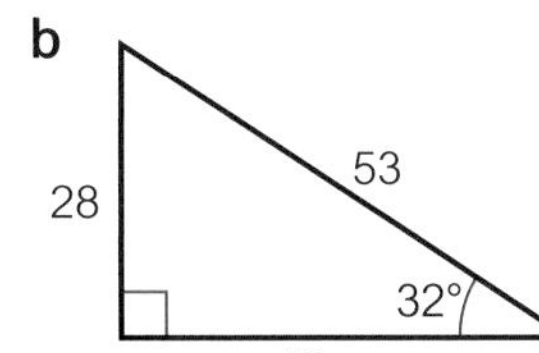

c

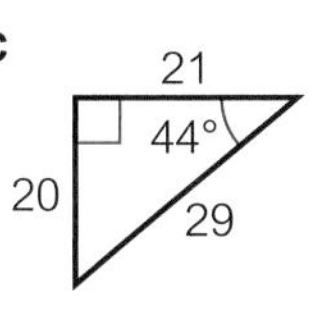

d

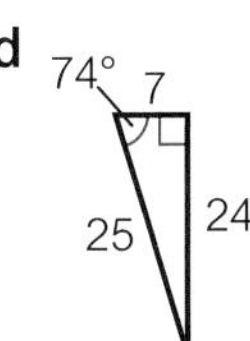

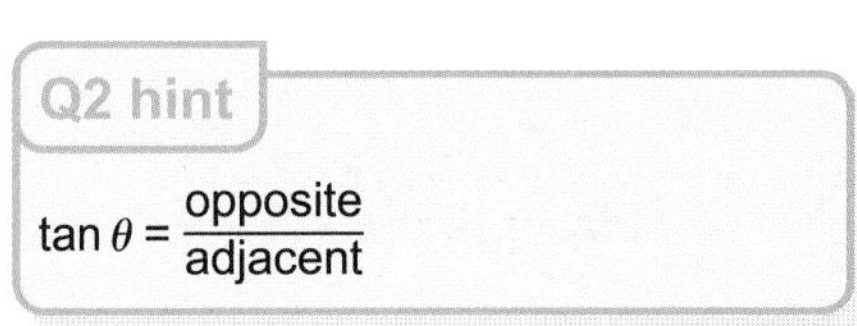
Q2 hint

$\tan\theta = \dfrac{\text{opposite}}{\text{adjacent}}$

3 Copy and complete to work out the missing length x, correct to 1 d.p.

a Write the tangent ratio

$\tan\square = \dfrac{\square}{\square}$

b Rearrange

$x = \square \times \tan\square$

c Use a calculator to find x.

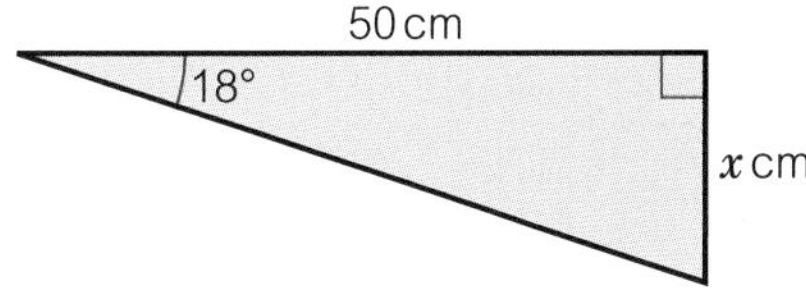

4 Copy and complete to work out the missing length x, correct to 1 d.p.

a Write the sine ratio

$\sin\square = \dfrac{x}{\square}$

b Rearrange

$x = \square \times \sin\square$

c Use a calculator to find x.

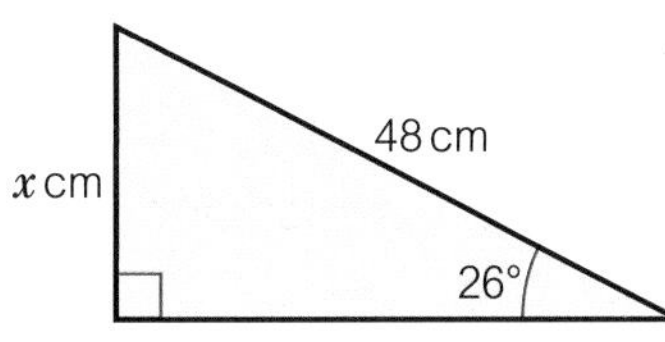

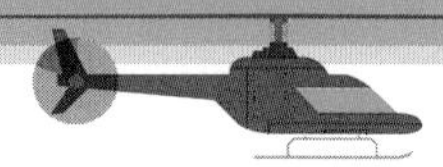

5 Copy and complete to work out the missing length x, correct to 1 d.p.

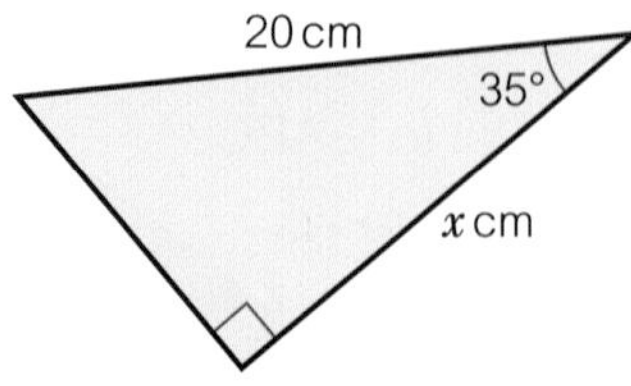

a Write the cosine ratio

$\cos\square = \frac{x}{\square}$

b Rearrange

$x = \square \times \cos\square$

c Use a calculator to find x.

6 Problem-solving An anchor on the seabed is at the end of a chain 40 m long that is secured at sea level to a boat.
The taut anchor chain makes an angle of 49° with the seabed.
Sketch the diagram and mark on the measurements you know.

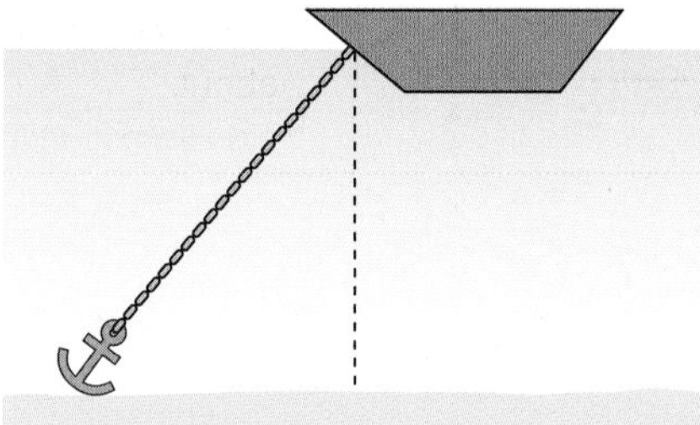

Use the sine ratio to work out the depth of the sea.

Enrichment

1 This pattern is part of a tessellation of small right-angled triangles.

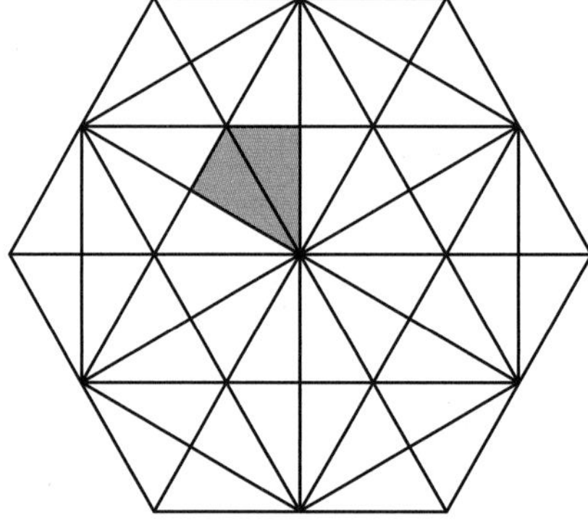

a Trace the pattern. Draw round a shape that is congruent with the pink kite.

b Draw round a shape that is similar to the pink kite.

c How many shapes can you find that are similar to the pink kite?

d Make another copy of the pattern. Choose another shape that you can see in the pattern. Draw round, or shade in your shape.

e How many shapes can you find that are similar to your shape?

Reflect

2 **Reflect**

a When looking at triangles, what can you tell from just the angles? Write down at least four things.

b When looking at right-angled triangles, what can you work out just from one other angle and the included side?
Write down at least four things.

Q2a hint

Think about what you can tell just by looking at the angles of one triangle. What about when comparing two triangles?

Q2b hint

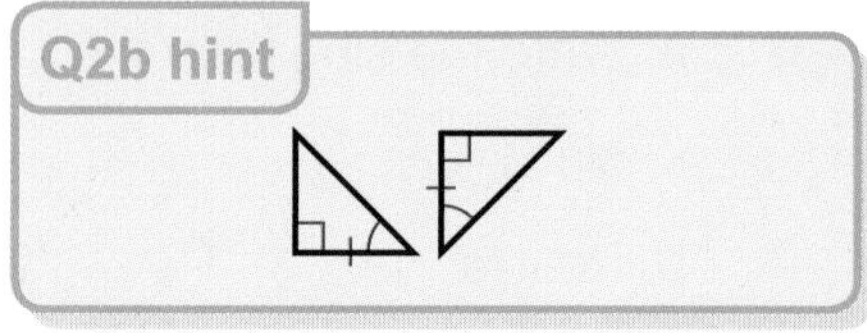

10 Extend

You will:

- Extend your understanding with problem-solving.

1 This rectangle is made up of four congruent right-angled triangles.

a Construct the diagram accurately.

b **Reasoning** What kind of triangle is triangle BFD? Explain how you know.

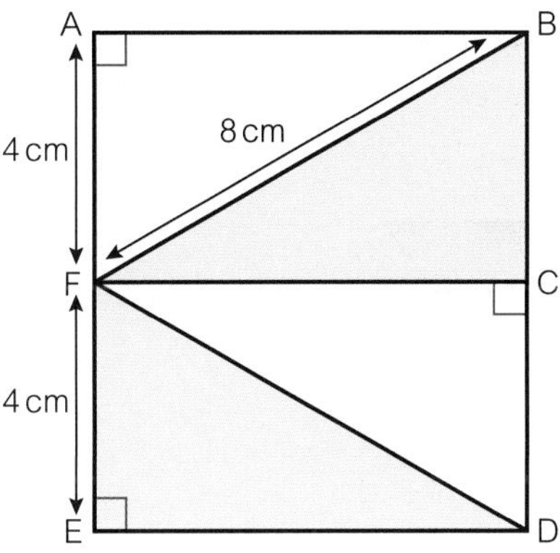

Q1a hint

Start with the triangle you know most about.

2 The line segment AC is split in the ratio 1 : 3.

a What fraction of AC is AB?

b Explain why triangles ABD and ABE are similar.

c Work out the scale factor.
AB × □ = AC

d Use the scale factor to work out x and y.

e Write the coordinates of B.

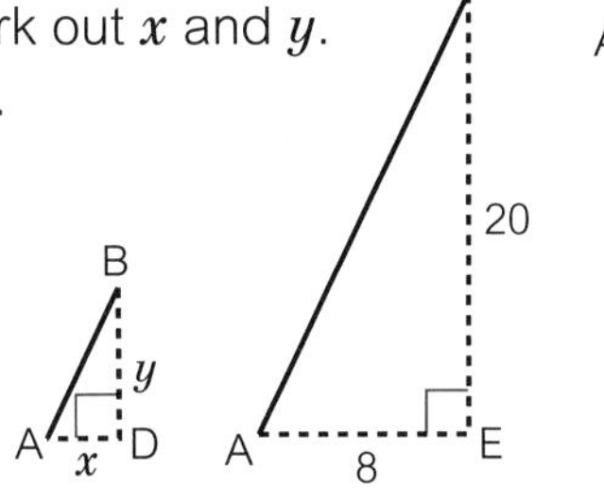

Q2b hint

Show they have equal angles.

Q2d hint

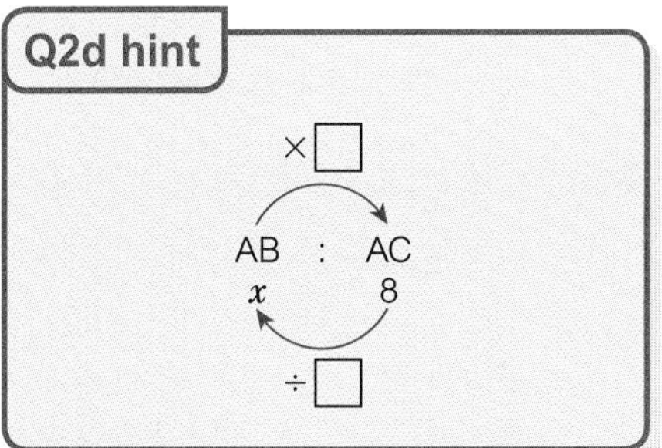

3 The line segment XZ is split in the ratio 2 : 3.

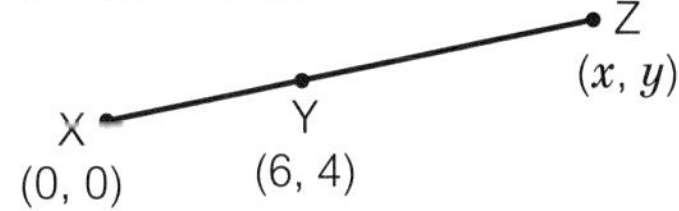

Work out the coordinates of Z.

Q3 hint

Draw similar triangles, as in Q2.

4 The four right-angled triangles in this diagram are all similar to each other.
Work out x, y and z.

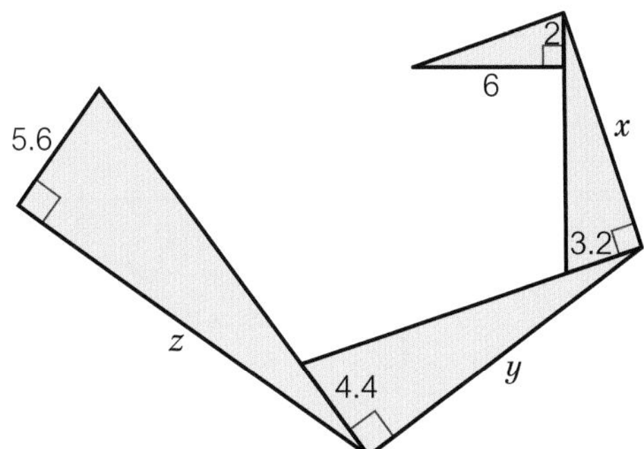

5 **Reasoning** Eight congruent isosceles right-angled triangles are arranged to make an octagon.

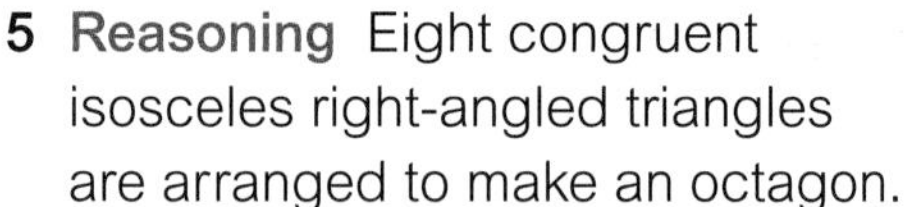

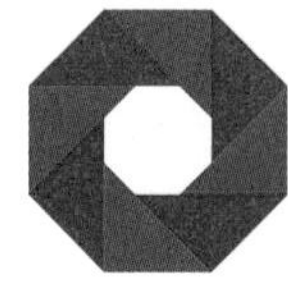

a Is the octagon a regular octagon?

b Is the hole in the centre a regular octagon? Explain how you know.

Q5 hint

Think about its exterior angles.

6 **Reasoning** By splitting the red parallelogram into congruent triangles, work out the fraction of the hexagon that is red.

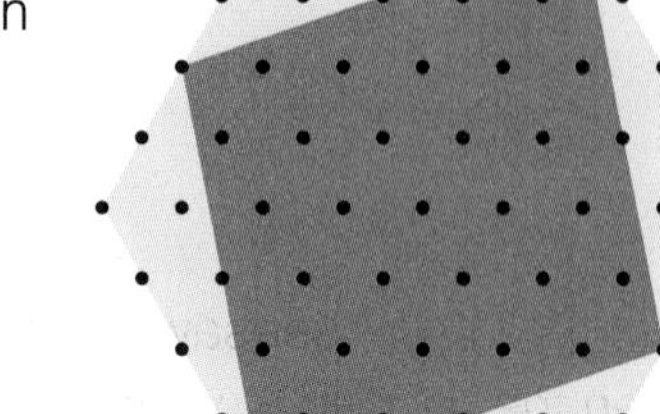

7 **Reasoning** a Show that kites ABCD and EFGH are similar.

b Find the value of x.

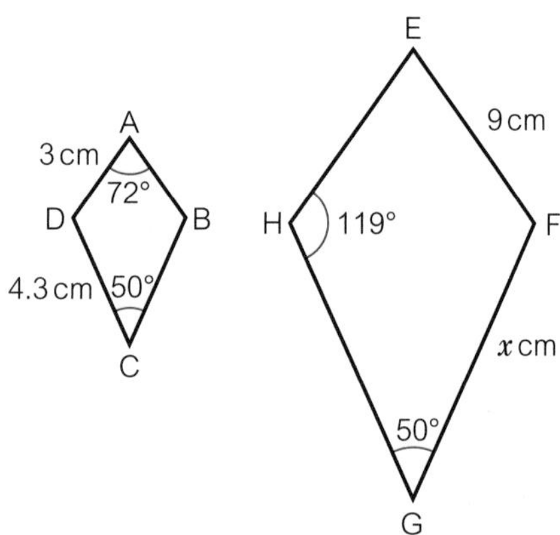

8 a Sketch the triangle and label the sides 'opposite', 'adjacent' and 'hypotenuse'.

b Which ratio do you need to use to find x, tangent, sine or cosine?

c Work out the value of x.

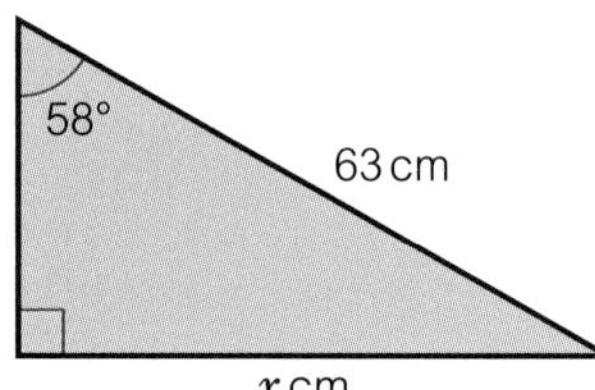

Q8b hint

Which ratio use the two sides labelled 63 cm and x cm?

$\sin \theta = \frac{\text{opp}}{\text{hyp}}$ $\cos \theta = \frac{\text{adj}}{\text{hyp}}$ $\tan \theta = \frac{\text{opp}}{\text{adj}}$

9 For each triangle, work out the value of x.

a

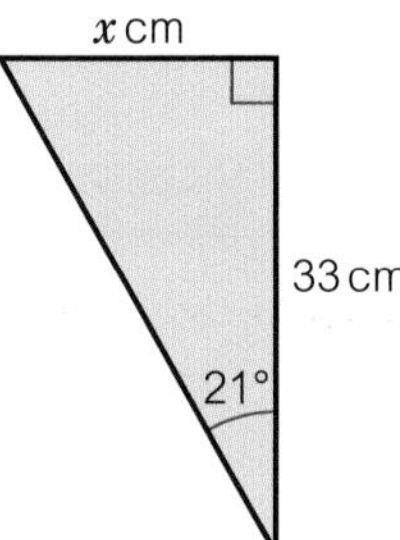

b

x cm

59°

47 cm

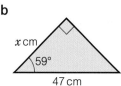

Q9 hint

Identify the labelled sides and choose the correct ratio.

10 **Real / Problem-solving** A flagpole is held in place by three wire ropes.
Each rope is attached to the ground 2 metres from the bottom of the flagpole. The rope makes an angle of 40° with the horizontal ground.
At what height does the rope attach to the flagpole?
Give your answer to the nearest centimetre.

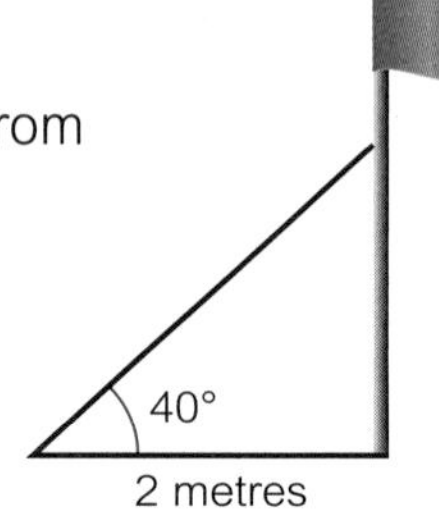

Q10 hint

Sketch the triangle and label the height x. Label opposite, adjacent and hypotenuse.

Topic links: 2D shapes, Construction, Coordinates, Pythagoras' theorem

11 **Real / Problem-solving** This roof truss is made from one equilateral triangle and four congruent triangles.

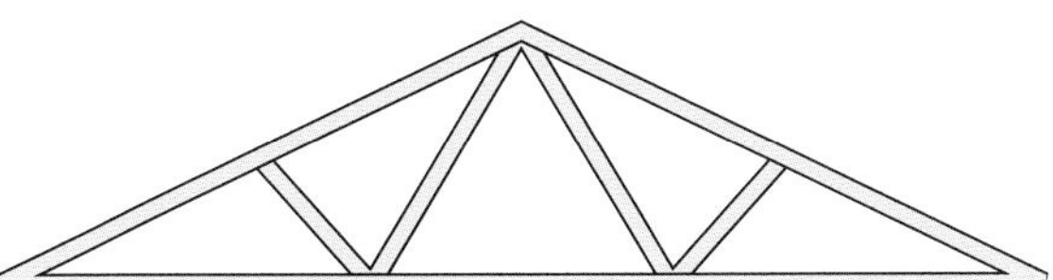

The truss is 4.8 m wide.

a Work out the total length of wood used to make the truss. Give your answer correct to 1 d.p.

b Work out the vertical height of the truss. Give your answer correct to 1 d.p.

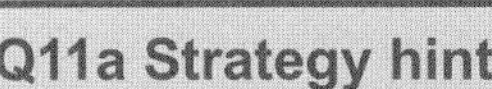

Q11a Strategy hint

Draw a sketch. Use what you know about equilateral triangles and congruent triangles to label as many angles and lengths as you can.

Q11b hint

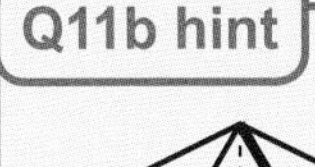

Use these lengths to find the height.

12 **Real / Problem-solving** The diagram shows a seesaw. The distance between the ground and the top of the seesaw is 84 cm.
The maximum angle between the seesaw and the horizontal is 20°.
The length of the seesaw is 3.6 m.

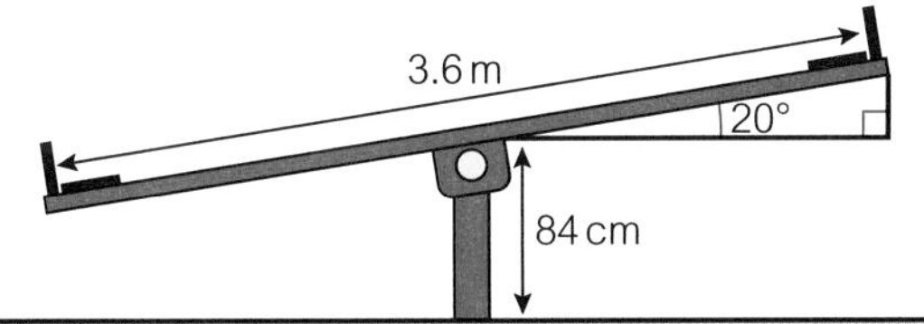

To meet safety regulations, when the seesaw is at the maximum angle of 20°, the end of each seat must be no less than 23 cm and no more than 150 cm from the ground.
Has the seesaw been safely installed? Give reasons for your answer.

13

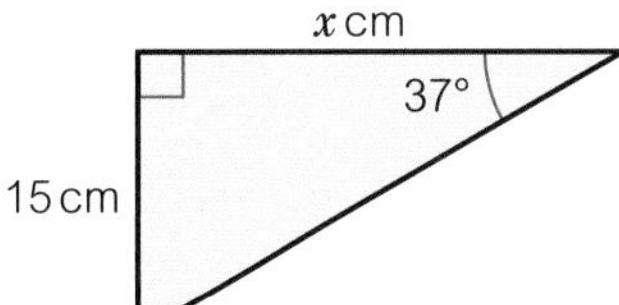

a Copy and complete.

$\tan 37° = \frac{\square}{\square}$

b Rearrange the equation to make x the subject.

c Solve the equation to find the value of x, correct to 1 d.p.

Q13a hint

$\tan \theta = \frac{\text{opposite}}{\text{adjacent}}$

14 For each triangle, find the value of x, correct to 1 d.p.

a

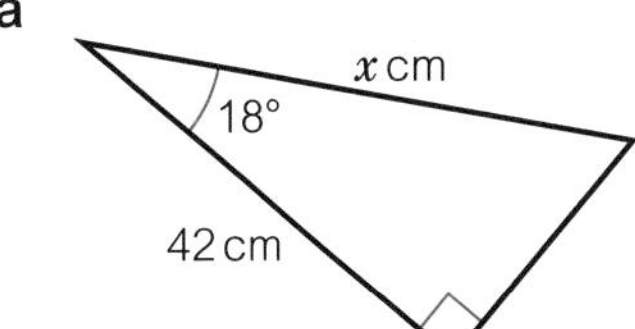

b

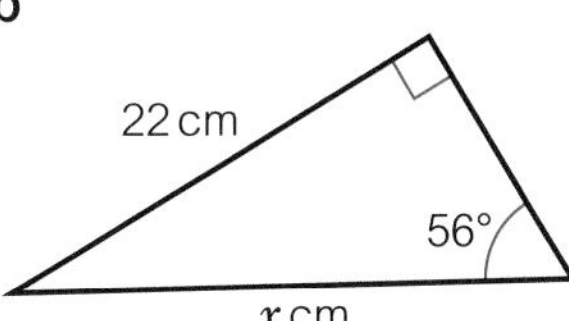

Q14 hint

First choose the correct ratio.

15 **Problem-solving** ABCD is a parallelogram.
Find the length of diagonal AC, correct to 1 d.p.

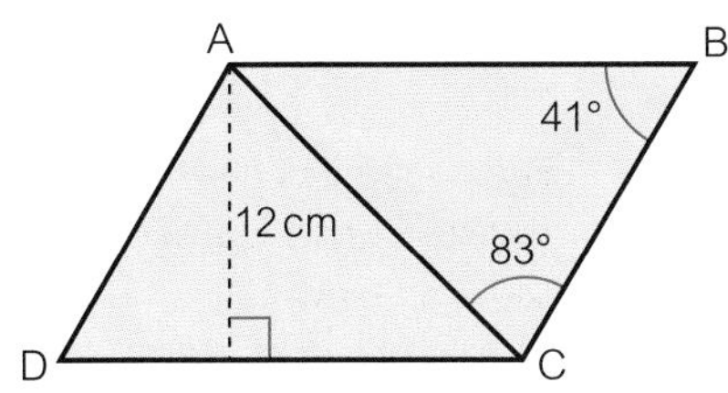

Q15 hint

First use angle facts to find ∠ACD and ∠DAC.

16 A small boat is caught in the beam of light from a lighthouse on a cliff.
The beam is at 23° to the horizontal.
The cliff top is 33 m above sea level. The lighthouse is 8 m tall.

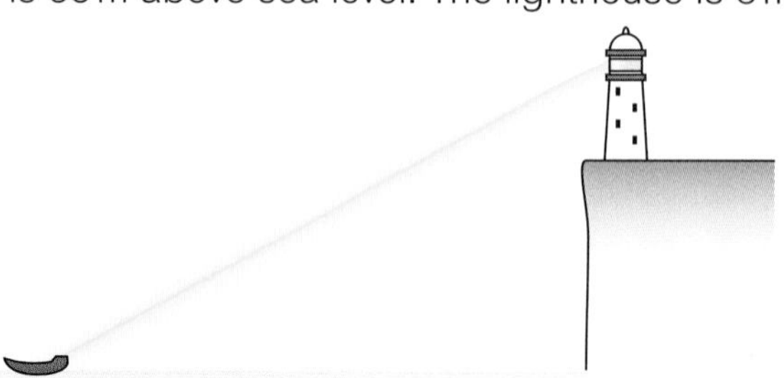

Find the horizontal distance of the boat from the lighthouse.
Give your answer to the nearest metre.

Literacy hint

'at 23° to the horizontal' means the angle between the beam and the horizontal is 23°.

Q16 hint

Sketch a diagram.

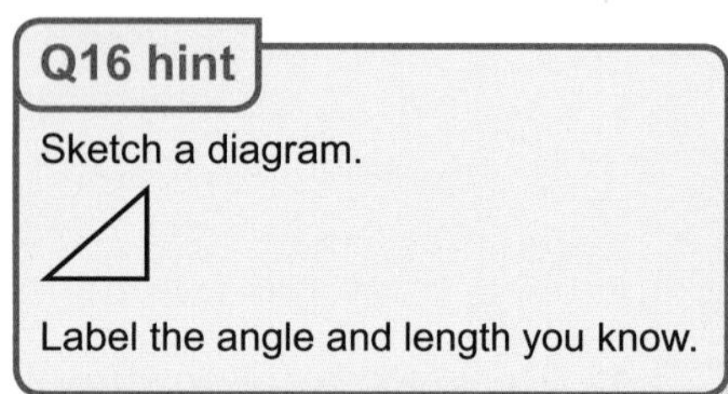

Label the angle and length you know.

17 **Real / Problem-solving** A fishing lodge wants to build a new boat ramp.
The slope of the ramp must be 8° to the horizontal.
The total height of the bank is 2.8 m.

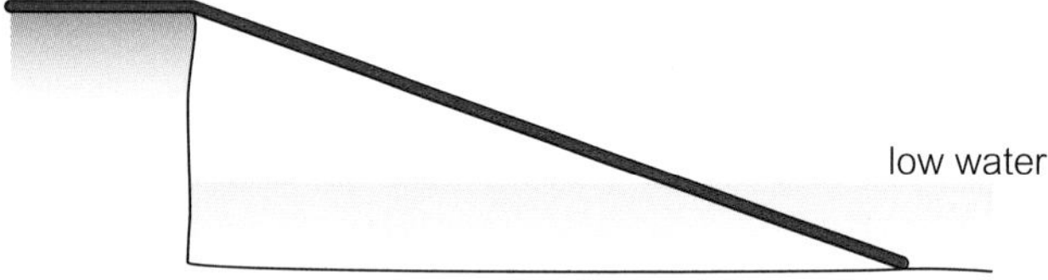

a How long must the sloping section of the ramp be?
Give your answer to the nearest centimetre.
At low water, the depth of water at the ramp site is 1.2 m.

b What length of the ramp will always be under water?
Give your answer to the nearest centimetre.

18

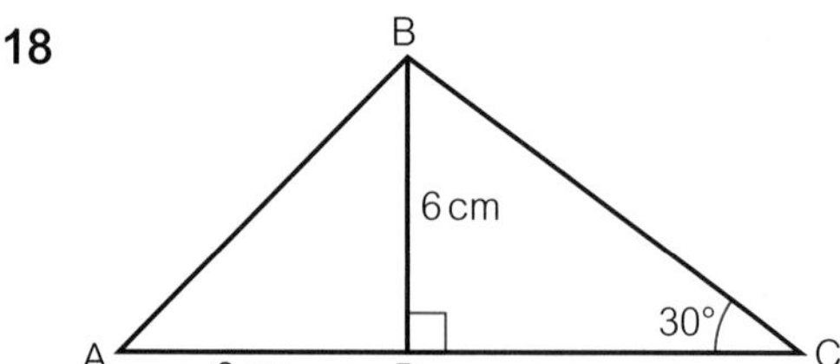

a Work out the length AB.
b Work out the length BC.
c Work out the length CD.
d **Reasoning** Is ABC a right-angled triangle? Explain your answer.

19 **Reasoning / Problem-solving** Two congruent circles fit exactly in a larger circle. They meet at the centre, P, of the large circle. PQR is a right-angled triangle, with Q on the circumference of the large circle. The third corner is at the centre, R, of one of the small circles.
What is the cosine of angle RPQ?
Explain your reasoning.

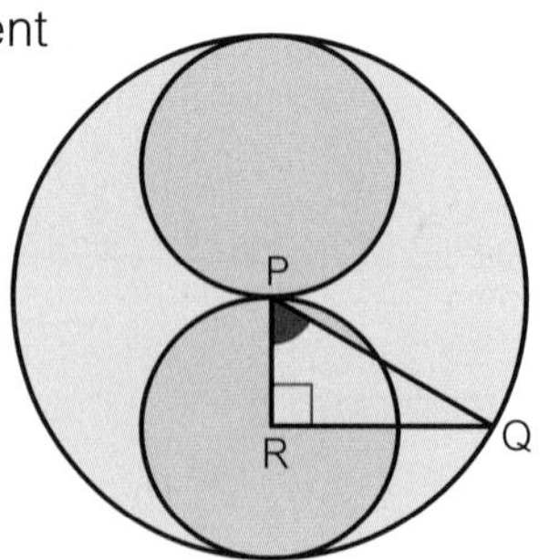

Q19 hint

Write PQ and PR in terms of the radius of the large circle.

Reflect

20 **Reflect** Copy and complete this paragraph.
Write at least three sentences.
'When I am given a mathematics problem to solve, this is what I do…'
Compare your paragraph with others in your class.

10 Unit test

Log how you did on your Student Progression Chart.

1 The three green right-angled triangles are congruent.
Is the white triangle congruent with each green triangle?
Give reasons for your answer.

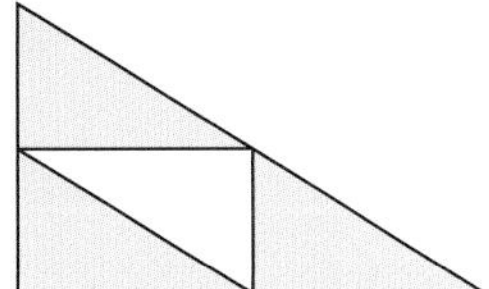

2 Which shapes are similar to shape A?

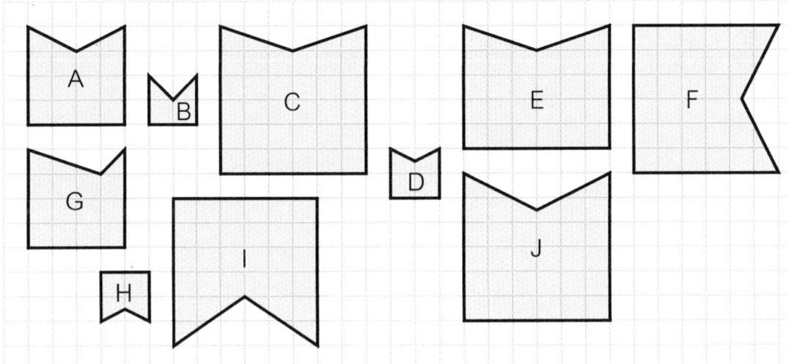

3 For each pair of triangles, decide whether the triangles are congruent, similar or neither.
Give reasons for your answers.

a PQ = AB, QR = BC, ∠PQR = ∠ABC

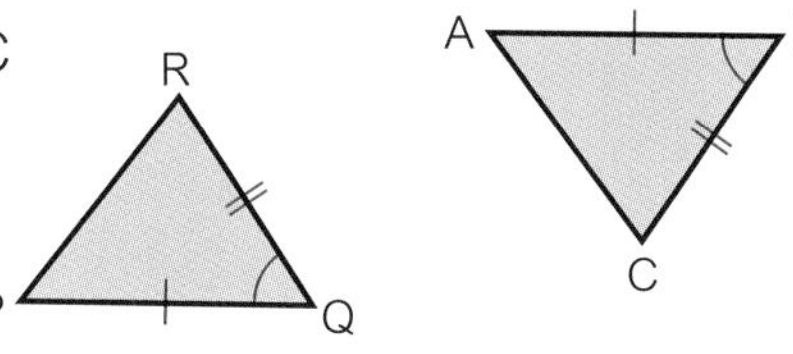

b ∠GHK = ∠XYZ, ∠HGK = ∠YXZ

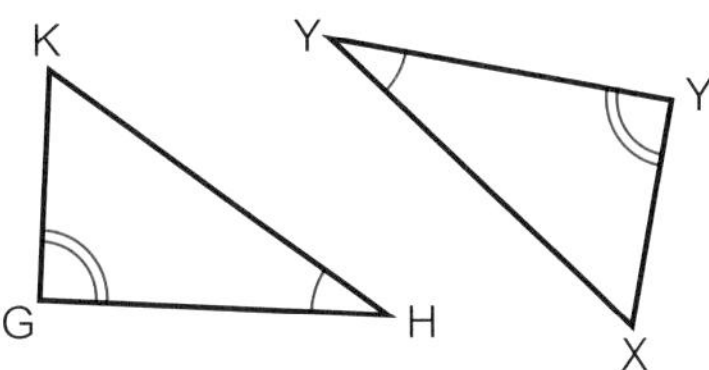

4 These triangles are all congruent. Work out the missing sides and angles.

a

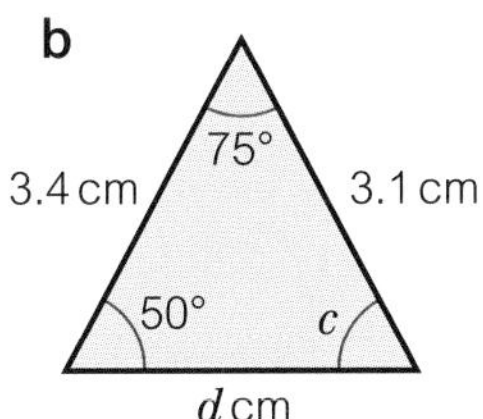

b

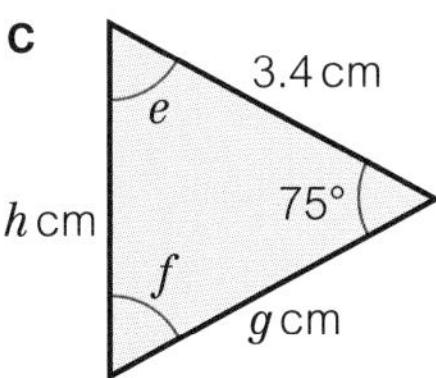

c

5 Triangles P and Q are similar.

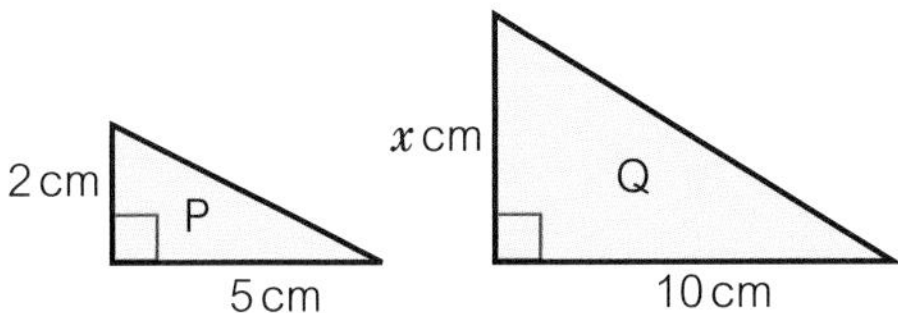

a State the scale factor from P to Q. **b** Find the missing length.

6 The line segment AC is split in the ratio 1 : 2.

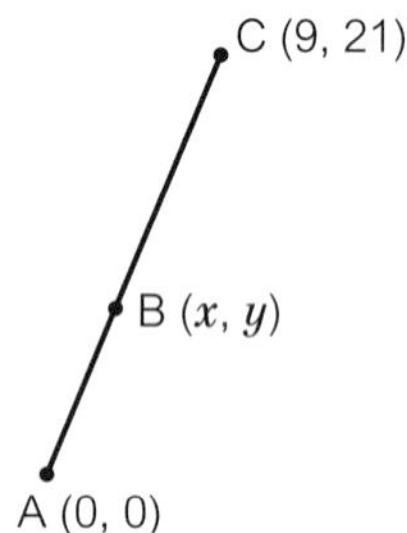

Work out the coordinates of B.

7 Use the tangent ratio to work out the missing length.
Give your answer to 1 d.p.

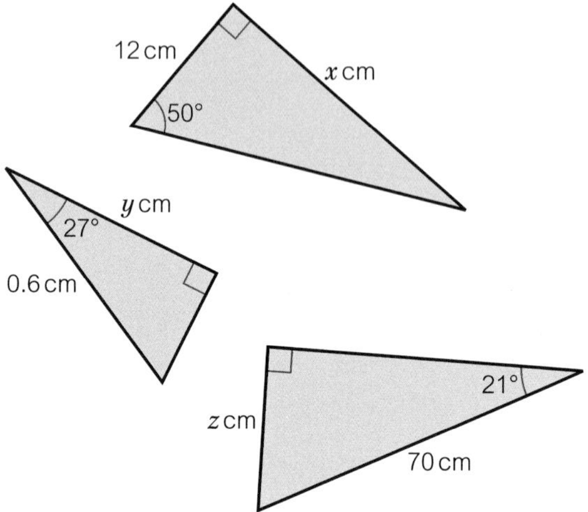

8 Use the cosine ratio to work out the missing length.
Give your answer to 1 d.p.

9 Use the sine ratio to work out the missing length.
Give your answer to 1 d.p.

10 A portable wedge ramp is 450 mm long and has a 9° slope.

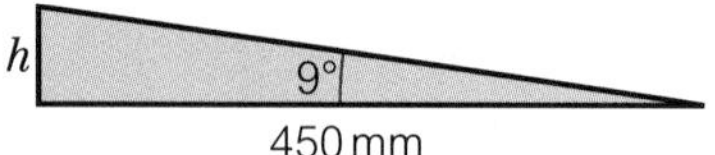

Work out the height (h) of the ramp, correct to the nearest millimetre.

11 Find the value of x. Give your answer to 1 d.p.

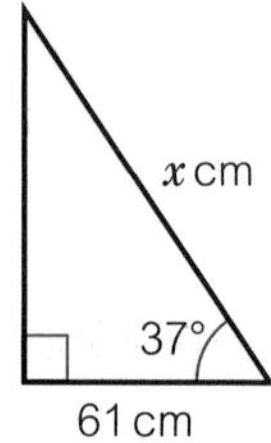

Challenge

12 Reflect

a For each statement A, B and C, choose a score:
1 – strongly disagree 2 – disagree 3 – agree 4 – strongly agree
A I always try hard in mathematics.
B Doing mathematics never makes me worried.
C I am good at mathematics.

b Look back at your answers to the reflect task in lesson 1.1.
It asked you the same question.

c Did your scores increase, decrease or stay the same? If your scores changed, why do you think this was?

d Did you do the things you wrote down in lesson 1.1 so that you might agree to statements A, B and C more strongly in future?

e Write down two other things you could do so you agree more strongly with these statements in future.

Reflect